The Princeton Review®

SAT®

PREP

2023 Edition

The Staff of The Princeton Review

PrincetonReview.com

Penguin
Random
House

The Princeton Review
110 East 42nd Street, 7th Floor
New York, NY 10017
Email: editorialsupport@review.com

Published in the United States by Penguin Random House LLC, New York, and in Canada by Random House of Canada, a division of Penguin Random House Ltd., Toronto.

ISBN: 978-0-593-45059-8
eBook ISBN: 978-0-593-45099-4
ISSN: 2687-9484

Editorial

Rob Franek, Editor-in-Chief
David Soto, Senior Director, Data Operations
Stephen Koch, Senior Manager, Data Operations
Deborah Weber, Director of Production
Jason Ullmeyer, Production Design Manager
Jennifer Chapman, Senior Production Artist
Selena Coppock, Director of Editorial
Aaron Riccio, Senior Editor
Meave Shelton, Senior Editor
Chris Chimera, Editor
Orion McBean, Editor
Patricia Murphy, Editor
Laura Rose, Editor
Alexa Schmitt Bugler, Editorial Assistant

Penguin Random House Publishing Team

Tom Russell, VP, Publisher
Alison Stoltzfus, Senior Director, Publishing
Brett Wright, Senior Editor
Emily Hoffman, Assistant Managing Editor
Ellen Reed, Production Manager
Suzanne Lee, Designer
Eugenia Lo, Publishing Assistant

Editor: Chris Chimera
Production Editors: Liz Dacey and Emily Epstein White
Production Artist: Jason Ullmeyer

Printed in the United States of America.

10 9 8 7 6 5 4 3 2 1

2023 Edition

Acknowledgments

An SAT course is much more than clever techniques and powerful computer score reports. The reason our results are great is that our teachers care so much about their students. Many teachers have gone out of their way to improve the course, often going so far as to write their own materials, some of which we have incorporated into our course manuals as well as into this book. The list of these teachers could fill this page.

Special thanks to all those who contributed to this year's edition: Sara Kuperstein, Amy Minster, Scott O'Neal, Cynthia Ward, Anne Bader, Gabby Budzon, Brittany Lee, Jomil London, Jason Morgan, Jess Thomas, and Chris Vakulchik.

We are also, as always, very appreciative of the time and attention given to each page by Jason Ullmeyer, Liz Dacey, Emily Epstein White.

Finally, we would like to thank the people who truly have taught us everything we know about the SAT: our students.

Contents

Foreword

Welcome to *Princeton Review SAT Prep!* The SAT is not a test of aptitude, how good of a person you are, or how successful you will be in life. The SAT simply tests how well you take the SAT. And performing well on the SAT is a skill, one that can be learned like any other. The Princeton Review was founded more than 35 years ago on this very simple idea, and—as our students' test scores show—our approach is the one that works.

Sure, you want to do well on the SAT, but you don't need to let the test intimidate you. As you prepare, remember two important things about the SAT:

- **It doesn't measure the stuff that matters.** It measures neither intelligence nor the depth and breadth of what you're learning in high school. It doesn't predict college grades as well as your high school grades do. Colleges know there is more to you as a student—and as a person—than what you do in a single 3-hour test administered on a random Saturday morning.

- **It underpredicts the college performance of women, minorities, and disadvantaged students.** Historically, women have done better than men in college but worse on the SAT. For a test that is used to help predict performance in college, that's a pretty poor record.

Your preparation for the SAT starts here. We at The Princeton Review spend millions of dollars every year improving our methods and materials so that students are always ready for the SAT, and we'll get you ready too.

However, there is no magic pill: just buying this book isn't going to improve your scores. Solid score improvement takes commitment and effort from you. If you read this book carefully and work through the problems and practice tests included in the book, not only will you be well-versed in the format of the SAT and the concepts it tests, you will also have a sound overall strategy and a powerful arsenal of test-taking strategies that you can apply to whatever you encounter on test day.

In addition to the comprehensive review in *SAT Prep*, we've included additional practice online, accessible through our website—PrincetonReview.com—to make it even more efficient at helping you to improve your scores. Before doing anything else, be sure to register your book at PrincetonReview.com/prep. When you do, you'll gain access to the most up-to-date information on the SAT, as well as more SAT and college admissions resources.

The more you take advantage of the resources we've included in this book and the online student tools that go with it, the better you'll do on the test. Read the book carefully and learn our strategies. Take the full-length practice tests under actual timed conditions. Analyze your performance and focus your efforts where you need improvement. Perhaps even study with a friend to stay motivated. Attend a free event at The Princeton Review to learn more about the SAT and how it is used in the college admissions process. Search our website for an event that will take place near you or take place online!

This test is challenging, but you're on the right track. We'll be with you all the way.

Good luck!

The Staff of The Princeton Review

Get More (Free) Content
at PrincetonReview.com/prep

As easy as 1·2·3

1 Go to PrincetonReview.com/prep or scan the **QR code** and enter the following ISBN for your book: **9780593450598**

2 Answer a few simple questions to set up an exclusive Princeton Review account. *(If you already have one, you can just log in.)*

3 Enjoy access to your **FREE** content!

Once you've registered, you can...

- Access and print out two more full-length practice tests as well as the corresponding answers and explanations
- Read our special "SAT Insider" and get valuable advice about the college application process, including tips for writing a great essay and where to apply for financial aid
- Download printable resources such as score conversion tables, extra bubble sheets, and essay lessons for students with required essays for SAT School Day administrations
- If you're still choosing between colleges, use our searchable rankings of *The Best 388 Colleges* to find out more information about your dream school
- Check to see if there have been any corrections or updates to this edition
- Get our take on any recent or pending updates to the SAT

Need to report a potential **content** issue?

Contact **EditorialSupport@review.com** and include:

- full title of the book
- ISBN
- page number

Need to report a **technical** issue?

Contact **TPRStudentTech@review.com** and provide:

- your full name
- email address used to register the book
- full book title and ISBN
- Operating system (Mac/PC) and browser (Chrome, Firefox, Safari, etc.)

Look For These Icons Throughout The Book

 ONLINE ARTICLES

 ONLINE PRACTICE TESTS

 PROVEN TECHNIQUES

 APPLIED STRATEGIES

 STUDY BREAK

 OTHER REFERENCES

 WATCH US CRACK IT

Part I
Orientation

LET'S GET THIS PARTY STARTED!

You are about to unlock a vast repertoire of powerful strategies that have one and only one purpose: to help you get a better score on the SAT. This book contains the collected wisdom of The Princeton Review, which has spent more than 35 years helping students achieve higher scores on standardized tests. We've devoted millions of dollars and years of our lives to beating the SAT. It's what we do (twisted as it may be), and we want you to benefit from our expertise.

WHAT IS THE PRINCETON REVIEW?

The Princeton Review is the leader in test prep. Our goal is to help students everywhere crack the SAT and a bunch of other standardized tests, including the PSAT and ACT as well as graduate-level exams like the GRE and GMAT. Starting from humble beginnings in 1981, The Princeton Review is now the nation's largest SAT preparation company. We offer courses in more than 500 locations in 20 different countries, as well as online; we also publish best-selling books, like the one you're holding, and online resources to get students ready for this test.

Our techniques work. We developed them after spending countless hours scrutinizing real SATs, analyzing them with computers, and proving our theories in the classroom.

The Princeton Review Way

This book will show you how to score higher on the SAT by teaching you to:

Study!

If you were getting ready to take a biology test, you'd study biology. If you were preparing for a basketball game, you'd practice basketball. So, if you're preparing for the SAT, you need to study and practice for the SAT. The exam can't test everything you learn in school (in fact, it tests very little), so concentrate on learning what it *does* test.

- extract important information from tricky test questions
- take full advantage of the limited time allowed
- systematically answer questions—even if you don't fully understand them
- avoid the traps that the SAT has laid for you (and use those traps to your advantage)

The test is written and administered by the College Board, and they know that our techniques work. For years, the test-writers claimed that the SAT couldn't be coached. But we've proven that view wrong, and they in turn have struggled to find ways of changing the SAT so that The Princeton Review won't be able to crack it—in effect, acknowledging what our students have known all along: that our techniques really do work. (In fact, the College Board has recently admitted that students can and should prepare for the SAT. So there!) The SAT has remained highly vulnerable to our techniques. And the current version of the SAT is even more susceptible to our methods. Read this book, work through the drills, take the practice tests, and you'll see what we mean.

Chapter 1
The SAT, The Princeton Review, and You

Welcome! Our job is to help you get the best possible score on the SAT. This chapter tells you what to expect from the SAT as well as some specifics about the test. It will also explain how to make the most of all your Princeton Review materials.

Wait, *Who* Writes This Test?
You may be surprised to learn that the people who write SAT test questions are NOT necessarily teachers or college professors. The people who write the SAT are professional test-writers, not super-human geniuses, so you can beat them at their own game.

Key Takeaway
What really matters to you as a test-taker is how the test is divided up and what YOU need to know to crack it!

GENERAL INFORMATION ABOUT THE SAT

You may have bought this book because you know nothing about the SAT, or perhaps you took the test once and want to raise your score. Either way, it's important to know about the test and the people who write it. Let's take a second to discuss some SAT facts: some of them may surprise you.

What Does the SAT Test?

Just because the SAT features math, reading, and writing questions doesn't mean that it reflects what you learned in school. You can ace calculus or write like Faulkner and still struggle with the SAT. The test-writers claim that the test predicts how well you will do in college by measuring "reasoning ability," but all the SAT really measures is how well you take the SAT. It does *not* reveal how smart—or how good—a person you are.

Who Writes the SAT?

Even though colleges and universities make wide use of the SAT, they're not the ones who write the test. That's the job of the College Board, the organization that creates the tests and decides how they will be administered and used.

The test-writers are often criticized for the SAT. Many educators have argued that the test does not measure the skills you really need for college. This led them in 2005 to overhaul the entire test, only to revise it all over again in early 2016. The important takeaway here is that the people who write the SAT are professional test-writers, and, with some practice, it's possible to beat them at their own game.

What's on the SAT?

The SAT is 3 hours long for most students. In some states, a 50-minute essay is also required as part of the SAT School Day administration. If you are taking such an administration, check to see whether the essay will be part of it. The SAT consists of the following:

- 1 multiple-choice Reading Test (52 questions, 65 minutes)
- 1 multiple-choice Writing and Language Test (44 questions, 35 minutes)
- 1 Math Test, consisting of a No Calculator section (20 questions, 25 minutes) and a Calculator section (38 questions, 55 minutes)

Both sections of the Math Test contain some student-produced-response questions called Grid-Ins, but all other questions on the exam are multiple choice. All multiple-choice sections on the SAT have four possible answer choices.

Each part of this book covers these tests in detail, but here's a brief rundown of what you can expect.

Reading Test

Your scores on the Reading Test and the Writing and Language Test (see below) together make up your Evidence-Based Reading and Writing score on the SAT. The Reading Test is 65 minutes long and consists of 52 questions, all of which are passage based and multiple choice. Passages may be paired with informational graphics, such as charts or graphs, and there will be a series of questions based on a pair of passages. The selected passages will be from previously published works in the areas of world literature, history/social studies, and science. Questions based on science passages may ask you to analyze data or hypotheses, while questions on literature passages will focus more on literary concepts like theme, mood, and characterization. The main goal of the Reading Test is to measure your ability to understand words in context as well as find and analyze evidence.

Want More?
For even more practice, check out *10 Practice Tests for the SAT.*

Writing and Language Test

The Writing and Language Test is 35 minutes long and consists of 44 questions, which are also multiple choice and based on passages. However, instead of asking you to analyze a passage, questions will require you to proofread and edit the passage. This means you will have to correct grammar and word choice, as well as make larger changes to the organization or content of the passage.

Math Test

You will have a total of 80 minutes to complete the Math Test, which, as mentioned earlier, is divided into two sections: No Calculator (Section 3; 25 minutes, 20 questions) and Calculator (Section 4; 55 minutes, 38 questions). Most questions are multiple choice, but there are also a handful of what College Board calls Student-produced Response questions, which are also known as Grid-Ins. For Grid-In questions, instead of choosing from four answer choices, you'll have to work through a question and then enter your answer on your answer sheet by bubbling in the appropriate numbers. We'll discuss this in more detail in Chapter 20. Exactly 13 of the 58 math questions will be Grid-Ins.

The Math Test covers four main content areas, which the College Board has named the following: (1) Heart of Algebra, (2) Problem Solving and Data Analysis, (3) Passport to Advanced Math, and (4) Additional Topics in Math. This last section includes complex numbers and topics in geometry and trigonometry. Part IV of this book covers each of these content areas in depth.

The Optional Essay is No Longer an Option

After June 2021, College Board stopped offering students the option to take the SAT essay. This means that no colleges require it (since it's not an option for most students), so ignore any outdated information you might see about the SAT essay. The only students who will take the essay are those who are required to do so during a School Day Administration—that is, when your school or district has you take the SAT during a school day rather than over the weekend. If you will be taking a School Day SAT, find out from your school whether the essay portion will be included. If it will be, you can find some sample prompts online in your free Student Tools.

Scoring on the SAT

The SAT is scored on a scale of 400 to 1600, which is a combination of your scores for Evidence-Based Reading and Writing (a combination of your Reading and Writing and Language scores, scored from 200 to 800) and Math (also scored from 200 to 800). The exam also has a detailed scoring system that includes cross-test scores and subscores based on your performance on each of the three tests. Your score report for the SAT will feature scores for each of the following:

- **Total Score (1):** The sum of the two section scores (Evidence-Based Reading and Writing, Math), ranging from 400 to 1600
- **Section Scores (2):** Evidence-Based Reading and Writing, ranging from 200 to 800; Math, also ranging from 200 to 800
- **Test Scores (3):** Reading Test, Writing and Language Test, Math Test, each of which is scored on a scale from 10 to 40
- **Cross-Test Scores (2):** Each is scored on a scale from 10 to 40 and based on selected questions from the three tests (Reading, Writing and Language, Math):
    1. Analysis in History/Social Studies
    2. Analysis in Science
- **Subscores (7):** Each of the following receives a score from 1 to 15:
    1. Command of Evidence (Reading; Writing and Language)
    2. Words in Context (Reading; Writing and Language)
    3. Expression of Ideas (Writing and Language)
    4. Standard English Conventions (Writing and Language)
    5. Heart of Algebra (Math)
    6. Problem Solving and Data Analysis (Math)
    7. Passport to Advanced Math (Math)

This scoring structure was designed to help provide a more holistic profile of students' skills and knowledge, as well as readiness for college. However, colleges aren't likely to look at the cross-test scores or the subscores.

Your Evidence-Based Reading and Writing score is determined in the following way:

Verbal Scaled Score out of 800 =

$$\left(\begin{array}{l} \text{Writing and Language test score out of 40} \\ \text{+ Reading test score out of 40} \end{array} \right) \times 10$$

Since the two verbal sections are tied together, an improvement in either area will increase your Evidence-Based Reading and Writing score. The Math score is a bit less complicated, with a direct relationship between the Math Test Score and the number of questions answered correctly in the Math sections. The scale may change slightly from test to test, but this chart will give you a good idea of the approximate score you would get with each number of raw points.

Math Scale Score	
Scaled Score	Raw Points
350	12
400	16
450	20
500	26
550	32
600	39
650	44
700	50
750	54
800	58

When Is the SAT Given?

The SAT schedule for the school year is posted on the College Board website at www.collegeboard.org. There are two ways to sign up for the test. You can either sign up online by going to www.collegeboard.org and clicking on the SAT link, or sign up through the mail with an SAT registration booklet, which may be available at your school guidance counselor's office.

Try to sign up for the SAT as soon as you know when you want to take the test. If you wait until the last minute to sign up, there may not be any open spots in the testing centers.

If you require any special accommodations while taking the test (including, but not limited to, extra time or assistance), www.collegeboard.org has information about applying for those accommodations. Make sure to apply early; we recommend applying six months before you plan to take the test.

Stay on Schedule
Although you may take the SAT any time starting freshman year, most students take it for the first time in the spring of their junior year and may retake it in the fall of their senior year. Sit down and plan a schedule.

HOW TO BEGIN

After this chapter, you will find Practice Test 1 and its answers and explanations. This will act as your "diagnostic" test. We recommend that you take this test before going any further in order to realistically determine:

Scoring Your Practice Tests

At the end of each Answers and Explanations chapter, we've provided a table and step-by-step equation to help you score your practice test and determine how your performance would translate to the actual SAT. You can also generate a detailed online score report in your Student Tools. Follow the steps on the "Get More (Free) Content" spread at the front of this book to access this awesome feature.

- your starting score right now
- which question types you're ready for and which you might need to practice
- which content topics you are familiar with and which you will want to carefully review

Once you have nailed down your strengths and weaknesses based on this exam, you can focus your test preparation, build a study plan, and be efficient with your time. Use the following steps to make the most of this first "diagnostic" test.

1. **Take a practice test.** To "diagnose" your strengths and weaknesses, take Practice Test 1 starting on page 11 of this book. Be sure to do so in one sitting, following the instructions that appear with each section of the test.
2. **Score your test online.** Once you register your book, you can enter the answers to your practice tests in your online tools. When you do so, you will get a score report that details your performance on a variety of question types. You will also get an approximate score, though the scale for the SAT does change a bit from test to test.
3. **Take stock and make a plan.** With the insights you'll gain from your score report, decide where to start with the content of this book. You may choose to use some parts of this book over others, or you may work through the entire book. The ways in which you use this book will depend on your needs and how much time you have.

Now let's look at how to make this determination.

When you enter your practice test answers online, you will get a score report that starts with your Total score, followed by a breakdown of the scores for each section of the test. You will also be able to see the various Cross-Section Scores and Subscores. Below that will be a breakdown of the questions by test section, with a tab for each one. Each question will be represented by a box with a mark to indicate if it was Correct, Incorrect, or Blank. Clicking on the box for a question brings up the explanation for it, which is also found in this book. Additionally, you can see the question category listed as "Concept Tested."

To see a section breakdown by concept, you can click the "View by Category" button. Use this view to determine the following:

- question types you are good at, to make sure you can find and correctly answer questions in these categories every time
- question types that have several questions in them but that you struggled with a bit, so you can work to improve your accuracy on these important questions
- question types that were either very difficult for you or had only one or two questions in them. Practice these question types only after you're mastered the others.

After you determine these things for Reading, you can do the same for Writing and Language and for Math by clicking on the respective tabs for each. There is also a guide at the bottom of the score report that indicates your Areas of Strength and Areas of Focus. Though this may point you to some areas to work on, make sure to verify that a given topic is worth the time it would take to master. For example, if there was only one Math question about Complex Numbers and you got it wrong, that may show up as an Areas of Focus. However, if each test has only 1 Complex Numbers question at most, studying that concept is not the best use of your time.

Your analysis of your performance on Practice Test 1 will affect how you engage with **Part II** (How to Crack the Reading Test), **Part III** (How to Crack the Writing and Language Test), **and Part IV** (How to Crack the Math Test). Each of these parts is designed to give a comprehensive review of the content tested on the SAT, including the level of detail you need to know and how the content is tested. At the end of each of these chapters, you'll have the opportunity to assess your mastery of the content covered through targeted drills that reflect the types of questions and level of difficulty you'll see on the actual exam. Answers and explanations can be found at the end of each chapter, so use those explanations to continue assessing your skills.

After you have mastered a few key concepts and strategies, take another practice test from **Part VI** and analyze it the same way to see where you've improved and where you have more work to do. Continue alternating working through the chapters of this book and taking practice tests until you feel fully prepared to conquer the SAT.

A FINAL THOUGHT BEFORE YOU BEGIN

The SAT does not measure intelligence, nor does it predict your ultimate success or failure as a human being. No matter how high or how low you score on this test initially, and no matter how much you may increase your score through preparation, you should never consider the score you receive on this or any other test a final judgment of your abilities.

Chapter 2
Practice Test 1

Reading Test

65 MINUTES, 52 QUESTIONS

Turn to Section 1 of your answer sheet to answer the questions in this section.

DIRECTIONS

Each passage or pair of passages below is followed by a number of questions. After reading each passage or pair, choose the best answer to each question based on what is stated or implied in the passage or passages and in any accompanying graphics (such as a table or graph).

Questions 1–10 are based on the following passage.

This passage is excerpted from George Gissing, *New Grub Street*. Originally published in 1891. Reardon was a newly successful author and had married, but soon found himself unable to write. Following a conversation with his wife, he takes a walk and thinks about the time just before his wedding.

And the words sang about him, filled the air with a mad pulsing of intolerable joy, made him desire to fling himself in passionate humility at her feet, to weep hot
Line tears, to cry to her in insane worship. He thought her
5 beautiful beyond anything his heart had imagined; her warm gold hair was the rapture of his eyes and of his reverent hand. Though slenderly fashioned, she was so gloriously strong. 'Not a day of illness in her life,' said Mrs. Yule, and one could readily believe it.
10 She spoke with such a sweet decision. Her 'I love you!' was a bond with eternity. In the simplest as in the greatest things she saw his wish and acted frankly upon it. No pretty petulance, no affectation of silly-sweet languishing, none of the weaknesses of woman. And
15 so exquisitely fresh in her twenty years of maidenhood, with bright young eyes that seemed to bid defiance to all the years to come.
He went about like one dazzled with excessive light. He talked as he had never talked before, recklessly,
20 exultantly, insolently—in the nobler sense. He made friends on every hand; he welcomed all the world to his bosom; he felt the benevolence of a god.
'I love you!' It breathed like music at his ears when he fell asleep in weariness of joy; it awakened him on
25 the morrow as with a glorious ringing summons to

renewed life. Delay? Why should there be delay? Amy wished nothing but to become his wife. Idle to think of his doing any more work until he sat down in the home of which she was mistress. His brain burned with
30 visions of the books he would henceforth write, but his hand was incapable of anything but a love-letter. And what letters! Reardon never published anything equal to those. 'I have received your poem,' Amy replied to one of them. And she was right; not a letter, but a
35 poem he had sent her, with every word on fire.
The hours of talk! It enraptured him to find how much she had read, and with what clearness of understanding. Latin and Greek, no. Ah! but she should learn them both, that there might be nothing
40 wanting in the communion between his thought and hers. For he loved the old writers with all his heart; they had been such strength to him in his days of misery.
They would go together to the charmed lands of
45 the South. No, not now for their marriage holiday— Amy said that would be an imprudent expense; but as soon as he had got a good price for a book. Will not the publishers be kind? If they knew what happiness lurked in embryo within their foolish cheque-books!
50 He woke of a sudden in the early hours of one morning, a week before the wedding-day. You know that kind of awaking, so complete in an instant, caused by the pressure of some troublesome thought upon the dreaming brain. 'Suppose I should not succeed
55 henceforth? Suppose I could never get more than this

CONTINUE ➡

poor hundred pounds for one of the long books which cost me so much labour? I shall perhaps have children to support; and Amy—how would Amy bear poverty?'

He knew what poverty means. The chilling of
60 brain and heart, the unnerving of the hands, the slow gathering about one of fear and shame and impotent wrath, the dread feeling of helplessness, of the world's base indifference. Poverty! Poverty!

1

Which choice best describes a major theme of the passage?

A) The internal battle between true love and self-doubt

B) The unequivocal joy of marital bliss

C) The destructive power of encroaching poverty

D) The fear of never reaching one's ultimate potential

2

According to the narrator, when the woman he loved learned of his feelings for her, she

A) pledged her undying affection in return.

B) dedicated herself to her maidenhood.

C) reconsidered her prior refusal of his advances.

D) wrote her own book of poetry.

3

Which choice provides the best evidence for the answer to the previous question?

A) Lines 7–8 ("Though . . . strong")

B) Lines 10–11 ("She spoke . . . eternity")

C) Lines 26–27 ("Amy wished . . . wife")

D) Lines 33–35 ("Amy replied . . . fire")

4

Which statement best describes a technique used to represent Amy's desire to marry the narrator?

A) The narrator describes in detail her youthful enthusiasm as a major motivating factor.

B) The narrator asks a hypothetical question that is immediately refuted.

C) The narrator applauds her decision as a reflection of an inner strength that is unparalleled.

D) The narrator stresses her sincerity as proof of a dedication fostered by her maidenhood.

5

As compared with his love letters, the narrator's book writing is portrayed as being

A) agreeable.

B) stalled.

C) fiery.

D) imaginative.

6

In describing the relationship between Amy and the narrator, the narrator highlights a distinction between Amy's

A) desire for marriage and his readiness.

B) beauty and his common appeal.

C) conventional education and his love of language.

D) distaste for spending and his ability to write.

7

Which choice provides the best evidence for the answer to the previous question?

A) Lines 4–7 ("He thought . . . hand")

B) Lines 11–13 ("In the . . . it")

C) Lines 38–41 ("Latin . . . hers")

D) Lines 45–47 ("No, not . . . book")

CONTINUE

8

As used in line 40, "wanting" most nearly means

A) lacking.

B) requesting.

C) pleasing.

D) desiring.

9

The narrator uses the phrase "what happiness lurked in embryo" (lines 48–49) to present the publishers as

A) kind.

B) wealthy.

C) influential.

D) foolish.

10

What function does the last paragraph (lines 59–63) serve in the passage as a whole?

A) It expands upon the overall theme of the narrator's never-ending love for Amy.

B) It lists the long-term effects that poverty could have on the narrator's relationship.

C) It provides evidence that the narrator cannot support his wife by revealing his hysteria.

D) It intensifies the narrator's growing concerns about his ability to support his marriage.

CONTINUE

Questions 11–21 are based on the following passage and supplementary material.

This passage is excerpted from Dan Glass, "What Happens if GPS Fails?" ©2016 by The Atlantic.

Despite its name, the Global Positioning System is not about maps; it's about time. Each satellite in the constellation (24 are needed, plus the U.S. has several spares) has multiple atomic clocks on board,

5 synchronized with each other and to Coordinated Universal Time (UTC)—the time standard used across the world—down to the nanosecond. The satellites continually broadcast their time and position information down to Earth, where GPS receivers in

10 equipment from iPhones to automated tractors acquire signals and use the minuscule differences in their arrival time to determine an exact position.

While GPS was initially conceived to aid navigation, globally synchronized time is now a much

15 more critical function of the system. Telecom networks rely on GPS clocks to keep cell towers synchronized so calls can be passed between them. Many electrical power grids use the clocks in equipment that fine-tunes current flow in overloaded networks. The finance

20 sector uses GPS-derived timing systems to timestamp ATM, credit card, and high-speed market transactions. Computer network synchronization, digital television and radio, Doppler radar weather reporting, seismic monitoring, even multi-camera sequencing for film

25 production—GPS clocks have a hand in all.

What if all these flying clock radios were wiped out, and everything on the ground started blinking 12:00? According to Mike Lombardi, a meteorologist at the National Institute for Standards and Technology,

30 "Nobody knows exactly what would happen." Since so many of these technologies were designed specifically with GPS in mind, the unsettling truth, he says, is "there's no backup."

The bulk of a more promising, comprehensive

35 backup system already exists, right here on the ground. After the sextant but before GPS, navigators around the world used Long Range Aids to Navigation, or "LORAN," a terrestrial system of transmitters and receiving equipment first developed during WWII.

40 By the mid-1990s, Loran "tower chains" provided coverage for North America, Europe, and other

regions in the Northern Hemisphere. Its use declined in favor of the much finer accuracy of GPS after it became available for civil use in 1995, but the U.S.

45 Coast Guard continued working on an improved system using the existing infrastructure. If adopted, "Enhanced" LORAN, or eLoran, could provide positioning accuracy comparable to GPS. Broadcast at hundreds of thousands of watts, the signal is virtually

50 un-jammable, and unlike GPS, can even be received indoors, underwater, and in urban or natural canyons. It also turns out that eLoran can provide a UTC time signal with sub-microsecond time resolution across a large geographical area.

55 The technology is available—the Coast Guard demonstrated a working prototype last year—so why isn't America using it? John Garamendi, a California congressman, asked this question at a July 2015 congressional hearing on the Federal

60 Radionavigation Plan, the nation's primary planning document for position, navigation, and timing (PNT). "There are two kinds of time," he opened, "real time … and then federal time, which seems to be the forever time. The eLoran system was identified as a backup 15

65 years ago, and here we are, federal time, not yet done."

Why is the sense of urgency among decision-makers so out of sync? Could some of it be similar to why people delay backing up their computers even though they've been telling themselves to for

70 weeks? How do we decide, when presented a risk with unknown odds, when it's time to sacrifice time and resources to prevent it?

Now is a critically important time to answer that question, as the world has actually been given odds on

75 another, even more catastrophic risk than GPS failure: destruction of the electrical power infrastructure itself. On July 23, 2012, a billion-ton cloud of electrified gases blasted off the far side of the sun at over six million miles per hour. According to professor Daniel Baker

80 at University of Colorado, this coronal mass ejection (CME) "was in all respects at least as strong as the 1859 Carrington Event," referring to the strongest solar storm ever recorded, which set fire to telegraph stations and caused auroras down to Cuba. As was

85 widely reported two years ago, if the 2012 CME had occurred one week later, it would have hit Earth.

CONTINUE ➡

Figure 1

Percent of Smartphone Users Who
Use Their Phones to get Location-Based Information,
over Time, by Age

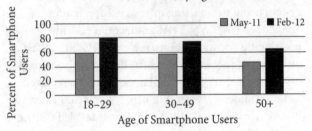

Figure 2

Commercial GPS Equipment Revenues in North America

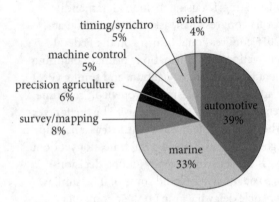

Data source: Pew Research Center

The main purpose of the passage is to

A) present a problem with a current technology and highlight a potential solution.

B) provide an overview of how clocks and satellites determine distance and location.

C) analyze the negative impacts of certain technologies across various industries.

D) praise developers for their ability to answer the hard questions.

As used in line 13, "conceived" most nearly means

A) designed.

B) understood.

C) absorbed.

D) accepted.

The primary purpose of the question in lines 26–28 ("What . . . 12:00") is to

A) introduce a problem.

B) correct a misconception.

C) reconsider a perspective.

D) undermine an idea.

Which of the following best characterizes Lombardi's attitude toward "flying clock radios" (line 26)?

A) He is confident about their ability to handle a multitude of tasks.

B) He is concerned about how they will interact with the eLoran systems.

C) He is annoyed that no one knows exactly how they work.

D) He is worried that they have no replacement systems in case of emergency.

Which choice provides the best evidence for the answer to the previous question?

A) Line 25 ("GPS clocks . . . all")

B) Line 30 ("Nobody . . . happen")

C) Lines 30–33 ("Since . . . backup")

D) Lines 34–35 ("The bulk . . . ground")

CONTINUE ▶

16

As used in line 34, "bulk" most nearly means

A) dimensions.

B) mass.

C) majority.

D) totality.

17

According to John Garamendi, the reason America isn't using the eLoran system even though the technology is available is that

A) the system doesn't use real time.

B) government approval takes longer than the development of the technology.

C) federal decision-makers are scared to change systems.

D) solar storms threaten the system.

18

Which choice provides the best evidence for the answer to the previous question?

A) Lines 48–51 ("Broadcast . . . canyons")

B) Lines 64–65 ("The eLoran . . . done")

C) Lines 70–72 ("How do . . . it")

D) Lines 73–76 ("Now is . . . itself")

19

According to figure 1, which group is closest in percentage to the percentage of users 18–29 in May 2011 who got location-based information on their smartphones?

A) Ages 50+ in Feb 2012

B) Ages 50+ in May 2011

C) Ages 30-49 in Feb 2012

D) Ages 18-29 in Feb 2012

20

Which statement is supported by figure 2?

A) Less than a third of North American GPS revenue comes from the Automotive industry.

B) GPS revenues for Surveying/Mapping are less than GPS revenues for Precision Agriculture.

C) GPS devices are less important for the Aviation industry than they are for the Marine industry.

D) The Automotive and Marine industries make up a greater percentage of North American GPS revenues than the rest of the industries combined.

21

Which additional information, if presented in figure 2, would be most useful in evaluating the statement in lines 13–15 ("While . . . system")?

A) The total number of GPS devices sold

B) The number of individuals in each industry using GPS devices

C) The percentage of the industry that relies on the GPS devices

D) The amount of revenue in dollars for each industry

CONTINUE ➤

Questions 22–31 are based on the following passage.

This passage is excerpted from Joshua Hammer, "The Dying of the Dead Sea." ©2005 by Smithsonian Magazine.

A refuge over the millennia for messiahs, martyrs and zealots, the Dead Sea region abounds with sites sacred to Islam, Christianity and Judaism. Some
Line Muslims believe that Moses, whom they regard as a
5 prophet, lies buried in a hilltop mosque just off the main road from Jerusalem. Jesus Christ was said to have been baptized in the Jordan River after traveling down to the Dead Sea from Galilee. And despite its name, the Dead Sea helps support one of the world's
10 most complex and vibrant ecosystems. Fed by fresh water springs and aquifers, a half-dozen oases along the shore harbor scores of indigenous species of plants, fish and mammals, including ibex and leopards. About 500 million birds representing at least 300 species,
15 including storks, pelicans, lesser spotted eagles, lesser kestrels and honey buzzards, take refuge here during a biannual great migration from Africa to Europe and back again. Ein Feshka, a lush expanse of tamarisk, papyrus, oleander and pools of crystal water, was
20 used by the late king Hussein of Jordan as a private playground in the 1950s and early '60s. But as the Dead Sea recedes, the springs that feed the oases are moving along with it; many experts believe that Ein Feshka and other oases could wither away within five years.
25   One reason for the decline, according to environmentalists and various government officials, is a water policy on the part of Israel, Jordan and Syria that encourages unrestricted agricultural use. From the first years of Israel's existence as a Jewish state, for
30 example, when collective farming transformed much of it into fertile vineyards and vegetable fields, both Labor and Likud governments have bestowed generous water subsidies on the nation's farmers. The results have been disastrous: today, agriculture accounts for
35 just 3 percent of Israel's gross national product and uses up to half of its fresh water. Recently, Uri Sagie, chairman of Israel's national water company, told a conference of Israeli farmers that a growing and irreversible gap between production and consumption
40 looms. "The water sources are being depleted without the deficit being restored," he warned. Jordan lavishes similar water subsidies on its farmers with similar consequences: the kingdom takes about 71 billion gallons of water a year from the Yarmouk River and

45 channels it into the King Abdullah Canal, constructed by USAID in the 1970s to provide irrigation for the Jordan Valley; Syria takes out another 55 billion gallons. So what is the answer?
       Environmental activists say that one solution is to
50 eliminate the water subsidies altogether. "Unless water is priced at its real costs," says Ra'ed Daoud, managing director of ECO Consult, a water-use consulting firm, "there's no way you're going to reduce agriculture." But because the region's agricultural lobby is strong
55 and the environmental movement weak, says Daoud, there has been insufficient leverage for change. Israel's water commissioner, Shimon Tal, recently spoke publicly about the need to reduce some subsidies, but he admitted that it would be a long and difficult
60 battle. Another approach is to encourage alternate water sources. Friends of the Earth Middle East is part of a coalition of 21 environmental groups that has developed proposals to conserve household water use (about 133 billion gallons a year, as much as that used
65 in agriculture) and to regulate the amount that can be taken out of Israel's springs. In addition, the Israeli government is promoting the building of wastewater treatment plants and desalination facilities; the first large one on the Mediterranean was completed this
70 past August. Over the next five years, the government says, these facilities will provide as much as 106 billion gallons of fresh water annually for agricultural and domestic consumption.
       Friends of the Earth is also taking its message to the
75 farmers themselves—encouraging them to plant crops that use less water and spelling out the advantages of renewed tourism in the area. "Israeli agriculture is incredibly mismanaged," Friends of the Earth director Gidon Bromberg says. "The farmers here could be
80 planting olives, flowers and other crops like dates that don't require fresh water. They could be using treated sewage water and allow fresh water to flow back into the Jordan River." Friends of the Earth cites a Haifa University study that argues that current uses of the
85 Jordan River make no sense. "The potential tourism-dollar return of a healthy river and a healthy Dead Sea outweighs the little return that agriculture offers," says Bromberg.

CONTINUE ▶

22

The primary purpose of the passage is to

A) discuss how the governments of Israel, Syria, and Jordan create water policy.

B) describe the many species of plants, fish, and mammals that live in the Dead Sea region.

C) explain the consequences of continuing current water policy in the Dead Sea region.

D) discuss one cause of the decline of the Dead Sea and outline a possible remedy.

23

As used in line 12, "harbor" most nearly means

A) nourish.

B) shelter.

C) entertain.

D) consider.

24

The author mentions Ein Feshka primarily in order to

A) describe a historical site in need of preservation.

B) transition from a description of the region to a discussion of a problem the region faces.

C) identify a need for recreation areas in the Dead Sea region.

D) indicate that environmental impacts vary with different types of land use.

25

What is the most likely reason the author includes "both Labor and Likud governments" in lines 28–33 ("From . . . farmers")?

A) To describe the level of cooperation between political parties in the Israeli government

B) To emphasize the popularity of current water policy among all political parties

C) To indicate broad political support for water subsidies

D) To criticize the politicization of natural resources

26

According to the passage, water laws favor

A) the tourism industry.

B) government.

C) environmental activists.

D) farmers.

27

What can reasonably be inferred about the agriculture industry in the Dead Sea region?

A) Its use of water is disproportionate to its impact on the economy.

B) It is an industry in decline.

C) The agriculture lobby is the most powerful influence on governments in the Dead Sea region.

D) It will soon use more than 100 billion gallons of water from treatment facilities.

28

Which choice provides the best evidence for the answer to the previous question?

A) Lines 34–36 ("today . . . water")

B) Lines 54–56 ("But . . . change")

C) Lines 70–73 ("Over . . . consumption")

D) Lines 77–79 ("Israeli . . . says")

29

What does the author suggest about tourism?

A) It was most vibrant in the mid-20th century.

B) Eco-tourism will be an important part of the future economy in the region.

C) Tourism may provide more benefit to the Dead Sea region's economy than agriculture currently does.

D) Officials in the tourism and agriculture industries should work together to create policy.

CONTINUE ➡

30

Which choice provides the best evidence for the answer to the previous question?

A) Lines 18–21 ("Ein Feshka . . . '60s")

B) Lines 66–68 ("the Israeli . . . facilities")

C) Lines 79–81 ("The farmers . . . water")

D) Lines 85–88 ("The potential . . . Bromberg")

31

What is the main idea of the final paragraph?

A) Farmers can adopt new practices to use less water and help maintain the Dead Sea.

B) Farmers should stop planting crops and focus on tourism.

C) Tourism will soon replace agriculture as the main industry of the region.

D) In the absence of policy change, farmers are adjusting their practices to conserve water.

CONTINUE

Questions 32–41 are based on the following passages.

Passage 1 is adapted from James Platt, *Poverty*. Originally published in 1884. Passage 2 is adapted from Will Reason, *Poverty*. Originally published in 1909. As societies became more industrialized and urban in the late nineteenth century, discussions arose regarding the root causes of poverty.

Passage 1

The aim of charitable persons should not be so much the giving with money in hand, or religious teaching on their lips, as the sympathetic, friendly
Line intercourse of man with man, woman with woman,
5 irrespective of class, and actuated by the desire to stimulate hope and energy, and to show the lowest outcast that the world, even to them, may be made more enjoyable, if they have the desire to live a life more in harmony with the better part of their nature;
10 and so in time, by degrees, as the child is taught to walk, step by step, we may improve the lowest types of humanity.

To obtain better dwellings for the poor, it is essential for the poorer class to feel a want for, and
15 a desire to have, houses better, cleaner, and more wholesome than those they now inhabit. Too many, at present, wantonly and maliciously, but more frequently, through neglect and apathy, injure the houses in which they live. Many of them prefer to be
20 uncomfortable.

The man or men that are wanted to solve this difficult question, the only true or real reformers, will be those who study how to alter the character, estimate of life, the ideal of existence amongst the poor. From
25 the clergy of all denominations, from every man who has influence over the masses, we want the moral courage to tell the poor not to marry until they are in a position to support a wife and family, to be reasonably industrious, uniformly thrifty, and unswervingly sober.
30 The real reformer, the only savior of society, is the man who will tell the poor how they may become less so, by teaching them how to earn more or spend less, not by robbing others of what they have.

We must raise the status of the poorer class,
35 improve their individuality, give them a higher character, and thus prepare the way for a well-working humanity that should result in well-working institutions. We must regenerate the entire social fabric, through the working of juster laws, purer aims,
40 nobler instincts—through individual cooperation of the many, as one, in contributing to the welfare of all.

Passage 2

It is clear, therefore, that the readjustment of distribution must be effected through a readjustment of the ownership and management of the essential
45 factors of production. It is not possible to effect this readjustment on the basis of unrestricted competition, because in the case on the prime factor of production, the land monopoly is caused, not by any artificial arrangement, but by the simple natural fact that it is
50 essential and restricted in quantity. The only course that remains is to find some way of democratizing the monopoly value, so that everyone benefits by his due share of what has not been made by the industry of any and is indispensable to the industry of all.

55 This cannot be effected by parceling it out to individuals, for very obvious reasons. It would have to be continually redistributed, it would be impossible to equate the value of the different parts, and such distribution would destroy its productive efficiency.

60 We therefore must look to some means of collective ownership and use of these natural forces, and also of all the value that accrues not from individual energy, industry or skill, but from the conditions which society itself affords. "To deal with causes we must strike at
65 the error of distribution, by gradually substituting public ownership for private ownership of the means of production. In no other way can we secure for each worker in the hive the full reward of his labor. So long as between the worker and his just wage stands the
70 private landlord and the private capitalist, so long will poverty remain, and not poverty alone, but the moral degradations which inevitably arise from the devotion of labor to the service of waste," [writes L.G. Chiozza in "Riches and Poverty."]

75 Here we touch the greatest controversy of the present time, and another volume would be needed to examine all the reasons for and against such a social adjustment. But it is clear that unless some way of effecting it is found, consistent with fairness to all,
80 poverty, undeserved and unavoidable, must be the lot of many, while equally undeserved income will continue to be reaped, without conscious or intentional fraud on their part, by many others. As the poverty reacts on the character for ill effect, so also it is to be
85 feared that the unearned riches also produce qualities, of a different and more subtle nature, but equally inimical to the true well-being both of the individuals concerned and of the community.

CONTINUE ▶

32

As used in line 1, "aim" most nearly means

A) focus.

B) shot.

C) gift.

D) ability.

33

In Passage 1, Platt suggests that one way a society can reduce poverty is to

A) provide in-demand technical training to citizens in need of marketable skills.

B) redistribute wealth directly from certain types of rich men.

C) teach that the benefits of budgeting outweigh the benefits of handouts.

D) instruct children in financial matters from a young age.

34

Which choice provides the best evidence for the answer to the previous question?

A) Lines 10–12 ("as the . . . humanity")

B) Lines 21–24 ("The man . . . poor")

C) Lines 30–33 ("The real . . . have")

D) Lines 38–41 ("We must . . . all")

35

In Passage 2, Reason implies that evenly distributing wealth and property among individuals would have what consequence?

A) Neither the rich nor the poor would reap benefits.

B) All parties to the economy would improve their position.

C) The rich would take advantage to create their own monopolies.

D) The poor would be able to purchase property at decreased value.

36

Which choice provides the best evidence for the answer to the previous question?

A) Lines 50–52 ("The only . . . value")

B) Lines 56–59 ("It would . . . efficiency")

C) Lines 60–64 ("We therefore . . . affords")

D) Lines 75–78 ("Here we . . . adjustment")

37

As used in line 69, "just" most nearly means

A) only.

B) strict.

C) equal.

D) fair.

38

Reason in Passage 2 would most likely characterize the position taken by Platt in lines 19–20 ("Many of . . . uncomfortable") as

A) an accurate description of the root cause of the current economic situation of the poorer class.

B) a flawed assumption that generalizes the negative behavior of a few.

C) a surprising but realistic statement consistent with the economic trends of the times.

D) an offensive characterization of the rich that is not applicable to other classes of society.

39

Both authors would most likely agree that any social changes undertaken to fight poverty would be

A) likely to completely solve the problems of financial inequality.

B) a stopgap measure needed to prevent the wealthy from keeping their money.

C) unsuccessful without a drastic change in the mindset of the poor.

D) partial solutions that would present new sets of challenges.

CONTINUE ▶

40

Which choice best describes the way the two authors characterize effective ways to reduce poverty?

A) Platt believes that financial education is the key to reducing poverty in a society, while Reason believes that financial education is irrelevant if individuals do not participate.

B) Platt believes that poverty will be reduced only if those who are poor truly desire to lift themselves out of poverty, while Reason believes that poverty will be reduced only if society's wealth is redistributed.

C) Platt believes wage regulation from major industry is a step in the right direction, while Reason believes that such regulation will be ineffective.

D) Platt believes training clergy to minister to the poor is the most effective way of improving the lives of those in poverty, while Reason believes that unearned riches are a necessary feature of a society.

41

Based on Passage 1, Platt would most likely say that the "readjustment of distribution" Reason mentions in lines 42–43 would have no effect unless

A) property were owned collectively by all members of society.

B) profits from property sales were distributed equally amongst all citizens.

C) those in poverty exhibited sufficient effort to better themselves.

D) the number of available jobs increased enough to significantly lower unemployment.

CONTINUE

Questions 42–52 are based on the following passage and supplementary material.

This passage is excerpted from Thomas Hayden, "What Darwin Didn't Know." ©2009 by Smithsonian Magazine.

[The] first public airing of Darwinian evolution caused almost no stir whatsoever. But when Darwin published his ideas in book form the following
Line year, the reaction was quite different. *On the*
5 *Origin of Species by Means of Natural Selection, or the Preservation of Favoured Races in the Struggle for Life* soon sold out its first press run of 1,250 copies, and within a year some 4,250 copies were in circulation. Allies applauded it as a brilliant unifying
10 breakthrough; scientific rivals called attention to the gaps in his evidence, including what would come to be known as "missing links" in the fossil record; and prominent clergymen, politicians and others condemned the work and its far-reaching implications.
15 In 1864 Benjamin Disraeli, later Britain's prime minister, famously decried the idea—barely mentioned in *Origin*—that human beings too had evolved from earlier species. "Is man an ape or an angel?" he asked rhetorically at a conference. "I, my lord, I am on the
20 side of the angels. I repudiate with indignation and abhorrence those newfangled theories."

Darwin knew that plant and animal species could be sorted into groups by similarity, such that birds clustered into songbirds and raptors, say, with each
25 group subdivided again and again down to dozens or hundreds of distinct species. He also saw that the individuals within any given species, despite many similarities, also differed from one another—and some of those differences were passed from parents to their
30 offspring. And Darwin observed that nature had a brutally efficient method of rewarding any variation that helped an individual live longer, breed faster or leave more progeny. The reward for being a slightly faster or more alert antelope? The lions would eat
35 your slower neighbors first, granting you one more day in which to reproduce. After many generations and a great deal of time, the whole population would run faster, and with many such changes over time eventually become a new species. Evolution, Darwin's
40 "descent with modification through natural selection," would have occurred.

But what was the source of variation and what was the mechanism for passing change from generation to generation? Darwin "didn't know anything about
45 why organisms resemble their parents, or the basis of heritable variations in populations," says Niles Eldredge, a paleontologist at the American Museum of Natural History in New York City.

In Darwin's era, the man who did make progress
50 on the real mechanism of inheritance was the Austrian monk Gregor Mendel. In his abbey garden in the late 1850s and early 1860s, Mendel bred pea plants and found that the transmission of traits such as flower color and seed texture followed observable rules. An
55 offspring inherits a set of these genetic units from each parent. Since the early 1900s, those units of inheritance have been known as genes.

The objection certainly applied to the paucity of ancestral human fossils in Darwin's time. Years
60 of painstaking work by paleontologists, however, have filled in many of the important gaps. There are many more extinct species to be discovered, but the term "missing link" has for the most part become as outdated as the idea of special creation
65 for each species. Anthropologists once depicted human evolution as a version of the classic "March of Progress" image—a straight line from a crouching proto-ape, through successive stages of knuckle draggers and culminating in upright modern
70 human beings. "It was a fairly simple picture, but it was a simplicity born of ignorance," says biological anthropologist William Jungers of Stony Brook University in New York. "The last 30 years have seen an explosion of new finds."
75 Asked about gaps in Darwin's knowledge, Francisco Ayala, a biologist at the University of California at Irvine, laughs. "That's easy," he says. "Darwin didn't know 99 percent of what we know." Which may sound bad, Ayala goes on, but "the 1 percent he did know was
80 the most important part."

CONTINUE

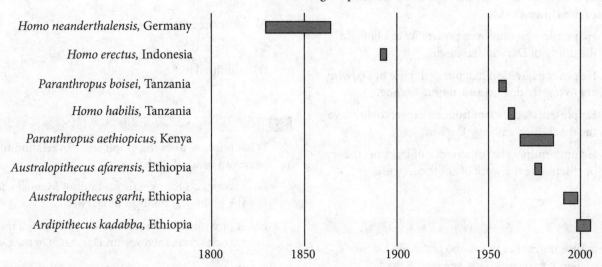

Human Fossil Discovery and Naming
*bars represent timespan between fossil discovery and initial naming of species

On the Origin of Species, published 1859

Over the course of the passage, the main focus shifts from

A) a description of Darwin's life to an overview of Darwin's published works.

B) detailed criticism of Darwin's controversial theory to qualified support for that theory.

C) Darwin's explanation of a scientific mystery to a summary of how other scientists facilitated that mystery's resolution.

D) the initial reception for Darwin's work to a broader discussion of how his findings continue to guide scientific research.

The author most strongly suggests that the largest reason Darwin's intellectual competitors took issue with his work was that it

A) didn't present a complete explanation of the hypothesized phenomenon.

B) presented ideas that didn't match what the church believed.

C) offended readers with its absurd questions.

D) unified what had been intentionally disparate ideas.

Which choice provides the best evidence for the answer to the previous question?

A) Lines 9–10 ("Allies . . . breakthrough")

B) Lines 10–12 ("scientific . . . record")

C) Lines 15–18 ("In 1864 . . . species")

D) Lines 20–21 ("I repudiate . . . theories")

The main purpose of the reference to lions in line 34 is to

A) disprove a questionable theory.

B) introduce a completely new idea.

C) reject a burgeoning controversy.

D) provide a clarifying example.

CONTINUE ➤

46

Which statement best describes the technique the author uses to advance the main point of the third paragraph (lines 42–48)?

A) He ponders an unproven possibility to highlight the utility of Darwin's research.

B) He poses a question that puzzled those of Darwin's era to foreshadow a forthcoming finding.

C) He presents a criticism from an expert to disprove the theory presented by Darwin.

D) He undermines the importance of Darwin's theory by discussing the work of another scientist.

47

The author notes that those who criticized Darwin's work when it first came out were

A) misguided in attacking scientific discovery based solely on the work of another scientist.

B) transparent in their jealous slander against his success.

C) mistaken because other scientists had already proven what Darwin had not.

D) correct in their complaints that his theory lacked sufficient supporting evidence.

48

Which choice provides the best evidence for the answer to the previous question?

A) Lines 4–8 ("*On the* . . . copies")

B) Lines 49–51 ("In Darwin's . . . Mendel")

C) Lines 58–59 ("The objection . . . time")

D) Lines 73–74 ("The last . . . finds")

49

As used in line 71, "born of" most nearly means

A) carried by.

B) generated from.

C) possessed by.

D) admitted to.

50

What purpose does the graph serve in relation to the passage as a whole?

A) It connects the genetic findings of Mendel with the biological findings of Darwin.

B) It provides indisputable evidence to prove the theories contained within Darwin's *On the Origin of Species*.

C) It reinforces a statement from an expert that much more has been learned since Darwin's scientific era.

D) It offers evidence that the fossils found by Darwin and his contemporaries were different from the fossils found in the next century.

CONTINUE

Which statement is best supported by the data presented in the graph?

A) Human fossils had been discovered in at least five locations by the time Darwin published *On the Origin of Species*.

B) Human fossils discovered in Tanzania were named more quickly than those found in Kenya.

C) Both *Paranthropus* species shown in the graph were discovered in the same country.

D) The more recently a new type of fossil was discovered, the less time it took scientists to name the species.

Based on information from both the graph and the passage, the anthropologists' depiction of the "March of Progress"

A) fails to address the discoveries of a variety of fossils from numerous human species.

B) accurately depicts the linear origin of modern man.

C) proves that Darwin's research on *Homo neanderthalensis* was accurate.

D) undermines the importance of fossil discoveries made around the world.

STOP
If you finish before time is called, you may check your work on this section only.
Do not turn to any other section in the test.

Writing and Language Test

35 MINUTES, 44 QUESTIONS

Turn to Section 2 of your answer sheet to answer the questions in this section.

DIRECTIONS

Each passage below is accompanied by a number of questions. For some questions, you will consider how the passage might be revised to improve the expression of ideas. For other questions, you will consider how the passage might be edited to correct errors in sentence structure, usage, or punctuation. A passage or a question may be accompanied by one or more graphics (such as a table or graph) that you will consider as you make revising and editing decisions.

Some questions will direct you to an underlined portion of a passage. Other questions will direct you to a location in a passage or ask you to think about the passage as a whole.

After reading each passage, choose the answer to each question that most effectively improves the quality of writing in the passage or that makes the passage conform to the conventions of standard written English. Many questions include a "NO CHANGE" option. Choose that option if you think the best choice is to leave the relevant portion of the passage as it is.

Questions 1–11 are based on the following passage.

NEH: A Human-Centered Agency

The National Endowment for the Humanities (NEH) is an independent federal agency that was created in 1965 to provide grants to humanities projects throughout the United States. Funding for the agency has been the **1** protagonist of debate for many years. Some critics **2** think the money that goes to the NEH would be better spent on infrastructure or job creation, while others object to the nature of some of the projects that receive funding.

1
A) NO CHANGE
B) significance
C) discipline
D) subject

2
A) NO CHANGE
B) thought
C) thinking
D) would think

CONTINUE

3 Therefore, the agency provides important services in all fifty states and has had a notable impact on American culture over the last fifty years.

    The NEH was founded as a direct response to an explosion in scientific research in the middle years of the 20th century. There was concern, especially among those in the fields of arts and humanities, that non-scientific pursuits were in danger of getting left behind or **4** overlooked. The NEH addresses this concern by distributing grant money in seven areas, including preservation, research, education, and digital humanities. Among the most notable projects that have been funded by the NEH over the last 50 years are the Ken Burns documentary *The Civil War*, the blockbuster Metropolitan Museum of Art exhibition "Treasures of **5** Tutankhamen"; and sixteen Pulitzer Prize-winning books.

3

A) NO CHANGE
B) Likewise,
C) However,
D) For instance,

4

A) NO CHANGE
B) in being overlooked.
C) of oversight.
D) to be overlooked.

5

A) NO CHANGE
B) Tutankhamen" and;
C) Tutankhamen," and
D) Tutankhamen" and,

CONTINUE

Although some critics of the NEH argue that the agency's spending is frivolous in an age when our country is in desperate need of spending on more concrete things like infrastructure, NEH grant money **6** which has a positive impact on local economies. Grants that support construction or renovation of facilities employ local construction workers, and the construction or expansion of a museum creates permanent jobs for staff. Preservation funds **7** likewise similarly create jobs for archivists and technicians. One striking example is the NEH-funded excavation of Historic Jamestown—the first permanent English colony in America—which has resulted in the creation of an entirely new local tourist industry. **8**

6

A) NO CHANGE

B) has

C) having

D) to have

7

A) NO CHANGE

B) in the same way

C) comparably

D) DELETE the underlined portion.

8

At this point, the writer is considering adding the following sentence.

> Jamestown was thought to be lost for hundreds of years—scholars knew where it should be, but found no evidence of it.

Should the writer make this addition here?

A) Yes, because it further explains why the discovery of Jamestown was important.

B) Yes, because it reinforces the importance of the NEH grant on the region's economy.

C) No, because it blurs the paragraph's focus on the far-reaching economic effects NEH grants can have.

D) No, because it undermines the idea that tourist attractions can contribute to the local economy.

CONTINUE

[1] As federal funding for scientific research and the military continues to increase, we should not forget Seaborg's words. [2] In the early 1960s, Glenn Seaborg, then head of the Atomic Energy Commission, expressed his support for establishing the NEH by **9** cautioning against an over-reliance on technology: "Science and technology are providing us with the means to travel swiftly. But what course do we take? This is the question that no computer can answer." [3] The issue should not be **10** weather to fund the NEH but how much. [4] NEH grants help inform the kind of cultural awareness that is vital to our roles as good citizens in a global community. **11**

9

Which choice most effectively sets up the quote that follows in this sentence?

A) NO CHANGE

B) emphasizing the importance of science over humanities:

C) lobbying for increased funding for computer research:

D) arguing for the importance of public art:

10

A) NO CHANGE

B) weather too

C) whether to

D) whether too

11

To make this paragraph most logical, sentence 1 should be placed

A) where it is now.

B) after sentence 2.

C) after sentence 3.

D) after sentence 4.

CONTINUE

Questions 12–22 are based on the following passage and supplementary material.

Tuition Reimbursement: A Mutual Benefit

All employers want a well-educated workforce, and one way to accomplish that goal is to provide tuition assistance benefits to employees. Tuition assistance programs are **12** commonplace; a 2019 study showed that 63% of U.S. employers offered undergraduate tuition assistance as a benefit—but their goals and guidelines vary widely. Companies that offer tuition assistance **13** see it as a benefit both to employees and to the company. Whether employees are taking classes that are related to their careers or not, tuition assistance programs result in improved morale, **14** also better job performance, and retention.

12
A) NO CHANGE
B) commonplace,
C) commonplace
D) commonplace—

13
A) NO CHANGE
B) seeing
C) have seen
D) sees

14
A) NO CHANGE
B) job performance,
C) job performance too,
D) additionally job performance,

CONTINUE

Those who are skeptical of tuition assistance programs argue that **15** the programs cost a lot and provide very little return on the investment. Some firms have instituted a requirement that employees receiving tuition benefits must stay with the company for a specific amount of time after completing their educations. **16** In any case, such clauses are hard to enforce, and research shows that they aren't necessary. Over 80% of workers who receive tuition benefits from their employers feel an increased sense of loyalty stemming from the investment, and they are in fact less likely to **17** leave—than the average employee is.

15

Which choice best establishes the argument that follows?

A) NO CHANGE

B) companies should place restrictions on the types of courses employees can be reimbursed for.

C) taking classes while working spreads employees too thin, resulting in lower productivity.

D) an employee may use the benefit to seek a position at a different company.

16

A) NO CHANGE

B) Consequently,

C) However,

D) Additionally,

17

A) NO CHANGE

B) leave;

C) leave,

D) leave

CONTINUE

Increased employee loyalty is not the only way that employers benefit from offering tuition assistance. The programs can also be powerful recruiting tools. Employers from the U.S. Armed Forces to Starbucks are able to attract workers who are interested in earning an education while they earn money, without having to [18] take out loans. Most companies require employees to earn a minimum grade in their classes, but student employees often find it easier to maintain their grades when they feel a responsibility to the company paying for their education, not just to themselves. Managers can also use tuition assistance programs to evaluate their employees. If an employee takes advantage of the optional benefit, the thinking [19] goes then he or she is likely to be a highly motivated and productive worker.

18

A) NO CHANGE

B) borrow money through educational loan programs.

C) go into debt by financing their educations with student loans.

D) take on the risky proposition of borrowing loan money that would leave them with a significant debt burden.

19

A) NO CHANGE

B) goes, then

C) goes; then

D) goes. Then

CONTINUE

Some companies are increasing the value of their investment in tuition assistance programs by restricting the benefit to classes that will provide their employees with necessary or helpful job skills. [20] In addition, some employers have even gone so far as to create custom degree or certification programs. The figure shows the ways in which a company can leverage its tuition assistance program to [21] make a killing on the company's investment in the program. As shown in the figure, the most effective programs will start with [22] a strategy to manage the workforce necessary for a particular field, which will lead to a secure workforce, will provide a reliable source of talent, and will ultimately make talent development proceed productively.

Benefits of Employee Tuition Assistance Programs

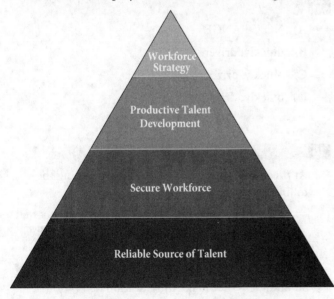

Workforce Strategy

Productive Talent Development

Secure Workforce

Reliable Source of Talent

20

A) NO CHANGE

B) By contrast,

C) In other words,

D) DELETE the underlined portion and begin the sentence with a capital letter.

21

A) NO CHANGE

B) provide the best return

C) make a whole lot of dough

D) earn a pile of money

22

Which choice makes the writer's description of the figure most accurate?

A) NO CHANGE

B) productive talent development, which will lead to strategies for managing the workforce necessary for a particular field, and will ultimately lead to a more stable source of talent and also a secure workforce.

C) productive talent development, which will create a secure workforce with a reliable source of talent, which will ultimately align with strategies for managing the workforce necessary for a particular field.

D) a reliable source of talented workers, which will contribute to a secure workforce, will productively develop that workforce, and will ultimately lead to strategies for managing the workforce necessary for a particular field.

CONTINUE →

Questions 23–33 are based on the following passage.

The Changing Face of Fast Food

Over the last three decades there [23] are a number of studies that have shown a strong correlation between the rise of fast food restaurants in the United States and the rise of obesity. Partly in response to this epidemic, a new trend has taken off in the restaurant business: "fast casual" food. It's difficult to precisely define what fast casual is, but it generally refers to restaurants that offer the traditional quick preparation and counter service of fast food at a slightly higher price point, with a focus on fresh, high-quality ingredients. Though many fast casual restaurants have menus that focus on a particular healthy type of food, such as salads or vegan foods, others offer the traditional burgers-and-fries fast food fare. But even fast casual burger joints [24] are often still cheaper than going to a sit-down restaurant.

It is generally agreed that Chipotle Mexican Grill started the fast casual trend when it opened its first restaurant in Denver in 1993. The chain grew [25] quickly. Driven by customers who were attracted to its fresh menu and sustainably sourced ingredients. Many within the fast food industry took notice—McDonald's even became a major investor—and the fast casual movement was born. [26]

[23]

A) NO CHANGE
B) have been
C) will be
D) had been

[24]

Which choice most effectively reinforces the definition of fast casual given earlier in the paragraph?

A) NO CHANGE
B) emphasize the higher quality and freshness of their ingredients.
C) serve salads as well as burgers and fries.
D) may contribute to the obesity epidemic.

[25]

A) NO CHANGE
B) quickly: driven
C) quickly, driven
D) quickly; driven

[26]

At this point, the writer is considering adding the following sentence.

It is somewhat unclear where the term fast casual came from—two different people are generally credited with coining the term, but it was trademarked in 1995 by Horatio Lonsdale-Hands.

Should the writer make this addition here?

A) Yes, because it provides important background for the information presented in the following paragraph.
B) Yes, because it clarifies the origins of the term "fast casual."
C) No, because it blurs the paragraph's focus on the beginnings of the fast casual movement.
D) No, because it distracts from the paragraph's main idea by introducing a figure whose role in the movement is unclear.

CONTINUE

Fast casual's focus on high-quality ingredients has been working. During the 2007–2009 recession, spending in the restaurant business declined for two **27** unbending years. **28** In fact, during that same period, fast casual business grew by double digits. Traditional fast food restaurants started changing in response. McDonald's, which is now a competitor of **29** Chipotle, having sold its interest in the burrito business in 2006, made the switch from frozen burger patties to fresh meat for its Quarter Pounders at most of its restaurants. This came after the company eliminated high fructose corn syrup from **30** they're buns and announced a plan to transition to using only eggs from cage-free chickens.

27

A) NO CHANGE
B) linear
C) even
D) straight

28

A) NO CHANGE
B) Unsurprisingly,
C) In other words,
D) In contrast,

29

A) NO CHANGE
B) Chipotle having sold its interest in the burrito business in 2006
C) Chipotle, having sold its interest in the burrito business in 2006
D) Chipotle having sold its interest, in the burrito business in 2006,

30

A) NO CHANGE
B) their
C) it's
D) its

CONTINUE

While the move to cage-free eggs has the potential to make a big impact on how chicken farms are run, it does nothing to address one of the bigger problems of fast food: [31] therefore, its lack of nutritional value. Critics also [32] question whether increasingly fast casual restaurants are actually healthy? The typical meal from Chipotle, for example, contains over 1,000 calories and a full-day's allowance of sodium. But [33] change is slowly coming. The pressure that fast casual restaurants are putting on their more traditional counterparts as well as the growing number that truly do serve healthy food are indications that consumers are paying more attention to what they put in their mouths and that the restaurant industry is responding.

31

A) NO CHANGE

B) indeed,

C) for instance,

D) specifically,

32

A) NO CHANGE

B) increasingly question whether fast casual restaurants are actually healthy?

C) question whether increasingly fast casual restaurants are actually healthy.

D) increasingly question whether fast casual restaurants are actually healthy.

33

A) NO CHANGE

B) slow changes are starting to arrive.

C) changes that take a long time are beginning to come.

D) arriving soon are those changes that never happen quickly.

CONTINUE

Questions 34–44 are based on the following passage.

Did the *Rite* Cause a Riot?

It is commonly understood that at the premiere of Igor Stravinsky's *The Rite of Spring* on May 29, 1913, the shocking nature of the ballet caused a riot to break out in the audience. The music started with an unnaturally high bassoon solo, which elicited shouts and jeers from the audience almost immediately. The furor only rose when the dancers from the Ballets Russes took the stage and began the jerky, convulsive movements of Vaslav Nijinsky's **34** choreography. The choreography was shocking because it was not characteristic of the grace and fluidity typically expected from ballet. A fight soon **35** broke up amidst the spectators, the orchestra was pelted with vegetables thrown by outraged audience members, and the police were called to restore order.

There are many theories **36** as to what caused the audience of *The Rite of Spring* to react so strongly. It may have been the dissonant nature of Stravinsky's music, with its constantly changing rhythms and jarring percussion, or the purposefully awkward, ungraceful movements of the dancers. The theme of the ballet **37** itself was a pagan ritual in which a virgin sacrifices herself to the god of spring, may also have upset some viewers. The negative reception was summed up by a **38** review, in *Le Figaro,* that proclaimed "We are sorry to see an artist such as M. Stravinsky involve himself in this disconcerting adventure."

34

Which choice most effectively combines the sentences at the underlined portion?

A) choreography, which was uncharacteristic through its lack of

B) choreography that lacked

C) choreography, because of it lacking in conveyance of

D) choreography through which Nijinsky tried not to convey

35

A) NO CHANGE

B) brought up among

C) broke out among

D) broke out between

36

Which choice best establishes the main idea of the paragraph?

A) NO CHANGE

B) about why Stravinsky composed such a controversial piece of music.

C) regarding the role of the police in the uproar.

D) surrounding which Russian folk traditions Stravinsky drew his inspiration from.

37

A) NO CHANGE

B) itself, being

C) itself

D) itself,

38

A) NO CHANGE

B) review, in *Le Figaro* that proclaimed,

C) review in *Le Figaro* that proclaimed,

D) review in *Le Figaro,* that proclaimed

CONTINUE ➡

Although several dozen eyewitness accounts of the evening exist, they are often contradictory and do little **39** to sort of exactly what happened in the Theatre des Champs-Elysees that night. In fact, if one makes a timeline of first-person accounts of the *Rite's* premiere, descriptions of the level of disruption and violence increase as the accounts get further away from the actual event. **40** On the other hand, it's likely that stories of the riot have gotten exaggerated over time.

39

A) NO CHANGE

B) to sort out

C) for sort out

D) for sort of

40

A) NO CHANGE

B) As a result,

C) At the same time,

D) In other words,

CONTINUE

[1] Scholars have also recently begun to suspect that the uproar may have been planned. [2] It is possible that he actually planted someone to start shouting, but more likely he simply set up an expectation for controversy. [3] There was impassioned debate in Paris in the early years of the 20th century between traditionalists and modernists that was **41** exemplified by the debate over the Eiffel Tower: modernists saw it as a mark of progress, while traditionalists saw it as a monstrosity. [4] Diaghilev likely caused members of both groups **42** that believed that others would react strongly to *The Rite of Spring*. [5] Serge Diaghilev, the founder of the Ballets Russes, was a savvy entrepreneur who understood that any publicity is good publicity. [6] From such charged expectations, it is **43** not unsurprising that controversy arose. **44**

41

The writer wants to add a supporting detail to explain the different views of the traditionalists and the modernists. Which choice best accomplishes this goal?

A) NO CHANGE

B) still going on today: *The Rite of Spring* remains a controversial piece of music in many circles.

C) not limited to music: people also argued over visual arts, architecture, and literature.

D) nothing new: there have always been people who will be upset by innovation of any kind, and there always will be.

42

A) NO CHANGE

B) believing

C) who believed

D) to believe

43

Which choice most effectively signals that the result the author mentions was expected?

A) NO CHANGE

B) surprising

C) not surprising

D) unusual

44

To make this paragraph most logical, sentence 5 should be placed

A) where it is now.

B) before sentence 2.

C) before sentence 3.

D) before sentence 4.

STOP

**If you finish before time is called, you may check your work on this section only.
Do not turn to any other section in the test.**

Math Test – No Calculator

25 MINUTES, 20 QUESTIONS

Turn to Section 3 of your answer sheet to answer the questions in this section.

CONTINUE →

1

Which of the following is equivalent to $10 + 2(x - 7)$?

A) $-14x + 10$

B) $2x + 24$

C) $2x + 3$

D) $2x - 4$

2

$$3x - \frac{y}{3} = 21$$

$$x = y + 7$$

Which ordered pair (x, y) satisfies the system of equations shown above?

A) $(0, -7)$

B) $(4, 27)$

C) $(7, 0)$

D) $(9, -16)$

3

$$a + b = 15$$

The equation above relates the number of hours, a, Kevin spends doing homework each week and the number of hours he spends watching television each week. If Kevin spends a total of 15 hours doing homework and watching television each week, what does the variable b represent?

A) The number of hours spent watching television for each hour spent doing homework

B) The number of hours spent watching television each week

C) The number of hours spent doing homework each week

D) The total number of hours spent doing homework and watching television each week

4

Josephine purchases a computer for $4,590. The computer decreases in value at a constant rate for 9 years, after which it is considered not to have any monetary value. How much is the computer worth 6 years after it is purchased?

A) $1,530

B) $2,295

C) $3,060

D) $4,080

CONTINUE

5

For $i = \sqrt{-1}$, which of the following complex numbers is equivalent to $(10i - 4i^2) - (7 - 3i)$?

A) $-11 + 7i$

B) $-3 + 13i$

C) $3 - 13i$

D) $11 - 7i$

6

What is the value of $f(-2)$ if $f(x) = \dfrac{x^2 + 4x - 8}{x - 2}$?

A) -3

B) -1

C) 1

D) 3

7

Heinrich must buy at least 100 shares of stock for his portfolio. The shares he buys will be from Stock X, which costs \$22 per share and Stock Y, which costs \$35 per share. His budget for buying stock is no more than \$4,500. He must buy at least 20 shares of Stock X and 15 shares of Stock Y. Which of the following represents the situation described if a is the number of shares of Stock X purchased and b is the number of shares of Stock Y purchased?

A) $22a + 35b \le 4{,}500$
   $a + b \ge 100$
   $a \le 20$
   $b \le 15$

B) $22a + 35b \le 4{,}500$
   $a + b \le 100$
   $a \le 20$
   $b \le 15$

C) $22a + 35b \le 4{,}500$
   $a + b \le 100$
   $a \ge 20$
   $b \ge 15$

D) $22a + 35b \le 4{,}500$
   $a + b \ge 100$
   $a \ge 20$
   $b \ge 15$

8

$$x^2 - 8x + 5$$

Which of the following is equivalent to the expression above?

A) $(x - 4)^2 - 11$

B) $(x - 4)^2 + 11$

C) $(x + 4)^2 - 11$

D) $(x + 4)^2 + 11$

CONTINUE

9

Juliet is selling photographs as part of a project for her entrepreneurship class. She sells the first 20 photographs for $10 each. Because the first 20 photographs sold so quickly, she raised the price of the photographs to $15 each for the rest of the project. After her expenses, Juliet earns a profit of 80% of the revenues from her sales. What is the least number of photographs she must sell for the rest of the project to earn a profit of at least $400 ?

A) 18

B) 20

C) 24

D) 32

10

$$\frac{p^{\frac{1}{4}} q^{-3}}{p^{-2} q^{\frac{1}{2}}}$$

Which of the following is equivalent to the expression above, where $p > 1$ and $q > 1$?

A) $\dfrac{p^2 \sqrt[4]{p}}{q^3 \sqrt{q}}$

B) $\dfrac{p^2 \sqrt{p}}{q^3 \sqrt{q}}$

C) $\dfrac{\sqrt[4]{p}}{q^3 \sqrt{q}}$

D) $\dfrac{\sqrt[4]{p}}{\sqrt[3]{q^2}}$

11

The graph of function g in the xy-plane is a parabola defined by $g(x) = (x - 2)(x - 4)$. Which of the following intervals contains the x-coordinate of the vertex of the graph?

A) $6 < x < 8$

B) $4 < x < 6$

C) $-2 < x < 4$

D) $-4 < x < -2$

12

$$xa^3 + ya^2 + za = 0$$

In the equation above, x, y, and z are constants. If the equation has roots -6, 0, and 4, which of the following is a factor of $xa^3 + ya^2 + za$?

A) $a - 2$

B) $a + 4$

C) $a - 6$

D) $a + 6$

CONTINUE

13

If the expression $\frac{1}{2}(x + c)(x - c)$, where c is a positive constant, can be rewritten as $\frac{1}{2}x^2 - 5$, what is the value of c ?

A) $\sqrt{5}$

B) $\sqrt{10}$

C) 5

D) 10

14

Which of the following is equivalent to $\dfrac{z^2 + 7z - 3}{z + 2}$?

A) $z + 5 - \dfrac{13}{z + 2}$

B) $z + 5 - \dfrac{7}{z + 2}$

C) $z + 9 - \dfrac{21}{z - 2}$

D) $z + 9 - \dfrac{15}{z - 2}$

15

A homeowners' association limits the dimensions of the pools that it will allow in a particular subdivision. The bylaws state that permits will only be granted for pools shaped like rectangular prisms, for which the sum of the length of the pool and the perimeter of the vertical side containing the ladder cannot exceed 200 meters. The perimeter of the ladder side is determined using the width and the depth of the pool. If a pool has a length of 75 meters and its width is 1.5 times its depth, which of the following shows the allowable depth a, in meters, of the pool?

A) $0 < a \le 62\dfrac{1}{2}$

B) $0 < a \le 50$

C) $0 < a \le 31\dfrac{1}{4}$

D) $0 < a \le 25$

CONTINUE

DIRECTIONS

For questions 16–20, solve the problem and enter your answer in the grid, as described below, on the answer sheet.

1. Although not required, it is suggested that you write your answer in the boxes at the top of the columns to help you fill in the circles accurately. You will receive credit only if the circles are filled in correctly.

2. Mark no more than one circle in any column.

3. No question has a negative answer.

4. Some problems may have more than one correct answer. In such cases, grid only one answer.

5. **Mixed numbers** such as $3\frac{1}{2}$ must be gridded as 3.5 or 7/2. (If 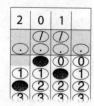 is entered into the grid, it will be interpreted as $\frac{31}{2}$, not as $3\frac{1}{2}$.)

6. **Decimal Answers:** If you obtain a decimal answer with more digits than the grid can accommodate, it may be either rounded or truncated, but it must fill the entire grid.

Answer: $\frac{7}{12}$ Answer: 2.5

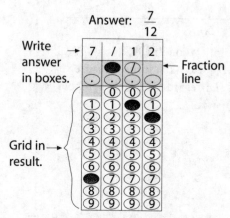

Write answer in boxes.   ← Fraction line

Grid in result.   ← Decimal point

Acceptable ways to grid $\frac{2}{3}$ are:

Answer: 201 – either position is correct

NOTE: You may start your answers in any column, space permitting. Columns you don't need to use should be left blank.

CONTINUE ▶

16

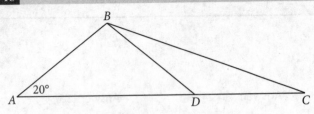

In the figure above, point D is on line AC, $AB = BD = CD$, and $AD = 15$. What is the measure, in degrees, of $\angle BCD$? (Disregard the degree symbol when gridding your answer.)

17

If $15 - 3b = 21$, what is the value of $5 - b$?

18

The graph of a line in the xy-plane passes through the point $(-2, k)$ and crosses the x-axis at the point $(-4, 0)$. The line crosses the y-axis at the point $(0, 12)$. What is the value of k?

CONTINUE

19

$$5(10x^2 - 300) + (9,844 + 50x^2)$$

The expression above can be rewritten in the form $cx^2 + d$, where c and d are constants. What is the value of $d - c$?

20

If n is a constant equal to the number of degrees in an angle measuring 3π radians, what is the value of n?

STOP
If you finish before time is called, you may check your work on this section only.
Do not turn to any other section in the test.

Math Test – Calculator

55 MINUTES, 38 QUESTIONS

Turn to Section 4 of your answer sheet to answer the questions in this section.

DIRECTIONS

For questions 1–30, solve each problem, choose the best answer from the choices provided, and fill in the corresponding circle on your answer sheet. **For questions 31–38,** solve the problem and enter your answer in the grid on the answer sheet. Please refer to the directions before question 31 on how to enter your answers in the grid. You may use any available space in your test booklet for scratch work.

NOTES

1. The use of a calculator **is permitted**.
2. All variables and expressions used represent real numbers unless otherwise indicated.
3. Figures provided in this test are drawn to scale unless otherwise indicated.
4. All figures lie in a plane unless otherwise indicated.
5. Unless otherwise indicated, the domain of a given function f is the set of all real numbers x for which $f(x)$ is a real number.

REFERENCE

$A = \pi r^2$
$C = 2\pi r$

$A = \ell w$

$A = \frac{1}{2}bh$

$c^2 = a^2 + b^2$

Special Right Triangles

$V = \ell wh$

$V = \pi r^2 h$

$V = \frac{4}{3}\pi r^3$

$V = \frac{1}{3}\pi r^2 h$

$V = \frac{1}{3}\ell wh$

The number of degrees of arc in a circle is 360.
The number of radians of arc in a circle is 2π.
The sum of the measures in degrees of the angles of a triangle is 180.

CONTINUE →

1

A certain homeowner uses a gas edger to clean up his lawn every time he mows. If the edger uses 160 milliliters of fuel each time, what is the maximum number of times the homeowner can edge his lawn with 8 liters of fuel? (1 liter = 1,000 milliliters)

A)   5

B)   50

C)   100

D) 1,000

2

Assignment Choice for Two Physics Classes

	Dr. Soper	Mr. Coelho	Total
Lab Report Only	17	21	38
Lab Report and Final Exam	3	2	5
Total	20	23	43

The table above shows the number of students who chose to be graded on lab reports only or on lab reports and final exams in Dr. Soper's and Mr. Coelho's physics classes. What fraction of the students in Dr. Soper's class chose to be graded on the lab report and final exam?

A) $\dfrac{3}{43}$

B) $\dfrac{5}{43}$

C) $\dfrac{3}{20}$

D) $\dfrac{3}{5}$

3

$$(4 - a^2) - (2a^2 - 6)$$

Which of the following expressions is equivalent to the one above?

A) $a^2 - 2$

B) $a^2 + 10$

C) $-3a^2 - 2$

D) $-3a^2 + 10$

4

The ordered pair $(3, -1)$ satisfies which of the following inequalities?

    I. $x + 3y > 0$

    II. $2x + 3y > 2$

    III. $x + y < 0$

A) I only

B) II only

C) I and III only

D) II and III only

CONTINUE

5

A psychology student randomly selected 300 people from a group of people who indicated that they preferred to work alone. Those 300 people were given a task to work on individually and then asked whether they were happy or unhappy while doing the task. Of those surveyed, 5% stated they were unhappy while doing the task. Which of the following inferences can appropriately be drawn from this survey result?

A) Few people who prefer working alone will be unhappy doing this task.

B) Few people who do not prefer working alone will be happy doing this task.

C) Less than 5% of people will be happy doing this task if they do not work alone.

D) Less than 5% of people will be unhappy doing this task if they work alone.

Questions 6 and 7 refer to the following information.

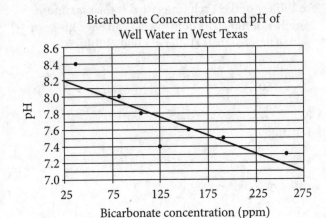

The scatterplot above shows the pH of seven well water samples in West Texas with respect to the bicarbonate concentration in ppm (parts per million). The line of best fit is also shown.

6

According to the scatterplot, which of the following statements about the relationship between a well's pH and its bicarbonate concentration is true?

A) A well with half as much bicarbonate as another well will have a pH twice that of the other well.

B) Wells that have more bicarbonate tend to have higher pH.

C) Wells that have more bicarbonate tend to have lower pH.

D) The bicarbonate concentration of the well water is unrelated to its pH.

CONTINUE

7

A new well is discovered in West Texas with a bicarbonate concentration of 225 ppm. According to the line of best fit, which of the following best approximates the pH of the well water?

A) 7.1

B) 7.3

C) 7.4

D) 8.4

8

$$25 = (ky - 1)^2$$

In the equation above, $y = -2$ is one solution. If k is a constant, what is a possible value of k ?

A) −13

B) −3

C)   0

D)   5

9

Andrew works out for 30 minutes every other day. If he spends 35% of his workout time one day waiting for the weight rack, how many seconds of that day's workout did he spend waiting for the weight rack?

A) 630

B)   35

C)   21

D)   10.5

10

If $8x - 8yz + 2 = 74$, what is the value of $x - yz$?

A)   2

B)   6

C)   9

D) 16

CONTINUE

11

A chef trimmed fat off a steak and was left with a steak weighing 8.80 ounces. If the weight of the fat was equal to 12 percent of the original weight, what was the original weight, in ounces, of the steak?

A) 8.92

B) 9.20

C) 10.00

D) 11.20

12

A backpacker is packing survival rations that consist of granola bars and packets of peanut butter. A granola bar has 470 food calories, and a packet of peanut butter has 90 food calories. The backpacker makes the survival rations using a total of 10 granola bars and packets of peanut butter combined, and the granola bars and packets of peanut butter have a total of 1,660 food calories. Which of the following systems of equations can be used to determine the number of granola bars, g, and packets of peanut butter, p, that are in the survival rations?

A) $280(g + p) = 1,660$
    $g - p = 10$

B) $90g + 470p = 1,660$
    $g - p = 10$

C) $90g + 470p = 1,660$
    $g = 10 - p$

D) $470g + 90p = 1,660$
    $g = 10 - p$

13

Ten floorboards with equal widths laid down side-to-side cover a width of approximately $7\frac{3}{4}$ feet. At this rate, which of the following is the closest to the number of boards laid side-to-side needed to cover a width of 32 feet?

A) 15

B) 20

C) 30

D) 40

CONTINUE

14

George's Distance from Home over Time

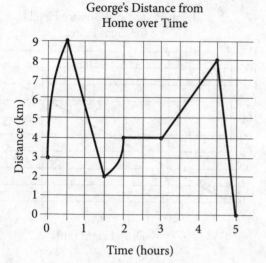

George recorded his distance from home over a five-hour period; his distance and time are shown in the graph above. According to the graph, which of the following is NOT true about the five-hour period?

A) George's distance from home increased at a constant rate during the first hour of the five-hour period.

B) George's distance from home reached its maximum during the first hour.

C) George remained a constant distance from his home for one hour.

D) George was moving further from his home for a longer period of time than he was moving closer to his home.

15

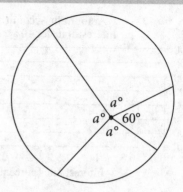

In the figure above, what is the value of a ?

A)   40

B)   60

C)   100

D)   130

16

$$y = -75x + 5,000$$

The equation above models the amount of money y, in dollars, remaining in Bo's bank account x days after the start of the fall semester. The amount of money in Bo's bank account is based on the money he earned over the summer and how much he spends per day during the fall semester. When the equation is graphed in the xy-plane, what does the slope of the graph represent in terms of the model?

A)   The total amount in Bo's bank account

B)   Daily spending of $5,000

C)   Daily spending of $75

D)   The amount of money Bo earned over the summer

CONTINUE ➤

17

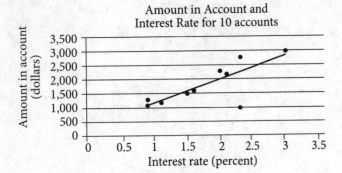

Amount in Account and
Interest Rate for 10 accounts

The scatterplot above shows data for ten accounts opened by a company, along with the line of best fit. For the account that contains the least amount of money, which of the following is closest to the difference of the actual amount and the amount predicted by the line of best fit?

A) $200

B) $500

C) $900

D) $1,200

18

If $\frac{x}{3} = 4$ and $x + y = 32$, what is the value of $x - y$?

A)   −24

B)   −8

C)   12

D)   32

19

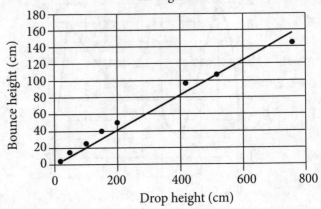

Drop Height and Bounce Height
for Eight Balls

The scatterplot above shows the height in centimeters for both the drop and bounce of eight different balls of the same type. The line of best fit for the data is also shown. According to the line of best fit, which of the following is closest to the predicted increase in bounce height, in centimeters, for every increase of 100 centimeters in drop height?

A)   25

B)   20

C)   15

D)   10

CONTINUE

Questions 20 and 21 refer to the following information.

Formula A: $BMI = \dfrac{w}{h^2}$

Formula B: $BMI = \dfrac{4w - 100}{5}$

The formulas above are used in nutrition to estimate the body mass index *BMI*, in kilograms per square meter, of adults whose weight *w* ranges between 50 and 100 kilograms and whose height *h* is measured in meters.

20

Based on Formula B, what is *w* in terms of *BMI* ?

A) $w = 5BMI + 25$

B) $w = 5BMI - 25$

C) $w = \dfrac{5BMI + 100}{4}$

D) $w = \dfrac{5BMI - 100}{4}$

21

If both Formulas A and B give the same estimate for *BMI*, which of the following expressions is equivalent to $4w - 100$?

A) $\dfrac{w}{h^2}$

B) $\dfrac{5w}{h^2}$

C) $\dfrac{5w}{4h^2}$

D) $\dfrac{5w + 100}{4h^2}$

22

The number of bacteria colonies *h* hours after the beginning of an experiment is given by the function $C(h) = 3^h - 2h + 20$. What does the number 20 represent in the function?

A) The final rate of growth, in colonies per hour

B) The initial rate of growth, in colonies per hour

C) One less than the initial number of bacteria colonies

D) One more than the final number of bacteria colonies

CONTINUE

23

Agricultural Land as a Percent of
Total Land Area, 2014

Country	Percent of Total Land Area
Brazil	33.8%
Canada	7.2%
Greenland	0.6%
Latvia	30.1%
Mexico	54.9%
New Zealand	42.2%
Russian Federation	13.3%
Turkey	50.1%
United States	44.6%

The World Bank measures the amount of land devoted to agriculture among all 196 countries in the world. The results from 9 of the countries are given in the table above. The median percent of agricultural land for all 196 countries is 34.95%. What is the difference between the median percent of agricultural land for these 9 countries and the median for all 196 countries?

A) 1.15%

B) 4.19%

C) 9.65%

D) 19.95%

24

To ship figurines, the figurines are placed in a rectangular box and then small packing pellets are added. The base of the box has an area of 4.4 in.^{2}, and the height of the box is 6.5 in. If the volume of the air in the box after the figures and pellets are added is 8.0 in.^{3}, which of the following is closest to the combined volume of the figurines and pellets in the box?

A) 1.9 in.^{3}

B) 20.6 in.^{3}

C) 28.6 in.^{3}

D) 117.84 in.^{3}

25

The economy of Argentina as measured by its Gross Domestic Product (GDP) is shrinking at a rate of 2.6% per year. In 2015, the GDP of Argentina was $630 billion. Which of the following functions represents Argentina's GDP, A, in billions of dollars, y years since 2015 ?

A) $A(y) = 630 - (1 - 0.26)y$

B) $A(y) = 630(1 - 0.26)^y$

C) $A(y) = 630 - (1 - 0.026)y$

D) $A(y) = 630(1 - 0.026)^y$

CONTINUE

Questions 26 and 27 refer to the following information.

Weights of Modern U.S. Coins

Coin	Grams	Drams
Penny	2.50	1.41
Nickel	5.00	2.82
Dime	2.25	1.27

The table above gives the average weight, expressed in both grams and drams, of three types of modern U.S. coins.

26

If y grams is equivalent to d drams, of the following, which best represents the relationship between y and d ?

A) $y = 1.8d$

B) $d = 1.8y$

C) $yd = 1.8$

D) $y = 0.56d$

27

If a bag of coins weighing 225 grams is filled with p pennies, n nickels, and d dimes, which of the following expresses d in terms of n and p ?

A) $100 - \dfrac{10}{9}(p + 2n)$

B) $100 + \dfrac{10}{9}(p + 2n)$

C) $100 - \dfrac{10}{9}(p - 2n)$

D) $100 + \dfrac{10}{9}(p - 2n)$

28

$$(x - 2)^2 + (y + 5)^2 = 36$$

If a circle in the xy-plane has the equation above, which of the following does NOT lie on the exterior of the circle?

A) $(2, 1)$

B) $(2, 5)$

C) $(5, 2)$

D) $(-1, 1)$

CONTINUE

Month	Number of Peppers
June	2,200
July	2,640

A farmer counted the number of peppers produced by a certain field in June and July. The number counted for each month was recorded in the table above. The farmer estimates that the percent increase from June to July would be half the percent increase from July to August. How many peppers does the farmer expect the field to produce in August?

A) 2,860

B) 2,904

C) 3,520

D) 3,696

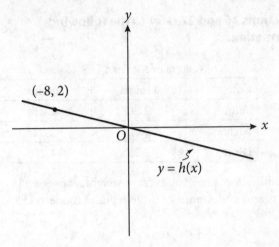

30

In the *xy*-plane above, a point (not shown) with coordinates (a, b) lies on the graph of the linear function h. If a and b are nonzero integers, what is the ratio of b to a ?

A) −4 to 1

B) −2 to 1

C) −1 to 2

D) −1 to 4

CONTINUE

DIRECTIONS

For questions 31–38, solve the problem and enter your answer in the grid, as described below, on the answer sheet.

1. Although not required, it is suggested that you write your answer in the boxes at the top of the columns to help you fill in the circles accurately. You will receive credit only if the circles are filled in correctly.

2. Mark no more than one circle in any column.

3. No question has a negative answer.

4. Some problems may have more than one correct answer. In such cases, grid only one answer.

5. **Mixed numbers** such as $3\frac{1}{2}$ must be gridded as 3.5 or 7/2. (If $\boxed{3\ 1\ /\ 2}$ is entered into the grid, it will be interpreted as $\frac{31}{2}$, not as $3\frac{1}{2}$.)

6. **Decimal Answers:** If you obtain a decimal answer with more digits than the grid can accommodate, it may be either rounded or truncated, but it must fill the entire grid.

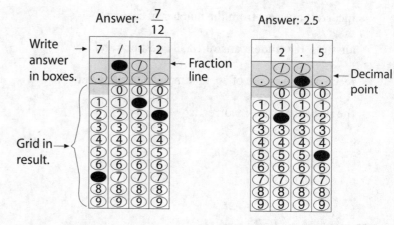

Acceptable ways to grid $\frac{2}{3}$ are:

Answer: 201 – either position is correct

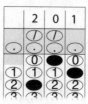 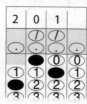

NOTE: You may start your answers in any column, space permitting. Columns you don't need to use should be left blank.

CONTINUE ➡

31

The raw score on a certain standardized test is determined by subtracting $\frac{1}{4}$ of the number of incorrect answers from the number of correct answers. If a student answered 30 questions and received a raw score of 20, how many questions did the student answer incorrectly?

32

One of the first diets to limit the intake of carbohydrates was prescribed by Dr. William Harvey in 1862. This diet consisted of three meals a day containing equal amounts of protein per meal. If protein contains 4 dietary calories per gram, and the diet consisted of 672 dietary calories of protein per meal, how much protein, to the nearest ounce, was in each meal? (1 ounce is approximately 28 grams.)

33

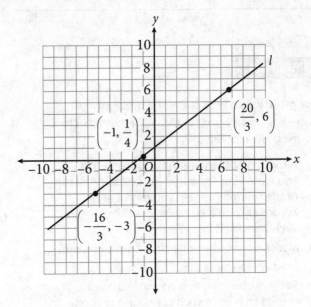

What is the slope of line l shown in the xy-plane above?

34

$$-9 - a = b$$
$$a^2 - 6a - 9 = b$$

If the ordered pair (a, b) satisfies the system of equations above, what is one possible value of a?

CONTINUE

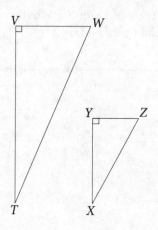

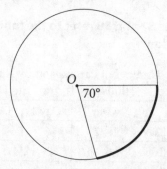

In the figure above, $\sin T = \dfrac{5}{13}$. If $TV = 24$, $XZ = 13$, and $\angle W \cong \angle Z$, what is $VW - YZ$?

Point O is the center of the circle above. What fraction of the circumference of the circle is the length of the bolded arc?

38

What is the mean number of bullseyes each participant threw on Day 2 ?

Questions 37 and 38 refer to the following information.

Number of Participants by Number of Bullseyes Thrown and Day

	Day 1	Day 2	Day 3	Total
0 Bullseyes	2	3	4	9
1 Bullseyes	1	3	1	5
2 Bullseyes	2	3	7	12
3 Bullseyes	5	2	1	8
4 Bullseyes	3	2	0	5
5 Bullseyes	2	2	2	6
Total	15	15	15	45

The same 15 participants, on each of 3 days, threw 5 darts in order to win a bullseye contest. The number of players throwing a given number of bullseyes on each day is shown in the table above.

37

No participant threw the same number of bullseyes on two different days. If a participant is selected at random, what is the probability that the selected participant threw 3 bullseyes on Day 1 or Day 2, given that the contestant threw 3 bullseyes on one of the three days?

END OF TEST

DO NOT RETURN TO A PREVIOUS SECTION.

Chapter 3
Practice Test 1:
Answers and
Explanations

DIAGNOSTIC TEST 1: MULTIPLE-CHOICE ANSWER KEY

Let's take a look at how you did on Diagnostic Test 1. Follow the two-step process in the scorecard below and go read the explanations for any questions you got wrong or you struggled with but got correct. Once you finish working through the scorecard and the explanations, go to the next chapter to make your study plan.

STEP 1 ▶ Check your answers and mark any correct answers with a ✔ in the appropriate column.

| Reading Comprehension |||||||||||
Q #	Ans.	✔	Chap. #	Section	Q #	Ans.	✔	Chap. #	Section
1	A		6	General Questions	27	A		6	Paired Questions
2	A		6	Paired Questions	28	A		6	Paired Questions
3	B		6	Paired Questions	29	C		6	Paired Questions
4	B		5	Using the Basic Approach	30	D		6	Paired Questions
5	B		5	Using the Basic Approach	31	A		5	Using the Basic Approach
6	C		6	Paired Questions	32	A		5	Vocabulary-in-Context
7	C		6	Paired Questions	33	C		6	Paired Questions
8	A		5	Vocabulary-in-Context	34	C		6	Paired Questions
9	C		6	Purpose Questions	35	A		6	Paired Questions
10	D		6	Purpose Questions	36	B		6	Paired Questions
11	A		6	General Questions	37	D		5	Vocabulary-in-Context
12	A		5	Vocabulary-in-Context	38	B		5	Using the Basic Approach
13	A		6	Purpose Questions	39	D		6	Dual Passages
14	D		6	Paired Questions	40	B		6	Dual Passages
15	C		6	Paired Questions	41	C		6	Dual Passages
16	C		5	Vocabulary-in-Context	42	D		6	General Questions
17	B		6	Paired Questions	43	A		6	Paired Questions
18	B		6	Paired Questions	44	B		6	Paired Questions
19	A		6	Charts and Graphs	45	D		6	Purpose Questions
20	D		6	Charts and Graphs	46	B		5	Using the Basic Approach
21	C		6	Charts and Graphs	47	D		6	Paired Questions
22	D		6	General Questions	48	C		6	Paired Questions
23	B		5	Vocabulary-in-Context	49	B		5	Vocabulary-in-Context
24	B		6	Purpose Questions	50	C		6	Charts and Graphs
25	C		6	Purpose Questions	51	B		6	Charts and Graphs
26	D		5	Using the Basic Approach	52	A		6	Charts and Graphs

Writing and Language

Q #	Ans.	✔	Chap. #	Section	Q #	Ans.	✔	Chap. #	Section
1	D		10	Vocabulary	23	B		10	Verbs
2	A		10	Verbs	24	B		11	Purpose
3	C		10	Transitions	25	C		12	STOP, GO, & the Vertical Line Test
4	A		10	Verbs	26	D		11	Adding and Deleting
5	C		12	Commas	27	D		10	Vocabulary
6	B		12	Punctuation Questions in Disguise	28	D		10	Transitions
7	D		10	Concision	29	A		12	A Slight Pause for Commas
8	C		11	Adding and Deleting	30	D		10	Pronouns
9	A		11	Purpose	31	D		10	Transitions
10	C		10	More Fun with Words	32	D		10	Precision
11	B		11	Order	33	A		10	Concision
12	D		12	STOP, GO, & the Vertical Line Test	34	B		11	Combining Sentences
13	A		10	Verbs	35	C		10	More Fun with Words
14	B		10	More Fun with Words	36	A		11	Purpose
15	D		11	Purpose	37	D		12	Punctuation Questions in Disguise
16	C		10	Transitions	38	C		12	A Slight Pause for Commas
17	D		12	STOP, GO, & the Vertical Line Test	39	B		10	More Fun with Words
18	A		10	Concision	40	D		10	Transitions
19	B		12	A Slight Pause for Commas	41	A		11	Purpose
20	D		10	Concision	42	D		10	Verbs
21	B		10	Vocabulary	43	C		11	Purpose
22	D		11	What Do Graphs Have to Do with Grammar?	44	B		11	Order

Math (No Calculator)

Q #	Ans.	✔	Chap. #	Section	Q #	Ans.	✔	Chap. #	Section
1	D		16	Plugging In Your Own Numbers	11	C		18	Root, Solutions, and x-intercepts
2	C		16	Plugging In the Answers (PITA)	12	D		18	Root, Solutions, and x-intercepts
3	B		16	Meaning In Context	13	B		16	Plugging In Your Own Numbers
4	A		17	Rates	14	A		16	Plugging In Your Own Numbers
5	B		15	Imaginary and Complex Numbers	15	D		15	Solving Inequalities
6	D		18	Function Fundamentals	16	10		19	Triangles
7	D		15	Write Your Own System of Equations	17	7		15	Solving for Expressions
8	A		16	Plugging In Your Own Numbers	18	6		18	Equations of a Line
9	B		16	Plugging In the Answers (PITA)	19	8,244		15	Simplifying Expressions
10	A		14	Exponents and Square Roots	20	540		19	Converting Degrees to Radians

				Math (Calculator)						
Q #	Ans.	✔	Chap. #	Section	Q #	Ans.	✔	Chap. #	Section
1	B		17	Ratios and Proportions	20	C		15	Fundamentals of SAT Algebra
2	C		14	How to Read Charts and Graphs	21	B		15	Simultaneous Equations
3	D		15	Fundamentals of SAT Algebra	22	C		16	Meaning In Context
4	B		15	Solving Inequalities	23	A		17	What Is a Median?
5	A		14	Surveys on the SAT	24	B		19	Volume
6	C		14	How to Read Charts and Graphs	25	D		17	Percentages: Advanced Principles
7	B		14	How to Read Charts and Graphs	26	A		15	SAT Algebra: Cracking the System
8	B		16	Plugging In the Answers (PITA)	27	A		15	SAT Algebra: Cracking the System
9	A		17	Ratios and Proportions	28	A		18	Equation of a Circle
10	C		15	Solving for Expressions	29	D		17	Percent Change
11	C		16	Plugging In the Answers (PITA)	30	D		18	The Coordinate Plane
12	D		15	Write Your Own System of Equations	31	8		15	SAT Algebra: Cracking the System
13	D		17	Ratios and Proportions	32	6		17	Ratios and Proportions
14	A		14	How to Read Charts and Graphs	33	$\frac{3}{4}$ or .75		18	Slope
15	C		19	Circles	34	0 or 5		15	Simultaneous Equations
16	C		16	Meaning In Context	35	5		19	Triangles
17	D		14	How to Read Charts and Graphs	36	$\frac{7}{36}$ or .194		19	Circles
18	B		15	Simultaneous Equations	37	$\frac{7}{8}$ or .875		17	Probability
19	B		14	How to Read Charts and Graphs	38	$\frac{11}{5}$ or .2.2		17	Averages

 To determine your score, follow the instructions in the flow chart below. To find the Scaled Score for any section, match the Raw Score (number of correct answers) from the left-hand column to the Scaled Score from the appropriate column for that section.

RAW SCORE CONVERSION TABLE SECTION AND TEST SCORES

Raw Score (# of correct answers)	Math Test Score	Reading Test Score	Writing and Language Test Score	Raw Score (# of correct answers)	Math Test Score	Reading Test Score	Writing and Language Test Score
0	200	10	10	30	530	28	29
1	200	10	10	31	540	28	30
2	210	10	10	32	550	29	30
3	230	11	10	33	560	29	31
4	240	12	11	34	560	30	32
5	260	13	12	35	570	30	32
6	280	14	13	36	580	31	33
7	290	15	13	37	590	31	34
8	310	15	14	38	600	32	34
9	320	16	15	39	600	32	35
10	330	17	16	40	610	33	36
11	340	17	16	41	620	33	37
12	360	18	17	42	630	34	38
13	370	19	18	43	640	35	39
14	380	19	19	44	650	35	40
15	390	20	19	45	660	36	
16	410	20	20	46	670	37	
17	420	21	21	47	670	37	
18	430	21	21	48	680	38	
19	440	22	22	49	690	38	
20	450	22	23	50	700	39	
21	460	23	23	51	710	40	
22	470	23	24	52	730	40	
23	480	24	25	53	740		
24	480	24	25	54	750		
25	490	25	26	55	760		
26	500	25	26	56	780		
27	510	26	27	57	790		
28	520	26	28	58	800		
29	520	27	28				

Please note that the numbers in the table may shift slightly depending on the SAT's scale from test to test; however, you can still use this table to get an idea of how your performance on the practice tests will translate to the actual SAT.

CONVERSION EQUATION SECTION AND TEST SCORES

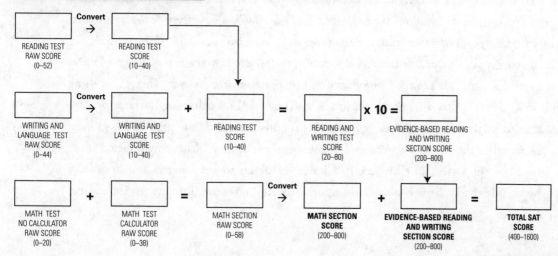

PRACTICE TEST 1 EXPLANATIONS

Section 1: Reading

1. **A** This question asks about a major theme of the passage. Because this is a general question, it should be done after the specific questions have been completed. Throughout the passage, the main character speaks of his love for Amy, discusses their relationship, and then worries about his ability to be a good husband because he might not have any money. Find an answer that's consistent with this prediction. Choice (A) is a solid paraphrase of this structure, so keep it. Choice (B) can be eliminated because the references to money and poverty make the passage about more than *unequivocal joy*. Choice (C) can be eliminated because it doesn't include any reference to the happiness and love from the first part of the passage. Choice (D) matches the narrator's fear of not succeeding, but like (C), it does not include any mention of love or happiness. Eliminate (D). The correct answer is (A).

2. **A** This question asks about the narrator's wife and how she responds to his declaration of love. Notice that it is the first question in a paired set, so it can be answered in tandem with Q3. Start with the answers to Q3 first. The lines for (3A) describe Amy as *slender fashioned* yet *gloriously strong*. These lines have nothing to do with the narrator's declaration of love, so eliminate (3A). The lines for (3B) say that she *spoke with such a sweet decision* and that her response was a *bond with eternity*. These lines support (2A), so draw a line connecting those two answers. Choice (3C) references Amy's wish *to become his wife*. These lines also might seem to support (2A), but there is no actual pledge in (3C) as there is in (3B). Eliminate (3C). The lines for (3D) reference a poem the narrator sent Amy. Although (2D) mentions writing poetry, it is the narrator who writes the poetry, not Amy. Eliminate (3D). Without support from Q3, (2B), (2C), and (2D) can be eliminated. The correct answers are (2A) and (3B).

3. **B** (See explanation above.)

4. **B** This question asks about a technique the author uses to express Amy's desire to marry the narrator. Lines 26–27 say that *Amy wished nothing but to become his wife*. Use those lines to find the window and read carefully. Within the window, the narrator asks *Delay? Why should there be delay?* He then goes on to say that *Amy wished nothing but to become his wife*, so he isn't actually asking for a reason to delay the marriage. Eliminate any answers that are not supported by the text. Choice (A) says that the narrator describes her *youthful enthusiasm* as a *major motivating factor*. There is nothing in the window to support that answer, so eliminate it. Choice (B) says that the narrator *presents a hypothetical question* that is *immediately refuted*. This is consistent with the prediction, so keep it. Choice (C) says that the narrator *applauds her decision* as a reflection of her unparalleled inner strength. This is not supported, so eliminate it. Choice (D) refers to her *sincerity* and *dedication* fostered by her maidenhood. This is also not supported by the text, so eliminate it. The correct answer is (B).

5. **B** This question asks about the narrator's book writing as compared with his love-letter writing. In lines 29–31, the narrator says that *his brain burned with visions of the books he would…write, but his hand was incapable of anything but a love-letter.* Therefore, compared to his love-letter writing, his book writing is not happening. Eliminate anything that is not consistent with this prediction. Choices (A), (C), and (D) can all be eliminated, because *agreeable, fiery,* and *imaginative* are not consistent with the prediction. Choice (B), *stalled,* is the only answer choice consistent with the idea of "not happening." The correct answer is (B).

6. **C** This question asks about a distinction made between Amy and the narrator. Notice that this is the first question in a paired set, so it can be done in tandem with Q7. Start with the answers to Q7 first. Choice (7A) describes how the narrator sees Amy, that she's *beautiful beyond anything his heart could imagine.* These lines could support (6B), so draw a line connecting those two answers. The lines for (7B) describe Amy's ability to see the narrator's wishes in *the simplest as in the greatest things* and then acting upon those. These lines describe Amy, but there's no contrast with the narrator. Eliminate (7B). The lines for (7C) refer to Latin and Greek and state that Amy should *learn both, that there might be nothing wanting in the communion….* These lines support (6C), so draw a line connecting those two answers. The lines for (7D) refer to Amy wanting to wait on their honeymoon until the narrator sells his book. Those lines show a contrast between the two characters, but they don't support any of the answers for Q6. Eliminate (7D). Go back to the two pairs of connected answers and read a little more around each set of lines given. Choices (6B) and (7A) initially seem to connect, but there's no mention of the narrator's *common appeal.* Choices (6C) and (7C) have a solid connection. The text refers to *how much she had read,* but not *Latin and Greek.* The lines go on to say that *she should learn them…*as *the old masters…had been such strength to him,* clearly supporting the contrast between her *conventional education* and his *love of language.* The correct answers are (6C) and (7C).

7. **C** (See explanation above.)

8. **A** This question asks what *wanting* most nearly means in line 40. Go back to the text, find the word *wanting,* and cross it out. Then read the window carefully, using context clues to determine another word that would fit in the text. The text refers to Amy's lack of knowledge about Latin and Greek, and then says that she should learn them, so *there might be nothing wanting in the communion between….* The missing word must mean something like "missing" or "failing." Choice (A), *lacking,* is consistent with this prediction. Choices (B) and (D) are both possible definitions for *wanting,* but they do not fit with the context of the passage. Eliminate both of them. Choice (C), *pleasing,* is not consistent with "missing" or "failing." Eliminate (C). The correct answer is (A).

9.   **C**   This question asks about the narrator's use of the phrase *what happiness lurked in embryo* as it refers to his publishers. Carefully read the window around lines 48–49 to determine what the narrator is saying about the publishers. He says that for his *marriage holiday* with Amy, he must get *a good price for a book* and that the publishers *must be kind*. He goes on to ask if they know what happiness lurks *within their foolish cheque-books*. The publishers, therefore, have a lot of power over whether or not Amy and the narrator will be happy, because their marriage holiday is totally dependent on whether or not they give the narrator a good price for his book. The correct answer should be consistent with the idea of "having power." Choice (A) can be eliminated because the narrator is hoping the publishers will be *kind*, but there's no evidence as to whether they actually are or not. They might be *wealthy*, but there's no mention of that in the text, so eliminate (B). Choice (C), *influential*, is consistent with the prediction, so keep it. Choice (D) might initially look good, because *foolish* is in the text, but it is not consistent with "having power." Eliminate (D). The correct answer is (C).

10.   **D**   This question asks about the function of the final paragraph. Carefully read the paragraph and determine its function in the context of the passage. Throughout the passage, the narrator talks about Amy and his love for her. Then, at the end, he suddenly starts to worry about poverty, finding himself very concerned about the *chilling of brain and heart* and *the dread feeling of helplessness*. This final paragraph describes a concern of the narrator. Eliminate any answer choices that aren't consistent with this prediction. Choice (A) can be eliminated because this paragraph shifts from the narrator's focus on Amy to his concern about poverty. Choice (B) can also be eliminated because there is no mention in the paragraph of *long-term effects…on [his] relationship*. Although the narrator worries that he *cannot support his wife*, he's worried about his ability to support her financially. There is nothing in the text to support *revealing his hysteria*. Eliminate (C). Choice (D) is consistent with the prediction. The correct answer is (D).

11.   **A**   This question asks about the main purpose of the passage. Because it is a general question, it should be done after all the specific questions have been completed. The passage begins with a description of GPS and how it works, and then introduces a problem with GPS. The passage continues by describing a more reliable alternative to GPS called the eLoran system. Eliminate any answer choices that are inconsistent with this prediction. Choice (A) is a clear paraphrase of the prediction, so keep it. Choice (B) can be eliminated because how *clocks and satellites determine distance and location* is a detail in the passage, not its main idea. Choice (C) can be eliminated because there are no discussions about problems within specific industries. Choice (D) can be eliminated because the main idea of the passage is not to *praise developers*. The correct answer is (A).

12. **A** This question asks what *conceived* most nearly means in line 13. Go back to the text, find the word *conceived*, and cross it out. Then read the window carefully, using context clues to determine another word that would fit in the text. The passage says that GPS was *initially conceived to aid navigation*, but that now it's a *much more critical function of the system*. There has been a change in how GPS is used since it was first developed. The missing word must mean something like "thought of" or "created." Choice (A) is consistent with this prediction, so keep it. While *understood* is a possible definition for *conceived*, the meaning does not fit with the context of the passage, so eliminate (B). The passage does not refer to GPS being either *absorbed* or *accepted*, so (C) and (D) can also be eliminated. The correct answer is (A).

13. **A** This question asks about the purpose of the lines provided. Go back to the window and read carefully to determine why the author included those lines. The lines ask a question about what would happen if GPS *were wiped out*. The text then goes on to answer that question with the response, "Nobody knows." These lines present a potential complication with GPS, so find an answer consistent with that prediction. Choice (A) is a solid paraphrase of "presenting a potential complication," so keep it. Choice (B) can be eliminated because no *corrections* are being made. Choice (C) can also be eliminated because nothing is being *reconsidered,* and (D) can be eliminated because no idea is being *undermined*. The correct answer is (A).

14. **D** This question asks about *Lombardi's attitude toward "flying clock radios."* Carefully read the window around line 28. After the *flying clock radios* are mentioned, Lombardi says, *"Nobody knows exactly what would happen."* He then goes on to say, *"there's no back-up."* Therefore, Lombardi is a bit concerned about potential problems with the current state of GPS. Eliminate answer choices that aren't consistent with this prediction. Choice (A) can be eliminated because *confident* is not consistent with *concerned*. Choice (B) does say that Lombardi is *concerned*, but then goes on to say that concern comes from not knowing how the radios will *interact with eLoran systems*. That's not consistent with the prediction, so eliminate (B). Choice (C) might initially look attractive because of the phrase *no one knows*, but the text says that no one knows what will happen if the GPS system is wiped out, whereas (C) says no one knows *exactly how they work*. Additionally, Lombardi is not *annoyed*. Eliminate (C). Choice (D) matches the prediction. The correct answer is (D).

15. **C** This question is the best evidence question in a paired set. Because Q14 was a specific question, choose the answer to Q15 that includes the lines used to make the prediction for Q14. The correct answer is (C).

16. **C** This question asks what *bulk* most nearly means in line 34. Go back to the text, find the word *bulk*, and cross it out. Then read the window carefully, using context clues to determine another word that would fit in the text. The text says *the bulk of a more promising…system already exists* and then goes on to explain that it's mostly finished. The missing word must mean something like "big part." Eliminate any answers that are not consistent with that prediction. Choices (A) and (B) are potential definitions of *bulk*, but they aren't consistent with the text. Eliminate both of them. There is evidence in the text to support the idea that the eLoran system is not completely and totally ready to be used, so (D), *totality*, is too strong. Choice (C) is consistent with the idea of "big part." The correct answer is (C).

17. **B** The question asks about the reason for a situation as given by John Garamendi. Use *John Garamendi* as lead words, and search for them in the window. Carefully read the window around line 57 to determine why Garamendi says *America isn't using the eLoran system*. In lines 62–65, he says *there are two kinds of time,…real time…and then federal time, which seems to be the forever time.* He goes on to say that although the *eLoran system was identified as a backup fifteen years ago…here we are, federal time, not yet done.* Therefore, although the technology exists, the federal government is moving slowly and preventing the technology from being used. Eliminate anything that isn't consistent with that prediction. Choice (A) mentions *real time*, but the problem is not with the eLoran system itself. Eliminate (A). Choice (B) is consistent with the prediction, so keep it. Choice (C) can be eliminated because there is no indication in the text that the decision-makers are *scared*. Choice (D) is not mentioned in the window at all, so eliminate it. The correct answer is (B).

18. **B** This is the best evidence question for Q17, which was a specific question containing lead words. The correct answer will be the lines that contain Garamendi's quote about federal time being slower than real time. The correct answer is (B).

19. **A** This question asks which group is closest in percentage to the percentage of users 18–29 in May 2011. Look at figure 1 to find that 18–29-year-olds in May 2011 are roughly 60%. Two other groups are close to that: 30–49 in May 2011 and 50+ in February 2012. Only one of those is an answer choice. The correct answer is (A).

20. **D** This question asks which statement is supported by figure 2. Go to the figure and eliminate any answer choices not supported by the data. Choice (A) can be eliminated because the Automotive industry accounts for 39%, which is greater than one-third. Choice (B) can be eliminated because Surveying/Mapping is 8%, which is greater than the 6% covered by Precision Agriculture. Choice (C) can be eliminated because there is no indication of levels of importance. Choice (D) is correct because Automotive and Marine add up to 72% and the other industries combined add up to only 28%. The correct answer is (D).

21. **C** This question asks what additional information would be useful in figure 2 to evaluate the claim that *globally synchronized time is a much more critical function of the system.* As written, figure 2 shows the percentage of GPS equipment revenue from each industry. There is no indication of how important GPS is to each industry, which would be the information needed to evaluate the claim. Choice (A) can be eliminated because that information would not show the importance of GPS in each industry. Choice (B) can also be eliminated, because although it would give information about each industry, the number of people using GPS doesn't give information about GPS's importance without additional information about the total number of people in each industry. Keep (C) because knowing that a high percentage of an industry relies on GPS would help evaluate the claim that GPS is a critical function. Choice (D) can be eliminated because the amount of revenue does not show how often GPS is used within an industry. The correct answer is (C).

22. **D** The question asks for the primary purpose of the passage. Because this is a general question, it should be done after all of the specific questions. The passage discusses the receding of the Dead Sea, suggests that water policy is a cause of the decline, and outlines some possible solutions. Eliminate (A) because it does not include any discussion of the Dead Sea. In addition, although the passage discusses water policy, it does not discuss *how* the governments *create water policy.* Eliminate (B) because *the many species of plants, fish, and mammals that live in the Dead Sea region* are discussed only in the first paragraph of the passage. Eliminate (C) because, although the passage does *explain the consequences of continuing current water policy in the Dead Sea region*, this choice does not include the passage's discussion of solutions. Keep (D) because it includes both the *cause of the decline* and *a possible remedy.* The correct answer is (D).

23. **B** The question asks what the word *harbor* means in line 12. Go back to the text, find the word *harbor*, and cross it out. Carefully read the surrounding text to determine another word that would fit in the blank based on the context of the passage. The first paragraph states that *a half-dozen oases along the shore harbor scores of indigenous species of plants, fish and mammals....* The next sentence states that many birds *take refuge here* during migration. The correct answer should mean something like "give refuge." Eliminate (A): although it might be true that the oases *nourish* these animal species, *nourish* does not mean "give refuge." Keep (B) because *shelter* is consistent with "give refuge." Eliminate (C) and (D) because the oases are neither "amusing" the animals, nor "thinking carefully" about them. The correct answer is (B).

24. **B** The question asks why the author mentions *Ein Feshka*. Look for *Ein Feshka*, which is first mentioned in line 18. The beginning of the paragraph briefly describes the history and *ecosystems of the Dead Sea region*. The last two sentences of the paragraph state that *Ein Feshka, a lush expanse of tamarisk, papyrus, oleander and pools of crystal water, was used by the late king Hussein of Jordan as a private playground in the 1950s and early '60s. But as the Dead Sea recedes, the springs that feed the oases are moving along with it; many experts believe that Ein Feshka and other oases could wither away within five years*. The author mentions Ein Feshka to transition from describing the area to talking about a specific problem. Eliminate (A) because Ein Feshka is not mentioned primarily as *a historical site*; the region's *ecosystems* are emphasized. Keep (B) because this choice describes the *transition from a description of the region to a discussion of a problem the region faces*. Eliminate (C) because the region's *ecosystems* are emphasized; the author's purpose is not to discuss *a need for recreation areas*. Eliminate (D) because the author is introducing an environmental problem, not arguing that *environmental impacts vary with different types of land use*. The correct answer is (B).

25. **C** The question asks why the author includes *both Labor and Likud governments* in lines 28–33. Use the given line reference to find the window. The second paragraph states that *[f]rom the first years of Israel's existence as a Jewish state...both Labor and Likud governments have bestowed generous water subsidies on the nation's farmers*. Eliminate (A) because, although governments of both parties have had similar water policies, the passage does not state that there was *cooperation between* the parties. Eliminate (B) because the passage mentions only two parties; there is not enough support for the statement that the policy is popular among *all political parties*. Keep (C) because the fact that *both Labor and Likud governments* have given the water subsidies indicates *broad political support*. Notice that this choice is similar to (B), but it does not contain wording as strong as *all political parties*. Eliminate (D) because, although the passage criticizes the current water policy, it does not criticize the *politicization of natural resources*. The correct answer is (C).

26. **D** The question asks who or what the *water laws favor*. Look for references to water laws in the passage. The second paragraph states that *both Labor and Likud governments have bestowed generous water subsidies on the nation's farmers*. Eliminate (A) because there is no mention of *the tourism industry* benefitting from the water laws. Eliminate (B): although the passage indicates that the *government* sets the water laws, it does not state that the water laws *favor* the government. Eliminate (C) because the passage indicates that *environmental activists* advocate for eliminating the current water subsidies. Keep (D) because *farmers* is supported by the second paragraph. The correct answer is (D).

27.   **A**   The question asks what can *be inferred about the agriculture industry in the Dead Sea region*. Notice that the following question is a best evidence question, so this question and Q28 can be answered in tandem. Look at the answers for Q28 first. The lines for (28A) state that *today, agriculture accounts for just 3 percent of Israel's gross national product and uses up to half of its fresh water*. Check the answers for Q27 to see if any of the answers are supported by those lines. They support (27A), which says that the agricultural industry's *use of water is disproportionate to its impact on the economy*, so connect those two answers. Next, consider the lines for (28B). Those lines state that *the region's agricultural lobby is strong*, so look to see if those lines support any of the answers for Q27. They are close to (27C), but that choice states that the agricultural industry is the *most powerful influence* on regional governments, which is not supported. Eliminate (28B). The lines in (28C) state that *these facilities will provide as much as 106 billion gallons of fresh water annually for agricultural and domestic consumption*. This is close to (27D), but it doesn't quite match: the lines in (28C) mention both *agricultural and domestic consumption*, while (27D) indicates that the agricultural industry alone *will soon use more than 100 billion gallons of water from treatment facilities*. Eliminate (28C). The lines in (28D) quote an environmental activist saying, *"Israeli agriculture is incredibly mismanaged."* These lines do not support any of the answers for Q27, so eliminate (28D). Without support from Q28, (27B), (27C), and (27D) can be eliminated. The correct answers are (27A) and (28A).

28.   **A**   (See explanation above.)

29.   **C**   The question asks what the author suggests *about tourism*. Notice that the following question is a best evidence question, so this question and Q30 can be answered in tandem. Look at the answers for Q30 first. The lines for (30A) discuss a location that *was used by the late king Hussein of Jordan as a private playground in the 1950s and early '60s*, but they do not reference *tourism*, so eliminate (30A). The lines for (30B) discuss *the building of wastewater treatment plants and desalination facilities*; they do not reference *tourism*, so eliminate (30B). The lines for (30C) discuss what farmers *could be planting*; they don't reference *tourism*, so eliminate (30C). The lines for (30D) say that the *potential tourism-dollar return of a healthy river and a healthy Dead Sea outweighs the little return that agriculture offers*. Check the answers for Q29 to see if any of the answers are supported by those lines. Choice (29C) is a paraphrase of this quote: *Tourism may provide more benefit to the Dead Sea region's economy than agriculture currently does*. Connect these two answers. Without support from Q30, (29A), (29B), and (29D) can be eliminated. The correct answers are (29C) and (30D).

30.   **D**   (See explanation above.)

31.　**A**　The question asks for the main idea of the final paragraph. Carefully read the last paragraph. The first sentence of this paragraph states that *Friends of the Earth is also taking its message to the farmers themselves—encouraging them to plant crops that use less water and spelling out the advantages of renewed tourism in the area.* The final sentence states that the *potential tourism-dollar return of a healthy river and a healthy Dead Sea outweighs the little return that agriculture offers.* Keep (A), since the paragraph discusses *new practices* that *farmers can adopt* to *use less water*, leading to a *healthy Dead Sea.* Eliminate (B) because the paragraph does not say that *farmers should stop planting crops;* it only says that farmers should *plant crops that use less water.* Eliminate (C) because the passage it does not make a prediction that *tourism will soon replace agriculture;* it says that the *potential tourism-dollar return* would be better than the return from agriculture, if the Dead Sea and Jordan River were healthy. Eliminate (D) because the paragraph discusses recommendations for farmers from environmental activists; it does not discuss how *farmers are adjusting their practices.* The correct answer is (A).

32.　**A**　This question asks what *aim* most nearly means in line 1. Go back to the text, find the word *aim*, and cross it out. Then read the window carefully, using context clues to determine another word that would fit in the text. The window talks about what *charitable people* should want: not so much *giving with money in hand or religious teaching*, but *friendly intercourse…and the desire to stimulate hope and energy.* The author is talking about what the people should want to do, so the missing word must mean something like "goal" or "end game." Eliminate any answers that aren't consistent with this prediction. Choice (A), *focus*, is consistent, so keep that answer. Choice (B) might initially look attractive because *aim* and *shot* seem to go together, but *shot* is not consistent with the prediction. Eliminate (B). Choices (C) and (D) can both be eliminated, because neither *gift* nor *ability* is a "goal" or "end game" that a person could work toward. The correct answer is (A).

33.　**C**　This question asks how Platt suggests society reduce poverty. Notice that this is the first question in a paired set, so it can be done in tandem with Q34. Begin with the answers to Q34. The lines for (34A) say that even the lowest types of humanity can be improved, but the author doesn't specify how. This answer does not support any of the answers for Q33, so eliminate (34A). The lines for (34B) talk about how those who want to be reformers will study the problem, but again, this does not support any of the answers for Q33. Eliminate (34B). The lines for (34C) say that someone who wants to be a reformer will *tell the poor how they may become less so,* and not rob *others of what they have.* These lines support (33C), so draw a line connecting those two answers. The lines for (34D) say that the problem can be solved by *regenerat[ing] the entire social fabric* through laws, aims, instincts, and individual cooperation. Although these lines address the question, they do not support any of the answers for Q33. Eliminate (34D). Without support from Q34, (33A), (33B), and (33D) can be eliminated. The correct answers are (33C) and (34C).

34.　**C**　(See explanation above.)

35. **A** This question asks for the consequence of evenly distributing wealth and property, according to Reason. Notice that this is the first question in a paired set, so it can be done in tandem with Q36. Consider the answers for Q36 first. The lines for (36A) say that the only remaining option is *democratizing the monopoly value*. This says nothing about a consequence of evenly distributing the wealth among individuals, so these lines do not support any of the answers for Q35. Eliminate (36A). The lines for (36B) say that *such distribution would destroy its productive efficiency*. These lines support (35A), so draw a line connecting those two answers. The lines for (36C) advocate for *collective ownership* and say nothing about individual ownership. Eliminate (36C). The lines for (36D) do not discuss any consequences of wealth distribution among individuals, so this answer does not support any of the answers for Q35. Eliminate (36D). Without support from Q36, (35B), (35C), and (35D) can all be eliminated. The correct answers are (35A) and (36B).

36. **B** (See explanation above.)

37. **D** This question asks what *just* most nearly means in line 69. Go back to the text, find the word *just*, and cross it out. Then read the window carefully, using context clues to determine another word that would fit in the text. The text refers to a worker's *just wage*, earlier referring to it as the *full reward of his labor*. Therefore, the missing word must mean something like "fair" or "earned." Choices (A) and (B) can be eliminated right away because neither *only* nor *strict* means "fair." Choices (C) and (D) might both initially look good, but there is no indication that all workers are receiving the same wage. The text says only that the worker will receive the *full reward of his labor*, or everything he earned for the work he did. This is *fair*, but not necessarily *equal*. Eliminate (C). The correct answer is (D).

38. **B** This question asks how Reason would characterize the position taken by Platt that *[m]any of [the poor] prefer to be uncomfortable*. Reason says that poverty is caused by men not earning a fair wage and by an uneven distribution of wealth and property. He says that *poverty, undeserved and unavoidable, must be the lot of many, while equally undeserved income will be reaped...by many others*. Reason sees poverty as a problem with society, not with individuals. Choices (A) and (C) can both be eliminated because Reason does not agree with Platt. Choice (B) is consistent with the text, so keep it. Choice (D) can be eliminated because Platt's statement is about the poor, not the rich. The correct answer is (B).

39. **D** This question asks which statement both authors would agree with. Because this is a general question that asks about both passages, it should be answered after all the questions about each individual passage, and after any specific questions about both passages have been completed. Choice (A) can be eliminated because neither man believed any solutions would *completely solve* the problems of poverty. Choice (B) can be eliminated because Platt did not believe any measures needed to be taken to redistribute wealth. Reason, on the other hand, did not believe a *change of mindset* for the poor was needed to solve the problem, so (C) can also be eliminated. Choice (D) is consistent with both authors. The correct answer is (D).

40.   **B**   This question asks how both authors would characterize effective ways to reduce poverty. Because it is a general question about both passages, it should be done after the questions for each individual passage and the specific questions for both passages have been completed. Platt believed that reducing poverty required education of the poor and a change in the way the poor perceive the world. Reason believed that the structure of society reinforced poor and rich classes, and that redistributing wealth and allowing for fair wages would alleviate the problems. Eliminate any answers that aren't consistent with that prediction. Choice (A) can be eliminated because, although the first part is consistent with Platt, the second part is not consistent with Reason. Choice (B) is consistent with the prediction, so keep it. Choice (C) can be eliminated because Reason advocated for a fair wage, not Platt. Choice (D) can also be eliminated because Reason did believe that unearned riches were a feature of society, but not that they were *necessary*. The correct answer is (B).

41.   **C**   This question asks what Platt would say was necessary for Reason's *readjustment of distribution* to be effective. Platt's focus in Passage 1 was about shifting the mindset of the poor and helping them learn that they don't actually want to be poor. The correct answer should be consistent with that viewpoint. Eliminate (A) because that is Reason's idea, not Platt's. Choice (B) can also be eliminated, because Platt does not say anything about evenly distributing profits from property sales. Choice (C) is consistent with Platt's point of view, so keep it. Choice (D) can be eliminated because Platt does not advocate for increasing the number of jobs. The correct answer is (C).

42.   **D**   This question asks how the main focus of the passage shifts. Because this is a general question, it should be done after the specific questions. The passage begins with a discussion of the *first public airing of Darwinian evolution* and how it *caused almost no stir whatsoever*. It continues with how Darwin finally managed to drum up some controversy, both with religious-leaning folks and other scientists who were less than thrilled with some of the missing pieces of Darwin's research. The passage ends with a discussion of how Darwin's work laid the foundation for other researchers to come along in later years and fill in the gaps. Find an answer choice that's consistent with that prediction. Choice (A) can be eliminated because the passage does not discuss *Darwin's life*. Choice (B) can be eliminated because, although the passage does contain both *criticism* and *support* for his theory, it does not shift from one to the other. Choice (C) can be eliminated because the other scientists did not *facilitate that mystery's resolution*. Choice (D) is consistent with the prediction. The correct answer is (D).

43.   **A**   This question asks why Darwin's *intellectual competitors took issue with his work*. Notice that although it's the first question in a paired set, it's a specific question. Q45 gives a line reference in the second paragraph, so you can be confident that questions 42 and 43 will be answered in the first paragraph, since questions go in consecutive order. So skim the first paragraph to find something about Darwin's *intellectual competitors*. Lines 11–12 say that *scientific rivals called attention to the gaps in his evidence*. Eliminate any answer choices that aren't consistent with this prediction. Choice (A) is a direct paraphrase of the prediction, so keep it. Choice (B) can be eliminated because although the text mentions *clergymen* who *condemned the work*, the question asks about the *intellectual competitors* rather than the *church*. Choice (C) can be eliminated because the passage does not discuss whether *readers* were *offended*. Choice (D) might initially look good, but read carefully. It was his *allies* who applauded it as a *unifying breakthrough*, not his *rivals*. Eliminate (D). The correct answer is (A).

44. **B**   This is the best evidence question for a specific question. Choose the answer that includes the lines used to predict the answer to Q43: *scientific rivals called attention to the gaps in his evidence.* The correct answer is (B).

45. **D**   This question asks about the purpose of the reference to the lions in the second paragraph. Use the line reference to find the window and read carefully. The text describes Darwin's theory of nature rewarding the faster and stronger, and then gives an example of an antelope that is *slightly faster or more alert.* Its neighbors would be eaten by lions first, *granting [the antelope] one more day to live and reproduce.* Over time, the fastest antelopes reproduce, making more of the faster antelopes. Thus, the lions are mentioned in order to provide a specific example of Darwin's theory. The correct answer should be consistent with this prediction. The reference is there neither to *disprove* nor *reject*, so eliminate (A) and (C). Choice (B) can be eliminated because no *completely new idea* is being introduced. Choice (D) matches the prediction. The correct answer is (D).

46. **B**   This question asks what technique the author uses to advance the main point of the third paragraph. Go back to the third paragraph and read carefully. The author begins the paragraph with a question, asking about *the source of variation* and the *mechanism for passing change from generation to generation.* He then goes on to say that *Darwin didn't know.* Eliminate any answer choices that aren't consistent with this prediction. Choice (A) can be eliminated because the author is not *ponder[ing] an unproven possibility.* Choice (B) is consistent with the text. Keep it. Choices (C) and (D) can be eliminated because the author is neither *presenting a criticism* nor *undermining the importance of Darwin's theory.* The correct answer is (B).

47. **D**   This question asks about those who criticized Darwin's work when it first came out. Notice that this is the first question in a paired set, so it can be done in tandem with Q48. Consider the answers to Q48 first. The lines for (48A) say that Darwin's book *sold out its first press run.* These lines have nothing to do with those who criticized Darwin's work, so eliminate (48A). The lines for (48B) say that the one who made real progress was Mendel. Although these lines mention another scientist, which could initially make (47A) look like a good match, there is no indication the critics were *misguided in attacking a scientific discovery.* Eliminate (48B). The lines for (48C) say that an objection *certainly applied to the paucity of...fossils.* These lines support the ideas in (47D), both that the critics had a point, and that there was a lack of evidence (*paucity* means "lack"). Draw a line connecting these two answers. The lines for (48D) state that there has been an explosion of finds in the last 30 years, which does not support any of the answers for Q47. Eliminate (48D). Without support from Q48, (47A), (47B), and (47C) can all be eliminated. The correct answers are (47D) and (48C).

48. **C**   (See explanation above.)

49. **B** This question asks what *born of* most nearly means in line 71. Go back to the text, find the phrase *born of*, and cross it out. Then read the window carefully, using context clues to determine another word or phrase that would fit in the text. The text talks about anthropologists who *depicted human evolution as...a straight line from a crouching proto-ape through successive stages...to modern human beings*. The text goes on to say it *was a fairly simple picture* that was *born from ignorance*, because in the last 30 years there has *been an explosion of new finds*. Therefore, the missing phrase must mean something like "came from" or "started with." Eliminate any answer choices that aren't consistent with this prediction. Choice (A) can be eliminated because the simplicity was not *carried by* ignorance. Choice (B) is consistent with the prediction, so keep it. Choices (C) and (D) can both be eliminated because the ignorance itself wasn't doing anything, and neither *possessed by* nor *admitted to* is consistent with the prediction. The correct answer is (B).

50. **C** This question asks what purpose the graph serves in relation to the passage as a whole. Consider the graph. It shows a timeline from 1800 to past 2000, indicating the timeframes between the discovery of a fossil and the naming of the species. The label indicates that Darwin's *On the Origin of Species* was published in 1859. Eliminate any answers that are inconsistent with the information provided. Choice (A) can be eliminated because there are no specifics in the graph about either Mendel's or Darwin's discoveries. Choice (B) can also be eliminated because there is nothing that provides *indisputable evidence* to prove Darwin's theories. Choice (C) is consistent with the graph, because the graph shows the discoveries of multiple species after Darwin published his work. Keep (C). Choice (D) can be eliminated because there is nothing on the graph that indicates similarities or differences between species. The correct answer is (C).

51. **B** This question asks which statement is best supported by the graph. Eliminate anything that is inconsistent with the information in the graph. Choice (A) can be eliminated because only one fossil discovery is marked on the graph before 1859. Choice (B) is consistent with the graph, because there was less time between discovery and naming of the fossils in Tanzania than there was for the fossils discovered in Kenya. Keep (B). Choice (C) can be eliminated because one *Paranthropus* was discovered in Tanzania and another was discovered in Kenya. Choice (D) can be eliminated because it took scientists longer to name *Australopithecus garhi* than it did for them to name *Australopithecus afarensis*, even though the *garhi* species was found after the *afarensis*. The correct answer is (B).

52. **A** This question asks what can be supported about anthropologists' depiction of the "March of Progress" based on the passage and the graph. Lines 65–70 say that *anthropologists once depicted human evolution as a version of the classic "March of Progress" image—a straight line from a crouching proto-ape...culminating in upright humans beings*. The text goes on to quote a contemporary biological anthropologist saying that it *was a fairly simple picture, but...it was a simplicity born of ignorance*. Choice (A) is consistent with both the graph and the passage, so keep it. Choice (B) can be eliminated because the text says that the image was *born of ignorance*. Choice (C) can also be eliminated because the image is incorrect, so it does not *prove* anything. Choice (D) can be eliminated because the image does not *undermine any discoveries*. The correct answer is (A).

Section 2: Writing and Language

1. **D** The vocabulary is changing in the answer choices, so the question is testing word choice. Look for a word whose definition is consistent with the other ideas in the sentence. The sentence discusses *funding for the agency* and that there is a *debate* about it, so the definition should mean "topic" or "focus." *Protagonist* means "the main character," so eliminate (A). *Significance* means "importance" or "meaning," so eliminate (B). *Discipline* can mean "punishment" or "branch of knowledge," so eliminate (C). *Subject* means "topic," so keep (D). The correct answer is (D).

2. **A** Verbs are changing in the answer choices, so the question is testing consistency of verbs. A verb must be consistent with its subject and with the other verbs in the sentence. The sentence says *while others object*, so the correct verb will be consistent with *object*, which is present tense. *Think* is consistent with *object*, so keep (A). *Thought* and *would think* are in the past tense, so eliminate (B) and (D). *Thinking* makes the idea incomplete, so eliminate (C). The correct answer is (A).

3. **C** Transitions are changing in the answer choices, so the question is testing consistency of transitions. The transition should connect the ideas in the previous and current sentences. The previous sentence discusses *critics* and *others* who *object to the nature of some of the projects that receive funding*. The current sentence says that *the agency provides important services* and *has had a notable impact on American culture*. The ideas in the sentences are opposite, so look for a transition that changes the direction of the ideas. *Therefore* and *likewise* keep the ideas in the same direction, so eliminate (A) and (B). *However* changes the direction, so keep (C). *For instance* introduces an example, so eliminate (D). The correct answer is (C).

4. **A** The number of words is changing in the answer choices, so the question is testing concision. First determine whether the phrases before *overlooked* are necessary. Removing the phrases does not change the meaning of the sentence, so the phrases are not necessary. Eliminate (B) and (D). *Oversight* is not consistent with *left behind*, so eliminate (C). The correct answer is (A).

5. **C** Punctuation is changing in the answer choices, so the question is testing STOP and GO punctuation. Use the Vertical Line Test to identify the ideas as complete or incomplete. Draw the vertical line between *Tutankhamen* and *and*. The phrase *Among the most notable projects that have been funded by the NEH over the last 50 years are the Ken Burns documentary* The Civil War, *the blockbuster Metropolitan Museum of Art exhibition "Treasures of Tutankhamen"* is an incomplete idea. The phrase *sixteen Pulitzer Prize-winning books* is an incomplete idea. STOP punctuation cannot be used for two incomplete ideas, so eliminate (A). Choice (B) places the STOP punctuation after *and*. Even with the new placement, both phrases are incomplete ideas, so eliminate (B). Comma placement in (C) and (D) is changing, so check for the four ways to use a comma. The sentence contains a list. The comma should go before *and*, so eliminate (D). The correct answer is (C).

6.   **B**   Verbs are changing in the answer choices, so the question is testing consistency of verbs. A verb must be consistent with its subject and with the other verbs in the sentence. The subject relating to the verb is *NEH grant money*, which is singular. This does not immediately eliminate any answer choices. The other verbs in the sentence are *argue* and *is*. *Which has* creates an incomplete idea, so eliminate (A). *Has* is consistent with the other verbs, so keep (B). *Having* and *to have* are not consistent with the other verbs, so eliminate (C) and (D). The correct answer is (B).

7.   **D**   The phrases are changing in the answer choices, so the question is testing word choice. There is also the option to DELETE; consider this choice carefully, as it's often the correct answer. The three choices—*likewise, in the same way,* and *comparably*—basically mean the same thing. The sentence already uses the word *similarly*, so there's no need to repeat the idea. The phrase should be deleted to make the sentence more concise. The correct answer is (D).

8.   **C**   Note the question! The question asks whether the sentence should be added, so it's testing consistency. If the content of the new sentence is consistent with the ideas surrounding it, then it should be added. The paragraph discusses the *NEH grant money's positive impact on local economie*s and the example of *Jamestown* and the *new local tourist industry*. The new sentence discusses the history of Jamestown, which is not consistent with the ideas in the text. Therefore, the sentence should not be added. Eliminate (A) and (B). Keep (C) because it states that the new sentence blurs the focus of the paragraph. Eliminate (D) because it does not undermine the ideas in the paragraph. The correct answer is (C).

9.   **A**   Note the question! The question asks which choice sets up the quote, so it's testing consistency. The correct choice should be consistent with the idea in the quote. The quote says *Science and technology are providing us with the means to travel swiftly. But what course do we take? This is the question that no computer can answer*. Look for the choice that is consistent with the idea of caution about technology. Choice (A) is consistent, so keep it. There is no mention of the *humanities*, so eliminate (B). The quote does not discuss *funding*, so eliminate (C). There is no mention of *public art* in the quote, so eliminate (D). The correct answer is (A).

10.   **C**   The vocabulary is changing in the answer choices, so the question is testing word choice. Look for a word whose definition is consistent with the other ideas in the sentence. *Weather* refers to conditions in the atmosphere, while *whether* indicates multiple options, so eliminate (A) and (B). *Too* means "also," so eliminate (D). The correct answer is (C).

11.   **B**   Note the question! The question asks where sentence 1 should be placed, so it's testing consistency. Determine the subject matter of the sentence, and find the other sentence that also discusses that information. Sentence 1 says that *we should not forget Seaborg's words*. Sentence 2 introduces *Glenn Seaborg* and his words. Therefore, sentence 1 should follow sentence 2. The correct answer is (B).

12.   **D**   The punctuation is changing in the answer choices, so the question is testing STOP and GO punctuation. Use the Vertical Line Test and identify the ideas as complete or incomplete. Draw the vertical line between *commonplace* and *a 2013 study*. The phrase *Tuition assistance programs are commonplace* is a complete idea. The phrase *a 2013 study showed that 61% of U.S. employers offered undergraduate tuition assistance as a benefit—but their goals and guidelines vary widely* is a complete idea. GO punctuation cannot be used between two complete ideas, so eliminate (B) and (C). Both STOP and HALF-STOP punctuation can be used so check to see if a dash is needed. Since *a 2013 study showed that 61% of U.S. employers offered undergraduate tuition assistance as a benefit* is an unnecessary idea, it needs a pair of dashes around it, similar to a pair of commas. The correct answer is (D).

13.   **A**   Verbs are changing in the answer choices, so the question is testing consistency of verbs. A verb must be consistent with its subject and with the other verbs in the sentence. The subject for the verb is *companies*, which is plural. *Sees* is singular and is not consistent with the subject, so eliminate (D). There are no other verbs in the sentence so check the sentences before and after. Other verbs in those sentences are *vary*, *are taking*, and *result,* which are in the present tense. *See,* which is also in the present tense, is consistent with the other verbs, so keep (A). *Seeing* and *have seen* are not consistent with the other verbs, so eliminate (B) and (C). The correct answer is (A).

14.   **B**   The number of words is changing in the answer choices, so the question is testing consistency and concision. The sentence contains a list; *improved morale, retention,* and the underlined item. Look for an answer choice that is consistent with the other two items and does not contain unnecessary words. Only (B) is consistent and concise. The correct answer is (B).

15.   **D**   Note the question! The question asks for a choice that establishes the argument that follows, so it's testing consistency. The following sentence says that *Some firms have instituted a requirement that employees receiving tuition benefits must stay with the company for a specific amount of time after completing their educations.* Look for an answer choice that is consistent with the argument. The argument does not discuss *cost, types of courses,* or *productivity,* so eliminate (A), (B), and (C). Requiring employees to *stay with the company* is a way to prevent employees from seeking *a position at a different company,* so the correct answer is (D).

16.   **C**   Transitions are changing in the answer choices, so the question is testing consistency of transitions. The transition should connect the ideas in the previous and current sentences. The previous sentence discusses *a requirement that employees receiving tuition benefits must stay with the company for a specific amount of time.* The current sentence says that *such clauses are hard to enforce*. The ideas in the sentences are opposite, so look for a transition that changes the direction of the ideas. *In any case, consequently,* and *additionally* keep the same direction, so eliminate (A), (B), and (D). *However* changes the direction of the ideas. The correct answer is (C).

17. **D** The punctuation is changing in the answer choices, so the question is testing STOP and GO punctuation. Use the Vertical Line Test and identify the ideas as complete or incomplete. Draw the vertical line between *leave* and *than*. The phrase *Over 80% of workers who receive tuition benefits from their employers feel an increased sense of loyalty stemming from the investment, and they are in fact less likely to leave* is a complete idea. The phrase *than the average employee is* is an incomplete idea. STOP punctuation cannot be used with an incomplete idea, so eliminate (B). The second phrase is not a list or an explanation, so there is no need for HALF-STOP punctuation. Eliminate (A). Check the reasons to use a comma. The sentence does not contain a list, so check for unnecessary information. The phrase *and they are in fact less likely to leave* cannot be removed from the sentence, so it is necessary. There is no reason to use a comma, so eliminate (C). The correct answer is (D).

18. **A** The number of words is changing, so the question is testing concision. Since all the choices discuss *loans* and basically mean the same thing, choose the answer choice that is most concise. The correct answer is (A).

19. **B** Punctuation is changing in the answer choices, so the question is testing STOP and GO punctuation. Use the Vertical Line Test and identify the ideas as complete or incomplete. Draw the vertical line between *goes* and *then*. The phrase *If an employee takes advantage of the optional benefit, the thinking goes* is an incomplete idea. The phrase *then he or she is likely to be a highly motivated and productive worker* is an incomplete idea. Only GO punctuation can be used between two incomplete ideas, so eliminate (C) and (D). Check to see if a comma is necessary. The phrase *the thinking goes* is unnecessary and needs a pair of commas around it. The correct answer is (B).

20. **D** The phrases are changing in the answer choices, so the question is testing precision and concision. There is also the option to DELETE; consider this choice carefully as it's often the correct answer. The three choices do not correctly connect the two ideas. The phrase should be deleted to make the sentence more concise. The correct answer is (D).

21. **B** The vocabulary in the phrases is changing in the answer choices, so the question is testing word choice. The correct choice will be consistent with the ideas and tone of the passage. Choices (A), (C), and (D) are too informal, so they are not consistent with the tone of the passage. The correct answer is (B).

22. **D** Note the question! The question asks for a description that is accurate based on the figure. Look at the figure and read the title and any labels. The figure shows a pyramid with four levels. Look for an answer choice that is consistent with the order of the levels. The base of the pyramid is *reliable source of talent*, so eliminate (A), (B), and (C). The correct answer is (D).

23. **B** Verbs are changing in the answer choices, so the question is testing consistency of verbs. A verb must be consistent with its subject and with the other verbs in the sentence. The other verb in the sentence is *have shown*, so the correct answer must be consistent with this verb. Only *have been* is consistent. The correct answer is (B).

24. **B** Note the question! The question asks for a choice that reinforces the definition of fast casual, so it's testing consistency. The paragraph states that *fast casual...generally refers to restaurants that offer the traditional quick preparation and counter service of fast food at a slightly higher price point, with a focus on fresh, high-quality ingredients.* Although fast casual has a slightly higher price point than fast food, no information is given about the cost of sit-down restaurants, so eliminate (A). *Higher quality and freshness of their ingredients* is consistent, so keep (B). There is no mention of *salads* or *burgers*, so eliminate (C). The definition does not discuss the *obesity epidemic*, so eliminate (D). The correct answer is (B).

25. **C** Punctuation is changing in the answer choices, so the question is testing STOP and GO punctuation. Use the Vertical Line Test and identify the ideas as complete or incomplete. Draw the vertical line between *quickly* and *driven*. The phrase *The chain grew quickly* is a complete idea. The phrase *Driven by customers who were attracted to its fresh menu and sustainably sourced ingredients* is an incomplete idea. STOP punctuation can only be used between two complete ideas, so eliminate (A) and (D). Between the colon and the comma, the comma is the correct choice because it continues the flow of the ideas, whereas the colon sets up a list or a cause and effect relationship, neither of which is present here. The correct answer is (C).

26. **D** Note the question! The question asks whether the sentence should be added, so it's testing consistency. If the content of the new sentence is consistent with the ideas surrounding it, then it should be added. The paragraph discusses the beginning of the fast casual movement and *Chipotle*. The new sentence discusses the *term fast casual* and *Horatio Lonsdale-Hands*, so it is not consistent with the ideas in the text; the sentence should not be added. Eliminate (A) and (B). Eliminate (C) because it does not entirely blur the focus of the paragraph, but rather adds extraneous details. Keep (D) because it does introduce a new figure in the movement. The correct answer is (D).

27. **D** The vocabulary is changing in the answer choices, so the question is testing word choice. Look for a word whose definition is consistent with the other ideas in the sentence. The sentence says that spending in the restaurant business declined for two years, so the definition should mean "consecutive" or "continuous." *Unbending* means "strict," so eliminate (A). *Linear* means "straight line," so eliminate (B). *Even* means "balanced," so eliminate (C). *Straight* is consistent with "consecutive." The correct answer is (D).

28. **D** Transitions are changing in the answer choices, so the question is testing consistency of transitions. The transition should connect the ideas in the previous and current sentences. The previous sentence says that *spending in the restaurant business declined*. The current sentence says that *during that same period, fast casual business grew by double digits*. The ideas in the sentences are opposite, so look for a transition that changes the direction of the ideas. *In fact, unsurprisingly,* and *in other words* keep the ideas in the same direction, so eliminate (A), (B), and (C). *In contrast* changes the direction, so the correct answer is (D).

29. **A** Commas are changing in the answer choices, so the question is testing the four ways to use a comma. The phrase *having sold its interest in the burrito business in 2006* is unnecessary information, so it should be surrounded by commas. Eliminate (B) because it contains no commas. Eliminate (C) and (D) because each contains only one comma. The correct answer is (A).

30. **D** Pronouns and apostrophes are changing in the answer choices, so the question is testing consistency of pronouns and apostrophe usage. A pronoun must be consistent in number with the noun it is replacing. The pronoun refers to the noun *company*, which is singular. Eliminate (A) and (B) because the pronouns are plural. When an apostrophe is attached to a pronoun, it indicates a contraction. The *buns* belong to the company, so the possessive pronoun is needed, which does not contain the apostrophe. The correct answer is (D).

31. **D** Transitions are changing in the answer choices, so the question is testing consistency of transitions. The transition should connect the ideas in the two parts of the sentence. The first part of the sentence introduces *one of the bigger problems of fast food*. The second part of the sentence names the problem: *lack of nutritional value*. Look for a transition that connects the example to the first part of the sentence. *Therefore* and *indeed* indicate a continuation, so eliminate (A) and (B). *For instance* is too general, so eliminate (C). *Specifically* indicates a particular example. The correct answer is (D).

32. **D** The punctuation and phrasing are changing in the answer choices, so the question is testing punctuation and precision. The sentence is a statement, so it should end in a period; eliminate (A) and (B). The restaurants are not becoming *increasingly fast*, so eliminate (C). The critics *increasingly question*, so keep (D). The correct answer is (D).

33. **A** The number of words is changing in the answer choices, so the question is testing concision. Since all the choices discuss changes over time, choose the answer choice that is most concise. The correct answer is (A).

34. **B** Note the question! The question asks which choice best combines the two sentences, so it's testing precision and concision. Start with the most concise option, which is (B). Choice (B) is the most concise and there are no errors in consistency or precision. The correct answer is (B).

35. **C** The phrases are changing in the answer choices, so the question is testing word choice. The sentence discusses *a fight* that involved *the spectators* so the correct choice will mean "started." *Amidst* means "in the middle of" but doesn't indicate that the spectators were involved, so eliminate (A). *Brought* is the past tense of "bring," so eliminate (B). *Broke out among* is consistent, so keep (C). *Between* is used for two things or groups, but there are more than two spectators, so eliminate (D). The correct answer is (C).

36. **A** Note the question! The question asks for the choice that best establishes the main idea of the paragraph, so it's testing consistency. Read the paragraph to find out the main idea. The paragraph discusses the *dissonant nature* of the *music*, the *awkward, ungraceful movements of the dancers, the theme* that *may also have upset some viewers*, and *the negative reception*. The *audience* reacting *strongly*

is consistent, so keep (A). There is no explanation for *why Stravinsky composed* the music, so eliminate (B). The police are mentioned in the previous paragraph but not in this one, so eliminate (C). The paragraph does not discuss *Russian folk traditions*, so eliminate (D). The correct answer is (A).

37. **D** Commas are one thing changing in the answer choices, so the question is testing the four ways to use a comma. Make sure to read all the way until the end of the sentence. The phrase *a pagan ritual in which a virgin sacrifices herself to the god of spring* is unnecessary information, so it should be surrounded by commas. Eliminate (A) and (C) because they contain no commas. *Being* is not needed, so eliminate (B). The correct answer is (D).

38. **C** Commas are changing in the answer choices, so the question is testing the four ways to use a comma. There are no lists or unnecessary information in the sentence. There should be a comma before the quote. The correct answer is (C).

39. **B** The phrases are changing in the answer choices, so the question is testing word choice. The sentence says that the *eyewitness accounts* are *contradictory,* so the phrase means "to understand." *Sort of* means "not quite right," which is not consistent, so eliminate (A) and (D). *To sort out* is consistent with "to understand," so keep (B). *For sort out* is not a correct phrase, so eliminate (C). The correct answer is (B).

40. **D** Transitions are changing in the answer choices, so the question is testing consistency of transitions. The transition should connect the ideas in the previous and current sentences. The previous sentence says that *descriptions of the level of disruption and violence increase as the accounts get further away from the actual event.* The current sentence says that *it's likely that stories of the riot have gotten exaggerated over time.* The ideas in the sentences are the same, so look for a transition that keeps the same direction of the ideas. *On the other hand* changes the direction, so eliminate (A). *As a result* indicates a consequence of an action, which is inconsistent, so eliminate (B). *At the same time* refers to events occurring simultaneously, which is not consistent, so eliminate (C). *In other words* is consistent with keeping the same ideas. The correct answer is (D).

41. **A** Note the question! The question asks for an answer choice that helps to explain the different views of the traditionalists and modernists, so it's testing consistency. Look for a choice that is consistent with the different views of the two groups. Choice (A) mentions both traditionalists and modernists and their different views of the Eiffel Tower, so keep (A). Choices (B), (C), and (D) do not mention the traditionalists and modernists, so eliminate them. The correct answer is (A).

42. **D** The phrases are changing in the answer choices, so the question is testing precision. The sentence says that *Diaghilev likely caused members of both groups,* which indicates an action that should have a result. The correct answer will complete the idea. Only *to believe* correctly finishes the idea by providing the result. The correct answer is (D).

43. **C** Note the question! The question asks for the choice that signals that the result was *expected* by the author, so it is testing precision. *Not unsurprising* is another way of saying "surprising," so eliminate (A). Both *surprising* and *unusual* indicate that the result was unexpected, so eliminate (B) and (D). The correct answer is (C).

44. **B** Note the question! The question asks where sentence 5 should be placed, so it's testing consistency. Determine the subject matter of the sentence, and find the other sentence that also discusses that information. Sentence 5 introduces *Serge Diaghilev*. Sentence 2 says that *he actually planted someone to start shouting*. Since there is no noun that *he* can refer to, sentence 5 must come before sentence 2. The correct answer is (B).

Section 3: Math (No Calculator)

1. **D** The question asks for an equivalent expression. There is a variable in the answer choices, which usually indicates an opportunity to plug in. However, the algebra is straightforward here, so it is probably better to solve this one. Start by distributing the 2 to get $10 + 2x - 14$, then combine like terms to get $2x - 4$. The correct answer is (D).

2. **C** The question asks for the ordered pair that satisfies the system of equations. Because there are possible ordered pairs in the choices, plug in the answers. Because the second equation is simpler, begin by plugging each of the choices into that equation. For (A), this becomes $0 = -7 + 7$. This is true, so keep (A). For (B), this becomes $27 = 4 + 7$. This is false, so eliminate (B). For (C), this becomes $7 = 0 + 7$. This is true, so keep (C). For (D), this becomes $9 = -18 + 7$. This is false, so eliminate (D). Plug each of the two remaining choices into the first equation. For (A), this becomes $3(0) - \dfrac{-7}{3} = 21$. This is false, so eliminate (A). For (C), this becomes $3(7) - \dfrac{0}{3} = 21$. This is true, so keep (C). The correct answer is (C).

3. **B** The question asks for the meaning of the variable *b* in the situation. Start by labelling the parts of the equation. The variable *a* represents *the number of hours...doing homework each week*, and the number 15 represents *hours doing homework or watching television each week*. This makes the equation *number of hours doing homework + b = hours doing homework or watching television each week*. Next, go through the answers and use POE. Choice (A) relates doing homework and watching television to each other, but no information is given about the specific number of hours spent on each activity. Eliminate (A). Choice (B) fits the labeling of the equation; keep (B). Choice (C) can be eliminated because the question states that this is represented by *a*. Choice (D) can be eliminated because the question states that this is 15. The correct answer is (B).

4. **A**   The question asks for the value of the computer after 6 years. Begin by ballparking. Since 6 is more than half of 9, after 6 years, the computer will have lost more than half its value. Thus, the value of the computer must be less than half of its original value. Half of the original value is $4,590 ÷ 2 = $2,295. Eliminate (B), which is exactly half, and (C) and (D), which are more than half. The only value that remains is (A), so it must be correct. To verify the value of the computer after 6 years, determine the constant rate by which it decreases in value. Since the computer has no monetary value after 9 years, it takes 9 years for it to lose its entire value of $4,590. Therefore, the rate of decrease in value is $\frac{\$4,590}{9\ years} = \$510$ per year. After 6 years, the value of the computer decreases by $510 × 6 = $3,060. The value after 6 years is obtained by subtracting this amount from the original value to get $4,590 − $3,060 = $1,530. The correct answer is (A).

5. **B**   The question asks for an equivalent expression. Rather than getting mixed up with all the negatives, work using Bite-Sized Pieces and use POE. All four answer choices have different i terms, so start there. The first part of the expression has $10i$, and the second part has $-3i$. There is a subtraction sign in between, so the i-terms become $10i - (-3i)$, or $10i + 3i = 13i$. The only answer with a positive $13i$ is (B). The correct answer is (B).

6. **D**   The question asks for the value of the function for a given x value. To find $f(-2)$, plug -2 into the function in place of x. Therefore, $f(-2) = \dfrac{(-2)^2 + 4(-2) - 8}{-2 - 2}$. Simplify to get $f(-2) = \dfrac{4 + (-8) - 8}{-4} = \dfrac{-4 - 8}{-4} = \dfrac{-12}{-4} = 3$. The correct answer is (D).

7. **D**   The question asks for the system of inequalities that describes the situation. Because there is a lot of information in the question, solve using Bite-Sized Pieces. Start with the most straightforward piece. The question states that Heinrich must buy at least 20 shares of Stock X. The term *at least* translates to ≥. Since a represents the number of shares of Stock X, the correct answer must include $a ≥ 20$. Eliminate the choices that do not include this inequality, which are (A) and (B). Look at the two remaining choices and find the differences between them. The only difference between (C) and (D) is that (C) includes the inequality $a + b ≤ 100$, while (D) includes the inequality $a + b ≥ 100$. According to the question, Heinrich must buy at least 100 total shares. Therefore, the total number of shares must be ≥ 100. Eliminate (C). The correct answer is (D).

8. **A**   The question asks for an equivalent expression. Since there is a variable in the choices, plug in. Let $x = 5$. If $x = 5$, then the original expression becomes $x^2 - 8x + 5 = 5^2 - 8(5) + 5$. Apply the exponent and multiply to get $25 - 40 + 5$, which equals -10. The target value is -10; circle it. Go through each choice, make $x = 5$, and eliminate any that doesn't equal -10. Choice (A) is $(5 - 4)^2 - 11$, which is $1^2 - 11$. This equals $1 - 11$ or -10. Keep (A), but check the remaining answers just in case. Choice (B) is $(5 - 4)^2 + 11$, which is $1^2 + 11$. This equals $1 + 11$ or 12. Eliminate (B). Choice (C) is $(5 + 4)^2 - 11$, which is $9^2 - 11$. This equals $81 - 11$ or 70. Eliminate (C). Choice (D) is $(5 + 4)^2 + 11$, which is $9^2 + 11$. This equals $81 + 11$ or 92. Eliminate (D). The correct answer is (A).

9.   **B**   The question asks for the least number of photographs Juliet must sell. Since the question asks for a specific value and there are numbers in the answer choices, plug in the answers. Start with the smallest value, which is in (A). According to the question, Juliet sells the first 20 photographs for $10 each. Therefore, she takes in a total of 20 × $10 = $200. If Juliet sells an additional 18 photographs for $15 each, she will bring in an additional 18 × $15 = $270. Therefore, she brought in a total of $200 + $270 = $470. She earns a profit of 80% of her revenues, so she earns $\frac{80}{100} \times \$470$, which is $\frac{4}{5} \times \frac{\$470}{1}$. This can be simplified to $\frac{4}{1} \times \frac{\$94}{1}$, which equals $376. She must earn at least $460 in profit, so this answer is too small. Eliminate (A). Try (B). She still makes $200 on the first 20 photographs. If she sells 20 additional photographs, she takes in an additional 20 × $15 = $300, for a total of $200 + $300 = $500 in revenues. She earns a profit of 80% of the revenues, which is $\frac{80}{100} \times \$500 = \frac{4}{5} \times \$500 = \$400$. This matches the goal of *at least $400*. Therefore, the correct answer is (B).

10.   **A**   The question asks for an equivalent expression. Solve this question using Bite-Sized Pieces, working with one variable at a time. Because the expression divides variables with exponents, use the MADSPM rule of Division-Subtract. Subtract the exponents on the p terms to get $\frac{p^{\frac{1}{4}}}{p^{-2}} = p^{\frac{1}{4}-(-2)} = p^{\frac{1}{4}+2}$. Both parts of the exponent are positive, so the p term should be in the numerator. Unfortunately, this doesn't eliminate any answers. MADSPM rules indicate that Addition means Multiplication, and a fractional exponent is a power over a root. Therefore, the numerator must include p^2 multiplied by $\sqrt[4]{p}$. Only (A) has $p^2\sqrt[4]{p}$ in the numerator. Eliminate the choices that do not include this: (B), (C), and (D). Only one choice remains, so there is no need to continue. However, to see why (A) is correct, follow the same process for q. Subtract the exponents in $\frac{q^{-3}}{q^{\frac{1}{2}}}$ to get $q^{-3-\frac{1}{2}}$. Both parts of the exponent are negative, so q term should be in the denominator. To determine what the denominator should be, factor a negative from the exponent to get $q^{-\left(3+\frac{1}{2}\right)}$. Once again, use MADSPM rules to get that the denominator must be q^3 multiplied by $\sqrt{q}$. Therefore, the expression simplifies to $\frac{p^2\sqrt[4]{p}}{q^3\sqrt{q}}$. The correct answer is (A).

11.   **C**   The question asks for the interval containing the x-coordinate of the vertex of a parabola. The vertex of a parabola is always on the axis of symmetry, which is located halfway between the roots of the parabola. To find the roots, set $g(x) = 0$ to get $0 = (x - 2)(x - 4)$. Set both factors equal to 0 to get $x - 2 = 0$ and $x - 4 = 0$. If $x - 2 = 0$, then $x = 2$. If $x - 4 = 0$, then $x = 4$. Since the axis of symmetry is halfway between the roots, it is $x = \dfrac{2+4}{2} = \dfrac{6}{2} = 3$. Therefore, the x-coordinate of the vertex is 3. Select the choice that includes $x = 3$. The correct answer is (C).

12.   **D**   The question asks for a factor of a polynomial. The equation is given as $xa^3 + ya^2 + za = 0$, but it is not necessary to deal with the equation in this question because the question asks for a factor of the equation, not to solve for x, y, or z. An equation is divisible by its factors, which means the factors multiply to each other to give the equation. If the equation has roots -6, 0, and 4, then when $a = -6$, 0, or 4, the equation is true (in this case, the left side is equal to 0). In order to make the left side equal to zero, at least one of the factors must be equal to zero. Therefore, to find a factor of the equation, plug the roots into the answer choices for a until one of the choices equals 0. It's easier to use positive numbers, so start with 4. Plugging 4 into each of the answer choices for a doesn't give 0 for any answer, so try -6 instead. When $a = -6$, (D) equals $-6 + 6$, which is 0. This means that $a + 6$ is a factor of the equation. The correct answer is (D).

13.   **B**   The question asks for the value of c when an expression containing c is rewritten into another form. Therefore, these two forms can be set as equal to get $\dfrac{1}{2}x^2 - 5 = \dfrac{1}{2}(x + c)(x - c)$. Since this is an equation with x and c, and the question asks for c, plug in for x. Let $x = 2$. Plug $x = 2$ into the equation to get $\dfrac{1}{2}(2^2) - 5 = \dfrac{1}{2}(2 + c)(2 - c)$. Simplify the left side to get $\dfrac{1}{2}(4) - 5 = \dfrac{1}{2}(2 + c)(2 - c)$, then multiply to get $2 - 5 = \dfrac{1}{2}(2 + c)(2 - c)$. Subtract on the left side to get $-3 = \dfrac{1}{2}(2 + c)(2 - c)$. Multiply both sides by 2 to get $-6 = (2 + c)(2 - c)$. Use FOIL on the right side to get $-6 = 4 - c^2$. Subtract 4 from both sides to get $-10 = -c^2$. Divide both sides by -1 to get $10 = c^2$. Take the square root of both sides to get $\pm\sqrt{10} = c$. Since the question specifies that c is a positive constant, the only possible value of c is $\sqrt{10}$. It is also possible to plug in the answers and simplify the equation, but that might be more time-consuming. The correct answer is (B).

14. **A** The question asks for an equivalent expression. Because there is a variable in the question and choices, plug in. Choose a value that makes the arithmetic easier. Let $z = -1$, because the denominators of most of the fractions will equal 1. If $z = -1$, then the original expression becomes $\dfrac{z^2 + 7z - 3}{z + 2} = \dfrac{(-1)^2 + 7(-1) - 3}{-1 + 2}$, which is equal to $\dfrac{1 - 7 - 3}{1} = -9$. This is the target value; circle it. Go through each choice, plugging in $z = -1$ and eliminating any choice that is not equal to -9. Choice (A) is $-1 + 5 - \dfrac{13}{-1 + 2} = 4 - 13 = -9$. Keep (A), but check the remaining answer just in case. Choice (B) is $-1 + 5 - \dfrac{7}{-1 + 2} = 4 - 7 = -3$. Eliminate (B). Choice (C) is $-1 + 9 - \dfrac{21}{-1 - 2} = 8 + 7 = 15$. Eliminate (C). Choice (D) is $-1 + 9 - \dfrac{15}{-1 - 2} = 8 + 5 = 13$. Eliminate (D). The correct answer is (A).

15. **D** The question asks for an inequality that shows the allowable depth of a pool. Set up an inequality that describes the restriction. Each of the choices indicates that $0 < a$, so it is only necessary to determine the upper limit of the inequality. The sum of the length of the pool and the perimeter of the vertical side cannot exceed 200 meters. The perimeter is $2w + 2d$, so the sum of the length and the perimeter is $l + 2w + 2d$. The term *cannot exceed* translates to $\le$, so $l + 2w + 2d \le 200$. The length of the pool is 75 and the depth is a, so $75 + 2w + 2a \le 200$. The width is 1.5 times the depth, so $75 + 2(1.5a) + 2a \le 200$. This simplifies to $75 + 2a + 3a \le 200$. Combine like terms to get $75 + 5a \le 200$, then subtract 75 from both sides to get $5a \le 125$. Divide both sides by 5 to get $a \le 25$. The correct answer is (D).

16. **10** The question asks for the degree measure of $\angle BCD$, which is part of triangle BCD. First, mark the information given by the question. Mark $AB = BD = CD$ and $AD = 15$ in the figure. Since $AB = BD$, triangle ABD is isosceles. Therefore, $\angle BDA$ is also equal to 20°. Since $\angle BDC$ is adjacent to $\angle BDA$, forming a straight angle, the measures of the two angles have a sum of 180°. This means that $\angle BDC = 180° - 20° = 160°$. Since $BD = DC$, triangle BCD is also isosceles. Label $\angle BCD$ and $\angle CBD$ as x. There are 180° in a triangle, so $160° + x + x = 180°$. Therefore, $2x = 20°$ and $x = 10°$. The correct answer is 10.

17. **7** The question asks for the value of an expression. There are two possible approaches to this question. One is to solve for b, and then plug that value into the expression $5 - b$. The other approach is to notice that the given expression $15 - 3b = 21$ can be factored to $3(5 - b)$. Therefore, the original equation can be rewritten in form $3(5 - b) = 21$. Divide both sides by 3 to get $5 - b = 7$. Using either approach, the correct answer is 7.

18. **6** The question asks for the value of k, which is the y-coordinate of a point on a line. Use the other two points to find the equation of the line, in the form $y = mx + b$, where m is the slope and b is the y-intercept. To find the slope, use formula $m = \dfrac{y_2 - y_1}{x_2 - x_1}$ to get $m = \dfrac{12 - 0}{0 - (-4)}$, which is $\dfrac{12}{4}$ or 3. Plug $m = 3$ into the line equation to get $y = 3x + b$. The y-intercept is the point where the line crosses

the y-axis, or where $x = 0$. The question gives this value as 12, so the full equation of the line is $y = 3x + 12$. To find the value of k, plug $(-2, k)$ into the equation to get $k = 3(-2) + 12$. Simplify the right side to get $k = -6 + 12 = 6$. The correct answer is 6.

19. **8,244** The question asks for the value of $d - c$, where d and c are coefficients in an equivalent form of the given expression. To simplify the expression, start by distributing 10 to get $50x^2 - 1,500 + 9,844 + 50x^2$. Combine like terms to get $100x^2 + 8,344$. Since the expression is now in the form $cx^2 + d$, $c = 100$ and $d = 8,344$. The value of the expression $d - c$ is $8,344 - 100 = 8,244$. The correct answer is 8,244.

20. **540** The question asks for the value of n, which is the number of degrees in an angle measuring 3π radians. To convert from degrees to radians, use the fact that 180 degrees is equal to π radians. Set up the proportion $\dfrac{n^\circ}{3\pi \text{ radians}} = \dfrac{180^\circ}{\pi \text{ radians}}$. Cross-multiply to get $540\pi = \pi n$. Divide both sides by π to get $n = 540$. The correct answer is 540.

Section 4: Math (Calculator)

1. **B** The question asks for the maximum number of times a homeowner can edge his lawn given a certain fuel requirement. Use proportions to determine the maximum number. There are 1,000 milliliters per 1 liter, and he has 8 liters of fuel. Set up a proportion to find how many milliliters of fuel he has: $\dfrac{1,000 \text{ milliliters}}{1 \text{ liter}} = \dfrac{x \text{ milliliters}}{8 \text{ liters}}$. Cross-multiply to get $x = 8,000$. Therefore, he has 8,000 milliliters of fuel. Next, set up a proportion to find how many times he can edge his lawn if the edger uses 160 milliliters of fuel each time: $\dfrac{160 \text{ milliliters}}{1 \text{ time}} = \dfrac{8,000 \text{ milliliters}}{y \text{ times}}$. Cross-multiply to get $160y = 8,000$. Divide both sides by 160 to get $y = 50$. The correct answer is (B).

2. **C** The question asks for the fraction of the students in Dr. Soper's class that chose to be graded on the lab report and final exam. A fraction is defined as $\dfrac{\text{part}}{\text{whole}}$. For this question, the "part" is the number of Dr. Soper's students who chose to be graded on the lab report and final exam, which is 3. The "whole" is Dr. Soper's class total, which is 20. Therefore, the fraction of Dr. Soper's class that chose to be graded on the lab report and final exam is $\dfrac{3}{20}$. The correct answer is (C).

3. **D**   The question asks for an equivalent expression to the one given. There are variables in the answer choices, so plugging in is an option. However, the question is straightforward enough to solve without plugging in. Use Bite-Sized Pieces and Process of Elimination. Start with the a^2 terms. Combine the terms: $-a^2 - (2a^2) = -3a^2$. Eliminate (A) and (B). Next, work the numbers: $4 - (-6)$, which is $4 + 6 = 10$. Eliminate (C). The correct answer is (D).

4. **B**   The question asks for the inequalities satisfied by the ordered pair $(3, -1)$, so make $x = 3$ and $y = -1$ in each of the inequalities. Roman numeral (I) becomes $3 + 3(-1) > 0$, which is $3 + (-3) > 0$ or $0 > 0$. This is false, so eliminate (A) and (C), which both contain (I). Both remaining answers include Roman numeral (II), so try Roman numeral (III). That inequality becomes $3 + (-1) < 0$, which is $2 < 0$. This is false, so eliminate (D). The correct answer is (B).

5. **A**   The question asks for an inference that can be made from a given survey. For questions like this, stick closely to the results of the survey and use Process of Elimination. Choice (A) concludes that few people who like working alone will be unhappy doing this task, which closely matches the group chosen *(a group of people who indicated that they preferred to work alone)* and the results *(5% stated they were unhappy while doing the task)*. This answer sticks closely to the survey; keep (A). Choice (B) makes an inference about people who do not like working alone; however, the survey collected data only on those who do like working alone, so there is no support for (B); eliminate it. Choices (C) and (D) are about people in general and whether they are working alone, but the survey considered only those people who like working alone; eliminate (C) and (D). The correct answer is (A).

6. **C**   The question asks for a true statement, so go through the answers and use Process of Elimination. Choice (A) compares the pH of two wells, one with half as much bicarbonate as the other, so choose two points on the scatterplot. The well with approximately 150 ppm of bicarbonate has a pH of 7.6, and the well with approximately 75 ppm of bicarbonate has a pH of 8. Since 8 is not twice 7.6, this statement is false; eliminate (A). Choice (B) says that wells with more bicarbonate tend to have a higher pH, but according to the line of best fit, pH decreases as bicarbonate increases; eliminate (B). Choice (C) is the opposite of (B) and is supported by the downward trend of the line of best fit; keep (C). Choice (D) is disproven by the clear trend shown by the line of best fit; eliminate (D). The correct answer is (C).

7. **B**   The question asks for the pH of a well with a bicarbonate concentration of 225 ppm, so look it up. Go along the horizontal axis to 225 ppm, and go up to the line of best fit. Now trace across the grid line to the vertical axis. It hits the vertical axis between 7.2 and 7.4, so the pH is approximately 7.3. The correct answer is (B).

8. **B** The question asks for a specific value, so plug in the answers. It is easy to plug in a value of 0, so start with (C). The value of y is given in the question, so if $k = 0$, the equation becomes 25 = $[(0)(-2) - 1]^2$. Multiply in the parentheses to get 25 = $(0 - 1)^2$, which is 25 = $(-1)^2$ or 25 = 1. This is not true, so eliminate (C). It might not be clear if a larger or smaller number is needed, so pick a direction to go in. Try (B). If $k = -3$, the equation becomes 25 = $[(-3)(-2) - 1]^2$. Multiply in the parentheses to get 25 = $(6 - 1)^2$, which is 25 = 5^2 or 25 = 25. This is true. The correct answer is (B).

9. **A** The question asks for the number of *seconds* Andrew waits for the weight rack. Start by converting 30 minutes to seconds by setting up a proportion: $\dfrac{1 \text{ minute}}{60 \text{ seconds}} = \dfrac{30 \text{ minutes}}{x \text{ seconds}}$. Cross-multiply to get $x = 1{,}800$ seconds. Next, take 35% of 1,800 seconds by multiplying: $\dfrac{35}{100} \times 1{,}800$ or $0.35 \times 1{,}800$ = 630 seconds. The correct answer is (A).

10. **C** The question asks for the value of $x - yz$ with the given equation. Try to isolate those terms. Start by subtracting 2 from both sides to get $8x - 8yz = 72$. Every term is divisible by 8, so divide both sides by 8 to get $x - yz = 9$. Another option is to plug in. Make $y = 2$ and $z = 3$, so the equation becomes $8x - 8(2)(3) + 2 = 74$. Simplify to get $8x - 48 + 2 = 74$ or $8x - 46 = 74$. Add 46 to both sides to get $8x = 120$, then divide both sides by 8 to get $x = 15$. Therefore, $x - yz = 15 - (2)(3) = 15 - 6 = 9$. The correct answer is (C).

11. **C** The question asks for a specific value and there are numbers in the answer choices, so plug in the answers. Choice (C) is easier to work with than (B), so start with (C). If the original weight of the steak is 10.00 ounces, then the weight of the fat trimmed off would be 12% of 10.00, which is $\dfrac{12}{100} \times 10.00$ or $0.12 \times 10.00 = 1.20$ ounces. Subtract this from 10.00 to find the weight after trimming the fat: $10.00 - 1.20 = 8.80$ ounces. This matches the information in the question. The correct answer is (C).

12. **D** The question asks for a system of equations that models a certain situation. Use Bite-Sized Pieces, translate from English to math, and use Process of Elimination. Start with the most straightforward piece of information. The backpacker uses *a total of 10 granola bars and packets of peanut butter*, and g represents granola bars and p represents packets of peanut butter. This means that $g + p = 10$. This is not part of any answer choice. In the answer choices, look at the equations that have the number 10. Choices (A) and (B) include the equation $g - p = 10$. This equation is definitely not the same as $g + p = 10$. However, (C) and (D) include the equation $g = 10 - p$. Add p to both sides of the equation to get $g + p = 10$, which matches the translation. Eliminate (A) and (B). Next, compare the remaining answer choices. Choices (C) and (D) only differ by what g and

p are multiplied by; both remaining equations equal 1,660, which is the *total…food calories*. The question states that *a packet of peanut butter has 90 food calories*, so 90 should be multiplied by *p*, not *g*. Eliminate (C). The correct answer is (D).

13. **D** The question asks for the number of boards needed to cover a certain floor width. Set up a proportion. Be sure to match the labels on the numerators and denominators: $\dfrac{10 \text{ boards}}{7\frac{3}{4} \text{ feet}} = \dfrac{x \text{ boards}}{32 \text{ feet}}$. Cross-multiply to get $7\frac{3}{4}x = 320$. Convert $7\frac{3}{4}$ to 7.75 to make the division easier. Then divide both sides by 7.75 to get $x \approx 41.3$. The question asks for the closest answer. The correct answer is (D).

14. **A** The question asks for the statement that is NOT true given the figure. Start by working the figure. The figure shows the time, in hours, along the horizontal axis and the distance from home, in kilometers, along the vertical axis. Note that the scales on each axis are different. Next, read the final question. The question asks for what is NOT true, so work each answer choice and eliminate any choice that IS true. Choice (A) states that George's distance from home increased at a constant rate for the first hour; however, the distance increased along a curved line, whereas a constant increase would result in a straight line. Furthermore, the increase is only for the first 30 minutes; the distance from home decreases after 30 minutes. Therefore, (A) is not true. This is likely the correct answer, but check the remaining ones to be sure. To check (B), look for the highest vertical value, which is at 0.5 hours. This is in the first hour, so (B) is true; eliminate it. For (C), a constant distance from home would appear as a horizontal line in the graph. The graph is horizontal between 2 and 3 hours, so the distance from home was constant for one hour. Choice (C) is true; eliminate it. To check (D), go through the graph and add up the time intervals George's distance from home was increasing and check that total against the total time intervals that his distance from home was decreasing. His distance from home was increasing from 0 to 0.5 hours, from 1.5 to 2 hours, and from 3 to 4.5 hours, for a total of 2.5 hours. His distance from home was decreasing from 0.5 to 1.5 hours and 4.5 to 5 hours, for a total of 1.5 hours. Choice (D) is true; eliminate it. The correct answer is (A).

15. **C** The question asks for the value of *a* in the given diagram. Start by ballparking any answer choice that clearly doesn't fit the figure. The angles with degree measure *a* are greater than the angle labeled 60°, so eliminate (A) and (B). The sum of the angles intersecting in the circle is 360°. Therefore, $a + a + a + 60 = 360$. Solve by first combining like terms to get $3a + 60 = 360$. Subtract 60 from both sides to get $3a = 300$. Divide both sides by 3 to get $a = 100$. The correct answer is (C).

16. **C** The question asks what the slope represents in the graph of a certain situation. When asked about the meaning of a constant or variable in context, start by reading the final question. In the given equation, the slope is the coefficient on the *x* term: –75. Next, label the information in the equation. The variable *y* represents *amount of money remaining*, and the variable *x* is *days after the start of the fall semester*. Therefore, the equation is *amount of money remaining* = –75(*days after the start*

of the fall semester) + 5,000. Next, go through the answer choices using Process of Elimination. Choice (A) references the total amount, which is *y*, not the slope. Eliminate (A). Choice (B) refers to the number 5,000, but the slope of the equation is –75. Eliminate (B). Choice (C) fits the equation; –75 is multiplied by the number of days since the beginning of the semester, so it would be consistent that Bo spent $75 per day. Keep (C). Choice (D) refers to the amount of money Bo earned over the summer. However, that is the starting point and wouldn't need to be multiplied by the number of days. Also, slope is a rate of change, and the amount he made over the summer is fixed. Eliminate (D). The correct answer is (C).

17. **D** The question asks about the *account that contains the least amount of money*, so look it up. The scatterplot shows the interest rate in percent along the horizontal axis and the amount in the account along the vertical axis. The point that represents the account with the least money is the point that is closest to the bottom of the graph, which is at about 2.3 percent and $1,000. The question asks for the *difference of the actual amount and the amount predicted by the line of best fit*. Trace up from the point to the line of best fit. Then, trace horizontally to the vertical axis to get a value of about $2,200, making the difference 2,200 – 1,000 = $1,200. The question asks for the answer choice that is the closest. The correct answer is (D).

18. **B** The question asks for the value of *x* − *y* given a system of equations. Start by multiplying both sides of the first equation by 3 to get *x* = 12. Next, plug *x* = 12 into the second equation to get 12 + *y* = 32. Subtract 12 from both sides to get *y* = 20. The question asks for the value of *x* − *y*, which is 12 – 20 or –8. The correct answer is (B).

19. **B** The question asks for the predicted increase in bounce height for every 100 centimeters in drop height, so choose two points from the line of best fit. At a drop height of 0 centimeters, the line of best fit gives a bounce height of 0 centimeters, and at a bounce height of 200 centimeters, the line of best fit gives a bounce height of about 40 centimeters. Therefore, the increase in drop height of 200 − 0 = 200 centimeters gives an increase in bounce height of 40 − 0 = 40 centimeters. Use a proportion to find the increase in bounce height for 100 centimeters: $\frac{40 \text{ cm bounce height}}{200 \text{ cm drop height}} = \frac{x \text{ cm bounce height}}{100 \text{ cm drop height}}$. Cross-multiply to get 4,000 = 200*x*. Divide both sides by 200 to get *x* = 20. The correct answer is (B).

20. **C** The question asks for *w*, and the answer choices are all equations solved for *w*, so isolate *w* in Formula B. Start by multiplying both sides by 5 to get 5*BMI* = 4*w* − 100. Next, add 100 to both sides to get 5*BMI* + 100 = 4*w*. Divide both sides by 4 to get $\frac{5BMI + 100}{4} = w$. The correct answer is (C).

21. **B** The question asks for an expression equivalent to $4w - 100$, and it states that both formulas give the same value for *BMI*. Therefore, the left sides of each equation are equal, so set the right sides equal and solve for $4w - 100$. The equation becomes $\frac{w}{h^2} = \frac{4w - 100}{5}$. Isolate $4w - 100$ by multiplying both sides by 5 to get $\frac{5w}{h^2} = 4w - 100$. Be sure to read the final question! The question asks for $4w - 100$, so the correct answer is (B).

22. **C** The question asks for the meaning of the number 20 in the context of the function. Label the parts of the function. $C(h)$ represents *the number of bacteria colonies* and *h* represents *hours*, so the function becomes *number of bacteria colonies* = $3^{hours} - 2(hours) + 20$. Next, go through the answers and use Process of Elimination. The number 20 is not affected by *hours*, so it cannot represent a rate of growth; eliminate (A) and (B). Next, plug in. Choice (C) asks about the initial number of colonies, so make $h = 0$. The function becomes $C(0) = 3^0 - 2(0) + 20$, which is $C(0) = 1 - 0 + 20$ or $C(0) = 21$. This fits (C). There's no way to determine the final number of bacteria colonies because the final time is not given; eliminate (D). The correct answer is (C).

23. **A** The question asks for the *difference between the median percent of agricultural land for these 9 countries* and the median for all countries, which is given as 34.95%. Find the median of the 9 countries given by crossing out the greatest and least values in pairs until only one value remains. Number the countries in order of increasing percent of land area. Then cross out in pairs of the highest and lowest numbers on the list. Cross out Greenland and Mexico, Canada and Turkey, Russian Federation and United States, and Latvia and New Zealand. The country remaining, Brazil, is the median. Therefore, the median percentage is 33.8. Find the difference by subtracting: $34.95 - 33.8 = 1.15\%$. The correct answer is (A).

24. **B** The question asks for the combined volume of the figurines and pellets in the box. Find the volume of the box and subtract the volume of the air in the box. To find the volume of the box, write down the formula for the volume of a rectangular solid: $V = lwh$. Next, plug in the given information into the formula. The question gives the area of the base of the box rather than the length and the width. There is not enough information to determine the length and width of the box, but length times width will equal the base of the box. Therefore, it is possible to plug in 4.4 for *lw* and 6.5 for *h* to get $V = (4.4)(6.5)$, which is 28.6 in.^{3}. Finally, subtract the volume of the air: $28.6 - 8.0 = 20.6$ in.^{3}. The correct answer is (B).

25. **D** The question asks for the equation that models a certain situation. Use Bite-Sized Pieces and Process of Elimination. Because the GDP is shrinking a certain percentage per year, the answer should use the exponential growth and decay formula. That formula is *final amount = original amount*$(1 \pm rate\ of\ change)^{number\ of\ changes}$, where *rate of change* is expressed as a decimal. Eliminate (A) and (C) because they do not have exponents and therefore are not in this form. The difference between (B) and (D) is *rate of change*. The value 2.6% expressed as a decimal is $\frac{2.6}{100}$ or 0.026. Eliminate (B). The correct answer is (D).

26. **A** The question asks for the relationship between two variables, so plug in. Use Nickel in the table because it has the most straightforward value for grams. Because y is grams and d is drams, make $y = 5.00$ and $d = 2.82$. Plug these values into the answer choices and eliminate any choice that is not true. Choice (A) becomes $5.00 = 1.8(2.82)$, which is $5.00 = 5.08$. This is close, so keep (A). Choice (B) becomes $2.82 = 1.8(5.00)$, which is $2.82 = 9.00$. This is false; eliminate (B). Choice (C) becomes $(5.00)(2.82) = 1.8$, which is $14.1 = 1.8$. This is false; eliminate (C). Choice (D) becomes $5.00 = 0.56(2.82)$, which is $5.00 = 1.58$. This is false; eliminate (D). The correct answer is (A).

27. **A** The question asks for d in terms of n and p, but there is no equation given. Therefore, start by translating English to math. The total weight is 225 grams, and p pennies will weigh $2.50p$ grams. Similarly, n nickels will weigh $5.00n$ grams, and d dimes will weigh $2.25d$ grams. Therefore, the equation will be $225 = 2.50p + 5.00n + 2.25d$. Next, solve the equation for d. Start by subtracting $2.50p$ and $5.00n$ from both sides to get $225 - 2.50p - 5.00n = 2.25d$. At this point, every answer has the same terms; the only differences are the addition and subtraction signs. Both the p and n terms need to be subtracted from the constant term, so eliminate (B) because both terms are added. Distributing the negative before $\frac{10}{9}$ in (C) results in $d = 100 - \frac{10}{9}p + \frac{20}{9}n$. Since this subtracts the p term but adds the n term, eliminate (C). Choice (D) adds the p term, so eliminate (D). The correct answer is (A).

28. **A** The question asks for a point that does NOT lie on the exterior of a circle, so the correct answer will be on the circle or inside it. Sketch a graph and ballpark. The standard form of the equation of a circle is $(x - h)^2 + (y - k)^2 = r^2$, where the center of the circle is (h, k) and the radius is r. Therefore, the center of this circle is at $(2, -5)$ and the radius is 6. Choices (B) and (C) are clearly outside the circle, so eliminate them. Choice (A) is 6 units directly up from the center of the circle, and the circle has a radius of 6. Therefore, the distance from $(2, 1)$ to the center of the circle is equal to the radius and must be on the circle. The correct answer is (A).

29. **D** The question asks for the number of peppers *the farmer expects…in August*. Work using Bite-Sized Pieces. The question states that *the percent increase from June to July would be half the percent increase from July to August*. First find the percent increase from June to July using the percent change formula: percent change = $\dfrac{\text{difference}}{\text{original}} \times 100$. Plug the numbers from the table into the formula to get $\dfrac{2{,}640 - 2{,}200}{2{,}200} \times 100$, which is $\dfrac{440}{2{,}200} \times 100$ or 20%. If this is *half the percent increase from July to August*, then the percent increase from July to August must be double 20%, or 40%. To find the number of peppers expected in August, find what 40% of July's amount would be. Multiply 2,640 by 40% to get $2{,}640 \times \dfrac{40}{100}$ or 1,056. Add this to 2,640 to get 3,696 peppers expected in August. The correct answer is (D).

30. **D** The question asks for the ratio of *b* to *a* given point (a, b) on a line. Because (a, b) isn't shown, any nonzero point will work. Use the given point $(-8, 2)$, which makes $a = -8$ and $b = 2$. Therefore, the ratio of *b* to *a* is 2 to -8, which can be reduced by dividing both terms by -2 to get -1 to 4. The correct answer is (D).

31. **8** The question asks for the number of incorrect answers a student had on a test. Translate the English to math, starting with the first sentence. The *raw score* equals *subtracting* $\dfrac{1}{4}$ *of the number of the incorrect answers* from *the number of correct answers*. Assign variables to the parts of the problem to make it easier to follow. If incorrect answers are *IA* and correct answers are *CA*, the equation becomes *raw score* $= CA - \dfrac{1}{4}(IA)$. Next, plug in the information given in the question. The *raw score* is 20, so $20 = CA - \dfrac{1}{4}(IA)$. The student answered 30 questions, which is the total of *CA* and *IA*, so this is another equation: $30 = CA + IA$. To find the number of *IA*, stack the equations and subtract to cancel out *CA*.

$$
\begin{array}{r}
30 = CA + IA \\
- \; [20 = CA - \dfrac{1}{4}(IA)] \\
\hline
10 = \dfrac{5}{4}(IA)
\end{array}
$$

Clear the fraction by multiplying both sides by 4 to get $40 = 5(IA)$. Divide both sides by 5 to get $IA = 8$. The correct answer is 8.

32. **6**   The question asks how much protein, in ounces, was in each meal of a given diet. Use proportions to determine the number of grams of protein, the total number of ounces of protein, and the ounces of protein per meal. There were 672 calories of protein in each meal, and there are 4 calories per gram. Set up a proportion to determine the weight of the protein in grams: $\dfrac{4 \text{ calories}}{1 \text{ gram}} = \dfrac{672 \text{ calories}}{x \text{ grams}}$. Cross-multiply to get $4x = 672$. Divide both sides by 4 to get $x = 168$ grams. Next, each ounce is 28 grams, so set up another proportion: $\dfrac{1 \text{ ounce}}{28 \text{ grams}} = \dfrac{x \text{ ounces}}{168 \text{ grams}}$. Cross-multiply to get $28x = 168$. Divide both sides by 28 to get $x = 6$ ounces. The correct answer is 6.

33. $\dfrac{3}{4}$ or .75

The question asks for the slope of a line in the xy-plane. Find the slope using the slope formula:

$m = \dfrac{y_2 - y_1}{x_2 - x_1}$, where m is the slope. There are three points given; to make working the slope formula more straightforward, choose two points that have fractions for the same values (either both for x or both for y). Use $\left(-\dfrac{16}{3}, -3\right)$ and $\left(\dfrac{20}{3}, 6\right)$. Plugging these points into the slope equation gives $m = \dfrac{-3 - 6}{-\dfrac{16}{3} - \dfrac{20}{3}}$. Subtract in both the numerator and denominator to get $m = \dfrac{-9}{-\dfrac{36}{3}}$. Reduce the fraction in the denominator to get $m = \dfrac{-9}{-12}$ or $\dfrac{9}{12}$. This fits in the Grid-In box, so the correct answer is $\dfrac{9}{12}$. Other equivalent responses, such as $\dfrac{3}{4}$ or .75, are also correct.

34. **0 or 5**   The question asks for a possible solution for a. To solve the system, substitute the left side of the first equation for b in the second equation to get $a^2 - 6a - 9 = -9 - a$. Solve the quadratic by setting the equation equal to 0. Add 9 to both sides to get $a^2 - 6a = -a$. Add a to both sides to get $a^2 - 5a = 0$. To solve, factor out an a to get $a(a - 5) = 0$. Two expressions multiplied together to equal 0 means that one of the terms must be equal to 0. Therefore, $a = 0$ or $a - 5 = 0$. Add 5 to both sides of the second equation to get $a = 5$. The correct answers are 0 and 5.

35.   **5**   The question asks for $VW - YZ$, so find the lengths of those sides. Follow the geometry basic approach. Start by labeling the given information onto the diagram, which is $TV = 24$, $XZ = 13$, and $\angle W \cong \angle Z$. Because both triangles are right triangles with another congruent angle, the triangles must be similar triangles. Next, write down formulas. SOHCAHTOA indicates that $\sin = \dfrac{\text{opposite}}{\text{hypotenuse}}$. Because the triangles are similar, the trigonometric functions for the corresponding angles are equal. Therefore, $\sin T = \sin X = \dfrac{5}{13} = \dfrac{YZ}{XZ} = \dfrac{VW}{TW}$. The question states that $XZ = 13$, so $YZ = 5$. When dealing with right triangles, keep an eye out for Pythagorean triples. This is a 5-12-13 right triangle, so $XY = 12$; otherwise, use the Pythagorean Theorem to find that $5^2 + 12^2 = 13^2$. Label each of these sides in the figure. Because the triangles are similar, the sides are in the same ratio. Create a ratio using the sides opposite the congruent angles: $\dfrac{TV}{XY} = \dfrac{24}{12}$, or $\dfrac{TV}{XY} = 2$, so $TV = 2XY$. Therefore, all the sides of triangle TVW are twice those of triangle XYZ. Thus, $TW = 26$ and $VW = 10$. Label each of these sides in the figure. The question asks for $VW - YZ$, which is $10 - 5$ or 5. The correct answer is 5.

36. $\dfrac{7}{36}$ or **.194**

The question asks what fraction of the circumference is the arc, which translates to $\dfrac{\text{arc}}{\text{circumference}}$.

The length of an arc compared to the circumference of the circle is proportional to the central angle over 360°, so $\dfrac{\text{arc}}{\text{circumference}} = \dfrac{\text{angle}}{360°}$. Plug in the given information to get $\dfrac{\text{arc}}{\text{circumference}} = \dfrac{70°}{360°}$. The fraction reduces to $\dfrac{7}{36}$. The correct answer is $\dfrac{7}{36}$ or .194.

37. $\dfrac{7}{8}$ or **.875**

The question asks for the probability that a selected participant threw 3 bullseyes on Day 1 or Day 2, provided that the participant threw 3 bullseyes on one of the three days. Probability is $\dfrac{\text{number of outcomes that fulfill requirements}}{\text{total number of possible outcomes}}$. On Day 1, 5 participants threw 3 bullseyes, and on Day 2, 2 participants threw 3 bullseyes, so there are 7 outcomes that fulfill the requirements. Because the question stipulates that the participants must have thrown 3 bullseyes on one of the three days, the total number of possible outcomes is the number of participants who threw 3 bullseyes, which is 8. Therefore, the probability that someone who threw 3 bullseyes did so on Days 1 or 2 is $\dfrac{7}{8}$. The correct answer is $\dfrac{7}{8}$ or .875.

38. $\dfrac{11}{5}$ or **2.2**

The question asks for the mean number of bullseyes on Day 2, so find the total number of bullseyes thrown and divide by the number of participants. To find the total number of bullseyes, multiply the number of participants who threw a certain number of bullseyes by the number of bullseyes and add those products. On Day 2, there were 3 participants who threw 0 bullseyes, 3 who threw 1 bullseye, 3 who threw 2 bullseyes, 2 who threw 3 bullseyes, 2 who threw 4 bullseyes, and 2 who threw 5 bullseyes. Therefore, the total number of bullseyes thrown on Day 2 is $(3 \times 0) + (3 \times 1) + (3 \times 2) + (2 \times 3) + (2 \times 4) + (2 \times 5)$, which is $0 + 3 + 6 + 6 + 8 + 10 = 33$. There are 15 participants, so the average bullseyes per participant is $\dfrac{33}{15}$, which is $\dfrac{11}{5}$ or 2.2. The correct answer is $\dfrac{11}{5}$ or 2.2.

Chapter 4
Cracking the SAT: Basic Principles

The first step to cracking the SAT is knowing how best to approach the test. The SAT is not like the tests you've taken in school, so you need to learn to look at it in a different way. This chapter provides and explains test-taking strategies that will immediately improve your score. Make sure you fully understand these concepts before moving on to Part II. Good luck!

BASIC PRINCIPLES OF CRACKING THE TEST

What the College Board Does Well

The folks at the College Board have been writing standardized tests for a long time. They have administered the SAT so many times that they know exactly how you will approach it. They know how you'll attack certain questions, what sort of mistakes you'll probably make, and even what answer you'll be most likely to pick. Freaky, isn't it?

However, this strength is also a weakness. Because the test is standardized, the SAT asks the same type of questions over and over again. Sure, the numbers or the words might change, but the basics don't. With enough practice, you can learn to think like the test-writers. But try to use your powers for good, okay?

The SAT Isn't School

Our job isn't to teach you math or English—leave that to your super smart school teachers. Instead, we're going to teach you what the SAT is and how to crack it. You'll soon see that the SAT involves a very different skill set.

No Wrong-Answer Penalty!

You will NOT be penalized on the SAT for any wrong answers. This means you should always guess, even if this means choosing an answer at random.

Be warned that some of the approaches we're going to show you may seem counterintuitive or unnatural. Some of these strategies may be very different from the way you learned to approach similar questions in school, but trust us! Try tackling the questions using our techniques, and keep practicing until they become easier. When you do this, you'll see a real improvement in your score.

Let's take a look at the questions.

Cracking Multiple-Choice Questions

What's the capital of Azerbaijan?

Give up?

Unless you spend your spare time studying an atlas, you may not even know that Azerbaijan is a real country, much less what its capital is. If this question came up on a test, you'd have to skip it, wouldn't you? Well, maybe not. To find out if you can figure out the answer anyway, let's turn this question into a multiple-choice question—just like all the questions on the SAT Reading Test and Writing and Language Test, and the majority of questions you'll find on the SAT Math Test.

1

What is the capital of Azerbaijan?

A) Washington, D.C.

B) Paris

C) London

D) Baku

The question doesn't seem that hard anymore, does it? Of course, we made our example extremely easy. (By the way, there won't actually be any questions about geography that aren't answered by an accompanying passage or figure on the SAT.) But you'd be surprised by how many people give up on SAT questions that aren't much more difficult than this one just because they don't know the correct answer right off the top of their heads. "Capital of Azerbaijan? Oh, no! I've never heard of Azerbaijan!"

These students don't stop to think that they might be able to find the correct answer simply by eliminating all of the answer choices they know are wrong.

You Already Know Almost All of the Answers

All but a handful of the questions on the SAT are multiple-choice questions, and every multiple-choice question has four answer choices. One of those choices, and only one, will be the correct answer to the question. You don't have to come up with the answer from scratch. You just have to identify it.

How will you do that?

Look for the Wrong Answers Instead of the Right Ones

Why? Because wrong answers are usually easier to find than the right ones. After all, there are more of them! Remember the question about Azerbaijan? Even though you didn't know the answer off the top of your head, you easily figured it out by eliminating the three obviously incorrect choices. You looked for wrong answers first.

In other words, you used Process of Elimination, which we'll call POE for short. This is an extremely important concept, one we'll come back to again and again. It's one of the keys to improving your SAT score. When you finish reading this book, you will be able to use POE to answer many questions that you may not understand.

The great artist Michelangelo once said that when he looked at a block of marble, he could see a statue inside. All he had to do to make a sculpture was to chip away everything that

It's Not About Circling the Right Answer
Physically marking in your test booklet what you think of certain answers can help you narrow down choices, take the best possible guess, and save time! Try using the following notations:

✔ Put a check mark next to an answer that seems correct.

∼ Put a squiggle next to an answer that seems kinda right.

? Put a question mark next to an answer you don't understand.

A̶ Cross out the letter of any answer choice you KNOW is wrong.

You can always come up with your own system. Just make sure you are consistent.

wasn't part of it. You should approach difficult multiple-choice questions on the SAT in the same way, by "chipping away" the answers that are not correct. By first eliminating the most obviously incorrect choices on difficult questions, you will be able to focus your attention on the few choices that remain.

PROCESS OF ELIMINATION (POE)

There won't be many questions on the SAT in which incorrect choices will be as easy to eliminate as they were on the Azerbaijan question. But if you read this book carefully, you'll learn how to eliminate at least one choice on almost any SAT multiple-choice question, if not two or even three choices.

What good is it to eliminate just one or two choices on a four-choice SAT question?

Plenty. In fact, for most students, it's an important key to earning higher scores. Here's another example:

2

What is the capital of Qatar?

A) Paris

B) Dukhan

C) Tokyo

D) Doha

On this question, you'll almost certainly be able to eliminate two of the four choices by using POE. That means you're still not sure of the answer. You know that the capital of Qatar has to be either Doha or Dukhan, but you don't know which.

Should you skip the question and go on? Or should you guess?

Close Your Eyes and Point

There is no guessing penalty on the SAT, so you should bubble something for every question. If you get down to two answers, just pick one of them. There's no harm in doing so.

You're going to hear a lot of mixed opinions about what you should bubble or whether you should bubble at all. Let's clear up a few misconceptions about guessing.

FALSE: Don't answer a question unless you're absolutely sure of the answer.

You will almost certainly have teachers and guidance counselors who tell you this. Don't listen to them! The SAT does not penalize you for wrong answers (though it used to). Put something down for every question: you might get a freebie.

FALSE: If you have to guess, guess (C).

This is a weird misconception, and obviously it's not true. Each answer choice appears roughly equally on the SAT (we've checked!). As a general rule, if someone says something really weird-sounding about the SAT, it's usually safest not to believe that person.

FALSE: Always pick the [fill in the blank].

Be careful with directives that tell you that this or that answer or type of answer is always right. It's much safer to learn the rules and to have a solid guessing strategy in place.

As far as guessing is concerned, we do have a small piece of advice. First and foremost, make sure of one thing:

> Answer every question on the SAT. There's no penalty.

LETTER OF THE DAY (LOTD)

Sometimes you won't be able to eliminate any answers, and sometimes there will be questions that you won't have time to look at. For those, we have a simple solution. Pick a "letter of the day," or LOTD (from A to D), and choose that answer choice for questions for which you can't eliminate any answers or do not have time to do.

This is a quick and easy way to make sure that you've answered every question. (Remember, you are not penalized for wrong answers!) It also has some potential statistical advantages. If all the answers show up about one-fourth of the time and you guess the same answer every time you have to guess, you're likely to get a couple of freebies.

LOTD should absolutely be an afterthought; it's far more important and helpful to your score to eliminate answer choices. But for those questions you don't know at all, LOTD is better than full-on random guessing or no strategy at all.

Are You Ready?
Check out *Princeton Review SAT Advanced* to practice some of those more challenging questions for the exam.

PACE YOURSELF

LOTD should remind you about something very important: there's a very good chance that you won't attempt every question on the test.

Think about it this way. There are 5 passages and 52 questions on the Reading Test. You've got 65 minutes to complete those questions. Now, everyone knows that the Reading Test is super long and boring, and 52 questions in 65 minutes probably sounds like a ton. The great news is that you don't have to work all 52 of these questions. After all, do you think you read most effectively when you're in a huge rush? You might do better if you worked only four of the passages and filled in your LOTD on the rest. There's nothing in the test booklet that says that you can't work at your own pace.

Let's say you do all 52 Reading questions and get half of them right. What raw score do you get from that? That's right: 26.

Now, let's say you do only three of the 10-question Reading passages and get all of them right. It's conceivable that you could because you've now got all this extra time. What kind of raw score would you get from this method? You bet: 30—and maybe even a little higher because you'll get a few freebies from your Letter of the Day.

In this case, and on the SAT as a whole, slowing down can get you more points. Unless you're currently scoring in the 650+ range on the two sections, you shouldn't be working all the questions. We'll go into this in more detail in the later chapters, but for now remember this:

> Slow down, score more. You're not scored on *how many questions you do*. You're scored on *how many questions you answer correctly*. Doing fewer questions can mean more correct answers overall!

EMBRACE YOUR POOD

Embrace your what now? POOD! It stands for "Personal Order of Difficulty." One of the things that SAT has dispensed with altogether is a strict Order of Difficulty—in other words, an arrangement of questions that places easy questions earlier in the test than hard ones. Even the supposed Order of Difficulty in the Math sections is very loose. In the absence of this Order of Difficulty (OOD), you need to be particularly vigilant about applying your *Personal Order of Difficulty (POOD)*.

Think about it this way. There's someone writing the words that you're reading right now. So what happens if you are asked, *What are the names of the people who worked on Princeton Review SAT Prep?* Do you know the answer to that question? Maybe not. Do we know the answer to that question? Absolutely.

So you can't exactly say that that question is "difficult," but you can say that certain people would have an easier time answering it.

As we've begun to suggest with our Pacing, POE, and Letter of the Day strategies, our strategies are all about making the test your own, to whatever extent that is possible. We call this idea POOD because we believe it is essential that you identify the questions that you find easy or hard and that you work the test in a way most suitable to your goals and strengths. Make sure you answer all the questions you find easier to do before you even think about tackling the ones that are harder for you.

As you familiarize yourself with the rest of our strategies, keep all of this in mind. You may be surprised to find out how you perform on particular question types and sections. The SAT may be standardized, but the biggest improvements are usually reserved for those who can treat the test in a personalized, non-standardized way.

A Note on Question Numbering
You may notice that the practice questions and drill questions found in this book, particularly the math chapters, are not always numbered sequentially. In other words, you may see a math drill with questions numbered 6, 7, 13, 32, and 37, for example. We've done this to indicate where a given question may show up on the actual exam, and thus help you anticipate where a certain topic may be tested and how.

Summary

- When you don't know the right answer to a multiple-choice question, look for wrong answers instead. They're usually easier to find.

- When you find a wrong answer, cross it off with your pencil. In other words, use Process of Elimination, or POE.

- There's no guessing penalty on the SAT, so there's no reason NOT to guess.

- There are bound to be at least a few questions you simply don't get to or ones on which you're finding it difficult to eliminate even one answer choice. When this happens, use the LOTD (Letter of the Day) strategy.

- Pace yourself. Remember, you're not scored on how many questions you answer, but on how many questions you answer correctly. Focus on working slowly and steadily.

- Make the test your own. When you can work the test to suit your strengths (and use our strategies to overcome any weaknesses), you'll be on your way to a higher score.

Part II
How to Crack the Reading Test

Chapter 5
The Reading Test: Basic Approach

Half of your Evidence-Based Reading and Writing score comes from the Reading Test, a 65-minute test that requires you to answer 52 questions spread out over five passages. The questions will ask you to do everything from determining the meaning of words in context to deciding an author's purpose for a detail to finding the main idea of a whole passage to pinpointing information on a graph. Each passage ranges from 500 to 750 words and has 10 or 11 questions. Time will be tight on this test. The purpose of this chapter is to introduce you to a basic approach that will streamline how you take the test and allow you to focus on only what you need to get your points.

SAT READING: CRACKING THE PASSAGES

You read every day. From street signs to novels to the back of the cereal box, you spend a good part of your day recognizing written words. So this test should be pretty easy, right?

Unfortunately, reading on the SAT is different from reading in real life. In real life, you read *passively*. Your eyes go over the words, the words go into your brain, and some stick and some don't. On the SAT, you have to read *actively*, which means trying to find specific information to answer specific questions. Once you've found the information you need, you have to understand what it's actually saying.

Reading on the SAT is also very different from the reading you do in school. In English class, you are often asked to give your own opinion and support it with evidence from a text. You might have to explain how Scout Finch and Boo Radley in *To Kill a Mockingbird* are, metaphorically speaking, mockingbirds. Or you might be asked to explain who is actually responsible for the tragedies in *Romeo and Juliet*. On the SAT, however, there is no opinion. You don't have the opportunity to justify why your answer is the right one. That means there is only *one* right answer, and your job is to find it. It's the weirdest scavenger hunt ever.

Your Mission:

Read five passages and answer 10 or 11 questions for each passage (or set of passages). Get as many points as you can.

Unless you are aiming for a top score, you should not be answering all the questions. See the chart below to determine how many questions you need to answer correctly to get your target Reading Test score.

For a Reading *Test Score* of:	You need about this many *Correct Answers*:
10	<3
12	5
14	7
16	10
18	14
20	18
22	21
24	26
26	29
28	33
30	37
32	41
34	44
36	47
38	50
40	52

Okay, so how do you get those points? Let's start with the instructions for the Reading Test.

DIRECTIONS

Each passage or pair of passages below is followed by a number of questions. After reading each passage or pair, choose the best answer to each question based on what is stated or implied in the passage or passages and in any accompanying graphics (such as a table or graph).

Great news! This is an open-book test. Notice the directions say *based on what is stated or implied in the passage.* This means that you are NOT being tested on whether you have read, studied, and become an expert on the Constitution, *The Great Gatsby*, or your biology textbook. All the test-writers care about is whether or not you can read a text and understand it well enough to correctly answer some questions about it. Unlike the Math and Writing and Language Tests, there are no formulas to memorize or comma rules to learn for the Reading Test. You just need to know how to approach the passages, questions, and answer choices in a way that maximizes your accuracy and efficiency. It's all about the text! (No thinking!)

Another awesome thing about an open-book test is that you don't have to waste time reading every single word of the passage and trying to become an expert on whatever the topic is. You have the passage right there in front of you. So, move back and forth between the passage and the questions, focusing only on what you need to know instead of getting mired down in all the little details.

POOD and the Reading Test

You will get all five of the reading passages at the same time, so use that to your advantage. Take a quick look through the whole section and figure out the best order in which to do the passages. Depending on your target score, you may be able to skip an entire passage or two, so figure out which passages are likely to get you the most points and do those first.

Consider the following:

- **Type of passage:** There will be 1 literature passage, 2 science passages, and 2 history/social studies passages. If you like to read novels and short stories, the literature passage may be a good place to start. If you prefer nonfiction, you might consider tackling the science and history/social studies passages first.
- **Topic of passage:** The blurb preceding the passage will give you some basic information about the passage, which may help you decide whether to do the passage or skip it.
- **Date of passage:** Older passages may be more challenging to understand than more modern passages.
- **Types of questions:** Do the questions have a good number of **line references** and **lead words**? Will you be able to find what you're looking for relatively quickly, or will you have to spend more time wading through the passage to find the information you need?

Don't forget: On any questions or passages that you skip, always fill in your LOTD!

Basic Approach for the Reading Test

Follow these steps for every Reading passage. We'll go over these in greater detail in the next few pages.

"Where the Money Is"

A reporter once asked notorious thief Willie Sutton why he robbed banks. Legend has it that his answer was, "Because that's where the money is." While reading comprehension is much safer and more productive than larceny, the same principle applies. Concentrate on the questions and answer choices because that's where the points are. The passage is just a place for the test-writers to stash facts and details. You'll find them when you need to. What's the point of memorizing all 67 pesky details about plankton if you're asked about only 12?

1. **Read the Blurb.** The short paragraph at the beginning of each passage may not contain a lot of information, but it can be helpful for identifying the type of passage, as well as the source.

2. **Select and Understand a Question.** For the most part, do the questions in order, saving the general questions for last and using your LOTD on any questions you want to skip.

3. **Read What You Need.** Don't read the whole passage! Use line references and lead words to find the reference for the question, and then carefully read a window of about 10–12 lines to find the answer to the question.

4. **Mark the Answer in the Passage.** Use your pencil to underline a sentence or phrase in the passage that answers the question. Don't create your own interpretation.

5. **Use POE.** Eliminate anything that isn't consistent with the text you underlined in the passage. Don't necessarily try to find the right answer immediately, because there is a good chance you won't see an answer choice that you like. If you can eliminate choices that you know are wrong, though, you'll be closer to the right answer. If you're left with more than one choice that seems to match the passage, use the POE criteria (which we'll talk about later on).

Let's see these steps in action!

What follows is a sample reading passage followed by a series of questions. Don't start working the passage right away. In fact, you can't, because we've removed the answer choices. Just turn to page 124, where we will begin going through each step of the Reading Basic Approach using this sample passage and questions.

SAMPLE PASSAGE AND QUESTIONS

Here is an example of an SAT Reading passage and questions. We will use this passage to illustrate the Reading Basic Approach throughout this chapter. You don't need to do the questions now, but you might want to paperclip this page so it's easy to flip back to later.

Questions 11–21 are based on the following passage.

This passage is adapted from Linton Weeks's "The Windshield-Pitting Mystery of 1954." ©2015 by NPR History Department.

The nationwide weirdness that was the Windshield-Pitting Mystery began in the spring of 1954. Looking back at the events today may give us
Line a window—OK, a windshield—on the makeup and
5 the mindset of mid-20th-century America.

The epidemic's epicenter, according to HistoryLink—an online compendium of Washington state history—was the town of Bellingham, where "tiny holes, pits, and dings...
10 seemingly appeared in the windshields of cars at an unprecedented rate" in late March.

"Panicked residents," the website reports, suspected "everything from cosmic rays to sand-flea eggs to fallout from H-bomb tests."
15 In Canton, Ohio, some 1,000 residents notified police that their windshields had been "blemished in a mysterious manner," the *Daily Mail* of Hagerstown, MD reported on April 17. And United Press in New York noted on April 20
20 that "new reports of mysterious windshield pittings came in today almost as fast as theories about what causes them." A Canadian scientist posited that the marks were made by the skeletons of minute marine creatures that had been propelled into
25 the air by hydrogen bomb testing in the Pacific Ocean. In Utah, someone suggested that acid from flying bugs might be the source of the windshield-denting, but a Brigham Young University biologist disproved the theory, the Provo *Daily Herald*
30 reported on June 27. As summer rolled on, reports of pitting decreased everywhere and the country moved on to building backyard fallout shelters.

But the question remains: What about those pitted windshields?
35 For guidance, we turn to Missouri State University sociologist David Rohall, who has taught courses in social movements and collective behavior for more than a decade. "Much of what happens in society is a numbers game," Rohall
40 says. "If you have more people, any phenomenon starts to appear more common if you focus on any one event or behavior. Even something that is very infrequent may start to appear to be a trend, he says, "when you aggregate those events. There are
45 millions of cars in Washington state but thousands of cases of pitting. While thousands sounds like a huge phenomenon, it represents less than 1 percent of cars. If everyone is looking for and reporting it, it would appear to be a conspiracy of some sort."
50 Windshield-pitting, Rohall says, "may be more like crop circles in which there is physical evidence that 'something' happened but no one is certain of the cause. Of course, we have since found evidence that, in some cases, people utilize special
55 equipment to make those crop circles. The cause of the pitting is different because it would be very difficult to capture someone creating them."

"Most people in the field no longer believe in mass hysteria as a cause of large-group behavior,"
60 Rohall says. "The idea came from Gustave Le Bon, a French theorist trying to explain the strange behavior of large groups during the French Revolution, in which average citizens began killing large numbers of people via the guillotine. What
65 would cause them to do such a heinous thing?"

Even if the theory were true, Rohall says, "it is designed to be applied to situations of heightened emotional arousal—for example: large crowds. While the ideas about pitting may have 'caught
70 on' among people in the region, I doubt it was an emotional contagion that drove them to act in a particular way."

"*War of the Worlds* is a wonderful example of how the media emphasizes the few 'real cases' of
75 hysteria without recognizing that the vast majority of people knew that the radio program was fictional and did nothing," Rohall adds. "Like crop circles, we know that some of them are man-made, so might these pits. However, the media may have
80 had people start noticing the pits that had already been there."

He likens the experience to this: "It is very common for people to believe that they have contracted an illness when they hear a doctor
85 describe a medical problem and the symptoms associated with that problem. I suspect that most people already had these pits all along and only attributed it to the mysterious cause when they heard other people doing it. Still others may have
90 resulted from vandalism or new cases from simple accidents—debris from the roads. Is this hysteria or simply logical thinking utilizing information from the media and their own situation—a pitted car? Some research about supposed 'hysteria' really
95 shows that people are not hysterical at all."

These are the questions for the passage. We've removed the answer choices because, for now, we just want you to see the different question types the SAT will ask. Don't worry about answering these here; we'll walk you through some of them in this chapter.

11

The central claim of the passage is that

12

According to the passage, residents of Bellingham, Washington attributed windshield pitting to

13

The author's statement that the "country moved on to building backyard fallout shelters" (lines 31–32) implies that Americans

14

As used in line 41, "common" most nearly means

15

The passage indicates that an effect of aggregating events is that

16

According to the passage, what percent of cars in Washington suffered damage?

17

Which choice provides the best evidence for the answer to the previous question?

18

The author most likely mentions *War of the Worlds* in line 73 in order to

19

The quotation marks around the word "hysteria" in line 94 most likely indicate

20

Based on the passage, the author most likely agrees that "pitting" is

21

Which choice provides the best evidence for the answer to the previous question?

STEPS OF THE BASIC APPROACH

Step 1: Read the Blurb

The Strategy
1. Read the Blurb

You should always begin by reading the blurb (the introductory material preceding the passage). The blurb gives you the title of the piece, as well as the author and the publication date. Typically, the blurb won't have much more information than that, but it'll be enough for you to identify whether the passage is literature, history/ social studies, or science. It will also give you a sense of what the passage will be about and can help you make a POOD (Personal Order of Difficulty) decision about when to do the passage.

Read the blurb at the beginning of the passage on page 121. Based on the blurb, is this a literature, history/social studies, or science passage? What will the passage be about?

_____

_____

Step 2: Select and Understand a Question

The Strategy
1. Read the Blurb
2. Select and Under-
   stand a Question

Select…

Notice that the steps of the Basic Approach have you jumping straight from the blurb to the questions. There is no "Read the Passage" step. You get points for answering questions, not for reading the passage, so go straight to the questions.

On a school test, you probably answer the questions in order. That seems logical and straightforward. However, doing the questions in order on a Reading passage can set you up for a serious time issue. According to the College Board, the order of the questions "is also as natural as possible, with general questions about central ideas, themes, point of view, overall text structure, and the like coming early in the sequence, followed by more localized questions about details, words in context, evidence, and the like." So to sum it up: the general questions come first, followed by the specific questions.

That question structure works well in an English class, when you have plenty of time to read and digest the text on your own. But when you're trying to get through five passages in just over an hour, you don't have time for that. So, instead of starting with the general questions and then answering the specific questions, we're going to flip that and do the specific questions first.

Look back at the questions on page 123.

What does the first question ask you about?

In order to answer that question, you'd have to read what part of the passage?

What you do *not* want to do is read the *whole* passage. So skip that first question. You'll come back to it, but not until you've done the specific questions. Once you go through and answer all (or most) of the specific questions, you'll have a really good idea what the test-writers think is important. You'll also have read most of the passage, so answering the general questions will be easy.

Look at the line references in the specific questions. What do you notice about them?

Yup; they're in sequential order! The specific questions (even the ones without line references) are written roughly in sequential order. So work through them as they're given, and you'll work through the passage from beginning to end. Avoid getting stuck on questions, though. If you find yourself stumped, use your LOTD and move on to the next question. You can always come back if you have time.

Based on that logic, let's skip the first question and move on to the second question.

…and Understand

Once you've selected a question, you need to make sure you understand what it's asking. Reading questions are often not in question format. Instead, they will make statements such as, "The author's primary reason for mentioning the gadfly is to," and then the answer choices will follow. Make sure that you understand the question by turning it into a question—that is, back into a sentence that ends with a question mark and begins with What/Why/How.

Watch Us Crack It

12 ██████████████████

According to the passage, residents of Bellingham, Washington attributed windshield pitting to

What is this question asking?

> **Rephrase the Question…**
> …so that it asks:
> What?
> Why?
> How?

Rephrase the question stem as an actual question starting with "What," "Why," or "How." Question 12 is a "what?" question. It asks what the residents of Bellingham, Washington thought was the cause of the windshield pitting.

Step 3: Read What You Need

The Strategy
1. Read the Blurb
2. Select and Understand a Question
3. Read What You Need

5 Above, 5 Below
5 is the magic number when it comes to specific questions. Read 5 lines above the line reference or lead word and then 5 lines below it to get all of the information you need in order to answer the question correctly.

Line References, Lead Words, and Question Order

Many questions will refer you to a specific set of lines or to a particular paragraph. Those are **line references**. Other questions may not give you a line reference, but may ask about specific names, quotes, or phrases that lead you to a certain place in the text. We'll call those **lead words**. The specific questions are presented roughly in order according to where they're discussed in the passage, so if you work the specific questions in order, you'll be working through the passage roughly in order. If you're looking for the window for a question without a line reference, you can use line references from questions that come before and after to help you know where to look.

It's important to remember that the line reference or lead word shows you where the question is mentioned in the passage, but you'll have to read more than that single line to find the answer in the passage. If you read a window of about five lines above and five lines below each line reference or lead word, you should find the information you need. It's important to note that while you do not need to read more than these 10–12 lines of text, you usually cannot get away with reading less. If you read only the lines from the line reference, you will very likely not find the information you need to answer the question.

> Read a window of about 5 lines above and 5 lines below the line reference to get the context for the question.

Since question 12 is the first specific question, its window is likely near the beginning of the passage. Additionally, the next question (question 13) asks about lines 31–32, so the window for question 12 is likely somewhere in the first 30 lines of the passage.

What are the lead words in this question?

What lines will you need to read to find the answer?

Once you locate the line reference or lead word in the passage, draw a bracket around the window. The more you can get out of your brain and onto the page, the better off you'll be. The lead word *Bellingham* appears in line 9, and you should read a window of about 10–12 lines. In this case, the paragraphs in lines 6–14 would be a good window.

Now it's time to read. Even though you're reading only a small chunk of the text, make sure you read it carefully.

Step 4: Mark the Answer in the Text

The test-writers do their best to distract you by creating tempting—but nevertheless wrong—answers. However, if you know what you're looking for in advance, you will be less likely to fall for a trap answer. Before you even glance at the answer choices, take the time to find the specific, stated information in your window that supplies the answer to the question. Be careful not to paraphrase too far from the text or try to analyze what you're reading. Remember, what might be a good "English class" answer may lead you in the wrong direction on the SAT! Stick with the text.

The Strategy
1. Read the Blurb
2. Select and Understand a Question
3. Read What You Need
4. Mark the Answer in the Text

As you read the window, look for specific lines or phrases that answer the question. Often what you're looking for will be in a sentence before or after the line reference or lead word, so it's crucial that you read the full window.

Once you've found text to answer the question, underline it if you can! Otherwise, jot down a prediction for the answer, sticking as closely to the text as possible.

Let's take a look at question 12 again, this time with the window.

12 ▆▆▆▆▆▆▆▆▆▆▆▆▆▆▆▆▆▆▆▆▆▆

According to the passage, residents of Bellingham, Washington attributed windshield pitting to

Here's your window from the passage. Read it and try to underline something that answers the question: what did the residents of Bellingham, Washington think was the cause of the windshield pitting?

> The epidemic's epicenter, according to
> HistoryLink—an online compendium of
> Washington state history—was the town of
> Bellingham, where "tiny holes, pits, and dings...
> 10 seemingly appeared in the windshields of cars at an
> unprecedented rate" in late March.
>   "Panicked residents," the website reports,
> suspected "everything from cosmic rays to sand-
> flea eggs to fallout from H-bomb tests."

Did you underline the phrase *"Panicked residents," the website reports, suspected "everything from cosmic rays to sandflea eggs to fallout from H-bomb tests"*?

The passage provides direct evidence that the Bellingham residents had many different theories about the cause of the windshield pitting, *everything from cosmic rays to sandflea eggs to fallout from H-bomb tests.*

Step 5: Use Process of Elimination

On a multiple-choice test, the right answer will always be on the page in front of you. All you have to do is eliminate the answer choices that are incorrect. On the Reading Test, it's often easier to find wrong answers that aren't supported by the passage than it is to find the right answer, which might not look the way you think it should.

Process of Elimination, or POE, may involve two steps. The first step requires asking yourself the question, "What can I eliminate that doesn't match the answer I marked in the text?"

For many of the more straightforward questions, this step will be enough to get down to the right answer.

The Strategy
1. Read the Blurb
2. Select and Understand a Question
3. Read What You Need
4. Mark the Answer in the Text
5. Use Process of Elimination

12

According to the passage, residents of Bellingham, Washington attributed windshield pitting to

Remember, in Step 4, you marked in the text that the Bellingham residents *suspected "everything from cosmic rays to sandflea eggs to fallout from H-bomb tests."*

Eliminate any choice that has nothing to do with that answer. When you eliminate an answer choice, use your pencil to cross off the letter. Here are the answers provided in the test.

A) a wide range of possible causes.

B) loose gravel on city roadways.

C) H-bombs dropped on the town.

D) acid from flying insects.

Did you eliminate all answer choices except (A)? The other answer choices are trap answers. We'll discuss them more in a moment.

Once you're down to one answer choice, use the text to make sure you can prove it. What's the *wide range of possible causes*? The text says, *everything from cosmic rays to sandflea eggs to fallout from H-bomb tests.*

POE Criteria

On many questions, you'll be able to eliminate three of the four answers simply by using the answer you marked in the text. On more difficult questions, however, you'll get rid of one or two answer choices, and then you'll need to consider the remaining answers a little more carefully. If you've narrowed it down to two answer choices and they both seem to make sense, you're probably down to the right answer and a trap answer. Luckily, we know some common traps that the test-writers use, and they include the following:

> **Traps and POE**
> Use these criteria after you have eliminated any answer choice that doesn't match the answer from the text.

- **Mostly Right/Slightly Wrong**: These answers look just about perfect, but they include a word or two that do not match what's in the text. Make sure every word of the answer choice is supported by the text.
- **Could Be True (But Not Supported)**: These answers might initially look good because they seem logical. You might even know they are true based on outside knowledge. However, they lack the concrete support from the text to make them correct SAT answers. Make sure you can underline proof for the answer choice in the passage.
- **Right Answer, Wrong Question**: You will see answer choices that are true but don't answer the question asked. Understand the question and keep it in mind. Don't simply pick something "true" from the passage.
- **Right Words, Wrong Meaning**: Finally, you'll be given answer choices that use words directly from the passage, but the meaning of the answer choice will be different from the passage's meaning. For example, the answer may reverse what is said in the passage or give a literal interpretation of figurative language. Make sure you are reading for the correct meaning and not just matching words.

In question 12, (B) was a Could Be True trap answer: *loose gravel* could damage windshields, but there is no mention of loose gravel in the passage. Choice (C) was a Right Words, Wrong Meaning trap answer: according to the passage, residents suspected the windshield pitting was caused by *fallout from H-bomb tests*, not by *H-bombs* that were *dropped on the town*. Choice (D) was a Right Answer, Wrong Question trap: the next paragraph states that someone in Utah suspected *acid from flying bugs*, but question 12 asked about the residents of *Bellingham, Washington*. A Mostly Right/Slightly Wrong trap answer to question 12 might say that the residents thought sandflea eggs were the *primary* cause of the pitting, or that they were *certain* that cosmic rays were the cause.

Being aware of these traps will help you spot them on the SAT and therefore avoid them.

USING THE BASIC APPROACH

Now that you know the steps of the Basic Approach, let's practice them on specific question types: infer/imply/suggest questions and vocabulary-in-context questions.

Infer/Imply/Suggest

When you see a question that contains the word *infer, imply,* or *suggest,* be extra careful. You may think that the test-writers want you to do some English-class-level reading between the lines, but they don't. It's still just a reading comprehension question. The answer may not be directly stated in the text as it usually is with detail questions, but there will still be plenty of evidence in the text to support the correct answer.

13

The author's statement that the "country moved on to building backyard fallout shelters" (lines 31–32) implies that Americans

A) were aware that the threat from bombs was more imminent than that from windshield pitting.

B) had lost interest in the windshield pitting phenomenon.

C) needed a place to be protected from nuclear fallout.

D) did not yet have fallout shelters in their backyards.

Here's How to Crack It

First, you need to go back to the text and find the line reference. Then mark and read your window. Make sure you know what the question is asking. In this case, you want to figure out what the line reference tells you about Americans. When you carefully read your window, you see that *as summer rolled on, reports of pitting decreased everywhere* and the *country moved on.* They are leaving the mystery of pitting behind. Now use POE to work through the answer choices. Choice (A) doesn't match the idea of Americans moving on, so eliminate it. Choice (B) looks pretty good, so hang on to it. Choice (C) might look good initially because we did see something earlier about nuclear fallout, but it has nothing to do with moving on from the pitting phenomenon, so you can eliminate it. Choice (D) might make sense—if they are building the shelters, they probably don't have them already—but it has nothing to do with the text we marked in the passage. That leaves (B), which answers the question and matches the answer from the text!

Line Reference Questions

On any line reference question, you need to go back to the passage and find the line reference, and then read your window.

Vocabulary-in-Context

Another way that your reading comprehension will be tested is with vocabulary-in-context (VIC) questions. The most important thing to remember is that these are **IN CONTEXT!** Gone are the days of "SAT vocabulary" when you had to memorize lists of obscure words like *impecunious* and *perspicacious*. Now the focus is on whether you can understand what a word means based on the context of the passage. You'll see words that look familiar, but are often used in ways that are a little less familiar. Do not try to answer these questions simply by defining the word in your head and looking for that definition. You have to go back to the text and look at the context for the word.

> **14**
>
> As used in line 41, "common" most nearly means
>
> A) tasteless.
>
> B) popular.
>
> C) frequent.
>
> D) inferior.

VIC Questions
For vocab questions, there's no need for you to read 10–12 lines to figure out the context in which the word is being used. Instead, read a few lines above and a few lines below the word to find context clues, and then apply POE, as shown here in question 14.

Here's How to Crack It

With VIC questions, you don't need to read a full 10–12 line window. Typically, a few lines before and a few lines after will give you what you need. Go to line 41 and find the word *common*. Cross it out. When you read before and after the word, the text talks about a *numbers game* and *more people*. The next sentence says that something *infrequent may start to appear to be a trend*. Based on those context clues, jot down a word or phrase that matches *numbers game* and *more people* and is the opposite of *infrequent*. Put in something like "often" and then use POE to eliminate (A), (B), and (D).

Be careful with VIC questions. As with the other questions, you have to rely heavily on the text, not your own opinions. You might be able to rather convincingly talk yourself into the idea that if something is common, it's popular, because if it's common, it's everywhere, and if it's everywhere, that must mean a lot of people like it. It can be easy to talk yourself into a tangle if you use your brain. Try to avoid that and instead focus on what the text actually says. In this case, you only have evidence for *common* having something to do with numbers and frequency, not how the general public feels about something.

Try another question.

15

The passage indicates that an effect of aggregating events is that

A) patterns seem to emerge more frequently.

B) the truth about a conspiracy is easier to find.

C) a tiny percent of the events are similar.

D) connections between unrelated events can be reported.

Here's How to Crack It

This question doesn't have a line reference, but notice that the question before it does. Since question 14 references line 41, the reference for question 15 most likely comes after that line. Start with line 42 and look for the lead words *aggregating events* to find your window. Carefully read the window, looking for the answer to the question, "What is an effect of aggregating events?" Within the window, you find *something that is very infrequent may start to appear to be a trend* and *[i]f everyone is looking for and reporting it, it would appear to be a conspiracy of some sort.* Go through the answer choices and eliminate those that have nothing to do with appearing to be a trend or conspiracy.

Choice (A) definitely seems to match an apparent *trend*, so hang on to it.

Choice (B) mentions finding a conspiracy, which might seem to match.

Choice (C) doesn't match at all, so eliminate it.

Choice (D) might be true, but doesn't match the answer in the text, so eliminate it.

Based on our first pass through the answer choices, you are now down to (A) and (B). Remember the POE criteria? Take a closer look at these two answer choices.

Choice (A): *patterns seem to emerge more frequently* is a close paraphrase of *something…may start to appear to be a trend*, so this one still looks pretty good.

Choice (B): Although the word *conspiracy* appears in both the text and the answer choice, don't forget that you need to read carefully. The text says that it would *appear to be a conspiracy*, which is much different from finding the *truth about a conspiracy*. Don't be deceived by answers with the right words but the wrong meaning! Match content, not just words. Choice (B) is out, leaving (A) as the correct answer.

POE in Action
Questions 15 and 18 are additional examples of how to apply POE for different types of questions.

So, you can see that by following the Basic Approach, you'll be in good shape to answer a majority of the Reading questions! You'll use your time more efficiently, focusing on the pieces of the test that will get you points, and your accuracy will be much higher. There are a few other question types which we'll look at in the next chapter.

Summary

- The Reading Test on the SAT makes up 50 percent of your Evidence-Based Reading and Writing score.

- Reading questions are *not* presented in order of difficulty. Don't be afraid to skip a hard question, and don't worry if you can't answer every question.

- Use your POOD to pick up the points you can get, and don't forget LOTD on the rest!

- The Reading Test is an open-book test! Use that to your advantage by focusing only on the text that is key to answering the questions.

- Translate each question into a *what, why,* or *how* question before you start reading your window.

- Use line references, lead words, and the sequence of the questions to help you find the answer in the passage. Always start reading a few lines above the line reference or the lead words and read until you have the answer.

- Mark the answer in the text before you look at the answer choices.

- Use POE to eliminate answers that don't match the answer in the text.

- If you have more than one answer left after you eliminate the ones that do not match the text, compare the remaining answer choices and decide whether any of them are trap answers:

  - mostly right/slightly wrong
  - could be true
  - right answer, wrong question
  - right words, wrong meaning

Chapter 6
More Question Types

In this chapter, we'll take a look at some other types of questions you will see on the Reading Test, including general questions, paired questions, and quantitative questions. For the most part, these questions will follow the Basic Approach, but the general paired questions and quantitative questions will look a little different.

MORE QUESTION TYPES ON THE READING TEST

In this chapter, we'll look at other question types you'll see on the SAT Reading Test, including paired questions, main idea questions, general questions, questions featuring charts and graphs, and questions based on dual passage sets.

Remember the "Windshield-Pitting Mystery" passage from the last chapter? We'll continue to use it for the questions in this chapter as well.

If you're feeling like you could use a little extra Reading prep, look no further than our *Reading and Writing Workout for the SAT,* which provides additional strategy advice and focused practice.

Questions 11–21 are based on the following passage.

This passage is adapted from Linton Weeks's "The Windshield-Pitting Mystery of 1954." ©2015 by NPR History Department.

The nationwide weirdness that was the Windshield-Pitting Mystery began in the spring of 1954. Looking back at the events today may give us
Line a window—OK, a windshield—on the makeup and
5 the mindset of mid-20th-century America.

The epidemic's epicenter, according to HistoryLink—an online compendium of Washington state history—was the town of Bellingham, where "tiny holes, pits, and dings...
10 seemingly appeared in the windshields of cars at an unprecedented rate" in late March.

"Panicked residents," the website reports, suspected "everything from cosmic rays to sand-flea eggs to fallout from H-bomb tests."

15 In Canton, Ohio, some 1,000 residents notified police that their windshields had been "blemished in a mysterious manner," the *Daily Mail* of Hagerstown, MD reported on April 17. And United Press in New York noted on April 20
20 that "new reports of mysterious windshield pittings came in today almost as fast as theories about what causes them." A Canadian scientist posited that the marks were made by the skeletons of minute marine creatures that had been propelled into
25 the air by hydrogen bomb testing in the Pacific Ocean. In Utah, someone suggested that acid from flying bugs might be the source of the windshield-denting, but a Brigham Young University biologist disproved the theory, the Provo *Daily Herald*
30 reported on June 27. As summer rolled on, reports of pitting decreased everywhere and the country moved on to building backyard fallout shelters.

But the question remains: What about those pitted windshields?

35 For guidance, we turn to Missouri State University sociologist David Rohall, who has taught courses in social movements and collective behavior for more than a decade. "Much of what happens in society is a numbers game," Rohall
40 says. "If you have more people, any phenomenon starts to appear more common if you focus on any one event or behavior. Even something that is very infrequent may start to appear to be a trend, he says, "when you aggregate those events. There are
45 millions of cars in Washington state but thousands

of cases of pitting. While thousands sounds like a huge phenomenon, it represents less than 1 percent of cars. If everyone is looking for and reporting it, it would appear to be a conspiracy of some sort."

50 Windshield-pitting, Rohall says, "may be more like crop circles in which there is physical evidence that 'something' happened but no one is certain of the cause. Of course, we have since found evidence that, in some cases, people utilize special
55 equipment to make those crop circles. The cause of the pitting is different because it would be very difficult to capture someone creating them."

"Most people in the field no longer believe in mass hysteria as a cause of large-group behavior,"
60 Rohall says. "The idea came from Gustave Le Bon, a French theorist trying to explain the strange behavior of large groups during the French Revolution, in which average citizens began killing large numbers of people via the guillotine. What
65 would cause them to do such a heinous thing?"

Even if the theory were true, Rohall says, "it is designed to be applied to situations of heightened emotional arousal—for example: large crowds. While the ideas about pitting may have 'caught
70 on' among people in the region, I doubt it was an emotional contagion that drove them to act in a particular way."

"*War of the Worlds* is a wonderful example of how the media emphasizes the few 'real cases' of
75 hysteria without recognizing that the vast majority of people knew that the radio program was fictional and did nothing," Rohall adds. "Like crop circles, we know that some of them are man-made, so might these pits. However, the media may have
80 had people start noticing the pits that had already been there."

He likens the experience to this: "It is very common for people to believe that they have contracted an illness when they hear a doctor
85 describe a medical problem and the symptoms associated with that problem. I suspect that most people already had these pits all along and only attributed it to the mysterious cause when they heard other people doing it. Still others may have
90 resulted from vandalism or new cases from simple accidents—debris from the roads. Is this hysteria or simply logical thinking utilizing information from the media and their own situation—a pitted car? Some research about supposed 'hysteria' really
95 shows that people are not hysterical at all."

PAIRED QUESTIONS

You will notice that on every passage there is at least one set of questions that are paired together. The first question looks and sounds just like a regular question. It may ask about a detail, it may be an inference question, or it may be a main idea question. The second question in the pair will always ask, "Which choice provides the best evidence for the answer to the previous question?" There are two types of paired questions: specific and general.

Specific Paired Questions

The specific paired questions are a fabulous two-for-one deal. If you're following all the steps of the Basic Approach, you'll find when you get to the "best evidence" question of a specific paired set, you've already answered it. This is because you've already found the best evidence when you carefully read your window and underlined the answer in the text. Let's take a look at a set.

16

According to the passage, what percent of cars in Washington suffered damage?

A) About 20%

B) Approximately 10%

C) Between 5% and 6%

D) Less than 1%

17

Which choice provides the best evidence for the answer to the previous question?

A) Lines 6–11 ("The epidemic's . . . March")

B) Lines 15–18 ("In Canton . . . April 17")

C) Lines 44–48 ("There . . . cars")

D) Lines 55–57 ("The cause . . . them")

Start with the first question. This question is very straightforward to answer by itself. All you need to do is find out what percent of the cars in Washington were damaged. Although there isn't a given line reference, you can still skim through the text looking for the lead words *Washington* and *percent*. You'll find these in the sixth paragraph, around lines 35–49. The text clearly states that less than 1% of cars suffered damage. Underline that line and choose (D) for question 16. Then, because you already have the "best evidence" underlined, when you get to question 17, you've already answered it. Just find your line reference in the answers (in this case (C)), bubble it in, and move on.

General Paired Sets and Parallel POE

Not all sets of paired questions will be as easy as specific paired sets, but they'll still be approachable. If you have a question that is a general question or a question without a clear line reference or lead word, Parallel POE is a very useful strategy.

Using Parallel POE, you'll be able to work through the questions at the same time! When you find yourself faced with a set of paired questions, you can start with the second question (the "best evidence" question) if (1) you aren't sure where to look for the answer, or (2) the first question is a general question about the passage. Because the second question in the pair asks which lines provide the *best evidence* for the previous question, you can use those lines to help work through the answers for the previous question. Let's take a look.

Best Evidence
Not sure where to find the answer? Let the "best evidence" lines help!

20

Based on the passage, the author most likely agrees that "pitting" is

A) a coincidence based on group observations.

B) the result of cosmic rays and nuclear fallout.

C) an example of mass hysteria similar to the Salem Witch trials.

D) the result of a streak of vandalism in the spring of 1954.

Which choice provides the best evidence for the answer to the previous question?

A) Lines 12–14 ("Panicked . . . tests")

B) Lines 30–32 ("As summer . . . shelters")

C) Lines 50–53 ("Windshield-pitting . . . cause")

D) Lines 86–89 ("I suspect . . . it")

Watch Us Crack It

When you read question 20, you might have an initial feeling of, "Well, that could be from anywhere in the passage." Sure could. Now you're faced with what is potentially the *worst* scavenger hunt ever. Instead of wading through the entire passage and trying to find something you think answers the question and then hope it's included in the "best evidence" question, go to the "best evidence" first! This is the Parallel POE strategy.

What's great about Parallel POE is that it gives you two possible reasons to eliminate an answer for the second question: if the lines don't answer the first question OR if the lines don't support an answer choice in the first question. Think for a moment about how paired questions operate. The correct answer to the first question *must* be supported by an answer to the evidence question, and the correct answer to the evidence question *must* support an answer to the first question. In other words, if there is an evidence answer that doesn't support an answer to the first question, it is wrong. Likewise, if there is an answer to the first question that isn't supported by an evidence answer, it too is wrong.

When you find a set of lines that does answer the first question, see if it supports one of the answers to the first question. If an evidence answer supports a first question answer, literally draw a line connecting them. You should not expect to have four connections. If you are lucky, you will have only one connection, and you will therefore have your answer pair. Otherwise, you might have two or three connections and will then start looking for trap answers. The important thing to remember is that any answer choice in the first question that isn't physically connected to an evidence answer—and any evidence answer that isn't connected to an answer in the first question—must be eliminated.

Let's take a look at how this first Parallel POE pass would look. (The paired questions have been arranged in two columns to help understand this, and the lines have been written out for your convenience. This does not represent what you will see on the official test.)

20. Based on the passage, the author most likely agrees that "pitting" is	21. Which choice provides the best evidence for the answer to the previous question?
A) a coincidence based on group observations.	A) "Panicked residents" suspected "everything from cosmic rays to sand-flea eggs to fallout from H-bomb tests."
B) the result of cosmic rays and nuclear fallout.	B) As summer rolled on, reports of pitting decreased everywhere and the country moved on to building backyard fallout shelters.
C) an example of mass hysteria similar to the Salem Witch trials.	C) Windshield-pitting, Rohall says, "may be more like crop circles in which there is physical evidence that 'something' happened but no one is certain of the cause.
D) the result of a streak of vandalism in the spring of 1954.	D) "I suspect that most people already had these pits all along and only attributed it to the mysterious cause when they heard other people doing it."

First, read and understand question 20. The question asks what the author would most likely agree that *pitting* is. Now, go to the "best evidence" lines.

- Choice (21A): *"Panicked residents" suspected "everything from cosmic rays to sand-flea eggs to fallout from H-bomb tests."* Do these lines provide an answer to what the author thinks that *pitting* is? No. These lines explain what "panicked residents" thought the pitting was caused by, not what the author thinks it was. This does not provide evidence to answer question 20, so eliminate (21A).
- Choice (21B): *As summer rolled on, reports of pitting decreased everywhere and the country moved on to building backyard fallout shelters.* This appears to be a fact that the author would agree with—he's reporting it in this text. Looking through the answers for question 20, you find nothing that is supported by these lines, so you can eliminate (21B). It doesn't matter that the lines could conceivably answer question 20; if there's no support, the answer cannot be right.

- Choice (21C): *Windshield-pitting, Rohall says, "may be more like crop circles in which there is physical evidence that 'something' happened but no one is certain of the cause."* Do these lines provide an answer to what the author thinks that *pitting* is? Yes. These lines include a quote from David Rohall, and in lines 35–36, the author says we are turning to David Rohall *for guidance*, indicating that the author agrees with Rohall. Now, check to see whether (21C) supports an answer to question 20. Looking through the answers for question 20, you find nothing that is supported by these lines, so you can eliminate (21C).
- Choice (21D): *"I suspect that most people already had these pits all along and only attributed it to the mysterious cause when they heard other people doing it."* Do these lines provide an answer to what the author thinks that *pitting* is? Yes. These lines also include a quote from David Rohall, with whom the author agrees. Now, check to see whether (21D) supports an answer to question 20. These lines support (20A). Draw a line physically connecting (21D) with (20A).

Without support from question 21, (20B), (20C), and (20D) can be eliminated.

At this point, the questions should look something like this:

20. Based on the passage, the author most likely agrees that "pitting" is	21. Which choice provides the best evidence for the answer to the previous question?
A) a coincidence based on group observations.	A) "Panicked residents" suspected "everything from cosmic rays to sand-flea eggs to fallout from H-bomb tests."
B) the result of cosmic rays and nuclear fallout.	B) As summer rolled on, reports of pitting decreased everywhere and the country moved on to building backyard fallout shelters.
C) an example of mass hysteria similar to the Salem Witch trials.	C) Windshield-pitting, Rohall says, "may be more like crop circles in which there is physical evidence that 'something' happened but no one is certain of the cause."
D) the result of a streak of vandalism in the spring of 1954.	D) "I suspect that most people already had these pits all along and only attributed it to the mysterious cause when they heard other people doing it."

At this point, you're done! Only (20A) and (21D) remain. For other questions, you may find that you're left with two (or, very rarely, three) pairs. In those cases, look for the common trap answers among the pairs that are left to narrow it down to the correct pair.

Parallel POE

Since you can't draw a full table on the actual exam, try making notations as shown in question 21; that is, create a column to the left of the "best evidence" answer choices listing the choices to the previous question.

On the actual test, it would be too complicated to draw a full table, so all you need to do is create a column to the left of the "best evidence" choices for the answers to the previous question. It should look something like this:

Q20   21

Which choice provides the best evidence for the answer to the previous question?

A A) Lines 12–14 ("Panicked . . . tests")

B B) Lines 30–32 ("As summer . . . shelters")

C C) Lines 50–53 ("Windshield-pitting . . . cause")

D D) Lines 86–89 ("I suspect . . . it")

PURPOSE QUESTIONS

So far, all the questions we've answered have been "what" questions. However, some questions ask "why?" The same Basic Approach applies, but it's important to answer the right question. Let's look at an example.

18

The author most likely mentions *War of the Worlds* in line 73 in order to

Notice the phrase *in order to* at the end of the question. That phrase lets you know the question can be rephrased as a "why" question. So, for this question, you want to figure out *why* the author mentions *War of the Worlds*. In other words, you need to determine the author's purpose.

Find your window and carefully read it, looking for the answer to the question, "Why does the author mention *War of the Worlds*?" When you read your window, you find that the author says, *War of the Worlds is a wonderful example of how the media emphasizes the few 'real cases' of hysteria without recognizing that the vast majority of people knew that the radio program was fictional and did nothing.*

You might not expect an author to come right out and tell you why they mentioned a certain detail, but on the SAT, there will be direct evidence in the text. Underline lines 73–77 and eliminate answer choices that don't match the answer provided by the text.

18

The author most likely mentions *War of the Worlds* in line 73 in order to

A) argue that some cases of mass hysteria are legitimate.

B) prove the media was responsible for people's reactions.

C) point out that most people were not upset by the broadcast.

D) criticize the media for failing to recognize that the program was fictional.

Choice (A): Don't be deceived by the Right Answer to the Wrong Question! Notice that, in the text, "real cases" is in quotation marks. This indicates that the author doesn't agree with the media's emphasis on these cases, so (A) is not the author's purpose.

Choice (B): This doesn't match the text. The passage discusses how the media portrayed people's reactions; it doesn't indicate that the media caused their reactions. The word "prove" is also too strong.

Choice (C): This is a close match for *the vast majority of people knew that the radio program was fictional and did nothing*, so hang on to it.

Choice (D): This doesn't match the text. The passage indicates there were just a few people who didn't know the program was fictional. It doesn't say that the media didn't know it was fictional.

That leaves (C) as the correct answer!

It's worth noting that the correct answer to a Purpose question often comes just before or just after the sentence that includes the line reference or lead word. When answering a "why" question, be sure to read the full 10- to 12-line window, then think about the relationship between the detail the question asks about and the larger point the author is making in that paragraph.

GENERAL QUESTIONS

For many of the Reading passages, the very first question will ask a general question about the passage. It might ask about the main idea or purpose of the passage, the narrative point of view, or a shift that occurs through the passage. Remember the Select a Question step? Those general questions are not good to do first because you haven't read the passage yet, but once you've done most of the other questions, you should have a really good idea of the overall themes of the text.

Main Idea Questions

Let's take a look at the first question from the "Windshield-Pitting Mystery" passage:

The central claim of the passage is that

Because this question asks about the *central claim* of the passage, there's no one place you can look. General questions don't have line references or lead words, so there's not a great way to mark the answer in the text. It's okay, though. By the time you get to answering this question, you've already answered almost all of the questions about the passage, so you know what the main idea of the passage is. Not only that, but you also have a good sense of what the test-writers found most interesting about the passage. While having this knowledge does not always help, it surely can sometimes. If there are answer choices that have nothing to do with either the questions or the answers you've seen repeatedly, you can probably eliminate them and instead choose the one that is consistent with those questions and answers.

Let's take a look at the answer choices:

A) windshield pitting was a major source of concern for most drivers in 1954.

B) windshield pitting turned out to be nothing but a prank.

C) widespread focus on a specific event can make random occurrences seem significant.

D) lack of consensus for an event's explanation can cause hysteria.

Remember: If it's a *central claim*, it's a main point of the text. What can you eliminate?

Choice (A) might look good initially because it has the words *windshield pitting, drivers,* and *1954,* but this is definitely not a *central claim* of the passage.

Choice (B) can be eliminated because the only mention of a prank was as a possible theory put forward by someone else.

Choice (C) looks pretty good. You've already answered several specific questions dealing with this idea.

Choice (D) might look pretty good at first too. When you go back to the text, though, you see that the author's *central claim* is not about the lack of consensus causing the hysteria. That's a part of it, but it's not a complete answer.

Choice (C) is best supported by the text and all of the other questions you've answered.

Question 11 was a main idea question. Next, we'll look at two other types of general questions. The following two questions were not included in the set on page 123. Each passage on the SAT Reading test has only 10–11 questions, but we're adding these two so that you can see examples of additional question types.

Analyzing Text Structure Questions

Which choice best describes the overall structure of the passage?

A) An introduction to an interesting phenomenon and evidence suggesting that it is man-made rather than natural

B) A comparison of two competing explanations of a puzzling circumstance, the observations supporting each theory, and a conclusion about which is more likely

C) A description of an unusual event, presentation of several possible theories explaining the event, and dismissal of one proposed explanation

D) A list of several events which have not been explained to the satisfaction of researchers

This question asks for a description of the passage as a whole. Like any general question, it is best left for after you have worked the specific questions. Use what you've learned while working the specific questions to help you with your Process of Elimination. The answer choices will probably include some abstract descriptions, so you'll need to match the abstract phrases back to the specific topics discussed in the passage. The answers are also likely to include multiple parts; take each answer choice in Bite-Sized Pieces.

Choice (A) states that the passage includes an *introduction to an interesting phenomenon*, and that's true—the *Windshield-Pitting Mystery* could be described as an *interesting phenomenon*. But then (A) says the passage provides *evidence suggesting that it is man-made rather than natural*. The author doesn't provide evidence that windshield-pitting was caused by people. Be careful—the passage mentions that *crop circles* are made by people, and it says that some of the pits might have been, but it doesn't provide evidence of this. Furthermore, the possibility that the pits were man-made is only one small detail in the passage and doesn't answer the question about the passage's overall structure. Eliminate (A).

Choice (B) has three parts, and they are all about *two competing explanations of a puzzling circumstance*. The passage describes **several** possible explanations about what caused the windshield pitting; it doesn't *compare two competing explanations*. Eliminate (B).

Choice (C) also has three parts. The first part says the passage includes a *description of an unusual event*. That's a match—the *Windshield-Pitting Mystery* can be described as an *unusual event*. The next part of (C) says that there's a *presentation of several possible theories explaining the event*. That's a match—as mentioned in the explanation of (B), the passage presents several theories about the cause of the windshield-pitting. For example, *cosmic rays*, *skeletons of minute marine creatures*, and *mass hysteria* are all mentioned. The final part of (C) says the passage includes *dismissal of one proposed explanation*. That's a match—several paragraphs are devoted to David Rohall's argument that the Windshield-Pitting Mystery was not an example of mass hysteria.

Choice (D) describes the passage as a *list of several events which have not been explained to the satisfaction of researchers*, but the passage isn't a *list*, and it doesn't give equal weight to *several events*. Instead, the passage is an exploration, and it's focused on how looking back on the Windshield-Pitting Mystery *may give us a window…on the makeup and the mindset of mid-20th-century America*. Eliminate (D).

The correct answer is (C).

Analyzing Point of View Questions

The passage is written from the point of view of a

A) journalist exploring reactions to unusual events.

B) sociologist debunking claims of supernatural causes.

C) car owner evaluating preventative measures.

D) data analyst explaining new approaches to research.

The question asks for the author's point of view. Like the general questions we've already discussed, it is best left for after you've worked the specific questions. Use what you've learned while working the specific questions to help you with your Process of Elimination. Consider the author's tone in addition to the passage's focus, and take the answer choices in Bite-Sized Pieces. The blurb may or may not be helpful for point-of-view questions.

Choice (A) describes the author as a *journalist exploring reactions to unusual events*. The passage does focus on *reactions to unusual events*, and the tone of the passage supports the idea that the author is a *journalist*. The language is formal, but not technical, and the reporting is from an outside perspective. You may find the blurb helpful if you know that *NPR* stands for National Public Radio, but you don't need to know that to answer the question. Keep (A).

Choice (B) describes the author as a *sociologist debunking claims of supernatural causes*. There is no mention of *supernatural causes* in the passage. Furthermore, although a *sociologist* (David Rohall) is quoted extensively in the passage, the question is about the author's point of view. Eliminate (B).

Choice (C) describes the author as a *car owner evaluating preventative measures*. The passage describes people whose car windshields got damaged, but there's no mention of *preventative measures*. Moreover, the reporting is objective—there's no indication that the author personally experienced these events as a *car owner*. And, okay, the author might own a car, but you know that's a Could Be True trap, right? The passage never gives us any evidence of that. Eliminate (C).

Choice (D) describes the author as a *data analyst explaining new approaches to research*. The passage doesn't describe *new approaches to research*. Moreover, the author doesn't analyze any data, so there is no evidence that the author is a *data analyst*. Eliminate (D).

The correct answer is (A).

When you see a general question, remember to leave it for later. Use what you learn from answering the specific questions to help with Process of Elimination. In addition, take the answers in Bite-Sized Pieces and match them back to the passage.

CHARTS AND GRAPHS

Two passages on the Reading Test will contain one or two of what the College Board calls *informational graphics,* which are charts, tables, and graphs. That means that two of the four history/social studies and science passages will be accompanied by one or two figures that will provide additional information related to the passages. These passages will include a few questions that ask about the data presented in the graphics, either alone or in relation to the information in the passage. These figures might seem like they'll require more work, but the charts, tables, and graphs and the questions about them are relatively straightforward. Let's look at an example.

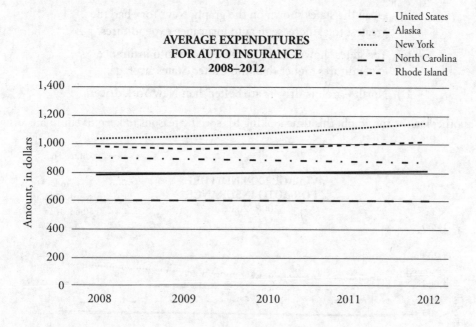

Data collected by Insurance Information Institute, http://www.iii.org/fact-statistic/auto-insurance.

Step 1: Read the graphic. Carefully look at the title, axis labels, and legend. Notice on this graph you're looking at *Average Expenditures for Auto Insurance* from 2008 to 2012. The years are listed across the horizontal axis, and the amount, in dollars, is listed on the vertical axis. According to the legend, the graph compares the entire country to Alaska, New York, North Carolina, and Rhode Island.

Step 2: Read the question.

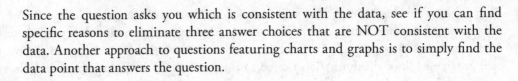

According to the graph, which of the following statements is most consistent with the data?

Watch Us Crack It

Since the question asks you which is consistent with the data, see if you can find specific reasons to eliminate three answer choices that are NOT consistent with the data. Another approach to questions featuring charts and graphs is to simply find the data point that answers the question.

Step 3: Read the answer choices.

A) Auto insurance expenditures have increased in all states from 2008 to 2012.

B) Of all the states shown on the graph, New York had the greatest total increase in auto insurance expenditures.

C) The states shown on the graph all have auto insurance expenditures higher than the United States' average.

D) North Carolina drivers are better than New York drivers.

Take another look at the graph, this time looking for specific reasons to keep or eliminate answers.

The line for New York goes up the most, so that looks good for (B).

This line for Alaska goes down instead of up, so you can eliminate (A).

The line for North Carolina is below the line for United States. Eliminate (C).

Although the line for New York is much higher than the line for North Carolina, that doesn't necessarily indicate quality of drivers. There's no data to support (D), so eliminate it.

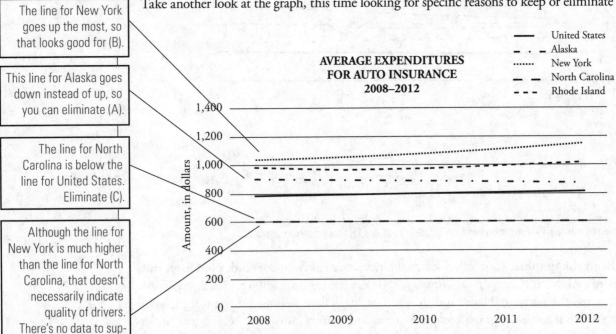

Based on the data shown, (B) is the correct answer.

Now you try one.

31

Data in the graph indicate that Rhode Island's average expenditure for auto insurance was closest to the national average in which year?

A) 2009

B) 2010

C) 2011

D) 2012

Here's How to Crack It

The question asks only about *Rhode Island* and the *national average* (which indicates the United States line). That means you need to worry about only those two lines. Find the place where those two lines are the closest and put your pencil on it. Notice how the Rhode Island line is just about parallel to the United States line, except where it dips down before it goes back up. That dip is where the lines are closest together, which is in 2009. The answer is (A)! As you may have noticed, there was no need to eliminate the three wrong answer choices because you were able to simply find the data point that answered the question. Sometimes it really will be that simple. Just make sure you have the information to support your answer.

DUAL PASSAGES

One of the science or history/social studies passages will be a set of dual passages, two shorter passages about one topic. Although the two passages will be about the same topic, there will also be differences that you'll need to pay attention to. Rather than attempting to read and understand both passages at the same time, just follow the Basic Approach and focus on one passage at a time.

The questions for Passage 1 will come before the questions for Passage 2, and the questions for each passage follow the order of the passage, just like single-passage questions. The questions about both passages will follow the questions for Passage 2.

Step 1: **Work the questions for Passage 1 using the Basic Approach.**
After working Passage 1, make a note of the main focus of the passage.

Step 2: **Work the questions for Passage 2 using the Basic Approach.**
After working Passage 2, make a note of main focus of the passage.

Step 3: **Make a note of the relationship between the passages.**
What is similar about the focus of the passages? What is different?
What do the authors agree about or disagree about?

Step 4: **Answer the questions about both passages.**

Two-Passage Questions

For questions that ask you to compare or contrast both passages, it's helpful to consider one passage at a time rather than trying to juggle both passages at the same time. First, find the answer for the first passage (or the second passage if that one is easier) and use POE to narrow down the answer choices. Then find the answer in the other passage and use POE to arrive at the correct answer. This will save time and keep you from confusing the two passages when you're evaluating the answer choices. Always keep in mind that the same POE criteria apply, no matter how two-passage questions are presented.

- If a question is about what is supported by both passages, make sure that you find specific support in both passages, and be wary of all the usual trap answers.

- If a question is about an issue on which the authors of the two passages disagree or on how the passages relate to each other, make sure you find support in each passage for the author's particular opinion.

- If the question asks how one author would respond to the other passage, find out what was said in that other passage, and then find out exactly what the author you are asked about said on that exact topic.

The bottom line: If you're organized and remember the Basic Approach for reading comprehension, you'll see that two-passage questions are no harder than single-passage questions! The following drill provides some practice with dual passages. Answers and explanations can be found at the end of the chapter.

Dual-Passage Drill

Questions 11–21 are based on the following passages.

Passage 1 is adapted from Louisa Twining, "Workhouses and Women's Work" ©1857 by The National Association for the Promotion of Social Science. Passage 2 is adapted from Florence Nightingale and William Rathbone, "Workhouse Nursing, the Story of a Successful Experiment" ©1867 by Macmillan and Co.

Passage 1

The evils of the employment of pauper nurses is dwelt upon by all who have considered the subject of workhouse management. When we
Line
5 consider the persons to whom such extensive power and responsibility are entrusted, in the care of 50,000 sick persons in the London workhouses alone, we can hardly wonder at what is told of the results of the system. The only way in which an employment of the inmates could
10 be successfully carried out, would be under the constant supervision of superior persons; but in the present system that is an impossibility. Efficient nurses, who could gain a living in any of our hospitals, would not be likely to offer
15 themselves for a post in which it is nearly all work of the hardest kind, and no pay. One of these pauper nurses boldly stated that she had been sixteen times in the House of Correction, and she was not ashamed of it. Of course such labor
20 is cheap, and it is desirable, if possible, to employ those who must be maintained at the cost of the parish; but in no case should they be left with the sole charge and responsibility of sick wards, as they continually are at present, without any other
25 control than the occasional visit of the matron, bestowed at the utmost once a day, in some cases only once a week.

Seeing how careful boards of guardians are in all matters of expense, it would have been well if
30 the recommendation of the poor law with regard to the employment of at least one paid nurse had been a law; as it is, many workhouses are without one. That such a person would always be all we could desire for so important a post we could
35 hardly hope, from what we know of the paid

nurses in hospitals, but at any rate there would be a better chance of efficiency and character than in the present plan.

Passage 2

But on the 18th of May, 1865, a Lady
40 Superintendent who had received a thorough training at Kaiserswerth and St. Thomas's, twelve Nightingale nurses from St. Thomas's, eighteen probationers, and fifty-two of the old pauper nurses were placed in charge of the patients in the
45 male wards of the Workhouse Infirmary.

With the exception of the failure of the nurses taken from the pauper class, the first year's trial was sufficiently successful to induce a continuance of the experiment. It was impossible,
50 however, to judge the result by statistics. None that were available could be considered as an evidence of success or failure, for several reasons. The season was very unhealthy, and to relieve the pressure on the space and resources of the
55 hospital, steps were taken to treat slight cases outside.

The endeavor to limit the admissions to serious cases would of course affect the returns, both as regards the time taken in curing, and the
60 proportion of deaths. Even had there been no exceptional disturbing element, there is a defect in the statistics of workhouse hospitals which affects all inferences from them, in the absence of any careful classified list of cases kept by the
65 medical officers, such as might fairly enable one to form a judgment from mere statistical tables. These, then, are not reliable as means of judgment, unless extending over a long period. The character of seasons, and nature of cases
70 admitted, varies so much from year to year as to invalidate any deductions, unless founded on minutely kept medical records. The following extracts, however, from the reports of the Governor, and the surgical and medical officers of
75 the Workhouse, bear decisive witness to the value of the "new system," especially as contrasted with the "old system," which in 1865–66 still prevailed in the female wards. All these reports bear

emphatic testimony to the merits and devotion
80 of the Lady Superintendent and her staff. The
medical men, it is noteworthy, speak strongly of
the better discipline and far greater obedience to
their orders observable where the trained nurses
are employed—a point the more important
85 because it is that on which, before experience has
reassured them, medical and other authorities
have often been most doubtful.

11

The primary purpose of Passage 1 is to

A) praise an effective structure.

B) criticize a social group.

C) examine the finances of a system.

D) advocate for a necessary change.

12

Which choice provides the best evidence for the
answer to the previous question?

A) Lines 13-16 ("Efficient . . . pay")

B) Lines 16-19 ("One of . . . it")

C) Lines 19-22 ("Of course . . . parish")

D) Lines 22-27 ("but in . . . week")

13

As used in line 21, "maintained" most nearly
means

A) provided for.

B) affirmed.

C) healed.

D) fixed.

14

The phrase in lines 34–35 ("we could hardly
hope") most directly suggests that

A) an ideal candidate should be found for a
position.

B) people who go to hospitals should be critical
of nurses.

C) allowances should be made, since no person
is perfect.

D) an improvement is still likely to have some
flaws.

15

Which choice provides the best evidence for the
answer to the previous question?

A) Lines 7-8 ("we can . . . system")

B) Lines 19-22 ("Of course . . . parish")

C) Lines 29-32 ("it would . . . law")

D) Lines 33-36 ("That such . . . hospitals")

16

The final sentence of Passage 1 has which effect?

A) It emphasizes that the current situation is
unpleasant.

B) It shares the author's despair over the
circumstances.

C) It casts an entirely optimistic light on a
proposal.

D) It evokes the generally low opinion held for a
certain group.

17

It can be most directly inferred from the second paragraph of Passage 2 (lines 46-56) that the first year of the experiment described in the passage was unusual in

A) having weather that caused an uncharacteristic amount of illness.

B) the overall number of people who required medical treatment.

C) that effective medical treatment exceeded statistical expectations.

D) the number of people who died from disease.

18

The authors of Passage 2 reference a "careful classified list of cases" (line 64) in order to

A) specify what will be required of all workhouses in the future, if the experiment continues.

B) explain a missing element that would have ensured an outcome.

C) reveal an inconsistency that made more accurate analysis impossible.

D) detail the extent to which records can be kept over a long period.

19

As used in line 69, the phrase "character of seasons" most nearly means

A) changes in morality.

B) weather patterns.

C) the overall health during a period.

D) the unpredictable nature of human behavior.

20

The author of Passage 1 would most likely respond to the phrase in lines 46-47 ("With the exception . . . class") of Passage 2 by

A) expressing surprise at an unexpected result that is inconsistent with prior observations.

B) acknowledging that an ideal situation may not be practical to attain.

C) noting that intervention earlier in life may have changed an outcome.

D) suggesting that the data may not be entirely representative.

21

Which choice best describes the relationship between the two passages?

A) Passage 2 describes a scenario that addresses some elements of the situation shown in Passage 1.

B) Passage 2 discusses potential results of the overall problem reviewed in Passage 1.

C) Passage 2 underscores the futility of attempts to resolve the concerns of Passage 1.

D) Passage 2 resolves the issues brought to light in Passage 1.

DUAL-PASSAGE DRILL ANSWERS AND EXPLANATIONS

11. **D**   The question asks about the *primary purpose of Passage 1*. Notice that this is the first question in a paired set, so it can be done in tandem with Q12. As this is a general question, it should be done after the specific questions. Look at the answers for Q12 first. The lines for (12A) state that *efficient nurses…would not be likely to offer themselves for a post in which it is nearly all work of the hardest kind, and no pay.* The passage recommends a change in the employment of pauper nurses in workhouses, saying that they should not have the sole responsibility for sick patients, and that it would be better to hire a paid nurse to supervise at each workhouse. The lines for (12A) give one detail in the argument, but they do not capture the passage's primary purpose. Additionally, none of the answer choices for Q11 mention the difficulty of the *work* or how much *pay* there is. Eliminate (12A). The lines for (12B) mention a *pauper nurse* who has *been sixteen times in the House of Correction.* These lines only mention an example of one person; they do not reflect the primary purpose of the passage. Eliminate (12B). The lines for (12C) state that *such labor is cheap, and it is desirable, if possible, to employ those who must be maintained at the cost of the parish.* These lines acknowledge what the author sees as a benefit of the current system, but the passage's main purpose is to advocate for a change. These lines don't capture the main idea of the passage, so eliminate (12C). The lines for (12D) state that *in no case should [the pauper nurses] be left with the sole charge and responsibility of sick wards, as they continually are at present.* These lines reflect the passage's purpose. Look to see whether these lines support any of the answer choices for Q11: they *advocate for a necessary change*, so draw a line connecting (12D) and (11D). Without any support in the answers in Q12, (11A), (11B), and (11C) can be eliminated. The correct answers are (12D) and (11D).

12. **D**   (See explanation above.)

13. **A**   The question asks what the word *maintained* most nearly means in line 21. Go back to the text, find the word *maintained*, and cross it out. Then read the window carefully, using context clues to determine another word that would fit in the text. The text says that *of course such labor is cheap, and it is desirable, if possible, to employ those who must be maintained at the cost of the parish.* Therefore, *maintained* must mean something like "financially supported." Choice (A), *provided for*, closely matches the text of the passage, so keep it. *Affirmed* means "encouraged by;" it does not match "financially supported." Eliminate (B). *Healed* does not match "financially supported," so eliminate (C). *Fixed* does not match "financially supported;" this is a Could Be True trap answer based on a different meaning of *maintained* than the one used in the text, so eliminate (D). The correct answer is (A).

14. **D**   The question asks what is most directly suggested by lines 34–35. This is the first question in a paired set, but it is a specific question, so it can be done on its own. Read a window around the line reference. Lines 33–38 state, *That such a person would always be all we could desire for so important a post we could hardly hope…but at any rate, there would be a better chance of efficiency and character than in the present plan.* In other words, the author acknowledges that the nurses hired won't be perfect, but hiring them will still be an improvement over the current situation. These

lines indicate that the plan should be implemented even though there is not an *ideal candidate*, so eliminate (A). Eliminate (B) because, although the author is critical, she never indicates what *people who go to hospitals* should do. Choice (C) states that *allowances should be made, since no person is perfect*. The passage does not indicate that *no person is perfect*; it only discusses nurses. It also does not state that *allowances should be made*; instead it says that the plan to hire the nurses would improve on the present situation. Eliminate (C). Choice (D) matches the text of the passage, as it correctly states that hiring the nurses would be an *improvement* even though they would *have some flaws*. The correct answer is (D).

15. **D** The question is the best evidence question in a paired set. Because Q14 was a specific question, simply look at the lines used to answer the previous question. The last sentence of the passage, lines 33–38, was the underlined text for the last question. Only one of the answers matches those lines. The correct answer is (D).

16. **A** The question asks for the effect of the *final sentence of Passage 1*. Read a window around the line reference. The last sentence states *that such a person would always be all we could desire for so important a post we could hardly hope, from what we know of the paid nurses in hospitals, but at any rate, there would be a better chance of efficiency and character than in the present plan.* The author is acknowledging that the solution has flaws, but it is nonetheless preferable to the current system. Since the last sentence indicates that even an imperfect plan would be better than the present situation, it implies that *the present situation is unpleasant*, so keep (A). Choice (B) uses the word *despair*, and while the author is not happy with the current situation, she does not completely lack hope. This answer choice is Mostly Right but Slightly Wrong; eliminate (B). Choice (C) mentions an *entirely optimistic light*, but the last sentence acknowledges flaws with the solution, so it is not completely *optimistic*. Eliminate (C). Choice (D) mentions *the generally low opinion held for a certain group*, but the last sentence is about finding solutions, however imperfect, to the current dilemma, not about criticizing a group of people. Eliminate (D). The correct answer is (A).

17. **B** The question asks what can be seen as *unusual* about *the first year of the experiment* described. Read a window around the line reference. Lines 49–50 indicate that the first year of the experiment could not be judged by statistics, for several reasons. Line 53 states that *the season was very unhealthy*, which means that an unusual number of people were sick that season. This is something unusual about the first year of the experiment. Choice (A) mentions *weather that caused an uncharacteristic amount of illnesses*. This answer is Mostly Right but Slightly Wrong: *an uncharacteristic amount of illness* matches the text in the passage, but the text never states that the illnesses were caused by *weather*. Eliminate (A). Choice (B) states that *the overall number of people who required medical treatment* was unusual that season. This matches the passage text closely, so keep (B). Choice (C) mentions that effective medical treatment *exceeded statistical expectations*. However, lines 49–50 state *it is impossible...to judge the results by statistics*. Eliminate (C). Choice (D) mentions *the number of people who died*, but no deaths are mentioned in paragraph two. Eliminate (D). The correct answer is (B).

18. **C** The question asks why the authors of Passage 2 reference a *careful classified list of cases*. Read a window around the line reference. In lines 60–67, the authors discuss a defect in the statistics of workhouse hospitals. They say that the absence of a careful classified list of cases kept by the medical officers is one reason it is not possible *to form a judgement from mere statistical tables*. Though the text in lines 64–67 makes it clear that the absence of the *careful classified list of cases* is problematic, the author never states that it would be *required of all workhouses in the future*. Eliminate (A). Choice (B) is a Mostly Right/Slightly Wrong trap answer: it mentions *a missing element*, which seems to match the absence of a *careful classified list of cases*. However, lines 65–67 say that having the list of cases *might* allow one to *form a judgment*. Choice (B) says that having the list of cases would have *ensured an outcome*; the passage does not support this much certainty. Eliminate (B). Choice (C) says *reveal an inconsistency that made more accurate analysis impossible*, which closely matches the text of the passage that indicates that it was not possible *to form a judgement from mere statistical tables*. Keep (C). Choice (D) mentions *a long period*. This phrase is used in line 68, but the text indicates that it's necessary to keep statistical tables over a long period to make accurate judgements; it doesn't discuss whether *records can be kept* for a long period. Eliminate (D). The correct answer is (C).

19. **C** The question asks what the phrase *character of seasons* most nearly means in line 69. Go back to the text, find the phrase *character of seasons*, and cross it out. Then read the window carefully, using context clues to determine another phrase that would fit in the text. The text says that *the character of seasons, and nature of cases admitted, varies so much from year to year as to invalidate any deductions, unless founded on minutely kept medical records*. Therefore, *character of seasons* must mean something like "seasonal changes in average health." Notice that (A) uses the word *morality*, not "mortality." The correct answer should refer to health, not morals, so eliminate (A). *Weather* is not mentioned in the sentence, so eliminate (B). Choice (C) closely matches the text of the passage, so keep it. While the *unpredictable nature* part of (D) seems to match the idea in the text, the text is talking about health, not *human behavior*. Eliminate (D). The correct answer is (C).

20. **B** The question asks how the *author of Passage 1 would most likely respond* to lines 46–47 of Passage 2. Consider the relationship between the passages. In Passage 1, the author recommends that the *pauper nurses* employed in the workhouses be supervised by *a paid nurse*. In Passage 2, the authors evaluate the success of a trial in which a trained nurse (*a Lady Superintendent*) was placed in charge of the patients in a workhouse. The authors agree on their criticism of the *pauper nurses*. Lines 46–47 of Passage 2 mention *the failure of the nurses taken from the pauper classes*. Choice (A) mentions that the author of Passage 1 would be *surprise[d] at an unexpected result*. But the author of Passage 1 clearly has a low view of the *pauper nurses*, as can be seen in the first line, which introduces *the evils of the employment of pauper nurses*. So, the author would be expecting failure from the *pauper nurses*. Eliminate (A). Choice (B), *acknowledging that an ideal situation may not be practical to attain*, matches Twining's attitude in lines 33–38, in which she states *that such a person would always be all we could desire for so important a post we could hardly hope*. In other words, she

acknowledges that even the solution she is proposing would not be perfect. Keep (B). As the author of Passage 1 never discussed an *intervention earlier in life*, (C) must be eliminated. The author of Passage 1 would most likely agree that poor performance would be *representative*, or typical, of pauper nurses. Eliminate (D). The correct answer is (B).

21. **A** The question asks for the *relationship between the two passages*. Consider the relationship. In Passage 1, the author recommends that the *pauper nurses* employed in the workhouses be supervised by *a paid nurse*. In Passage 2, the authors evaluate the success of a trial in which a trained nurse (*a Lady Superintendent*) was placed in charge of the patients in a workhouse. Choice (A) states that *Passage 2 describes a scenario that addresses some elements of the situation shown in Passage 1*. This choice matches the passage text: the experiment described in Passage 2 is the scenario, and it does discuss some elements that are addressed in Passage 1, including trained nurses and pauper nurses. Keep (A). Choice (B) states that *Passage 2 discusses the potential results of the overall problem reviewed in Passage 1*. The *overall problem reviewed in Passage 1* is the lack of supervision of the *pauper nurses*. Though Passage 2 mentions *pauper nurses*, it does not discuss *the potential results of the* problem; in fact, it discusses a trial of the solution recommended in Passage 1. Eliminate (B). Choice (C) states that *Passage 2 underscores the futility of attempts to resolve the concerns of Passage 1*. Passage 2 does not *underscore the futility* of attempts to resolve the problem of supervision of pauper nurses—it recounts a relatively successful attempt. Note the positive tone of lines 78–80: *All these reports bear emphatic testimony to the merits and devotion of the Lady Superintendent and her staff*. Eliminate (C). Choice (D) states that *Passage 2 resolves the issues brought to light in Passage 1*. Passage 2 does not entirely *resolve the issues brought to light in Passage 1*; note lines 46–49, which state, *With the exception of the failure of the nurses taken from the pauper class, the first year's trial was sufficiently successful to induce a continuance of the experiment*. In other words, the trial was successful enough to continue, but not completely successful. Eliminate (D). The correct answer is (A).

Summary

- o For paired questions, make sure you're following the right strategy.
  - • Specific paired questions simply require you to follow the Basic Approach, making sure you've underlined the answer in the text.
  - • General paired questions will be much more straightforward if you use Parallel POE to consider the "best evidence" in tandem with the previous question.

- o For dual passages, do questions about the first passage first, questions about the second passage second, and dual questions last. Remember that even with dual questions, you must find support in the passages.

- o Save main idea or general questions until the end of the passage. POE will be much more efficient once you've done all of the other questions.

- o Don't get bogged down by hard or time-consuming questions! If you find yourself stuck or running short on time, use LOTD and move on.

Chapter 7
Advanced Reading Skills

In this chapter, we'll cover skills to use when you encounter more difficult passages, questions, or answer choices.

WHEN THE GOING GETS TOUGH

SAT Reading passages cover a wide variety of topics and time periods. You may encounter passages on topics you find unfamiliar and difficult, or passages from as long ago as the 18th century. Likewise, you may encounter questions with confusing language in the answer choices. Your POOD should tell you to leave these passages and questions for last, or possibly to use your Letter of the Day. However, if your pacing goal requires you to work the toughest passages and questions, you will need a strategy to tackle them. In this chapter, we will look at skills for dealing with difficult passages and answer choices.

TRANSLATING

If you read the window for a question in the passage and you don't understand what you've read, what can you do?

First, break the section of text down using **Bite-Sized Pieces:** focus on one sentence, or even one phrase, at a time. Start with whichever piece you find most straightforward, and work your way forward or backward from there, translating as you go.

Let's look at an excerpt from a text written in 1774.

> The following passage is excerpted from a speech given by Edmund Burke in 1774. Burke was a member of the British Parliament.

And, of course, the question to go with it:

12

> In line 1, the words, "I am sorry" most nearly express the author's regret that

And then our window:

> I am sorry I cannot conclude without saying a word on a topic touched
> upon by my worthy colleague. I wish that topic had been passed by at a time
> when I have so little leisure to discuss it. But since he has thought proper to
> Line throw it out, I owe you a clear explanation of my poor sentiments on that
> 5 subject.

Imagine if you tried to just jump in and read this passage without a question to work on! Even with the question to guide your thought process, these few sentences are still a challenge to understand. So, let's break this down using Bite-Sized Pieces.

Which part of this paragraph do you find most straightforward? You might start with the phrase *I cannot conclude without saying a word on a topic*. What does this tell you about what the author is doing? He is introducing a topic that he is going to speak about, and he says he *cannot conclude* without doing so, which indicates that this passage comes from the end of a longer speech or piece of writing.

Work forward or backward from this phrase. The sentence starts with *I am sorry*. Why does he feel sorry about speaking on this topic? Asking yourself **questions** about the text is an important reading comprehension skill. It tells you what to look for in the text and can help you understand the text more quickly and completely. As you read the rest of the paragraph, look for clues as to why the author is sorry.

Now consider the end of the first sentence: it says that the topic was *touched upon by my worthy colleague*. It sounds as though someone the speaker works with brought up the topic. What kind of work do the author and the colleague do? The blurb says that the speaker, Edmund Burke, was a member of British Parliament, so he and his colleague are politicians. Don't forget to check the **blurb**! It may include information that will help you understand the passage.

In the next sentence, Burke states, *I wish that topic had been passed by at a time when I have so little leisure to discuss it*. What does this sentence tell you? It expresses the author's *wish* about the topic and indicates that he has *so little leisure to discuss it*. The word *leisure* means something like "free time," so the author is saying that he does not have much time to discuss the topic now. Now consider the phrase *had been passed by*—since the author does not have time to discuss the topic, he must be saying that he wishes they had skipped over it. Now, we understand why the author is sorry about having to speak on the topic—he doesn't have as much time as he would like to talk about it now.

Now consider the final sentence: *But since he has thought proper to throw it out, I owe you a clear explanation of my poor sentiments on that subject*. The sentence starts with the transition word *but*. **Transition words** are important clues in understanding the text. Just before this, the author said that he does not have time to discuss the topic and wishes they had skipped over it. The word *but* indicates a change in direction, so it's likely that the author is going to say that he will speak on the topic anyway. (This prediction is supported by the first sentence too.)

Who do the pronouns *he* and *it* in this sentence refer to? Matching **pronouns** back to the nouns they replace is another important skill in translating convoluted text. Look at the previous sentences: *he* refers to Burke's *colleague*, and *it* refers to the topic he brought up.

When you see the phrase *throw it out*, you may think about taking out the garbage, but use the **context**: we know the colleague brought up the topic, so it's logical that *throw it out* means "bring it up." The word *proper* means "right" or "correct." Putting it all together, this phrase means, "But, since he thought it was right to bring it up…"

Finally, look at the last phrase: *I owe you a clear explanation of my poor sentiments on that subject*. What does *my poor sentiments on that subject* mean? *Sentiments* are feelings, or possibly thoughts. Burke is a politician: is it likely that he is about to share thoughts that he actually believes are *poor*? Probably not—he is likely just trying to sound humble. Who does *you* refer to? We don't know yet who he is speaking to; this is another question to keep in mind as you read. We can also make a good guess based on the fact that he is a politician: he might be speaking to other politicians or to the people he represents.

As you translate, try to summarize periodically. Thinking about the **main idea** or **purpose of each paragraph** will help you understand the structure of the passage. Putting all the pieces together, what is Burke doing in this paragraph? He is introducing the topic he will speak on.

What do we know so far? We don't know the topic of the speech yet, but we know it's a subject that his colleague brought up, that Burke would rather have more time to talk about it, and that he is going to explain his thoughts on the topic anyway.

Now let's use the translation to answer the question.

12

In line 1, the words, "I am sorry" most nearly express the author's regret that

A) he is imposing on his audience by asking them to continue listening.

B) his colleague has dismissed an important topic.

C) he does not have more time to discuss his next subject.

D) he is a poor speaker and cannot express himself clearly.

Which answers can you eliminate based on your translation? Choice (A) implies that Burke is making an apology to the audience. This does not match the text: he regrets that he doesn't have more time to speak. Eliminate (A). Choice (B) is a Right Words, Wrong Meaning trap based on the phrase *throw it out*. Based on the context, we translated that phrase as "bring up the topic," so this answer is not supported by the text. Eliminate (B). Choice (C) is a good match for our translation: Burke regrets that he doesn't have as much time as he would like to talk about this topic. Keep (C). Choice (D) is also a Right Words, Wrong Meaning trap based on the phrase *I owe you a clear explanation of my poor sentiments*, but we noted that Burke used the word *poor* to be humble, not because he actually thinks he is a poor speaker. Eliminate (D). The correct answer is (C).

Now try answering some questions based on the rest of this passage. Use the Basic Approach. As you Read What You Need, translate one bite-sized piece at time, starting with the piece that seems most straightforward. Don't forget to underline the answer in the text.

13

The "topic of instructions" can best be characterized as

He tells you that "the topic of instructions has occasioned much altercation and uneasiness in this city;" and he expresses himself (if I understand him rightly) in favour of the coercive authority of such instructions.

What is your translation?

_____

_____

_____

_____

14

As used in line 12, the word "weight" most nearly means

Certainly, gentlemen, it ought to be the happiness and glory of a
10 representative to live in the strictest union, the closest correspondence, and
the most unreserved communication with his constituents. Their wishes ought
to have great weight with him; their opinion, high respect; their business,
unremitted attention. It is his duty to sacrifice his repose, his pleasures, his
satisfactions, to theirs; and above all, ever, and in all cases, to prefer their
15 interest to his own. But his unbiassed opinion, his mature judgment, his
enlightened conscience, he ought not to sacrifice to you, to any man, or to any
set of men living. These he does not derive from your pleasure; no, nor from
the law and the constitution. They are a trust from Providence, for the abuse of
which he is deeply answerable. Your representative owes you, not his industry
20 only, but his judgment; and he betrays, instead of serving you, if he sacrifices it
to your opinion.

What is your translation?

_____

_____

_____

_____

_____

15

The fourth paragraph (lines 22–29) suggests Burke would be most
likely to agree that legislation should

My worthy colleague says, his will ought to be subservient to yours. If that
be all, the thing is innocent. If government were a matter of will upon any side,
yours, without question, ought to be superior. But government and legislation
25 are matters of reason and judgment, and not of inclination; and what sort of
reason is that, in which the determination precedes the discussion; in which
one set of men deliberate, and another decide; and where those who form the
conclusion are perhaps three hundred miles distant from those who hear the
arguments?

What is your translation?

_____

_____

_____

_____

_____

16

As used in line 36, "a fundamental mistake" most nearly refers to

30   To deliver an opinion, is the right of all men; that of constituents is a
weighty and respectable opinion, which a representative ought always to
rejoice to hear; and which he ought always most seriously to consider. But
authoritative instructions; mandates issued, which the member is bound
blindly and implicitly to obey, to vote, and to argue for, though contrary to the
35   clearest conviction of his judgment and conscience,—these are things utterly
unknown to the laws of this land, and which arise from a fundamental mistake
of the whole order and tenor of our constitution.

What is your translation?

_____

_____

_____

_____

Now, with your translations in mind, try the following questions on your own before reading
the explanations.

———————————○———————————

13

The "topic of instructions" can best be characterized as

A) a popular policy.

B) a controversial subject.

C) an authoritative statement.

D) a settled matter.

Here's How to Crack It

The question asks how best to characterize the *topic of instructions*. The paragraph states that
the topic of instructions has occasioned much altercation and uneasiness in this city. Translate
this phrase, starting with the most straightforward part: *uneasiness* indicates that something
about the topic makes people uncomfortable. You may not know what *altercation* means, but
the word *and* indicates that it goes in the same direction as *uneasiness*. Therefore, the *topic of
instructions* has caused some kind of discomfort or disruption in the city. This paragraph also
answers one of the questions that was brought up by the first paragraph: the *topic of instructions*
is the subject that Burke is going to discuss.

Choice (A) is positive, and doesn't match the negative tone of *uneasiness*, so eliminate it.

Choice (B) matches: *a controversial subject* could cause *uneasiness*, so keep it.

Choice (C) may be tempting because *authoritative* seems to match the idea of giving *instructions*, but use the text you underlined: *authoritative* doesn't match *uneasiness*. In addition, one *statement* is not a *topic*. Eliminate (C).

Choice (D) does not match the text; if the topic is causing uneasiness, it must not be *settled*. Eliminate (D).

The correct answer is (B).

14

As used in line 12, the word "weight" most nearly means

A) significance.

B) heaviness.

C) measure.

D) burden.

Here's How to Crack It

This is a vocabulary in context question that asks about the word *weight*. Go back to the passage, cross out the word *weight*, and use the surrounding lines to determine another word that would match the meaning. The previous phrase talks about communication between a *representative* and his *constituents* (the people he represents). The sentence with the word *weight* says, *Their wishes ought to have great weight with him; their opinion, high respect; their business, unremitted attention.* Use the next part of the sentence to help determine the meaning: it pairs the constituents' opinion with *high respect* and the constituents' business with *attention*. The text is saying that the representative should give the constituents his respect and attention, so the word *weight* must mean something like "importance."

Choice (A), *significance*, matches "importance," so keep it.

Choice (B), *heaviness*, does not match "importance," so eliminate it. This is a Could Be True trap answer, based on another meaning of *weight* that is not supported by the context.

Choices (C) and (D) are also Could Be True trap answers: neither of these words matches "importance," so eliminate both choices.

The correct answer is (A).

In your translation, did you notice that this paragraph also answers the question of whom Burke is speaking to? He discusses what a representative should and should not sacrifice to his constituents, and then he switches to the pronoun *you*. The last sentence says, *Your representative owes you, not his industry only, but his judgment; and he betrays, instead of serving you, if he sacrifices it to your opinion.* Burke is speaking to his constituents.

15

The fourth paragraph (lines 22–29) suggests Burke would be most likely to agree that legislation should

A) follow guidelines established by the Magna Carta.

B) always reflect the opinions of those who correspond with their representatives.

C) reflect representatives' knowledge of legal precedent.

D) be decided following debate of the relevant issues.

Here's How to Crack It

The question asks which statement about *legislation* Burke would most likely agree with. In this paragraph, Burke begins by telling the audience what his colleague thinks: *his will ought to be subservient to yours*. Then, he makes a couple of statements that begin with the word *if*. *If that be all, the thing is innocent. If government were a matter of will upon any side, yours, without question, ought to be superior.* It sounds like, in some respects, Burke agrees with his colleague. However, in the next sentence, he uses the opposite-direction transition word *but*. *But government and legislation are matters of reason and judgment, and not of inclination.* Therefore, Burke does not agree entirely. In these lines, he echoes the statement he made at the end of the last paragraph: the representative should not sacrifice his judgement to the constituents' opinion. He goes on to say, *and what sort of reason is that, in which the determination precedes the discussion; in which one set of men deliberate, and another decide; and where those who form the conclusion are perhaps three hundred miles distant from those who hear the arguments?* He supports his argument by pointing out that it doesn't make sense to have one group of people (the legislators) debate an issue after another group of people (the constituents) has already made the decision.

Choice (A) is a Could Be True trap answer. It's possible, even likely, that Burke does support following the Magna Carta's guidelines. However, this is not discussed in the text, and on the SAT, the correct answer must be supported by the text. Eliminate (A).

Choice (B) says that legislation should *always* reflect the opinions of constituents. Burke does think that legislators should consider their constituents' opinions, but he does not think they should sacrifice their judgement to the constituents' opinions, so the word *always* is not supported. Eliminate (B).

Choice (C) is a Mostly Right/Slightly Wrong trap answer: Burke does think that legislation should reflect representatives' judgement and reason, but he does not mention *legal precedent*. Eliminate (C).

Choice (D) matches the last sentence of the paragraph: Burke believes that decisions about legislation should be made after deliberation. The correct answer is (D).

16

As used in line 36, "a fundamental mistake" most nearly refers to

A) disregarding the opinions of constituents.

B) a misunderstanding of the constitution.

C) disobeying instructions.

D) a law that should be amended.

Here's How to Crack It

The question asks what the phrase *a fundamental mistake* refers to. In this paragraph, Burke reiterates his argument. Representatives should consider and respect their constituents' opinions but should not ignore good judgement and conscience to obey instructions from their constituents. He ends by saying that these approaches to governing are *utterly unknown to the laws of this land,* and that they *arise from a fundamental mistake of the whole order and tenor of our constitution*. In other words, the idea that legislators are meant to follow instructions from their constituents is not supported by the law; if people think so, they misunderstand.

Choice (A) is a Right Words, Wrong Meaning trap. Burke does state that representatives should consider their constituents' opinions, but disregarding them is not the *fundamental mistake* that he discusses.

Choice (B) matches the passage, so keep it.

Choice (C) is another Right Words, Wrong Meaning trap. *Obey* and *instructions* appear in the passage, but Burke does not think it's a mistake to disobey instructions. In fact, it's just the opposite: he thinks representatives should not be expected to obey instructions.

Choice (D) mentions a law that needs to be changed, but the law is not a mistake; the *mistake* refers to misunderstanding the law. Eliminate (D).

The correct answer is (B).

And now try a general Paired Evidence question about this passage.

11

The central question that Burke and his colleague disagree over is whether

A) representatives should prioritize the will of their constituents.

B) important topics have been given due consideration in Parliament.

C) members of Parliament should vote according to constituents' directives.

D) voters possess the reason and judgement necessary to make policy decisions.

12

Which choice provides the best evidence for the previous question?

A) Lines 3–5 ("But since . . . subject")

B) Line 22 ("My worthy . . . yours")

C) Lines 24–29 ("But government . . . arguments")

D) Lines 30–32 ("To deliver . . . consider")

Here's How to Crack It

Since this is a general Paired Evidence question, use Parallel Process of Elimination. Question 11 asks for the central point of disagreement between Burke and his colleague.

The lines for (12A) say, *But since he has thought proper to throw it out, I owe you a clear explanation of my poor sentiments on that subject.* In these lines, Burke does not mention the topic he will discuss: he only says that his colleague has mentioned the topic and that he is going to talk about it. Therefore, these lines can't give evidence of the central point of disagreement. They don't address question 11, so eliminate (12A).

The lines for (12B) say, *My worthy colleague says, his will ought to be subservient to yours.* This certainly mentions the colleague's opinion. However, Burke agrees with his colleague on this point. Burke says, *If that be all, the thing is innocent. If government were a matter of will upon any side, yours, without question, ought to be superior.* Therefore, these lines don't provide evidence about a point of disagreement between the two men. They don't address question 11, so eliminate (12B).

The lines for (12C) say, *But government and legislation are matters of reason and judgment, and not of inclination; and what sort of reason is that, in which the determination precedes the discussion; in which one set of men deliberate, and another decide; and where those who form the conclusion are perhaps three hundred miles distant from those who hear the arguments?* The opposite-direction transition *But* at the beginning of these lines indicates disagreement. In these lines, Burke states his argument against his colleague on the topic of instructions: government is a matter of reason, so representatives should deliberate issues and then make decisions. They should not have to follow instructions from constituents, who have made decisions ahead of time without the benefit of deliberation. This addresses the central point of disagreement between Burke and his colleague. Look to see if this supports an answer choice for question 11. It supports (11C), the question of whether *members of Parliament* (the representatives) should follow their *constituents' directives*, or instructions. Draw a line connecting (12C) and (11C).

The lines for (12D) say, *To deliver an opinion, is the right of all men; that of constituents is a weighty and respectable opinion, which a representative ought always to rejoice to hear; and which he ought always most seriously to consider.* These lines convey a point of agreement between Burke and his colleague, who believes that a representative should put the constituents' will above his own. These lines don't address question 11, so eliminate (12D).

Without support from question 12, (11A), (11B), and (11D) can be eliminated. The correct answers are (11C) and (12C).

―――――――――――○―――――――――――

MATCHING BACK ANSWER CHOICES

Sometimes, even the answer choices require translation. This is especially true for answer choices that use very general language. Let's look at some examples, based on the following passage.

This passage is from Charles Petit, "Hazy Days in Our Parks," which originally appeared in *Smithsonian* magazine. ©2005 by Charles Petit

Ever since Congress created the first national park, at Yellowstone in 1872, the parks have enjoyed special legal protections. In 1916, the
Line National Park Service was set up to maintain
5 areas "unimpaired for the enjoyment of future generations." Additional legal backing came in 1977 when amendments to the Clean Air Act gave parks the highest priority, designating them as Class I areas. The law is emphatic: "Congress
10 hereby declares as a national goal the prevention of any future, and the remedying of any existing, impairment of visibility in mandatory class I Federal areas which impairment results from manmade air pollution."
15 "It was visionary to try to protect these areas without even knowing how difficult it would be," says air resources division director Chris Shaver. The division has outfitted most major parks with filters to gather aerosols, or ultrafine solid
20 and liquid particles in the air; nephelometers to measure how haze scatters sunlight; and transmissometers that gauge scattering and absorption of light by pollution, dust, mist or other material in the air. Chemical samplers
25 scrutinize the concentration of such problematic molecules as ozone, which can be harmful to humans at ground level.
Shaver remembers standing on the rim of the Grand Canyon with her then 6-year-old
30 daughter, Courtney, in 1990. The girl looked at the barely visible cliffs on the other side and said, "Mom, I don't know how to tell you this, because I know how hard you are working, but you're not doing a very good job." Courtney graduated
35 from college this year, and Shaver still sees haze in the park system. When researchers started measuring the Grand Canyon's air quality in the 1970s, "Congress and most people thought we had a problem with [only] a few power plants in
40 the four corners," she says of the region where Arizona, New Mexico, Colorado and Utah meet.

Since then, while these power plants have slashed their overall sulfur emissions by 72 percent, the canyon's haze remains—evidence that the
45 problem isn't merely local.
The Clear Skies Initiative aims to replace the strict limits governing an individual power plant's emissions of sulfur dioxide and nitrogen oxides with a "cap-and-trade" system. A plant
50 that exceeds a limit for a pollutant would buy or trade credits from an operator that was under the limit for the same compound, keeping the nation's overall pollution in check. Proponents say the plan is simpler, allows companies to be
55 flexible, and lets some stay in business without buying expensive clean-up equipment. If a plant goes over its limit and has no credits to buy its way clear, EPA officials can levy fines with fewer hearings and lawsuits.
60 But opponents see Clear Skies as a sellout to industry. They say the proposal is less aggressive than current regulations, and they complain that it would let dirty power plants operate as long as their owners buy credits elsewhere. Many
65 environmental organizations have attacked the proposals. "Why is the Administration bragging about a plan that will actually result in more pollution than if we simply enforced the existing Clean Air Act?" the Sierra Club asks.
70 Clear Skies opponents also say the plan would put park air at risk because the cap-and-trade credit system takes the teeth out of the parks' Class I designation. Park superintendents would no longer have clear authority to demand that
75 the EPA or other agencies go after individual polluters. The Clear Skies legislation is currently stalled in a Senate committee.
Bartering has worked in the past. Since 1990, power plants have been allowed to use a cap-and-
80 trade system to help reduce acid rain, produced largely by coal-fired plants spewing nitrogen and sulfur. Consequently, sulfur emissions went from 17.3 million tons in 1980 to 10.6 million tons in 2003.
85 Park service expert Mark Scruggs is guardedly optimistic about the Clear Skies Initiative. "If the

caps are stiff enough, sure, it will help a
lot," he says. "A 70 percent cut in sulfur
dioxide is going to make a difference,
90 especially for the East Coast parks."
But Scruggs says that when the current
system is at its best—when agencies
work together to prosecute individual
polluters—results are impressive. EPA
95 pressure on industry led to improvements
in scrubber technologies, which reduce
smokestack emissions, with 95 to 98
percent elimination of some pollutants
now commonplace. Scruggs says similar
100 improvements are possible for other
pollutants.

23

The reference to amendments to the Clean Air Act primarily
serves to

A) cite changes that had detrimental effects.

B) provide support for a previous statement.

C) introduce a controversial hypothesis.

D) offer an alternative proposal.

**Watch Us
Crack It**

Here's How to Crack It

Note that the answer choices contain general words such as *effects*, *previous statement*, *hypothesis*,
and *explanation*, rather than naming specific things that were discussed in the passage. The key
with these answers is to match the general terms back to specifics in the passage, eliminating
answers that do not match up. Let's try to **match back** the general terms. The *amendments to
the Clean Air Act* are discussed in line 7, so the window for this question is the first paragraph.

Choice (A) mentions *changes* and *detrimental effects*. The word *changes* matches *amendments*, but
the passage indicates that the effect of the amendments was to *make the parks the highest priority*.
Therefore, the effects were not *detrimental* (harmful). Only part of (A) matches the passage.

Choice (B) mentions a *previous statement* and says that the amendments are referenced to
support it. The first sentence states that *the parks have enjoyed special legal protections*. The passage
also describes the amendments as *additional legal backing* for the protection provided by the
National Park Service. This supports the previous statement that the parks have enjoyed special
legal protections. Choice (B) matches the specifics of the paragraph.

Choice (C) mentions a *hypothesis*. A hypothesis provides an explanation for something and is an
idea that has not been proven. However, this paragraph is not trying to explain anything, and
the statements about the amendments are facts, not unproven ideas. Choice (C) does not match
the passage.

Choice (D) mentions an *alternative proposal*, but this paragraph does not offer any proposals—it discusses past events. This answer does not match the passage.

The correct answer to this question is (B).

Matching back from the answer choices to the passage can be helpful when a question is very open-ended, making it difficult to identify a specific answer in the text. Careful matching back will also help you avoid trap answers. Work the following questions using the Basic Approach. Try matching back the answers when you get to Step 5: Process of Elimination.

24

The reference to Shaver's daughter's graduation in lines 34–36 primarily serves to

A) highlight the scale of a problem.

B) celebrate progress made over time.

C) demonstrate the futility of continued efforts.

D) offer hope for the future.

Here's How to Crack It

The question asks for the purpose of the reference to Shaver's daughter's graduation. Use the line reference to find the window for the question. Lines 28–34 indicate that when Shaver's daughter was six years old, the cliffs at the Grand Canyon were *barely visible* because of the haze from air pollution, and that Shaver had been working hard. According to the previous paragraph, Shaver is working to reduce the air pollution in national parks. The reference to the daughter's graduation says that she *graduated from college this year, and Shaver still sees haze in the park system*. The reference to the daughter's graduation indicates that people have been working on the problem for more than a decade, and there is still haze from air pollution in the parks.

Choice (A), *highlight the scale of a problem*, matches the specifics in the text: the *problem* is air pollution in the national parks, and these lines *highlight the scale* of it by showing how long it is taking to solve.

Choice (B), *celebrate progress made over time*, does not match the specifics in the text. There has not been much *progress* made, since there is still haze in the park system. Notice that *graduation* might make you think of progress over time, so if you did not carefully read the window, this Right Words, Wrong Meaning trap answer might tempt you.

Choice (C), *demonstrate the futility of continued efforts*, does not match the specifics in the text. This paragraph indicates that the problem is not solved yet, but it does not indicate that it is *futile*, or useless, to keep trying to solve the problem. In fact, there's no discussion of what will happen in the future in this paragraph.

Choice (D), *offer hope for the future*, does not match the specifics in the text. Again, there's no discussion of what will happen in the future in this paragraph. Additionally, this paragraph talks about lack of progress, so it doesn't *offer hope*. Notice that this choice might also be tempting if you read *graduation* without the context provided by the window.

The correct answer is (A).

25

Proponents of the Clear Skies Initiative would most likely agree with which of the following statements?

A) It puts strict limits on individual power plants' emissions.

B) Its "cap-and-trade" system is less complex than current regulations.

C) It is the best option for reducing air pollution.

D) It supports both businesses and the environment by providing clean-up equipment.

Here's How to Crack It

The question asks which statement *proponents of the Clear Skies Initiative would most likely agree with*. This question doesn't have a line reference, but you can use the sequence of the questions, together with the lead words *proponents* and *Clear Skies Initiative* to help you find the window. The previous question asked about lines 34–36, so start with line 36 and scan for the lead words. The *Clear Skies Initiative* appears in line 46 and *proponents* appears in line 53. Read a window around these lines. This paragraph indicates that the Clear Skies Initiative proposes a cap-and-trade system to fight pollution. It states, *Proponents say the plan is simpler, allows companies to be flexible, and lets some stay in business without buying expensive clean-up equipment.*

Choice (A) says that proponents of the Clear Skies Initiative would agree that the initiative *puts strict limits on individual power plants' emissions*. Match this answer back to the passage. The passage says, *The Clear Skies Initiative aims to replace the strict limits governing an individual power plant's emissions* with a cap-and-trade system. Did you notice the word *replace*? Choice (A) is contradicted by the passage, but it is a Mostly Right/Slightly Wrong trap answer, and the difference between the answer and the passage comes down to one word. Careful matching back can help you avoid traps like this one.

Choice (B) says proponents would agree that the initiative's *"cap-and-trade" system is less complex than current regulations*. Match this answer back to the text, which says, *Proponents say the plan is simpler*. *Simpler* matches *less complex*. Although the author doesn't explicitly state what he is comparing the plan with, the first sentence of the paragraph says that *The Clear Skies Initiative aims to replace the strict limits governing an individual power plant's emissions*, so it is reasonable to infer that the author is comparing the proposed plan to current emissions regulations.

Choice (C) says proponents would agree that the initiative *is the best option for reducing air pollution*. It's certainly possible that people who support this plan think it is the best option, but match this answer back to the text. There is nothing in the text you can point to as evidence that proponents think this is the *best* plan. We only know that they think it is better than the current plan. This is a Could Be True trap answer; matching back to the passage can help you avoid traps like this one.

Choice (D) says proponents would agree that the initiative *supports both businesses and the environment by providing clean-up equipment*. Match this answer back to the text. The text says that the initiative's cap-and-trade system *lets some stay in business without buying expensive clean-up equipment*. Choice (D) uses many of the same words from the passage, but it doesn't quite match the meaning: the initiative doesn't *provide* the equipment; instead it allows businesses to buy credits for pollution, so they don't have to buy equipment to reduce the pollution. This is a Right Words, Wrong Meaning trap answer; careful matching back can help you avoid traps like this one.

The correct answer is (B).

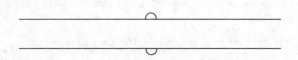

26

Which choice best supports the claim that the Clean Air Act can successfully reduce air pollution?

A) Lines 15–17 ("It was . . . Shaver")

B) Lines 42–45 ("Since . . . local")

C) Lines 88–90 ("A 70 . . . parks")

D) Lines 91–99 ("But . . . commonplace")

Here's How to Crack It

The question asks which lines from the passage provide evidence that *the Clean Air Act can successfully reduce air pollution*. Consider the lines for each answer choice, and match them back to the claim in the question.

The lines for (A) state, *"It was visionary to try to protect these areas without even knowing how difficult it would be," says air resources division director Chris Shaver*. Do these lines refer to the Clean Air Act? Yes. Widen the window for this line reference to include the previous paragraph: the protection that Shaver mentions came from the Clean Air Act. Do these lines support the claim that *the Clean Air Act can successfully reduce air pollution*? No. They indicate that it was visionary *to try* to provide protection, but that it was *difficult*. There is no evidence here that the Clean Air Act could successfully reduce air pollution.

The lines for (B) state, *Since then, while these power plants have slashed their overall sulfur emissions by 72 percent, the canyon's haze remains—evidence that the problem isn't merely local.* The beginning of these lines sounds promising: power plants have cut their sulfur emissions. However, there is a change in direction: *the canyon's haze remains.* Despite some positive results, this does not demonstrate that the Clean Air Act *can successfully reduce air pollution.*

The lines for (C) state, *"A 70 percent cut in sulfur dioxide is going to make a difference, especially for the East Coast parks."* Do these lines refer to the Clean Air Act? No. Widen the window to include the beginning of the paragraph: this quote refers to the promise of the *Clear Skies Initiative.*

The lines for (D) state, *But Scruggs says that when the current system is at its best—when agencies work together to prosecute individual polluters—results are impressive. EPA pressure on industry led to improvements in scrubber technologies, which reduce smokestack emissions, with 95 to 98 percent elimination of some pollutants now commonplace.* Do these lines refer to the Clean Air Act? Yes. These lines refer to the *current system,* and the passage as a whole indicates that the Clean Air Act is the legislation that created the current system. (The Clear Skies Initiative is a proposed plan to replace part of the current system.) These lines indicate that the current system has had *impressive* results, including reducing *smokestack emissions* by up to *98 percent.*

The correct answer is (D).

———————————◯———————————

Now, try a general question.

———————————◯———————————

22

Which choice best reflects the overall structure of the passage?

A) A change in legislation is proposed; historical examples are given in support of the legislation; the legislation is favorably compared with an alternative policy.

B) A theoretical dilemma is outlined; two possible outcomes are compared; the outcomes are illustrated with real-life examples.

C) Ongoing efforts to solve a problem are discussed; opposing views on a proposed solution are described; an authority's point of view is presented.

D) A challenge is presented; past attempts to solve the problem are analyzed; a new remedy is considered and dismissed.

Here's How to Crack It

The question asks for *the overall structure of the passage.* Match the general language in each answer back to the specifics in the passage.

Choice (A) says, *A change in legislation is proposed; historical examples are given in support of the legislation; the legislation is favorably compared with an alternative policy.* Is a change in legislation discussed in the passage? Yes. The Clear Skies Initiative would create a change in legislation. Is the Clear Skies Initiative proposed at the beginning of the passage? No, it isn't mentioned until the fourth paragraph. The first three paragraphs are about the history of efforts to reduce air pollution in the national parks. There's another problem with this answer as well: the *historical examples* that are given illustrate the efforts made under the current legislation—the Clean Air Act—not the proposed legislation.

Choice (B) says, *A theoretical dilemma is outlined; two possible outcomes are compared; the outcomes are illustrated with real-life examples.* Does the passage begin by describing a theoretical dilemma? No. The dilemma, air pollution in the national parks, is a real problem, not a theoretical one. There are other problems with this answer as well: two approaches to solving the problem (the Clean Air Act and the Clear Skies Initiative) are compared, not two outcomes. Finally, only the outcomes from the Clean Air Act are illustrated with real-life examples; the text states that the *Clear Skies legislation is currently stalled in a Senate committee*, so it hasn't produced any outcomes yet.

Choice (C) says, *Ongoing efforts to solve a problem are discussed; opposing views on a proposed solution are described; an authority's point of view is presented.* The first three paragraphs describe the history of efforts to reduce air pollution in the national parks; this matches *ongoing efforts to solve a problem*. The next two paragraphs discuss what *proponents* and *opponents* think about the *Clear Skies Initiative*; this matches *opposing views on a proposed solution*. The final paragraph presents the views of Mark Skruggs, a *park service expert*; this matches *an authority's point of view*. Choice (C) matches the structure of the passage.

Choice (D) says, *A challenge is presented; past attempts to solve the problem are analyzed; a new remedy is considered and dismissed.* Parts of this answer match the passage fairly well: the *challenge* of air pollution in the parks and *past attempts to solve the problem* are both discussed in the passage. The *Clear Skies Initiative* matches *a new remedy*. However, the Clear Skies Initiative is not *dismissed*. The passage offers both positive and negative views on the initiative, and the expert quoted in the last passage is *guardedly optimistic* about it.

The correct answer is (C).

Summary

○ When **translating** difficult text, keep the following in mind:
  - Translate using **Bite-Sized Pieces.** Start with the most straightforward piece.
  - Ask yourself **questions** about the text.
  - Don't forget to check the **blurb.**
  - Consider the relationships between ideas indicated by **transition words**.
  - Match **pronouns** back to the nouns they replace.
  - Note the **main idea** or **purpose of each paragraph** you translate.

○ **Match back** the answers to the text.

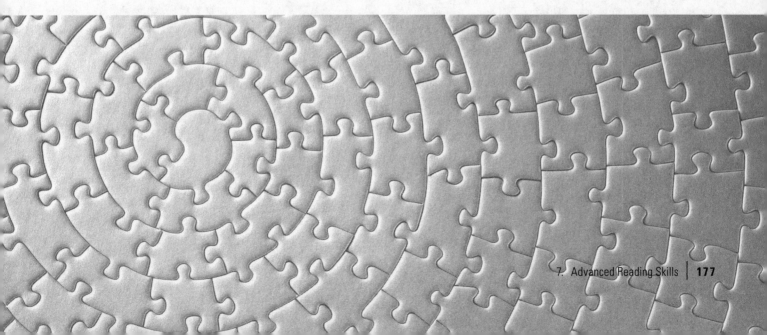

Chapter 8
Reading Drills

Use your new reading comprehension and test-taking skills on two Reading drills (one in the book and one online), which contain passages on science and literature topics. Then check your responses against the answers and explanations provided at the end of the chapter.

Reading Drill 1

Questions 1–10 are based on the following passage.

This passage is an excerpt from the 1854 book *Walden* by Henry David Thoreau, which details Thoreau's experiences living in a cabin alone for two years.

I think that I love society as much as most, and am ready enough to fasten myself like a bloodsucker for the time to any full-blooded man
Line that comes in my way. I am naturally no hermit,
5 but might possibly sit out the sturdiest frequenter of the bar-room, if my business called me thither.

I had three chairs in my house; one for solitude, two for friendship, three for society. When visitors came in larger and unexpected
10 numbers there was but the third chair for them all, but they generally economized the room by standing up. It is surprising how many great men and women a small house will contain. I have had twenty-five or thirty souls, with their bodies,
15 at once under my roof, and yet we often parted without being aware that we had come very near to one another.

One inconvenience I sometimes experienced in so small a house, the difficulty of getting to
20 a sufficient distance from my guest when we began to utter the big thoughts in big words. You want room for your thoughts to get into sailing trim and run a course or two before they make their port. The bullet of your thought must have
25 overcome its lateral and ricochet motion and fallen into its last and steady course before it reaches the ear of the hearer, else it may plow out again through the side of his head. Also, our sentences wanted room to unfold and form
30 their columns in the interval. Individuals, like nations, must have suitable broad and natural boundaries, even a considerable neutral ground, between them. I have found it a singular luxury to talk across the pond to a companion on the
35 opposite side. In my house we were so near that we could not begin to hear—we could not speak low enough to be heard; as when you throw two stones into calm water so near that they break each other's undulations. As the conversation
40 began to assume a loftier and grander tone, we gradually shoved our chairs farther apart till they

touched the wall in opposite corners, and then commonly there was not room enough.

My "best" room, however, my withdrawing
45 room, always ready for company, on whose carpet the sun rarely fell, was the pine wood behind my house. Thither in summer days, when distinguished guests came, I took them, and a priceless domestic swept the floor and dusted the
50 furniture and kept the things in order.

If one guest came he sometimes partook of my frugal meal, and it was no interruption to conversation to be stirring a hasty-pudding, or watching the rising and maturing of a loaf
55 of bread in the ashes, in the meanwhile. But if twenty came and sat in my house there was nothing said about dinner, though there might be bread enough for two, more than if eating were a forsaken habit; but we naturally practised
60 abstinence; and this was never felt to be an offence against hospitality, but the most proper and considerate course. The waste and decay of physical life, which so often needs repair, seemed miraculously retarded in such a case, and the vital
65 vigor stood its ground. I could entertain thus a thousand as well as twenty; and if any ever went away disappointed or hungry from my house when they found me at home, they may depend upon it that I sympathized with them at least. So
70 easy is it, though many housekeepers doubt it, to establish new and better customs in the place of the old. You need not rest your reputation on the dinners you give.

As for men, they will hardly fail one
75 anywhere. I had more visitors while I lived in the woods than at any other period in my life; I mean that I had some. I met several there under more favorable circumstances than I could anywhere else. But fewer came to see me on trivial business.
80 In this respect, my company was winnowed by my mere distance from town. I had withdrawn so far within the great ocean of solitude, into which the rivers of society empty, that for the most part, so far as my needs were concerned, only the finest
85 sediment was deposited around me.

1

The main narrative point of view of the passage is of

A) a man adjusting to life in a big city after growing up on a farm.

B) a discussion of visitors to a small house away from city life.

C) a sailor discussing the pond on which he grew up and how it affected his friendships.

D) a man discussing the potential of big thoughts and their need to be expressed.

2

The passage suggests which of the following about the author?

A) He moved to the country to avoid being disturbed by a large number of visitors.

B) He had more visitors to his home in the country than at any other time in his life.

C) He felt that having more than three people in his house was too many.

D) He needed to throw dinner parties to entice guests to come from town to his home.

3

Which choice provides the best evidence for the answer to the previous question?

A) Lines 7–11 ("I had . . . all")

B) Lines 33–35 ("I have . . . side")

C) Lines 72–73 ("You need . . . give")

D) Lines 75–76 ("I had . . . life")

4

As used in line 11, "economized" most nearly means

A) wasted.

B) used efficiently.

C) squandered.

D) purchased.

5

It can be inferred from the passage that "big thoughts" (line 21) must

A) become violent before settling down.

B) bounce around and break out of one's head.

C) be mulled over and formulated before being heard.

D) have time to move around before being heard.

6

In the context of the passage, the phrase "as when you throw two stones into calm water so near that they break each other's undulations" (lines 37–39) is best described as

A) a reference to the author's childhood days when he threw stones into a lake.

B) an analogy used to elaborate on a previous statement.

C) a way to expand on the reasons national boundaries are always changing.

D) a reason that the author and his companion had to continually move their chairs to be heard.

7

What happens when the author does not have enough food for his guests?

A) He shares.

B) He turns them away.

C) He buys more food.

D) They refrain from eating.

8

The passage suggests that housekeepers most likely

A) are stuck in their ways and unable to change.

B) may be hesitant to change some traditions.

C) believe there is a certain protocol that must always be followed when hosting guests.

D) feel that pudding and bread are not a suitable meal.

9

What does the author mean when he says that "only the finest sediment was deposited around me" (lines 84–85)?

A) He was living far from town and his visitors were of a higher caliber.

B) He was covered in a fine dust while living in the woods.

C) The pond near his home frequently flooded, leaving sediment in his "best" room.

D) Many people came to see him about the dirty business of trivial matters.

10

What choice provides the best evidence for the answer to the previous question?

A) Lines 48–50 ("a priceless . . . order")

B) Lines 70–72 ("though . . . old")

C) Lines 75–77 ("I had . . . some")

D) Line 79 ("But fewer . . . business")

CHAPTER DRILL ANSWERS AND EXPLANATIONS

Reading Drill 1

1. **B** The question asks about the main *point of view of the passage*. Since this is a general question, it should be answered after the specific questions. The narrator discusses what it was like for him to receive guests. He states in lines 33–35, *I have found it a singular luxury to talk across the pond to a companion*, and, in lines 44–47, *My "best" room…was the pine wood behind my house*. The blurb states that the narrator lived in a cabin. Therefore, the narrator lives in a cabin next to a pond and near the woods. Look for an answer choice that matches this information. Choice (A) is incorrect because the narrator is not in the *city*; eliminate it. Keep (B) because it matches the prediction. There is no evidence that the author was a *sailor*, so eliminate (C). Although the author does discuss *big thoughts* in the third paragraph, it is not the main subject of the passage. This is the Right Answer to the Wrong Question; eliminate (D). The correct answer is (B).

2. **B** The question asks what the passage suggests *about the author*. Notice that this is the first question in a paired set, so it can be done in tandem with Q3. Look at the answer choices for Q3 first. The lines for (3A) say that the author *had three chairs in [his] house* and *when visitors came in larger and unexpected numbers there was but the third chair*. Look to see whether these lines support any of the answers for Q2. Although these lines mention that there were not enough chairs for more than three people, they do not indicate that the author *felt that having more than three people in his house was too many*. These lines do not support any of the answers for Q2; eliminate (3A). The lines for (3B) state that the author *found it a singular luxury to talk across the pond to a companion*; they do not support any of the answers for Q2; eliminate (3B). The lines for (3C) say that *you need not rest your reputation on the dinners you give*. These lines don't support any of the answer choices in Q2. Eliminate (3C). The lines for (3D) state that the author *had more visitors while [he] lived in the woods than at any other period in [his] life*. This information matches (2B), which states that *he had more visitors to his home in the country than at any other time in his life*. Draw a line connecting (3D) and (2B). Without any support in the answers from Q3, (2A), (2C), and (2D) can be eliminated. The correct answers are (2B) and (3D).

3. **D** (See explanation above.)

4. **B** The question asks what the word *economized* most nearly means in line 11. Go back to the text, find the word *economized,* and cross it out. Then read the window carefully, using context clues to determine another word that would fit in the text. The text says that if there were more than three people in the room, they *economized the space by standing*. Therefore, *economized* must mean something like "used wisely" or "saved." *Wasted* and *squandered* are both opposites of "saved" or "used wisely," so eliminate (A) and (C). *Used efficiently* matches "used wisely" or "saved," so keep (B). *Purchased* means "bought," and does not match "used wisely," so eliminate (D). The correct answer is (B).

5. **C** The question asks what *can be inferred from the passage* about *big thoughts*. Use the given line reference to find the window. Lines 21–28 state that *you want room for your thoughts to get into sailing trim and run a course or two before they make their port* and *your thought must have overcome its lateral and ricochet motion and fallen into its last and steady course before it reaches the ear of the hearer*. These statements figuratively express the idea that a person needs space to think big thoughts. There is no evidence in the passage that the big thoughts need to be *violent*; this is a Right Words, Wrong Meaning trap answer based on the figurative reference to a *bullet*. Eliminate (A). Eliminate (B) because the author does not state that big thoughts need to *break out of one's head*; this is a literal interpretation of figurative language. Furthermore, the author says that the thoughts could break out of the listener's head if they are not given enough time to develop, so this is not something big thoughts *must* do. Choice (C) matches the text, so keep it. Choice (D) is a literal interpretation of the figurative description of a thought *overcoming its lateral and ricochet motion*; eliminate (D). The correct answer is (C).

6. **B** The question asks how to describe the phrase *as when you throw two stones into calm water so near that they break each other's undulations*. Read a window around the line reference. Lines 18–43 express the need for space when discussing big ideas. Lines 35–36 say, *In my house we were so near that we could not begin to hear*; therefore, the phrase illustrates what happens when things are too close. The author has made no reference to his *childhood* in this passage, and this phrase is used figuratively, not literally, so eliminate (A). Choice (B) matches the text; keep it. While *national boundaries* are mentioned in this paragraph, they are just another analogy by which the author describes his experience; eliminate (C). Eliminate (D) because the analogy about the stones is not the reason the author and his companion move their chairs; furthermore, they moved their chairs to give themselves more space, not because they had to in order *to be heard*. The correct answer is (B).

7. **D** The question asks *what happens when the author does not have enough food for his guests*. Use the sequence of the questions and the lead words *guests* and *food* to find the window. Q7 asked about line 27, so the window for Q8 most likely comes after line 27. Scan the passage beginning with line 28, looking for references to *guests* and *food*. Lines 51–52 state that *if one guest came he sometimes partook of my frugal meal,* and lines 56–60 say, *if twenty came and sat in my house there was nothing said about dinner...we naturally practiced abstinence.* Therefore, if there are many guests and not much food, the guests do not eat. Choice (A) is the Right Answer to the Wrong Question, as the author shares his food when there is only one guest. Eliminate (A). There is no mention of the author turning guests away or buying more food for those who come, so eliminate (B) and (C). Choice (D) matches the text; keep it. The correct answer is (D).

8. **B**   The question asks what is most likely true of *housekeepers*. Use the sequence of the questions and the lead word *housekeepers* to find the window. The support for Q8 came from lines 51–60, so the window for Q9 most likely comes after line 60. Scan the passage beginning with line 61, looking for the lead word *housekeepers*. Lines 69–72 say, *so easy is it, though many housekeepers doubt it, to establish new and better customs in the place of the old*. Choice (A) is a Mostly Right/Slightly Wrong trap answer; the passage indicates that housekeepers are doubtful about change, but not that they are *unable to change*. Eliminate (A). The housekeepers doubt that it is *easy to establish new and better customs in place of the old*, which indicates that they *may be hesitant to change some traditions*; keep (B). The passage does not state that housekeepers have *a certain protocol* that they must *always* follow for guests: the passage indicates that they have certain customs they follow, but the extreme words *must* and *always* and the focus on one *certain protocol* make this answer Mostly Right but Slightly Wrong; eliminate (C). While the author mentions *pudding* and *bread*, there is no indication that housekeepers disapprove of such a meal; eliminate (D). The correct answer is (B).

9. **A**   The question asks what the phrase *only the finest sediment was deposited around me* means in context. This is the first question in a paired set, but because Q10 is a specific question, it can be answered on its own. Use the given line reference to find the window. Lines 79–85 discuss the narrator's visitors. Lines 79–81 state that *fewer came...on trivial business,* and his *company was winnowed by mere distance from town*. The last sentence is a metaphor about the ocean and rivers, and it says that *only the finest sediment was deposited around me*. In other words, the narrator believes that because he lived far from town, fewer people came to see him about unimportant things, so the quality of the visits was better. Choice (A) matches the text; keep it. Both (B) and (C) refer to the literal meaning of *sediment*, but that word is used figuratively in context, so eliminate (B) and (C). Choice (D) contradicts the passage; the author says *fewer came to see me on trivial business;* eliminate it. The correct answer is (A).

10. **D**   The question is the best evidence question in a paired set. Because Q10 was a specific question, simply look at the lines used to answer the previous question. Lines 79–81 state that *fewer came to see me on trivial business*, and the author's company *was winnowed by [his] mere distance from town*. Of these lines, only line 79 is an answer choice. The correct answer is (D).

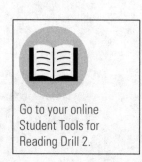

Go to your online
Student Tools for
Reading Drill 2.

Part III
How to Crack the Writing and Language Test

Chapter 9
Introduction to Writing and Language Strategy

The Writing and Language Test consists of 44 multiple-choice questions that you'll have 35 minutes to complete. The questions test a few select grammar, punctuation, and style topics. In this chapter, we'll introduce you to the format of Writing and Language Test, the types of the questions and passages you'll encounter, and the overall strategies you need to ace this section.

CAN YOU REALLY TEST WRITING ON A MULTIPLE-CHOICE EXAM?

We would say no, but College Board seems to think the answer is yes. To that end, you will have 35 minutes to answer 44 multiple-choice questions that ask about a few select grammar, punctuation, and style topics. If you like to read and/or write, the SAT may frustrate you a bit because it seems to boil writing down to a couple of dull rules. But the next few chapters will introduce a method that keeps things simple for pro- and anti-grammarians alike.

Before you begin, though, think about how many questions you will be answering in the Writing and Language section. Unless you are aiming for a top score, you can likely use LOTD on some of the harder questions in each passage.

WHERE DID ALL OF THE QUESTIONS GO?

One thing that can seem a little strange about the Writing and Language Test is that most of the questions are not technically, well, questions. Instead, most of the questions look something like this:

Watch Us Crack It

The history of **1** language although it may sound like a boring subject, is a treasure trove of historical, cultural, and psychological insights.

1

A) NO CHANGE

B) language, although it may sound like a boring subject

C) language, although it may sound, like a boring subject,

D) language, although it may sound like a boring subject,

How are you supposed to choose an answer when there's no question?

Well, actually, what you'll find throughout this chapter and the next two chapters is that you're given a *lot* of information in this list of answer choices.

Look at these pairs, and you'll see just what we mean. As you read through these pairs of answer choices, think about what each question is probably testing.

i. A) could of
    B) could have

ii. A) tall, dark, and handsome
    B) tall, dark, and, handsome

iii. A) let them in
     B) let Sister Susie and Brother John in

iv. A) We arrived in Paris on a Sunday. Then we took the train to Nantes. Then we took the train to Bordeaux.
    B) We arrived in Paris on a Sunday. Then we took the train to Bordeaux. Then we took the train to Nantes.

If you were able to see the differences in these answer choices, you're already more than halfway there. Now, notice how the differences in these answers can reveal the question that is lurking in the heart of each list of answer choices.

i. The difference between the word "of" and "have" means that this question is asking, *Is the correct form "could of" or "could have"?*

ii. The difference between having a comma after the word "and" and not having one there means that this question is asking, *How many commas does this sentence need, and where do they belong?*

iii. The difference between "them" and "Sister Susie and Brother John" means that this question is asking, *Is "them" adequately specific, or do you need to refer to people by name?*

iv. The difference between the order of these sentences asks, *What order should the sentences be in?*

Therefore, what we have noticed in these pairs of answer choices is something that may seem fairly simple but which is essential to success on the SAT.

THE ANSWER CHOICES ASK THE QUESTIONS

At some point in English class, you've almost certainly had to do an exercise called "peer editing." In this exercise, you are tasked with "editing" the work of one of your fellow students. But this can be really tough, because what exactly does it mean to "edit" an entire essay or paper when you aren't given any directions? It's especially tough when you start getting into the subtleties of writing and language, namely, whether a piece of grammar is definitely wrong or could merely be improved.

For example, look at these two sentences:

It was a beautiful day outside birds were singing cheerful songs.

It was a beautiful day outside; birds were singing cheerful songs.

You'd have to pick the second one in this case because the first has a grammatical error: it's a run-on sentence. Or for the non-grammarians out there, you have to break that thing up.

Now, look at these next two sentences:

The weather was just right, so I decided to play soccer.

Just right was how I would describe the weather, so a decision of soccer-playing was made by me.

In this case, the first sentence is obviously better than the second, but the second technically doesn't have any grammatical errors in it. The first may be better, but the second isn't exactly wrong.

What made each of these pairs of sentences relatively easy to deal with, though, is the fact that you could compare the sentences to each other. In doing so, you noted the differences between those sentences, and you picked the *better* answer accordingly.

Let's see how this looks in a real SAT situation.

Language is a living **2** document shows how people think and communicate.

2

A) NO CHANGE
B) document it shows
C) document that shows
D) document, which showing

Here's How to Crack It

First, look at what's changing in the answer choices. The word *document* remains the same in each, but what comes after it changes each time. This question is asking *Which words will best link the two ideas in the sentence?*

Choices (A) and (D) make the sentence incomplete, so eliminate them. Choice (B) creates a run-on sentence, so that should also be eliminated. Only (C) appropriately links the ideas without adding new errors.

Notice that the entire process started with asking, "What's changing in the answer choices?" With that question, we figured out what was being tested, and we used POE to do the rest.

Let's try another.

A community's very soul, we might say, is communicated through **3** their language.

A) NO CHANGE
B) they're language.
C) their languages.
D) its language.

Here's How to Crack It

As always, start by figuring out what's changing in the answer choices. One change is between the words *their, they're,* and *its,* and there's another change between the words *language* and *languages.* As such, this question is asking, *What is the appropriate pronoun to use in this context, and just how many "languages" are we talking about?*

Start wherever is easiest. In this case, it's difficult to say for sure whether the sentence is talking about one language or about a bunch of languages, so start with the pronoun. What does it refer back to? In this sentence, the pronoun refers back to *a community,* which is a singular noun (even though it describes a lot of people). Therefore, the only possible answer that could work is (D), which contains the singular pronoun *its.*

Notice that you didn't need to figure out whether the sentence is talking about one language or many languages. Sometimes fixing one problem will make others irrelevant!

LEARN FROM THE ANSWER CHOICES

Let's think about the previous question a bit more. If someone said to you *A community's very soul, we might say, is communicated through their language,* you probably wouldn't hear that as wrong. That's because the way we speak is often very different from the way we write. On the SAT, however, the test-writers are more concerned with how we write and the stricter set of rules that go along with writing.

Therefore, the answer choices not only indicate what a particular question is testing, but can also reveal mistakes that you might not have otherwise seen (in the original sentence) or heard (in your head). In the previous question, for example, we might not have noted the mistake at all if we hadn't looked at what was changing in the answer choices.

Try another example.

For all **4** intensive purposes, any social, cultural, or historical study *must* start with an analysis of language.

4

A) NO CHANGE

B) intents and purposes,

C) intent's and purpose's,

D) intensive purpose's,

Here's How to Crack It

As always, start by checking what's changing in the answer choices. In this case, this step is especially important because you can't hear the error. People misuse this expression all the time because they so rarely see it written, and all four of the answer choices sound basically the same.

Now use POE. There's no good reason to have apostrophes anywhere (there are neither contractions nor possessions), so eliminate (C) and (D). Then, if you're still not sure, take a guess. The correct form of the expression is (B).

Notice that looking at the answer choices revealed an error that you might not have otherwise been able to see or hear. POE took you the rest of the way.

POE DOES THE BIG WORK

Once you have a sense of what the question is testing, POE can get you closer and closer to the answer. POE is especially helpful when you're dealing with sentences that have lots of issues, like this one.

It may seem that how people speak is distinct from how they **5** are acting; however, there's something that most historians will tell you is wrong.

5

A) NO CHANGE

B) act, however, there's

C) are acting, however, that's

D) act; however, that's

Here's How to Crack It

Check what's changing in the answer choices. Here, there are three things changing: *act* and *are acting*, *that's* and *there's*, and a comma versus a semicolon. Lots of changes means lots of opportunity to use POE! Start with the difference you find easiest and work backward from there.

Start with the difference between *that's* and *there's*. *That's* refers to something mentioned already, and *there's* refers to something that will be introduced next. Since the *wrong* idea is what was mentioned in the beginning of the sentence, the correct word here is *that's*. Eliminate (A) and (B). Now, choose between the last two: *they act* is more concise and more consistent with the words *people speak* than is *they are acting*, which makes (D) better than (C).

Notice that you didn't have to make a decision on the punctuation, and focusing on one thing at a time was easier than trying to decide whether all aspects of each answer choice are correct or not. POE saves the day!

ALL OF THE QUESTIONS CAN'T BE WRONG ALL OF THE TIME

Now that you know the strategy, try a more difficult question.

---

6 Your knowledge of grammar and vocabulary may be shaky, but you can learn a lot from some basic tenets of linguistics.

6

A) NO CHANGE

B) You're knowledge of grammar or vocabulary might be shaky,

C) Your knowledge of grammar and vocabulary might be shakily,

D) You're knowledge of grammar and vocabulary might be shaky,

Here's How to Crack It

As always, check the answer choices first. In this case, here's what's changing: the answers are switching between *your* and *you're*, *and* and *or*, and *shaky* and *shakily*. Do the easy parts first!

Start with the apostrophe. *You're* is a contraction of *you are*, which doesn't make sense in the context of the sentence; eliminate (B) and (D). The difference between (A) and (C) is *shaky* versus *shakily*. *Your knowledge* can't be described as *shakily*, so eliminate (C). The answer has to be (A).

Remember, NO CHANGE is right sometimes! If you've done the other steps in the process and have eliminated all of the other choices, go ahead and pick (A)!

HOW TO ACE THE WRITING AND LANGUAGE TEST: A STRATEGY

Here's a step-by-step breakdown of the process we've been following:

Step 1: Check what's changing in the answer choices.

Step 2: Figure out what the question is testing and let the differences in the answer choices reveal potential errors. (More on this later.)

Step 3: Use POE.

Step 4: If you can't eliminate three answer choices, pick the shortest answer that is most consistent with the rest of the sentence.

The next few chapters will cover some of the more technical issues related to the Writing and Language Test, but this strategy will be used throughout. Try the drill on the next page to get the basics down.

Writing and Language Drill 1

The purpose of this drill is to practice identifying what each question is testing from only the answer choices. Check your answers on page 198.

1

A) NO CHANGE
B) babies' favorite bottles
C) baby's favorite bottle's
D) babies' favorite bottles'

What's changing in the answer choices?

_____

What is this question testing?

_____

2

A) NO CHANGE
B) did
C) does
D) have done

What's changing in the answer choices?

_____

What is this question testing?

_____

3

A) NO CHANGE
B) Although
C) While
D) Because

What's changing in the answer choices?

_____

What is this question testing?

_____

4

A) NO CHANGE
B) was notable for their
C) were notable for its
D) were notable for their

What's changing in the answer choices?

_____

What is this question testing?

_____

5

A) NO CHANGE
B) beautiful, as in super pretty.
C) beautiful, like easy on the eyes.
D) beautiful.

What's changing in the answer choices?

_____

What is this question testing?

_____

WRITING AND LANGUAGE DRILL 1 ANSWER KEY

1. Apostrophes; apostrophes and where they go
2. Verbs; verb tense and number
3. Words; transition words (direction)
4. Was/were and their/its; verb number and pronoun number
5. Number of words; concision

Summary

○ The Writing and Language Test on the SAT is 35 minutes long and contains 44 questions.

○ Many of the questions on the Writing and Language Test are not in traditional question form. Instead, you'll be presented with a series of passages with underlined portions, and your job is to determine whether the underlined portion is correct or if it should be replaced with one of the given choices.

○ The first step is always to determine what's changing in the answer choices. They not only tell you what a particular question is testing, but also reveal mistakes that you might not have otherwise noticed.

○ Use POE to get rid of incorrect answers and narrow down your options. If you can't eliminate three choices, pick the shortest one that is most consistent with the rest of the sentence.

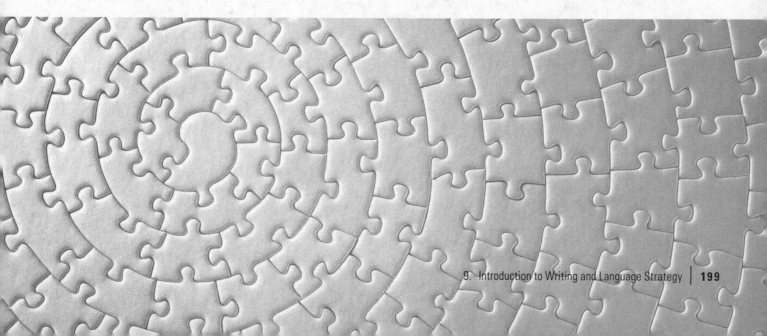

Chapter 10
Words

Many questions on the Writing and Language test focus on words—mainly transitions, verbs, and pronouns. While we will discuss a few grammar rules along the way, this chapter will boil these concepts down to three main terms: consistency, precision, and concision. With less minutiae to remember, you will be able to work through Words questions with confidence and ease.

THE WORDS CHANGE, BUT THE SONG REMAINS THE SAME

Most of the questions you'll see on the Writing and Language test have words changing in the answers. "Words" is a broad term, but most of the questions deal with three specific types of words: transitions, verbs, and pronouns. In order to figure out what's being tested, you'll want to stick with the basic approach from the previous chapter.

> Check what's changing in the answer choices and use POE.

Achieve Grammar Greatness

While you don't need to be a grammar expert to do well on the Writing and Language test, you may want to brush up on your grammar terms, especially if you're feeling a bit rusty. Pick up a copy of *Grammar Smart* for a quick refresher!

Throughout this chapter, we talk a lot about certain parts of speech, but we don't use a lot of grammar terms. That's because we find that on the SAT, the correct answers across a lot of different parts of speech can be summed up more succinctly with three basic terms: *consistency, precision,* and *concision*.

You don't need to know a ton of grammar if you can remember these three basic rules.

> **CONSISTENCY:** Correct answers are consistent with the rest of the sentence and the passage.
>
> **PRECISION:** Correct answers make the meaning of the sentence as precise as possible.
>
> **CONCISION:** Barring other errors, correct answers are as concise as possible.

Let's look at some examples of how to apply these concepts to transitions, verbs, and pronouns.

TRANSITIONS

The term "English" seems, on the surface, to apply to just one language. On closer examination, **1** therefore, it refers to many different languages, the most obvious of which are the versions spoken within different English-speaking countries.

1

A) NO CHANGE

B) for example,

C) however,

D) moreover,

Here's How to Crack It

First, as always, check what's changing in the answer choices. In this case, transition words change. That means this question is testing transitions.

When you see transitions changing in the answer choices, look at the ideas that the transition word connects. The transition should be consistent with the relationship between those ideas. In this case, the two ideas are that English is *just one language* and that it is *many different languages*. These ideas contrast with each other, so you need a transition that indicates a contrast. Choices (A), (B), and (D) all indicate that ideas agree with each other, so get rid of them. Only (C) indicates a contrast, so that's the only choice that is consistent with the ideas here.

Whenever transitions change in the answers, the first thing to figure out is whether the ideas being connected agree or contrast.

Take a look at another example.

Even within a single English-speaking country there are many different dialects of English. In the United States, **2** consequently, distinct regional dialects include those spoken in Boston, the Mid-Atlantic, Southern states, the Upper Midwest, and California.

2

A) NO CHANGE

B) additionally,

C) by contrast,

D) for instance,

Watch Us Crack It

Here's How to Crack It

Check what's changing in the answer choices. The transitions change, so first establish whether the ideas agree or contrast. The first sentence is about the *many different dialects*, and the second sentence gives a list of *distinct regional dialects*. These ideas agree, so you want a same-direction transition. Eliminate (C) because it's an opposite-direction transition.

Choices (A), (B), and (D) are all same-direction transitions, but they indicate different things. Use POE to choose the one that indicates the correct relationship. *Consequently* indicates a conclusion, which isn't what the second sentence is here, so eliminate (A). *Additionally* indicates a new point is being introduced, which also isn't the case here, so eliminate (B). *For instance* introduces an example, which is exactly what's going on here. That means (D) is consistent with the ideas in these sentences.

After you eliminate transitions that indicate the wrong direction, use POE to get rid of the ones that don't work in the particular context. Remember, with transitions, keep things consistent.

Here's a list of some of the most common same-direction and opposite-direction transitions that appear on the SAT.

Same-Direction	Opposite-Direction
For example	Conversely
In addition	Despite this
Likewise	However
Therefore	Instead
Thus	Nevertheless
Similarly	Nonetheless
Subsequently	On the other hand

When you see transitions changing in the answer choices, first check whether the ideas being connected agree or disagree. Then, make sure the transition is

- CONSISTENT with the relationship between the ideas.

VERBS

The speakers of what has come to be known as Appalachian English **3** has used a form of English that few can explain.

3

A) NO CHANGE

B) uses

C) use

D) using

Here's How to Crack It

First, as always, check what's changing in the answer choices. In this case, the forms of the verb *to use* change. Therefore, because the verbs change, you know that the question is testing verbs.

When you see verbs changing in the answer choices, the first thing to check is the subject of the sentence. Is the verb consistent with the subject? In this case, it's not. The subject of this sentence is *speakers*, which is plural. Therefore, (A) and (B) have to be eliminated, because both are singular verbs. Eliminate (D) because it makes the sentence incomplete. Only (C) works in this context.

Thus, when you see verbs changing in the answer choices, check the subject first. Subjects and verbs need to be consistent with each other.

Take a look at another.

Many scholars believe Appalachian pronunciation comes from Scots-Irish immigration, but some theorizes that this dialect of English may be closer to what Londoners spoke in Elizabethan times.

4

A) NO CHANGE

B) theorized

C) have theorized

D) theorize

Here's How to Crack It

Check what's changing in the answer choices. The verbs are changing. Remember from the previous question that whenever you see verbs changing, make sure the verb is consistent with the subject. Because the subject of this sentence is *some*, which is plural, you can eliminate (A), which is singular. Therefore, the verb in (A) is not consistent with the subject.

Then, because all of the other choices are consistent with the subject, make sure they are consistent with the other verbs. All the other verbs in this sentence—*believe, comes, may be*—are in the present tense, so the underlined verb should be as well, as it is in (D). Eliminate (B) and (C) because they're both past tense. The correct answer is (D).

As you can see, verbs are all about consistency.

When you see verbs changing in the answer choices, make sure those verbs are

- CONSISTENT with their subjects
- CONSISTENT with other verbs in the sentence and surrounding sentences

Let's try one that has a little bit of everything.

Trying to understand these changes [5] demonstrate that although we all technically speak English, we speak very different languages indeed.

5

A) NO CHANGE

B) demonstrate that although we all technically spoke English, we speak

C) demonstrates that although we all technically speak English, we might have been speaking

D) demonstrates that although we all technically speak English, we speak

Here's How to Crack It

Check what's changing in the answer choices. It looks like lots of verbs!

First, determine whether *demonstrate* or *demonstrates* is consistent with the subject. That subject is *Trying*, which is singular, thus eliminating (A) and (B).

Then, you have to choose between *speak* and *might have been speaking*. Since both of these are consistent with the subject *we*, pick the one that is most consistent with other verbs. The only other verbs are *demonstrates* and *speak*, both of which are in the present tense and don't use the odd *might have been* form. Therefore, eliminate (C) because it isn't consistent. The correct answer is (D).

PRONOUNS

Speakers of Appalachian English and [6] there families communicate in a way that shows just how influential diversity can be on the language we speak.

6

A) NO CHANGE

B) its family communicates

C) their families communicate

D) it's family communicates

Here's How to Crack It

Check what's changing in the answers. Everything changes: the pronoun, *family* versus *families,* and *communicate* versus *communicates.* Start with the pronoun. A pronoun must be consistent with the noun it refers to, so identify that noun. In this case, the pronoun refers to *speakers,* which is plural, so the underlined pronoun also has to be plural. Eliminate (B) and (D) because *its* and *it's* are both singular.

Their and *there* both sound the same, but *there* indicates a location, which doesn't work here. Eliminate (A). *Their* is a possessive pronoun that indicates that the *families* belong to the *speakers,* so (C) is the best choice.

As with transitions and verbs, consistency is the first thing to check when pronouns change in the answer choices.

Take a look at another pronoun question.

Scholars today are not sure whether Appalachian English belongs to the category of European dialects or American dialects. Really, 7 most are collections of many influences, but the Appalachian dialect seems unique.

7

A) NO CHANGE

B) most of them

C) most of those

D) most American dialects

> On the SAT, if you have a choice between a pronoun and an actual noun, go with the actual noun. A pronoun may be more concise, but the actual noun is more precise—and that's more important than being concise.

Here's How to Crack It

Check what's changing in the answer choices. Choices (B) and (C) have pronouns, so find the noun that the pronoun refers back to. The previous sentence mentions *European dialects* and *American dialects,* but the pronouns (or the word *most* in (A)) could refer to either or both. If it's at all unclear what a pronoun refers to on the SAT, you can't use one! So eliminate (A), (B), and (C) because the meaning of the sentence isn't precise with any of those options. Choice (D) makes it absolutely clear what *most* refers to, so that's the best choice.

> When you see pronouns changing in the answer choices, make sure the pronouns:
>
> • are CONSISTENT with the nouns they refer to
> • are as PRECISE as possible; if they could refer to more than one thing, eliminate them!

VOCABULARY

Another way that the SAT tests the idea of precision is with vocabulary. If you've heard stories from your parents or older siblings about memorizing obscure SAT vocabulary words, don't worry—the way that the SAT tests vocabulary these days isn't with difficult words. Instead, it's usually with more common words that are synonyms of each other but that don't all work in the same context. Your job is to find the word that gives the most precise meaning in context.

Take a look at this example.

The Appalachian region's ⬛8⬛ solitude from major urban centers has led to some hypotheses that its dialect has remained intact from the days of its earliest settlers.

8

A) NO CHANGE

B) withdrawal

C) isolation

D) aloneness

Here's How to Crack It

Check what's changing in the answer choices. In this case, it's vocabulary. All the words are similar in meaning, so look for the one that's most consistent with the other ideas in the sentence and that gives the most precise meaning in context. Both *solitude* and *aloneness* describe the state of being alone, which doesn't work in this context with *from major urban centers*, so eliminate (A) and (D).

Withdrawal suggests an action, which also doesn't make sense here—a region can't *withdraw from* someplace. Eliminate (B). *Isolation* works here—it means that the region is separated from the big cities. So (C) gives the most precise meaning in context.

When you see vocabulary changing in the answer choices, make sure the word you choose

- is CONSISTENT with the ideas in the sentence
- provides the most PRECISE meaning in context

CONCISION

Ever hear the saying "less is more"? Concision has its advantages. For example, if you were to ask for directions, which answer would you rather receive?

> *Turn right at Main Street and walk four blocks.*

or

> *Since this street, Elm Street, is facing in a northerly direction, and your destination is due northeast, go east when you arrive at the intersection of Elm and Main. Going east will entail making a right turn in quite that easterly direction. After having made this turn and arrived on the perpendicular street…*

The first one, obviously.

That's because concision is key when you want to communicate meaning. As long as the sentence is otherwise consistent and precise, the correct answer is typically the shortest one.

Let's see an example.

It is precisely this isolation that has led many scholars to believe that Appalachian English is **9** alike and similar to the English spoken in Shakespeare's time.

9

A) NO CHANGE

B) similar

C) likely similar

D) similarly alike

Here's How to Crack It

Check what's changing in the answer choices. In this case, the word *similar* appears in all the answer choices, and in some it is paired with the word *alike*. Typically, if you see a list of answer choices wherein one answer is short and the rest mean the same thing but are longer, the question is testing concision.

What, after all, is the difference between the words *similar* and *alike*? There isn't one, so there's no use in saying both of them, as in (A), or pairing them awkwardly, as in (D). In fact, the shortest answer choice, (B), does everything the other choices do, but it does so in the fewest words. Therefore, (B) is the correct answer.

Let's see one more.

Unfortunately for linguists, such dialects tend to gradually disappear **10** over time and must therefore be studied before they no longer exist.

10

A) NO CHANGE

B) as time goes on

C) bit by bit

D) DELETE the underlined portion.

Here's How to Crack It

As always, check what's changing in the answer choices. The phrasing of the underlined portion changes, but notice something different: the option to DELETE the underlined portion. When given this option, try it first. The sentence still makes sense and works grammatically, so hold on to (D). Consider whether there is any reason to use the additional words in (A), (B), or (C). The fact that they all mean essentially the same thing is a good clue that the question is testing concision. The sentence already says *gradually*, which means the same thing as *over time, as time goes on*, and *bit by bit*, so there is no reason to include those words. Therefore, the correct answer is (D).

The option to DELETE isn't always right, but try it! If the sentence still works and is consistent and precise without the word or phrase, then chances are that's the answer.

MORE FUN WITH WORDS

Transitions, verbs, pronouns, precision, and concision are some of the most commonly tested grammar topics. There are a few more that tend to come up no more than once per test. If you're aiming for a top Writing and Language score, though, you'll want to master the following grammar rules.

Modifiers

Consider the following sentence:

Hoping for success, the chef's newest creation would satisfy guests who were looking to eat local, seasonal ingredients.

Do you spot the error? While you might understand that the chef is hoping for success, the way this sentence is written makes it sound like *the chef's newest creation* is hoping for success. Unless the food has a brain with hopes and dreams, this sentence doesn't make logical sense. This grammar error is called a misplaced modifier. According to this rule, a describing phrase or "modifier" (in this case, *hoping for success*) needs to come as close as possible to the thing it's describing. Here are two ways the sentence above could be rewritten.

Hoping for success, the chef had created a dish to satisfy guests who were looking to eat local, seasonal ingredients.

The chef hoped her newest creation would successfully satisfy guests who were looking to eat local, seasonal ingredients.

As you can see, the sentence can be rewritten so the thing being described comes right before or after the modifying phrase. Another option is to rewrite the sentence entirely to get rid of the modifier.

Having gotten lost and without an idea of where to go, **5** nobody was around to ask for directions.

5

A) NO CHANGE

B) I wanted to find someone to ask for directions.

C) someone nearby could have given me directions.

D) directions from someone nearby would have been helpful.

Watch Us Crack It

Here's How to Crack It

Check what's changing in the answer choices. The options provide similar meanings, but the order of the words changes. This is a good clue the question is testing modifiers. The beginning of the sentence contains a modifier: *Having gotten lost and without an idea of where to go*. Who was lost? Not *nobody*, so eliminate (A). Not *someone*, so eliminate (C). And *directions* can't be lost, so eliminate (D). *I* was the one who was lost, so the correct answer is (B).

Parallelism and Comparisons

Learning a new skill, be it painting a still-life, **23** to pitch a softball, or speaking another language, requires time and dedication as well as regular reflection on how to improve.

23

A) NO CHANGE

B) pitching a softball,

C) when people pitch a softball,

D) softball pitching,

Here's How to Crack It

Check what's changing in the answer choices. The four options provide the same meaning but appear in different forms. This question is testing consistency. Notice that the sentence includes a list of three things. The other two phrases are *painting a still-life* and *speaking another language*. The underlined phrase needs to be in the same form. Only (B), like the other phrases, uses an *-ing* verb with a noun after. The correct answer is (B).

You might notice you didn't have to learn any new rules for that one! We can figure out the answer using one of the big three rules we already discussed: consistency. To be more specific, however, this rule is called parallelism. It's typically tested in a list of two or more things. Every item in that list should be in the same form to be consistent.

———○———

Let's take a look at another one that follows a related rule.

———○———

The study found that children who were offered raw, cut-up vegetables twenty minutes before dinner typically accepted the snack; those children then were more willing to eat the provided dinner **9** than were children who were not offered the pre-dinner vegetables.

9

A) NO CHANGE

B) compared with children

C) than food eaten by children

D) than children

> One reason the comparison word is needed is because a phrasing like (D) could mean that the children ate more dinner than they ate *children*, which is a much more sinister meaning than what was intended!

Here's How to Crack It

Look at the answers to see what's changing. They involve different phrasings of a comparison. Remember that everything on the Writing and Language must be consistent. The comparison is between two groups of children. The first group was *more willing to eat the provided dinner*. The second group must have been less willing to eat the dinner. The sentence must make that clear by making the underlined portion parallel. Choice (A) does that by using the word *were* before *children* to refer back to *more willing* from the first part of the comparison. Choices (B), (C), and (D) don't use the verb *were*, so they're not parallel. The correct answer is (A).

The shorter option might seem better, but in a case like the sentence above, more words are needed to make the comparison consistent and precise. These comparison errors can be tough to notice. Watch for words like *more*, *less*, *than*, or *as* and ask yourself the following questions: what are the two things being compared, and is the comparison consistent?

———○———

Frequently Confused Words and Idioms

Do you know the difference between *then* and *than*? How about *affect* and *effect*? Occasionally, you'll see questions involving these and other frequently confused words. Let's take a look at an example.

The new medication may have a negative **34** affect on oral health by causing a reduction in tooth enamel.

34

A) NO CHANGE

B) effect on

C) affects

D) effect with

Here's How to Crack It

Look for what's changing in the answer choices. The most obvious difference is *affect* versus *effect*. For the purposes of the SAT and how the words are used most commonly, *affect* is a verb and *effect* is a noun. In this sentence, a noun is needed. Eliminate (A) and (C) because they use the verb *affect*. Now, prepositions are changing. Which is correct: *effect on* or *effect with*? The correct idiom is *effect on*. The correct answer is (B).

Throughout this lesson, you have generally been able to apply the rules of consistent, precise, and concise to a variety of questions. For frequently confused words and idioms, however, those ideas probably won't help you to find the answer. Unfortunately, these questions require you to simply know the correct form of the word or phrase. Luckily, you won't see many of these on the test. We recommend using POE based on what you might know and how the idioms sound, and if needed—guess.

Here's another example.

---

20 According with the author of the book, healthcare debts affect a significant portion of Americans and prevent them from engaging in the economy.

20

A) NO CHANGE

B) In accordance to

C) According by

D) According to

Here's How to Crack It

The correct idiom is *according to,* so eliminate (A) and (C). Another idiom is *in accordance with,* so (B) is incorrect and should be eliminated. The correct answer is (D).

———————————◯———————————

Many idioms involve prepositions (those little directional words like *of, with, in, for,* and *by*). Why do we say "according to" and not "according with?" No real reason—it's just an idiom. The SAT rarely, if ever, tests the same idiom twice, so it's not worth trying to memorize lists of idioms. Remember that an idiom question is likely to appear only once on each test, if at all.

As we have seen in this chapter, when SAT is testing *words* (any time the words are changing in the answer choices), make sure that those words are

- **Consistent**—Verbs, nouns, and pronouns should agree within sentences and passages.
- **Precise**—The writing should communicate specific ideas and events.
- **Concise**—When everything else is correct, the shortest answer choice is correct.

Writing and Language Drill 2

Answers can be found starting on page 218.

Time: 7–8 minutes

War and Peace and History

    War and Peace (1869) is **1** well-known and famous mainly for its length. Not many readers, especially in the modern day, **2** has the time or the patience to work through Leo Tolstoy's 1,400 pages, countless characters, and plot twists. **3** They are missing a major opportunity, not only because the novel is more fun than its page count suggests, but also because it marks the end of a particular moment in history.

1

A) NO CHANGE
B) famous and well-known
C) famously well-known
D) well-known

2

A) NO CHANGE
B) have
C) are having
D) do have

3

A) NO CHANGE
B) Those readers
C) Many of them
D) Some

Czech novelist Milan Kundera cited Tolstoy as the last novelist who **4** was possessing the sum of his era's human knowledge. This may seem like an odd claim. Some people may be very intelligent, others may be know-it-alls, but is it really possible to know everything? **5** Neighboring Tolstoy's other great novels and non-fiction writings, a book like *War and Peace* makes the case that it is possible to know it all, or at least that it *was* possible. Shakespeare **6** seemed to have an emotional vocabulary that was advanced for his age, but Tolstoy lived in an era of facts and discoveries, and his novels show the fruits of his vast study. **7** Thus, it is conceivable that a man with Tolstoy's leisure, intelligence, and curiosity **8** learns about his age's most current findings in literature, politics, religion, and science.

4

A) NO CHANGE

B) will possess

C) possess

D) possessed

5

A) NO CHANGE

B) Alongside

C) Touching

D) Bordering

6

A) NO CHANGE

B) seems having

C) has

D) seemingly has

7

A) NO CHANGE

B) Surprisingly,

C) Nevertheless,

D) Instead,

8

A) NO CHANGE

B) learn

C) could have learned

D) are learning

The very fact that such an achievement is impossible now shows us just how much things have changed since Tolstoy's death in 1910. This was the year, **9** however, that Virginia Woolf cited in her oft-quoted remark, "On or about 1910 human character changed." If we at least entertain the idea that she is correct, we can begin to see why she would be willing to make such a grandiose remark. After 1910, the twentieth century started in earnest. Knowledge became more complex as it became more specialized, and although airplanes seemed to make the world a smaller place, the differences among all the places in that small world truly emerged.

War and Peace is the great document of that pre-1910 era, of a moment when the great scientists were also the **10** famous and great philosophers and when the great mathematicians were also the great theologians. A great discovery in one field could also be a great discovery for another. Although it was certainly remarkable, it was also possible for a man like Tolstoy to have a fundamental grasp of all that united the many branches of knowledge. Tolstoy's achievement is impossible today, but it is a wonderful reminder of the value of intellectual curiosity and cosmopolitanism. No matter how brilliant and refined **11** you may become, you can always stand to be reminded that there is a world outside of our immediate circle.

9
A) NO CHANGE
B) in fact,
C) consequently,
D) nonetheless,

10
A) NO CHANGE
B) best and
C) famously
D) DELETE the underlined portion.

11
A) NO CHANGE
B) you may become, one
C) we may become, we
D) one may become, you

WRITING AND LANGUAGE DRILL 2: ANSWERS AND EXPLANATIONS

1. **D** The length of the phrase is changing in the answer choices, so the question is testing concision. Since *well-known* appears in every answer choice, determine whether any additional words are necessary. *Famous* and *well-known* mean the same thing, so there is no reason to use both words in the phrase. Eliminate (A), (B), and (C) because they are not concise. The correct answer is (D).

2. **B** Verbs are changing in the answer choices, so the question is testing consistency of verbs. A verb must be consistent with its subject and with the other verbs in the sentence. The subject of the verb is *readers*, which is plural. To be consistent, the underlined verb must also be plural. Eliminate (A) because it is singular. Since the remaining verbs are plural and all in the present tense, look for the most concise answer. Eliminate (C) and (D) because they are not concise. The correct answer is (B).

3. **B** Pronouns and nouns are changing in the answer choices, so the question is testing precision. A pronoun can only be used if it is clear what the pronoun refers to. The pronouns *they*, *them*, and *some* could refer to *readers, pages, characters,* or *plot twists*, so the pronouns are not precise; eliminate (A), (C), and (D). The correct answer is (B).

4. **D** Verbs are changing in the answer choices, so this question is testing consistency of verbs. A verb must be consistent with its subject and with the other verbs in the sentence. The subject of the verb is *the last novelist*, which is singular. To be consistent, the underlined verb must also be singular. Eliminate (C) because it is plural. The other verb in the sentence is *cited*, which is in the past tense. To be consistent, the underlined verb must also be in the past tense. Eliminate (B) because it is not in past tense. Between *was possessing* and *possessed*, *possessed* is more concise, so eliminate (A). The correct answer is (D).

5. **B** Vocabulary is changing in the answer choices, so this question is testing precision of word choice. Look for a word with a definition that is consistent with the other ideas in the sentence. The sentence says that *War and Peace makes the case that it is possible to know it all* with *Tolstoy's other great novels and non-fiction writings*, so the correct word should mean "with." *Neighboring, touching,* and *bordering* all mean "next to" physically, which is not consistent with the meaning of the sentence, so eliminate (A), (C), and (D). *Alongside* means "with." The correct answer is (B).

6. **A** Verbs are changing in the answer choices, so this question is testing consistency of verbs. The answers are in different tenses, so look for a clue in the sentence or surrounding sentences to determine what tense the underlined portion should be in. The other verb in the sentence is *was*, which is in the past tense. To be consistent, the underlined verb must also be in the past tense. Eliminate (B), (C), and (D) because they are not in the past tense. The correct answer is (A).

7. **A** Transitions are changing in the answer choices, so this question is testing consistency of ideas. A transition must be consistent with the relationship between the ideas it connects. The sentence before the transition states that *Tolstoy lived in an era of facts and discoveries, and his novels show the fruits of his vast study,* and the sentence that starts with the transition states that *it is conceivable*

Tolstoy learned *about his age's most current findings in literature, politics, religion, and science.* These ideas agree, so eliminate (B), (C), and (D), which contain opposite-direction transitions. Choice (A) appropriately uses the same-direction transition *thus.* The correct answer is (A).

8. **C** Verbs are changing in the answer choices, so this question is testing consistency of verbs. A verb must be consistent with its subject and with the other verbs in the sentence. The subject of the verb is *man,* which is singular. To be consistent, the underlined verb must also be singular. Eliminate (B) and (D) because they are plural. Although the other verb in the sentence is *is,* which is in the present tense, the sentence is about what Tolstoy could have done while he was alive. To be consistent with the sentence's meaning, the underlined verb must be in the past tense. Eliminate (A) because it is not in the past tense. The correct answer is (C).

9. **B** Transitions are changing in the answer choices, so this question is testing consistency of ideas. A transition must be consistent with the relationship between the ideas it connects. The sentence before the transition says *how much things have changed since Tolstoy's death in 1910,* and the sentence with the transition includes a quote from Virginia Woolf: *"On or about 1910 human character changed."* These ideas agree, so eliminate (A) and (D), which both contain opposite-direction transitions. *Consequently* indicates a conclusion based on previous evidence, but the quote is not a conclusion, so eliminate (C). Choice (B) appropriately uses the transition *in fact* to support the previous sentence. The correct answer is (B).

10. **D** Vocabulary is changing in the answer choices, so this question is testing precision of word choice. There is also the option to DELETE; consider this choice carefully as it is often the correct answer. Choices (A), (B), and (C)—*famous, best,* and *famously*—all mean the same thing in this context. The sentence already uses the word *great,* so there's no need to repeat the idea. The underlined portion should be deleted to make the sentence more concise. The correct answer is (D).

11. **C** Pronouns are changing in the answer choices, so this question is testing consistency of pronouns. A pronoun must be consistent with other pronouns in the sentence. The sentence includes the pronoun *our,* so the underlined portion needs to be consistent with *our.* Eliminate (A), (B), and (D) because *you* and *one* are not consistent with *our.* *We* is consistent with *our.* The correct answer is (C).

Summary

- On Writing and Language questions, the first step is always to check what's changing in the answer choices and then use POE.

- The correct answers across many different parts of speech can be summed up succinctly with three basic terms: consistency, precision, and concision. You don't need to know a ton of grammar if you can remember these three basic rules:
  - Correct answers are *consistent* with the rest of the sentence and the passage.
  - Correct answers are as *precise* as possible.
  - Barring other errors, correct answers are as *concise* as possible.

- When you see transitions changing in the answer choices, make sure those transitions are consistent with the ideas they connect.

- When you see verbs changing in the answer choices, make sure those verbs are consistent with their subjects as well as with other verbs in the sentence and surrounding sentences.

- When the nouns are changing in the answer choices, make sure those nouns are consistent with the other nouns in the sentence and the paragraph.

- When you see vocabulary changing in the answer choices, choose the word that is consistent with the other ideas in the sentence and that gives the most precise meaning in context.

- Concision is key when you want to communicate meaning. Eliminate options that add additional words that do not contribute to the meaning of the sentence.

Chapter 11
Questions

Most of the questions you will see on the Writing and Language Test are not in question form, but there are some that appear as traditional multiple-choice questions. It's important to read these carefully so you know exactly what is being asked and do not jump to conclusions. This chapter covers some typical questions you might see and strategies you can use to approach and simplify them.

AND THEN SAT WAS LIKE, "HEY, CAN I ASK YOU A QUESTION?"

As you have seen, many "questions" on the Writing and Language test aren't questions at all, grammatically speaking. They're just lists of answer choices, and you start the process of answering them by asking a question of your own: "What's changing in the answer choices?"

Because you need to move quickly through this test, you may fall into the habit of not checking for actual questions. Even when you do read the questions, you may read them too hastily to understand what you are being asked. Well, we are here to tell you that neither of these approaches will work.

> The most important thing about Writing and Language questions is that you *notice* those questions and then *answer* those questions.

This may seem like just about the most obvious advice you've ever been given, but you'd be surprised how much less precise your brain is when you're working quickly.

Here's an example. Do these next 10 questions as quickly as you can.

1. $2 + 1 =$

2. $1 + 2 =$

3. $3 + 1 =$

4. $3 + 2 \neq$

5. $1 + 2 =$

6. $2 - 1 <$

7. $2 \pm 2 =$

8. $3 + 1 =$

9. $3 + 2 =$

10. $3 + 3 \neq$

Now check your answers.

1. 3

2. 3

3. 4

4. Anything but 5

5. 3

6. Any number greater than 1 (but not 1!)

7. 0 or 4

8. 4

9. 5

10. Anything but 6

Now, it's very possible that you got at least one of those questions wrong. What happened? It's not that the questions are difficult. In fact, the questions are about as easy as can be. So why did you get some of them wrong? You were probably moving too quickly to notice that the signs changed a few times.

This is a lot like the Writing and Language test. You might miss some of the easiest questions on the test by not reading carefully enough.

As you will see throughout this chapter, most of the questions will test concepts with which we are already familiar.

PURPOSE

Many Writing and Language questions that have actual questions ask you to do something specific. Remember the ideas of consistent and precise from the Words chapter? Those are in play here too. Purpose questions can ask about a main idea or a detail, but either way your job is to identify the purpose and choose the answer that is most consistent with that purpose.

Here's an example.

---

1 World War II is often cited as a turning point for women in the workforce in the U.S. What most people don't realize is just how persistent that pay gap has been. The size of the gap may have narrowed in recent years, but we still have a long way to go. The problem has certainly gained a good deal of traction in public debates, which raises the question of why more isn't being done to combat the gap.

1

Which choice best establishes the main idea of the paragraph?

A) NO CHANGE

B) When child labor laws were first enacted, many of them included provisions for mandatory schooling.

C) Most people are familiar with the idea of a gender pay gap.

D) Women still make up the vast majority of workers in fields associated with traditional female roles, such as child care, healthcare, and education.

Here's How to Crack It

The purpose stated in this question is to *establish the main idea of the paragraph*. Before you can choose an answer for this type of question, you have to read the paragraph! Once you've read the paragraph, use POE, eliminating any answer choices that aren't consistent with the topic of the paragraph.

The paragraph focuses on a *pay gap*, which you may infer has something to do with gender, but the idea of *women in the workforce* doesn't directly connect with the idea of a *pay gap;* eliminate (A). The paragraph also doesn't say anything about *child labor*, so eliminate (B). Choice (C) introduces the idea of *a gender pay gap*, which directly connects to the rest of the paragraph, so keep (C) while you check (D). The paragraph is not about the number of workers in particular fields, so eliminate (D). The correct answer is (C).

Try another example.

The question of unequal pay for women draws on many other broader social issues. The gender disparities persist in areas other than pay. **2** However, there are a few select fields in which women earn slightly more than men do. **3** There is a long history of misogyny written into the very cultural and social fabric of the United States.

2

Which choice best supports the idea in the previous sentence?

A) NO CHANGE

B) Women did not gain the right to vote in the U.S. until 1920, and they could not freely apply for credit cards until 1974.

C) The removal of the military's ban on women serving in combat marked the demise of one of the last official barriers to women's ability to work in any field.

D) The field of financial services has one of the largest gender pay gaps in the United States.

Here's How to Crack It

The purpose stated in the question is to *support the idea in the previous sentence*. The previous sentence talks about *gender disparities in areas other than pay*, so eliminate answer choices that aren't consistent with that purpose. Choice (A) is about pay, so eliminate it. Choice (B) gives examples of *gender disparity* in an *area other than pay*, so keep it. Choice (C) is about an *area other than pay*, but it talks about the *removal* of *barriers to women's ability to work*, which is not a *disparity*. Eliminate (C). Choice (D) is about *pay gaps*, so eliminate (D). Choice (B) is most consistent with the purpose stated in the question, so it's the correct answer.

Whether a purpose question asks about a main idea or about a detail, your approach should be the same: look for the answer that's most consistent with the purpose stated in the question, and always use POE!

ADDING AND DELETING

Sometimes, questions ask you whether information should be added to or deleted from a paragraph. When you run into one of these questions, ask yourself two questions: Is the information to be added or deleted consistent with the rest of the paragraph? And if it is consistent, does it make the paragraph more precise? If the answer to either question is no, it doesn't belong. If the answer to both questions is yes, it should be included.

Let's check out another question in the same paragraph.

The question of unequal pay for women draws on many other broader social issues. The gender disparities persist in areas other than pay. **2** However, there are a few select fields in which women earn slightly more than men do. **3** There is a long history of misogyny written into the very cultural and social fabric of the United States.

3

At this point, the writer is considering adding the following true statement:

> The year that women's suffrage became legal in the United States was also the year that the American Football League was formed under the leadership of Jim Thorpe.

Should the writer make this addition here?

A) Yes, because it gives a broader context to the achievement of women's suffrage.

B) Yes, because it helps to ease some of the political rhetoric in the rest of the passage.

C) No, because it does not contribute in a significant way to the discussion of the gender pay gap.

D) No, because the question of gender pay is irrelevant when all football players are men.

Here's How to Crack It

The first thing to ask yourself is whether the new sentence is relevant to the paragraph. In this case, the paragraph is about how *gender disparities persist in areas other than pay*. The new sentence is about the formation of the *American Football League*. It doesn't say anything about *gender disparities*, so it shouldn't be added—eliminate (A) and (B).

If you're saying to yourself, "but wait—isn't football a prime example of gender disparity?" take a deep breath. Read the sentence literally; there's no interpreting required in SAT Writing and Language. Football *could* be an example of gender disparity, but since this sentence doesn't say anything about it, it isn't relevant here.

Now look more closely at the reasons given in (C) and (D). The best reasons on questions like this have to do with the ideas of consistency and precision. Choice (C) accurately describes the new sentence by saying, essentially, that it's not relevant. Choice (D) could arguably be true, though football cheerleaders are a pretty compelling example of gender pay disparity…oh, but there we go interpreting! Stop! Thinking about an answer choice in that way isn't helpful in Writing and Language. The real problem with (D) is that it doesn't relate to the role the sentence would play in the paragraph, so eliminate it. The correct answer is (C).

If you run into a question that asks you whether to delete a sentence from a paragraph, approach it in exactly the same way we just did.

ORDER

Another type of question you're likely to see asks for the best placement of a sentence within a paragraph. Once again, consistency is the name of the game. The sentence in question needs to be consistent with the ideas in the sentences before and after it.

Take a look at an example.

---

[1] One need look no further than to the idea of the "traditional" family. [2] The shift, however, has yet to produce a substantive increase in how women, who are now nearly as likely to work as men, are paid. [3] In this idea, the father of the family earns the family wage while the mother tends to the children and the home. [4] With such an idea bolstering what many consider to be the goal inherent in the "American dream," it is no wonder that women in the workplace should have a somewhat degraded position. [5] Shifting social and economic roles have begun to change how people think about gender roles within the family. **4**

4

To make this paragraph most logical, sentence 2 should be placed

A) where it is now.

B) before sentence 1.

C) after sentence 4.

D) after sentence 5.

Here's How to Crack It

When you're placing a sentence within a paragraph, look for words or phrases that can connect the sentence to other sentences. In this case, sentence 2 refers to *the shift*, which should logically follow after some explanation of a *shift*. That mention comes in sentence 5, which mentions *shifting social and economic roles*, so sentence 2 belongs after sentence 5. The correct answer is (D).

COMBINING SENTENCES

So far in all the examples we've looked at, the key guidelines have been consistency and precision. We haven't mentioned grammar or concision at all in relation to questions. There is one type of question, however, that has to do with those concepts.

Take a look at this example.

The gender pay gap has no correlation to overall 5 salary. The gender pay gap appears in fields at both ends of the salary spectrum, from CEO to housekeeper.

5

Which choice most effectively combines the sentences at the underlined portion?

A) salary: this gap appears

B) salary; it appears

C) salary, appearing as it does

D) salary, although it appears

Here's How to Crack It

The question asks how to most effectively combine the sentences. Think about the overall goal of combining sentences—it's to make things shorter, so start by looking at the shortest answer. Double-check that the sentence is consistent and precise and that the punctuation is correct. If everything checks out, the shortest answer is the best option.

In this case, (B) is the shortest, the punctuation is correct, and the sentence is consistent and precise, so that's the best answer.

> Unsure how to tell if the punctuation is correct? Read on—the next chapter is all about punctuation!

Questions that ask you to combine sentences are almost always about concision, but occasionally an answer choice has incorrect punctuation, or something like (D) here, which has an opposite-direction transition when there's no actual contrast in the sentence. So be sure to check the answers carefully—the shortest one may not *always* be right.

WHAT DO GRAPHS HAVE TO DO WITH GRAMMAR?

The short answer is nothing. But charts and graphs do appear in SAT Writing and Language, so be prepared! As with graphs in any section of the test, you'll want to read the labels (title, axes, and key or legend) carefully, and then choose the answers that are most consistent with the data shown.

Take a look at an example.

Even as women's roles in high-level positions, such as Congress, have increased almost five-fold since 1989, **6** the pay that women receive relative to men has increased by only approximately 15 percentage points.

6

Which of the following choices gives information consistent with the graph?

A) NO CHANGE

B) women's wages have increased by over 80%.

C) the wages of women in Congress have decreased.

D) the efforts of women in Congress to raise wages have failed.

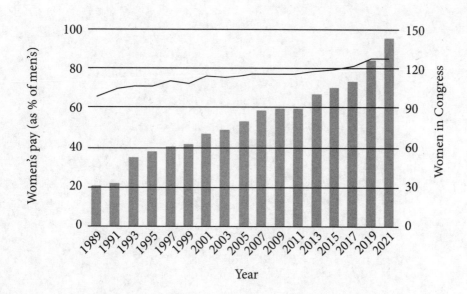

Women in Congress and Women's Pay

■ Women in Congress — Women's pay (as % of men's)

Here's How to Crack It

The question asks you to find which choice agrees with the graph. It looks like "Women in Congress" goes up significantly where "Women's Pay" remains relatively consistent. The only choice that reflects that trend is (A). Choice (B) misreads the graph, and (C) and (D) can't be supported one way or the other. Choice (A) is therefore the correct answer.

In general, graphs on the SAT Reading and Writing and Language Tests are very straightforward, and the fundamental question they ask is, "Can you read a graph?" These are easy points as long as you read the graphs carefully and use POE.

CONCLUSION

As you have seen in this chapter, the SAT can ask a lot of different kinds of questions, but you're not going to have anything really crazy thrown at you. The most important rules to remember are *consistency* and *precision*. If you choose answers that are precise and consistent with other information in the passage, you should be good to go.

Writing and Language Drill 3

Answers can be found starting on page 236.

Time: 10–11 minutes

Zombies in the Movies

[1] With the rise of movie streaming, the number of movies that are never shown in theaters increases every year. Horror, Western, and Sci-Fi movies are made every year, but the number of movies produced in each genre fluctuates annually. For example, as the number of Westerns has stayed at or below about 25 per year since the 1960s, the number of Zombie and Vampire films has [2] risen, with Zombie films increasing approximately ten-fold.

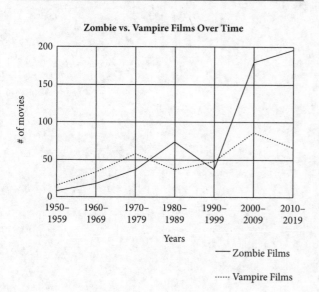

Zombie vs. Vampire Films Over Time

1

Which of the following choices would best introduce the main point of the essay?

A) NO CHANGE

B) While many movie genres are staples in Hollywood, the popularity of these genres has changed over time.

C) Everyone knows that the highest form of Hollywood film is the drama.

D) There's a lot that you may not know about how films are made in Hollywood.

2

Which of the following gives information consistent with the graph?

A) NO CHANGE

B) risen, with Vampire films increasing approximately ten-fold.

C) declined, with Zombie film production decreasing by a tenth.

D) declined, with Vampire film production decreasing by a tenth.

While the saying goes that there's "no accounting for the public's taste," **3** lots of people like lots of different things. Why should the number of Westerns have remained relatively low while the number of Zombie films has skyrocketed? Maybe we should ask the question another way: what do people today get from Zombie films that they don't from Westerns?

3

Which of the following choices would offer the most effective transition between the previous paragraph and the current one?

A) NO CHANGE

B) these trends nonetheless invite us to try

C) a lot of people don't even care about Zombie movies

D) science has not yet shown that zombies exist

Westerns dominated the 1920s. Zombie films have dominated the 2000s and 2010s. **4** Beginning with these facts alone, we can start to see why these films might have been popular in different eras. The 1920s, for instance, was an American moment of crusade. **5** These were crusades altogether distinct from those conducted by the Catholic Church starting in 1095. Only a tough sheriff, the kind one might get in an old-west town, could find the perfect balance between **6** legit action and foul play. Thus, if the world could not be contained by law and order, at least here was an imaginary space that could be in the West.

4

The writer is considering deleting the underlined sentence. Should the sentence be kept or deleted?

A) Kept, because it provides a logical transition between ideas in the paragraph.

B) Kept, because it explains why Westerns are now less popular than Zombie films are.

C) Deleted, because it is not directly related to the paragraph's focus on Zombie films.

D) Deleted, because it undermines the passage's claim about the declining popularity of Westerns.

5

Which choice best supports the idea in the previous sentence?

A) NO CHANGE

B) The United States is still interested in crusades today, so it's hard to see why they don't make as many Westerns anymore.

C) Led by Woodrow Wilson's plan for a U.S.-led League of Nations, the world, reeling from World War I, wanted justice among the outlaws.

D) The stock market wouldn't crash for another nine years, at which point people would really freak out.

6

Which choice best maintains the style and tone of the passage?

A) NO CHANGE

B) integrity and harshness

C) being lit and cruelty

D) justice and brutality

[1] The 2000s and 2010s, dominated as they are by Zombie films, show that contemporary conflicts are not so far away. [2] Instead, we are interested in and suspicious of the people around us. [3] Although we now have the world at the click of a button, Zombie films show that we are not all that interested in that world. [4] Whether coworkers or fellow students, the people around us, especially when viewed as a mass, can seem almost "dead." [5] And the reasons for this are fairly obvious: our private or online personalities have become so robust that **7** we end up spending a lot of time designing avatars that match our personalities. **8**

7

Which choice would most effectively conclude the sentence and the paragraph?

A) NO CHANGE

B) sometimes it's hard to have face-to-face conversations with people

C) many people now struggle with addictions to their Internet devices

D) the "real world" outside cannot help but seem dull by comparison

8

To make this paragraph most logical, sentence 2 should be placed

A) where it is now.

B) before sentence 1.

C) before sentence 4.

D) before sentence 5.

9 It may seem that genre conventions never change. Because they never change, it probably seems like a Western today follows the same set of rules as a Western from 100 years ago. What the rise in Zombie films shows, however, is that the genres themselves change, and they provide different things to different eras. **10** This is not to say that one genre is better than the other—that it's better, for instance, to watch a tough cowboy fight off a gang of cattle rustlers—but it is to say that these genres hold a lot more than their **11** bloodthirsty entertainment value.

9

Which choice most effectively combines the underlined sentences?

A) It may seem that genre conventions never change; because they never change, it probably seems like a Western today follows the same rules as a Western from 100 years ago.

B) It may seem that genre conventions never change; because of it, it could be argued that a Western today follows the same set of rules as a Western from 100 years ago.

C) It may seem that genre conventions never change: a Western today follows the same set of rules as a Western from 100 years ago.

D) Because Westerns today follow the same set of rules as they did 100 years ago, it seems to most outside observers that genre conventions never change.

10

At this point, the author is considering adding the following true statement:

For what it's worth, my personal favorite is Jacques Tourneur's *I Married a Zombie,* which is based loosely on *Jane Eyre.*

Should the writer make this addition here?

A) Yes, because the essay as a whole is filled with these kinds of examples and personal preferences.

B) Yes, because the author's quirky choice shows that he has an off-beat perspective.

C) No, because the author's strange choice disqualifies the author from discussing popular taste.

D) No, because the essay as a whole is not primarily focused on the author's personal preferences.

11

Which choice most effectively suggests that Westerns offer more than what they seem superficially to represent?

A) NO CHANGE

B) mere

C) wholesome

D) engaging

WRITING AND LANGUAGE DRILL 3: ANSWERS AND EXPLANATIONS

1. **B** Note the question! The question asks which choice *would best introduce the main point of the essay*, so it's testing consistency of ideas. Save this question for later, after reading the whole passage. Determine the subject of the passage and find the answer that is consistent with that idea. The paragraph says *Horror, Western, and Sci-Fi movies are made every year, but the number of movies produced in each genre fluctuates annually*. The rest of the passage continues this discussion of movie genres. Eliminate (A) because *movie streaming* or *theaters* are not consistent with the main idea. Keep (B) because it focuses on *movie genres*, which is consistent with the main idea. Eliminate (C) because *drama* is not one of the genres mentioned. Eliminate (D) because *how films are made in Hollywood* is not consistent with *movie genres*. The correct answer is (B).

2. **A** Note the question! The question asks which choice *gives information consistent with the graph*, so it's testing consistency. Read the labels on the graph carefully, and look for an answer that is consistent with the information given in the graph. Choices (C) and (D) are not consistent with the figure since the number of *Zombie* and *Vampire* films has risen, so eliminate (C) and (D). Choice (B) is not consistent with the figure since the number of Vampire films has increased from around 30 to 70, which is not a ten-fold increase, so eliminate (B). The graph does show that the number of Zombie films has increased ten-fold since it goes from about 20 in the 1960s to nearly 200 in the 2010s. The correct answer is (A).

3. **B** Note the question! The question asks which choice *would offer the most effective transition between the previous paragraph and the current one*, so it's testing consistency of ideas. Determine the subjects of the previous and current paragraphs and find the answer that is consistent with those ideas. The previous paragraph states that *the number of movies produced in each genre fluctuates annually* and *the number of Westerns* has not increased, while *the number of Zombie and Vampire movies has risen*. The current paragraph asks questions about that trend, like *Why should the number of Westerns have remained relatively low while the number of Zombie films has skyrocketed?* A consistent transition will link the trend and the discussion of the trend. Choice (A) is not consistent with either paragraph, so eliminate (A). Choice (B) mentions *trends,* and the phrase *invites us to try* to account for people's taste is consistent with the questions in the paragraph, so keep (B). Choice (C) mentions *Zombie movies* but says that *people don't care*, which is not consistent with the information in the previous paragraph, so eliminate (C). Choice (D) mentions *zombies*, but not *Zombie movies*, so eliminate (D). The correct answer is (B).

4. **A** Note the question! The question asks whether a sentence should be deleted, so it's testing consistency. If the content of the underlined sentence is consistent with the ideas surrounding it, then it should be kept. The previous sentences state that *Westerns dominated the 1920s. Zombie films have dominated the 1990s and 2000s.* The following sentence states that *The 1920s, for instance, was an American moment of crusade.* The sentence in question is consistent with the discussion of film genres and when they were popular, so the sentence should be kept; eliminate (C) and (D). Keep (A) because the sentence does provide *a logical transition*. Eliminate (B) because the sentence does not explain *why Westerns are now less popular than Zombie films are*. The correct answer is (A).

5. **C** Note the question! The question asks which choice *best supports the idea in the previous sentence*, so it's testing consistency. Eliminate answers that are inconsistent with the previous sentence. The previous sentence states that *The 1920s, for instance, was an American moment of crusade.* Look for an answer choice that is consistent with and supports the idea of the 1920s being an American moment of crusade. Eliminate (A) because *the Catholic Church* and *1095* do not support America in the 1920s. Eliminate (B) because the *United States today* does not support the 1920s. Keep (C) because *the world, reeling from World War I, wanted justice among the outlaws* supports the 1920s being a moment of crusade. Eliminate (D) because it discusses what happened after the 1920s. The correct answer is (C).

6. **D** Note the question! The question asks which choice *best maintains the style and tone of the passage*, so it's testing consistency. Eliminate answers that are inconsistent with the style and tone of the passage. The passage is written in a formal tone, so eliminate any answers that use slang or informal language. Eliminate (A) and (C) because *legit* and *being lit* are slang terms. Between (B) and (D), *brutality* is more consistent with the tone than *harshness*. The correct answer is (D).

7. **D** Note the question! The question asks which choice would *most effectively conclude the sentence and the paragraph*, so it's testing consistency of ideas. Determine the subject of the sentence and the paragraph and find the answer that is consistent with that idea. The paragraph says *Zombie films show that we are not all that interested in that world* and that *the people around us, especially when viewed as a mass, can seem almost "dead."* The last sentence of the paragraph starts by saying *our private or online personalities have become so robust.* Eliminate (A) because *designing avatars* is not a contrast to *online personalities.* Eliminate (B) because *face-to-face conversations* being hard is not consistent with the main idea of the paragraph. Eliminate (C) because *addictions to…Internet devices* is not consistent with the main idea of the paragraph. Keep (D) because *the real world* seeming *dull* is a contrast to *robust online personalities* and is consistent with *people around us* seeming *almost "dead."* The correct answer is (D).

8. **C** Note the question! The question asks where sentence 2 should be placed, so it's testing consistency of ideas. The sentence must be consistent with the ideas that come both before and after it. Sentence 2 says that *Instead, we are interested in and suspicious of the people around us.* Therefore, that sentence must come after some mention of being *interested.* Sentence 3 says *we are not all that interested in that world.* Therefore, sentence 2 should follow sentence 3 and come before sentence 4. The correct answer is (C).

9. **C** Note the question! The question asks how to effectively combine the underlined sentences, so it's testing precision and concision. Look for a sentence that is concise and maintains the meaning of the sentence. Eliminate (A) because it repeats the word *change*, which is not concise. Eliminate (B) because it repeats the word *it*, which is not concise. Keep (C) because it is concise, and the meaning is precise. Eliminate (D) because it is not as concise as (C). The correct answer is (C).

10. **D** Note the question! The question asks whether a sentence should be added, so it's testing consistency. If the content of the new sentence is consistent with the ideas surrounding it, then it should be added. The paragraph discusses movie genres changing. The new sentence discusses the author's favorite Zombie film, so it is not consistent with the ideas in the text; the sentence should not be added. Eliminate (A) and (B). Eliminate (C) because there is no indication that the author's favorite movie is a *strange choice*, and the reason provided does not relate to the content of the passage. Keep (D) because it correctly states that *the essay as a whole is not primarily focused on the author's personal preferences*. The correct answer is (D).

11. **B** Note the question! The question asks which choice *most effectively suggests that Westerns offer more than what they seem superficially to represent*, so it's testing consistency. Eliminate answers that are inconsistent with the purpose stated in the question. The sentence says *it is to say that these genres hold a lot more than their…entertainment value.* Look for an answer choice that is consistent with the idea that the films offer more than what they seem to represent. Eliminate (A), (C), and (D) because *bloodthirsty*, *wholesome*, and *engaging* do not suggest that there is more to the Western films than entertainment. Keep (B) because *mere* suggests the films are more than just entertainment. The correct answer is (B).

Summary

o   The most important thing to remember about Writing and Language questions is that you must *notice* those questions and then *answer* those questions. Don't miss out on some of the easiest points on the whole test by not reading carefully enough.

o   Always choose the answer that is most consistent with the task in the question and with the passage.

o   When answering questions, keep this general rule in mind: Writing and Language passages should be judged on what they *do* say, not on what they *could* say. When dealing with style, tone, and focus, work with the words and phrases the passage has already used.

o   There will be charts or graphs on the Writing and Language Test, but don't let that throw you off. Just read the graphs with as much precision as you would a passage and choose the most precise answers possible.

o   Even though some questions can be easy, many of these will be more time-consuming because they require more reading. Your POOD may tell you to skip some of the longer ones if you have trouble finishing the section in time.

Chapter 12
Punctuation

Punctuation is the focus of many questions on the Writing and Language test. But how do you know when to use the punctuation marks that are being tested? This chapter will answer that question as well as highlight some of the SAT's rules for using punctuation and the strategies you can use to outsmart the test-writers.

WAIT, THE SAT WANTS ME TO KNOW HOW TO USE A SEMICOLON?

Kurt Vonnegut once wrote, "Here is a lesson in creative writing. First rule: Do not use semicolons.... All they do is show you've been to college." Unfortunately, this does not apply to the SAT. For the SAT, you'll need to know how to use the semicolon and a few other types of weird punctuation. This chapter covers all the punctuation you need to know how to use on the Writing and Language Test. Learn these few simple rules, and you'll be all set on the punctuation questions.

First and foremost, stick to the strategy! Start by asking,

> What's changing in the answer choices?

If you see punctuation marks—commas, periods, apostrophes, semicolons, colons—changing, then the question is testing punctuation. As you work the problem, make sure to ask the big question:

> Does this punctuation need to be here?

The particular punctuation mark you are using, no matter what it is, must have a specific role within the sentence. You wouldn't use a question mark without a question, would you? Nope! Well, all punctuation works that way on the SAT, and in this chapter we'll give you examples of specific instances in which you would use a particular type of punctuation. Otherwise, let the words do their thing unobstructed!

STOP, GO, AND THE VERTICAL LINE TEST

Let's get the weird punctuation out of the way first. Everyone knows that a period ends a sentence, but once things get more complicated, even a particularly nerdy grammarian can get lost. Because of this confusion, we've created a chart that summarizes the different situations in which you might use what the SAT calls "end-of-sentence" and "middle-of-sentence" punctuation. We call them STOP, HALF-STOP, and GO.

When you are linking ideas, you must use one of the following:

STOP	HALF-STOP	GO
• Period (.)	• Colon (:)	• Comma (,)
• Semicolon (;)	• Long dash (—)	• No punctuation
• Comma (,) + **FANBOYS**		
• Question Mark (?)		
• Exclamation Mark (!)		

> **FANBOYS** stands for **F**or, **A**nd, **N**or, **B**ut, **O**r, **Y**et, and **S**o.

> STOP punctuation can link *only* complete ideas.
>
> HALF-STOP punctuation must be *preceded* by a complete idea.
>
> GO punctuation can link anything *except* two complete ideas.

Let's see how these work. Here is a complete idea:

Samantha studied for the SAT.

Notice that we've already used one form of STOP punctuation at the end of this sentence: a period.

Now, if we want to add a second complete idea, we'll keep the period.

Samantha studied for the SAT. She ended up doing really well on the test.

In this case, the period is linking these two complete ideas. But the nice thing about STOP punctuation is that you can use any of the punctuation in the list to do the same thing, so we could also say this:

Samantha studied for the SAT; she ended up doing really well on the test.

What the list of STOP punctuation shows us is that essentially, a period and a semicolon are the same thing. We could say the same for the use of a comma plus one of the FANBOYS.

Samantha studied for the SAT, and she ended up doing really well on the test.

You can also use HALF-STOP punctuation to separate two complete ideas, so you could say

Samantha studied for the SAT: she ended up doing really well on the test.

or

Samantha studied for the SAT—she ended up doing really well on the test.

There's a subtle difference, however, between STOP and HALF-STOP punctuation: for STOP punctuation, both ideas have to be complete, but for HALF-STOP punctuation, only the first one does.

You might notice that authors of books and articles do not always follow these punctuation (or grammar!) rules. Writers have "poetic license" to deviate from the rules. On the SAT, however, the punctuation and grammar rules in this book are always followed.

Let's see what this looks like. If you want to link a complete idea and an incomplete idea, you can use HALF-STOP punctuation as long as the complete idea comes first. For example,

Samantha studied for the SAT: all three sections of it.

or

Samantha studied for the SAT: the silliest test in all the land.

When you use HALF-STOP punctuation, there has to be a complete idea before the punctuation. So, these examples are NOT correct:

Samantha studied for: the SAT, the ACT, and every AP Exam in between.

The SAT—Samantha studied for it and was glad she did.

When you are not linking two complete ideas, you can use GO punctuation. So you could say, for instance,

Samantha studied for the SAT, the ACT, and every AP Exam in between.

or

Samantha studied for the SAT, all three sections of it.

These are the three types of mid-sentence or end-of-sentence punctuation: STOP, HALF-STOP, and GO. You'll notice that there is a bit of overlap between the concepts, but the SAT couldn't possibly make you get into the minutia of choosing between, say, a period and a semicolon. All you need to be able to do is figure out which of the big three categories (STOP, HALF-STOP, and GO) you'll need.

Let's see what this looks like in context.

Jonah studied every day for the big test he was taking the SAT that Saturday.

1

A) NO CHANGE

B) test, he was taking

C) test, he was taking,

D) test; he was taking

Here's How to Crack It

As always, check what's changing in the answer choices. In this case, the only thing changing is the punctuation; the words stay the same. Notice the types of punctuation that are changing: STOP and GO.

When you see different types of punctuation in the answer choices, you can use the Vertical Line Test to help you determine which type of punctuation to use.

To use the Vertical Line Test, draw a line where you see STOP or HALF-STOP punctuation—in this case, between the words *test* and *he*. First, read up to the vertical line: *Jonah studied every day for the big test.* That's a complete idea. Now, read after the vertical line: *he was taking the SAT that Saturday.* That's also a complete idea.

So, there are two complete ideas here. What kind of punctuation do you need? STOP or HALF-STOP. It looks like STOP is the only one available, so choose (D).

Vertical Line Test
You can use this test when you see STOP or HALF-STOP punctuation changing in the answer choices, as in this question.

Let's try another.

It was very important for him to do
2 well. High scores in all the subjects.

2

A) NO CHANGE

B) well; high

C) well: high

D) well, he wanted high

**Watch Us
Crack It**

Here's How to Crack It

Check the answer choices. What's changing? The punctuation is changing, and some of that punctuation is STOP and HALF-STOP. Use the Vertical Line Test. Draw a vertical line where you see the punctuation changing: between *well* and *high* or *well* and *he*.

What's before the vertical line? *It was very important for him to do well* is a complete idea. Then, *high scores in all the subjects* is not a complete idea. Therefore, because you have one complete idea (the first) and one incomplete idea (the second), you can't use STOP punctuation, thus eliminating (A) and (B).

A colon doesn't have to come before a list. It can come before any related information, such as a list, explanation, or definition.

Now, what's different between the last two? Choice (C) contains HALF-STOP punctuation, which can work, so keep that. Choice (D) adds some words. Adding those words makes the second idea *he wanted high scores in all the subjects*, which is a complete idea. That means (D) has two complete ideas separated by a comma, but can you use GO punctuation between two complete ideas? Nope. Eliminate (D)! Only (C) is left.

Let's see one more.

Whenever Jonah had a free
3 moment—he was studying.

3
A) NO CHANGE
B) moment; he
C) moment, he,
D) moment, he

Here's How to Crack It

The punctuation is changing in the answer choices, and there's some STOP and HALF-STOP punctuation, so use the Vertical Line Test. Put the line between *moment* and *he*. The first idea, *Whenever Jonah had a free moment*, is an incomplete idea, and the second idea, *he was studying*, is a complete idea. Therefore, you can't use STOP (which needs two complete ideas) or HALF-STOP (which needs a complete idea before the punctuation), thus eliminating (A) and (B). Then, because there is no good reason to put a comma after the word *he*, the correct answer must be (D).

A SLIGHT PAUSE FOR COMMAS

Commas can be a little tricky. In question 3, we narrowed it down to two answer choices, (C) and (D), after completing the Vertical Line Test. But then how do you decide whether to keep a comma in or not? It seems a little arbitrary to say that you use a comma "every time you want to pause," so let's make it a little more concrete.

> If you can't cite a reason to use a comma, *don't use one.*
>
> On the SAT, there are only four reasons to use a comma:
> * in STOP punctuation, with one of the FANBOYS
> * in GO punctuation, to separate incomplete ideas from other ideas
> * in a list of three or more things
> * in a sentence containing unnecessary information

We've already seen examples of the first two scenarios, so let's look at the other two.

Try this one.

His top-choice schools were

4 Harvard, Yale; and Princeton.

4
A) NO CHANGE
B) Harvard, Yale, and Princeton.
C) Harvard, Yale, and, Princeton.
D) Harvard Yale and Princeton.

Here's How to Crack It

First, check what's changing in the answer choices. The punctuation is changing, and there's STOP punctuation in a couple of the answers. But there's also a list in this sentence, and when you see that, there's no need for the Vertical Line Test—lists of three or more items on the SAT are punctuated by commas. That means you can eliminate (A), because the semicolon has no place here.

Next, eliminate (D) because the items in the list should be separated by commas, and (D) doesn't have any commas. The difference between (B) and (C) is the comma after the word *and,* which is never necessary in a list—eliminate (C). That means (B) is the correct answer.

Note that it may seem that (B) incorrectly uses STOP punctuation (if you paid attention to FANBOYS, a comma followed by the word *and* is STOP), but the *, and* at the end of a list doesn't count as STOP punctuation.

Let's try another.

5 Jonah, everyone seemed fairly certain, was going to get into one of those schools.

5
A) NO CHANGE
B) Jonah everyone seemed fairly certain
C) Jonah, everyone seemed fairly certain
D) Jonah everyone seemed fairly certain,

Here's How to Crack It

First, check what's changing in the answer choices: just the commas. And those commas are circling around the words *everyone seemed fairly certain*. When you've got a few commas circling around a particular word or phrase in a sentence, the question is usually testing necessary versus unnecessary information.

A good way to test whether the idea is necessary to the meaning of the sentence is to take it out. Read the original sentence again. Now read this one: *Jonah was going to get into one of those schools.*

Is the sentence still complete? Yes. Has the meaning of the sentence changed? No, we just lost a little extra description. Therefore, the idea is *unnecessary* to the meaning of the sentence and should be set off with commas, as it is in (A).

———————○———————

Let's try a few more. Try to figure out whether the word or idea in italics is necessary to the meaning of the sentence, and whether or not commas need to surround the italics. The answers are on page 253.

1. The student *with the best GPA* will be admitted to the best college.
2. Edward wants to go to Pomona College *which is a really good school.*
3. The car *that was painted red* drove off at a hundred miles an hour.
4. Charles Chesnutt *who wrote a lot of great stories* was also a lawyer.
5. Philadelphia Flyers goalie *Steve Mason* is an underappreciated player.

Now let's put it all together in the next question.

———————○———————

Everyone **6** hoped, he would get in, after his brother and two sisters had gone to their first-choice schools.

6

A) NO CHANGE
B) hoped, he would get in, after his brother, and
C) hoped, he would get in after his brother, and,
D) hoped he would get in after his brother and

Here's How to Crack It

Check what's changing in the answer choices. Commas are changing in a bunch of places. Remember, the rule of thumb with commas is that if you can't cite a reason to use a comma, *don't use one.*

In (A) and (B), *he would get in* is set off by commas. Determine whether it's necessary or unnecessary information. Read the original sentence, and then read the sentence again without that piece of information: *Everyone hoped after his brother and two sisters had gone to their first-choice schools*. The sentence isn't complete anymore. Therefore, that bit of information is necessary to the meaning of the sentence, so it doesn't need commas; eliminate (A) and (B). There are no good reasons to put commas in the phrase *after his brother and two sisters*, so eliminate (C).

In the end, there's no reason to put commas anywhere in this sentence. The correct answer is (D). Sometimes the SAT will test "unnecessary punctuation" explicitly, so make sure you can cite one of the four comma rules when you choose an answer with commas!

———————————○———————————

YOUR GOING TO BE TESTED ON APOSTROPHE'S (AND INTERNET SPELLING IS A TERRIBLE GUIDE!)

Like commas, apostrophes have a very limited set of applications. Apostrophes are a little trickier, though, because you can't hear them in speech, so people misuse them all the time. Think about the header of this section. There's one missing apostrophe and one apostrophe misused. Here's the correct way of punctuating it: *You're going to be tested on apostrophes*. Can you hear the difference? Neither can we, but you can definitely see the difference.

As with commas, if you can't cite a reason to use an apostrophe, don't use one. There are only two reasons to use an apostrophe on the SAT:

> - Possessive nouns (NOT pronouns)
> - Contractions

Let's see some examples.

———————————○———————————

Some of those very selective
7 schools' require really high score's.

7
A) NO CHANGE
B) school's require really high scores'.
C) schools require really high score's.
D) schools require really high scores.

Here's How to Crack It

Check what's changing in the answer choices. In this case, the words are all the same, but the apostrophes are changing. Remember, don't use apostrophes at all if you can't cite a good reason to do so.

Does anything belong to *schools* or *score*? No! Are they forming contractions like *school is* or *score is*? No! Therefore, there's no reason to use apostrophes, and the only possible answer is (D), which dispenses with the apostrophes altogether.

As in the previous question, there's no need for any punctuation, and in a question like this, you're being tested on whether you can spot unnecessary punctuation.

Sometimes apostrophes are necessary. Look at the following example.

8 It's tough to get in to you're top-choice schools.

8
A) NO CHANGE
B) Its tough to get in to your
C) Its tough to get in to you're
D) It's tough to get into your

Here's How to Crack It

Check what's changing in the answer choices. The apostrophes change, in two places: the words *its/it's* and *your/you're*.

The first word, *its/it's*, needs an apostrophe. It creates the contraction *it is*, which is necessary in this sentence. Therefore, get rid of (B) and (C). As for the other, this word is possessive (as in, the *top-choice schools* belonging to *you*), but remember, possessive *nouns* need an apostrophe, but possessive *pronouns* don't. Therefore, because *you* is a pronoun, this word should be spelled *your*, as it is in (D).

Phew! These apostrophes can get a little tricky, so let's try a few more. On these questions, you'll find that using your ear and sounding things out doesn't help much—knowing the rules is the way to go here.

Circle the option that works. The big question is, apostrophes or no apostrophes? You can find the answers on page 253.

1. *Tinas/Tina's* boss said *shes/she's* allowed to take the next few *days/day's* off.
2. If *your/you're* not coming to my party, *its/it's* really fine with me.
3. *There/They're* are really no good *reasons/reason's* for *your/you're* bad attitude.
4. *Well/We'll* get back to you as soon as *your/you're* application is received.
5. *Its/It's his/his'* guacamole, and he said we *cant/can't* have any because *its/it's* not *ours/our's*.

PUNCTUATION QUESTIONS IN DISGUISE

Occasionally you'll see a question in which the punctuation doesn't change, but it actually is testing you on punctuation. You can recognize this if subjects and verbs are changing in the answer choices, and you'll want to use the Vertical Line Test to determine whether you need complete or incomplete ideas to match the punctuation in the sentence. Take a look at the following example.

Consider attending a college fair, **9** <u>they are</u> where you can find out about more schools that could be good fits.

9

A) NO CHANGE
B) those being
C) these fairs are
D) DELETE the underlined portion.

Here's How to Crack It

Check what's changing in the answer choices. Some options have a subject and a verb, or a verb and no subject, or no verb or subject (delete). Even though punctuation doesn't change in the answers, when you see subjects and verbs changing, it's a good idea to use the Vertical Line Test where there is already punctuation of any type or where the ideas shift. Draw the line after *fair*. The first part of the sentence, *Consider attending a college fair*, is a complete idea. With the underlined portion, the second part of the sentence is also complete. You might remember that it's never allowed to just put a comma between two complete ideas, so (A) is wrong. Choice (C) also has a subject and verb, so eliminate both (A) and (C). The phrase *where you can find out about more schools that could be good fits* describes *a college fair*, so there is no reason to use any additional words. Eliminate (B). The correct answer is (D).

Treat Yourself

You've reached the end of the Writing and Language section! Give yourself a little relaxation time by going for a walk, reading a book (not this one!), or listening to some music or your favorite podcast. Your brain deserves a break!

CONCLUSION

We've now covered all of the punctuation you will ever need to know on the SAT. It's not that much, and you probably knew a lot of it already. In general, checking what's changing in the answer choices can help reveal mistakes that you may not have noticed otherwise, and POE can help you narrow down your options.

Punctuation rules are easy to learn, as is the biggest rule of all about punctuation.

> Know why you are using punctuation, whether that punctuation is STOP, HALF-STOP, GO, commas, or apostrophes. If you can't cite reasons to use these punctuation marks, don't use them!

Try out these skills in the drill starting on page 254.

Answers to Questions on Page 248:

1. NECESSARY to the meaning of the sentence (no commas). If you remove the italicized part, the sentence is not adequately specific.
2. UNNECESSARY to the meaning of the sentence (commas). If you remove the italicized part, the sentence is still complete and the main meaning does not change.
3. NECESSARY to the meaning of the sentence (no commas). If you remove the italicized part, the sentence is not adequately specific.
4. UNNECESSARY to the meaning of the sentence (commas). If you remove the italicized part, the sentence is still complete and the main meaning does not change.
5. NECESSARY to the meaning of the sentence (no commas). If you remove the italicized part, the sentence is no longer complete.

Answers to Questions on Page 251:

1. Tina's, she's, days
2. you're, it's
3. There, reasons, your
4. We'll, your
5. It's, his, can't, it's, ours

Writing and Language Drill 4

Use what you've learned in this chapter in the drill questions that follow. Answers can be found starting on page 257.

Time: 7–8 minutes

Human Versus Machine

More and more of our lives are mechanized, and at some point, we have to start wondering, what's the limit of that mechanization? Many factory workers in the 19th century thought their jobs were **1** safe but we know now that they were wrong. Many people in **2** today's world believe there jobs are safe, but how safe are those jobs really?

Studies abound that ask whether man or machine is better at particular tasks, and the results are not always so obvious. Sure, a machine is obviously better **3** at say, welding huge pieces of steel together, but what would you say if someone told you people are more likely to open up to a machine than to a psychologist? Or that a machine could write a quicker, more efficient news story than an experienced reporter could?

1

A) NO CHANGE
B) safe, but
C) safe,
D) safe. But,

2

A) NO CHANGE
B) todays world believe their
C) todays world believe they're
D) today's world believe their

3

A) NO CHANGE
B) at, say
C) at, say,
D) at say

These questions may seem overly pessimistic (or overly optimistic depending on **4** your point of view); however, some recent studies have been truly remarkable. Take Ellie, a computer program used primarily to diagnose patients with depression, **5** PTSD and, other mood disorders. Many patients found it easier to talk to "Ellie" than to a real **6** person: she didn't react in some of those seemingly judgmental ways that a person would, and her voice never **7** broke on top of that she could help psychologists to diagnose mental illnesses better than human observation could. She could detect facial movements or voice tones that a person might have not heard or ignored.

4

A) NO CHANGE
B) your point of view),
C) you're point of view),
D) you're point of view);

5

A) NO CHANGE
B) PTSD, and other
C) PTSD, and, other
D) PTSD, and other,

6

A) NO CHANGE
B) person, she
C) person; but she
D) person she

7

A) NO CHANGE
B) broke, on top of that,
C) broke. On top of that,
D) broke; on top, of that,

Whether Ellie is the way of the future is yet to be determined. We can't know right now, but there is no question that she raises some interesting questions, not only about **8** psychologists' method's but also about all of what we think are definitively human activities.

On the other side of the discussion, however, there's some evidence that humans may have the upper hand. In some of the more basic **9** tasks those learned before the age of about 10 humans have a huge upper hand. Computers can do the complex thinking, but one thing with which they have a lot of trouble is, paradoxically, simplicity. Sure, a computer can tell **10** your washer's and dryer's what a perfect washing and drying cycle is, but can it fold your laundry? Your GPS can tell you the fastest route to the next state, but can it tell you the prettiest way to go or the best restaurants along the way? Not without humans!

While the battle of man against machine rages **11** on. The questions will persist. No matter who wins, though, humans will almost assuredly find ways to adapt: that's something we've been doing for thousands of years, which is something that no computer can say.

8

A) NO CHANGE
B) psychologists method's
C) psychologists' methods
D) psychologists methods

9

A) NO CHANGE
B) tasks those learned before the age of about 10,
C) tasks, those learned before the age of about 10
D) tasks, those learned before the age of about 10,

10

A) NO CHANGE
B) your washer and dryer
C) you're washers and dryers
D) you're washer and dryer

11

A) NO CHANGE
B) on; the
C) on—the
D) on, the

WRITING AND LANGUAGE DRILL 4: ANSWERS AND EXPLANATIONS

1. **B** Punctuation is changing in the answer choices, so this question is testing STOP, HALF-STOP, and GO punctuation. Use the Vertical Line Test and identify the ideas as complete or incomplete. Draw the vertical line through the word *but* and consider the ideas before and after the FANBOYS word. The first part of the sentence, *Many factory workers in the 19th century thought their jobs were safe*, is a complete idea. The second part, *we know now that they were wrong*, is a complete idea. To connect two complete ideas, STOP punctuation is needed. Eliminate (A) and (C) because a FANBOYS word alone and a comma alone can't link two complete ideas. Keep (B) because *but* with a comma is STOP punctuation. Choice (D) has a period, which is STOP punctuation, but placing the word *but* after the period makes the second idea incomplete. Eliminate (D) because a period cannot be used between a complete and an incomplete idea. The correct answer is (B).

2. **D** Apostrophes are changing in the answer choices, so the question is testing apostrophe usage. When used with a noun on the SAT, an apostrophe indicates possession. In this sentence, the *world* belongs to *today*, so an apostrophe is needed. Eliminate (B) and (C) because they do not contain an apostrophe. Next, pronouns are changing. The jobs belong to *many people*, so a possessive plural pronoun is needed. Eliminate (A) because *there* does not correctly show possession of the *jobs*. Choice (D) correctly uses the possessive pronoun *their* to show possession of the *jobs*. The correct answer is (D).

3. **C** Commas are changing in the answer choices, so this question is testing the four ways to use a comma. The word *say* is unnecessary information, so it should have commas both before and after it. Eliminate (A) and (B) because they both only have one comma each. Keep (C) because it correctly places commas before and after *say*. Eliminate (D) because it has no commas. The correct answer is (C).

4. **A** Apostrophes are changing in the answer choices, so this question is testing apostrophe usage. When used with a pronoun, an apostrophe indicates a contraction. *You're* means "you are." In this sentence, the *point of view* belongs to someone, so an apostrophe should not be used. A possessive pronoun is needed instead. Eliminate (C) and (D). Next, punctuation is changing in the answer choices, so this question is testing STOP, HALF-STOP, and GO punctuation. Use the Vertical Line Test and identify the ideas as complete or incomplete. Draw the vertical line between the words *view* and *however*. The first part of the sentence, *These questions may seem overly pessimistic (or overly optimistic depending on your point of view)*, is a complete idea. The second part, *however, some recent studies have been truly remarkable*, is a complete idea. To connect two complete ideas, STOP punctuation is needed. Eliminate (B) because a comma alone is GO punctuation. The correct answer is (A).

5. **B**   Commas are changing in the answer choices, so this question is testing the four ways to use a comma. The sentence contains a list of three things: 1) *depression*, 2) *PTSD*, and 3) *other mood disorders*. There should be a comma after each item in the list. Eliminate (A) because it does not have a comma after *PTSD* and incorrectly adds a comma after *and*. Keep (B) because it has a comma after each item in the list. Eliminate (C) because it incorrectly adds a comma after *and*. Eliminate (D) because it incorrectly adds a comma after *other*. The correct answer is (B).

6. **A**   Punctuation is changing in the answer choices, so this question is testing STOP, HALF-STOP, and GO punctuation. Use the Vertical Line Test and identify the ideas as complete or incomplete. Draw the vertical line between the words *person* and *she*. The first part of the sentence, *Many patients found it easier to talk to "Ellie" than to a real person*, is a complete idea. The second part, *she didn't react in some of those seemingly judgmental ways that a person would, and her voice never broke*, is a complete idea. To connect two complete ideas, STOP or HALF-STOP punctuation is needed. Keep (A) because a colon is HALF-STOP punctuation. Eliminate (B) and (D) because a comma and no punctuation are both GO punctuation. Eliminate (C) because adding *but* to the second idea makes it incomplete, and STOP punctuation cannot be used to connect a complete idea and an incomplete idea. The correct answer is (A).

7. **C**   Punctuation is changing in the answer choices, so this question is testing STOP, HALF-STOP, and GO punctuation. Use the Vertical Line Test and identify the ideas as complete or incomplete. Draw the vertical line between the words *broke* and *on*. The first part of the sentence, *she didn't react in some of those seemingly judgmental ways that a person would, and her voice never broke*, is a complete idea. The second part, *on top of that she could help psychologists to diagnose mental illnesses better than human observation could*, is a complete idea. To connect two complete ideas, STOP punctuation is needed. Eliminate (A) and (B) because no punctuation and a comma alone are both GO punctuation. Keep (C) because a period is STOP punctuation. Eliminate (D) because it incorrectly places a comma after *top*. The correct answer is (C).

8. **C**   Apostrophes are changing in the answer choices, so the question is testing apostrophe usage. When used with a noun on the SAT, an apostrophe indicates possession. In this sentence, the *methods* belong to *psychologists*, so an apostrophe is needed. Eliminate (B) and (D) because they do not contain the apostrophe on *psychologists*. Eliminate (A) because the word *but* does not belong to *methods*, so there should not be an apostrophe on *methods*. The correct answer is (C).

9. **D**   Commas are changing in the answer choices, so this question is testing the four ways to use a comma. The phrase *those learned before the age of about 10* is unnecessary information, so it should have commas both before and after it. Eliminate (A) because it contains no commas. Eliminate (B) and (C) because they both contain only one comma. Keep (D) because it correctly places commas before and after the phrase. The correct answer is (D).

10. **B** Apostrophes are changing in the answer choices, so the question is testing apostrophe usage. The *washers and dryers* belong to *you*. When used with a pronoun, an apostrophe indicates a contraction. *You're* is equal to "you are," which is not correct in this sentence; eliminate (C) and (D). When used with a noun on the SAT, an apostrophe indicates possession. In this sentence, the *washers and dryers* do not possess anything, so no apostrophe is needed. Eliminate (A) because it contains apostrophes on *washers* and *dryers*. The correct answer is (B).

11. **D** Punctuation is changing in the answer choices, so this question is testing STOP, HALF-STOP, and GO punctuation. Use the Vertical Line Test and identify the ideas as complete or incomplete. Draw the vertical line between the words *on* and *The*. The first part of the sentence, *While the battle of man against machine rages on*, is an incomplete idea. The second part, *The questions will persist*, is a complete idea. To connect an incomplete idea to a complete idea, GO punctuation is needed. Eliminate (A), (B), and (C) because they contain STOP or HALF-STOP punctuation. The correct answer is (D).

Summary

- o Remember STOP, HALF-STOP, and GO punctuation.
  - STOP punctuation can link *only* complete ideas.
  - HALF-STOP punctuation must be *preceded* by a complete idea.
  - GO punctuation can link anything *except* two complete ideas.

- o When you see STOP or HALF-STOP punctuation changing in the answer choices, use the Vertical Line Test.

- o On the SAT, there are only four reasons to use a comma:
  - STOP punctuation (with one of the FANBOYS)
  - GO punctuation
  - after every item in a list of three or more items
  - to set off unnecessary information

- o On the SAT, there are only two reasons to use an apostrophe:
  - possessive nouns (NOT pronouns)
  - contractions

- o Know why you are using punctuation, whether that punctuation is STOP, HALF-STOP, GO, commas, or apostrophes. If you can't cite reasons to use these punctuation marks, don't use them!

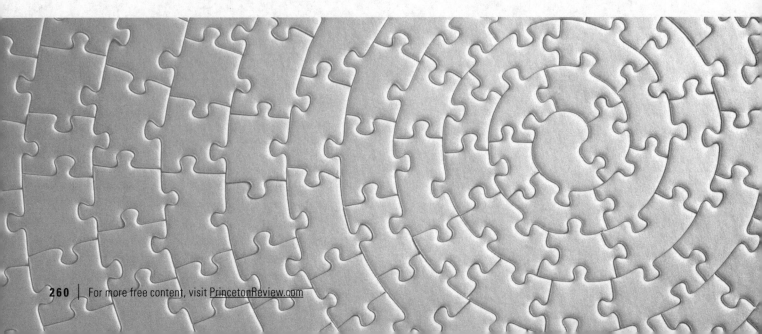

Part IV
How to Crack
the Math Test

A FEW WORDS ABOUT SAT MATH

As we've mentioned before, the SAT isn't your typical school test. This also goes for the Math sections of the SAT. There are two types of questions that you'll run into: multiple-choice and student-produced response questions. We've already discussed multiple-choice questions, so let's talk about these strange questions known as student-produced response questions. These questions are the only non-multiple-choice questions on the SAT. Instead of selecting the correct answer from among several choices, you will have to find the answer on your own and mark it in a grid (which is why we call them Grid-Ins). The Grid-In questions on the SAT will be drawn from arithmetic, algebra, and geometry, just like the multiple-choice math questions. However, the grid-in format has special characteristics, so we will treat these questions a bit differently. You'll learn more about them later in this book.

What Does the SAT Math Test Measure?

The College Board says that the Math Test covers "all mathematical practices," with a strong focus on problem solving, using tools appropriately, and using structure to manipulate expressions. Fortunately for you, there is no way one test can cover *all* mathematical concepts. The SAT Math Test is actually a brief test of arithmetic, algebra, and a bit of geometry—when we say a "bit," we mean it. There are only 6 geometry questions at most on the test. We'll show you which geometry concepts are important. We will also give you the tools you need to do well on the Math Test as a whole, and the skills to use those tools appropriately.

The Math Breakdown

No Need to Know

Here are a few things you won't need to know to answer SAT Math questions: calculus, logarithms, matrices, and geometric proofs. Essentially, the SAT tests a whole lot of algebra and some arithmetic, statistics, and geometry.

The SAT includes two scored Math sections: one on which calculator use is allowed and one on which it is not. The No Calculator section, or Section 3, is 25 minutes long and includes 20 questions. The Calculator section, or Section 4, is 55 minutes long and includes 38 questions.

According to the College Board, the Math questions on the SAT fall into the following cleverly named categories:

1. Heart of Algebra
2. Passport to Advanced Math
3. Problem Solving and Data Analysis
4. Additional Topics

The first three will give you some of your test subscores, but the names of all four categories don't really mean anything. This is what will really be tested:

1. Algebra I and II
2. Arithmetic/Probability/Data Analysis
3. Plane Geometry/Coordinate Geometry/Trigonometry

That's it! Of these categories, Algebra makes up the majority of the Math Test, accounting for more than half of the questions. Plane Geometry and Trigonometry make up the smallest part—there will be a maximum of only 6 questions from that category on the SAT.

The Math questions on your SAT will appear in two different formats:

1. Regular multiple-choice questions
2. Grid-Ins

The Grid-Ins will appear at the end of each Math section: 5 questions in the No Calculator section and 8 questions in the Calculator section. (See Chapter 20 for more on the Grid-In questions.)

You Don't Have to Finish

We've all been taught in school that when you take a test, you have to finish it. If you answered only two-thirds of the questions on a high school math test, you probably wouldn't get a very good grade. But as we've already seen, the SAT is not at all like the tests you take in school. Most students don't know about the difference, so they make the mistake of doing all of the questions on both Math sections of the SAT.

Because they have only a limited amount of time to answer all the questions, most students rush through the questions they think are easy to get to the harder ones as soon as possible. At first, it seems reasonable to save more time for the more challenging questions, but think about how the test is scored for a minute. All correct answers are worth the same amount, no matter how difficult they are or how long they take to answer. So when students rush through a Math Test, they're actually spending less time on the easier questions (which they have a good chance of getting right), just so they can spend more time on the harder questions (which they have less chance of getting right). Does this make sense? Of course not.

Here is the secret: on the Math Test, you don't have to answer every question in each section. In fact, unless you are aiming for a top score, you should intentionally skip some harder questions in each section. Most students can raise their Math scores by concentrating on correctly answering all of the questions that they find easy and of medium difficulty. In other words...

> **Quick Note**
> Remember, this is not a math test in school! It is not scored on the same scale your math teacher uses. You don't need to get all the questions right to get an above-average score.

Slow Down!

Most students do considerably better on the Math Test when they slow down and spend less time worrying about the more complex questions (and more time working carefully on the more straightforward ones). Haste causes careless errors, and careless errors can ruin your score. In most cases, you can actually raise your score by answering fewer questions. That doesn't sound like a bad idea, does it? If you're shooting for an 800, you'll have to answer every question correctly. But if your target is 550, you should ignore the hardest questions in each section and use your limited time wisely.

The chart below will tell you exactly how many questions to attempt on each part of the Math sections. Notice that for all scores less than 750, some room for error is built into the number of questions to attempt.

To get: (scaled score)	You need to earn: (raw points)	Answer this many questions				Total # of questions to attempt
		Section 3: No Calculator		Section 4: Yes Calculator		
		15 questions MC	5 questions Grid-Ins	30 questions MC	8 questions Grid-Ins	
350	12	5	1	9	1	16
400	16	7	2	11	2	22
450	20	9	2	13	3	27
500	26	10	2	18	3	33
550	32	11	2	21	5	39
600	39	12	3	24	6	45
650	44	13	4	26	7	50
700	50	14	5	29	8	56
750	54	15	5	30	8	58
800	58	15	5	30	8	58

POOD and the Math Test

The questions in both sections of the Math Test (No Calculator and Calculator) are arranged in a loose order of difficulty. The earlier questions are generally easier and the last few are harder, but the level of difficulty may jump around a little. Also, "hard" on the SAT means that a higher percentage of students tend to get it wrong, often due to careless errors or lack of time.

The difficulty level resets with the Grid-In questions, so the first Grid-In question on each section will often be much easier than the last multiple-choice question. You don't want to miss a chance to get an easy Grid-In question right simply because you got stuck on harder multiple-choice questions and ran out of time.

Because difficulty levels can go up and down a bit, don't worry too much about how hard the test-writers think a question is. Focus instead on the questions that are easiest for you, and do your best to get those right—no matter where they appear—before moving on to the tougher ones. So which will be the easy ones for you? It is *personal* order of difficulty, but here are some things to consider:

- **Math knowledge:** Do you know the topic cold? Do you see exactly how to start solving it? Then the question is worth attempting, but read and work carefully!
- **SAT knowledge:** Is there a Princeton Review technique from this book that would be perfect for this question? Then now is the time to put your skills to use.

Remember!
Practice questions and drill questions throughout the Math section are each assigned a question number. At first glance, these numbers might seem random, but they are actually meant to show where you might see a similar question on the test.

- **Self-knowledge:** Do your eyes glaze over at a word problem that takes up half a page? Do imaginary numbers make you imagine doing literally anything else? Then come back to that question later or just pick your Letter of the Day (LOTD).
- **Take the first bite:** A great way to decide whether a question deserves your time is to think about Bite-Sized Pieces. If you know immediately how to start a question, there's a good chance you'll be able to finish it and get it right.

> Don't forget: Fill in your LOTD for questions you decide to skip, and bubble in an answer for every question.

Calculators

Calculators are permitted (but not required) on Section 4 of the SAT. You should definitely take a calculator to the test. It will be extremely helpful to you on many questions, as long as you know how and when to use it and don't get carried away. In this book, questions that would likely appear in the Calculator section will have a calculator symbol next to them. If there is no symbol by a question, it is more likely to be found in the No Calculator section of the test. We'll tell you more about calculators as we go along, as well as teach you how to manage without one.

The Princeton Review Approach

We're going to give you the tools you need to handle the easier questions on the SAT Math Test, along with several great techniques to help you crack some of the more difficult ones. But you must concentrate first on getting the easier questions correct. Don't worry about the questions you find difficult on the Math sections until you've learned to work carefully and accurately on the easier questions.

When it does come time to look at some of the harder questions, use Process of Elimination to help you avoid trap answers and to narrow down your choices if you have to guess. Just as you did in the other sections of the test, you'll learn to use POE to improve your odds of finding the answer by getting rid of answer choices that can't possibly be correct.

Generally speaking, each chapter in this section begins with the basics and then gradually moves into more advanced principles and techniques. If you find yourself getting lost toward the end of the chapter, don't worry. Concentrate your efforts on principles that are easier to understand but that you still need to master.

Chapter 13
SAT Math: The Big Picture

In this chapter, you'll see a few ways you can eliminate bad answer choices, avoid traps, improve your odds of answering correctly if you have to guess, and maximize your Math score. You'll also learn how to best make use of your calculator, when it is permitted, and how to get along without it.

THE BIG PICTURE

In the Reading section of this book, you learned about various ways to eliminate wrong answers on hard questions. Well, that idea comes into play on the SAT Math Test as well. This chapter provides an overview of the strategies you should know to maximize your Math score, as well as some tips on how to use your calculator wisely (and how to work without it!).

BALLPARKING

One way to eliminate answers on the Math Test is by looking for ones that are the wrong size, or that are not "in the ballpark." We call this strategy **Ballparking.** Although you can use your calculator on the following question, you can also eliminate one answer without doing any calculations.

25

Joy plants three rows of corn in her garden. The row on the south edge of the garden receives more sunlight than the row on the north edge of the garden. Therefore, the corn on the north edge of the garden is 30% shorter than that on the south. If the corn on the south edge of the garden is 50 inches tall, how tall is the corn on the north edge of the garden, in inches?

A) 30

B) 33

C) 35

D) 65

Here's How to Crack It

The question asks for the height of the corn on the north edge of the garden and states that the corn there is shorter than the corn on the south edge, which is 50 inches tall. You are asked to find the height of the corn on the north edge, so the correct answer must be less than 50. Eliminate (D), which is too high. Often, one or more of the bad answers on these questions is the result you would get if you applied the percentage to the wrong value. To find the right answer, take 30% of 50 by multiplying 0.3 by 50 to get 15; then subtract that from 50. The corn on the north edge would be 35 inches tall. The correct answer is (C).

READ THE FINAL QUESTION

You never know what a question is going to ask you to do, so make sure to always read the final question before solving. Underline what you are actually solving for and any key words you think you might forget about as you solve the question. Then, try to ballpark before you solve.

Watch Us Crack It

7

If $16x - 2 = 30$, what is the value of $8x - 4$?

A) 12

B) 15

C) 16

D) 28

Here's How to Crack It

The question asks for the value of an expression, but don't just dive in and solve for the variable. First, see if you can eliminate answers by Ballparking, which can also work on algebra questions. To go from $16x$ to $8x$, you would just divide by 2. Dividing 30 by 2 gives you 15, so 28 is way too big. Eliminate it. The correct answer is not likely to be 15, either, because that ignores the –2 and the –4 in the question.

To solve this one, add 2 to each side of the equation to get $16x = 32$. Divide both sides by 2, which gives you $8x = 16$. But don't stop there! The final question asks for $8x - 4$, so (C) is a trap answer. You have to take the last step and subtract 4 from both sides to find that $8x - 4 = 12$. The correct answer is (A).

RTFQ:
Read
The
Final
Question

Get started faster and avoid trap answers by reading and underlining the actual question being asked.

ONE PIECE AT A TIME

When dealing with complicated math questions, take it one little piece at a time. We call this strategy Bite-Sized Pieces. If you try to do more than one step at a time, especially if you do it in your head, you are likely to make mistakes or fall for trap answers. After each step, take a look at the answer choices and determine whether you can eliminate any.

Try the following question.

9

A paper airplane is thrown from the top of a hill and travels horizontally at 9 feet per second. If the plane descends 1 foot for every 3 feet traveled horizontally, how many feet has the plane descended after 5 seconds of travel?

A)   3

B)   10

C)   15

D)   20

Bite-Sized Piece:
Do one small, manageable piece at a time and keep writing things down.

Here's How to Crack It

The question asks how many feet the plane has descended after 5 seconds. There are a few things going on here. The plane is traveling horizontally, and it is also descending. Start by figuring out how far it travels horizontally. It moves in that direction at 9 feet per second for 5 seconds, so it moves horizontally $9 \times 5 = 45$ feet. It descends 1 foot for every 3 traveled horizontally. If it goes 45 feet horizontally, it will descend more than 3 feet, so eliminate (A). Now figure out how many "3 feet" are in 45 feet—for each one of them, the plane will descend 1 foot. Since $45 \div 3 = 15$, the plane descends 15 feet. The correct answer is (C).

You may also have noticed that all the numbers in the question are odd. This makes it unlikely that the answer would be 10 or 20, which are even. If you see things like that, use them as opportunities to eliminate.

Here's another example.

6

$$(5jk^2 + 5j^2 - 2j^2k) - (jk^2 + 2j^2k + 5j^2)$$

Which of the following is equivalent to the expression above?

A) $4jk^2$

B) $4jk^2 - 4j^2k$

C) $5j^2k^4 - 10j^4k$

D) $8j^2k^3 + 7j^2k - 5j^2$

Here's How to Crack It

The question asks for an expression that is equivalent to the difference of two polynomials. In math class, your teacher would want you to combine all like terms and show your work, but this isn't math class. Start with one tiny piece of this ugly-looking question. The first set of parentheses starts with a term containing jk^2. Check the second set of parentheses for the same combination of variables and exponents. The first term there matches, so the first step to take is $5jk^2 - jk^2 = 4jk^2$. There are no other terms with jk^2, so the correct answer must contain $4jk^2$. Eliminate (C) and (D). Now you have a fifty-fifty chance of getting it right, so you can guess and go, *or* you can do one more step to determine if the answer is (A) or (B). The difference between the two answers is the $-4j^2k$ term, so focus on the terms in the expression that contain j^2k. In the first set of parentheses, you have $-2j^2k$, and then you subtract the $2j^2k$ term in the second set of parentheses to get $-2j^2k - 2j^2k = -4j^2k$. The correct answer is (B).

Word Problems

The last two Big Picture strategies are a large part of the approach to tackling word problems on the SAT. The test-writers will make things difficult to understand by making the questions wordier and sometimes even adding extraneous information. To make sure you have the best shot at reaching the correct answer quickly and accurately, follow this basic approach.

> ### WORD PROBLEM BASIC APPROACH
>
> 1. Read the Final Question—Read and underline the actual question that is being asked.
> 2. Let the Answers Help—Look for clues on how to approach the question and opportunities to use POE.
> 3. Work using Bite-Sized Pieces—Start with the most straightforward piece of information.

WRITE STUFF DOWN

As you solve questions in small pieces, write down the steps. Don't keep track of things in your head—your test booklet is there for your notes. If a figure is given, write the information from the question right on it.

Here's an example.

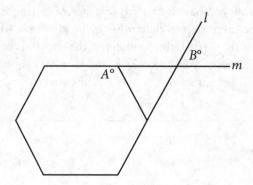

12

Lines *l* and *m* extend from two sides of the regular hexagon as shown above. If *A* = 120, what is the value of *B*, in degrees?

A)   30

B)   60

C)   90

D)   140

Here's How to Crack It

The question asks for the value of *B* in the figure. Sometimes Ballparking can help even on geometry questions. Not all pictures are drawn to scale, so don't assume the figure is exact. You can, however, use what the question tells you about the figure to estimate angles, line lengths, areas, and points on graphs in the *xy*-plane.

If the previous figure is drawn to scale, the angle with measurement *B* appears to be acute, making (A) or (B) a good bet. The question says the hexagon is "regular," which means that all the interior angles have the same measure, and the drawing looks like this is the case. Start by marking the angle that is *A*° as 120° on the figure. This angle looks like 120°, so *B* can't possibly equal 90° or 140°. Eliminate (C) and (D). To find the exact value of *B*, you need to find the measure of the angle opposite it, which is one of the angles from the triangle. The angle of the upper-left corner of the triangle is formed by drawing a straight line from the angle that is *A*°, or 120°. There are 180° in a straight line, so the upper-left corner of the triangle measures 180° − 120° = 60°. Label this measure on the figure as well. The fact that the hexagon is regular means that all the interior angles are 120°, so label the angle next to the bottom corner of the triangle. Since this corner of the triangle is formed in the same way as the upper-left corner, the bottom corner also measures 60°. Label it. There are 180° in a triangle, so the upper-right angle is also 60°. The angle measuring *B*° is opposite this, so *B* is 60°.

By the time you're done, your figure should look like this:

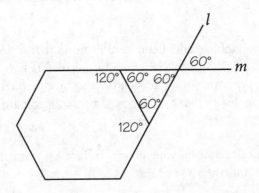

The correct answer is (B).

THE CALCULATOR

As you already know, the Math Test is divided into a shorter section in which calculator use is not permitted (Section 3) and a longer section in which it is permitted (Section 4). This affects the way you do the questions in each of these sections. The No Calculator section will lean more toward fluency and understanding of mathematical concepts, but that doesn't mean you won't have to calculate anything. On the Calculator section, using the calculator is not always helpful. In this book, if you see a calculator symbol next to a question, it means you may use your calculator as needed to arrive at the answer. If there is no calculator symbol next to a question, leave that calculator alone! The rest of this chapter will give you general information about how to use your calculator when you can and what to do when you can't. Other Math chapters will provide information about using your calculator in specific situations. Even if you now use a calculator regularly in your math class at school, you should still read this chapter and the other Math chapters carefully and practice the techniques we describe.

You'll need to take your own calculator to the testing center. Make sure that your calculator is either a scientific or a graphing calculator and can perform the order of operations correctly. To test your calculator, try the following problem, typing it in exactly as written without hitting the ENTER or "=" key until the end: $3 + 4 \times 6 =$. The calculator should give you 27. If it gives you 42, it's not a good calculator to use.

Section 3: No Calculator

The College Board says that the purpose of the No Calculator section is to test your "fluency" and "conceptual understanding" of math topics. While you may have to rearrange some terms and do some manipulation to answer questions correctly, you won't be expected to do anything too crazy, like calculate $\sqrt{2{,}789}$ to three decimal places—so have no fear!

Section 4: Calculator

A calculator can be an obstacle at times. The test-writers have designed this section of the test in the hopes of assessing your "appropriate use of tools," and they freely admit that a calculator can slow you down on some of the questions. So, by all means, use that calculator if you need it to avoid making careless errors, but don't forget that using your brain and pencil can often be a faster way to get to the right answer.

Many students already own a graphing calculator. If you have one, great; if you don't, don't sweat it. A graphing calculator is not necessary for the SAT, though it may help simplify certain graphing questions.

If you do decide to use a graphing calculator, keep in mind that it *cannot* have a QWERTY-style keyboard (like the TI-95). Most of the graphing calculators have typing capabilities, but because they don't have typewriter-style keyboards, they are perfectly legal. To see the full College Board calculator policy, visit collegereadiness.collegeboard.org/sat/taking-the-test/calculator-policy.

Also, you *cannot* use the calculator on your phone. In fact, on test day, you will have to turn your phone off and put it underneath your seat.

The only danger in using a calculator on the SAT is that you may be tempted to use it in situations in which it won't help you. Some students believe that their calculator will solve many difficulties they have with math. It won't. This type of thinking may even occasionally cause students to miss a question they might have otherwise answered correctly on their own. Remember that your calculator is only as smart as you are. But if you practice and use a little caution, you will find that your calculator will help you a great deal.

What a Calculator Is Good at Doing

Here is a complete list of what a calculator is good at on the SAT:

- arithmetic
- decimals
- fractions
- square roots
- percentages
- graphs (if it is a graphing calculator)

We'll discuss the calculator's role in most of these areas in the next few chapters.

Calculator Arithmetic

Adding, subtracting, multiplying, and dividing integers and decimals is easy on a calculator. But, you need to be careful when you key in the numbers. A calculator will give you an incorrect answer to an arithmetic calculation only if you press the wrong keys.

Calculators Don't Think for You
A calculator crunches numbers and often saves you a great deal of time and effort, but it is not a substitute for your problem-solving skills.

The main thing to remember about a calculator is that it can't help you find the answer to a question you don't understand. If you wouldn't know how to solve a particular problem using pencil and paper, you won't know how to solve it using a calculator either. Your calculator will help you, but it won't take the place of a solid understanding of basic SAT mathematics.

Use Your Paper First

Whether or not calculator use is permitted, the first step should be to set up the problem or equation on paper; this will keep you from getting lost or confused. This is especially important when solving the problem involves a number of separate steps. The basic idea is to use the extra space in your test booklet to make a plan, and then use your calculator to execute it.

Working on paper first will also give you a record of what you have done if you change your mind, run into trouble, or lose your place. If you suddenly find that you need to try a different approach to a question, you may not have to go all the way back to the beginning. This will also make it easier for you to check your work, if you have time to do so.

Don't use the memory function on your calculator (if it has one). Because you can use your test booklet as scratch paper, you don't need to juggle numbers within the calculator itself. Instead of storing the result of a calculation in the calculator, write it on your scratch paper, clear your calculator, and move to the next step of the question. A calculator's memory is fleeting; scratch paper is forever.

> **Write Things Down**
> You paid for the test booklet, so make the most of it. Keep track of your progress through each question by writing down each step.

Order of Operations

In the next chapter, we will discuss the proper order of operations for solving equations that require several operations to be performed. Be sure you understand this information, because it applies to calculators as much as it does to pencil-and-paper computations. You may remember PEMDAS from school. PEMDAS is the order of operations. You'll learn more about it and see how questions on the SAT require you to know the order of operations. You must always perform calculations in the proper order.

Fractions

Most scientific calculators have buttons that will automatically simplify fractions or convert fractions from decimals. (For instance, on the TI-81, TI-83, and TI-84, hitting "Math" and then selecting the first option, "Answer → Fraction," will give you the last answer calculated as a fraction in the lowest terms.) Find out if your calculator has this function! If it does, you can use it to simplify messy fractions on the Calculator section. This function is also very useful when you get an answer as a decimal, but the answer choices given are all fractions. For the No Calculator section, you will have to be able to do these things by hand, so practice these skills in the next chapter. (For Grid-In questions, it is not necessary to reduce a fraction to its simplest form if it fits in the grid, and the decimal equivalent will also be accepted as a correct answer.)

Batteries

Change the batteries on your calculator a week before the SAT so that you know your calculator won't run out of power halfway through the test. You can also take extra batteries with you, just in case. Although it isn't very likely that the batteries will run out on your calculator on the day of the test, it could happen—so you want to be prepared.

Final Words on the Calculator

Remember that the test-writers are trying to test your ability to use your calculator wisely. As such, they have purposely created many questions in which the calculator is worthless. (There are questions that are so wordy and deceptive that reading carefully is a much more important skill than properly using a calculator.) So be sure to Read the Final Question—there may be some serious surprises in there. Finally, remember that on Section 3 you won't be able to use it at all. Practice your math skills so that you can solve questions with or without your calculator.

Summary

o   Look for ways to eliminate answer choices that are too big or too small. Ballparking can help you find the right answer without extensive paper-and-pencil calculations when calculator use is not allowed. Even when you can use your calculator, Ballparking can help you avoid trap answers and improve your chances of getting the question right if you have to guess.

o   When ballparking answers on geometry questions, use a bit of caution. The figures are not always drawn to scale. Use the given information to determine if you can trust your figure before using it to eliminate answers.

o   After you've set up the question on the page, you should definitely use the calculator when allowed to avoid careless mistakes from doing math in your head.

o   Take your own calculator when you take the test. You don't need a fancy one. Make sure your calculator doesn't beep or have a typewriter-style keyboard.

o   Even if you already use a calculator regularly, you should still practice with it before the test.

o   Be careful when you key in numbers on your calculator. Check each number on the display as you key it in. Clear your work after you finish each question or after each separate step.

o   A calculator can't help you find the answer to a question you don't understand. (It's only as smart as you are!) Be sure to use your calculator as a tool, not a crutch.

o   Set up the question or equation on paper first. By doing so, you will eliminate the possibility of getting lost or confused.

o   Don't use the memory function on your calculator (if it has one). Writing things down on paper works better.

o   Whether you are using your calculator or paper and pencil, you must always perform calculations in the proper order.

o   If your calculator runs on batteries, make sure it has fresh ones at test time! Change them a week before.

o   Make sure your math skills are solid, so you can tackle questions in the No Calculator section with confidence.

Chapter 14
Fun with Fundamentals

Although we'll show you which mathematical concepts are most important to know for the SAT, this book relies on your knowledge of basic math concepts. If you're a little rusty, though, this chapter is for you. Read on for a quick review of the math fundamentals you'll need to know before you continue.

THE BUILDING BLOCKS

As you go through this book, you might discover that you're having trouble with stuff you thought you already knew—like fractions or square roots. If this happens, it's probably a good idea to review the fundamentals. That's where this chapter comes in. Our drills and examples will refresh your memory if you've gotten rusty. Always keep in mind that the math tested on the SAT is different from the math taught in school. If you want to raise your score, don't waste time studying math that the SAT never tests.

Let's talk first about what you should expect to see on the test.

The Instructions

Both of the Math sections on the SAT will begin with the same set of instructions. We've reprinted these instructions, just as they appear on the SAT, in the Math sections of the practice tests in this book. These instructions include a few formulas and other information that you may need to know in order to answer some of the questions. You should learn these formulas ahead of time so you don't have to waste valuable time flipping back to them during the test.

Still, if you do suddenly blank out on one of the formulas while taking the test, you can always refresh your memory by glancing back at the instructions. Be sure to familiarize yourself with them thoroughly ahead of time, so you'll know which formulas are there.

Standard Symbols

The following standard symbols are used frequently on the SAT:

Formulas and Definitions
Go to your online Student Tools for a complete list of the math terms and formulas that you'll need to know for the SAT.

SYMBOL	MEANING
=	is equal to
≠	is not equal to
<	is less than
>	is greater than
≤	is less than or equal to
≥	is greater than or equal to

THERE ARE ONLY SIX OPERATIONS

There are only six arithmetic operations that you will ever need to perform on the SAT:

1. Addition (3 + 3)
2. Subtraction (3 − 3)
3. Multiplication (3 × 3 or 3 · 3)
4. Division (3 ÷ 3 or 3/3)
5. Raising to a power (3^3)
6. Finding a root ($\sqrt{9}$ and $\sqrt[3]{8}$)

If you're like most students, you probably haven't paid much serious attention to these topics since junior high school. You'll need to learn about them again if you want to do well on the SAT. By the time you take the test, using them should be automatic. All the arithmetic concepts are fairly basic, but you'll have to know them cold. You'll also have to know when and how to use your calculator, which will be quite helpful.

What Do You Get?

You should know the following arithmetic terms:

> - The result of addition is a *sum* or *total*.
> - The result of subtraction is a *difference*.
> - The result of multiplication is a *product*.
> - The result of division is a *quotient*.
> - In the expression 5^2, the 2 is called an *exponent*.

The Six Operations Must Be Performed in the Proper Order

Very often, solving an equation on the SAT will require you to perform several different operations, one after another. These operations must be performed in the proper order. In general, the questions are written in such a way that you won't have trouble deciding what comes first. In cases in which you are uncertain, you need to remember only the following sentence:

Please **E**xcuse **M**y **D**ear **A**unt **S**ally;
she limps from *left* to *right*.

That's **PEMDAS**, for short. It stands for **P**arentheses, **E**xponents, **M**ultiplication, **D**ivision, **A**ddition, and **S**ubtraction. First, do any calculations inside the parentheses; then take care of the exponents; then perform all multiplication and division, from *left* to *right*, followed by addition and subtraction, from *left* to *right*.

Do It Yourself

Some calculators automatically take order of operations into account, and some don't. Either way, you can very easily go wrong if you are in the habit of punching in long lines of arithmetic operations. The safe, smart way is to clear the calculator after every individual operation, performing PEMDAS yourself. When calculator use is not allowed, make sure to write out all the steps on your paper to avoid careless errors.

The following drill will help you learn the order in which to perform the six operations. First, set up the equations on paper. Then, use your calculator for the arithmetic. Make sure you perform the operations in the correct order.

DRILL 1

Solve each of the following problems by performing the indicated operations in the proper order. Answers can be found on page 306.

1. $107 + (109 - 107) =$ _____

2. $(7 \times 5) + 3 =$ _____

3. $6 - 3(6 - 3) =$ _____

4. $2 \times [7 - (6 \div 3)] =$ _____

5. $10 - (9 - 8 - 6) =$ _____

Whichever Comes First
For addition and subtraction, solve from left to right. The same is true of multiplication and division. And remember: if you don't solve in order from left to right, you could end up with the wrong answer!
Example:
$24 \div 4 \times 6 = 24 \div 24 = 1$ wrong
$24 \div 4 \times 6 = 6 \times 6 = 36$ right

Parentheses Can Help You Solve Equations

Using parentheses to regroup information in SAT arithmetic problems can be very helpful. In order to do this, you need to understand a basic law that you have probably forgotten since the days when you last took arithmetic—the **Distributive Law.** You don't need to remember the name of the law, but you do need to know how to use it to help you solve problems.

The Distributive Law

If you're multiplying the sum of two numbers by a third number, you can multiply each number in your sum individually. This comes in handy when you have to multiply the sum of two variables.

If a question gives you information in "factored form"—$a(b + c)$—then you should distribute the first variable before you do anything else. If you are given information that has already been distributed—$(ab + ac)$—then you should factor out the common term, putting the information back in factored form. Very often on the SAT, simply doing this will enable you to spot the answer.

Here are some examples:

Distributive: $6(53) + 6(47) = 6(53 + 47) = 6(100) = 600$

Multiplication first: $6(53) + 6(47) = 318 + 282 = 600$

You get the same answer each way, so why get involved with ugly arithmetic? If you use the Distributive Law for this problem, you don't even need to use your calculator.

The drill on the following page illustrates the Distributive Law.

DRILL 2

Rewrite each problem by either distributing or factoring and then solve. (Hint: For questions 1, 2, 4, and 5, try factoring.) Questions 3, 4, and 5 have no numbers in them; therefore, they can't be solved with a calculator. Answers can be found on page 306.

1. $(6 \times 57) + (6 \times 13) =$ _____

2. $51(48) + 51(50) + 51(52) =$ _____

3. $a(b + c - d) =$ _____

4. $xy - xz =$ _____

5. $abc + xyc =$ _____

FRACTIONS

A Fraction Is Just Another Way of Expressing Division

The expression $\dfrac{x}{y}$ is exactly the same thing as $x \div y$. The expression $\dfrac{1}{2}$ means nothing more than $1 \div 2$. In the fraction $\dfrac{x}{y}$, x is known as the **numerator,** and y is known as the **denominator.**

Adding and Subtracting Fractions with the Same Denominator

To add two or more fractions that all have the same denominator, simply add the numerators and put the sum over the common denominator. Consider the following example:

$$\frac{1}{100} + \frac{4}{100} = \frac{1+4}{100} = \frac{5}{100}$$

Subtraction works exactly the same way:

$$\frac{4}{100} - \frac{1}{100} = \frac{4-1}{100} = \frac{3}{100}$$

Fractions and Your Calculator

When calculator use is not allowed, be sure to write out all the steps on your paper to avoid careless errors. When calculator use is allowed, you can use your calculator to solve fraction problems. When you do, ALWAYS put each of your fractions in a set of parentheses. This will ensure that your calculator knows that they are fractions. Otherwise, the order of operations will get confused. On a scientific calculator, you can write the fraction in two different ways:

1. You will have a fraction key, which looks similar to "$a\,{}^{b}\!/_{c}$." If you wanted to write $\dfrac{5}{6}$, you'd type "5 $a\,{}^{b}\!/_{c}$ 6."

2. You can also use the division key, because a fraction bar is the same as "divided by." Be aware that your answer will be a decimal for this second way, so we recommend the first.

On a graphing calculator, you'll use the division bar to create fractions. Keep in mind that, whatever calculator you are using, you can always turn your fractions into decimals before you perform calculations with them. Just be aware that the answer won't always be exact.

Adding and Subtracting Fractions with Different Denominators

In school you were taught to add and subtract fractions with different denominators by finding the common denominator. To do this, you have to multiply each fraction by a number that makes all the denominators the same. Most students find this process annoying.

Fortunately, we have an approach to adding and subtracting fractions with different denominators that simplifies the entire process. Use the example below as a model. Just multiply in the direction of each arrow, and then either add or subtract across the numerator. Lastly, multiply across the denominator.

$$\frac{1}{3}+\frac{1}{2}=$$

$$\frac{1}{3} \overset{\textbf{2} \quad \textbf{3}}{\underset{}{\times}} \frac{1}{2} \quad \textbf{6}$$

$$\frac{2+3}{6}=\frac{5}{6}$$

We call this procedure the **Bowtie** because the arrows make it look like a bowtie. Use the Bowtie to add or subtract any pair of fractions without thinking about the common denominator, just by following the steps above.

Calculating Fractions

Let's say you wanted to find $\frac{1}{3}+\frac{1}{2}=$ using your calculator. For a scientific calculator, you'd type in "(1 $a\frac{b}{c}$ 3) + (1 $a\frac{b}{c}$ 2) =" The answer will come up looking like something similar to 5⌐6, which means 5/6. On a graphing calculator, you'd type in (1/3) + (1/2) [ENTER]. This gives you the repeating decimal .833333. Now hit the [MATH] button and hit the [>FRAC] button and press [ENTER]. The calculator will now show "5/6." The shortcut to turn a decimal into a fraction on a TI-80 series graphic calculator is [MATH][ENTER][ENTER]. Remember those parentheses for all fraction calculations!

Multiplying All Fractions

Multiplying fractions is easy. Just multiply across the numerator; then multiply across the denominator.

Here's an example.

$$\frac{4}{5}\times\frac{5}{6}=\frac{20}{30}$$

When you multiply fractions, all you are really doing is performing one multiplication problem on top of another.

You should never multiply two fractions before looking to see if you can reduce either or both. If you reduce first, your final answer will be in the form that the test-writers are looking for. Here's another way to express this rule: *Simplify before you multiply*.

$$\frac{63}{6} \times \frac{48}{7} = \frac{\cancel{63}^{9}}{6} \times \frac{48}{\cancel{7}_{1}} = \frac{\cancel{63}^{9}}{\cancel{6}_{1}} \times \frac{\cancel{48}^{8}}{\cancel{7}_{1}} =$$

$$\frac{9}{1} \times \frac{8}{1}$$

$$\frac{72}{1} = 72$$

Dividing All Fractions

To divide one fraction by another, flip over (or take the reciprocal of) the second fraction and multiply.

Here's an example.

$$\frac{2}{3} \div \frac{4}{3} =$$

$$\frac{2}{3} \times \frac{3}{4} = \frac{6}{12} = \frac{1}{2}$$

Be careful not to cancel or reduce until after you flip the second fraction. You can even do the same thing with fractions whose numerators and/or denominators are fractions. These problems look quite frightening but they're actually easy if you keep your cool.

Here's an example.

$$\frac{\frac{4}{4}}{\frac{4}{3}} =$$

$$\frac{4}{1} \div \frac{4}{3} =$$

$$\frac{4}{1} \times \frac{3}{4} =$$

$$\frac{\cancel{4}}{1} \times \frac{3}{\cancel{4}} =$$

$$\frac{3}{1} = 3$$

Just Flip It
Dividing by a fraction is the same thing as multiplying by the reciprocal of that fraction. So just flip over the fraction you are dividing by and multiply instead.

Start Small

It is not easy to see that 26 and 286 have a common factor of 13, but it's pretty clear that they're both divisible by 2. So start from there.

Fast Reduction

When calculator use is allowed, reducing fractions can be pretty easy. To reduce fractions in your scientific calculator, just type in the fraction and hit the equals key. If you are using a graphing calculator, type in the fraction, find the [>FRAC] function, and hit ENTER.

Reducing Fractions

When you add or multiply fractions, you will very often end up with a big fraction that is hard to work with. You can almost always reduce such a fraction into one that is easier to handle.

To reduce a fraction, divide both the numerator and the denominator by the largest number that is a factor of both. For example, to reduce $\frac{12}{60}$, divide both the numerator and the denominator by 12, which is the largest number that is a factor of both. Dividing 12 by 12 yields 1; dividing 60 by 12 yields 5. The reduced fraction is $\frac{1}{5}$.

If you can't immediately find the largest number that is a factor of both, find any number that is a factor of both and divide both the numerator and denominator by that number. Your calculations will take a little longer, but you'll end up in the same place. In the previous example, even if you don't see that 12 is a factor of both 12 and 60, you can no doubt see that 6 is a factor of both. Dividing numerator and denominator by 6 yields $\frac{2}{10}$. Now divide both numbers by 2. Doing so yields $\frac{1}{5}$. Once again, you have arrived at the answer.

Converting Mixed Numbers to Fractions

A **mixed number** is a number such as $2\frac{3}{4}$. It is the sum of an integer and a fraction. When you see mixed numbers on the SAT, you should usually convert them to ordinary fractions.

Here's a quick and easy way to convert mixed numbers.

- Multiply the integer by the denominator.
- Add this product to the numerator.
- Place this sum over the denominator.

For practice, let's convert $2\frac{3}{4}$ to a fraction. Multiply 2 (the integer part of the mixed number) by 4 (the denominator). That gives you 8. Add that to the 3 (the numerator) to get 11. Place 11 over 4 to get $\frac{11}{4}$.

The mixed number $2\frac{3}{4}$ is exactly the same as the fraction $\frac{11}{4}$. We converted the mixed number

to a fraction because fractions are easier to work with than mixed numbers.

DRILL 3

Try converting the following mixed numbers to fractions. Answers can be found on page 306.

1. $8\frac{1}{3}$

2. $2\frac{3}{7}$

3. $5\frac{4}{9}$

4. $2\frac{1}{2}$

5. $6\frac{2}{3}$

Just Don't Mix

For some reason, the test-writers think it's okay to give you mixed numbers as answer choices. On Grid-Ins, however, if you use a mixed number, you won't get credit. You can see why. In your Grid-In box, $3\frac{1}{4}$ will be gridded in as 3 1 / 4, which looks like $\frac{31}{4}$.

Fractions Behave in Peculiar Ways

Fractions don't always behave the way you might want them to. For example, because 4 is obviously greater than 2, it's easy to forget that $\frac{1}{4}$ is less than $\frac{1}{2}$. It's particularly confusing when the numerator is something other than 1. For example, $\frac{2}{7}$ is less than $\frac{2}{5}$. Finally, you should keep in mind that when you multiply one fraction by another, you'll get a fraction that is smaller than either of the first two. Study the following example:

$$\frac{1}{2} \times \frac{1}{4} = \frac{1}{8}$$

$$\frac{1}{8} < \frac{1}{2}$$

$$\frac{1}{8} < \frac{1}{4}$$

A Final Word About Fractions and Calculators

Throughout this section, we've given you some hints about your calculator and fractions. Of course, you still need to understand how to work with fractions the old-fashioned way for the No Calculator section. On the Calculator section, your calculator can be a tremendous help if you know how to use it properly. Make sure that you practice with your calculator so that working with fractions on it becomes second nature before the test.

DRILL 4

Work these problems with the techniques you've read about in this chapter so far. Then check your answers by solving them with your calculator. If you have any problems, go back and review the information just outlined. Answers can be found on page 306.

1. Reduce $\dfrac{18}{6}$. _____

2. Convert $6\dfrac{1}{5}$ to a fraction. _____

3. $2\dfrac{1}{3} - 3\dfrac{3}{5} =$ _____

4. $\dfrac{5}{18} \times \dfrac{6}{25} =$ _____

5. $\dfrac{3}{4} \div \dfrac{7}{8} =$ _____

6. $\dfrac{\frac{2}{5}}{5} =$ _____

7. $\dfrac{\frac{1}{3}}{\frac{3}{4}} =$ _____

DECIMALS

A Decimal Is Just Another Way of Expressing a Fraction

Fractions can be expressed as decimals. To find a fraction's decimal equivalent, simply divide the numerator by the denominator. (You can do this easily with your calculator.)

$$\frac{3}{5} =$$
$$3 \div 5 = 0.6$$

Adding, Subtracting, Multiplying, and Dividing Decimals

Manipulating decimals is easy with a calculator. Simply punch in the numbers—being especially careful to get the decimal point in the right place every single time—and read the result from the display. A calculator makes these operations easy. In fact, working with decimals is one area on the SAT in which your calculator will prevent you from making careless errors. You won't have to line up decimal points or remember what happens when you divide. The calculator will keep track of everything for you, as long as you punch in the correct numbers to begin with. Just be sure to practice carefully before test day.

What can you do when the math decimals get ugly on the No Calculator section? Never fear—you can still answer these questions. Just round the awkward numbers to ones that are easier to work with. As long as you aren't rounding things too far, like rounding 33 to 50, the answers are likely to be spread far enough apart that only one or maybe two will be close to your estimated answer.

DRILL 5

Calculate each of the answers to the following questions on paper with your pencil, rounding any awkward numbers to make the math easier to handle. Then check your answers with your calculator. Answers can be found on page 306.

1. $0.43 \times 0.87 =$ _____

2. $\dfrac{43 + 0.731}{0.03} =$ _____

3. $3.72 \div 0.02 =$ _____

4. $0.71 - 3.6 =$ _____

EXPONENTS AND SQUARE ROOTS

Exponents Are a Kind of Shorthand

Many numbers are the product of the same value multiplied over and over again. For example, $32 = 2 \times 2 \times 2 \times 2 \times 2$. Another way to write this would be $32 = 2^5$, or "thirty-two equals two to the fifth power." The little number, or **exponent,** denotes the number of times that 2 is to be used as a factor. In the same way, $10^3 = 10 \times 10 \times 10$, or 1,000, or "ten to the third power," or "ten cubed." In this example, the 10 is called the **base** and the 3 is called the **exponent.** (You won't need to know these terms on the SAT, but you will need to know them in order to understand our explanations.)

Warning #1

The rules for multiplying and dividing exponents do not apply to addition or subtraction:

$2^2 + 2^3 = 12$

$(2 \times 2) + (2 \times 2 \times 2) = 12$

It does not equal 2^5 or 32.

Multiplying Numbers with Exponents

To multiply two numbers with the same base, simply add the exponents. For example, $2^3 \times 2^5 = 2^{3+5} = 2^8$.

Dividing Numbers with Exponents

To divide two numbers with the same base, simply subtract the exponents. For example, $\dfrac{2^5}{2^3} = 2^{5-3} = 2^2$.

Warning #2

Parentheses are very important with exponents, because you must remember to distribute powers to everything within them.

For example, $(3x)^2 = 9x^2$,

not $3x^2$. Similarly,

$\left(\dfrac{3}{2}\right)^2 = \dfrac{3^2}{2^2}$, not $\dfrac{9}{2}$.

But the Distributive Law

applies only when you

multiply or divide:

$(x + y)^2 = x^2 + 2xy + y^2$,

not $x^2 + y^2$.

Raising a Power to a Power

When you raise a power to a power, you multiply the exponents. For example, $(2^3)^4 = 2^{3 \times 4} = 2^{12}$.

MADSPM

To remember the exponent rules, all you need to do is remember the acronym **MADSPM**. Here's what it stands for:

- **M**ultiply → **A**dd
- **D**ivide → **S**ubtract
- **P**ower → **M**ultiply

Whenever you see an exponent question, you should think MADSPM. The three MADSPM rules are the only rules that apply to exponents.

Here's a typical SAT exponent question.

14

For the equations $\dfrac{a^x}{a^y} = a^{10}$ and $(a^y)^3 = a^x$, if $a > 1$, what is the value of x ?

A) 5

B) 10

C) 15

D) 20

Here's How to Crack It

The question asks for the value of x, but it looks pretty intimidating with all those variables. In fact, you might be about to cry "POOD" and go on to the next question. That might not be a bad idea, but before you skip the question, pull out those MADSPM rules.

For the first equation, you can use the Divide-Subtract Rule: $\dfrac{a^x}{a^y} = a^{x-y} = a^{10}$. In other words, the first equation tells you that $x - y = 10$.

For the second equation, you can use the Power-Multiply Rule: $\left(a^y\right)^3 = a^{3y} = a^x$. So, that means that $3y = x$.

Now, it's time to substitute: $x - y = 3y - y = 10$. So, $2y = 10$ and $y = 5$. Be careful, though! Don't choose (A). That's the value of y, but the question wants to know the value of x. Since $x = 3y$, $x = 3(5) = 15$. The correct answer is (C).

If calculator use were allowed on this one, you could also do this question by using Plugging In the Answers, or PITA, which will be discussed in more detail later in this book. Of course, you still need to know the MADSPM rules to do the question that way.

Exponents and Your Calculator

Raising a number to a power is shown in two different ways on your calculator, depending on the type of calculator you have. A scientific calculator will use the y^x button. You'll have to type in your base number first, then hit the y^x key, and then type the exponent. So 4^3 will be typed in as "$4\ y^x\ 3 =$" and you'll get 64. If you have a calculator from the TI-80 series, your button will be a $\wedge$ sign. You'll enter the same problem as "$4\wedge3$ [ENTER]." Think of these two keys as the "to the" button, because you say "4 to the 3rd power."

The Peculiar Behavior of Exponents

Raising a number to a power can have quite peculiar and unexpected results, depending on what sort of number you start out with. Here are some examples.

- If you square or cube a number greater than 1, it becomes larger.
  For example, $2^3 = 8$.
- If you square or cube a positive fraction smaller than one, it becomes smaller.
  For example, $\left(\dfrac{1}{2}\right)^3 = \dfrac{1}{8}$.
- A negative number raised to an even power becomes positive.
  For example, $(-2)^2 = 4$.
- A negative number raised to an odd power remains negative.
  For example, $(-2)^3 = -8$.

You should also have a feel for relative sizes of exponential numbers without calculating them. For example, 2^{10} is much larger than 10^2 ($2^{10} = 1{,}024$; $10^2 = 100$). To take another example, 2^5 is twice as large as 2^4, even though 5 seems only a bit larger than 4.

Square Roots

The radical sign ($\sqrt{}$) indicates the **square root** of a number. For example, $\sqrt{25} = 5$. Note that square roots cannot be negative. If the test-writers want you to think about a negative solution, they won't use the radical sign; instead they'll say $x^2 = 25$ because then $x = 5$ or $x = -5$.

The Only Rules You Need to Know

Here are the only rules regarding square roots that you need to know for the SAT.

1. $\sqrt{x}\sqrt{y} = \sqrt{xy}$. For example, $\sqrt{3}\sqrt{12} = \sqrt{36} = 6$.

2. $\sqrt{\dfrac{x}{y}} = \dfrac{\sqrt{x}}{\sqrt{y}}$. For example, $\sqrt{\dfrac{5}{4}} = \dfrac{\sqrt{5}}{\sqrt{4}} = \dfrac{\sqrt{5}}{2}$.

3. $\sqrt{x}$ = positive root only. For example, $\sqrt{16} = 4$.

Note that rule 1 works in reverse: $\sqrt{50} = \sqrt{25} \times \sqrt{2} = 5\sqrt{2}$. This is really a kind of factoring.

You are using rule 1 to factor a large, clumsy radical into numbers that are easier to work with.

Rule 2 works in reverse as well. $\sqrt{75}$ divided by $\sqrt{3}$ looks ugly, but $\sqrt{\dfrac{75}{3}} = \sqrt{25} = 5$. And

remember that radicals are just fractional exponents, so the same rules of distribution apply.

We'll get to fractional exponents on the next page.

Careless Errors

The SAT will try to confuse you with the behavior of roots. Remember that the square root of a number between 0 and 1 is *larger* than the original number. For example, $\sqrt{\dfrac{1}{4}} = \dfrac{1}{2}$, and $\dfrac{1}{2} > \dfrac{1}{4}$.

Negative and Fractional Exponents

So far we've dealt with only positive integers for exponents, but they can be negative integers as well as fractions. The same concepts and rules apply, but the numbers just look a little weirder. Keep these concepts in mind:

- Negative exponents are a fancy way of writing reciprocals:

$$x^{-n} = \frac{1}{x^n}$$

- Fractional exponents are a fancy way of taking roots and powers:

$$x^{\frac{y}{z}} = \sqrt[z]{x^y}$$

Roots and Your Calculator

Another important key is the root key. On a scientific calculator, it is often the same button as y^x, but you'll have to hit shift first. The symbol is $\sqrt[x]{y}$. So "the 4th root of 81" would be "81 $\sqrt[x]{y}$ 4 = ." Sometimes the calculator will have y^x or $\sqrt[x]{y}$ as x^y or $\sqrt[y]{x}$. They mean the same thing. Just know which number you're supposed to type in first.

The root key in the TI-80 graphing calculator series varies, but the most common symbol is the square root sign, which you can get to by pressing "[SHIFT] x^2." In case you want to find the 3rd, 4th, or other root of a number, there is a button in the [MATH] directory for $\sqrt[3]{}$ or $\sqrt[x]{}$. In the case of the $\sqrt[x]{}$, you have to type in the root you want, then hit [MATH] and $\sqrt[x]{}$, and finally hit your base number. For example, if you wanted to find the 4th root of 81, you'd type "4 [MATH]," then select $\sqrt[x]{}$, then type 81, and press [ENTER]. If you look at it on the screen, it will appear as "4 $\sqrt[x]{}$ 81," which is similar to how you'd write it. You can also use the ^ symbol if you remember that a root is the same as the bottom part of a fractional exponent. So the fourth root of 81 would be written as "81 ^ (1/4)" on your calculator.

Here's an example.

14

If $x > 0$, which of the following is equivalent to $\sqrt{x^3}$?

I. $x + x^{\frac{1}{2}}$

II. $\left(x^{\frac{1}{2}}\right)^3$

III. $\left(x^2\right)\left(x^{-\frac{1}{2}}\right)$

A) None
B) I and II only
C) II and III only
D) I, II, and III

Here's How to Crack It

The question asks for an equivalent form of a root and gives three expressions with exponents, so it really tests your knowledge of exponents. First, convert $\sqrt{x^3}$ into an exponent to more easily compare it to the choices in the Roman numeral statements. (Plus, exponents are easier to work with because they have those nice MADSPM rules.) Therefore, according to the definition of a fractional exponent, $\sqrt{x^3} = x^{\frac{3}{2}}$. You want the items in the Roman numerals to equal $x^{\frac{3}{2}}$.

Now, it's time to start working with the Roman numerals. In (I), the test-writers are trying to be tricky. (There's a surprise.) There's no exponent rule for adding exponent expressions with like bases. So, $x + x^{\frac{1}{2}}$ does *not* equal $x^{\frac{3}{2}}$. (If you want to be sure, you could try a number for x: If $x = 4$, then $\sqrt{4^3} = 8$, but $4 + 4^{\frac{1}{2}} = 4 + 2 = 6$.) So, cross off any answer that includes (I): (B) and (D) are gone.

Now, since you are down to either (A) or (C), all you really need to do is try either (II) or (III). If either one works, the answer is (C). Try (II). Use the Power-Multiply Rule: $\left(x^{\frac{1}{2}}\right)^3 = x^{\left(\frac{1}{2}\right)(3)} = x^{\frac{3}{2}}$. Since (II) works, (C) is the correct answer.

Notice that you didn't even need to check (III). Using POE on a Roman numeral question often means that you won't need to check all of the Roman numerals.

HOW TO READ CHARTS AND GRAPHS

Another basic math skill you will need for the SAT is the ability to interpret data from charts, graphs, tables, and more. This section will cover the basics of reading these figures. How to answer questions related to charts and other figures in detail will be discussed in Chapter 17.

What's Up with All of These Figures?

The SAT includes charts, graphs, and tables throughout the test (not just in the Math sections) to present data for students to analyze. The College Board believes this will better reflect what students learn in school and what they need to understand in the real world. Questions will typically include real-life scenarios, such as finance and business situations, social science issues, and scientific matters.

Since you'll be seeing graphics throughout the test, let's look at the types you may encounter and the skills you'll need to work with to analyze charts and graphs.

Types of Graphics

The Scatterplot

A **scatterplot** is a graph with distinct data points, each representing one piece of information. On the scatterplot below, each dot represents the number of televisions sold at a certain price point.

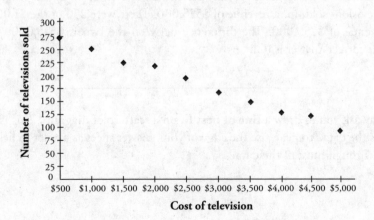

Here's How to Read It

To find the cost of a television when 225 televisions are sold, start at 225 on the vertical axis and draw a horizontal line to the right until you hit a data point. Use the edge of your answer sheet as a straight-edge if you have trouble drawing your own straight lines. Once you hit a point, draw a straight line down from the point to the horizontal axis and read the number the line hits, which should be $1,500. To determine the number of televisions sold when they cost a certain amount, reverse the steps—start at the bottom, draw up until you hit a point, and then move left until you intersect the vertical axis.

Now try a question based on that scatterplot.

9

A certain store sells televisions ranging in price from $500 to $5,000 in increments of $500. The graph above shows the total number of televisions sold at each price during the last 12 months. Approximately how much more revenue did the store collect from the televisions it sold priced at $3,500 than it did from the televisions it sold priced at $1,000 ?

A) $175,000

B) $250,000

C) $275,000

D) $350,000

Here's How to Crack It

The question asks for the difference in revenue from selling televisions at two different prices. The revenue is the *cost of television × number of televisions sold*. You need the information from the graph only for the television that costs $3,500 and for the television that costs $1,000 in order to determine how much more revenue the $3,500 television produced. There were 150 of the $3,500 televisions sold, for a revenue of $525,000. There were 250 of the $1,000 televisions sold, for a revenue of $250,000. The difference between the two is $525,000 − $250,000 = $275,000. The correct answer is (C).

A question may ask you to draw a **line of best fit** on a scatterplot diagram. This is the line that best represents the data. You can use the edge of your answer sheet as a ruler to help you draw a line that goes through most of the data.

The Line Graph

A **line graph** is similar to a scatterplot in that it shows different data points that relate the two variables. The difference with a line graph, though, is that the points have been connected to create a continuous line.

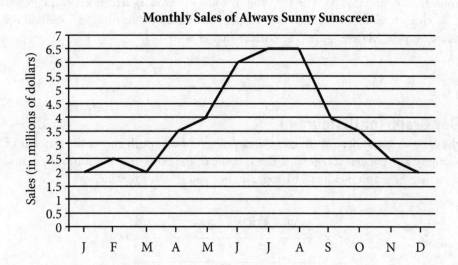

Monthly Sales of Always Sunny Sunscreen

Here's How to Read It

Reading a line graph is very similar to reading a scatterplot. Start at the axis that represents the data given, and draw a straight line up or to the right until you intersect the graph line. Then move left or down until you hit the other axis. For example, in February, indicated by an F on the horizontal axis, Always Sunny Sunscreen had $2.5 million in sales. Be sure to notice the units on each axis. If February sales were only $2.50, rather than $2.5 million, then this company wouldn't be doing very well!

Let's look at a question about this line graph.

2

The forecasted monthly sales of Always Sunny Sunscreen are presented in the figure above. For which period are the forecasted monthly sales figures strictly decreasing and then strictly increasing?

A) January to March

B) February to April

C) June to August

D) September to November

Here's How to Crack It

The question asks for a period during which the forecasted sales are decreasing and then increasing. Look up the values for each period in question and use Process of Elimination to get rid of those that don't fit. For (A), January sales are forecasted to be $2 million, February $2.5 million, and March $2 million. This is an increase followed by a decrease, not the other way around, so eliminate (A). For (B), you already know sales decreased from February to March, so check for a following increase in April. The figure for April is $3.5 million, which is an increase over the March figure. The correct answer is (B).

The Bar Graph (or Histogram)

Instead of showing a variety of different data points, a **bar graph** shows the number of items that belong to a particular category. If the variable at the bottom is given in ranges instead of distinct items, the graph is called a **histogram,** but you read it the same way.

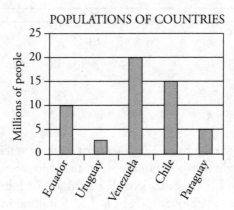

Here's How to Read It

The height of each bar corresponds to a value on the vertical axis. In this case, the bar above Chile hits the line that intersects with 15 on the vertical axis, so there are 15 million people in Chile. Again, watch the units to make sure you know what the numbers on the axes represent. On this graph, horizontal lines are drawn at 5 unit intervals, making the graph easier to read. If these lines do not appear on a bar graph, use your answer sheet to determine the height of a given bar.

Here's an example of a bar graph question, which is based on the Populations of Countries graph on the previous page.

14

The populations of five countries are shown in the graph above.

If population density is defined as $\dfrac{\text{population}}{\text{area}}$, and the area of Paraguay is 400,000 square kilometers, what is the population density of Paraguay, in people per square kilometer?

A)   0.08

B)   0.8

C)   1.25

D) 12.5

Here's How to Crack It

The question asks for the population density of Paraguay. Start by determining the population of Paraguay. The bar hits right at the horizontal line for 5, which is in millions, so there are 5 million people in Paraguay. Now use the definition of population density in the question.

$$\frac{\text{population}}{\text{area}} = \frac{5,000,000}{400,000}$$

Be very careful with the number of zeroes you put in the fraction—the answer choices are pairs that vary by a factor of 10, meaning the test-writers expect you to miss a zero. The answer must be greater than 1, since your numerator is bigger than your denominator, so eliminate (A) and (B). Choice (C) also seems too small, but check the math on your calculator (carefully). You should get 12.5 people per square kilometer. The correct answer is (D).

The Two-Way Table

A **two-way table** is another way to represent data without actually graphing it. Instead of having the variables represented on the vertical and horizontal axes, the data will be arranged in rows and columns. The top row will give the headings for each column, and the left-most column will give the headings for each row. The numbers in each box indicate the data for the category represented by the row and the column the box is in.

Computer Production

	Morning Shift	Afternoon Shift
Monday	200	375
Tuesday	245	330
Wednesday	255	340
Thursday	250	315
Friday	225	360

Here's How to Read It

If you want to find the number of computers produced on Tuesday morning, you can start in the Morning Shift column and look down until you find the number in the row that says Tuesday, or you can start in the row for Tuesday and look to the right until you find the Morning Shift column. Either way, the result is 245. Some tables will give you totals in the bottom row and/or the right-most column, but sometimes you will need to find the totals yourself by adding up all the numbers in each row or in each column. More complicated tables will have more categories listed in rows and/or columns, or the tables may even contain extraneous information.

Give this one a try.

3

Computer production at a factory occurs during two shifts, as shown in the chart above. If computers are produced only during the morning and afternoon shifts, on which of the following pairs of days is the greatest total number of computers produced?

A) Monday and Thursday

B) Tuesday and Thursday

C) Wednesday and Friday

D) Tuesday and Friday

Here's How to Crack It

The question asks for the pair of days on which the greatest number of computers were produced. This is a perfect calculator question. Just add the Morning Shift and the Afternoon Shift for each day and see which total is the greatest. Write each total down next to the day on the chart, so you don't have to keep track of it all in your head. Monday is 200 + 375 = 575, Tuesday is 245 + 330 = 575, Wednesday is 255 + 340 = 595, Thursday is 250 + 315 = 565, and Friday is 225 + 360 = 585. According to these calculations, Wednesday and Friday have the two greatest totals, so the greatest number of computers is produced on those two days together. The correct answer is (C).

Figure Facts

Every time you encounter a figure or graphic on the SAT, you should make sure you understand how to read it by checking the following:

- What are the variables for each axis or the headings for the table?
- What units are used for each variable?
- Are there any key pieces of information (numbers, for example) in the legend of the chart that you should note?
- What type of relationship is shown by the data in the chart? For instance, if the chart includes curves that show an upward slope, then the graph shows a **positive association,** while curves that show a downward slope show a **negative association.**
- You can use the edge of your answer sheet as a ruler to help you make sure you are locating the correct data in the graph or to draw a line of best fit if necessary.

Surveys on the SAT

Some SAT math questions will appear to be about data, but there's no figure and the question has a lot of words about survey results. These questions are usually about a biased sample, meaning that the group doing the survey asked people who are likely to already be in favor of or opposed to the issue, but then drew a conclusion about a larger group. For example, we couldn't survey people who read this book to ask whether they read the final question and take bite-sized pieces and then assume that everyone who takes the SAT does the same thing.

The best way to perform a survey is to ask a random sample rather than asking a group that's probably already picked a side. Questions about surveys might include numbers, and there's a chance that there is a problem with the sample size, meaning the survey asked too few people to get an accurate result. But usually the number is a distraction, so focus on using POE and crossing out answers that don't fit the information given in the question.

Here's an example of what these questions will look like.

24

Guests at the filming of a televised cake decorating competition were invited to taste the cakes and vote for their favorite cake. After the votes were counted, 49% voted for the wedding cake and 40% voted for the sweet sixteen cake. The results are unlikely to represent the opinion of all those who saw the competition due to which of the following reasons?

A) The votes were not split evenly among the types of cake.

B) The poll is invalid because the percentages do not add up to 100%.

C) There were not enough samples for every guest to taste the cakes before voting.

D) The votes were not a random sample of all those who had watched the competition.

Here's How to Crack It

The question asks for the factor that best explains why the results of a survey are unlikely to represent the opinion of everyone who saw the competition. Read each answer carefully and use Process of Elimination. Choice (A) says that the poll is not reliable because there wasn't an even split. This is illogical because polls rarely end with equal results, and that is not a requirement for a poll to be legitimate. Eliminate (A). Choice (B) refers to the fact that the results do not add up to 100%. The question did not specify that only two types of cake were part of the vote and, even if there were only two types, some people could have chosen not to answer. Eliminate (B). Choice (C) states that not every guest was able to taste the cakes due to the availability of the samples. No information was given about this, so it is not necessarily a problem. Eliminate (C). Choice (D) refers to the fact that the respondents were not randomly selected. Since the vote was only among people who attended the event in person and had a chance to taste the samples, the results are likely to be different than they would be if randomly selected viewers were chosen. The correct answer is (D).

Fundamentals Drill 1: No Calculator Section

Work these questions without your calculator, using the skills you've learned so far. Answers and explanations can be found on page 307.

1

Which of the following represents the statement "the sum of the squares of x and y is equal to the square root of the difference of x and y"?

A) $x^2 + y^2 = \sqrt{x - y}$

B) $x^2 - y^2 = \sqrt{x + y}$

C) $(x + y)^2 = \sqrt{x} - \sqrt{y}$

D) $\sqrt{x + y} = (x - y)^2$

4

If $a = -2$, then $a + a^2 - a^3 + a^4 - a^5 =$

A) -22

B) -18

C) 32

D) 58

6

If $9^{-2} = \left(\dfrac{1}{3}\right)^x$, what is the value of x?

A) 1

B) 2

C) 4

D) 6

7

$$\frac{1}{8} + \frac{1}{10} = \frac{a}{b}$$

In the equation above, if a and b are positive integers and $\dfrac{a}{b}$ is in its simplest reduced form, what is the value of a?

A) 2

B) 9

C) 18

D) 40

Fundamentals Drill 2:
Calculator-Permitted Section

These questions are similar to those that might appear on the Calculator section of the Math Test. Be sure to use your calculator when necessary to avoid careless calculation errors. Don't forget, though, that using it may slow you down when doing the math on paper would be faster. Answers and explanations can be found starting on page 307.

1

If 7 times a number is 84, what is 4 times the number?

A) 16

B) 28

C) 48

D) 56

4

If $3x = 12$, what is the value of $\dfrac{24}{x}$?

A) $\dfrac{1}{6}$

B) $\dfrac{2}{3}$

C) 4

D) 6

6

Which of the following graphs shows a strong positive association between x and y?

A)
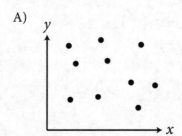

B)
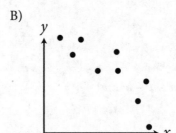

C)
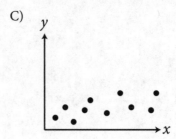

D)
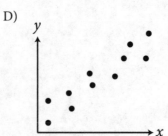

9

If $\sqrt{x} + 22 = 38$, what is the value of x?

A)   4

B)   16

C)   32

D) 256

14

If each number in the following sum were increased by t, the new sum would be 4.22. What is the value of t?

$$\begin{array}{r} 0.65 \\ 0.85 \\ 0.38 \\ + \ 0.86 \\ \hline 2.74 \end{array}$$

A) 0.24

B) 0.29

C) 0.33

D) 0.37

20

If $4^x \cdot n^2 = 4^{x+1} \cdot n$ and x and n are both positive integers, what is the value of n?

A) 2

B) 4

C) 6

D) 8

CHAPTER DRILL ANSWERS AND EXPLANATIONS

Drill 1
1. 109
2. 38
3. −3
4. 10
5. 15

Drill 2
1. $6(57 + 13) = 6 \times 70 = 420$
2. $51(48 + 50 + 52) = 51(150)$
   $= 7,650$
3. $ab + ac - ad$
4. $x(y - z)$
5. $c(ab + xy)$

Drill 3
1. $\dfrac{25}{3}$
2. $\dfrac{17}{7}$
3. $\dfrac{49}{9}$
4. $\dfrac{5}{2}$
5. $\dfrac{20}{3}$

Drill 4
1. 3
2. $\dfrac{31}{5}$
3. $-1\dfrac{4}{15}$ or $-\dfrac{19}{15}$
4. $\dfrac{1}{15}$
5. $\dfrac{6}{7}$
6. $\dfrac{2}{25}$
7. $\dfrac{4}{9}$

Drill 5

	Estimated Answer	Calculator Answer
1.	$0.4 \times 0.9 = 0.36$	0.3741
2.	$44 \div 0.03 = 1,466$	1,457.7
3.	$3.7 \div 0.02 = 185$	186
4.	$0.7 - 3.6 = -2.9$	−2.89

Fundamentals Drill 1: No Calculator Section

1. **A** The question asks for an algebraic expression. Translate the English into math by taking it one phrase at a time. "Sum" means you will add two things. The "squares of x and y" means to square x and square y, or x^2 and y^2. Add these to get $x^2 + y^2$. Cross out any choice that does not have $x^2 + y^2$ as the first part of the equation. Eliminate (B), (C), and (D). The correct answer is (A).

4. **D** The question asks for the value of an expression for a certain value of the variable. Plug in the number given for a in the expression to find the value: $-2 + (-2)^2 - (-2)^3 + (-2)^4 - (-2)^5$. Remember PEMDAS, the order of operations. The first thing to do here is deal with the **E**xponents, then take care of the **A**ddition and **S**ubtraction: $-2 + 4 - (-8) + 16 - (-32)$, which simplifies to $-2 + 4 + 8 + 16 + 32 = 58$. The correct answer is (D).

6. **C** The question asks for the value of x in an equation with exponents. Negative exponents mean to take the reciprocal and apply the positive exponent. So $9^{-2} = \left(\dfrac{1}{9}\right)^2 = \dfrac{1}{81}$. Now find what power of $\dfrac{1}{3}$ equals $\dfrac{1}{81}$. Because $3^4 = 81$, $\left(\dfrac{1}{3}\right)^4 = \dfrac{1}{81}$, and x must be 4. The correct answer is (C).

7. **B** The question asks for the value of a in an equation with fractions. The lowest number that both 8 and 10 are factors of is 40. Convert the fractions to a denominator of 40: $\dfrac{5}{40} + \dfrac{4}{40} = \dfrac{9}{40}$. There is no factor that 9 and 40 have in common, so the fraction cannot be reduced. The number in place of a in $\dfrac{a}{b}$ is 9. Be careful not to choose (D), which contains the value of b. The correct answer is (B).

Fundamentals Drill 2: Calculator-Permitted Section

1. **C** The question asks for the value of 4 times an unknown number. Translate the English into math, calling the number n, to get $7n = 84$. Divide both sides by 7 to get $n = 12$. Finally, $4n = 4(12) = 48$. The correct answer is (C).

4. **D** The question asks for the value of $\dfrac{24}{x}$. First, solve for x. Divide both sides of the equation by 3, and you get $x = 4$. Then divide 24 by 4, which gives you 6. The correct answer is (D).

6. **D** The question asks for the graph that shows a strong positive association between x and y. A "strong positive association" means that as one variable increases, the other one increases. This will be shown as a line that angles through the graph from the lower left to the upper right. These scatterplots don't have any lines of best fit drawn on them, so imagine the line that would go through most of the points on each graph. In (A), the points are all over the place, so no line of best fit can even be drawn. Eliminate (A). In (B), the line that hits most of the points would go from the upper left to the lower right. This is a negative association, not a positive one, so eliminate (B). In (C), the line would go straight across, parallel to the x-axis. This is not a positive association, so eliminate (C). The correct answer is (D).

9. **D** The question asks for the value of x. To solve this equation, get $\sqrt{x}$ by itself by subtracting 22 from both sides. The result is $\sqrt{x} = 16$, so square both sides: $(\sqrt{x})^2 = 16^2$, so $x = 256$. The correct answer is (D).

14. **D** The question asks for the value of t. To figure out how much you need to add to 2.74 to get to 4.22, find $4.22 - 2.74$ on your calculator. The difference between the two numbers is 1.48. This increase reflects the same number, t, added to each of the four numbers on the list. Divide 1.48 by 4 to find that $t = 0.37$. The correct answer is (D).

20. **B** The question asks for the value of n. First, simplify the equation $4^x \cdot n^2 = 4^{x+1} \cdot n$ by dividing both sides by n to get $4^x \cdot n = 4^{x+1}$, and then try an easy number for x. If $x = 2$, then $4^2 \cdot n = 4^{2+1}$. Since $16n = 4^3$, then $16n = 64$ and $n = 4$. The correct answer is (B).

Summary

- There are only six arithmetic operations tested on the SAT: addition, subtraction, multiplication, division, exponents, and square roots.

- These operations must be performed in the proper order (PEMDAS), beginning with operations inside parentheses.

- Apply the Distributive Law whenever possible. This is often enough to find the answer.

- A fraction is just another way of expressing division.

- You must know how to add, subtract, multiply, and divide fractions. Don't forget that you can also use your calculator in the section where it is permitted.

- If any questions involving large or confusing fractions appear, try to reduce the fractions first. Before you multiply two fractions, for example, see if it's possible to reduce either or both of the fractions.

- If you know how to work out fractions on your calculator, use it when it is allowed to help you with questions that involve fractions. If you intend to use your calculator for fractions, be sure to practice. You should also know how to work with fractions the old-fashioned way with paper and pencil.

- A decimal is just another way of expressing a fraction.

- When a calculator is permitted, use it to add, subtract, multiply, and divide decimals. When the calculator is not allowed, try rounding and estimating before doing the math with your pencil and paper.

- Exponents are a kind of shorthand for expressing numbers that are the product of the same factor multiplied over and over again.

- To multiply two exponential expressions with the same base, add the exponents.

- To divide two exponential expressions with the same base, subtract the exponents.

○   To raise one exponential expression to another power, multiply the exponents.

○   To remember the exponent rules, think MADSPM.

○   When you raise a positive number greater than 1 to a power greater than 1, the result is larger. When you raise a positive fraction less than 1 to an exponent greater than 1, the result is smaller. A negative number raised to an even power becomes positive. A negative number raised to an odd power remains negative.

○   When you're asked for the square root of any number, $\sqrt{x}$, you're being asked for the positive root only.

○   Here are the only rules regarding square roots that you need to know for the SAT:

$$\sqrt{x} \times \sqrt{y} = \sqrt{xy}$$

$$\sqrt{\frac{x}{y}} = \frac{\sqrt{x}}{\sqrt{y}}$$

○   The rule for fractional exponents is this:
$$x^{\frac{y}{z}} = \sqrt[z]{x^{y}}$$

○   The rule for negative exponents is this:
$$x^{-n} = \frac{1}{x^{n}}$$

○   When you encounter questions with charts, carefully check the chart for important information. Remember that you can use your answer sheet as a ruler to help you locate information or to draw a line of best fit.

Chapter 15
Algebra: Cracking the System

In the last chapter, we reviewed some fundamental math concepts featured on the SAT. Many questions on the SAT Math Test combine simple arithmetic concepts with more complex algebraic concepts. This is one way the test-writers raise the difficulty level of a question—they replace numbers with variables, or letters that stand for unknown quantities. This chapter covers multiple ways to answer these algebraic questions.

SAT ALGEBRA: CRACKING THE SYSTEM

The SAT generally tests algebra concepts that you most likely learned in eighth or ninth grade. So, you are probably pretty familiar with the level of algebra on the test. However, the test-writers are fairly adept at wording algebra questions in a way that is confusing or distracting in order to make the questions more difficult than the mathematical concepts that are being tested.

In this way, the SAT Math Test is not only a test of your math skills, but also, and possibly even more important to your score improvement, your reading skills. It is imperative that you read the questions carefully and translate the words in the question into mathematical symbols.

ENGLISH	MATH EQUIVALENTS
is, are, were, did, does, costs	=
what (or any unknown value)	*any variable (x, y, k, b)*
more, sum	+
less, difference	−
of, times, product, per (sometimes)	× *(multiply)*
ratio, quotient, out of, per (other times)	÷

"Per" is tricky: depending on the context, it can mean to divide (1 pizza per 3 people) or to multiply ($15 per pizza).

A Little Terminology

Here are some words that you will need to know to understand the explanations in this chapter. These words may even show up in the text of a question, so make sure you are familiar with them.

Term: An equation is like a sentence, and a **term** is the equivalent of a word. It can be just a number, just a variable, or a number multiplied by a variable. For example, 18, −2x, and 5y are the terms in the equation $18 − 2x = 5y$.

Expression: If an equation is like a sentence, then an **expression** is like a phrase or a clause. An expression is a combination of terms and mathematical operations with no equals or inequality sign. For example, $9 × 2 + 3x$ is an expression.

Polynomial: A **polynomial** is any expression containing two or more terms. Binomials and trinomials are both examples of polynomials. Binomials have two terms, and trinomials have three terms.

FUNDAMENTALS OF SAT ALGEBRA

Many questions on the SAT require you to work with variables and equations. In your math classes, you probably learned to solve equations by "solving for x" or "solving for y." To do this, you isolate x or y on one side of the equals sign and put everything else on the other side. The good thing about equations is that to isolate the variable you can do anything you want to them—add, subtract, multiply, divide, square—provided you perform the same operation to both sides of the equation.

Thus, the golden rule of equations:

> Whatever you do to the terms on one side of the equals sign, you must do to the terms on the other side of it as well.

Let's look at a simple example of this rule, without the distraction of answer choices.

Problem: If $2x - 15 = 35$, what is the value of x ?

Solution: The question asks for the value of x, so you want to isolate the variable. First, add 15 to each side of the equation. Now you have the following:

$$2x = 50$$

Divide each side of the equation by 2. Thus, x equals 25.

The skills for algebraic manipulation work just as well for more complex equations. The following question is another example of the way the SAT may ask you to manipulate equations. Don't panic when you see a question like this; just use the skills you already have and work carefully so you don't make an avoidable mistake in your algebra.

10

The wave velocity of a vibrating string can be determined using

the formula $v = \sqrt{\dfrac{T}{\dfrac{m}{L}}}$, where T is the tension of the string, m is

the mass of the string, and L is the length of the string. Which of

the following expresses the length of the string in terms of v, T,

and m ?

A) $L = \dfrac{T}{v^2 m}$

B) $L = \dfrac{v^2 m}{T}$

C) $L = v\sqrt{\dfrac{m}{t}}$

D) $L = \sqrt{\dfrac{T}{vm}}$

Here's How to Crack It

The question asks for an equation that expresses the length of a string, which is represented by L, so the goal is to get L by itself. Anything you do to one side of the equation, you must also do to the other side of the equation. Start by squaring both sides of the equation to get rid of the square root on the right side.

The equation becomes

$$v^2 = \frac{T}{\dfrac{m}{L}}$$

Next, multiply both sides by $\dfrac{m}{L}$ to get the fraction out of the denominator.

$$\frac{v^2 m}{L} = T$$

To finish isolating L, multiple both sides by L to get

$$v^2 m = TL$$

Now divide both sides by T to get L by itself.

$$\frac{v^2 m}{T} = L$$

The correct answer is (B).

———————○———————

SOLVING RADICAL EQUATIONS

Radical equations are just what the name suggests: an equation with a radical ($\sqrt{\ }$) in it. Not to worry, just remember to get rid of the radical first by raising both sides to that power.

Here's an example.

———————○———————

7

If $7\sqrt{x} - 24 = 11$, what is the value of x?

A) $\sqrt{5}$

B) $\sqrt{7}$

C) 5

D) 25

Here's How to Crack It

The question asks for the value of x, so start by adding 24 to both sides to get $7\sqrt{x} = 35$. Now, divide both sides by 7 to find that $\sqrt{x} = 5$. Finally, square both sides to find that $x = 25$. The correct answer is (D).

———————○———————

SOLVING RATIONAL EQUATIONS

Since you are not always allowed to use your calculator on the SAT, there will be some instances in which you will need to solve an equation algebraically. Even when calculator use is permitted, you may find it more efficient to use your mathematical skills to answer a question. Another way the test-writers may make your calculator less effective is by asking you to solve for an expression. Algebraic manipulation will often be the means by which you can solve that problem.

Here's an example.

5

If $\dfrac{18}{r+10} = \dfrac{3}{r}$, what is the value of $\dfrac{r}{3}$?

A) $\dfrac{2}{3}$

B) $\dfrac{3}{2}$

C) 2

D) 3

Here's How to Crack It

The question asks for the value of $\dfrac{r}{3}$. This question appears in the No Calculator section, so you must use your math skills to solve for r. You can cross-multiply to get $18r = 3(r + 10)$ or $18r = 3r + 30$. Subtracting $3r$ from both sides gives you $15r = 30$, so $r = 2$. Finally, $\dfrac{r}{3} = \dfrac{2}{3}$. The correct answer is (A).

Extraneous Solutions

Sometimes solving a rational or radical expression makes funny things happen. Look at the following example.

○

───────────────────────────

29

$$\sqrt{t+4} = t - 2$$

Which of the following contains the solution set to the equation above?

A) {0, 5}

B) {0, 4, 5}

C) {0}

D) {5}

Here's How to Crack It

The question asks for the solution set to the equation, so solve it for t. Start by squaring both sides of the equation to get rid of the radical. The equation becomes

$$t + 4 = (t - 2)^2$$

Use FOIL (First, Outer, Inner, Last) to multiply the right side of the equation to get $t^2 - 2t - 2t + 4$ or $t^2 - 4t + 4$. Now the equation is

$$t + 4 = t^2 - 4t + 4$$

Subtract t and 4 from both sides to get

$$0 = t^2 - 5t$$

The right side factors to $t(t - 5)$, so $t = 0$ or 5. Eliminate (B), since 4 is not a solution at all, extraneous or otherwise. Now plug 0 and 5 back into the original equation to see if they work. If both do, the answer is (A). If one of them does not, that one is an extraneous solution.

$\underline{t = 0}$	$\underline{t = 5}$
$\sqrt{0 + 4} = 0 - 2$	$\sqrt{5 + 4} = 5 - 2$
$\sqrt{4} = -2$	$\sqrt{9} = 3$
$2 \neq -2$	$3 = 3$

Since the equation is false when $t = 0$, eliminate (A) and (C). The correct answer is (D).

○

───────────────────────────

SOLVING FOR EXPRESSIONS

Some algebra questions on the SAT ask you to find the value of an expression rather than the value of a variable. In most cases, you can find the value of the expression without finding the value of the variable.

5

If $4x + 2 = 4$, what is the value $4x - 6$?

A) -6

B) -4

C) 4

D) 8

Math Class Solution

In math class, you would find the value of x and then plug that value into the provided expression. You would subtract 2 from both sides to find that $4x = 2$. Then divide both sides by 4 to find that $x = \frac{1}{2}$. Then, $4x - 6 = 4\left(\frac{1}{2}\right) - 6 = -4$. So, the answer is (B).

Here's How to Crack It

The question asks for the value of an expression. This is where reading the final question (RTFQ) can save time. Since the question doesn't ask for the value of x, there may be a shortcut. The term $4x$ is in both expressions, so instead of solving for x, you can solve for $4x$. Subtract 2 from both sides of $4x + 2 = 4$ to get $4x = 2$. Now, plug $4x = 2$ into $4x - 6$ to get $(2) - 6 = -4$. The correct answer is (B).

This approach will save you time—provided that you see it quickly. So, while you practice, you should train yourself to look for these sorts of direct solutions whenever you are asked to solve for the value of an expression.

However, don't worry too much if you don't always see the faster way to solve a problem like this one. The math class way will certainly get you the right answer.

Here's another example.

9

If $\sqrt{5} = x - 2$, what is the value of $\left(x - 2\right)^2$?

A) $\sqrt{5}$

B) $\sqrt{7}$

C) 5

D) 25

Here's How to Crack It

The question asks for te value of an expression. If you were to attempt the math class way, you'd find that $x = \sqrt{5} + 2$ and then you would have to substitute that into the provided expression. There's got to be an easier way!

The question is much easier if you read the final question and look for a direct solution. Then, you notice that all the question wants you to do is to square the expression on the right of the equals sign. Well, if you square the expression on the right, then you'd better square the expression on the left too. Therefore, $\left(\sqrt{5}\right)^2 = 5 = (x - 2)^2$, and the correct answer is (C). That was pretty painless by comparison.

SOLVING SIMULTANEOUS EQUATIONS

Some SAT questions will give you two or more equations involving two or more variables and ask for the value of an expression or one of the variables. These questions are very similar to the questions containing one variable. The test-writers would like you to spend extra time trying to solve for the value of each variable, but that is not always necessary.

Here's an example of this type of question as a Grid-In. We'll look at Grid-Ins in more detail in Chapter 20.

16

If $4x + y = 14$ and $3x + 2y = 13$, what is the value of $x - y = ?$

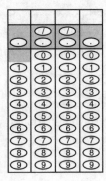

Here's How to Crack It

The question asks for the value of an expression. You've been given two equations here. But read the final question: instead being asked to solve for a variable (x or y), you've been asked to solve for $x - y$. Why? Because there must be a direct solution.

Learn Them, Love Them

Don't get bogged down looking for a direct solution. Always ask yourself if there is a simple way to find the answer. If you train yourself to think in terms of shortcuts, you won't waste a lot of time. However, if you don't see a quick solution, get to work. Something may come to you as you labor away.

In math class, you're usually taught to solve one equation for one variable in terms of a second variable and to substitute that value into the second equation to solve for the first variable.

Forget it. These methods are far too time consuming to use on the SAT, and they put you at risk of making mistakes. There's a better way. Just stack them on top of each other, and then add or subtract the two equations; either addition or subtraction will often produce an easy answer. Let's try it.

Adding the two equations gives you this:

$$\begin{array}{r} 4x + y = 14 \\ + 3x + 2y = 13 \\ \hline 7x + 3y = 27 \end{array}$$

Unfortunately, that doesn't get you anywhere, so try subtracting:

$$\begin{array}{r} 4x + y = 14 \\ - (3x + 2y = 13) \end{array}$$

When you subtract equations, just change the signs of the second equation and add. So the equation above becomes

$$\begin{array}{r} 4x + y = 14 \\ +(-3x - 2y = -13) \\ \hline x - y = 1 \end{array}$$

The value of $(x - y)$ is precisely what you are looking for. The correct answer is 1.

You can also use this method to solve problems in which you are asked to solve for an expression but you are given fewer equations than variables. If you have dealt with simultaneous equations in your math classes, you may know that that puts you in a bind since it may be impossible to solve for each individual variable.

Did you notice something about the three questions you just saw? In every case, reading the final question made it much simpler to solve. Try that again on the next one.

27

$$3a - 7b = 4d - 9$$
$$-4c + 10a = 6b + 7$$
$$-2a + 3c - 4d = 10$$

Given the system of equations above, what is the value of $-10a - 2b + 2c$?

A) −52

B) −26

C)   8

D)   26

Here's How to Crack It

The question asks for the value of a specific expression. Read the final question to see that it's not necessary to solve for individual variables. Notice that the test-writers have made this question harder by mixing up the variables. Your first step is to line up the variables on the left side of the equation and arrange them in alphabetical order; move the constants to the right side of the equation. Combine like terms in each equation, and use a placeholder for any variables that are missing in each equation.

Step 1:

$$3a - 7b + 0c - 4d = -9$$
$$10a - 6b - 4c + 0d = 7$$
$$-2a + 0b + 3c - 4d = 10$$

Once you have the variables aligned, complete this question just like the previous question by adding and subtracting the equations until you get something that looks like the expression in the question.

IF YOU ADD:

$$3a - 7b + 0c - 4d = -9$$
$$+ (10a - 6b - 4c + 0d = 7)$$
$$+ \underline{(-2a + 0b + 3c - 4d = 10)}$$
$$11a - 13b - 1c - 8d = 8$$

"Nothing" is Helpful

In these equations, the placeholders are $0c$, $0d$, and $0b$, respectively. Because 0 times any number is 0, nothing has been added to the equation; these 0's are simply acting as placeholders, so that all of the variables line up vertically. You may also choose to leave these areas blank.

Don't Forget to Share the Love

Don't forget that when you subtract an entire equation, you need to subtract each component of the equation—in simpler terms, change each sign to the opposite operation, and then add the equations.

IF YOU SUBTRACT:

$$3a - 7b + 0c - 4d = -9$$
$$+ (-10a + 6b + 4c - 0d = -7)$$
$$+ (\underline{ 2a - 0b - 3c + 4d = -10)}$$
$$-5a - 1b + 1c + 0d = -26$$

Neither of these answers appears to be what the test-writers are asking for, but on closer inspection, the equation that resulted from subtraction can be multiplied by 2 to get the expression in the question.

$$2(-5a - 1b + 1c) = 2(-26)$$

$$-10a - 2b + 2c = -52$$

The correct answer is (A).

○

Solving for Variables in Simultaneous Equations

Shortcuts are awesome, so take them whenever you can on the SAT. But occasionally, you won't have the option of using a shortcut with simultaneous equations, so knowing how to solve for a variable is crucial.

Here's an example.

○

17

If $3x + 2y = 17$ and $5x - 4y = 21$, what is the value of y?

Here's How to Crack It

The question asks for the value of y. Look for the most direct way to get there. In this case, the stack and solve method doesn't give you an immediate answer:

IF YOU ADD: **IF YOU SUBTRACT:**

$$
\begin{array}{r}
3x + 2y = 17 \\
+\ 5x - 4y = 21 \\
\hline
8x - 2y = 38
\end{array}
$$

$$
\begin{array}{r}
3x + 2y = 17 \\
+\ (-5x + 4y = -21) \\
\hline
-2x + 6y = -4
\end{array}
$$

Neither of these methods gives you the value of y. The best way to approach this question is to try to eliminate one variable. To do this, multiply one or both of the equations by a number that will cause the other variable to have a coefficient of 0 when the equations are added or subtracted.

Since the question is asking you to solve for y, try to make the x terms disappear. You want to make the coefficient of x zero, so you can quickly find the value of y.

Use the coefficient of x in the second equation, 5, to multiply the first equation:

$$5(3x + 2y) = 5(17)$$

$$15x + 10y = 85$$

Then use the original coefficient of x in the first equation to multiply the second equation:

$$3(5x - 4y) = 3(21)$$
$$15x - 12y = 63$$

Now stack your equations and subtract (or flip the signs and add, which is less likely to lead to a mistake).

$$
\begin{array}{r}
15x + 10y = 85 \\
+\ (-15x + 12y = -63) \\
\hline
0x\ + 22y = 22
\end{array}
$$

Simplify your equation and you have your answer.

$$22y = 22$$
$$y = 1$$

————————————○————————————

SOLVING INEQUALITIES

In an equation, one side equals the other. In an **inequality,** one side does not equal the other. The following symbols are used in inequalities:

Hungry Gator
Think of the inequality sign as the mouth of a hungry alligator. The alligator eats the bigger number.

SYMBOL	MEANING
>	is greater than
<	is less than
≥	is greater than or equal to; at least
≤	is less than or equal to; no more than

Solving inequalities is pretty similar to solving equations. You can collect like terms, and you can simplify by performing the same operation to both sides. All you have to remember is that if you multiply or divide both sides of an inequality by a negative number, the direction of the inequality symbol changes. For example, here's a simple inequality:

$$x > y$$

Now, just as you can with an equation, you can multiply both sides of this inequality by the same number. But if the number you multiply by is negative, you have to change the direction of the symbol in the result. For example, if you multiply both sides of the inequality above by -2, you end up with the following:

$$-2x < -2y$$

When you multiply or divide an inequality by a negative number, you must reverse the inequality sign.

Here's an example of how an inequality question may be framed on the test.

2

If $-3x + 6 \geq 18$, which of the following must be true?

A) $x \leq -4$

B) $x \leq 8$

C) $x \geq -4$

D) $x \geq -8$

Here's How to Crack It

The question asks for a true statement based on the inequality, and the answers are all possible values of x. Isolate the x by simplifying the inequality like any other equation:

$$-3x + 6 \geq 18$$

$$-3x \geq 12$$

Remember to change the direction of the inequality sign!

$$x \leq -4$$

The correct answer is (A).

A Range of Values

You may also be asked to solve inequalities for a range of values. In these instances, you can simplify the process by initially treating the inequality as two separate problems.

Here's an example.

33

If $-8 < -\dfrac{3}{5}m + 1 \leq -\dfrac{16}{5}$, what is one possible value of m?

Here's How to Crack It

The question asks for a possible value of m, so solve the inequality for m. First, work on the left side of the inequality: $-8 < -\dfrac{3}{5}m + 1$.

$$5(-8) < 5\left(-\frac{3}{5}m + 1\right)$$

$$-40 < -3m + 5$$

$$-40 - 5 < -3m + 5 - 5$$

$$-45 < -3m$$

$$\frac{-45}{-3} > \frac{-3m}{-3}$$

$$15 > m$$

Then, work on the right side of the inequality: $-\frac{3}{5}m + 1 \le -\frac{16}{5}$.

$$-\frac{3}{5}m + 1 - 1 \le -\frac{16}{5} - 1$$

$$-\frac{3}{5}m \le -\frac{21}{5}$$

$$5\left(-\frac{3}{5}m\right) \le 5\left(-\frac{21}{5}\right)$$

$$-3m \le -21$$

$$\frac{-3m}{-3} \ge \frac{-21}{-3}$$

$$m \ge 7$$

Once you have both pieces of the inequality simplified, you just need to put them back together.

If $15 > m$ and $m \ge 7$, then $15 > m \ge 7$, but this inequality doesn't make logical sense. Generally, inequalities are written with the smaller number on the left and the larger number on the right, so when you solve an inequality like this, you may need to rearrange the equation. This isn't difficult; just make sure the "arrows" are still pointing at the same numbers when you change the order.

$15 > m \ge 7$ becomes $7 \le m < 15$

So, a correct answer to this question would be any number between 7 and 15, which includes 7, but does NOT include 15.

Writing Your Own System of Equations

Sometimes you'll be asked to take a word problem and create a system of equations or inequalities from that information. In general, you will not be asked to solve this system of equations/inequalities, so if you are able to locate and translate the information in the question, you have a good shot at getting the correct answer. Always start with the most straightforward piece of information. What is the most straightforward piece of information? Well, that's up to you to decide. Consider the following question.

9

Aubrie, Bera, and Kea are running a lemonade and snack stand to earn money. They are selling lemonade for $1.07 a cup and chocolate chip cookies for $0.78 each. Their customers arrive on foot or by car. During a three-hour period, they had 47 customers each buying only one item and made $45.94. Aubrie, Bera, and Kea need to determine if they have enough supplies for tomorrow. Solving which of the following system of equations will let them know how many cups of lemonade, x, and how many cookies, y, they sold today?

Watch Us Crack It

A) $x + y = 45.94$
   $1.07x + 0.78y = 47$

B) $x + y = 47$
   $1.07x + 0.78y = 45.94$

C) $x + y = 47$
   $0.78x + 1.07y = 45.94$

D) $x + y = 47$
   $107x + 78y = 45.94$

Here's How to Crack It

The question asks for a system of equations that describes the situation, so translate the English to math one piece at a time. For some people, the most straightforward piece of information deals with the number of items being sold. For others, it may be the price of the items being sold. Whichever piece of information you choose, use the math to English translations in this chapter to help you identify the mathematical operations you will need to write your equation.

Now work through the question.

You may have noticed that the question provides background information that isn't really necessary to solve the problem. Lightly striking through the unnecessary information will make the question look less intimidating.

9

~~Aubrie, Bera, and Kea are running a lemonade and snack stand to earn money.~~ They are selling lemonade for $1.07 a cup and chocolate chip cookies for $0.78 each. ~~Their customers arrive on foot or by car. During a three-hour period~~ they had 47 customers each buying only one item and they made $45.94. ~~Aubrie, Bera, and Kea need to determine if they have enough supplies for tomorrow.~~ ~~Solving~~ which of the following system of equations will let them know how many cups of lemonade, x, and how many cookies, y, they sold today?

The shortened question makes it a lot easier to recognize important information. Start by identifying a straightforward piece of information to work with.

They are selling lemonade for $1.07 a cup and chocolate chip cookies for $0.78 each.

Once you identify which variable represents lemonade and which one represents cookies, you can begin to write your equation. In this question, the very last sentence gives you the needed information.

…how many glasses of lemonade, x, and how many cookies, y…

The number of cups of lemonade they sold, multiplied by $1.07 per cup, will give you the amount of money they made selling lemonade, and the number of cookies they sold, multiplied by $0.78, will give you the amount of money they made selling cookies. Since the question also gives you the total amount of money they made, $45.94, and states that customers were "each buying only one item," you can use the information above to write your first equation.

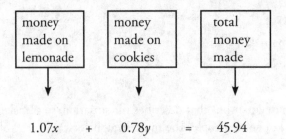

money made on lemonade	money made on cookies	total money made
↓	↓	↓
1.07x	+ 0.78y	= 45.94

Once you have your first equation, go to your answer choices to determine which answers you can eliminate. You'll quickly see that (A), (C), and (D) are all wrong, so you don't even need to construct the second equation. The correct answer is (B).

Now try one on your own.

13

A seamstress is ordering red and blue ribbon to use when creating a set of dresses. The seamstress wants to include at least 200 meters of ribbon in her order, and she will order no more than 3 times as much blue ribbon as red ribbon. Each spool of red ribbon contains 22.86 meters, and each spool of blue ribbon contains 18.29 meters. If r and b are nonnegative integers and represent the number of spools of red and blue ribbon, respectively, that the seamstress will order, which of the inequalities below best represents this scenario?

A) $22.86r + 18.29b \geq 200$

   $3b \leq r$

B) $22.86r + 54.87b \geq 200$

   $3b \leq r$

C) $22.86r + 18.29b \geq 200$

   $b \leq 3r$

D) $22.86r + 54.87b \geq 200$

   $b \leq 3r$

Here's How to Crack It

The question asks for a system of inequalities that describes the situation. Start with the most straightforward piece of information and translate it into math. In this case, the most straightforward information is about the total meters of ribbon, 200 meters. However, all of the answers include ≥ 200, so look for something else. The answers also all include $22.86r$ for the red ribbon, so work with the blue ribbon. The question states that *each spool of blue ribbon contains 18.29 meters* and that b represents the number of spools of blue ribbon. Therefore, the equation should include $18.29b$. Eliminate (B) and (D) because they have the wrong number multiplied by b.

Next, look at the relationship between the blue and red ribbon. The question states that *she will order no more than 3 times as much blue ribbon as red ribbon*. The phrase *no more than*, is indicated by the symbol $\leq$, and the amount of blue ribbon is being compared to 3 times the amount of red ribbon. The correct equation to depict this information is $b \leq 3r$. Eliminate (A). The correct answer is (C).

SIMPLIFYING EXPRESSIONS

If a question contains an expression that can be factored, it is very likely that you will need to factor it to solve the question. So, you should always be on the lookout for opportunities to factor. For example, if a question contains the expression $2x + 2y$, you should see if factoring it to produce the expression $2(x + y)$ will help you to solve the problem.

If a question contains an expression that is already factored, you should consider using the Distributive Law to expand it. For example, if a question contains the expression $2(x + y)$, you should see if expanding it to $2x + 2y$ will help.

Here are five examples that we've worked out:

1. $4x + 24 = 4(x) + 4(6) = 4(x + 6)$

2. $\dfrac{10x - 60}{2} = \dfrac{10(x) - 10(6)}{2} = \dfrac{10(x - 6)}{2} = 5(x - 6) = 5x - 30$

3. $\dfrac{x + y}{y} = \dfrac{x}{y} + \dfrac{y}{y} = \dfrac{x}{y} + 1$

4. $2(x + y) + 3(x + y) = (2 + 3)(x + y) = 5(x + y)$

5. $p(r + s) + q(r + s) = (p + q)(r + s)$

> **Something to Hide**
> Because factoring or expanding is usually the key to finding the answer on such questions, learn to recognize expressions that could be either factored or expanded. This will earn you more points. The test-writers will try to hide the answer by factoring or expanding the result.

Here's how this might be tested on the SAT.

───────────────○───────────────

10

Which of the following is equivalent to $\dfrac{f^2}{g} + f$?

A) $\dfrac{f}{g}(f + g)$

B) $f\left(\dfrac{f}{g} + f\right)$

C) $f^2\left(\dfrac{1}{g} - \dfrac{1}{f}\right)$

D) $f^2\left(\dfrac{1}{g} + 1\right)$

Here's How to Crack It

The question asks for an expression that is equivalent to the given one. Depending on what you see when you approach this question, you may choose to solve by distribution or factoring. You may notice that there is an f in each term of the expression. In this case, you may choose to factor the expression to $f\left(\dfrac{f}{g}+1\right)$, but that doesn't give you a possible answer; however, you can eliminate (B), since $f\left(\dfrac{f}{g}+f\right)$ is not equivalent to your expression. Now you are left with an expression you may find hard to manipulate. Go back and look at the mathematics behind the initial factorization so the next step in the process will make more sense.

When you factor an f out of the expression, what you are really doing is multiplying the expression by 1 so that you do not change the expression.

$$\frac{f}{f}\left(\frac{f^2}{g}+f\right)$$

$$f \times \frac{1}{f}\left(\frac{f^2}{g}+f\right)$$

Distribute the $\dfrac{1}{f}$.

$$f\left(\frac{f^2}{g}\times\frac{1}{f}+f\times\frac{1}{f}\right)$$

Cancel where possible.

$$f\left(\frac{f}{g}+1\right)$$

You can follow the exact same steps to factor an $\dfrac{f}{g}$ like you see in (A).

$$\frac{\dfrac{f}{g}}{\dfrac{f}{g}}\left(\frac{f^2}{g}+f\right)$$

$$\frac{f}{g} \times \frac{g}{f}\left(\frac{f^2}{g} + f\right)$$

$$\frac{f}{g}\left(\frac{f^2}{g} \times \frac{g}{f} + f \times \frac{g}{f}\right)$$

$$\frac{f}{g}(f + g)$$

This leaves you with the same expression as (A).

If you notice that the answers are all expressions themselves, you may choose to distribute the variable in front of the parentheses instead of trying to factor the expression.

Start with (A): $\frac{f}{g}(f + g)$

Distribute to each term within the binomial: $f \times \frac{f}{g} + g \times \frac{f}{g}$

Cancel where you can: $\frac{f^2}{g} + f$

Either way, the correct answer is (A).

Both methods give you the same answer; however, this type of algebra leaves you open to making mistakes. In the next chapter, you will discover a third way to approach this question that you may find even easier than the previous methods.

Multiplying Binomials

Multiplying binomials is easy. Just be sure to use **FOIL** (First, Outer, Inner, Last).

$$(x + 2)(x + 4) = (x + 2)(x + 4)$$
$$= (x \times x) + (x \times 4) + (2 \times x) + (2 \times 4)$$
$$\quad\text{FIRST}\quad\text{OUTER}\quad\text{INNER}\quad\text{LAST}$$
$$= x^2 + 4x + 2x + 8$$
$$= x^2 + 6x + 8$$

Combine Similar Terms First

When manipulating long, complicated algebraic expressions, combine all similar terms before doing anything else. In other words, if one of the terms is $5x$ and another is $-3x$, simply combine them into $2x$. Then you won't have as many terms to work with. Here's an example:

$$(3x^2 + 3x + 4) + (2 - x) - (6 + 2x) =$$
$$3x^2 + 3x + 4 + 2 - x - 6 - 2x =$$
$$3x^2 + (3x - x - 2x) + (4 + 2 - 6) =$$
$$3x^2$$

Evaluating Expressions

Sometimes you will be given the value of one of the variables in an algebraic expression and asked to find the value of the entire expression. All you have to do is plug in the given value and see what you come up with.

Here is an example:

Problem: If $2x = -1$, then $(2x - 3)^2 = ?$

Solution: Don't solve for x; simply plug in -1 for $2x$, like this:

$$(2x - 3)^2 = (-1 - 3)^2$$
$$= (-4)^2$$
$$= 16$$

SOLVING QUADRATIC EQUATIONS

To solve quadratic equations, remember everything you've learned so far: look for direct solutions and either factor or expand when possible.

Here's an example.

16

If $(x - 3)^2 = (x + 2)^2$, what is the value of x ?

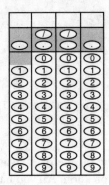

Here's How to Crack It

The question asks for the value of x. Expand both sides of the equation using FOIL:

$$(x - 3)(x - 3) = x^2 - 6x + 9$$

$$(x + 2)(x + 2) = x^2 + 4x + 4$$

$$x^2 - 6x + 9 = x^2 + 4x + 4$$

Now you can simplify. Eliminate the x^2 terms, because they are on both sides of the equals sign. Now you have $-6x + 9 = 4x + 4$, which simplifies to

$$-10x = -5$$
$$x = \frac{1}{2}$$

Factoring Quadratics

To solve a quadratic, you might also have to factor the equation. Factoring a quadratic basically involves doing a reverse form of FOIL.

For example, suppose you needed to know the factors of $x^2 + 7x + 12$. Here's what you would do:

1. Write down 2 sets of parentheses and put an x in each one because the product of the first terms is x^2.

$$x^2 + 7x + 12 = (x \quad)(x \quad)$$

2. Look at the number at the end of the expression you are trying to factor. Write down its factors. In this case, the factors of 12 are 1 and 12, 2 and 6, and 3 and 4.

3. To determine which set of factors to put in the parentheses, look at the coefficient of the middle term of the quadratic expression. In this case, the coefficient is 7. So, the correct factors will also either add or subtract to get 7. The only factors that work are 3 and 4. Write these factors in the parentheses.

$$x^2 + 7x + 12 = (x \_\_ 3)(x \_\_ 4)$$

4. Finally, determine the signs for the factors. To get a positive 12, the 3 and the 4 are either both positive or both negative. But, since 7 is also positive, the signs must both be positive.

$$x^2 + 7x + 12 = (x + 3)(x + 4)$$

> **Factoring**
> When factoring an equation like $x^2 + bx + c$, think "**A.M.**" Find two numbers that **A**dd up to the middle term (b) and **M**ultiply to give the last term (c).

You can always check that you have factored correctly by using FOIL on the factors to see if you get the original quadratic expression.

Try an example.

16

In the expression $x^2 + kx + 12$, k is a negative integer. Which of the following is a possible value of k ?

A) −13

B) −12

C) −6

D) 7

Here's How to Crack It

The question asks for a possible value of k, which is the coefficient on the x term in the quadratic. Since the question told you that k is a negative integer, you can immediately eliminate (D) because it is a positive integer. To solve the question, you need to factor. This question is just a twist on the example used above. Don't worry that you don't know the value of k. The question said that k was an integer, so you need to consider only the integer factors of 12. The possible factors of 12 are 1 and 12, 2 and 6, and 3 and 4. Since 12 is positive and k is negative, then you'll need subtraction signs in both factors.

The possibilities are as follows:

$$x^2 + kx + 12 = (x - 1)(x - 12)$$

$$x^2 + kx + 12 = (x - 2)(x - 6)$$

$$x^2 + kx + 12 = (x - 3)(x - 4)$$

If you use FOIL on each of these sets of factors, you'll get the following expressions:

$$(x - 1)(x - 12) = x^2 - 13x + 12$$

$$(x - 2)(x - 6) = x^2 - 8x + 12$$

$$(x - 3)(x - 4) = x^2 - 7x + 12$$

Of the coefficients on the x terms above, -13 is the only value from above included in the answers. Of course, you didn't need to write them all out if you started with 1 and 12 as your factors. The correct answer is (A).

SAT Favorites

The test-writers play favorites when it comes to quadratic equations. There are three equations that they use often. You should memorize these and be on the lookout for them. Whenever you see a quadratic that contains two variables, it is frequently one of these three.

$$(x + y)(x - y) = x^2 - y^2$$

$$(x + y)^2 = x^2 + 2xy + y^2$$

$$(x - y)^2 = x^2 - 2xy + y^2$$

Here's an example of how these equations will likely be tested on the SAT.

7

If $2x - 3y = 5$, what is the value of $4x^2 - 12xy + 9y^2$?

A) $\sqrt{5}$

B) 12

C) 25

D) 100

Here's How to Crack It

The question asks for the value of an expression. Since the expression seems kind of random, see if there is a way to get from the given equation to the expression.

In this case, work with $2x - 3y = 5$. If you square the left side of the equation, you get

$$(2x - 3y)^2 = 4x^2 - 12xy + 9y^2$$

That's precisely the expression for which you need to find the value. It's also the third of the equations from the box. Now, since you squared the left side, all you need to do is square the 5 on the right side of the equation to discover that the expression equals 25. The correct answer is (C).

Did you notice that this question was just another version of being asked to solve for the value of an expression rather than for a variable? Quadratics are one of the test-writers' favorite ways to do that.

Solving Quadratics Set to Zero

Before factoring most quadratics, you need to set the equation equal to zero. Why? Well, if $ab = 0$, what do you know about a and b? At least one of them must equal 0, right? That's the key fact you need to solve most quadratics.

Here's an example.

———————————○———————————

9

If $3 - \dfrac{3}{x} = x + 7$, and $x \neq 0$, which of the following is a possible

value for x?

A) -7
B) -1
C) 1
D) 3

Here's How to Crack It

The question asks for a possible value of x. Here, the test-writers have tried to hide that the equation is actually a quadratic. Start by multiplying both sides of the equation by x to get rid of the fraction.

$$x\left(3 - \frac{3}{x}\right) = x(x + 7)$$

$$3x - 3 = x^2 + 7x$$

Rearrange the terms to set the quadratic equal to 0. You'll get $x^2 + 4x + 3 = 0$. Now it's time to factor:

$$x^2 + 4x + 3 = (x + 1)(x + 3) = 0$$

So, at least one of the factors must equal 0. If $x + 1 = 0$, then $x = -1$. If $x + 3 = 0$, then $x = -3$. Only one of these values appears in the answer choices. The correct answer is (B).

———————————○———————————

The Quadratic Formula and the Discriminant

In addition to solving easily factorable quadratics, the test-writers would also like to see you demonstrate your understanding of the quadratic formula. We know what you're thinking: "Not that thing *again!* Can't I just solve it with that nifty program I have on my graphing calculator?" Why yes, yes you can, but only if the question appears in the calculator-permitted section of the test. Trust us on this one; the test-writers are not always going to put these types of questions in the calculator section. Knowing the quadratic formula is an easy way to gain points on a question the test-writers intend to be "hard."

For a quadratic equation in the form $y = ax^2 + bx + c$, the quadratic formula is

$$x = \frac{-b \pm \sqrt{b^2 - 4ac}}{2a}$$

To find the roots of a quadratic, or the points where $y = 0$, simply plug your values for a, b, and c into the quadratic formula.

Here's an example:

$$7x^2 - 5x - 17 = 0$$

So $a = 7$, $b = -5$, and $c = -17$. Plugging the constants into the quadratic equation, you get

$$x = \frac{5 \pm \sqrt{(-5)^2 - 4(7)(-17)}}{2(7)}$$

$$x = \frac{5 \pm \sqrt{25 + 476}}{14}$$

$$x = \frac{5 \pm \sqrt{501}}{14}$$

$$x = \frac{5}{14} + \frac{\sqrt{501}}{14} \text{ and } x = \frac{5}{14} - \frac{\sqrt{501}}{14}$$

The Signs They Are a Changin'
The quadratic formula works for quadratics in the form $y = ax^2 + bx + c$. There is only addition in that form, so be careful when your quadratic has negative signs in it.

Let's put your quadratic skills to work with a question you may see on the SAT.

> **12**
>
> What is the product of all the solutions to the equation
> $3z^2 - 12z + 6 = 0$?
>
> A) $\sqrt{2}$
>
> B) 2
>
> C) 4
>
> D) $4\sqrt{2}$

Here's How to Crack It

The question asks for the product of the solutions to a quadratic. The radicals in the answer choices are a clue that the quadratic may be hard to factor. Simplify the equation first by dividing both sides by 3 to get

$$z^2 - 4z + 2 = 0$$

To find the solutions using the quadratic formula $x = \dfrac{-b \pm \sqrt{b^2 - 4ac}}{2a}$, you would do the following:

$$x = \frac{-(-4) \pm \sqrt{(-4)^2 - 4(1)(2)}}{2(1)}$$

$$x = \frac{4 \pm \sqrt{16 - 8}}{2} = \frac{4 \pm \sqrt{8}}{2}$$

$$x = \frac{4 \pm \sqrt{4 \times 2}}{2} = \frac{4 \pm 2\sqrt{2}}{2}$$

$$x = 2 \pm \sqrt{2}$$

So $x = 2 + \sqrt{2}$ *or* $2 - \sqrt{2}$. "Product" means to multiply, so use FOIL to multiply $\left(2 + \sqrt{2}\right) \times \left(2 - \sqrt{2}\right)$ to get $4 - 2\sqrt{2} + 2\sqrt{2} - \left(\sqrt{2}\right)^2 = 4 - 2 = 2$. The correct answer is (B).

Wow, that was a lot of work! Wouldn't it be great if there were a shortcut? Actually, there is! When a quadratic is in the form $y = ax^2 + bx + c$, the product of the roots is equal to the value of c divided by the value of a. In this case, that's $6 \div 3 = 2$! It's the same answer for a lot less work. (See the inset "The Root of the Problems" for this and another handy trick—they're worth memorizing.)

There is one more useful thing that can be determined from just a piece of the quadratic formula. The part under the root symbol in the formula is called the *discriminant*. The value of the discriminant can tell you the number of roots the quadratic has, be they real or imaginary, without having to solve for them.

> **The Root of the Problems**
> Sometimes you'll be asked to solve for the sum or the product of the roots of a quadratic equation. You can use the quadratic formula and then add or multiply the results, but it's quicker to just memorize these two expressions.
>
> sum of the roots: $-\dfrac{b}{a}$
>
> product of the roots: $\dfrac{c}{a}$

> The discriminant of a quadratic in the standard form $ax^2 + bx + c = 0$ is $b^2 - 4ac$.
>
> - If the discriminant is positive, the quadratic has 2 real solutions.
>
> - If the discriminant equals 0, the quadratic has 1 real solution.
>
> - If the discriminant is negative, the quadratic has 2 imaginary solutions.

IMAGINARY AND COMPLEX NUMBERS

So far you have been working with **real numbers,** which are any numbers that you can place on a number line. The SAT will also ask you to do mathematical operations with imaginary or complex numbers.

Imaginary Numbers

An **imaginary number,** very simply, is the square root of a negative number. Since there is no way to have a real number that is the square root of a negative number, mathematicians needed to come up with a way to represent this concept when writing equations. They use an italicized lowercase "I" to do that: $i = \sqrt{-1}$, and the SAT will likely tell you that in any question involving imaginary numbers.

Complex Numbers

Complex numbers are another way in which the SAT may test the concept of imaginary numbers. A **complex number** is one that has a real component and an imaginary component connected by addition or subtraction. $8 + 7i$ and $3 - 4i$ are two examples of complex numbers.

Complex numbers might be tested in a variety of ways. You may be asked to add or subtract the complex numbers. When you are completing these operations, you can treat i as a variable. Just combine the like terms in these expressions and then simplify. (Don't forget to distribute the subtraction sign.)

Here's an example.

○

2

For $i = \sqrt{-1}$, what is the result of subtracting $(2 + 4i)$ from $(-5 + 6i)$?

A) $-7 + 2i$

B) $-3 - 10i$

C) $3 + 2i$

D) $7 - 10i$

Here's How to Crack It

The question asks for the result of subtracting one complex number from another. Set up the subtraction:

$$(-5 + 6i) - (2 + 4i)$$

Distribute the negative sign to both terms in the second set of parentheses to get

$$-5 + 6i - 2 - 4i$$

Combine like terms to get $-7 + 2i$. The correct answer is (A).

Since you never ended up with an i^2 term, you never even needed to worry about the fact that $i = \sqrt{-1}$. You just treat i as a regular variable.

○

The SAT may also test your ability to multiply complex numbers. Again, you can treat *i* as a variable as you work through the multiplication as if you were multiplying binominals. In other words, use FOIL to work through the problem. The only difference is that you substitute −1 for i^2.

$$\begin{array}{cccc} F & O & I & L \\ \downarrow & \downarrow & \downarrow & \downarrow \end{array}$$

$$(4 + 8i) \times (3 - 2i) = 12 - 8i + 24i - 16i^2 = 12 + 16i - 16(-1) = 12 + 16i + 16 = 28 + 16i$$

Finally, you may be asked about fractions with complex numbers in the denominator. Don't worry—you won't need polynomial or synthetic division for this. You just need to rationalize the denominator, which is much easier than it may sound.

To rationalize the denominator of a fraction containing complex numbers, you need to multiply the numerator and denominator by the conjugate of the denominator. To create the conjugate of a complex number, switch the addition or subtraction sign connecting the real and imaginary parts of the number for its opposite.

For example, the conjugate of 8 + 7*i* is 8 − 7*i*, and the conjugate of 3 − 4*i* is 3 + 4*i*.

Just like when you expand the expression $(x + y)(x - y)$ to get $x^2 - y^2$, you can do the same with a complex number and its conjugate. The Outer and Inner terms will cancel out, giving you $(x + yi)(x - yi) = (x^2 - i^2y^2) = (x^2 + y^2)$.

$(8 + 7i) \times (8 - 7i) = 8^2 - 7^2i^2$, and substituting $i^2 = -1$ gives you $8^2 + 7^2 = 113$.

Here's an example of how the SAT will test your knowledge that $i^2 = -1$.

6

$$(13i^2 + 2i) - (-7 + 4i)$$

When $i = \sqrt{-1}$, which of the following complex numbers is equivalent to the expression above?

A) −20 − 6*i*

B) −6 − 2*i*

C) 6 + 2*i*

D) 20 + 6*i*

Multiplying by One (in Disguise)

In order to keep the value of a fraction the same, you must multiply by 1. If you multiply the numerator of a fraction by the conjugate, you must do that same operation to the denominator or you have changed the fraction:

$$\frac{18}{8+7i} \times \left(\frac{8-7i}{8-7i}\right)$$

is the same thing as multiplying $\frac{18}{8+7i} \times 1$.

Here's How to Crack It

The question asks for an expression that is equivalent to an expression that contains imaginary numbers. Follow the order of operations, rewrite i^2 appropriately, and be very careful with signs. First, distribute the minus sign so you can remove the parentheses. The expression becomes

$$13i^2 + 2i + 7 - 4i$$

When i is not squared, it can be treated like a variable, so combine the two terms that have i to get

$$13i^2 - 2i + 7$$

Rewrite i^2 as -1 and multiply it by 13 to get

$$13(-1) - 2i + 7 = -13 - 2i + 7$$

Finally, combine the integer terms and the expression becomes

$$-6 - 2i$$

The correct answer is (B).

WHEN VALUES ARE ABSOLUTE

Absolute value is a measure of the distance between a number and 0. Since distances are always positive, the absolute value of a number is also always positive. The absolute value of a number is written as $|x|$.

When solving for the value of a variable inside the absolute value bars, it is important to remember that the variable could be either positive or negative. For example, if $|x| = 2$, then $x = 2$ or $x = -2$, as both 2 and -2 are a distance of 2 from 0.

Here's an example.

12

Which of the following is the value of $|y + z|$ if y and z are the solutions to the equation $|-4x - 2| = 6$?

A) -3

B) -2

C) 1

D) 3

Here's How to Crack It

The question asks for the value of an expression with an absolute value given an equation with an absolute value. Start with the equation and find the two solutions. Remember that the expression inside the absolute value symbols could be positive or negative and will still yield a positive result. Set that expression, $-4x - 2$, equal to 6 and -6, and solve for the two solutions.

$$-4x - 2 = 6 \qquad\qquad\qquad -4x - 2 = -6$$
$$-4x = 8 \qquad\qquad \textbf{and} \qquad\qquad -4x = -4$$
$$x = -2 \qquad\qquad\qquad\qquad x = 1$$

Thus, the solutions y and z are -2 and 1. There's no way to know which is y and which is z, but it doesn't matter. Replace the variables in the expression $|y + z|$ with those values in either order, and calculate the result.

$$|-2 + 1| = |-1| = 1$$

If you're curious, try the other order for y and z to see that, because of the absolute value, it still works.

$$|1 + (-2)| = |1 - 2| = |-1| = 1$$

In either case the result is 1. The correct answer is (C).

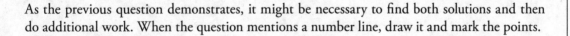

As the previous question demonstrates, it might be necessary to find both solutions and then do additional work. When the question mentions a number line, draw it and mark the points.

Try this example.

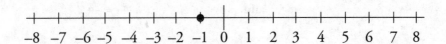

27

A number line contains two distinct points that are both 7 units away from a point with coordinate –1. Which of the following equations gives the coordinates of both points as the solutions?

A) $|x - 7| = 1$

B) $|x + 7| = 1$

C) $|x - 1| = 7$

D) $|x + 1| = 7$

Here's How to Crack It

The question asks for an equation that can be solved to find two coordinates. The question describes a number line and a point, so start by drawing it.

$$-8 \quad -7 \quad -6 \quad -5 \quad -4 \quad -3 \quad -2 \quad -1 \quad 0 \quad 1 \quad 2 \quad 3 \quad 4 \quad 5 \quad 6 \quad 7 \quad 8$$

The points that are 7 away from –1 on the number line are at –8 and 6, so label those points, too.

$$-8 \quad -7 \quad -6 \quad -5 \quad -4 \quad -3 \quad -2 \quad -1 \quad 0 \quad 1 \quad 2 \quad 3 \quad 4 \quad 5 \quad 6 \quad 7 \quad 8$$

Now solve the equations in the answer choices to find out which one gives both –8 and 6 as solutions. Keep in mind that the expression inside the absolute value symbol could be positive or negative. Choice (A) yields

$$\begin{aligned} x - 7 &= 1 \qquad \textbf{and} \qquad x - 7 = -1 \\ x &= 8 \qquad\qquad\qquad\qquad\quad x = 6 \end{aligned}$$

Only one of those values is a correct solution, so eliminate (A). Try the same thing with the other answer choices. Choice (B) results in –6 and –8, so eliminate (B). Choice (C) results in 8 and –8, so eliminate (C). Choice (D) results in 6 and –8, so keep it. The correct answer is (D).

Algebra Drill 1: No Calculator Section

Work these questions without your calculator using the skills you've learned so far. Answers and explanations can be found starting on page 350.

5

$$y = 3x - 1$$

$$\frac{1}{2}y + x = 1$$

In the system of equations above, if (x, y) is the solution to the system, what is the value of $\dfrac{x}{y}$?

A) $\dfrac{3}{8}$

B) $\dfrac{2}{5}$

C) $\dfrac{3}{4}$

D) $\dfrac{4}{3}$

8

For the equation $\sqrt{mx - 5} = x + 3$, the value of m is –3. What is the solution set for the equation?

A) $\{-3, 3\}$

B) $\{-2\}$

C) $\{-2, -7\}$

D) $\{3, 6\}$

11

If $i = \sqrt{-1}$, what is the product of $(4 + 7i)$ and

$\left(\dfrac{1}{2} - 2i\right)$?

A) $16 - \dfrac{9}{2}i$

B) $14 + \dfrac{9}{2}i$

C) $2 - 8i - 14i^2$

D) $i\left(8 + \dfrac{9}{2}\right)$

14

$$rx^2 = \frac{1}{s}x + 3$$

A quadratic equation is provided above, where r and s are constants. What are the solutions for x ?

A) $x = \dfrac{1}{2sr} \pm \dfrac{\sqrt{\dfrac{1}{s^2} + 12r}}{2r}$

B) $x = \dfrac{1}{2sr} \pm \dfrac{\sqrt{-\dfrac{1}{s^2} - 12r}}{2sr}$

C) $x = \dfrac{s}{2r} \pm \dfrac{\sqrt{\dfrac{1}{s^2} - 12r}}{2r}$

D) $x = \dfrac{s}{2r} \pm \dfrac{\sqrt{s^2 - 12sr}}{2sr}$

---

15. Algebra: Cracking the System | **347**

Algebra Drill 2: Calculator-Permitted Section

Work these questions using your calculator as needed and applying the skills you've learned so far. Answers and explanations can be found starting on page 352.

4

If $x + 6 > 0$ and $1 - 2x > -1$, which of the following values of x is NOT a solution?

A) -6

B) -4

C) 0

D) $\dfrac{1}{2}$

7

If $\dfrac{2x}{x^2 + 1} = \dfrac{2}{x + 2}$, what is the value of x ?

A) $-\dfrac{1}{4}$

B) $\dfrac{1}{2}$

C) 0

D) 2

10

If the product of x and y is 76, and x is twice the square of y, which of the following pairs of equations could be used to determine the values of x and y ?

A) $xy = 76$

$x = 2y^2$

B) $xy = 76$

$x = (2y)^2$

C) $x + y = 76$

$x = 4y^2$

D) $xy = 76$

$x = 2y$

12

If $-6 < -4r + 10 \le 2$, what is the least possible value of $4r + 3$?

A) 2

B) 5

C) 8

D) 11

16

How many solutions exist to the equation $|x| = |2x - 1|$?

A) 0

B) 1

C) 2

D) 3

25

The sum of three numbers, *a, b,* and *c,* is 400. One of the numbers, *a,* is 40 percent less than the sum of *b* and *c.* What is the value of *b + c* ?

A) 40

B) 60

C) 150

D) 250

CHAPTER DRILL ANSWERS AND EXPLANATIONS

Algebra Drill 1: No Calculator Section

5. **C** The question asks for the value of $\dfrac{x}{y}$ in the system of equations. Start by multiplying the second equation by 2 to clear the fraction. The equation becomes $y + 2x = 2$. To get it into the same form as the other equations, subtract $2x$ from both sides to get $y = -2x + 2$. Set the two x expressions equal to get $3x - 1 = -2x + 2$. Add $2x$ and 1 to both sides, so the equation becomes $5x = 3$. Then divide by 5 to find that $x = \dfrac{3}{5}$. Plug this value into the $y = 3x - 1$ to get $y = 3\left(\dfrac{3}{5}\right) - 1 = \dfrac{9}{5} - 1 = \dfrac{9}{5} - \dfrac{5}{5} = \dfrac{4}{5}$. Finally, find the value of $\dfrac{x}{y}$: $\dfrac{\frac{3}{5}}{\frac{4}{5}} = \dfrac{3}{5} \times \dfrac{5}{4} = \dfrac{3}{4}$. The correct answer is (C).

8. **B** The question asks for the solution set to the equation. Since the question gives the value of m, the first step is to plug that value into the original equation to get $\sqrt{-3x - 5} = x + 3$. Now square both sides of the equation to remove the square root: $\left(\sqrt{-3x - 5}\right)^2 = (x + 3)^2$ or $-3x - 5 = x^2 + 6x + 9$. Now combine like terms. If you combine the terms on the right side of the equation, you can avoid having a negative x^2 term. The equation becomes $0 = x^2 + 9x + 14$. Factor the equation to find the roots: $0 = (x + 2)(x + 7)$. The possible solutions to the quadratic are -2 and -7. Don't forget to plug these numbers back into the original equation to check for extraneous solutions. Begin by checking $x = -2$. When you do this, you get $\sqrt{(-3)(-2) - 5} = (-2) + 3$, or $\sqrt{6 - 5} = 1$, or $\sqrt{1} = 1$, which is true. Now, check $x = -7$. Set it up as $\sqrt{(-3)(-7) - 5} = (-7) + 3$, and start simplifying to get $\sqrt{21 - 5} = -4$. You can technically stop simplifying here, as there is a negative number on the right-hand side of the equals sign. Remember, when taking a square root with a radical provided, it will yield the positive root only. So -7 cannot be part of the solution set. Be very careful of (C), which is a trap answer. The correct answer is (B).

11.   **A**   The question asks for the product of two binomials. "Product" means to multiply, so use FOIL to

multiply the two binomials together. The expression becomes $4\left(\dfrac{1}{2}\right) - 8i + 7i\left(\dfrac{1}{2}\right) - 14i^2$. Simplify

the result by multiplying through where you can to get $2 - 8i + \dfrac{7}{2}i - 14i^2$. To combine the i terms,

multiply 8 by $\dfrac{2}{2}$ to get $\dfrac{16}{2}$. Now the expression is $2 - \dfrac{16}{2}i + \dfrac{7}{2}i - 14i^2$, which can be further

simplified to $2 - \dfrac{9}{2}i - 14i^2$. Substitute -1 for i^2 and combine like terms: $2 - \dfrac{9}{2}i + 14 = 16 - \dfrac{9}{2}i$.

The correct answer is (A).

14.   **A**   The question asks for the solutions for x in a quadratic. The first step is to get the equation into the

standard form of a quadratic equation by moving all terms to the left or right side of the equation

and setting it equal to zero, like this: $rx^2 - \dfrac{1}{s}x - 3 = 0$. Now that you have the equation in standard

form, you can begin to solve for the roots. Since you are given variables instead of numbers, factoring

this quadratic would require higher-level math, if it were even possible. You may have noticed the

familiar form of the answer choices. They are in a form similar to the quadratic equation.

Remember that a quadratic in standard form is represented by the equation $ax^2 + bx + c = 0$, and

the quadratic formula is $x = \dfrac{-b \pm \sqrt{b^2 - 4ac}}{2a}$. In this equation, $a = r$, $b = -\dfrac{1}{s}$, and $c = -3$. There-

fore, $x = \dfrac{\dfrac{1}{s} \pm \sqrt{\left(-\dfrac{1}{s}\right)^2 - 4r(-3)}}{2r} = \dfrac{\dfrac{1}{s} \pm \sqrt{\dfrac{1}{s^2} + 12r}}{2r}$. This exact format is not present in the answer

choices, but the root part matches only the one in (A), so that is likely the answer. You will have to do a little more manipulation before you can get the equations to match exactly. The fractions need

to be split up, so rewrite the equation as $x = \dfrac{\frac{1}{s}}{2r} \pm \dfrac{\sqrt{\frac{1}{s^2}+12r}}{2r}$ or $x = \dfrac{1}{2sr} \pm \dfrac{\sqrt{\frac{1}{s^2}+12r}}{2r}$. The correct

answer is (A).

Algebra Drill 2: Calculator-Permitted Section

4. **A**   The question asks for the value of x that is not a solution. Solve the first inequality by subtracting 6 from each side so that $x > -6$. You are looking for values that won't work for x, and x cannot equal -6. Therefore, the answer must be (A). Just to be sure, solve the next inequality by subtracting 1 from each side to get $-2x > -2$. Divide by -2, remembering to switch the sign because you are dividing by a negative number, to get $x < 1$. The values in (B), (C), and (D) fit this requirement as well, so they are values for x and not the correct answer. The correct answer is (A).

7. **B**   The question asks for the value of x. To solve this equation, use cross-multiplication to get $(2x)(x + 2)$ $= (x^2 + 1)(2)$. Expand the equation to get $2x^2 + 4x = 2x^2 + 2$. Once you combine like terms, the result is $2x^2 - 2x^2 + 4x = 2$ or $4x = 2$. Solve for x by dividing both sides by 4 to get $x = \dfrac{1}{2}$. The correct answer is (B).

10. **A**   The question asks for a pair of equations to represent the situation. Translate each statement, piece by piece. The first part tells you that "the product of x and y is 76." Since *product* means multiplication, the first equation must be $xy = 76$, so you can eliminate (C). The second part says that "x is twice the square of y," which translates to $x = 2y^2$, so eliminate (B) and (D), and (A) is the only choice left. Notice that only the y needs to be squared, which is why (B) is wrong. The second equation for (B) would be written as "the square of twice y," which is not what the question states. The correct answer is (A).

12. **D**   The question asks for the least possible value of $4r + 3$. Notice that this question is asking for an expression instead of a variable, so manipulate the inequality so that you get $4r + 3$ in the inequality. Treat each side of the inequality separately to avoid confusion. Starting with the $-6 < -4r + 10$ part, multiply both sides of the inequality by -1, remembering to switch the sign, to get $6 > 4r - 10$. Add 13 to each side to get $19 > 4r + 3$. Then solve the right side of the inequality. Again, multiply both sides of the inequality by -1, switching the sign to get $4r - 10 \geq -2$. Now add 13 to each side of the equation: $4r + 3 \geq 11$. Finally, combine the equations to get the range for $4r + 3$. The least possible value of the expression is 11. If you see the answer before the last step above, you don't need to combine the equations. The correct answer is (D).

16. **C** The question asks for the number of solutions to an equation. If $|x| = |2x - 1|$, either $x = 2x - 1$ or $-x = 2x - 1$. The solutions to these equations are 1 and $\frac{1}{3}$, respectively. However, the only thing you need to recognize is that the equation has two different solutions. The correct answer is (C).

25. **D** The question asks for the value of $b + c$. This is a system of equations question in disguise. First, locate a piece of information in this question that you can work with. "The sum of three numbers, a, b, and c, is 400," seems very straightforward. Write the equation $a + b + c = 400$. Now the question tells you that "one of the numbers, a, is 40 percent less than the sum of b and c." Translate this piece by piece to get $a = (1 - 0.4)(b + c)$, or $a = 0.6(b + c)$. Distribute the 0.6 to get $a = 0.6b + 0.6c$. Arrange these variables so they line up with those in the first equation as $a - 0.6b - 0.6c = 0$. To solve for $b + c$, stack the equations and multiply the second equation by –1:

$$a + b + c = 400$$
$$-1(a - 0.6b - 0.6c) = 0(-1)$$

Now solve:

$$\begin{aligned} a + \quad b + \quad c &= 400 \\ \underline{-a + 0.6b + 0.6c} &= \underline{0\quad} \\ 1.6b + 1.6c &= 400 \end{aligned}$$

Simplify by dividing both sides by 1.6 to get $b + c = 250$. The correct answer is (D).

Summary

- Don't "solve for *x*" or "solve for *y*" unless you absolutely have to. (Don't worry; your math teacher won't find out.) Instead, look for direct solutions to SAT questions. Math Test questions rarely require time-consuming computations or endless fiddling with big numbers. There's almost always a trick—if you can spot it.

- If a question contains an expression that can be factored, factor it. If it contains an expression that already has been factored, multiply it out.

- To solve simultaneous equations, simply add or subtract the equations. If you don't have the answer, look for multiples of your solutions. When the simultaneous equation question asks for a single variable and addition and subtraction don't work, try to make something disappear. Multiply the equations to make the coefficient(s) of the variable(s) you don't want go to zero when the equations are added or subtracted.

- Some SAT questions require algebraic manipulation. Use tricks when you can, but if you have to manipulate the equation, take your time and work carefully to avoid unnecessary mistakes. You don't get partial credit for getting the question mostly correct.

- When working with inequalities, don't forget to flip the sign when you multiply and divide by negative numbers.

- When working with inequalities over a range of values, treat each side of the inequality as a separate question. Then combine the parts in a logical order with the smaller number on the left, making sure the "arrows" are pointing to the correct numbers.

- When asked to create a system of equations, start with the most straightforward piece of information. You can also use the equations in the answer choices to help you narrow down the possibilities for your equations. Eliminate any answers in which an equation doesn't match your equation.

- When a question asks for an extraneous solution, first solve the equation, and then plug the answers back into the equation. If the equation is not true when solved with the solution, then that solution is extraneous.

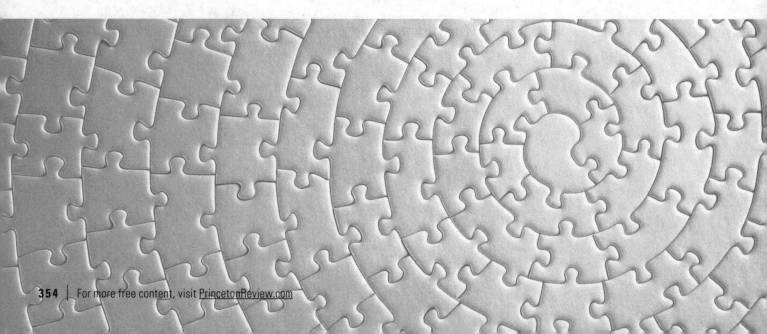

o   When solving quadratic equations, you may need to use FOIL or factor to get the equation into the easiest form for the question task. Don't forget about the common equations that the test-writers use when writing questions about quadratics.

o   To solve for the roots of a quadratic equation, set it equal to zero by moving all the terms to the left side of the equation, then factor and solve, or use the quadratic formula:

$$x = \frac{-b \pm \sqrt{b^2 - 4ac}}{2a}$$

When solving for the sum or product of the roots, you can also use these formulas:

- sum of the roots: $-\dfrac{b}{a}$

- product of the roots: $\dfrac{c}{a}$

o   The discriminant of a quadratic in the form $ax^2 + bx + c = 0$ is the value of $b^2 - 4ac$. If this value is positive, there are 2 real roots; if it is 0, there is 1 real root; if it is negative, there are two imaginary roots.

o   The imaginary number i is equal to $\sqrt{-1}$, so $i^2 = -1$. When doing algebra with i, treat it as a variable, unless you are able to substitute -1 for i^2 when appropriate.

o   A complex number is a number with a real and an imaginary component joined by addition or subtraction. In order to rationalize a fraction with a complex denominator, you need to multiply it by its conjugate, or the same complex number with the addition or subtraction sign switched to the opposite sign. Make sure to also multiply the numerator by the same thing to keep the value of the fraction the same.

o   The absolute value of a number is its distance from zero; distances are always positive. When working inside the | |, remember to consider both the positive and the negative values of the expression. Also remember that | | work like ( ); you need to complete all the operations inside the | | before you can make the value positive.

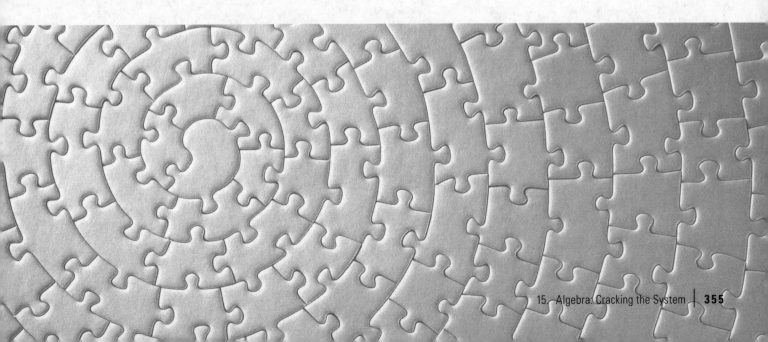

Chapter 16
Other SAT
Algebra Strategies

Now that you're familiar with the basics of algebra, it's time to learn how to avoid using algebra on the SAT. Yes, you read that correctly. Algebra questions on the SAT are filled with traps carefully laid by the test-writers, so you need to know how to work around them. This chapter gives you the strategies you need to turn tricky algebra questions into simple arithmetic.

PRINCETON REVIEW ALGEBRA—AKA HOW TO AVOID ALGEBRA ON THE SAT

Now that you've reviewed some basic algebra, it's time for something we call Princeton Review algebra. At The Princeton Review, we know that the SAT isn't your math class at school. It's the SAT, and on the SAT the best way to do some questions that looks like algebra is to *not* do the algebra. So we're going to show you how to avoid doing algebra on the SAT whenever possible. Now, before you start crying and complaining that you love algebra and couldn't possibly give it up, just take a second to hear us out. We have nothing against algebra—it's very helpful for solving problems, and it impresses your friends. But on the SAT, using algebra can actually hurt your score, and we don't want that.

We know it's difficult to come to terms with this. But if you use only algebra on the SAT, you're doing exactly what the test-writers want you to do. You see, when the test-writers design the questions on the SAT, they expect the students to use algebra to solve them. Many SAT problems have built-in traps meant to take advantage of common mistakes that students make when using algebra. But if you don't use algebra, there's no way you can fall into those traps.

Plus, when you avoid algebra, you add one other powerful tool to your tool belt: if you are on Section 4, you can use your calculator! Even if you have a super fancy calculator that plays games and doubles as a global positioning system, chances are it doesn't do algebra. (And if it can, chances are College Board won't let you use it on the SAT!) Arithmetic, on the other hand, is easy for your calculator. It's why calculators were invented. Our goal, then, is to turn algebra on the SAT into arithmetic. We do that using techniques we call Plugging In and Plugging In the Answers (PITA).

PLUGGING IN THE ANSWERS (PITA)

Algebra uses letters to stand for numbers. You don't go to the grocery store to buy x eggs or y gallons of milk. Most people think about math in terms of numbers, not letters that stand for numbers.

You should think in terms of numbers on the SAT as much as possible. On many SAT algebra questions, even very difficult ones, you will be able to find the correct answer without using any algebra at all. You will do this by working backward from the answer choices instead of trying to solve the problem using your standard math-class methods.

Plugging In the Answers is a technique for solving word problems in which the answer choices are all numbers. Using this powerful technique can solve many algebra problems on the SAT simply and quickly.

In algebra class at school, you solve word problems by using equations. Then, you check your solution by plugging in your answer to see if it works. Why not skip the equations entirely by simply checking the four possible solutions on the multiple-choice questions? One of these is the correct answer. You don't have to do any algebra, you will seldom have to try more than two choices, and you will never have to try all four. Note that you can use this technique only for questions that ask for a specific amount.

Here's an example.

Here's an example of using PITA instead of writing equations.

9

Zoë won the raffle at a fair. She will receive the prize money in 5 monthly payments. If each payment is half as much as the previous month's payment and the total of the payments is $496, what is the amount of the first payment?

A) $256

B) $96

C) $84

D) $16

Watch Us
Crack It

Here's How to Crack It

The question asks for the amount of Zoë's first prize payment. The test-writers would like you to go through all of the effort of setting up this equation:

$$p + \frac{1}{2}p + \frac{1}{4}p + \frac{1}{8}p + \frac{1}{16}p = 496$$

Representation
Make sure you know what the numbers in the answer choices represent. Be sure to label them!

Then, of course, they want you to solve the equation. But, look at all those fractions! There are plenty of opportunities to make a mistake, and you can bet that the test-writers have figured most of them out so they can have a trap answer waiting. So, let's work with the answers instead.

To work with the answer choices, first you need to know what they represent so that you can label them. In this case, the question asks for the first payment, so write something like "first payment" over the answers.

Now, it's time to start working the steps of the problem. But first, notice that the answer choices are in numerically descending order. The SAT test-writers like to keep their questions organized so they will always put the answers in order. You can use that to your advantage by starting with one of the middle answer choices. First try (C).

Grab (C) and ask yourself, "If the first payment is $84, what's the next thing I can figure out?" In this case, you could figure out the second payment.

So, make a chart and write down 42 (half of 84) next to the 84. Keep doing that to find the values of the third, fourth, and fifth payments. When you have worked all the steps, your problem should look like this:

9

Zoë won the raffle at a fair. She will receive the prize money in 5 monthly payments. If each payment is half as much as the previous month's payment and the total of the payments is $496, what is the amount of the first payment?

	1st Payment	2nd Payment	3rd Payment	4th Payment	5th Payment
(A)	$256				
(B)	$96				
(C)	$84	42	21	10.50	5.25
(D)	$16				

You need to determine if that is the correct answer. The question says that the total is supposed to be $496, so add up the payments: 84 + 42 + 21 + 10.50 + 5.25 = 162.75, which is much smaller than 496. So, cross off (C) and (D), because (D) will result in an even smaller number.

Now, all you need to do is try (B). If (B) works, then you're done. And, if (B) doesn't work, you're still done because the answer must be (A). That's putting your POE to good use! If the first payment is $96, then the payments are 96 + 48 + 24 + 12 + 6 = 186, which is still too small. Eliminate (B) as well. Only one answer remains, so there is no need to check it. The correct answer is (A).

Here are the steps for solving a problem using the PITA approach:

To solve a problem by plugging in the answers:

1. Label the answer choices.
2. Starting with one of the middle answer choices, work the steps of the problem. Be sure to write down a label for each new step.
3. Look for something in the question that tells you what must happen for the answer to be correct.
4. When you find the correct answer, STOP.

6

$$2x + y = 6$$
$$7x + 2y = 27$$

The system of equations above is satisfied by which of the following ordered pairs (x, y) ?

A) $(-5, 4)$

B) $(4, -2)$

C) $(5, 4)$

D) $(5, -4)$

Here's How to Crack It

The question asks for the coordinates of the point that satisfies the system of equations. When you feel the urge to do a whole lot of algebra, it is a good time to check whether it would be possible to just plug in the answers instead. In this case, trying your answer choices will be not only effective but also incredibly fast.

It doesn't seem like you will be able to tell whether to move up or down this time, as the ordered pairs don't really have an ascending or descending order, but start in the middle anyway. Even if you end up trying three of the four, you will be saving time by plugging in the answers instead of solving.

Starting with (B) gives you 4 for x and -2 for y. Try that out in the first equation: $2(4) + (-2) = 6$. That matches the first equation, so this is a possibility. Try it out in the second equation: $7(4) + 2(-2) = 24$. That does not match the second equation, so you can eliminate (B).

Try out (C) next. If $x = 5$ and $y = 4$, then $2(5) + 4 = 14$, and you wanted it to be 6, so you can eliminate this answer choice as well.

Move on to (D). That would give you $2(5) + (-4) = 6$. So far so good! Try the second equation to see if this choice satisfies both: $7(5) + 2(-4) = 27$. This works, so the correct answer is (D).

Which Way?
Sometimes, it's hard to tell if you need a larger number or a smaller number if the first answer you tried didn't work. Don't fret. Just pick a direction and go! Spend your time trying answers rather than worrying about going in the wrong direction.

You may recall that we covered questions like this in the last chapter. It is important to know how to solve these, in case a question like this comes up in one of the Grid-In sections. When you have answers available to you, though, don't be afraid to use them!

One last thing about PITA: Here's how to determine whether you should use this approach to solve a problem.

Three ways to know that it's time for PITA:

1. There are numbers in the answer choices.
2. The question asks for a specific amount, such as "what was the first payment."
3. You have the urge to write an algebraic equation to solve the problem.

Here's an example of using PITA instead of writing equations.

12

A bakery sold exactly 85% of the cupcakes it baked on Tuesday. Which of the following could be the total number of cupcakes baked on Tuesday?

A) 150

B) 145

C) 140

D) 130

Here's How to Crack It

The question asks for a possible total number of cupcakes. Is your first reaction that there isn't nearly enough information here to start on this question? That makes it a great opportunity to plug in the answers! Start with one of the middle answer choices and test it out. Sometimes, even if you can't see how a question works ahead of time, it starts to make a lot more sense once you plug real numbers into it.

Choice (B) is 145, but 145 what? Read the question very carefully. The question asks for the total number of cupcakes baked on Tuesday, so label the column of answer choices "Total."

Next, work your way through the problem. If 145 is the total number of cupcakes baked on Tuesday, the number the bakery sold on Tuesday is 85% of 145, or 123.25. Have you ever bought 0.25 cupcakes at a bakery? It would be really weird for a bakery to sell fractions of cupcakes, so this answer could not be the total number baked on Tuesday.

In this particular question, it is hard to tell whether you should try bigger or smaller numbers next, but you have learned two things from your first attempt: you can get rid of (B), and the correct answer will be the one that gives you a whole number of cupcakes. Instead of spending time trying to predict which direction to go for the answer, just get to work on the other answer choices.

Try (C) next. If the bakery baked 140 cupcakes on Tuesday, they sold 85% of 140, or 119. Is there anything wrong with selling 119 cupcakes? No! Since the bakery sold only whole cupcakes, the correct answer is (C).

Plugging In the Answers: Advanced Principles

Plugging In the Answers works the same way on difficult questions as it does on easy and medium ones. You just have to watch your step and make certain you don't make any careless mistakes.

Here's one example.

23

Mrs. Besitka is planning to give colored pencils to children at a party and has a basket containing p pencils. She will need an additional 17 pencils in order to give each child 8 colored pencils. She will have 13 pencils left over if she gives each child 6 colored pencils. How many children are at the party?

A) 4

B) 15

C) 17

D) 28

Here's How to Crack It

The question asks for the number of children at the party given different scenarios and numbers of pencils. The question asks for a specific value and there are numbers in the answers, so recognize this as a PITA question and start to plug in the answers. Start with one of the middle answers and try (C), 17. If there are 17 children, and Mrs. Besitka gives each student 8, she will need $17 \times 8 = 136$ pencils. She would need an additional 17 pencils in this scenario, meaning she currently has $136 - 17 = 119$ pencils. If each child receives 6 pencils, she needs $17 \times 6 = 102$ pencils. In this scenario, she has 13 left over, meaning she started with $102 + 13 = 115$ pencils. The total numbers of pencils that Mrs. Besitka started with in the two scenarios do not equal each other, so eliminate (C).

The totals of 119 and 115 are pretty close, so try plugging in 15 next. If there are 15 children, and Mrs. Besitka gives each student 8, she will need $15 \times 8 = 120$ pencils. Account for the extra 17 pencils she needs, and she currently has $120 - 17 = 103$ pencils. If each child receives 6 pencils, the teacher needs $15 \times 6 = 90$ pencils. Add the 13 left over, and she started with $90 + 13 = 103$ pencils. These starting totals are equal, so 15 is the number of students. The correct answer is (B).

Here's another example.

7

For what value of x is $|2x + 3| + 5 = 0$?

A) -4

B) 0

C) 4

D) There is no such value of x.

Here's How to Crack It

The question asks for the value of x. Although we covered it in the last chapter, solving algebraically on an absolute value question can be treacherous. There are so many ways to go wrong with those signs! Luckily, this absolute value question comes complete with answer choices, so we can simply plug in the answers to get a solution.

Start with (C). When you put 4 in for x, you get $|2(4) + 3| + 5 = 0$, or $16 = 0$. This is clearly not true, so cross off (C) and move on to (B). If x is 0, then the original equation becomes $|2(0) + 3| + 5 = 0$ or $8 = 0$, so you can eliminate (B) as well. Next, try (A): $|2(-4) + 3| + 5 = 0$ could be rewritten as $|-8 + 3| + 5 = 0$, or $|-5| + 5 = 0$. As long as you remember that the absolute value of a number is always positive, it is clear that this gives you $5 + 5 = 0$. Since this is also clearly untrue, eliminate (A). Apparently, there is no such value of x! The correct answer is (D).

SOLVING RATIONAL EQUATIONS

A rational equation is basically an equation in which one (or more) of the terms is a fractional one. Rational equations look scary, but there are very simple ways of solving them. One way is to factor out like terms and then cancel. All in all, the test-writers can't get too messy here, so they will keep the math nice and tidy. Try the following question.

9

$$x - 3 = \frac{5}{x - 3}$$

Which of the following is a possible value of $x - 3$ in the equation

above?

A) $\sqrt{5}$

B) 5

C) $3 + \sqrt{5}$

D) 25

Watch Us Crack It

Here's How to Crack It

The question asks for a possible value of x in an equation with fractions and binomials. You could use your skills with quadratics from the last chapter, but it's much simpler to use PITA! After all, there are numbers in the answers and the question asks for a specific value, so it sure looks like a PITA question. This approach will also avoid the issue of extraneous solutions.

Follow the PITA approach: start by labeling the answers as "$x - 3$" and then start with one of the middle answer choices. The value in (C) looks complicated, so start with (B), 5. When $x - 3 = 5$, the equation becomes

$$5 = \frac{5}{5} \text{ or } 5 = 1$$

This is not true, so eliminate (B). Plugging in 25 would make the fraction too small, so ballpark out (D). Try the next simplest answer, (A). When $x - 3 = \sqrt{5}$, the equation becomes

$$\sqrt{5} = \frac{5}{\sqrt{5}}$$

Multiply both sides by $\sqrt{5}$ to get $5 = 5$, or use your calculator to find out that the two sides are equal. This makes the equation accurate, so $\sqrt{5}$ is a possible value of $x - 3$. The correct answer is (A).

SOLVING RADICAL EQUATIONS

We covered this topic in the previous chapter, but here's another example of solving radical equations with PITA.

11

$$\sqrt{2x - k} = 3 - x$$

If $k = 3$, what is the solution set of the equation above?

A) $\{-2\}$

B) $\{2\}$

C) $\{2, 6\}$

D) $\{6\}$

Here's How to Crack It

The question asks for a solution set, which is just a fancy way of asking for all possible values of x. In the last chapter, we showed you how to solve these—a necessary skill if there are no answer choices to plug in. Here, using PITA is definitely the way to go, as it will allow you to sidestep any extraneous solutions. Start by plugging in the value given for k, which is 3. The equation becomes $\sqrt{2x - 3} = 3 - x$.

Now pick a value for x from the answer choices and plug it into the equation to see if it works. Rather than starting with a specific answer choice, start with a number that appears more than once in the answers, such as $x = 2$. The equation becomes $\sqrt{2(2) - 3} = 3 - 2$, then $\sqrt{4 - 3} = 1$, and $1 = 1$. That's true, so eliminate (A) and (D), which don't include 2.

Try it again with $x = 6$ to see if the correct answer is (B) or (C). You get $\sqrt{2(6) - 3} = 3 - 6$ or $\sqrt{12 - 3} = -3$. This doesn't work, so eliminate (C). The correct answer is (B).

PLUGGING IN YOUR OWN NUMBERS

Plugging In the Answers enables you to find the answer to questions whose answer choices are all numbers. What about questions that have answer choices containing variables? On these questions, you will usually be able to find the answer by plugging in your own numbers.

> Plugging In is easy. It has three steps:
>
> 1. Pick numbers for the variables in the question.
> 2. Use your numbers to find an answer to the questions. Circle your answer.
> 3. Plug your number(s) for the variable(s) into the answer choices and eliminate choices that don't equal the answer you found in Step 2.

The Basics of Plugging In Your Own Numbers

This sort of Plugging In is simple to understand. Here's an example.

13

Which of the following is equivalent to the expression $\frac{7x-4}{x+9}$?

A) $7 - \dfrac{4}{x+9}$

B) $7 - \dfrac{67}{x+9}$

C) $7 - \dfrac{4}{9}$

D) $\dfrac{7-4}{9}$

Get Real

Trying to imagine how numbers behave in the abstract is a waste of time. So, if the question says that Tina is *x* years old, why not plug in your own age? That's real enough. You don't have to change your name to Tina.

Here's How to Crack It

The question asks for an expression that is equivalent to the one given. Rather than do complicated algebra, try plugging in. First, pick a number for x. Pick something easy to work with, like 2. In your test booklet, write $x = 2$, so you won't forget. If $x = 2$, then $7x - 4 = 10$, and $x + 9 = 11$. So, when $x = 2$, the expression in the question equals $\frac{10}{11}$. Circle it! That is your target answer. When you find the answer choice that also gives you $\frac{10}{11}$ when you plug in $x = 2$, you will know you have found an equivalent expression.

Start with the easier answer choices: (C) and (D). For (C), does $7 - \frac{4}{9} = \frac{10}{11}$? No! Eliminate it and move on to (D): $\frac{7-4}{9}$ also does not equal your target answer, so it cannot be an equivalent expression.

Now try (B). When you put in 2 for x, you get $7 - \frac{67}{2+9} = 7 - \frac{67}{11} = \frac{77}{11} - \frac{67}{11} = \frac{10}{11}$. This is the number that you are looking for. Unlike using PITA, when you plug in your own numbers, you must check all four answer choices, just in case more than one works. Go ahead and try the last answer just to make sure that you're right. Choice (A) does not give you your target answer. The correct answer is (B).

Here's another example.

19

During a special sale at a furniture store, Erica bought a floor lamp at a 10% discount. She paid a total of t dollars, which included the discounted price of the floor lamp and a 6% sales tax on the discounted price. In terms of t, what was the original price of the floor lamp?

A) $\dfrac{t}{0.96}$

B) $(0.9)(1.06)t$

C) $\dfrac{t}{(0.9)(1.06)}$

D) $0.96t$

Here's How to Crack It

The question asks for an expression to represent the situation. This could be a pretty tricky algebra question, but if you read the question carefully and plug in easy numbers, it will be a breeze.

Start at the beginning. When Erica bought that floor lamp on sale, what did you really wish you knew? It would be very helpful to start this problem knowing the original price of the floor lamp. So, start plugging in there. Plug in a number that you know how to take a percentage of, like 100. Write down "original = 100" and move on the next step of the problem. Erica got a 10% discount, so take 10% of the original price. That means she got a $10 discount, and the discounted price of her floor lamp was $90. Write that down and move on to the sales tax. If you read carefully, it is clear that the sales tax is 6% of the discounted price. So, you need to take 6% of the $90 discounted price, or $5.40. To get her total, add the $5.40 of tax to the $90 for the discounted floor lamp, and you get $95.40. This is where the careful reading comes in. The variable t in this question is supposed to be the total amount she paid, so make sure that you label this "t = $95.40."

Next, read the last sentence of the question again to be sure you know which of the answers is your target answer. The question asks for the original price of the floor lamp, so circle the number you plugged in for the original price. Your target answer is 100.

On to the answer choices! When you put $95.40 in for t in (A), you get 99.375. This is not your target answer, so you can eliminate (A). Choice (B) gives you 91.0116, so that will not work either. Plugging in $95.40 into (C) yields the target of 100, so hang on to it while you check (D) just in case. When you plug in for (D), you get 91.584. Since that does not match your target, you can eliminate (D). The correct answer is (C).

Be Good

"Good" numbers make a problem less confusing by simplifying the arithmetic. This is your chance to make the SAT easier for you.

Which Numbers?

Although you can plug in any number, you can make your life much easier by plugging in "good" numbers—numbers that are simple to work with or that make the problem easier to manipulate. Picking a small number, such as 2, will usually make finding the answer easier. If the question asks for a percentage, plug in 100. If the question has to do with minutes, try 30 or 120.

Except in special cases, you should avoid plugging in 0 and 1; these numbers have weird properties. Using them may allow you to eliminate only one or two choices at a time. You should also avoid plugging in any number that appears in the question or in any of the answer choices. Using those numbers could make more than one answer match your target. If more than one answer choice matches your target, plug in a new number and check those answer choices. You may have to plug in more than once to eliminate all three incorrect answers.

Many times you'll find that there is an advantage to picking a particular number, even a very large one, because it makes solving the problem more straightforward.

Here's an example.

14

If 60 equally priced downloads cost *x* dollars, then how much do 9 downloads cost?

A) $\dfrac{20}{3x}$

B) $\dfrac{20x}{3}$

C) $60x + 9$

D) $\dfrac{3x}{20}$

Here's How to Crack It

The question asks for the cost of 9 downloads. Since the question is asking you to arrive at a number (how much 9 downloads cost) in terms of variable x, try plugging in. Should you plug in 2 for x? You could, but plugging in 120 would make the math easier. After all, if 60 downloads cost a total of \$120, then each download costs \$2. Write $x = 120$ in your test booklet.

If each download costs \$2, then 9 downloads cost \$18. Write an 18 in your test booklet and circle it. You are looking for the answer choice that works out to 18 when you plug in \$120 for x. Try each choice:

A) $\dfrac{20}{3(120)} \neq 18$

B) $\dfrac{20(120)}{3} \neq 18$

C) $60(120) + 9 \neq 18$

D) $\dfrac{3(120)}{20} = 18$

That last one matches the target answer, so the correct answer is (D).

───────────◯───────────

Let's try another example.

───────────◯───────────

20

A watch loses x minutes every y hours. At this rate, how many <u>hours</u> will the watch lose in one week?

A) $7xy$

B) $\dfrac{5y}{2x}$

C) $\dfrac{14y}{5x}$

D) $\dfrac{14x}{5y}$

Here's How to Crack It

The question asks for the number of hours lost in one week and gives information about minutes. This is an extremely difficult question for students who try to solve it using math-class algebra. You'll be able to find the answer easily, though, if you plug in carefully.

What numbers should you plug in? As always, you can plug in anything. However, if you think just a little bit before choosing the numbers, you can make the question easier to understand. There are three units of time—minutes, hours, and weeks—and that's a big part of the reason this question is hard to understand. If you choose units of time that are easy to think about, you'll make the question easier to handle.

Start by choosing a value for x, which represents the number of minutes that the watch loses. You might be tempted to choose $x = 60$ and that would make the math pretty easy. However, it's usually not a good idea to choose a conversion factor such as 60, the conversion factor between minutes and hours, for plugging in. When a question deals with time, 30 is usually a safer choice. So, write down $x = 30$.

Next, you need a number for y, which represents the number of hours. Again, you might be tempted to use $y = 24$, but that's the conversion factor between hours and days. Therefore, $y = 12$ is a safer choice. Write down $y = 12$.

Now, it's time to solve the problem to come up with a target. If the watch loses 30 minutes every 12 hours, then it loses 60 minutes every 24 hours. Put another way, the watch loses an hour each day. In one week, the watch will lose 7 hours. That's your target, so be sure to circle it.

Now, you just need to check the answer choices to see which one gives you 7 when $x = 30$ and $y = 12$.

A) $7xy = 7(30)(12) =$ Something too big! Cross it off.

B) $\dfrac{5y}{2x} = \dfrac{5(12)}{2(30)} = \dfrac{60}{60} = 1$. Also wrong.

C) $\dfrac{14y}{5x} = \dfrac{14(12)}{5(30)} = \dfrac{168}{150} = \dfrac{28}{25}$. Cross it off.

D) $\dfrac{14x}{5y} = \dfrac{14(30)}{5(12)} = \dfrac{420}{60} = 7$. Choose it!

The correct answer is (D).

Inequalities

Plugging In works on questions containing inequalities, but you will have to follow some different rules. Plugging in one number is often not enough; let's look at an example in which this is the case.

6

Mammoth Printing Company charges a fee of $28 to print an oversized poster, and $7 for each color of ink used in the poster. Colossal Printing charges a fee of $34 to print an oversized poster and $5.50 for each color of ink used. If x represents the number of colors of ink used to print a poster, what are all the values of x for which Mammoth Printing Company would charge more to print the poster than Colossal Printing?

A) $x < 4$

B) $2 \leq x \leq 4$

C) $4 \leq x \leq 7$

D) $x > 4$

Here's How to Crack It

The question asks for the values of x that satisfy the situation. Since you are looking for an amount that would make the Mammoth Printing Company's price *greater than* Colossal Printing's price, you have an inequality.

Using Plugging In on an inequality question means selecting a value for x that answers the question, and then comparing it to the inequalities in the answer choices. You may have to try more than one number with inequality questions, since the number you try first may satisfy the inequality in more than one answer choice!

Start out by trying a small number, like $x = 2$. Since x is the number of colors of ink used, Mammoth Printing Company would charge $28 to print the poster, plus $7 for each of the 2 colors, for a total of $42. Colossal Printing would charge $34 to print the poster, plus $5.50 for each of the 2 colors, or $45 total. That means that when $x = 2$, Mammoth Printing Company would charge less than Colossal Printing, and 2 is not a number that works as a solution to this problem.

Try a bigger number, such as $x = 5$. If the poster had 5 colors, Mammoth Printing Company would charge $28 to print the poster, plus $7 for each of the 5 colors, for a total of $63. Colossal Printing would charge $34 to print the poster, plus $5.50 for each of the 5 colors, or $61.50 total. That means that when $x = 5$, the price Mammoth charges would be more than Colossal's price, so this is a possible value for x.

Once you have a value for *x* that satisfies the question, it's time to move to the answer choices. You should eliminate (A) and (B), because *x* = 5 does not satisfy either of those inequalities. Choices (C) and (D) are satisfied when *x* = 5, so they are still possible.

Next, you need to find a number that will satisfy the inequality in one of the remaining answer choices but not the other, so you can determine whether (C) or (D) is your final answer. Looking at the answer choices, you can see that you will have to think about plugging in a number that will eliminate one answer choice but not the other. Try out *x* = 4, because it satisfies (C) but not (D). Mammoth Printing Company would charge $56 for a 4-color poster.

$$\$28 + \$7(4) = \$56$$

Colossal Printing would also charge $56 for a 4-color poster.

$$\$34 + \$5.50(4) = \$56$$

Since Mammoth would not charge more to print the poster than Colossal, you can eliminate (C). The correct answer is (D).

Weird Numbers
As you may have noticed, some numbers have uncommon properties. Because of this, you should plug them in only under certain circumstances, like solving inequalities, for example.

Using different integers got you down to one answer choice on that question. Sometimes, to find the answer, you may have to plug in several numbers, including weird numbers like –1, 0, 1, $\frac{1}{2}$, and $-\frac{1}{2}$.

The five numbers just mentioned all have special properties. Negatives, fractions, 0, and 1 all behave in peculiar ways when, for example, they are squared. Don't forget about them!

Plugging In: Advanced Principles

If there are variables in the answer choices, you should definitely consider plugging in. However, sometimes a question will be a Plug In question that doesn't have variables in the answer choices. It is, instead, a Hidden Plug In question. It will refer to some unknown amount, but never actually give you a number. So, you're going to have to make up your own number.

Here's an example.

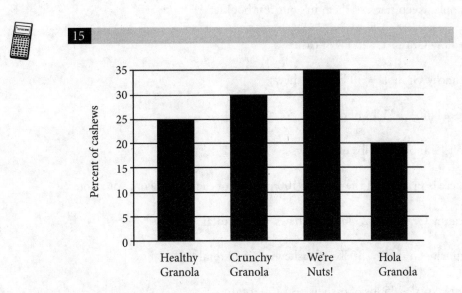

15

Vik is deciding which brand of granola to buy. He prefers granola with a lot of cashews, so he has made a chart (above) showing the cashew content, as a percentage of the total weight of the granola, of each of the 4 leading brands of bulk granola. If Healthy Granola costs $4 a pound, Crunchy Granola costs $5.40 a pound, We're Nuts! Granola costs $7.00 a pound, and Hola Granola costs $5 a pound, which brand of granola would offer Vik the greatest amount of cashews per dollar?

A)   Healthy Granola

B)   Crunchy Granola

C)   We're Nuts!

D)   Hola Granola

Here's How to Crack It

The question asks for the granola brand that has the greatest amount of cashews per dollar. This is one of those questions that has so much information in it, it is almost impossible to know where to start. It doesn't help that all the amounts are percentages, and you don't even know the total amount of granola Vik is going to buy. That feeling that you wish you had some real amount to start with tells you that this is a great opportunity to use Pluging In, even though there are no variables in the answer choices. This is a Hidden Plug In.

You have already realized that the most helpful thing to know here would be how much granola Vik will buy, so start by plugging in for that amount. The easiest number to plug in when you will be using percentages is 100, so even though it is a pretty ridiculous amount of granola for one guy, find out what happens if Vik buys 100 pounds of granola. Write down "total = 100 pounds" in your test booklet, and start to work the problem one piece at a time.

Once you have a 100 pound total, it is relatively simple to come up with the amount of cashews in each granola. Keep track of them in your test booklet:

100 lbs Healthy Granola = 25 lbs of cashews

100 lbs Crunchy Granola = 30 lbs of cashews

100 lbs We're Nuts! = 35 lbs of cashews

100 lbs Hola Granola = 20 lbs of cashews

The next piece is price. Add the price of 100 pounds of each granola to your notes:

100 lbs Healthy Granola = 25 lbs of cashews = $400 total

100 lbs Crunchy Granola = 30 lbs of cashews = $540 total

100 lbs We're Nuts! = 35 lbs of cashews = $700 total

100 lbs Hola Granola = 20 lbs of cashews = $500 total

With this information, you can start to figure out how much Vik is paying per pound of cashews.

Healthy Granola contains 25 lbs of cashews for $400. If you do the math, that is $400 ÷ 25 lbs cashews or $16 per pound of cashews. Crunchy Granola costs $540 for 30 lbs of cashews or $540 ÷ 30 lbs cashews = $18/lb cashews. Since this is more expensive, you can eliminate (B). This is not how Vik is going to get the greatest amount of cashews per dollar. We're Nuts!, besides having a great name, also has a really high percentage of cashews. You might think that would be Vik's best buy, but when you do the math, $700 for 35 lbs of cashews is $700 ÷ 35 lbs cashews or $20/lb cashews. This is less cashew per dollar than (A), so eliminate (C). Hola Granola costs $500 for 20 lbs of cashews, and $500 ÷ 20 lbs cashews is going to come out to a whopping $25/lb cashews. That is definitely not the best deal on cashews, so eliminate (D).

The correct answer is (A).

MEANING IN CONTEXT

Some questions, instead of asking you to come up with an equation, just want you to recognize what a part of the equation stands for. It sounds like a simple enough task, but when you look at the equation, the test-writers have made it really hard to see what is going on. For this reason, meaning-in-context questions are a great opportunity to plug in real numbers and start to see how the equation really works!

First things first, though, you want to think about your POOD. Does this question fit into your pacing goals? It might take a bit of legwork to get an answer, and you may need that time to go collect points on easier, quicker questions.

If this question does fit into your pacing plan, you should read carefully, label everything you can in the equation, and use POE to get rid of any answer choices that are clearly on the wrong track. Then, it's time to plug some of your own numbers in to see what is going on in there.

Here's an example.

7

$$n = 1{,}273 - 4p$$

The equation above was used by the cafeteria in a large public high school to model the relationship between the number of slices of pizza, *n*, sold daily and the price of a slice of pizza, *p*, in dollars. What does the number 4 represent in this equation?

A) For every $4 the price of pizza decreases, the cafeteria sells 1 more slice of pizza.

B) For every dollar the price of pizza decreases, the cafeteria sells 4 more slices of pizza.

C) For every $4 the price of pizza increases, the cafeteria sells 1 more slice of pizza.

D) For every dollar the price of pizza increases, the cafeteria sells 4 more slices of pizza.

Here's How to Crack It

The question asks for the meaning of the number 4 in the context of the situation. First, read the question very carefully, and use your pencil to label the variables. You know that *p* is the price of pizza, and *n* is the number of slices, so you can add that information to the equation. If you can, eliminate answer choices that don't make sense. But what if you can't eliminate anything, or you can eliminate only an answer choice or two?

Even with everything labeled, this equation is difficult to decode, so it's time to plug in! Try a few of your own numbers in the equation, and you will get a much better understanding of what is happening.

Try it out with *p* = 2. When you put 2 in for *p*, *n* = 1,273 – 4(2) or 1,265.

So, when *p* = 2, *n* = 1,265. In other words, at $2 a slice, the cafeteria sells 1,265 slices.

When *p* = 3, *n* = 1,261, so at $3 a slice, the cafeteria sells 1,261 slices.

When *p* = 4, *n* = 1,257, so at $4 a slice, the cafeteria sells 1,257 slices.

Now, use POE. First of all, is the cafeteria selling more pizza as the price goes up? No, as the price of pizza goes up, the cafeteria sells fewer slices of pizza. That means you can eliminate (C) and (D).

Choice (A) says that for every $4 the price goes down, the cafeteria sells 1 more slice of pizza. Does your plugging in back that up? No. The cafeteria sells 8 more slices of pizza when the price drops from $4 to $2, so (A) is no good.

Now take a look at (B). Does the cafeteria sell 4 more slices of pizza for every dollar the price drops? Yes! The correct answer is (B).

Here are the steps for using Plugging In to solve meaning-in-context questions:

Meaning in Context

1. Read the question carefully. Make sure you know which part of the equation you are being asked to identify.
2. Use your pencil to label the parts of the equation you can identify.
3. Eliminate any answer choices that clearly describe the wrong part of the equation, or go against what you have labeled.
4. Plug in! Use your own numbers to start seeing what is happening in the equation.
5. Use POE again, using the information you learned from plugging in real numbers, until you can get it down to one answer choice. Or get it down to as few choices as you can, and guess.

Let's look at a slightly different one now.

10

$$7x + y = 133$$

Jeffrey has set a monthly budget for purchasing frozen blended mocha drinks from his local SpendBucks coffee shop. The equation above can be used to model the amount of his budget, y, in dollars that remains after buying coffee for x days in a month. What does it mean that (19, 0) is a solution to this equation?

A) Jeffrey starts the month with a budget of $19.

B) Jeffrey spends $19 on coffee every day.

C) It takes 19 days for Jeffrey to drink 133 cups of coffee.

D) It takes 19 days for Jeffrey to run out of money in his budget for purchasing coffee.

Here's How to Crack It

The question asks about a point that is the solution to an equation in the context of the situation. Start by labeling the x and the y in the equation to keep track of what they stand for. Use your pencil to write "days" above the x and "budget" above the y. So 7 × days + budget = 133. Hmm, still not very clear, is it? One way to approach this is to plug in the point. If x = days = 19 when y = budget = 0, then Jeffrey will have no budget left after 19 days. This matches (D).

If you have trouble seeing this, you can use the answer choices to help you plug in. If (A) is true, the budget at the start of the month, when days = 0, is \$19. Plug these values into the equation to see if it is true. Is 7 × 0 + 19 = 133? Not at all, so eliminate (A). If (B) is true, Jeffrey drinks a lot of coffee! Try some numbers and see if it works. For x = 1, the equation becomes 7(1) + y = 133 or y = 126, and for x = 2, it is 7(2) + y = 133 or y = 119. The difference in y, the budget remaining, is 126 − 119 = 7, so that's not \$19 per day. Eliminate (B) so only (C) and (D) remain. These both have 19 for the number of days, and the point (19, 0) would indicate that 19 is the x-value, or days. If you saw that right away—great! That would allow you to skip right to testing (C) and (D).

For (C), you can plug in 19 for days in the equation to get 7 × 19 + budget = 133, or budget = 0. Does that tell you how many cups of coffee Jeffrey drank? You have no information about the cost of a single cup of coffee, so the answer can't be (C). It does tell you, however, that after 19 days, Jeffrey has no budget left. The correct answer is (D).

SAT Algebra Strategies Drill 1: No Calculator Section

Work these algebra questions without your calculator, using Plugging In or PITA. Answers and explanations can be found on page 383.

5

The length of a certain rectangle is twice the width. If the area of the rectangle is 128, what is the length of the rectangle?

A) 4

B) 8

C) 16

D) $21\dfrac{1}{3}$

10

If $xy < 0$, which of the following must be true?

   I. $x + y = 0$

  II. $2y - 2x < 0$

 III. $x^2 + y^2 > 0$

A) I only

B) III only

C) I and III

D) II and III

13

If $\dfrac{\sqrt{x}}{2} = 2\sqrt{2}$, what is the value of x ?

A) 4

B) 16

C) $16\sqrt{2}$

D) 32

15

If $y = 3^x$ and x and y are both integers, which of the following is equivalent to $9^x + 3^{x+1}$?

A) y^3

B) $3y + 3$

C) $y(y + 3)$

D) $y^2 + 3$

SAT Algebra Strategies Drill 2: Calculator-Permitted Section

Feel free to use your calculator as needed to apply the Plugging In skills you've learned so far. Answers and explanations can be found on page 384.

8

If Alex can fold 12 napkins in x minutes, how many napkins can he fold in y <u>hours</u>?

A) $\dfrac{720}{xy}$

B) $\dfrac{xy}{720}$

C) $\dfrac{720y}{x}$

D) $\dfrac{720x}{y}$

12

Nails are sold in 8-ounce and 20-ounce boxes. If 50 boxes of nails were sold and the total weight of the nails sold was less than 600 ounces, what is the greatest possible number of 20-ounce boxes that could have been sold?

A) 33

B) 25

C) 17

D) 16

18

If a is 63% of x and c is $\dfrac{3}{8}$ of x, which of the following is the closest to the ratio of a to c ?

A) 0.236

B) 0.381

C) 0.595

D) 1.680

21

If $c = \dfrac{1}{x} + \dfrac{1}{y}$ and $x > y > 0$, then which of the following is equal to $\dfrac{1}{c}$?

A) $x + y$

B) $x - y$

C) $\dfrac{x + y}{xy}$

D) $\dfrac{xy}{x + y}$

24

A gas station sells regular gasoline for $2.39 per gallon and premium gasoline for $2.79 per gallon. If the gas station sold a total of 550 gallons of both types of gasoline in one day for a total of $1,344.50, how many gallons of premium gasoline were sold?

A)   25

B)   75

C)   175

D)   475

25

There are k gallons of gasoline available to fill a tank. After d gallons have been pumped, in terms of k and d, what percent of the gasoline has been pumped?

A) $\dfrac{100d}{k}\%$

B) $\dfrac{k}{100d}\%$

C) $\dfrac{100k}{d}\%$

D) $\dfrac{100(k-d)}{k}\%$

CHAPTER DRILL ANSWERS AND EXPLANATIONS

SAT Algebra Strategies Drill 1: No Calculator Section

5. **C** The question asks for the length of the rectangle. This is a specific value, and there are numbers in the answer choices, so plug in the answers. If you start with (B), the length is 8, and the width is half that, or 4. Area is length × width. The area of this rectangle is 8 × 4, which is nowhere near 128. Eliminate (A) and (B), as both are too small. Try (C). If the length is 16, the width is 8. So, does 128 = 16 × 8? You could write it all out, since you can't use your calculator, but you can also estimate. 16 × 10 = 160, so 16 × 8 would be about 130. The number in (D) is too large and will give a weird fraction. The correct answer is (C).

10. **B** The question asks which statements must be true. A question with unknown variables indicates a good place to plug in. You need numbers for x and y that will give you a negative product. Try $x = 1$ and $y = -2$. If you plug these into the statements in the Roman numerals, you find that (I) is false, but (II) and (III) are true. You can eliminate any answer choice that contains (I). This leaves (B) and (D). Now try different numbers to see if you can eliminate another choice. If you try $x = -1$ and $y = 2$, you find that (II) is false and (III) is still true. The correct answer is (B).

13. **D** The question asks for the value of x. This is a specific amount, and there are numbers in the answer choices, so plug in the answers, starting with (B). If $x = 16$, the left side of the equation is $\frac{\sqrt{16}}{2} = \frac{4}{2} = 2$. Does that equal $2\sqrt{2}$? No—it's too small. Choice (C) is ugly to work with, so try (D) next. If it is too big, (C) is your answer. For (D), $x = 32$, and the left side of the equation becomes $\frac{\sqrt{32}}{2} = \frac{\sqrt{16 \times 2}}{2} = \frac{4\sqrt{2}}{2} = 2\sqrt{2}$. It's a match. The correct answer is (D).

15. **C** The question asks for an expression that is equivalent to the given one. There are variables in the answer choices, which means this is a perfect question to use Plugging In. Since you can't use a calculator, make up an easy value for x, such as 2. Therefore, $9^x + 3^{x+1}$ becomes $9^2 + 3^{2+1} = 81 + 27 = 108$. Use the number you plugged in for x to find y: $y = 3^x$, so $y = 3^2 = 9$. Now plug in $y = 9$ to each answer choice to see which one gives you 108. Choice (C) is $y(y + 3)$, which is $9(12) = 108$ and the only answer that matches the target. The correct answer is (C).

SAT Algebra Strategies Drill 2: Calculator-Permitted Section

8. **C** The question asks for the number of napkins that can be folded in y hours. Two variables tells you this is a great place to plug in. Pick numbers that make the math easy. You can try $x = 30$ and $y = 2$. So in 2 hours there are 4 periods of 30 minutes each: $12 \times 4 = 48$. Alex can fold 48 napkins in 2 hours, so 48 is your target. Plug the values for x and y into the answer choices to see which one matches the target. Only (C) works, so the correct answer is (C).

12. **D** The question asks for the greatest possible number of 20-ounce boxes. Because this is a specific amount and there are numbers in the answer choices, this is a perfect opportunity to use PITA. Start with (B). If there are twenty-five 20-ounce boxes, then there are twenty-five 8-ounce boxes because a total of 50 boxes was purchased. In this case, the twenty-five 20-ounce boxes weigh 500 ounces, and the twenty-five 8-ounce boxes weigh 200 ounces; the total is 700 ounces. This is too big because the question says the total weight was less than 600. If (B) is too big, (A) must also be too big; eliminate both answers. If you try (C), the total weight is 604 ounces, which is still too big. Thus, the correct answer is (D).

18. **D** The question asks for the ratio of a to c and defines both in terms of x. Since you are never told what x is, and there is no way to find it, plug in for x. Say that $x = 100$. Then, 63% of 100 is 63, and $\frac{3}{8}$ of 100 is 37.5. The ratio of a to c is $\frac{a}{c}$. So, $\frac{63}{37.5} = 1.68$. To save time, you can ballpark the answer, since $a > c$ and (D) is the only choice greater than 1. The correct answer is (D).

21. **D** The question asks for the value of $\frac{1}{c}$. Here's yet another chance to plug in because of the variables in the answer choices. In this case, you have several variables. You should start by plugging in values for x and y, and then work out c. Because $x > y > 0$, say $x = 6$ and $y = 3$. There-fore, $c = \frac{1}{6} + \frac{1}{3} = \frac{1}{6} + \frac{2}{6} = \frac{3}{6} = \frac{1}{2}$. Now that you have the value of c, find the value of $\frac{1}{c}$, which is the reciprocal of $\frac{1}{2}$, or 2. This is your target answer. If you plug $x = 6$ and $y = 3$ into all of the answer choices, you'll find that only (D) equals 2. The correct answer is (D).

24. **B** The question asks for the number of gallons of premium gasoline that were sold. When asked for a specific value, try plugging in the answers. Label them as gallons of premium and start with the value in (B). If 75 gallons of premium were sold, the station would make $75(\$2.79) = \$209.25$ for those sales. A total of 550 gallons was sold, so the station would have sold $550 - 75 = 475$ gallons of regular gasoline. The sales for the regular gasoline would be $475(\$2.39) = \$1,135.25$. The total sales for both types of gasoline would be $\$209.25 + \$1,135.25 = \$1,344.50$. That matches the information in the question, so the correct answer is (B).

25. **A** The question asks for the percent of the gasoline that has been pumped. There are variables in the answer choices, so plug in. This is a percent question, so make $k = 100$ and $d = 40$. If 40 out of the 100 gallons have been pumped, that equals 40%. So 40% is your target answer. When you plug $k = 100$ and $d = 40$ into the answers, only (A) gives you 40, so the correct answer is (A). Remember, Plugging In can turn a difficult question into a much more straightforward one.

Summary

o   When an algebra question asks for a specific amount and has numbers in the answer choices, plug each of the answer choices into the problem until you find one that works.

o   If you start with one of the middle numbers, you may be able to cut your work. The answer choices will be in order, so if your number is too high or too low, you'll know what to eliminate.

o   When the question has variables in the answer choices, you can often plug in your own amounts for the unknowns and do arithmetic instead of algebra.

o   When you plug in, use "good" numbers—ones that are simple to work with and that make the problem easier to manipulate: 2, 5, 10, or 100 are generally easy numbers to use.

o   Plugging In works on questions containing inequalities, but you will have to be careful and follow some different rules. Plugging in one number is often not enough; to find the answer, you may have to plug in several numbers.

o   Not every Plug In question has variables in the answer choices. For some questions, there will be some unknown amount. In that case, try making up a number.

o   Plugging In can also be used on meaning-in-context questions. If a question asks you to identify a part of an equation, plug your own amounts into the equation so you can start to see what is going on.

Chapter 17
Advanced
Arithmetic

Now that we have reviewed some mathematical fundamentals and some algebra, it is time to jump into our review of the more advanced arithmetic concepts you will find on the SAT. Many questions on the Math sections test concepts you learned in junior high school, such as averages and proportions. Some difficult questions build on these basic concepts by requiring you to use charts and data to obtain your numbers or to combine multiple techniques. In this chapter, we will review the arithmetic concepts you'll need to know for the SAT and show you how to apply these concepts when working with charts and data. *All of the questions in this chapter represent the kinds of questions that appear in the calculator-permitted section of the test.*

RATIOS AND PROPORTIONS

A Ratio Is a Comparison

Many students get extremely nervous when they are asked to work with ratios. But there's no need to be nervous. A **ratio** is a comparison between the quantities of ingredients you have in a mixture, be it a class full of people or a bowl of cake batter. Ratios can be written to look like fractions—don't get them confused.

The ratio of *x* to *y* can be expressed in the following three ways:

> 1. $\dfrac{x}{y}$
>
> 2. the ratio of *x* to *y*
>
> 3. *x*:*y*

Part, Part, Whole

Ratios are a lot like fractions. In fact, anything you can do to a fraction (convert it to a decimal or percentage, reduce it, and so on), you can do to a ratio. The difference is that a fraction gives you a part (the top number) over a whole (the bottom number), while a ratio typically gives you two parts (boys to girls, cars to trucks, sugar to flour), and it is your job to come up with the whole. For example, if there is one cup of sugar for every two cups of flour in a recipe, that's three cups of stuff. The ratio of sugar to flour is 1:2. Add the parts to get the whole.

Ratios vs. Fractions
Keep in mind that a ratio compares part of something to another part. A fraction compares part of something to the whole thing.

Ratio: $\dfrac{\text{part}}{\text{part}}$

Fraction: $\dfrac{\text{part}}{\text{whole}}$

Ratio to Real

If a class contains 3 students and the ratio of boys to girls in that class is 2:1, how many boys and how many girls are there in the class? Of course, there are 2 boys and 1 girl.

Now, suppose a class contains 24 students and the ratio of boys to girls is still 2:1. How many boys and how many girls are there in the class? This is a little harder, but the answer is easy to find if you think about it. There are 16 boys and 8 girls.

How did we get the answer? We added up the number of "parts" in the ratio (2 parts boys plus 1 part girls, or 3 parts all together) and divided it into the total number of students. In other words, we divided 24 by 3. This told us that the class contained 3 equal parts of 8 students each. From the given ratio (2:1), we knew that two of these parts consisted of boys and one of them consisted of girls.

The test-writers will often combine ratios with diagrams or data from charts and graphs. Don't let them intimidate you with these: just work in bite-sized pieces and write down the part-to-part relationships that you need to solve the question.

Try this example.

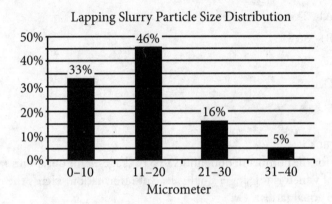

Lapping Slurry Particle Size Distribution

A lapping slurry contains microbeads suspended in a solution and is used to polish a silicon wafer by abrasion of the surface. The distribution of the particle size, in micrometers, is shown above. If the particle size distribution ranges were changed to 0–20 micrometers and 21–40 micrometers, which of the following is the closest to the ratio of the number of 0–20 micrometer microbeads to the number of 21–40 micrometer microbeads?

A) 3:1

B) 4:1

C) 5:2

D) 9:1

Here's How to Crack It

The question asks for the ratio of 0–20 micrometer microbeads to 21–40 micrometer micro-beads. Read carefully, look up the right information in the graph, and set up the part-to-part relationship. To create the new ranges, add the percentages for the 0–10 and 11–20 ranges. This means that 33% + 46% = 79% of the particles are in the 0–20 micrometer range. Do the same thing with the 21–30 and 31–40 ranges to find that 16% + 5% = 21% of the particles are in the 21–40 micrometer range. That is a ratio of 79:21. Because the question is asking for the closest ratio, round the numbers to get a ratio of 80:20, or 4:1. The correct answer is (B).

Proportions Are Equal Ratios

Some SAT math questions will contain two proportional, or equal, ratios from which one piece of information is missing.

Here's an example.

5

If 2 packages contain a total of 12 doughnuts, how many doughnuts are there in 5 packages?

A) 24

B) 30

C) 36

D) 60

Here's How to Crack It

The question asks for the number of doughnuts in 5 packages. This question simply describes two equal ratios, one of which is missing a single piece of information. Here's the given information represented as two equal ratios:

$$\frac{2 \text{ (packages)}}{12 \text{ (doughnuts)}} = \frac{5 \text{ (packages)}}{x \text{ (doughnuts)}}$$

Because ratios can be written so they look like fractions, you can treat them exactly like fractions. To find the answer, all you have to do is figure out what you could plug in for x that would make $\frac{2}{12} = \frac{5}{x}$. Now cross-multiply:

$$\frac{2}{12} \diagdown\!\!\!\!\diagup \frac{5}{x}$$

so, $2x = 60$

$x = 30$

The correct answer is (B).

Many proportion questions will also involve unit conversion. Be sure to pay attention to the units and have the same units in both numerators and the same units in both denominators.

Let's look at an example.

21

Gary is using a 3-D printer to create a miniature version of himself. The scale of the miniature is 0.4 inches to 1 foot of Gary's actual height. If Gary is 5 feet and 9 inches tall, what will be the height of his 3-D printed miniature? (12 inches = 1 foot)

A) 2.0 inches

B) 2.3 inches

C) 2.6 inches

D) 2.9 inches

Here's How to Crack It

The question asks for the height of the 3-D miniature. The scale of the 3-D printer is in inches and feet—0.4 inches on the miniature for every 1 foot in real life. Start by converting every measurement to inches. There are 12 inches in each foot, so the scale will be 0.4 inches = 12 inches in real life. Now convert Gary's height into inches. Begin by setting up a proportion to find out how many inches are in 5 feet.

$$\frac{12 \text{ inches}}{1 \text{ foot}} = \frac{x \text{ inches}}{5 \text{ feet}}$$

Cross-multiply to find that 5 feet equals 60 inches. Gary is 5 feet and 9 inches tall, so he is 60 + 9 = 69 inches tall. Now set up a proportion with the scale of the miniature and Gary's height in inches.

$$\frac{0.4 \text{ inches}}{12 \text{ inches}} = \frac{x \text{ inches}}{69 \text{ inches}}$$

Cross-multiply to get $12x = 27.6$, and then divide both sides by 12 to find that $x = 2.3$ inches. The correct answer is (B).

Direct and Inverse Variation

Questions dealing with **direct variation** (a fancy term for *proportion*) are exactly what you've just seen. If one quantity grows or decreases by a certain amount (a factor), the other quantity grows or decreases by the same amount. **Inverse variations** (also known as *inverse proportions*) are just the opposite of that. As one quantity grows or decreases, the other quantity decreases or grows by the same factor.

> **What's in a Name?**
> When you see *variation*, think *proportion*.

The main formula you want to remember for inverse proportions is

$$x_1 y_1 = x_2 y_2$$

Try one!

> **Translate!**
> *Direct* means divide. Since *inverse* is the opposite, inverse means multiply.

15

The amount of time it takes to consume a buffalo carcass is inversely proportional to the number of vultures. If it takes 12 vultures 3 days to consume a buffalo, how many fewer hours will it take if there are 4 more vultures?

A) $\dfrac{1}{4}$

B) $\dfrac{3}{4}$

C) 18

D) 54

Here's How to Crack It

The question asks for the difference in time with a new number in an inverse proportion. For inverse proportions, follow the formula. First, convert the days to hours: 3 days is equal to 72 hours. Now set up the equation: (12 vultures)(72 hours) = (16 vultures)(x). Solve to get $x = 54$, which is 18 fewer hours. The correct answer is (C).

PERCENTAGES

Percentages Are Fractions

There should be nothing frightening about a percentage. It's just a convenient way of expressing a fraction with a denominator of 100.

Percent means "per 100" or "out of 100." If there are 100 questions on your math test and you answer 50 of them, you will have answered 50 out of 100, or $\frac{50}{100}$, or 50 percent. To think of it another way:

$$\frac{\text{part}}{\text{whole}} = \frac{x}{100} = x \text{ percent}$$

Memorize These Percentage-Decimal-Fraction Equivalents

These show up all the time, so go ahead and memorize them.

$0.01 = \frac{1}{100} = 1$ percent $\qquad 0.25 = \frac{1}{4} = 25$ percent

$0.1 = \frac{1}{10} = 10$ percent $\qquad 0.5 = \frac{1}{2} = 50$ percent

$0.2 = \frac{1}{5} = 20$ percent $\qquad 0.75 = \frac{3}{4} = 75$ percent

Converting Percentages to Fractions

To convert a percentage to a fraction, simply put the percentage over 100 and reduce:

$$80 \text{ percent} = \frac{80}{100} = \frac{8}{10} = \frac{4}{5}$$

Converting Fractions to Percentages

Because a percentage is just another way to express a fraction, you shouldn't be surprised to see how easy it is to convert a fraction to a percentage. To do so, simply use your calculator to divide the top of the fraction by the bottom of the fraction, and then multiply the result by 100. Here's an example:

Another Way
You can also convert fractions to percentages by cross-multiplying:

$\frac{3}{4} = \frac{x}{100}$

$4x = 3(100)$

$x = \frac{3(100)}{4}$

$x = 75$

Problem: Express $\dfrac{3}{4}$ as a percentage.

Solution: $\dfrac{3}{4} = 0.75 \times 100 = 75$ percent.

Converting fractions to percentages is easy with your calculator, and all percent questions will appear in the section on which calculator use is allowed.

Converting Percentages to Decimals

To convert a percentage to a decimal, simply move the decimal point *two places to the left*. For example, 25 percent can be expressed as the decimal 0.25; 50 percent is the same as 0.50 or 0.5; 100 percent is the same as 1.00 or 1.

Converting Decimals to Percentages

To convert a decimal to a percentage, just do the opposite of what you did in the preceding section. All you have to do is move the decimal point *two places to the right*. Thus, 0.5 = 50 percent; 0.375 = 37.5 percent; 2 = 200 percent.

The following drill will give you practice working with fractions, decimals, and percentages.

FRACTIONS, DECIMALS, AND PERCENTS DRILL

Fill in the missing information in the following table. Answers can be found on page 430.

	Fraction	Decimal	Percent
	$\dfrac{1}{5}$	0.2	20%
1.	$\dfrac{1}{2}$		
2.		3.0	
3.			0.5%
4.	$\dfrac{1}{3}$		

Translation, Please!

Word problems can be translated into arithmetic symbols. Learning how to translate from English to math will help you immensely on the SAT Math Test. Here are some of the most common terms you will see in word problems and their math symbol equivalents:

Word	Symbol
is, are, costs	=
greater than, more than	+
fewer than, less than	−
of	× (multiply)
percent	÷ 100
what	n (variable)

Do You Speak Math?

Problem: What number is 5 more than 10 percent of 20?

Students often make careless errors on questions like this because they aren't sure how to translate the words they are reading into math. You won't make mistakes if you take the words slowly, one at a time, and translate each one into a mathematical symbol. Use the chart above to write this question in math. *What number* means "variable," so you can write that as n (or x or whatever letter works for you). *Is* means "equals," so now you have $n =$. Next you are given the number 5, so write that in your equation and you get $n = 5$. *More than* translates to +, and *10 percent* is $\dfrac{10}{100}$. That gives you $n = 5 + \dfrac{10}{100}$. Finally, *of 20* means multiply by 20, so now you have the equation:

$$n = 5 + \frac{10}{100}(20)$$

$$n = 5 + 2$$

$$n = 7$$

You will see the words *of, is, product, sum,* and *what* pop up a lot in math questions on the SAT. Don't let these words fool you because they all translate into simple math functions. Memorize all of these terms and their math equivalents. It will save you time on the test and make your life with the SAT much less unpleasant.

What Percent of What Percent of What?

On more challenging SAT questions, you may be asked to determine the effect of a series of percentage increases or decreases. The key point to remember on such questions is that each successive increase or decrease is performed on the result of the previous one.

Here's an example.

15

A business paid $300 to rent a piece of office equipment for one year. The rent was then increased by 10% each year thereafter. How much will the company pay for the first three years it rents the equipment?

A) $920

B) $960

C) $990

D) $993

Bite-Sized Pieces
Always handle percentage problems using Bite-Sized Pieces: one piece at a time.

Here's How to Crack It

The question asks for the cost of the equipment over three years. This question is a great place to use Bite-Sized Pieces. You know that the business paid $300 to rent the piece of office equipment for the first year. Then, you were told that the rent increases by 10 percent for each year thereafter. That's a sure sign that you're going to need the rent for the second year, so go ahead and calculate it. For the second year, the rent is $300 + \left(\dfrac{10}{100} \times 300 \right) = 330$.

Now, the question tells you that the business rents the equipment for three years. So, you need to do the calculation one more time. At this point, you might want to set up a chart to help keep track of the information.

Year 1: $300

Year 2: $330 = 300 + \left(\dfrac{10}{100} \times 300 \right)$

Year 3: $363 = 330 + \left(\dfrac{10}{100} \times 330 \right)$

To find the answer, all you need to do is add up the costs for each of the three years.

Year 1: $300
Year 2: $330
Year 3: $363
$993

The correct answer is (D).

What Percent of What Percent of . . . Yikes!

Sometimes you may find successive percentage questions in which you aren't given actual numbers to work with. In such cases, you need to plug in some numbers.

Here's an example.

17

A number is increased by 25 percent and then decreased by 20 percent. The result is what percent of the original number?

A) 80

B) 100

C) 105

D) 120

> **Careful!**
> Number 17 is a tricky question. Beware of percentage change problems in the later questions. The answers to these problems almost always defy common sense. Unless you are careful, you may fall for a trap answer.

Here's How to Crack It

The question asks for the result of a percent increase and a percent decrease on an original number. You aren't given a particular number to work with in this question—just "a number." Rather than trying to deal with the problem in the abstract, you should immediately plug in a number to work with. What number would be easiest to work with in a percentage question? Why, 100, of course.

1. 25 percent of 100 is 25, so 100 increased by 25 percent is 125.
2. Now you have to decrease 125 by 20 percent; 20 percent of 125 is 25, so 125 decreased by 20 percent is 100.
3. 100 (the result) is 100 percent of 100 (the number you plugged in). The correct answer is (B).

Remember, never try to solve a percentage problem by writing an equation if you can plug in numbers instead. Using Plugging In on percentage questions is faster, easier, and more accurate. Why work through long, arduous equations if you don't have to?

> **Plugging Away at Relationships**
> Questions dealing with percents, fractions, and other ways of expressing relationships among numbers are great chances to plug in!

PERCENT CHANGE

There's one more fundamental concept that you should know about percents. Some questions will ask for a **percent increase** or **percent decrease.** For these questions, use the following formula.

$$\% \text{ change} = \frac{\text{Difference}}{\text{Original}} \times 100$$

Most of the time that you use the formula, it will be pretty clear which number you should use for the original. However, if you're not sure, remember that you should use the *smaller* number for the original if you are finding a percent *increase*. You should use the *larger* number for the original if you are finding a percent *decrease*.

Here's an example of how to use the formula.

8

VISITATION AT ARCHES NATIONAL PARK, 2003–2006

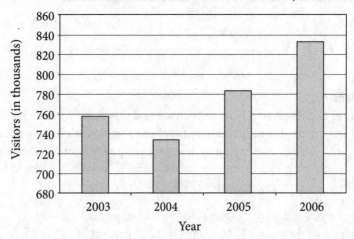

The chart above shows the number of visits, in thousands, at Arches National Park for the years 2003 to 2006. Which of the following is the closest approximation of the percent increase in the number of visits from 2004 to 2006 ?

A)   5%

B)   15%

C)   20%

D)   115%

Here's How to Crack It

The question asks about the percent increase in visits over a certain time period. First, you need to get the data from the chart. In 2004, the chart shows that there were approximately 730,000 visitors to Arches. In 2006, the chart shows that there were about 830,000 visitors to the park. Now, it's time to use the percent change formula. The difference is about 100,000 and the original is the 730,000 visitors in 2004:

$$\% \ increase = \frac{100,000}{730,000} \times 100 \approx 15\%$$

The correct answer is (B).

PERCENTAGES: ADVANCED PRINCIPLES

Another aspect of percent questions may relate to things that increase or decrease by a certain percent over time. This is known as **growth and decay.** Real-world examples include population growth, radioactive decay, and credit payments, to name a few. While plugging in can help on these, it is also useful to know the growth and decay formula.

> When the growth or decay rate is a percent of the total population:
>
> *final amount = original amount* $(1 \pm rate)^{number \ of \ changes}$

Let's see how this formula can make quick work of an otherwise tedious question.

23

Becca deposits $100 into a bank account that earns an annual interest rate of 4%. If she does not make any additional deposits and makes no withdrawals, how long will it take her, in years, to increase the value of her account by at least 60% ?

A) 12

B) 15

C) 25

D) 30

Here's How to Crack It

The question asks for the number of years it will take for Becca's account to reach a certain value. You could add 4% to the account over and over again until you get to the desired amount, but that would take a long time. Knowing the formula will make it a lot easier. First, set up the equation with the things you know. The original amount is 100, and the rate is 4%, or 0.04. The account is increasing, so you add the rate, and you can put in "years" for the number of changes. The formula becomes

$$\textit{final amount} = 100(1 + 0.04)^{\textit{years}}$$

Now you need to figure out what you want the final amount to be. Translate the English to math: the value of her account (100) will increase (+) by 60 percent (0.6) of the current value (×100). This becomes 100 + (0.6)(100) = 100 + 60 = 160. Now the formula is

$$160 = 100(1.04)^{\textit{years}}$$

SAT Math ≠ Math
Look for chances to PITA or Plug In throughout the math sections. These kinds of questions are everywhere, and using a good strategy will save you time and avoid mistakes.

The answer choices represent the number of years Becca keeps her money in the account. Now you are all set to easily plug in the answers. Start with (B), so *years* = 15. Is $100(1.04)^{15}$ = 160? Use your calculator to check, making sure to follow PEMDAS rules and do the exponent before you multiply by 100. The result is $180.09. That is a bit too much money, so the answer will likely be (A), but let's just check it. $100(1.04)^{12}$ = $160.10, which is at least $160. The correct answer is (A).

A final note on growth and decay: sometimes the population is tripling or halving instead of changing by a certain percent. In that case, the formula changes to

$$\textit{final amount} = \textit{original amount} \, (\textit{multiplier})^{\textit{number of changes}}$$

Two more topics related to percentages may be tested. You may be given a sample of a population that fits a certain requirement and asked to determine how many members of the general population will also be expected to fit that requirement. You may also be given the results of a study or poll and told that there is a margin of error of a certain percentage.

Let's look at an example that tests both of these advanced ideas.

29

A summer beach volleyball league has 750 players in it. At the start of the season, 150 of the players are randomly chosen and polled on whether games will be played while it is raining, or if the games should be canceled. The results of the poll show that 42 of the polled players would prefer to play in the rain. The margin of error on the poll is ±4%. What is the range of players in the entire league that would be expected to prefer to play volleyball in the rain rather than cancel the game?

A) 24–32

B) 39–48

C) 150–195

D) 180–240

Here's How to Crack It

The question asks for the range of players that would prefer to play in the rain. The first step is to determine the percent of polled players that wanted to play in the rain.

$$\frac{42}{150} = 0.28 \text{ or } 28\%$$

Now apply this percent to the entire population of the league. Since 28% of the polled players wanted to play in the rain, 28% of all players should want to play in the rain.

$$\frac{28}{100} \times 750 = 210$$

The only range that contains this value is (D), so that is the correct answer. To actually calculate the margin of error, add and subtract 4% to the actual percent of 28% to get a range of 24–32% of the total.

$$24\% \text{ of } 750 = 180$$

$$32\% \text{ of } 750 = 240$$

Therefore, the entire range is 180 to 240. The correct answer is (D).

AVERAGES

What Is an Average?

The **average,** also called the **arithmetic mean,** of a set of n numbers is simply the sum of all the numbers divided by n. In other words, if you want to find the average of three numbers, add them up and divide by 3. For example, the average of 3, 7, and 8 is $\frac{(3+7+8)}{3}$, which equals $\frac{18}{3}$, or 6.

That was an easy example, but average questions on the SAT won't always have clear solutions. That is, you won't always be given the information for averages in a way that is easy to work with. For that reason, use the formula $T = AN$, in which T is the *total*, A is the *average*, and N is the *number of things*. The total is the sum of all the numbers you're averaging, and the number of things is the number of elements you're averaging. Plug in the information you've been given, then you can solve the equation for the quantity that you don't know.

Here's what the formula looks like using the simple average example we just gave you.

$$T = AN$$

$$3 + 7 + 8 = (A)(3)$$

$$18 = (A)(3)$$

$$A = 6$$

Total
When calculating averages and means, always find the total. It's the one piece of information that the SAT loves to withhold.

Here's another simple example:

Problem: If the average of three test scores is 70, what is the total of all three test scores?

Solution: Just put the average (70) and the number of things (3 tests) into the formula for get $T = (70)(3)$. Then multiply to find the total, which is 210.

Averages: Advanced Principles

To solve most difficult average questions, all you have to do is use the formula more than once. Most of the time you will use it to find the total of the number being averaged. Here's an example.

Mark It!
Make sure you're using the formula $T = AN$ each time you see the word *average* in a question.

> **10**
>
> Maria has taken four chemistry tests and has an average (arithmetic mean) score of 80. If she scores a 90 on her fifth chemistry test, what is her average for these five tests?
>
> A) 80
>
> B) 81
>
> C) 82
>
> D) 84

Here's How to Crack It

The question asks for the average score Maria received on all 5 tests. Start by writing out $T = AN$ and filling in what you know. You can put 80 in for the average and 4 in for the number of things to get $T = (80)(4)$. You can calculate that Maria has gotten 320 total points on her first four tests.

Now, since the question mentions another average, write the formula again and fill in the new information. This time, there are five tests, making the formula $T = (A)(5)$. The question asks for the average, so you also need to find the total. The total for all five tests is the total from the first four tests plus the score from the fifth test: $320 + 90 = 410$. Put that into the formula to get $410 = (A)(5)$ and divide to find the average: 82. The correct answer is (C).

Averages, and many other arithmetic topics, may be tested using charts and data. To find the numbers to average, look them up on the graphic provided and watch out for mismatched units.

24

Charge No.	Battery Life
1	1:11
2	1:05
3	0:59
4	0:55
5	0:55
6	0:54
7	0:54

A toy drone is opened and charged to full battery life. The table above shows the duration of the battery life in hours and minutes between charges. What is the average battery life for the first five charges?

A) 55 minutes

B) 58 minutes

C) 1 hour and 1 minute

D) 1 hour and 5 minutes

Here's How to Crack It

The question asks for the average battery life for the first 5 charges. To find the average, add up the battery life values for the first 5 charges and divide by 5. Make sure that you convert the battery charge time for charges 1 and 2 into minutes before calculating: 1:11 = 60 + 11 = 71 minutes, and 1:05 = 60 + 5 = 65 minutes. The average is equal to $\frac{71+65+59+55+55}{5} = \frac{305}{5} = 61$ minutes, which is equal to 1 hour and 1 minute. The correct answer is (C).

Don't forget that you can also plug in when answering average questions.

16

The average (arithmetic mean) of a list of 5 numbers is *n*. When an additional number is added to the list, the average of all 6 numbers is *n* + 3. Which of the following is the value, in terms of *n*, of the number added to the list?

A) 6*n* + 18

B) 5*n*

C) *n* + 18

D) *n* + 6

Here's How to Crack It

The question asks for the value of a number added to the list. There are variables in the answers, so plug in for the value of *n*, which is the average. If *n* = 20, then you can use the average formula to find the total of the five numbers on the list.

$$T = AN$$

$$T = (20)(5)$$

$$T = 100$$

Now, a number is added and there is a new average, so it's time to write out the formula again. For this one, you know that there are 6 numbers and that their average is *n* + 3 = 20 + 3 = 23.

$$T = AN$$

$$T = (23)(6)$$

$$T = 138$$

Since the difference in the two totals was caused by the addition of the sixth number, the sixth number must be 138 − 100 = 38. That's the target, so be sure to circle it. Now check the answer choices. Choice (A) becomes 6(20) + 18 = 120 + 18 = 138. This does not match the target, so eliminate it. The value with (A) was much too large, so (B) will also be large. Try (C) and (D) next: (C) becomes 20 + 18 = 38, and (D) becomes 20 + 6 = 26. Only (C) matches the target, so the correct answer is (C).

On the SAT, you'll also need to know three other statistical topics related to averages: *median*, *mode*, and *range*. These topics have pretty straightforward definitions. One way the SAT will complicate the issue is by presenting the data in a chart or graph, making it harder to see the numbers you are working with.

Missing the Middle?
To find the median of a set containing an even number of items, take the average of the two middle numbers.

WHAT IS A MEDIAN?

The **median** of a list of numbers is the number that is exactly in the middle of the list when the list is arranged from smallest to largest, as on a number line. For example, in the group 3, 6, 6, 6, 6, 7, 8, 9, 10, 10, 11, the median is 7. Five numbers come before 7 in the list, and 5 come after. Remember it this way: median sounds like *middle*.

Let's see how this idea might be tested.

23

Milligrams of Gold					
	1	2	3	4	5
Limestone	0.45	0.58	0.55	0.42	0.41
Granite	0.94	0.87	0.82	0.55	0.73
Gneiss	0.38	0.60	0.37	0.40	0.34

Five samples of each of three different rock types were collected on a hiking trip in Colorado. Each sample was analyzed for its gold content. The milligrams of gold found in each sample are presented in the table above. How much larger is the median of the amount of gold in the granite samples than that of the limestone samples?

A) 0.00

B) 0.37

C) 0.45

D) 0.55

Here's How to Crack It
The question asks for a comparison of the medians of data for limestone and granite. Start by putting the gold weights for limestone in order to get

$$0.41, 0.42, 0.45, 0.55, 0.58$$

The median for limestone is the middle number: 0.45 mg.

Next, place the gold weights for granite in order to get

$$0.55, 0.73, 0.82, 0.87, 0.94$$

The median for granite is 0.82.

Therefore, the difference between the median amount of gold in the granite and limestone samples is 0.82 – 0.45 = 0.37. The correct answer is (B).

———————◯———————

WHAT IS A MODE?

The **mode** of a group of numbers is the number in the list that appears most often. In the list 3, 4, 4, 5, 7, 7, 8, 8, 8, 9, 10, the mode is 8, because it appears three times while no other number in the group appears more than twice. Remember it this way: *mode* sounds like "most."

Mode is often tested with bar graphs or points on a scatterplot. Look for the tallest bar on the bar graph or the vertical or horizontal line with the most points in a scatterplot to find the mode.

———————◯———————

6

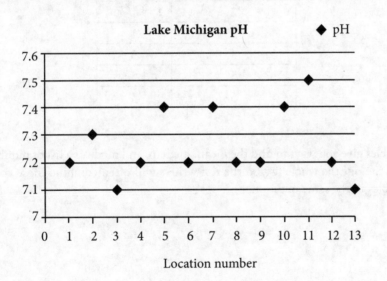

The pH of the water in Lake Michigan was tested at 13 locations along the Illinois shoreline. The data is presented in the scatterplot above. Which of the following best represents the mode of the pH in the collected data?

A) 7.2

B) 7.3

C) 7.4

D) 7.5

Here's How to Crack It

The question asks for the mode of the data in the scatterplot. The mode is the data point that occurs most frequently. Each diamond is a data point, so look for the line with the most diamonds on it. That line is 7.2, which means that when the lake was tested, the pH level most often read 7.2. The correct answer is (A).

WHAT IS A FREQUENCY TABLE?

A **frequency table** is just what it sounds like: a table to show how frequently something happens. One column shows numbers of something, like ages or scores on a test, and the other column shows how often that thing occurs. If you wanted to show, for example, how many meetings each member of a 15-person club attended, you could use the table below.

Meeting Attendance for this Cool Club I'm In

Meetings attended	Frequency
1	2
2	1
3	1
4	3
5	5
6	3

Frequency tables give you ways to find the mean, median, and mode of a list of numbers without needing to write out the whole list, so the test-writers will often combine those concepts with frequency tables in the same question.

Try out an example of this below.

18

Number of Ice Cream Scoops for Customers at an Ice Cream Parlor

Number of Ice Cream Scoops	Frequency
8	1
5	2
4	2
3	7
2	6
1	6

The distribution of Ice Cream Scoops for 24 customers at an ice cream parlor is displayed in the table above. Which of the following orders the mean, median, and mode correctly?

A) mode < median < mean

B) median < mode < mean

C) median < mean < mode

D) mean < median < mode

Here's How to Crack It

The question asks for the correct order of the mean, median, and mode of the data from least to greatest. Start with the mode, which is easiest to determine from the table. In a frequency table, the column labeled Frequency shows how often each value in the other column happened. Because the greatest number in the Frequency column is 7, the corresponding number of scoops is the mode. Thus, the mode is 3.

Next, find the median, which is the middle number of an ordered list. You could write out all 24 numbers in this list and count up to the middle number(s), but there's a better way. When a list has an even number of terms, the median is the average of the two middle terms. Since $\frac{24}{2} = 12$, the median is the average of the 12th and 13th terms. To confirm this, notice that there are $12 - 1 = 11$ terms to the left of the 12th term and $24 - 13 = 11$ terms to the right of the 13th term. Now, use the frequency table to find the 12th and 13th terms. The table shows that 6 customers chose 1 scoop and 6 customers chose 2 scoops, so the 12th term is 2. The next 7 customers chose 3 scoops, so the 13th term is 3. The average of 2 and 3 is $\frac{2 + 3}{2} = 2.5$. Thus, the median is 2.5, and the mode of 3 is greater than the median of 2.5. Eliminate (A), which says the median is greater than the mode.

Now find the average. Write the $T = AN$ equation and fill in what you know. The number of things is given in the question as 24, so fill that in for N. Rather than adding up all 24 numbers using your calculator and taking the risk that you'll miss one, use the frequency table to speed things up. Because 1 customer took 8 scoops, that's a total of $1 \times 8 = 8$ scoops. Do the same thing for every row.

$$1 \times 8 = 8$$
$$2 \times 5 = 10$$
$$2 \times 4 = 8$$
$$7 \times 3 = 21$$
$$6 \times 2 = 12$$
$$6 \times 1 = 6$$

Now add the totals to get $8 + 10 + 8 + 21 + 12 + 6 = 65$. Fill that in for T in the average formula. Now $65 = (A)(24)$. Divide both sides of the equation by 24 to get an average of a little more than 2.7.

Finally, put the three values in order: $2.5 < 2.7 < 3$. The order is median < mean < mode. The correct answer is (C).

WHAT IS A RANGE?

The **range** of a list of numbers is the difference between the greatest number on the list and the least number on the list. For the list 4, 5, 5, 6, 7, 8, 9, 10, 20, the greatest number is 20 and the least is 4, so the range is 20 − 4 = 16.

3

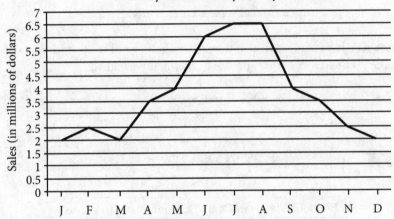

Monthly Sales of Always Sunny Sunscreen

The forecasted monthly sales of Always Sunny Sunscreen are presented in the figure above. Which of the following best describes the range of monthly sales, in millions of dollars, throughout the year shown?

A) 2.5

B) 3.5

C) 4.0

D) 4.5

Here's How to Crack It

The question asks for the range in monthly sales based on the graph. The range of a set of values is the difference between the greatest and the smallest value. The lowest monthly sales number for Always Sunny can be found where the line dips closest to the bottom of the graph. This happens in both January and March, when the forecasted sales are 2 million. Make sure to read the units carefully. The highest point is where the line goes closest to the top of the graph. This happens in July and August, when the forecasted monthly sales are 6.5 million. Therefore, the range is 6.5 million – 2 million = 4.5 million. The correct answer is (D).

By the way, you may recognize this graph from Chapter 14. On the SAT, the same chart or figure may be used for two different questions. We'll talk more about sets of questions later in this chapter.

The SAT might even have a question that tests more than one of these statistical concepts at the same time. Take it one step at a time and use POE when you can.

23

Precious Metals in Catalytic Converters, in grams					
1	2	2	3	4	6
6	6	9	9	10	10
11	13	14	14	15	17

The grams of precious metals in recycled catalytic converters were measured for a variety of automobiles. The data is presented in the table above. If the lowest data point, 1 gram, and highest data point, 17 grams, are removed from the set, which of the following quantities would change the most?

A) Mode

B) Mean

C) Range

D) Median

Here's How to Crack It

The question asks for the measure of the data that will change the most if a certain data point is removed. Start by evaluating the easier answer choices and save mean for last. The mode of the current list is 6, and removing 1 and 17 from the list won't change that. Eliminate (A). The range is the difference between the smallest number and the largest number on the list. Right now, the range is 17 − 1 = 16. If those extremes are removed from the list, the new range is 15 − 2 = 13, and the range changed by 3 units. Keep (C) for now. The median is the middle number in the list, or the average of the middle two numbers. Currently, both middle numbers are 9, so the median is 9. This won't change if 1 and 17 are removed, so eliminate (D). The mean of a list is not likely to change dramatically with the removal of the numbers at the extremes, so (C) is likely correct. To actually evaluate the mean, you need to add up all the numbers on the list and divide by the number of items in the list. For the current list, the total is 152 for the 18 items, so the average is $8.\overline{44}$. To find the new total if 1 and 17 are removed, don't re-add everything; just subtract 18 from the previous total. The new list will have only 16 items, so the new average is 8.375. This is only slightly different than the previous mean, so eliminate (B). The correct answer is (C).

WHAT IS STANDARD DEVIATION?

In real world applications, **standard deviation** is a measure of how numbers are distributed around the mean, and the calculations can get complicated. But SAT math is not the real world! The SAT considers standard deviation similar to range in that it shows the spread of a group of numbers. When the numbers are more spread out around the mean, the standard deviation is greater. When the numbers are clumped closer together around the mean, the standard deviation is smaller.

Take a look at this example of how an SAT question might combine standard deviation with another statistical concept you already know.

13

Data Set 1	Data Set 2
6	4
4	3
3	7
8	8
4	2
6	5
5	6

The table above shows two sets of data. Of the following statements comparing Data Set 1 to Data Set 2, which is true?

A) The standard deviations are the same, and the medians are the same.

B) The standard deviations are the same, and the medians are different.

C) The standard deviations are different, and the medians are the same.

D) The standard deviations are different, and the medians are different.

Here's How to Crack It

The question asks which statement is true about the medians and standard deviations of two data sets. Start by finding the median of each data set, recalling that the median of a group of numbers is the middle number when all values are arranged in order. Start by putting the lists in order. Data Set 1 is 3, 4, 4, 5, 6, 6, 8, and Data Set 2 is 2, 3, 4, 5, 6, 7, 8. Both Data Set 1 and Data Set 2 have 7 numbers, so the median will be the 4th number. The median of Data Set 1 is 5, and the median of Data Set 2 is 5. The medians are the same, so eliminate (B) and (D).

Standard deviation is a measure of the spread of a group of numbers. In Data Set 1, the numbers are clustered toward the middle. In Data Set 2, each number appears once and the numbers are evenly spread throughout the list. Thus, Data Set 1 has a smaller standard deviation than does Data Set 2. Eliminate (A), which says the standard deviations are the same. The correct answer is (C).

RATES

Rate is a concept related to averages. Cars travel at an average speed. Work gets done at an average rate. Because the ideas are similar, the formulas you can use for rate problems are similar to the one for averages you learned about earlier. These formulas are $D = RT$ for distance and $W = RT$ for work.

Here's a simple example:

Problem: If a fisherman can tie 9 flies for fly fishing in an hour and a half, how long does it take him to tie one fly, in minutes?

Solution: First, convert the hour and a half to 90 minutes, so your units are consistent. Then, fill in the formula with the work or amount done (9 flies) and the time (90 minutes).

$$W = RT$$

$$9 = (R)(90)$$

Divide 9 by 90 to get $R = \dfrac{1}{10}$, so the rate is one fly every 10 minutes.

Rates: Advanced Principles

Just as with complicated average questions, more challenging rate questions will also require more than one rate equation to solve. Here's an example.

29

Chef Desai's Cooking Times in a Day

Meal	Number of meals	Average cooking time with no delays (meals per hour)
Breakfast	51	36
Lunch	48	12
Dinner	90	6

Chef Desai and his crew cooks meals every Saturday for his catering company. The table above shows the number of meals and the average cooking time, in meals per hour, for each part of the schedule on a normal Saturday. If Chef Desai and his crew start to cook breakfast at 8:45 a.m., they can complete cooking all three types of meals on time without a delay in sending out orders. If they start cooking at 7:45 a.m., the time it takes to cook breakfast will decrease by 20%, but the times for the other meals will not change. Based on the table above, how many <u>minutes</u> will Chef Desai's crew save if they start cooking at 7:45 a.m. ?

A) 0.28

B) 17

C) 21

D) 29

Here's How to Crack It

The question asks for the difference in minutes between two different times to cook some meals. According to the question, the only meal that is cooked faster with the earlier start time is breakfast. Ignore the other two meals because their cooking times remain the same.

To determine how long it takes Chef Desai and his crew to cook breakfast, use the rate given in the question and set up an equation. If they cook 51 meals at a rate of 36 meals per hour, the equation will look like this:

$$\frac{51 \text{ meals}}{36 \text{ meals per hour}} = 1.41\overline{6} \text{ hours}$$

The question asks for the result in minutes, so use the rate of $\frac{60 \text{ minutes}}{1 \text{ hour}}$ and multiply by 60 to get $1.41\overline{6}(60) = 85$ minutes.

Next, find out what happens if Chef Desai decreases this time by 20%. Take 20% of the initial time of 85 minutes to get (0.20)(85) = 17 minutes. To avoid doing unnecessary work, read the final question. The question asks how much time he will save, which is 17 minutes. The correct answer is (B).

PROBABILITY

Probability is a mathematical expression of the likelihood of an event. The basis of probability is simple. The likelihood of any event is discussed in terms of all of the possible outcomes. To express the probability of a given event, *x,* you would count the number of possible outcomes, count the number of outcomes that give you what you want, and arrange them in a fraction, like this:

$$\text{Probability of } x = \frac{\text{number of outcomes that give you what you want}}{\text{total number of possible outcomes}}$$

Every probability is a fraction. The largest a probability can be is 1; a probability of 1 indicates total certainty. The smallest a probability can be is 0, meaning that it's something that cannot happen. Furthermore, you can find the probability that something WILL NOT happen by subtracting the probability that it WILL happen from 1. For example, if the weatherman tells you that there is a 0.3 probability of rain today, then there must be a 0.7 probability that it won't rain, because 1 − 0.3 = 0.7. Figuring out the probability of any single event is usually simple. When you flip a coin, for example, there are only two possible outcomes, heads and tails; the probability of getting heads is therefore 1 out of 2, or $\frac{1}{2}$. When you roll a die, there are six possible outcomes, 1 through 6; the odds of getting a 6 are therefore $\frac{1}{6}$. The odds of getting an even result when rolling a die are $\frac{1}{2}$ because there are 3 even results in 6 possible outcomes.

Here's an example of a probability question.

2

A bag contains 7 blue marbles and 14 marbles that are not blue. If one marble is drawn at random from the bag, what is the probability that the marble is blue?

A) $\dfrac{1}{3}$

B) $\dfrac{1}{2}$

C) $\dfrac{2}{3}$

D) $\dfrac{3}{7}$

Here's How to Crack It

The question asks for the probability that a selected marble is blue. To make the probability, find the number of blue marbles and the total number of marbles. Here, there are 21 marbles in the bag, 7 of which are blue. The probability that a marble chosen at random would be blue is therefore $\dfrac{7}{21}$, or $\dfrac{1}{3}$. The correct answer is (A).

Let's look at a probability question based on a chart. Again, getting to the correct answer involves reading the chart carefully to find the right numbers to use.

26

Size of College Manhattan High Students Plan to Attend

	Small (Fewer than 5,000 students)	Medium (From 5,000 to 10,000 students)	Large (More than 10,000 students)	Total
Manhattan High East	25	155	75	255
Manhattan High West	39	112	98	249
Total	64	267	173	504

At two high schools, those planning to attend college after graduation were polled. The sizes of the colleges they planned to attend based on student body sizes were tabulated in the table above. The 255 polled students from Manhattan High East had an average SAT score above 1100, and the 249 polled students from Manhattan High West had an average SAT score below 1100. If a poll respondent were chosen at random from those planning to attend a college with at least 5,000 students, what is the probability that the respondent would be enrolled at Manhattan High West?

A) $\dfrac{210}{249}$

B) $\dfrac{210}{440}$

C) $\dfrac{230}{440}$

D) $\dfrac{440}{504}$

Here's How to Crack It

The question asks for the probability that a respondent chosen from a certain group fits an even more specific qualification. Read the graph very carefully to find the correct numbers to use, as you are not choosing from among all students. The respondent is chosen from among those planning to attend colleges with "at least 5,000 students." That means that the total number of possible outcomes includes the 267 respondents who plan to attend medium schools and the 173 who plan to attend large schools, for 440 total. That is the denominator of the probability fraction, and the answer choices aren't reduced, so the answer must be (B) or (C). To find the number from among these 440 respondents who are enrolled at Manhattan High West, look in that row and add the 112 from the medium column to the 98 from the large column to get 210 for the numerator. The correct answer is (B).

Did the average SAT scores of the students at these two schools affect the answer at all? No! Watch out for extraneous information on the SAT. The test-writers may include it to distract you.

SETS OF QUESTIONS

Sometimes, two questions will refer to the same information. These will usually be found in the calculator-permitted section, where there will likely be one set in the Grid-In part and about three sets in the multiple-choice part of that section. Often, these sets are about arithmetic concepts, but they can also cover things like functions or exponential growth.

Try the following arithmetic set.

Questions 4 and 5 refer to the following information.

Grade	Activity	Price per item	Funds raised from activity
9th	Car Wash	$5.00 per car	$255.00
10th	Bake Sale	$2.00 per cookie	$360.00
11th	Magazine Sales	$2.50 per magazine	$337.50
12th	Bake Sale	$1.50 per cookie	$180.00

4

How many cars did the 9th grade class wash during the car wash?

A)   5

B)   51

C) 122

D) 180

Here's How to Crack It

The question asks for a specific value from the chart. Look up the numbers you need on the chart, ignoring all the extraneous information. To find out how many cars the 9th graders washed, take the *Funds raised* and divide by the *Price per item* in the row for the 9th graders to get $\dfrac{\$255.00}{\$5.00} = 51$. The correct answer is (B).

5

How many more cookies were sold by the 10th grade than were sold by the 12th grade?

A)   60

B)   90

C) 120

D) 150

Here's How to Crack It

The question asks for the difference between the number of cookies sold by two grades. First, find the number of cookies sold by 10th graders, again dividing *Funds raised* by *Price per item:* $\frac{\$360.00}{\$2.00} = 180$. Now find the number of cookies sold by 12th graders: $\frac{\$180.00}{\$1.50} = 120$. Finally, subtract to find out how many more cookies the 10th graders sold: $180 - 120 = 60$. The correct answer is (A).

ANALYSIS IN SCIENCE

If some of these questions are reminding you of science class, you're not crazy. One of the "Cross-Test scores" the SAT aims to measure is called Analysis in Science. It supposedly uses the science-based questions from Reading and Writing passages and Math questions to say something about your scientific ability. It doesn't. Treat these questions like any other question that asks if a conclusion can be reached based on the chart—review the chart or graph, carefully look up the numbers in the question, do the required calculations, and eliminate answers that aren't true.

You may also be asked to graph the data presented in a table. Your knowledge of positive and negative relationships from Chapter 11 will help—you can eliminate things with the wrong relationship.

Take a look at this next example.

7

Temperature in °C (t)	Vapor Pressure in kPa (p)
10	4
20	9
30	37
40	66
50	100

A student conducting experiments in class noticed that the temperature of a given liquid affected the vapor pressure of the liquid, as shown in the table above. Which of the following graphs best represents the relationship between the temperature, *t*, and the vapor pressure, *p*, as indicated by the table?

A)

B)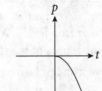

C)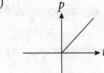

D)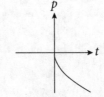

Here's How to Crack It

The question asks for the graph that shows the relationship between temperature and vapor pressure. Notice that the vapor pressure increases as the temperature increases. The line of best fit will go up as you follow the graph from left to right, so eliminate (B) and (D). To determine if the correct graph is (A) or (C), try roughly plotting the data points, and then look at your graph. Notice that the vapor pressure does not increase by the same number for each 10-degree temperature increase. This is an exponential increase, not a linear increase. Therefore, the graph will be curved. Eliminate (C). The correct answer is (A).

Sometimes you will be asked to draw conclusions without much data at all. The following question from the calculator section has only one number in it, making the calculator pretty useless. Just stick to the facts of the study and be sure not to take a conclusion too far.

14

When trees become iron deficient, their leaves will turn yellow prematurely. A botanist is testing iron-doped fertilizers on maple trees with iron deficiencies. The botanist has selected 200 maple trees in the state of Wisconsin that have been identified as having an iron deficiency. Half of the trees are randomly chosen to receive the iron-doped fertilizer, while the other half are given a fertilizer without iron. The results from the test show that trees administered the iron-doped fertilizer had fewer premature yellow leaves, indicating an increase in their iron levels. Which of the following statements best describes the results of the test?

A) The iron-doped fertilizer will improve iron levels in any tree.

B) The iron-doped fertilizer reduces premature yellow leaves better than any other fertilizer.

C) The iron-doped fertilizer will cause a significant increase in iron levels.

D) The iron-doped fertilizer will result in fewer premature yellow leaves in maple trees in Wisconsin.

Here's How to Crack It

The question asks for a statement to describe the results of a study. For this type of question, underline key words about how the study was conducted and what the study found. In this case, the study was on 200 maples trees with iron deficiencies in Wisconsin, and the conclusion is *The results from the test show that trees administered the iron-doped fertilizer had fewer premature yellow leaves, indicating an increase in their iron levels.* Eliminate answers that don't hit this mark or go too far. In (A), it says that this treatment will help *any tree.* You are told only about *200 maples trees in the state of Wisconsin,* so you can't draw conclusions about other trees. Eliminate (A). In (B), the fertilizer used is compared to other fertilizers, which you also don't know about. Choice (C) sounds good, but it is hard to say what qualifies as *a significant increase in iron levels.* The statement in (D) matches the key words you underlined perfectly without taking any aspect too far. Therefore, the correct answer is (D).

Advanced Arithmetic Drill: Calculator-Permitted Section

Work these questions using the advanced arithmetic techniques covered in this chapter. These questions are similar to those you will see on the Calculator section of the test. Answers and explanations can be found starting on page 430.

5

$$20 - 2x$$
$$20 - x$$
$$20$$
$$20 + x$$
$$20 + 2x$$

What is the average (arithmetic mean) of the list of numbers above?

A) 20

B) 100

C) $20 + \dfrac{x}{5}$

D) $\dfrac{100}{x}$

11

Steve ran a 12-mile race at an average speed of 8 miles per hour. If Adam ran the same race at an average speed of 6 miles per hour, how many minutes longer did Adam take to complete the race than did Steve?

A) 12

B) 16

C) 24

D) 30

15

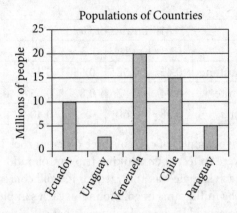

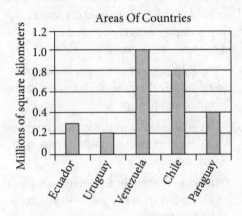

The populations and areas of five countries are shown in the graphs above. If population density is defined as $\dfrac{\text{population}}{\text{area}}$, which of the five countries has the highest population density?

A) Ecuador

B) Uruguay

C) Venezuela

D) Chile

19

The amount of time that Amy walks is directly proportional to the distance that she walks. If she walks a distance of 2.5 miles in 50 minutes, how many miles will she walk in 2 hours?

A) 4.5

B) 5

C) 6

D) 6.5

20

A total of 140,000 votes was cast for two candidates, Skinner and Whitehouse. If Skinner won by a ratio of 4 to 3, how many votes were cast for Whitehouse?

A) 30,000

B) 40,000

C) 60,000

D) 80,000

23

Spice Prices of Distributor D	
Spice	Price Per Pound
Cinnamon	$8.00
Nutmeg	$9.00
Ginger	$7.00
Cloves	$10.00

The owner of a spice store buys 3 pounds each of cinnamon, nutmeg, ginger, and cloves from distributor D. She then sells all of the spices at $2.00 per ounce. What is her total profit, in dollars?

(1 pound = 16 ounces)

A) $192

B) $282

C) $384

D) $486

25

Milligrams of Gold					
	1	2	3	4	5
Limestone	0.45	0.58	0.55	0.42	0.41
Granite	0.94	0.87	0.82	0.55	0.73
Gneiss	0.38	0.60	0.37	0.40	0.34

Five samples of each of three different rock types were collected on a hiking trip in Colorado. Each sample was analyzed for its gold content. The milligrams of gold found in each sample are presented in the table above. What is the percent difference of the average gold content in the granite samples when compared to the average gold content of the gneiss samples?

A) The gold content in the gneiss samples is 62% higher than the gold content in the granite samples.

B) The gold content in the granite samples is 62% higher than the gold content in the gneiss samples.

C) The gold content in the gneiss samples is 87% higher than the gold content in the granite samples.

D) The gold content in the granite samples is 87% higher than the gold content in the gneiss samples.

26

Of all the houses in a certain neighborhood, 80% have garages. Of those houses with garages, 60% have two-car garages. If there are 56 houses with garages that are not two-car garages, how many houses are there in the neighborhood?

A) 93

B) 117

C) 156

D) 175

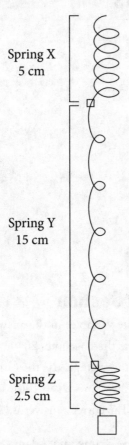

Spring X
5 cm

Spring Y
15 cm

Spring Z
2.5 cm

The ratio of the lengths, in centimeters, that two springs stretch is given by the ratio $x:z$. The ratio of the spring constant (force per length) of two springs is $z:x$. In the diagram above, a mass is hung from Spring Z, making it stretch. Spring X and Spring Y also stretch when Spring Z is stretched. If Spring X has a spring constant of 2 N/cm, what is the spring constant of Spring Z ?

A) 1

B) 4

C) 4.5

D) 5

On Tuesday, a watchmaker made 4 more watches than he made during the previous day. If he made 16% more watches on Tuesday than on Monday, how many watches did he make on Tuesday?

A) 20

B) 21

C) 25

D) 29

CHAPTER DRILL ANSWERS AND EXPLANATIONS

Fractions, Decimals, and Percents Drill

1. $\dfrac{1}{2}$ 0.5   50

2. $\dfrac{3}{1}$ 3.0   300

3. $\dfrac{1}{200}$ 0.005   0.5

4. $\dfrac{1}{3}$ $0.333\overline{3}$ $33\dfrac{1}{3}$

Advanced Arithmetic Drill: Calculator-Permitted Section

5. **A** The question asks for the average of a list of numbers. There are variables in the answer choices, so plug in. Make up a value for x. Say that x is 3. The list of numbers then becomes $20 - 2(3)$, $20 - 3$, 20, $20 + 3$, $20 + 2(3)$, so the list is 14, 17, 20, 23, and 26. To find the average, use the formula $T = AN$. You know the number of things (5) and the total ($14 + 17 + 20 + 23 + 26 = 100$), so the formula becomes $100 = (A)(5)$. Therefore, the average is $100 \div 5 = 20$. The correct answer is (A).

11. **D** The question asks for the difference in minutes between Steve's time and Adam's time. Use the formula $D = RT$ to calculate the time for each runner. Steve runs 12 miles at 8 miles per hour, so the formula becomes $12 = (8)(T)$. To find Steve's time, divide his distance by his rate, which means that he runs for $1\dfrac{1}{2}$ hours (or 1.5 if you're using your calculator). Adam runs the same 12 miles at 6 miles per hour, so the formula becomes $12 = (6)(T)$. This means that Adam runs for 2 hours. Adam takes half an hour longer to complete the race, and half an hour is 30 minutes. The correct answer is (D).

15.   **A**   The question asks for the country with the greatest population density based on two graphs. The top graph is of the countries' populations, and the bottom graph is of the countries' areas. Find the population density, $\dfrac{\text{population}}{\text{area}}$, for each country by taking its number from the top graph and dividing that by its number from the bottom graph:

$$\text{Ecuador} = \frac{10}{0.3}\text{, which equals } 33.33$$

$$\text{Uruguay} = \frac{2.5}{0.2}\text{, which equals } 12.5$$

$$\text{Venezuela} = \frac{20}{1.0}\text{, which equals } 20$$

$$\text{Chile} = \frac{15}{0.8}\text{, which equals } 18.75$$

The highest value among the countries is that of Ecuador. The correct answer is (A).

19.   **C**   The question asks for the distance Amy can walk in two hours if she walks at a given rate. Since you know the time that Amy walked and the distance she walked are directly proportional, you can set up a proportion to show her distance ÷ time. The time it took her to walk 2.5 miles is given in minutes and the requested time is in hours, so match the units in the proportion by putting 120 (60×2) minutes in the second half of the ratio: $\dfrac{2.5}{50} = \dfrac{x}{120}$. To solve, cross-multiply, and you'll get $50x = 2.5 \times 120$; $50x = 300$; $x = 6$ miles. The correct answer is (C).

20.   **C**   The question asks for the number of votes Whitehouse received. You know the ratio for the votes is 4 for Skinner to every 3 for Whitehouse, so the proportion of votes Whitehouse received is 3 out of every 7 or $\dfrac{3}{7}$ of the total votes. There were 140,000 votes all together, so Whitehouse received $\dfrac{3}{7}$ (140,000) = 60,0000 votes. The correct answer is (C).

23.   **B**   The question asks for the profit the owner made by selling the spices. This is a hard question, so you have to stay on your toes. If the owner buys 3 pounds of each spice, that means she pays the following amounts for each spice:

cinnamon: $8 × 3 = $24
nutmeg: $9 × 3 = $27
ginger: $7 × 3 = $21
cloves: $10 × 3 = $30

So she pays a total of 24 + 27 + 21 + 30, or $102 for 12 pounds of spices. She then sells the spices per *ounce*, so you have to figure out first how many ounces of spices she has. If 1 pound is 16 ounces, then 12 pounds is 12 × 16, or 192 ounces. She sells all the spices at $2 per ounce, so she makes

192 × \$2, or \$384. To figure out her profit, subtract the amount she paid for the spices from the amount she made selling them: \$384 − \$102 = \$282. The correct answer is (B).

25. **D** The question asks for the percent difference of average gold content in granite as compared to the average gold content in gneiss. Start by finding the average for each material. The average gold content in the granite samples can be calculated as follows:

$$\frac{0.94 + 0.87 + 0.82 + 0.55 + 0.73}{5} = 0.782$$

The average gold content in the gneiss samples can be calculated as

$$\frac{0.38 + 0.60 + 0.37 + 0.40 + 0.34}{5} = 0.418$$

Because the average gold content in the granite samples is higher, you can eliminate (A) and (C). Ballpark to find the right answer: 0.782 is almost twice as much as 0.418. Therefore, granite contains, on average, almost 100% more gold than gneiss does. The correct answer is (D).

26. **D** The question asks for the number of houses in the neighborhood. Start by figuring out what percent of the houses do not have two-car garages. Since 60% of the houses with garages have two-car garages, 40% of the houses with garages do not have two-car garages. In other words, 40% of 80% of the houses do not have two-car garages. Translate that into math to get $\frac{40}{100} \times \frac{80}{100} = 0.32$, or 32% of the houses. The question states that 56 houses do not have two-car garages, which means 32% of the houses equals 56. Translating into math gives $\frac{32}{100} \times x = 56$. Solve for x, and you'll get 175. The correct answer is (D).

27. **B** The question asks for the spring constant of one spring given the spring constant of another spring and information about ratios. The question states that the ratio of the spring constants of two springs ($z{:}x$) is the reciprocal of the ratio of their lengths when stretched ($x{:}z$). The ratio of the length of Spring X to that of Spring Z is 5:2.5, which simplifies to 2:1. Therefore, the ratio of the spring constants of Spring X to Spring Z is the reciprocal of that value, or 1:2. Given that Spring X has a spring constant of 2, Spring Z must have a spring constant of 4 because 1:2 and 2:4 are the same ratio. Notice how you didn't use Spring Y for anything! The test-writers sometimes include extraneous information in word problems. If you read the final question and work in bite-sized pieces, you won't waste time doing unnecessary work. The correct answer is (B).

28. **D** The question asks for number of watches a watchmaker made on Tuesday. This is a specific amount, and there are numbers in the answer choices, so plug in the answers. Start with (B). If the watchmaker made 21 watches on Tuesday, then he must have made 17 watches on Monday. You know that he should have made 16% more watches on Tuesday than on Monday, so use the percent change formula $\left(\dfrac{\text{difference}}{\text{original}} \times 100 \right)$ to see if you get 16%: $\dfrac{4}{17} \times 100 = 23.5\%$, which is too big. Eliminate (B). You want the 4 watches to be a smaller percent of the total, so you need a bigger total. Try a bigger answer choice, like (D). If he made 29 watches on Tuesday, then he made 25 watches on Monday. Now the percent change is $\dfrac{4}{25} = 0.16 = 16\%$, which is exactly what you want. The correct answer is (D).

Summary

o   A ratio can be expressed as a fraction, but ratios are not fractions. A ratio compares parts to parts; a fraction compares a part to the whole.

o   Direct proportion is $\dfrac{x_1}{y_1} = \dfrac{x_2}{y_2}$. Inverse proportion is $x_1 y_1 = x_2 y_2$.

o   A percentage is just a convenient way of expressing a fraction with a denominator of 100.

o   To convert a percentage to a fraction, put the percentage over 100 and reduce.

o   To convert a fraction to a percentage, use your calculator to divide the top of the fraction by the bottom of the fraction. Then multiply the result by 100.

o   To convert a percentage to a decimal, move the decimal point two places to the left. To convert a decimal to a percentage, move the decimal point two places to the right.

o   In questions that require you to find a series of percentage increases or decreases, remember that each successive increase or decrease is performed on the result of the previous one.

o   If you need to find the percent increase or decrease, use % change $= \dfrac{\text{difference}}{\text{original}} \times 100$.

o   To find the average (arithmetic mean) of several values, add up the values and divide the total by the number of values.

o   Use the formula $T = AN$ to solve questions involving averages. The key to most average questions is finding the total.

o   The median of a group of numbers is the number that is exactly in the middle of the group when the group is arranged from smallest to largest, as on a number line. If there is an even number of numbers, the median is the average of the two middle numbers.

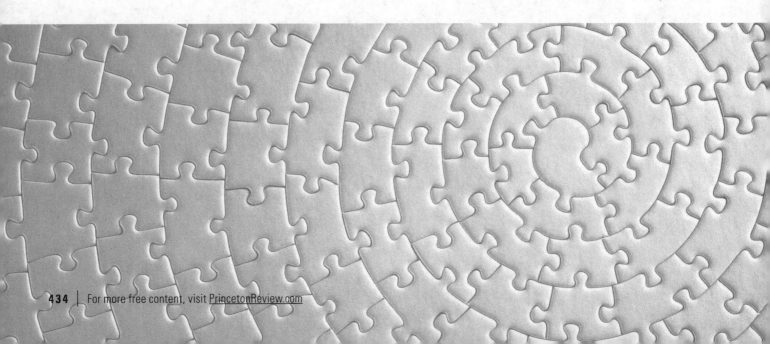

o   The mode of a group of numbers is the number in the group that appears most often.

o   The range of a group of numbers is the difference between the greatest number in the group and the least number.

o   On questions about rates, use the formulas $D = RT$ and $W = RT$. Be careful with the units—the SAT will often require you to do a unit conversion such as minutes to hours or inches to feet.

o   Probability is expressed as a fraction:

- Probability $= \dfrac{\text{number of outcomes that give you what you want}}{\text{total number of possible outcomes}}$

Chapter 18
Functions and Graphs

In the last chapter, you looked at a few different types of charts and graphs likely to show up on the Math Test. Another way data can be represented is with a graph in the *xy*-plane. This chapter will give you the tools you need to understand these graphs and other representations of functions.

FUNCTION FUNDAMENTALS

Think of a **function** as just a machine for producing ordered pairs. You put in one number and the machine spits out another. The most common function is an $f(x)$ function. You've probably dealt with it in your algebra class.

Let's look at a question.

———————————○———————————

3

If $f(x) = x^3 - 4x + 8$, what is the value of $f(5)$?

A)   67

B)   97

C)   113

D)   147

What's This?

Anytime you see the notation $f(x)$, know that f isn't a variable; it's the name of the function. When you say it out loud it's "f of x." Though $f(x)$ is the most common way to show that an equation is a mathematic function, any letter can be used. So you may see $g(x)$ or $h(d)$. Know that you're still dealing with a function.

Here's How to Crack It

The question asks for the value of $f(5)$ for the given function. Any time you see a number inside the parentheses, such as $f(5)$, plug in that number for x. The question is actually telling you to use Plugging In! Let's do it:

$f(5) = 5^3 - 4(5) + 8$
$f(5) = 125 - 20 + 8$
$f(5) = 113$

The correct answer is (C).

———————————○———————————

The previous question gave you a number to put into the function, which made it a Plugging In question. If the question gives you information about what comes out of the function and asks what should go in, it's a PITA question!

Here's an example of using PITA on a function question.

8

$$f(a) = -6a$$

$$g(a) = a^2$$

Two functions are defined above. For which of the following values of a does $f(a) + g(a) = -9$

A) −3

B) $\dfrac{2}{3}$

C) 3

D) 6

Use PITA!
Don't forget that you can often plug in the answer choices on function questions! Noticing a pattern yet? Just a few easy tricks can unlock a lot of easy points.

Here's How to Crack It

The question asks for the value of a that goes into two functions to produce a specific result. There are numbers in the answers, and the question is asking for a specific value, so this is a good chance to Plug In The Answers. Label the answers as "a" and start with one of the middle answer choices. An integer will be easier to work with than a fraction, so try (C), 3. Plug $a = 3$ into both functions to get

$$f(3) = -6(3) = -18$$

$$g(3) = (3)^2 = 9$$

Plug those results into the equation given at the end of the question to find that

$$f(3) + g(3) = -18 + 9 = -9$$

This matches the information in the question, so the correct answer is (C).

Now that you know the basics of functions on the SAT, try the next one.

14

If $f(x) = x^2 + 2$, which of the following could be a value of $f(x)$?

A) −1

B) 0

C) 1

D) 2

Here's How to Crack It

The question asks for a possible value of the function. Therefore, the question is asking which of these values could be spit out of the $f(x)$ machine. Think about what is going in. No matter what you put in as a value for x, the value of x^2 has to be positive or zero. So, the lowest possible value of $x^2 + 2$ is 2. The correct answer is (D).

Note that you could also approach this question by plugging in the answers. If you plugged in 1 for $f(x)$, for instance, you would get $1 = x^2 + 2$, which becomes $x^2 = -1$, which is impossible.

Sometimes you'll get more complicated questions. As long as you know that when you put in x, your function will spit out another number, you'll be fine. Now try another one.

25

What is the value of c if $g(x) = 4x^2 - 6$ and $g(x - c) = 4x^2 + 40x + 94$?

A) −40

B) −5

C)   5

D) 40

Here's How to Crack It

The question asks for the value of *c*. In function notation, the number inside the parentheses is the *x*-value that goes into the function. This question might seem complicated, but look beyond the math and use your Princeton Review SAT knowledge. The question asks for a specific value and has numbers in the answers, so try PITA! Label the answer choices as "*c*" and start in the middle with (C), 5. Plug *c* = 5 into the question, and the value to put into the function becomes $x - 5$.

$$g(x - 5) = 4(x - 5)^2 - 6$$

FOIL the quadratic to get

$$g(x - 5) = 4(x^2 - 10x + 25) - 6$$

Distribute and combine like terms to get

$$g(x - 5) = 4x^2 - 40x + 100 - 6$$
$$g(x - 5) = 4x^2 - 40x + 94$$

Set the results equal to the quadratic given in the question.

$$4x^2 - 40x + 94 = 4x^2 + 40x + 94$$

This is not true, so eliminate (C). The middle term has the right coefficient but the wrong sign, so try (B), –5. The function becomes

$$g(x + 5) = 4(x + 5)^2 - 6.$$

Carry out the same steps as before to get

$$g(x + 5) = 4(x^2 + 10x + 25) - 6$$
$$g(x + 5) = 4x^2 + 40x + 100 - 6$$
$$g(x + 5) = 4x^2 + 40x + 94$$

This is equal to the quadratic given in the question, so –5 is the value of *c*. The correct answer is (B).

———————————○———————————

Another way the SAT can make functions more complicated is to give you two functions to deal with together. If you approach these question one piece at a time, they will be easier to handle.

Here's an example.

———————————○———————————

14

$$p(x) = 2 + q(x)$$
$$q(x) = 2 - 2x$$

What is the value of $p(-1)$ given the functions defined above?

A) 6

B) 2

C) 1

D) −1

Here's How to Crack It

The question asks for the value of a function given the value of x. When given the value to input into the function, plug in that value and solve in bite-sized pieces. Since $p(x)$ contains $q(x)$, first solve for $q(-1)$. Plug $x = -1$ into the q function to get

$$q(-1) = 2 - 2(-1) = 2 + 2 = 4$$

Now plug $x = -1$ and $q(-1) = 4$ into the p function. That function becomes

$$p(-1) = 2 + 4 = 6$$

This question might have looked complicated, but it can be solved by working in bite-sized pieces and applying the basics of working with functions twice. The correct answer is (A).

———————————○———————————

Sometimes you may see a word problem that describes a function and then asks you to "build a function" that describes the real-world situation presented in the question. Take the following question, for example.

15

Rock climbing routes are rated on a numbered scale with the highest number representing the most difficult route. Sally tried a range of shoe sizes on each of several routes of varying difficulty and found that when she wore smaller shoes, she could climb routes of greater difficulty. If D represents the difficulty rating of a route Sally successfully climbed and s represents the size of the shoes she wore on such a route, then which of the following could express D as a function of s ?

A) $D(s) = s^2$

B) $D(s) = \sqrt{s}$

C) $D(s) = s - 3.5$

D) $D(s) = \dfrac{45}{s}$

Here's How to Crack It

The question asks for a function that best represents a situation. Start by thinking about the relationship described in the question: the smaller the shoes, the greater the difficulty. This is an inverse relationship. So, look for an inverse function. Only (D) is an inverse function.

If you aren't sure, try plugging in numbers to try it out. Plug in $s = 8$ and then $s = 10$ to see if the result for D is smaller when you use a larger shoe size. Since only (D) results in a smaller difficulty for a larger shoe size, the correct answer is (D).

What's the Point?

Why did math folks come up with functions? To graph them, of course! When you put in a value for x, and your machine (or function) spits out another number, that's your y. You now have an ordered pair. Functions are just another way to express graphs. Knowing the connection between functions and graphs is useful, because you will most likely see questions involving graphs on the SAT.

THE COORDINATE PLANE

A **coordinate plane,** or the **xy-plane,** is made up of two number lines that intersect at a right angle. The horizontal number line is called the **x-axis,** and the vertical number line is the **y-axis.**

The four areas formed by the intersection of the axes are called **quadrants.** The location of any point can be described with a pair of numbers (x, y), just the way you would point on a map:
(0, 0) are the coordinates of the intersection of the two axes (also called the **origin**);
(1, 2) are the coordinates of the point one space to the right and two spaces up;
(–1, 5) are the coordinates of the point one space to the left and five spaces up;
(–4, –2) are the coordinates of the point four spaces to the left and two spaces down. All of these points are located on the following diagram.

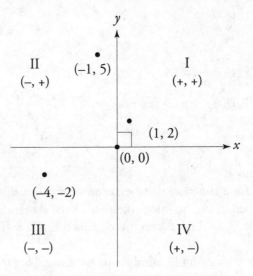

Some of the questions on the SAT may require you to know certain properties of lines on the xy-plane. Let's talk about them.

POINTS ON A LINE

You may be asked if a point is on a line or on the graph of any other equation. Just plug the coordinates of the point into the equation of the line to determine if that point makes the equation a true statement.

3

In the xy-plane, which of the following ordered pairs is a point on the line $y = 2x - 6$?

A) (6, 7)

B) (7, 7)

C) (7, 8)

D) (8, 7)

Quadrants

A coordinate plane has four distinct areas known as quadrants. The quadrants are numbered counterclockwise, starting from the top right. They help determine generally whether x and y are positive or negative. Sometimes knowing what quadrant a point is in and what that means is all you need to find the answer.

Ways to Remember

Having trouble remembering that the x-coordinate comes before the y-coordinate in an ordered pair? Just remember the phrase "x before y, walk before you fly." The letter x also comes before y in the dictionary.

Here's How to Crack It

The question asks for point that is on the given line. Plug in the answers, starting with (B). The (x, y) point is $(7, 7)$, so plug in 7 for x and 7 for y. The equation becomes $7 = 2(7) - 6$ or $7 = 8$. This isn't true, so eliminate (B). The result was very close to a true statement, and the point in (C) has the same x-coordinate and a larger y-coordinate, so try that next. Because $8 = 2(7) - 6$, the correct answer is (C).

SLOPE

You always read a graph from left to right. As you read the graph, how much the line goes up or down is known as the slope. **Slope** is the rate of change of a line and is commonly known as "rise over run." It's denoted by the letter m. Essentially, it's the change in the y-coordinates over the change in x-coordinates and can be found with the following formula:

$$m = \frac{(y_2 - y_1)}{(x_2 - x_1)}$$

This formula uses the points (x_1, y_1) and (x_2, y_2).

For example, if you have the points $(2, 3)$ and $(7, 4)$, the slope of the line created by these points would be

$$m = \frac{(4 - 3)}{(7 - 2)}$$

So the slope of a line with points $(2, 3)$ and $(7, 4)$ would be $\frac{1}{5}$, which means that every time you go up 1 unit, you travel to the right 5 units.

EQUATIONS OF A LINE

Slope-Intercept Form

The equation of a line can take multiple forms. The most common of these is known as the **slope-intercept form.** If you know the slope and the y-intercept, you can create the equation of a given line. A slope-intercept equation takes the form $y = mx + b$, where m is the slope and b is the **y-intercept** (the point where the function crosses the y-axis).

Let's say that you know that a certain line has a slope of 5 $\left(\text{which is the same as } \frac{5}{1} \right)$ and a y-intercept of 3. The equation of the line would be $y = 5x + 3$. You could graph this line simply by looking at this form of the equation. First, draw the y-intercept, $(0, 3)$. Next, plug in a number for *x* and solve for *y* to get a coordinate pair of a point on the line. Then connect the point you just found with the *y*-intercept you already drew, and voilà, you have a line. If you want more points, you can create a table such as the following:

x	y
–2	–7
–1	–2
0	3
1	8

Take a look at the finished product:

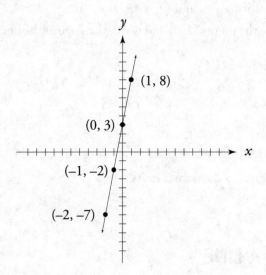

One way the SAT can test your understanding of lines is to show you a graph and ask you which equation describes that graph.

Here's an example.

―――――――――○―――――――――

4

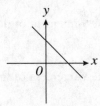

Which of the following could be the equation of the line
represented in the graph above?

A) $y = 2x + 4$

B) $y = 2x - 4$

C) $y = -2x - 1$

D) $y = -2x + 4$

Here's How to Crack It

The question asks for the equation of a line based on the graph. Remember that the equation of
a line is $y = mx + b$, where m is the slope and b is the y-intercept. Look at the graph and think
about what the equation should look like. Since the line is sloping downward, it should have a
negative slope, so you can eliminate (A) and (B). Next, since the line has a positive y-intercept,
you can eliminate (C). The correct answer is (D).

―――――――――○―――――――――

Standard Form

Another way the equation of a line can be written is the **standard form** of $Ax + By = C$, where
A, B, and C are constants and A and B do not equal zero. The test-writers will sometimes
present equations in this form in the hopes that you will waste time putting it in slope-intercept
form. If you know what to look for, the standard form can be just as useful as the slope-
intercept form.

In standard form $Ax + By = C$:

- the slope of the line is $-\dfrac{A}{B}$

- the y-intercept of the line is $\dfrac{C}{B}$

- the x-intercept of the line is $\dfrac{C}{A}$

The equation $y = 5x + 3$ in the previous example would be $-5x + y = 3$ when written in the standard form. Using the information above, you can see that:

$$\text{slope} = -\left(\dfrac{-5}{1}\right) = 5$$

$$y\text{-intercept} = \dfrac{3}{1} = 3$$

$$x\text{-intercept} = \dfrac{3}{-5} = -\dfrac{3}{5}$$

The answers for the slope and the y-intercept were the same as when the slope-intercept form was used. Depending on the form of the equation in the question or in the answers, knowing these line equation facts can help save time on the test.

Let's look at how this may be tested.

15

The graph of which of the following equations is parallel to the line with equation $y = -\dfrac{1}{3}x - \dfrac{1}{6}$?

A) $x - \dfrac{1}{3}y = 3$

B) $x - 3y = 2$

C) $x + 6y = 4$

D) $x + 3y = 5$

Here's How to Crack It

The question asks for the equation of a line that has a slope parallel to the slope of the line given. In the form $y = mx + b$, m represents the slope. The equation in the question is in that form, so the slope is $-\frac{1}{3}$. All you need to do now is find the answer choice that also has a slope of $-\frac{1}{3}$.

One way to do that would be to rewrite each answer in the $y = mx + b$ form.

However, notice that the equations in the answer choices are in the $Ax + By = C$ form, and in that form the slope is equal to $-\frac{A}{B}$. Find the slope of each answer choice, and eliminate the ones that are not $-\frac{1}{3}$. The slope of the line in (A) is $-\frac{1}{-\frac{1}{3}} = 3$.

This is not the correct slope, so eliminate (A). The slope of the line in (B) is $-\frac{1}{-3} = \frac{1}{3}$. This is also the wrong slope, so eliminate (B). The slope of the line in (C) is $-\frac{1}{6}$, which is also the wrong slope, so eliminate (C). The slope of the line in (D) is $-\frac{1}{3}$. This is the same slope as the line given in the question. The correct answer is (D).

PARALLEL AND PERPENDICULAR LINES

So now you know that **parallel lines** have the same slope. Whenever the SAT brings up **perpendicular lines,** just remember that a perpendicular line has a slope that is the *negative reciprocal* of the other line's slope. For instance, if the slope of a line is 3, then the slope of a line perpendicular to it would be $-\frac{1}{3}$. Combine this with the skills you've already learned to attack a question about perpendicular lines. Here's an example.

> **Parallel vs. Perpendicular**
> Parallel lines have the same slope and never intersect. Perpendicular lines have slopes that are negative reciprocals and intersect at a right angle.

18

Which of the following is the graph of a line perpendicular to the line defined by the equation $2x + 5y = 10$?

A)

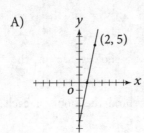

B)

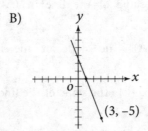

C)

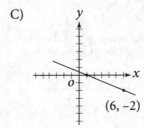

D)

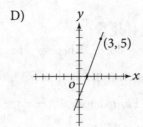

Here's How to Crack It

The question asks for a line perpendicular to the line $2x + 5y = 10$. Therefore, you need to find the slope of the line and then take the negative reciprocal to find the slope. You can convert the equation into the $y = mx + b$ format in order to find the slope, or simply remember that when an equation is presented in the form $Ax + By = C$, the slope is equal to $-\dfrac{A}{B}$. So the slope of this line is $-\dfrac{2}{5}$, and the slope of a perpendicular line would be $\dfrac{5}{2}$.

Look at the answer choices for one with a positive (upward) slope. Choices (B) and (C) slope downward, so eliminate them. Next, use points in the graph to find the slope of each answer. Eliminate (A); it has points at (1, 0) and (2, 5), for a slope of 5—too steep. The only remaining choice is (D), so the correct answer is (D).

———————————◯———————————

TWO EQUATIONS WITH INFINITELY MANY SOLUTIONS

In the previous chapters on algebra, we discussed equations with one or multiple solutions. Now imagine an equation in which any value of x would create a viable solution to the equation.

$$x + 3 = x + 3$$

In this case, it is fairly obvious that any number you choose to put in for x will create a true equation. But what does it mean when two lines have infinitely many solutions? Let's look at an example.

———————————◯———————————

20

$$gx - hy = 78$$
$$4x + 3y = 13$$

In the system of equations above, g and h are constants. If the system has infinitely many solutions, what is the value of gh ?

A) −432

B) −6

C) 6

D) 432

> **To Infinity…and Beyond!**
> When given two equations with infinitely many solutions, find a way to make them equal. The equations represent the same line.

Here's How to Crack It

The question asks for the value of gh, where g and h are coefficients in the system of equations. This question may have you scratching your head and moving on to the next question, but explore what you can do to solve this before you decide it's not worth your time. You may be surprised by how easy it is to solve a problem like this.

When they say that these equations have infinitely many solutions, what they are really saying is that these are the same equation, or that one equation is a multiple of the other equation. In other words, these two equations represent the same line. With that in mind, try to determine what needs to be done to make these equations equal. Since the right side of the equation is dealing with only a constant, first determine what you would need to do to make 13 equal to 78.

In this case, you need to multiply 13 by 6. Since you are working with equations, you need to do the same thing to both sides of the equation in order for the equation to remain equal.

$$6(4x + 3y) = 6 \times 13$$

$$24x + 18y = 78$$

Since both equations are now equal to 78, you can set them equal to each other, giving you this equation:

$$24x + 18y = gx - hy$$

You may know that when you have equations with the same variables on each side, the coefficients on those variables must be equal, so you can deduce that $g = 24$ and $h = -18$. (Be cautious when you evaluate this equation. The test-writers are being sneaky by using addition in one equation and subtraction in another.) Therefore, gh equals $24 \times -18 = -432$. The correct answer is (A).

TWO EQUATIONS WITH NO SOLUTIONS

You saw above that a system of equations can have infinitely many solutions. When solving equations, you likely assume, as most people do, that there will be at least one solution to the equation, but that is not always the case. Look at the following example.

$$3x - 6 = 3x + 7$$

If you solve this equation, you will find that $-6 = 7$. Since -6 can never equal 7, there is no value of x that can be put into this equation to make it true. In this case, the equation has no solutions.

What does it mean if two equations of lines have no solutions? Here's one to try.

5

Which of the following accurately represents the set of solutions

for the lines $6x + 12y = -24$ and $y = -\dfrac{1}{2}x + 2$?

A) (0, –4)

B) (0, 4)

C) There are no solutions.

D) There are infinitely many solutions.

There's Just No Solution
When given two equations with no solutions, find a way to compare slopes. The equations represent parallel lines.

Here's How to Crack It

The question asks for the solution to the system of equations. If the lines intersect, this will be

the point of intersection. The answers in (C) and (D), though, suggest that the lines may be the

same or parallel. Rather than plugging in the points in (A) and (B), look for a way to compare

slopes. Start by putting the first line into $y = mx + b$ form: $12y = -6x - 24$. Divide the whole

equation by 12, so $y = -\dfrac{1}{2}x - 2$. Since these lines have the same slope but different y-intercepts,

the lines are parallel, and they will never intersect. Therefore, the correct answer is (C).

If two lines had different slopes, the lines would intersect at a single point such as (A) or (B).
If the equations were identical, then they would be the same line and therefore have infinitely
many solutions.

POINTS OF INTERSECTION

Earlier in this book you learned how to find the solution to a system of equations. There are
several ways to do this, including stacking up the equations and adding or subtracting, setting
them equal, or even plugging in the answers. The SAT may also ask about the intersection of
the graphs of two equations in the xy-plane, which is a similar idea.

Let's try one.

14

In the *xy*-plane, which of the following is a point of intersection between the graphs of $y = x + 2$ and $y = x^2 + x - 2$?

A) $(0, -2)$

B) $(0, 2)$

C) $(1, 0)$

D) $(2, 4)$

Here's How to Crack It

Here's how you would apply PITA in a point of intersection question.

The question asks for the point of intersection for two equations. This is a point that is on the graphs of both equations. Therefore, the point would actually work if plugged into the equation of the line and the equation of the parabola.

So, use PITA by testing the answer choices: start with one of the answers in the middle and plug in the point to each equation to see if it is true. The correct point of intersection will work in both functions. Try (C) in the first equation: does $0 = (1) + 2$? No. So, (C) is not the answer. Try (D) in the first equation: does $4 = (2) + 2$? Yes. So, try (D) in the second equation: does $4 = (2)2 + 2 - 2$? Yes. Since $(2, 4)$ works in both equations, the correct answer is (D).

OTHER THINGS YOU CAN DO TO A LINE

The **midpoint formula** gives the midpoint of *ST*, with points $S(x_1, y_1)$ and $T(x_2, y_2)$. It's simply

the average of the *x*-coordinates and the *y*-coordinates. In our example, the midpoint would be

$\left(\dfrac{x_1 + x_2}{2}, \dfrac{y_1 + y_2}{2} \right)$.

Let's see an example of a midpoint question.

2

In the *xy*-plane, what is the midpoint of the line segment with endpoints at (3, 4) and (0, 0) ?

A) (1.5, 2)

B) (5, 0)

C) (2.5, 0)

D) (3.5, 3.5)

Here's How to Crack It

The question asks for the midpoint of the line segment formed by two points in the coordinate plane. You can use the formula for the midpoint of a line segment: $\left(\dfrac{x_1 + x_2}{2}, \dfrac{y_1 + y_2}{2} \right)$. If you forget it, try to remember that you are just taking the average of the *x*-coordinates of the two points to get the *x*-coordinate of the midpoint, and doing the same for the *y*-coordinates. For the *x*-coordinates, the average of 3 and 0 is (3 + 0) ÷ 2 = 1.5. Only one answer has this for the *x*-coordinate: (A). Don't waste time calculating the *y*-coordinate if you don't have to! The correct answer is (A).

The **distance formula** looks quite complicated. The easiest way to solve the distance between two points is to connect them and form a triangle. Then use the Pythagorean Theorem. Many times, the triangle formed is one of the common Pythagorean triplets (3-4-5 or 5-12-13).

Let's try a distance formula question.

3

Which of the following points lies the greatest distance from the origin in the *xy*-plane?

A) $(\sqrt{2}, \sqrt{2})$

B) $(-1, -1)$

C) $(\sqrt{2}, 0)$

D) $(0, 1)$

Here's How to Crack It

The question asks for a point that will be farthest away from the origin. Draw the line between the origin and the point in each answer choice and use the technique described above to see which has the longest hypotenuse. Choice (A) would look like this:

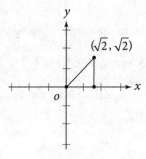

This creates a triangle with legs of $\sqrt{2}$ and $\sqrt{2}$. Use the Pythagorean Theorem to find the hypotenuse.

$$\left(\sqrt{2}\right)^2 + \left(\sqrt{2}\right)^2 = c^2$$
$$2 + 2 = c^2$$
$$4 = c^2$$
$$2 = c$$

Thus, the distance between the point in (A) and the origin is 2. Do the same thing for the other three points. The distance from the origin to the point in (B) is $\sqrt{2}$. The points in (C) and (D) lie on a straight line right and up from the origin, respectively, so the distance from the origin to the point in (C) is $\sqrt{2}$, and the distance from the origin to the point in (D) is 1. The longest distance is 2, which is the distance from the origin to the point in (A). The correct answer is (A).

ROOTS, SOLUTIONS, AND *x*-INTERCEPTS

We've talked about *y*-intercepts in the discussion of the slope-intercept form of a line, and we talked about solutions when we covered systems of equations. But what about *x*-intercepts, or the solution for just one equation? A **solution,** sometimes called a **root,** is simply any point where a line or curve intersects the *x*-axis. Similarly, just as the *y*-intercept was the point where a line crossed the *y*-axis, an ***x*-intercept** is a point where a line or curve intersects the *x*-axis.

Keep these terms straight and you'll be in great shape!

Let's try a question that requires knowledge of intercepts and distance in the *xy*-plane.

15

What is the distance between the *x*-intercept and the *y*-intercept of the line $y = \frac{2}{3}x - 6$?

A)   9

B)   15

C) $\sqrt{89}$

D) $\sqrt{117}$

Here's How to Crack It

The question asks for the distance between the intercepts of a line, so start by finding the

x- and *y*-intercepts of the line. When an equation is in $y = mx + b$ form, the *y*-intercept is *b*.

So, the *y*-intercept is at the point $(0, -6)$. To find the *x*-intercept, you need a point where the

y-value is 0, just like how the *y*-intercept has an *x* value of 0. So, plug in 0 for *y* in the equation:

$0 = \frac{2}{3}x - 6$, so $\frac{2}{3}x = 6$, and $x = 6\left(\frac{3}{2}\right) = 9$. The *x*-intercept, then, is (9, 0).

Now draw a right triangle with a base of 9 (the difference between the *x*-coordinates) and a height of 6 (the difference between the *y*-coordinates), and use the Pythagorean Theorem (more on this in the next chapter) to calculate the distance: $6^2 + 9^2 = c^2$, so $c^2 = 117$, and the distance is $\sqrt{117}$. The correct answer is (D).

---

y = f(x)

Sometimes, instead of seeing the typical $y = mx + b$ equation, or something similar, you'll see $f(x) = mx + b$. Look familiar? Graphs are just another way to show information from a function. Functions show information algebraically and graphs show functions geometrically (as pictured).

Here's an example. The function $f(x) = 3x - 2$ is shown graphically as the following:

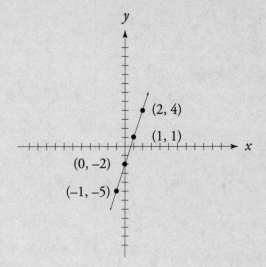

The reason the SAT includes function questions is to test whether you can figure out the relationship between a function and its graph. To tackle these questions, you need to know that the independent variable, the x, is on the x-axis, and the dependent variable, the $f(x)$, is on the y-axis. For example, if you see a function of $f(x) = 7$, then you need to understand that this is a graph of a horizontal line where $y = 7$.

GRAPHING FUNCTIONS

One type of function question you might be asked is how the graph of a function would shift if you added a value to it.

Here is a quick guide for the graph of $f(x) = x^2$, as seen below:

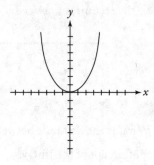

For $f(x) + c$, where c is a constant, the graph will shift up c units, as shown in the diagram below:

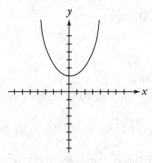

Conversely, $f(x) - c$ will shift the graph down by c units:

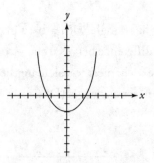

For $f(x + c)$, the graph will shift c units to the left:

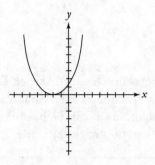

For $f(x - c)$, the graph will shift to the right by c units:

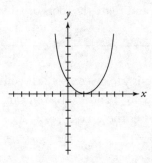

You may have realized how easy these questions would become if you simply put them into your graphing calculator. If calculator use is allowed, type in the function; if not, remember the four simple rules for transforming graphs.

You can also plug in points to find the correct graph.

EQUATIONS OF A PARABOLA

Standard Form

The SAT will ask questions using three different forms of the equation for a parabola.

> The standard form of a parabola equation is
>
> $$y = ax^2 + bx + c$$

In the standard form of a parabola, the value of a tells whether a parabola opens upward or downward (if a is positive, the parabola opens upward, and if a is negative, the parabola opens downward).

Factored Form

We looked at equations for parabolas in Chapter 13 when we solved quadratics. The factored form of a quadratic equation reveals the roots of the parabola. These are also the solutions of x. Given a question about roots or solutions, it can be helpful to know the relationship between the equation and the graph of the parabola in the xy-plane.

> The factored form of a parabola equation is
>
> $$y = a(x - r_1)(x - r_2)$$
>
> In the factored form, r_1 and r_2 are the roots or x-intercepts of the parabola.

For the next question, the equation is $y = x^2 - 4x - 12$. If you factored this, you'd get $y = (x + 2)(x - 6)$, and the roots would be at $x = -2$ and $x = 6$. You can see that those are the exact points on the graph that the parabola crosses the x-axis.

Vertex Form

> The vertex form of a parabola equation is
>
> $$y = a(x - h)^2 + k$$
>
> In the vertex form, the point (h, k) is the vertex of the parabola.

In vertex form, the value of a still indicates which way the parabola opens. Simply knowing what the vertex form looks like may help you answer a question, like the following example.

29

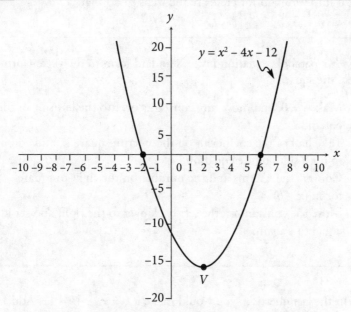

$y = x^2 - 4x - 12$

Which of the following is an equivalent form of the equation of the graph shown in the *xy*-plane above, from which the coordinates of vertex *V* can be identified from constants in the equation?

A) $y = (x - 2)^2 - 16$

B) $y = x(x - 4) - 12$

C) $y = (x - 6)(x + 2)$

D) $y = (x + 6)(x - 2)$

Here's How to Crack It

The question asks for the equation that contains the coordinates of the vertex. The graph tells you that the vertex of the parabola is at about (2, –16). Only (A) has the numbers 2 and 16 in it, so it must be the correct answer. If more than one choice had these constants, you could use your knowledge of the vertex form. If you recognize that the question asks for the vertex form of the equation of the parabola, you can simply select (A), the only choice that actually uses that form. (If the question had asked about the roots or solutions, you would pick (C) or (D), which are in the factored form.) Finally, if you forget the form, you can multiply out the answers to see which of them matches the original equation. Of course, the test-writers have written the answers such that all but (D) are equivalent, so you would still have to guess from among the remaining three answer choices. No matter which approach you take, the correct answer is (A).

Knowing the vertex of a parabola can help you more easily answer questions about the minimum or maximum value a parabolic function will reach, or the *x*-value that results in that minimum or maximum *y*-value. Say the last question was a Grid-In on the No Calculator section that asked for the *x*-coordinate of the vertex. You couldn't graph it to find the vertex, so you'd have to get it into vertex form. Here are the steps to do that.

> To convert a parabola equation in the standard form to the vertex form, complete the square.
>
> 1. Make $y = 0$, and move any constants over to the left side of the equation.
> 2. Take half of the coefficient on the *x*-term, square it, and add it to both sides of the equation.
> 3. Convert the *x* terms and the number on the right to square form: $(x - h)^2$.
> 4. Move the constant on the left back over to the right and set it equal to *y* again.

For the equation in the last question, you would make it $0 = x^2 - 4x - 12$. Add 12 to both sides to get $12 = x^2 - 4x$. You'd add 4 to both sides to get $16 = x^2 - 4x + 4$, and then convert the right side to the square form to get $16 = (x - 2)^2$. Finally, you'd move the 16 back over and set it equal to *y* to get $y = (x - 2)^2 - 16$.

EQUATION OF A CIRCLE

The SAT will also ask questions about the equation of a circle in the *xy*-plane.

> The equation of a circle is
>
> $$(x - h)^2 + (y - k)^2 = r^2$$
>
> In the circle equation, the center of the circle is the point (h, k), and the radius of the circle is *r*.

Let's look at a question that tests the use of the circle equation.

28

What is the radius of a circle graphed in the xy-plane and given by the equation $3x^2 + 15x + 3y^2 - 3y = 28.5$?

A) 3

B) 4

C) $\sqrt{35}$

D) $\sqrt{48}$

Here's How to Crack It

The question asks for the radius of a circle given an equation for its graph. The equation in standard form of a circle in the xy-plane is

$$(x - h)^2 + (y - k)^2 = r^2$$

where (h,k) is the center of the circle and r is the radius. The equation given in the question is not in standard form. To put it into standard form, complete the squares. Start by dividing the entire equation by 3 to remove the coefficients on the x^2 and y^2 terms. This leaves

$$x^2 + 5x + y^2 - y = 9.5$$

Next, take half the coefficient on the x term, or 2.5, square it to get 6.25, and add 6.25 to both sides. Now the equation is

$$x^2 + 5x + 6.25 + y^2 - y = 15.75$$

Do the same with the coefficient on the y term to get

$$x^2 + 5x + 6.25 + y^2 - y + 0.25 = 16$$

The standard form equation for this circle is thus

$$(x + 2.5)^2 + (y - 0.5)^2 = 16$$

The question didn't ask for the center of the circle, so focus on the radius. If $r^2 = 16$, then $r = 4$. The correct answer is (B).

Just as you may be given a parabola in standard form and expected to convert it into vertex form, you may also be given an equation for a circle that is not in the form $(x - h)^2 + (y - k)^2 = r^2$ and expect you to figure out the radius or center. To do so, you just need to complete the square as you did with the equation of a parabola. You will need to do it twice, though—once for the x-terms and again for the y-terms.

Got all of that? Now test your knowledge of functions and graphing with the following drills.

Functions and Graphs Drill 1: No Calculator Section

Use your new knowledge of functions and graphs to complete these questions, but don't use your calculator! Answers and explanations can be found on page 468.

3

Let the function f be defined such that $f(x) = x^2 - c$, where c is a constant. If $f(-2) = 6$, what is the value of c ?

A) -10

B) -2

C) 0

D) 2

7

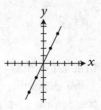

The graph above shows $y = 2x$. Which of the following graphs represents $y = |2x|$?

A)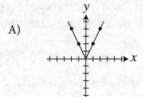

B)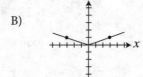

C)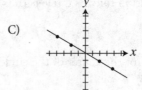

D)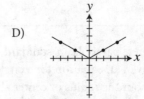

10

The graph of line *l* in the *xy*-plane passes through the points (2, 5) and (4, 11). The graph of line *m* has a slope of –2 and an *x*-intercept of 2. If point (*x*, *y*) is the point of intersection of lines *l* and *m*, what is the value of *y* ?

A) $\dfrac{3}{5}$

B) $\dfrac{4}{5}$

C) 1

D) 2

15

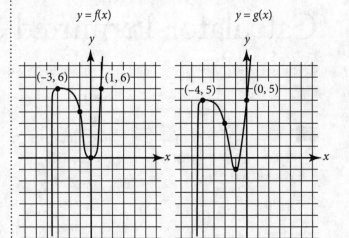

The figures above show the graphs of the functions *f* and *g*. The function *f* is defined by $f(x) = 2x^3 + 5x^2 - x$. The function *g* is defined by $g(x) = f(x - h) - k$, where *h* and *k* are constants. What is the value of *hk* ?

A) –2

B) –1

C) 0

D) 1

Functions and Graphs Drill 2: Calculator-Permitted Section

Calculator use is allowed on these questions, so use it wisely. Answers and explanations can be found starting on page 469.

6

If $f(x) = \sqrt{3x-2}$, what is the smallest possible value of $f(x)$?

A) 0

B) $\frac{2}{3}$

C) 1

D) 2

10

x	y
−3	−7
−1	−3
2	3

Based on the chart above, which of the following could express the relationship between x and y?

A) $y = x - 4$

B) $y = 2x - 1$

C) $y = 2x + 2$

D) $y = 3x - 3$

13

Line l contains points (3, 2) and (4, 5). If line m is perpendicular to line l, then which of the following could be the equation of line m?

A) $x + 5y = 15$

B) $x + 3y = 15$

C) $3x + y = 5$

D) $-5x + y = \frac{1}{3}$

18

If $f(x) = 2x^2 + 4$ for all real numbers x, which of the following is equal to $f(3) + f(5)$?

A) $f(4)$

B) $f(6)$

C) $f(10)$

D) $f(15)$

21

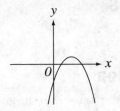

The graph of $y = g(x)$ is shown in the figure above. If $g(x) = ax^2 + bx + c$ for constants a, b, and c, and if $abc \neq 0$, then which of the following must be true?

A) $ac > 1$

B) $c > 1$

C) $ac > 0$

D) $a > 0$

26

Carlos and Katherine are estimating acceleration by rolling a ball from rest down a ramp. At 1 second, the ball is moving at 5 meters per second (m/s); at 2 seconds, the ball is moving at 10 m/s; at 3 seconds, the ball is moving at 15 m/s; and at 4 seconds, it is moving at 20 m/s. When graphed on an xy-plane, which equation best describes the ball's estimated acceleration where y expresses speed and x expresses time?

A) $y = 5x + 5$

B) $y = 25x$

C) $y = 5x$

D) $y = (4x + 1)^2 + 5$

CHAPTER DRILL ANSWERS AND EXPLANATIONS

Functions and Graphs Drill 1: No Calculator Section

3. **B** The question asks for the value of c. Start by plugging in what you know into the given function. If $f(x) = x^2 - c$, and $f(-2) = 6$, then plug in -2 for x in the function: $f(-2) = (-2)^2 - c$. Solve and replace $f(-2)$ with 6: $6 = 4 - c$; $2 = -c$; and $c = -2$. If you picked (A), you forgot that $(-2)^2$ is positive 4. The correct answer is (B).

7. **A** The question asks for the graph of the equation. Try plugging in a value for x to see if the graphs include that point. If $x = 0$, then $y = 0$, so $(0, 0)$ should be a point on the graph. Unfortunately, this doesn't eliminate any answer choices; try another value. If $x = 1$, then $y = 2$, so $(1, 2)$ should be a point on the graph. Eliminate (B), (C), and (D). The correct answer is (A).

10. **D** The question asks for the value of y. First, find the slope of line l by using the slope formula: $\dfrac{y_2 - y_1}{x_2 - x_1} = \dfrac{11 - 5}{4 - 2} = \dfrac{6}{2} = 3$. Plug this slope and one of the points on line l into the slope-intercept form $y = mx + b$ to solve for b, giving you the full equation of the line. If you use the point $(2, 5)$, you get $5 = 3(2) + b$ or $5 = 6 + b$, so $b = -1$. Therefore, the equation for line l is $y = 3x - 1$. For line m, the slope is given as -2, and the x-intercept is 2. Be very careful not to jump to the conclusion that the equation of line m is $y = -2x + 2$. In the form $y = mx + b$, the b is the y-intercept, not the x-intercept. The x-intercept is where $y = 0$, so you know that $(2, 0)$ is a point on line m. Use this point and the slope to find the equation of line m in the same way you did for line l: $0 = -2(2) + b$, so $b = 4$ and the equation is $y = -2x + 4$. Now set the x parts of the equations equal to find the point of intersection. If $3x - 1 = -2x + 4$, then $5x = 5$ and $x = 1$. Again, be careful! The question asked for the value of y! Plug $x = 1$ into one of the line equations to find y. For line l, the equation becomes $y = 3(1) - 1 = 3 - 1 = 2$. The correct answer is (D).

15. **B** The question asks for the value of hk. The second graph moves down 1 and to the left 1. Remember that when a graph moves to the left, it is represented by $(x + h)$, which would be the same as $x - (-1)$. So $h = -1$. Because a negative k represents moving down, $k = 1$. Therefore, $hk = (-1) \times (1) = -1$, and the correct answer is (B).

Functions and Graphs Drill 2: Calculator-Permitted Section

6. **A** The question asks for the smallest value of $f(x)$. This is a specific value, so you can use Plugging In the Answers. The numbers in the answer choices replace the $f(x)$ portion of the equation, so you can just write out the rest of it, $\sqrt{3x-2}$, next to each to see if it can be true. Start with (A) since you are looking for the smallest value of $f(x)$. If $0 = \sqrt{3x-2}$, then $0 = 3x - 2$ when you square both sides. Add 2 to both sides to get $2 = 3x$, and then divide both sides by 3. You get $x = \frac{2}{3}$. Since this is a real value, the equation works, so the smallest value of $f(x)$ is 0. The correct answer is (A).

10. **B** The question asks for the equation that best models a set of points. Plug in the values from the chart. Use the pair $(-3, -7)$ from the top of the chart and eliminate answers that are not true. Choice (A) becomes $-7 = -3 - 4$, which is true. Keep it. Keep (B): $-7 = 2(-3) - 1$ is true. Get rid of (C), which becomes $-7 = 2(-3) + 2$: -7 does not equal -4. Get rid of (D): $-7 = 3(-3) - 3$, and -7 does not equal -12. Now use another pair just to test (A) and (B). Using $(-1, -3)$, (A) gives $-3 = -1 - 4$, which is not true, so eliminate it. The correct answer is (B).

13. **B** The question asks for the equation of line m. First, find the slope of line l by using the slope formula: $\frac{y_2 - y_1}{x_2 - x_1} = \frac{5-2}{4-3} = \frac{3}{1}$. A line perpendicular to line l must have a slope that is the negative reciprocal of l's slope. So, its slope should be $-\frac{1}{3}$. In the standard form of a line $Ax + By = C$, the slope is $-\frac{A}{B}$. Only (B) has a slope of $-\frac{1}{3}$. If you didn't remember the rule about the slope of perpendicular lines in standard form, you could have converted the answers to slope-intercept form and sketched out each of the lines to look for the answer that looked perpendicular to l. The correct answer is (B).

18. **B** The question asks for the value of $f(3) + f(5)$, so find the values of $f(3)$ and $f(5)$ separately: $f(3) = 2(3)^2 + 4 = 22$ and $f(5) = 2(5)^2 + 4 = 54$. So $f(3) + f(5) = 76$. Now evaluate the answers to see which one will give a result of 76. You can tell that $f(4)$ will be between 22 and 54, so you can cross out (A). If you ballpark (C) and (D), putting 10 or 15 in the function will give you a number bigger than 100, and you're looking for 76, so (C) and (D) are too big. The correct answer is (B).

21. **C** The question asks for a true statement about the coefficients of a quadratic equation based on its graph. Use the graph transformation rules. Whenever a parabola faces down, the quadratic equation has a negative sign in front of the x^2 term. It always helps to plug in! For example, if your original equation was $(x - 2)^2$, putting a negative sign in front would make the parabola open

downward, so you'll have $-(x-2)^2$. If you expand it out, you get $-x^2 + 4x - 4$. Notice that the value of a in this equation is -1. Also notice that the value of c is -4. This allows you to eliminate (B) and (D). Now you must plug in differently to distinguish between (A) and (C). Be warned: you must use fractions to help discern which is correct. Say the x-intercepts take place at $x = \dfrac{1}{2}$ and $x = \dfrac{3}{4}$. Rewriting those two expressions means that the factors are $\left(x - \dfrac{1}{2}\right)$ and $\left(x - \dfrac{3}{4}\right)$. If you use FOIL on the terms, you end up with $x^2 - \dfrac{5}{4}x + \dfrac{3}{8}$. Remember, the parabola opens downward, so you must multiply each term by -1 to yield $-x^2 + \dfrac{5}{4}x - \dfrac{3}{8}$. Your values of a and c are now -1 and $-\dfrac{3}{8}$, respectively. Multiply the two values and you get $\dfrac{3}{8}$, which allows you to eliminate (A). The correct answer is (C).

26. **C**   The question asks for the equation that best models the ball's acceleration. Figure out the points that will be on the graph from the data given: (0, 0), (1, 5), (2, 10), (3, 15), (4, 20). Draw a line through or close to these points to get an idea of what the graph will look like. Then use POE. The line is linear, not quadratic, so you can eliminate (D). It is also clear that the line begins at the origin, so the y-intercept will be 0. This will eliminate (A). A slope of 25 is far too big—ballpark— so you can eliminate (B). The correct answer is (C).

Summary

o   Given a function, you put an *x*-value in and get an *f*(*x*) or *y*-value out.

o   Look for ways to use Plugging In and PITA on function questions.

o   For questions about the graphs of functions, remember that *f*(*x*) = *y*.

o   If the graph contains a labeled point or the question gives you a point, plug it into the equations in the answers and eliminate any that aren't true.

o   The equation of a line can take two forms. In either form, (*x*, *y*) is a point on the line.
   •   In slope-intercept form, *y* = *mx* + *b*, the slope is *m* and the *y*-intercept is *b*.

   •   In standard form, *Ax* + *By* = *C*, the slope is $-\dfrac{A}{B}$ and the *y*-intercept is $\dfrac{C}{B}$.

o   Given two points on a line, (x_1, y_1) and (x_2, y_2), the slope is $\dfrac{(y_2 - y_1)}{(x_2 - x_1)}$.

o   Two linear equations with infinitely many solutions actually represent the same line.

o   Parallel lines have the same slopes and no points of intersection.

o   Perpendicular lines have slopes that are negative reciprocals and intersect at a right angle.

o   To find a point of intersection, plug the point into both equations to see if it works or graph the lines on your calculator when it is allowed.

o   To find the midpoint between two points, average the *x*-coordinates and average the *y*-coordinates.

o   To find the distance between two points, make them the endpoints of the hypotenuse of a right triangle and use the Pythagorean Theorem.

o   The roots of a function, also known as solutions, zeroes, or *x*-intercepts, are the points where the graph crosses the *x*-axis and where *y* = 0.

- o Graphs of functions can be moved up or down if a number is added to or subtracted from the function, respectively. They can move left if a number is added inside the parentheses of the function or move right if a number is subtracted inside the parentheses.

- o The standard form of a parabola is $y = ax^2 + bx + c$, where c is the y-intercept. If a is positive, the parabola opens up, and if a is negative, it opens down.

- o The factored form of a parabola equation is $y = a(x - r_1)(x - r_2)$, where r_1 and r_2 are the roots or x-intercepts of the parabola.

- o The vertex form of a parabola equation is $y = a(x - h)^2 + k$, where (h, k) is the vertex. To get a parabola in the standard form into vertex form, complete the square.

- o The standard form of a circle equation is $(x - h)^2 + (y - k)^2 = r^2$, where (h, k) is the center and r is the radius. To get a circle equation into the standard form, complete the square for both the x-terms and the y-terms.

Chapter 19
Geometry

Now that you've had some review and practice in coordinate geometry, it's time to learn a few more geometry rules. The SAT Math Test contains five or six questions that test your basic geometry knowledge on topics like lines and angles, triangles, and circles. This chapter covers each of these topics and more and provides a step-by-step walk-through for each type of question.

GEOMETRY ON THE SAT

We covered coordinate geometry in Chapter 18. But in addition to coordinate geometry questions, there will be five or six questions on the SAT that test your knowledge of basic geometry rules. Well, kinda. At the beginning of each Math section, you are provided with the following reference table:

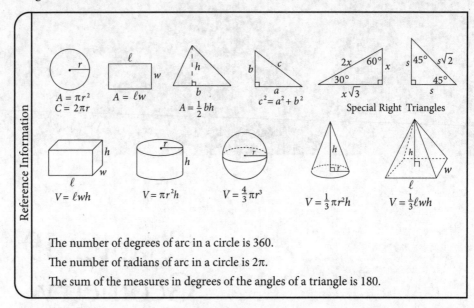

Reference Information

$A = \pi r^2$
$C = 2\pi r$

$A = \ell w$

$A = \frac{1}{2} bh$

$c^2 = a^2 + b^2$

Special Right Triangles

$V = \ell w h$

$V = \pi r^2 h$

$V = \frac{4}{3} \pi r^3$

$V = \frac{1}{3} \pi r^2 h$

$V = \frac{1}{3} \ell w h$

The number of degrees of arc in a circle is 360.

The number of radians of arc in a circle is 2π.

The sum of the measures in degrees of the angles of a triangle is 180.

This box of information contains *some* of what you'll need to tackle geometry on the SAT. In this chapter, we'll cover how to approach geometry questions and other information you will need to know in order to handle geometry questions on the SAT.

Geometry: Basic Approach

For the handful of non-coordinate geometry questions that appear on the SAT, we recommend the following step-by-step approach:

1. **Draw a figure** if a figure is not provided. Also, if there is a figure provided, but the question contains the note "Figure not drawn to scale," you might want to redraw the figure using the information in the question.
2. **Label the figure** with any information given in the question. Sometimes you can plug in for parts of the figure as well.
3. **Write down formulas** that you might need for the question.
4. **Ballpark** if you're stuck or running short on time.

These four steps, combined with the techniques you've learned in the rest of this book and the geometry concepts this chapter will cover, will enable you to tackle any geometry question you might run across on the SAT.

Before we dive in to the nitty-gritty, let's try a question using this approach.

25

In $\triangle ABC$ (not shown), $\angle ABC = 60°$ and $AC \perp BC$. If $AB = x$, then what is the area of $\triangle ABC$, in terms of x?

A) $\dfrac{x^2\sqrt{3}}{8}$

B) $\dfrac{x^2\sqrt{3}}{4}$

C) $\dfrac{x^2\sqrt{3}}{2}$

D) $x^2\sqrt{3}$

Here's How to Crack It

The question asks for the area of the triangle. Follow the steps outlined on the previous page. Start by drawing the figure. If $AC \perp BC$, then $\triangle ABC$ is a right triangle with the right angle at point C:

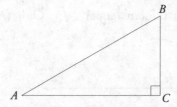

The next step is to label what you know. $\angle ABC = 60°$ can go right into the diagram. Because $AB = x$, you can plug in for x; make $x = 4$. Label this information in the diagram:

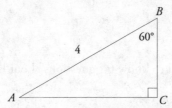

Next, figure out what other information you know. Because there are 180° in a triangle, $\angle BAC = 180 - 90 - 60 = 30°$. This is a 30°-60°-90° special right triangle, which you are given information about in the box at the start of each Math section. Based on the figure given in the box, the hypotenuse is equal to $2x$. (Note that this is a different x from the one you plugged in for; the test-writers are trying to confuse you.) So, if the hypotenuse is 4, then $x = \dfrac{4}{2} = 2$; this is the side opposite the 30° angle, BC. The remaining side, AC, is $x\sqrt{3}$, which is $2\sqrt{3}$. Label this information in your diagram:

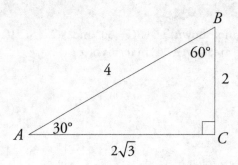

Now write down the formula you need. The question is asking for the area, so use the area of a triangle formula from the box: $A = \dfrac{1}{2}bh$. Fill in what you know. Because this is a right triangle, you can use the two legs of the triangle as the base and the height. Make $b = 2\sqrt{3}$ and $h = 2$ in the equation and solve: $A = \dfrac{1}{2}\left(2\sqrt{3}\right)(2) = 2\sqrt{3}$. This is your target; circle it. Now plug in $x = 4$ (that's the x from the question, NOT the x from the information in the box!) into each answer choice and eliminate what doesn't equal $2\sqrt{3}$. Only (A) works, so the correct answer is (A).

Now that we've covered how to approach geometry questions, let's look more closely at some of the geometry concepts you'll need for these questions.

LINES AND ANGLES

Here are the basic rules you need to know for questions about lines and angles on the SAT.

1. **A circle contains 360 degrees.**

   Every circle contains 360 degrees. Each degree is $\dfrac{1}{360}$ of the total distance around the outside of the circle. It doesn't matter whether the circle is large or small; it still has exactly 360 degrees.

2. When you think about angles, remember circles.
An angle is formed when two line segments extend from a common point. If you think of the point as the center of a circle, the measure of the angle is the number of degrees enclosed by the lines when they pass through the edge of the circle. Once again, the size of the circle doesn't matter; neither does the length of the lines. Refer to the following figure.

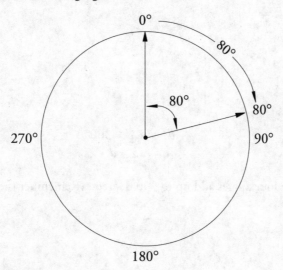

3. A line is a 180-degree angle.
You probably don't think of a line as an angle, but it is one. Think of it as a flat angle. The following drawings should help:

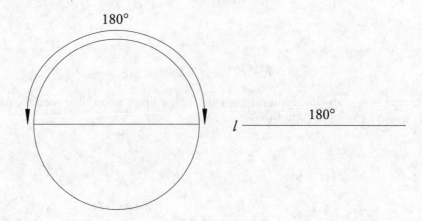

4. When two lines intersect, four angles are formed.
The following diagram should make this clear. The four angles are indicated by letters.

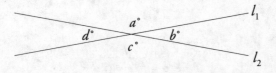

5. **When two lines intersect, the angles opposite each other will have the same measures.**
    Such angles are called **vertical angles.** In the following diagram, angles *a* and *c* are equal; so are angles *b* and *d*.

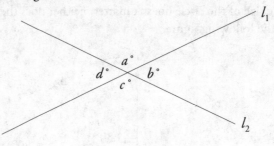

$$a + b + c + d = 360°$$
$$a = c, b = d$$

The measures of these four angles add up to 360 degrees. (Remember the circle.)

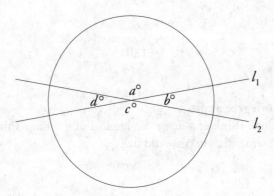

$$a + b + c + d = 360°$$

It doesn't matter how many lines you intersect through a single point. The total measure of all the angles formed will still be 360 degrees.

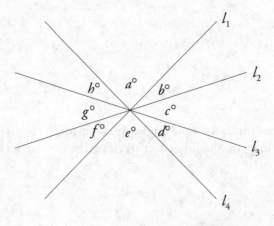

$$a + b + c + d + e + f + g + h = 360°$$
$$a = e, b = f, c = g, d = h$$

6. **If two lines are perpendicular to each other, each of the four angles formed is 90 degrees.**

A 90-degree angle is called a **right angle**.

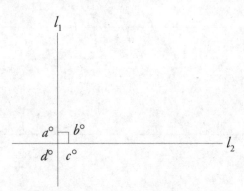

Angles *a*, *b*, *c*, and *d* all equal 90 degrees.

The little box at the intersection of the two lines is the symbol for a right angle. If the lines are not perpendicular to each other, then none of the angles will be right angles. Don't assume that an angle is a right angle unless you are specifically told that it is a right angle, either in the question or with the 90° symbol.

7. **When two parallel lines are cut by a third line, all of the small angles are equal, all of the big angles are equal, and the sum of any big angle and any small angle is 180 degrees.**

Parallel lines are two lines that never intersect, and the rules about parallel lines are usually taught in school with lots of big words. But we like to avoid big words whenever possible. Simply put, when a line cuts through two parallel lines, two kinds of angles are created: big angles and small angles. You can tell which angles are big and which are small just by looking at them. All the big angles look equal, and they are. The same is true of the small angles. Lastly, any big angle plus any small angle always equals 180 degrees. (The test-writers like rules about angles that add up to 180 or 360 degrees.)

In any geometry question, never assume that two lines are parallel unless the question or diagram specifically tells you so. In the following diagram, angle *a* is a big angle, and it has the same measure as angles *c, e,* and *g*, which are also big angles. Angle *b* is a small angle, and it has the same measure as angles *d, f,* and *h*, which are also small angles.

Perpendicular:
Meeting at right (90°) angles

Flip and Negate
If two lines are perpendicular, then their slopes are negative reciprocals; i.e., if l_1 has a slope of 2 and l_2 is perpendicular to l_1, then l_2 must have a slope of $-\dfrac{1}{2}$.

Parallel Lines
Parallel lines have the same slope.

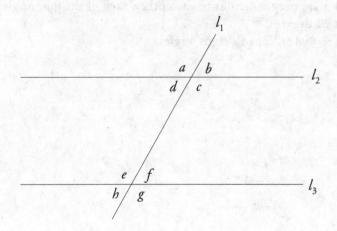

$$l_2 \parallel l_3$$
$$a = c = e = g$$
$$b = d = f = h$$

You should be able to see that the degree measures of angles a, b, c, and d add up to 360 degrees. So do those of angles e, f, g, and h. If you have trouble seeing it, draw a circle around the angles. What is the degree measure of a circle? Also, the sum of any small angle (such as d) and any big angle (such as g) is 180°.

Let's see how these concepts might be tested on the SAT.

12

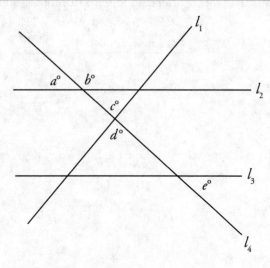

Note: Figure not drawn to scale.

In the figure above, $l_2 \parallel l_3$. Which of the following *could* be false?

A) $a = e$

B) $b + e = 180$

C) $l_1 \perp l_4$

D) $c = d$

Here's How to Crack It

The question asks for a statement that could be false. Use the geometry basic approach: start by marking l_2 and l_3 as parallel lines. Next, because you're looking for what could be false, consider each answer choice and use POE. For (A), if l_2 and l_3 are parallel, then l_4 transects both lines and creates sets of equal angles. All small angles around l_4 that are formed by l_2 or l_3 are equal, so a must be equal to e; eliminate (A). Choice (B) is based on the same set of intersecting lines; because l_2 and l_3 are parallel and l_4 transects both lines, then any big angle plus any small angle equals 180°. Therefore, (B) must be true; eliminate it. For (C), you don't know the value of any angles, so you cannot determine if these lines are perpendicular. Since (C) could be false, choose (C). Choice (D) must be true because opposite angles created by two lines are always equal. The correct answer is (C).

Converting Degrees to Radians

Some geometry questions will ask you to convert an angle measurement from degrees to radians. While this may sound scary, doing this conversion requires only that you remember that 180 degrees = π radians. Use this relationship to set up a proportion (see Chapter 17) and convert the units.

27

$\dfrac{54}{7}\pi$ radians is approximately equal to how many degrees?

A) 8°

B) 694°

C) 1,389°

D) 2,777°

Here's How to Crack It

Use the relationship between radians and degrees to set up a proportion. If 180 degrees = π radians, then the proportion will look like the following:

$$\frac{180\,\text{degrees}}{\pi\,\text{radians}} = \frac{x\,\text{degrees}}{\dfrac{54}{7}\pi\,\text{radians}}$$

Cross-multiply to get $180 \times \dfrac{54}{7}\pi = \pi x$. Divide both sides by π to get $180 \times \dfrac{54}{7} = x$. Finally, use your calculator, and you find that x is approximately 1,389. The correct answer is (C).

TRIANGLES

Here are some basic triangle rules you'll need to know for the SAT.

1. **Every triangle contains 180 degrees.**
    The word *triangle* means "three angles," and every triangle contains three interior angles. The measure of these three angles always adds up to exactly 180 degrees. You don't need to know why this is true or how to prove it. You just need to know it. And we mean *know* it.

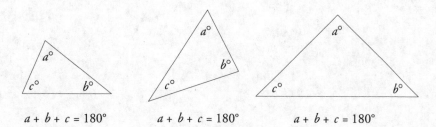

$a + b + c = 180°$ $a + b + c = 180°$ $a + b + c = 180°$

2. **An isosceles triangle is one in which two of the sides are equal in length.**
    The angles opposite those equal sides are also equal because angles opposite equal sides are also equal.

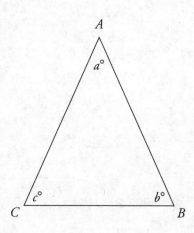

$$AB = AC \quad AB \neq BC$$
$$c = b \quad c \neq a$$

Your Friend the Triangle
If ever you are stumped by a geometry question that deals with a quadrilateral, hexagon, or other polygon, look for the triangles that you can form by drawing lines through the figure.

3. **An equilateral triangle is one in which all three sides are equal in length.**

Because the angles opposite equal sides are also equal, all three angles in an equilateral triangle are equal too. (Their measures are always 60 degrees each.)

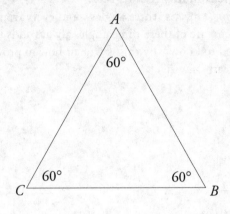

$$AB = BC = AC$$

4. **A right triangle is a triangle in which one of the angles is a right angle (90 degrees).**

The longest side of a right triangle, which is always opposite the 90-degree angle, is called the **hypotenuse.**

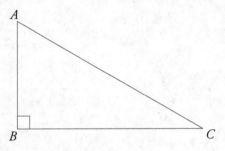

AC is the hypotenuse.

Some right triangles are also **isosceles.** The angles in an isosceles right triangle always measure 45°, 45°, and 90°.

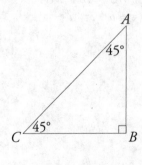

$$AB = BC$$

5. **The perimeter of a triangle is the sum of the lengths of its sides.**

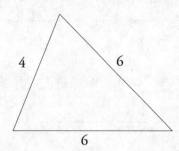

perimeter = 4 + 6 + 6 = 16

6. **The area of a triangle is** $\frac{1}{2}$ **(base × height).**

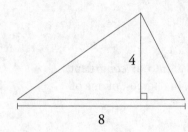

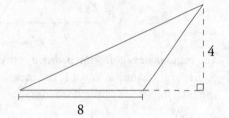

area = $\frac{1}{2}(8 \times 4)$ = 16   area = $\frac{1}{2}(8 \times 4)$ = 16

In or Out
The height can be found
with a line dropped
inside or outside the
triangle—just as long
as it's perpendicular to
the base.

Try a question testing some of these concepts.

3

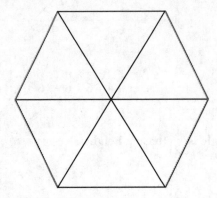

The regular hexagon shown above is divided into six congruent equilateral triangles. What is the measure, in degrees, of one of the interior angles of the hexagon?

A) 60°

B) 120°

C) 180°

D) 360°

Here's How to Crack It

The question asks for the measure of an angle in the diagram. First, you can ballpark and eliminate (C) and (D). Choice (C) would be a straight line, and (D) is all the way around a circle, so neither of those can be the interior angle of this figure. Next, label what you know. If each of the triangles in the figure is equilateral, then all of the angles within the triangles are equal to 60°. The interior angles of the hexagon are comprised of two angles of the triangles, so the interior angles of the hexagon must be 2 × 60 = 120°. The correct answer is (B).

SOHCAHTOA

Trigonometry will likely appear on the SAT Math Test. But fear not! Many trigonometry questions you will see mostly require you to know the basic definitions of the three main trigonometric functions. **SOHCAHTOA** is a way to remember the three functions.

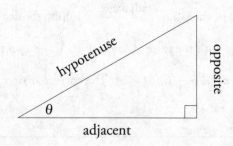

$$\text{sine } \theta = \frac{\text{opposite}}{\text{hypotenuse}} \qquad \text{cosine } \theta = \frac{\text{adjacent}}{\text{hypotenuse}} \qquad \text{tangent } \theta = \frac{\text{opposite}}{\text{adjacent}}$$

Check out this next example.

11

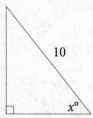

In the triangle above, sin $x = 0.8$ and cos $x = 0.6$. What is the area of the triangle?

A)   0.48

B)   4.8

C)   24

D)   48

Here's How to Crack It

The question asks for the area of the triangle. Use the definitions of sine and cosine to find the two legs of the triangle. Sine is $\dfrac{\text{opposite}}{\text{hypotenuse}}$, so if sin x = 0.8, then $0.8 = \dfrac{\text{opposite}}{10}$. Multiply both sides by 10 and you find the side opposite the angle with measure $x°$ is 8. Similarly, cosine is $\dfrac{\text{adjacent}}{\text{hypotenuse}}$, so if cos x = 0.6, then $0.6 = \dfrac{\text{adjacent}}{10}$. Multiply both sides by 10 to determine the side adjacent to the angle with measure $x°$ is 6. With those two sides, find the area. The formula for area is $A = \dfrac{1}{2}bh$, so $A = \dfrac{1}{2}(6)(8) = 24$. The correct answer is (C).

Pythagorean Theorem

The **Pythagorean Theorem** states that in a right triangle the square of the hypotenuse equals the sum of the squares of the other two sides. As mentioned earlier, the hypotenuse is the longest side of a right triangle; it's the side opposite the right angle. The square of the hypotenuse is its length squared. Applying the Pythagorean Theorem to the following drawing, we find that $a^2 + b^2 = c^2$.

> **Pythagorean Theorem**
> $a^2 + b^2 = c^2$, where c is the hypotenuse of a right triangle. Learn it; love it.

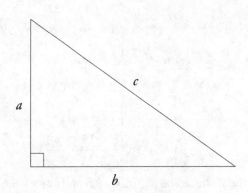

If you forget the Pythagorean Theorem, you can always look it up in the box at the beginning of the Math sections.

The test-writers love to ask you questions involving the Pythagorean Theorem along with SOHCAHTOA. See the following question.

15

In $\triangle ABC$ (not shown), $AC \perp BC$ and $\cos \angle ABC = \dfrac{12}{13}$. What is the value of $\tan \angle ABC$?

A) $\dfrac{5}{13}$

B) $\dfrac{5}{12}$

C) $\dfrac{12}{13}$

D) $\dfrac{12}{5}$

Here's How to Crack It

The question asks for the value of the tangent of an angle. Use the geometry basic approach: start by drawing triangle ABC.

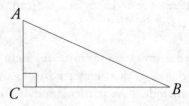

Next, label what you can. You don't know the actual side lengths, but because $\cos \angle ABC = \dfrac{12}{13}$,

you do know the relationship between the side adjacent to angle ABC and the hypotenuse.

You can plug in for this relationship: make BC (the side adjacent to the angle) 12 and AB (the

hypotenuse) 13:

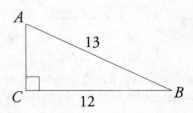

You need to find tan $\angle ABC$, which means you need $\dfrac{\text{opposite}}{\text{adjacent}}$. You already know the adjacent side is 12, but you still need the side opposite, AC. Use the Pythagorean Theorem to find the missing side:

$$a^2 + b^2 = c^2$$
$$12^2 + b^2 = 13^2$$
$$144 + b^2 = 169$$
$$b^2 = 25$$
$$b = 5$$

Therefore, $AC = 5$, and tan $\angle ABC = \dfrac{5}{12}$, so the correct answer is (B).

Special Right Triangles

Both of the previous questions you worked also used special right triangles. While in the last question we used the Pythagorean Theorem to find the missing side, if you memorize these special triangles, you can avoid using the Pythagorean Theorem in a lot of cases.

When it comes to geometry questions involving right triangles, the SAT Math Test is often fairly predictable, as questions tend to focus on certain relationships. In these questions, the triangles have particular ratios. There are two different types of special right triangles. The first involves the ratio of sides, and the second involves the ratio of angles.

The most common special right triangles with side ratios are known as **Pythagorean triplets.** Here are the test-writers' favorites:

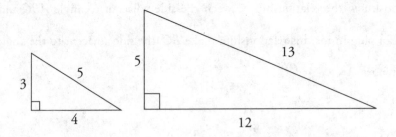

If you memorize these two sets of Pythagorean triplets (3-4-5 and 5-12-13), you'll often be able to find the answer without using the Pythagorean Theorem. If you're given a right triangle with a side of 3 and a hypotenuse of 5, you know right away that the other side has to be 4. Likewise, if you see a right triangle with sides of 5 and 12, you know the hypotenuse must be 13.

Your Friend the Rectangle

Be on the lookout for questions in which the application of the Pythagorean Theorem is not obvious. For example, every rectangle contains two right triangles. That means that if you know the length and width of the rectangle, you also know the length of the diagonal, which is the hypotenuse of both triangles.

Relax; It's Just a Ratio

A 3-4-5 triangle may be hiding, disguised as 6-8-10 or 18-24-30. It's all the same ratio, though, so be on the lookout.

The test-writers also like to use right triangles with sides that are simply multiples of the common Pythagorean triplets. For example, you might see a 6-8-10 or a 10-24-26 triangle. These sides are simply the sides of the 3-4-5 and 5-12-13 triangles multiplied by 2.

There are two types of special right triangles that have a specific ratio of angles. They are the **30°-60°-90° triangle** and the **45°-45°-90° triangle.** The sides of these triangles always have the same fixed ratio to each other. The ratios are as follows:

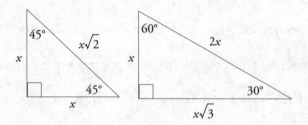

Let's talk about a 45°-45°-90° triangle first. Did you notice that this is also an isosceles right triangle? The legs will always be the same length. And the hypotenuse will always be the length of one leg times $\sqrt{2}$. Its ratio of side to side to hypotenuse is always $1:1:\sqrt{2}$. For example, if you have a 45°-45°-90° triangle with a leg length of 3, then the second leg length will also be 3 and the hypotenuse will be $3\sqrt{2}$.

Now let's talk about a 30°-60°-90° triangle. The ratio of shorter leg to longer leg to hypotenuse is always $1:\sqrt{3}:2$. For example, if the shorter leg of a 30°-60°-90° triangle is 5, then the longer leg would be $5\sqrt{3}$ and the hypotenuse would be 10.

Similar Triangles

Similar triangles have the same shape, but they are not necessarily the same size. Having the same shape means that the angles of the triangles are identical and that the corresponding sides have the same ratio. Look at the following two similar triangles:

Symbols

Here's a list of symbols you might see on the SAT Math Test, along with a translation of each one into English. Learn these symbols and keep an eye out for them!

Symbol	Meaning
$\triangle ABC$	triangle ABC
$\overline{AB}$	line segment AB
AB	the length of line segment AB

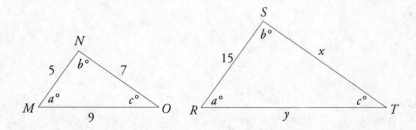

These two triangles both have the same set of angles, but they aren't the same size. Whenever this is true, the sides of one triangle are proportional to those of the other. Notice that sides *NO* and *ST* are both opposite the angle that is *a*°. These are called corresponding sides, because they correspond to the same angle. So the lengths of $\overline{NO}$ and $\overline{ST}$ are proportional to each other. In order to figure out the lengths of the other sides, set up a proportion: $\dfrac{MN}{RS} = \dfrac{NO}{ST}$. Now fill in the information that you know: $\dfrac{7}{x} = \dfrac{5}{15}$. Cross-multiply and you find that $x = 21$. You could also figure out the length of *y*: $\dfrac{NO}{ST} = \dfrac{MO}{RT}$. Therefore, $\dfrac{5}{15} = \dfrac{9}{y}$, and $y = 27$. Whenever you have to deal with sides of similar triangles, just set up a proportion.

Finally, there's a special relationship between similar triangles and trigonometry. Side lengths in similar triangles are proportional, and the trigonometric functions give the proportions of the sides of a triangle. Therefore, if two triangles are similar, the corresponding trigonometric functions are equal! Let's look at how this might work in a question.

16

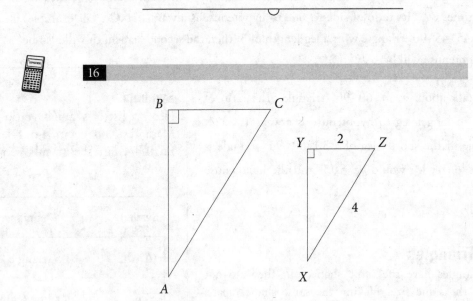

In the figure above, $\triangle ABC$ is similar to $\triangle XYZ$. What is the value of cos *A* ?

A) $\dfrac{1}{2}$

B) $\dfrac{\sqrt{3}}{2}$

C) $\sqrt{3}$

D) 2

Here's How to Crack It

The question asks for the value of cos *A* but gives measurements on triangle *XYZ*. Because the two triangles are similar, the value of corresponding trigonometric functions will be equal. Therefore, cos *A* = cos *X*. The value of cos *X* is $\dfrac{\text{adjacent}}{\text{hypotenuse}}$ or $\dfrac{XY}{XZ}$. You could use the Pythagorean Theorem to find *XY*, but it's easier to use the special right triangle discussed earlier. Because the hypotenuse is twice one of the legs, you know this is a 30°-60°-90° triangle. *YZ* is the shortest side (*x*), so *XY* is $x\sqrt{3}$ or $2\sqrt{3}$. Therefore, $\cos X = \dfrac{2\sqrt{3}}{4}$, which reduces to $\dfrac{\sqrt{3}}{2}$. Because cos *X* = cos *A*, cos *A* also equals $\dfrac{\sqrt{3}}{2}$. The correct answer is (B).

CIRCLES

Here are the rules you'll need to tackle circle questions on the SAT.

1. **The circumference of a circle is $2\pi r$ or πd, where *r* is the radius of the circle and *d* is the diameter.**

   You'll be given this information in your test booklet, so don't stress over memorizing these formulas. You will always be able to refer to your test booklet if you forget them. Just keep in mind that the diameter is always twice the length of the radius (and that the radius is half the diameter).

> **A Few Formulas**
> Area = πr^2
> Circumference = $2\pi r$
> or πd
> Diameter = $2r$

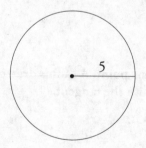

circumference = $2 \times \pi \times 5 = 10\pi$

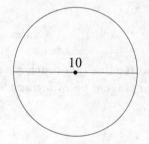

circumference = 10π

In math class you probably learned that π = 3.14 (or even 3.14159). On the SAT, π = 3⁺ (a little more than 3) is a good enough approximation. Even with a calculator, using π = 3 will give you all the information you need to solve difficult SAT multiple-choice geometry questions.

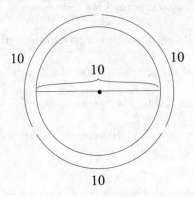

circumference = about 30

2. **The area of a circle is πr^2, where r is the radius of the circle.**

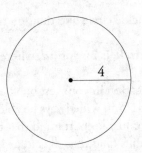

area = $\pi(4)^2 = 16\pi$

3. **A tangent is a line that touches a circle at exactly one point. A radius drawn from that tangent point forms a 90-degree angle with the tangent.**

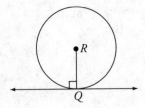

Let's see how these rules can show up on the SAT.

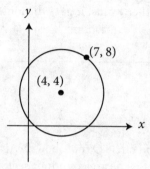

The circle defined by the equation $(x - 4)^2 + (y - 4)^2 = 25$ has its center at point (4, 4) and includes point (7, 8) on the circle. This is shown in the figure above. What is the area of the circle shown?

A) 5π

B) 10π

C) 16π

D) 25π

Here's How to Crack It

The question asks for the area of the circle, so write down the formula for area of a circle: $A = \pi r^2$. That means you need to determine the radius of the circle. If you remember the circle formula from the previous chapter, you simply need to recall that $r^2 = 25$ and just multiply by π to find the area. If not, you can find the distance between (4, 4) and (7, 8) by drawing a right triangle. The triangle is a 3-4-5 right triangle, so the distance between (4, 4) and (7, 8) (and thus the radius) is 5. If the radius is 5, then the area is $\pi(5)^2$, or 25π. The correct answer is (D).

Arcs and Sectors

Many circle questions on the SAT will not ask about the whole circle. Rather, you'll be asked about arcs or sectors. Both arcs and sectors are portions of a circle: arcs are portions of the circumference, and sectors are portions of the area. Luckily, both arcs and sectors have the same relationship with the circle, based on the central angle (the angle at the center of the circle that creates the arc or sector):

$$\frac{\text{part}}{\text{whole}} = \frac{\text{central angle}}{360°} = \frac{\text{arc length}}{2\pi r} = \frac{\text{sector area}}{\pi r^2}$$

Note that these relationships are all proportions. Arcs and sectors are proportional to the circumference and area, respectively, as the central angle is to 360°.

Questions on the Math Test sometimes refer to "minor" or "major" arcs or sectors. A minor arc or sector is one that has a central angle of less than 180°, whereas a major arc or sector has a central angle greater than 180° (in other words, it goes the long way around the circle). Let's see how arcs and sectors might show up in a question.

———————————————◯———————————————

15

Points A and B lie on circle O (not shown). $AO = 3$ and $\angle AOB = 120°$. What is the area of minor sector AOB ?

A) $\dfrac{\pi}{3}$

B) π

C) 3π

D) 9π

Here's How to Crack It

The question asks for the area of minor sector AOB in circle O. Because O is the name of the circle, it's also the center of the circle, so AO is the radius. $\angle AOB$ is the central angle of sector AOB, so you have all the pieces you need to find the sector. Put them into a proportion:

$$\frac{120°}{360°} = \frac{x}{\pi (3)^2}$$

Cross-multiply to get $360x = 1{,}080\pi$ (remember to not multiply out π). Divide both sides by 360, and you get $x = 3\pi$. The correct answer is (C).

———————————————◯———————————————

Relationship Between Arc and Angle in Radians

Sometimes you'll be asked for an arc length, but you'll be given the angle in radians instead of degrees. Fear not! Rather than making the question more complicated, the test-writers have actually given you a gift! All you need to do is memorize this formula:

$$s = r\theta$$

In this formula, s is the arc length, r is the radius, and θ is the central angle in radians. If you know this formula, these questions will be a snap!

RECTANGLES AND SQUARES

Here are some rules you'll need to know about rectangles and squares:

1. **The perimeter of a rectangle is the sum of the lengths of its sides.**
   Just add them up.

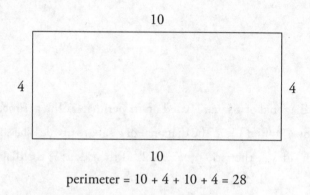

perimeter = 10 + 4 + 10 + 4 = 28

2. **The area of a rectangle is length × width.**
   The area of the preceding rectangle, therefore, is 10 × 4, or 40.

3. **A square is a rectangle whose four sides are all equal in length.**
   The perimeter of a square, therefore, is four times the length of any side. The area is the length of any side squared.

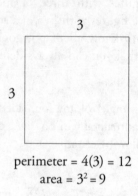

perimeter = 4(3) = 12
area = 3^2 = 9

4. **In rectangles and squares all angles are 90-degree angles.**
   It can't be a square or a rectangle unless all angles are 90 degrees.

Little Boxes

Here's a progression of quadrilaterals from least specific to most specific:

quadrilateral is any 4-sided figure
↓
parallelogram is a quadrilateral in which opposite sides are parallel
↓
rectangle is a parallelogram in which all angles = 90 degrees
↓
square is a rectangle in which all sides are equal

Let's check out an example.

6

If the perimeter of a square is 28, what is the length of the diagonal of the square?

A) $2\sqrt{14}$

B) $7\sqrt{2}$

C) $7\sqrt{3}$

D) 14

Here's How to Crack It

The question asks for the diagonal of a square based on its perimeter. The perimeter of a square is $4s$. So, $28 = 4s$. Divide by 4 to find $s = 7$. The diagonal of a square divides the square into two $45°$-$45°$-$90°$ triangles, with sides in the ratio of $x:x:x\sqrt{2}$. If the side is 7, the diagonal is $7\sqrt{2}$. The correct answer is (B).

POLYGONS

Polygons are two-dimensional figures with three or more straight sides. Triangles and rectangles are both polygons. So are figures with five, six, seven, eight, or any greater number of sides. The most important fact to know about polygons is that any one of them can be divided into triangles. This means that you can always determine the sum of the measures of the interior angles of any polygon.

For example, the sum of the interior angles of any four-sided polygon (called a *quadrilateral*) is 360 degrees. Why? Because any quadrilateral can be divided into two triangles, and a triangle contains 180 degrees. Look at the following example:

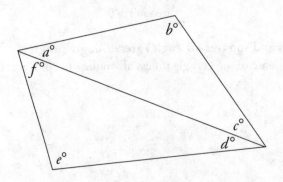

In this polygon, $a + b + c = 180$ degrees; so does $d + e + f$. That means that the sum of the interior angles of the quadrilateral must be 360 degrees ($a + b + c + d + e + f$).

A **parallelogram** is a quadrilateral whose opposite sides are parallel. In the following parallelogram, side AB is parallel to side DC, and AD is parallel to BC. Because a parallelogram is made of two sets of parallel lines that intersect each other, we know that the two big angles are equal, the two small angles are equal, and a big angle plus a small angle equals 180 degrees. In the figure below, big angles A and C are equal, and small angles B and D are equal. Also, because A is a big angle and D is a small angle, $A + D = 180$ degrees.

> **Need the Formula?**
> You may have learned the formula for this in math class. If so, you can use it: the sum of the degrees in an n-sided polygon is $180(n-2)$. If you don't know the formula, don't worry about memorizing it. It doesn't come up much, and when it does come up, you can always break up the polygon into triangles.

Let's try an example.

12

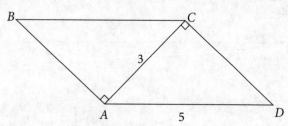

Note: Figure not drawn to scale.

In parallelogram $ABCD$ above, $AC = 3$ and $AD = 5$. What is the area of $ABCD$?

A) 12

B) 15

C) 18

D) 20

Here's How to Crack It

The question asks for the area of the parallelogram. Rather than worry about a formula for that, the trick is to notice that this parallelogram is actually made of two equal triangles. By finding the area of the triangles, you can find the area of the parallelogram. The triangles are both right triangles, and the two sides given in the figure follow the 3-4-5 pattern. If you look at triangle ACD with $\overline{AC}$ as the base, the base is 3 and the height is 4. Now use the formula for area of a triangle:

$$A = \frac{1}{2} \times 3 \times 4 = 6$$

That means the parallelogram is $2 \times 6 = 12$.

Also, if you estimate the area, the base is 5 and the height is less than 3, so the area is less than 15. The only answer less than 15 is (A), so the correct answer is (A).

○

VOLUME

Volume questions on the SAT can seem intimidating at times. The test-writers love to give you questions featuring unusual shapes such as pyramids and spheres. Luckily, at the beginning of the Math sections (and the beginning of this chapter), you're given a box with all the formulas you will ever need for volume questions on the SAT. Simply apply the Basic Approach for geometry using the given formulas and you'll be in good shape (pun entirely intended)!

Let's look at an example.

○

15

A sphere has a volume of 36π. What is the surface area of the sphere? (The surface area of a sphere is given by the formula $A = 4\pi r^2$.)

A) 3π

B) 9π

C) 27π

D) 36π

Here's How to Crack It

The question asks for the surface area of a sphere given its volume. Start by writing down the formula for volume of a sphere from the beginning of the chapter: $V = \frac{4}{3}\pi r^3$. Put what you know into the equation: $36\pi = \frac{4}{3}\pi r^3$. From this you can solve for r. Divide both sides by π to get $36 = \frac{4}{3}r^3$. Multiply both sides by 3 to clear the fraction: $36(3) = 4r^3$. Note we left 36 as 36, because the next step is to divide both sides by 4, and 36 divided by 4 is 9, so $9(3) = r^3$ or $27 = r^3$. Take the cube root of both sides to get $r = 3$. Now that you have the radius, use the formula provided to find the surface area: $A = 4\pi(3)^2$, which comes out to 36π. The correct answer is (D).

BALLPARKING

You may be thinking, "Wait a second, isn't there an easier way?" By now, you should know that of course there is, and we're going to show you. On many SAT geometry questions, you won't have to calculate an exact answer. Instead, you can estimate an answer choice. We call this **Ballparking,** a strategy mentioned earlier in this book.

Ballparking is extremely useful on SAT geometry questions. At the very least, it will help you avoid careless mistakes by immediately eliminating answers that could not possibly be correct. On many questions, Ballparking will allow you to find the answer without even working out the problem at all.

For example, on many SAT geometry questions, you will be presented with a drawing in which some information is given and you will be asked to find some of the information that is missing. In most such questions, you're expected to apply some formula or perform some calculation, often an algebraic one. But you'll almost always be better off if you look at the drawing and make a rough estimate of the answer (based on the given information) before you try to work it out.

The basic principles you just learned (such as the number of degrees in a triangle and the fact that $\pi \approx 3$) will be enormously helpful to you in ballparking on the SAT. You should also know the approximate values of several common square roots. Be sure to memorize them before moving on. Knowing them cold will help you solve problems and save time, especially when calculator use is not allowed.

> **Rocket Science?**
> The SAT is a college admissions test, not an exercise in precision. Because 45 of its 58 Math questions are multiple-choice, you can afford to approximate numbers like π, $\sqrt{2}$, and $\sqrt{3}$ (3+, 1.4, and 1.7+, respectively).

Square Roots

$\sqrt{1}$ = 1

$\sqrt{2}$ ≈ 1.4

$\sqrt{3}$ ≈ 1.7+

$\sqrt{4}$ = 2

You will also find it very helpful if you have a good sense of how large certain common angles are. Study the following examples.

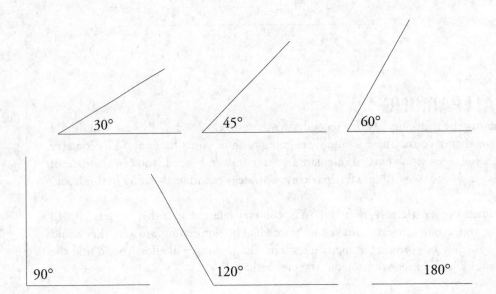

How High Is the Ceiling?

If your friend stood next to a wall in your living room and asked you how high the ceiling was, what would you do? Would you get out your trigonometry textbook and try to triangulate using the shadow cast by your pal? Of course not. You'd look at your friend and think something like this: "Dave's about 6 feet tall. The ceiling's a couple of feet higher than he is. It must be about 8 feet high."

Your Ballpark answer wouldn't be exact, but it would be close. If someone later claimed that the ceiling in the living room was 15 feet high, you'd be able to tell her with confidence that she was mistaken.

You'll be able to do the same thing on the SAT. Every geometry figure on your test will be drawn exactly to scale unless there is a note in that question telling you otherwise. That means you can trust the proportions in the drawing. If line segment *A* has a length of 2 and line segment *B* is exactly half as long, then the length of line segment *B* is 1. All such questions are ideal for Ballparking.

> **The Correct Choice**
> Remember that the SAT is a multiple-choice test. This means that you don't always have to come up with an answer; you just have to identify the correct one from among the four choices provided.

PLUGGING IN

As you learned already, Plugging In is a powerful technique for solving SAT algebra questions. It is also very useful on geometry problems. For some questions, you will be able to plug in ballpark values for missing information and then use the results either to find the answer directly or to eliminate answers that cannot be correct.

Here's an example.

20

The base of triangle *T* is 40 percent less than the length of rectangle *R*. The height of triangle *T* is 50 percent greater than the width of rectangle *R*. The area of triangle *T* is what percent of the area of rectangle *R* ?

A)   10

B)   45

C)   90

D)   110

**Watch Us
Crack It**

Here's How to Crack It

The question asks for the relationship between the areas of triangle T and rectangle R. This is a challenging question. Don't worry—you'll still be able to find the right answer by sketching and plugging in.

When plugging in, always use numbers that are easy to work with. Say the length of the rectangle is 10; that means that the base of the triangle, which is 40 percent smaller, is 6. If you plug 4 in for the width of rectangle R, the height of triangle T is 6. You should come up with two sketches that look like this:

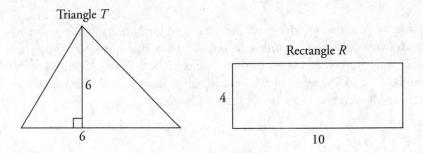

T has an area of $\frac{1}{2}bh$, or 18. R has an area of 40. Now set up the translation: $18 = \frac{x}{100}(40)$, where x represents what percent the triangle is of the rectangle.

Solve for x and you get 45. The correct answer is (B).

———————————◯———————————

Geometry Drill 1: No Calculator Section

Work these Geometry questions without your calculator. Answers and explanations can be found on page 509.

2

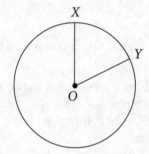

In the figure above, circle O has a radius of 8, and angle XOY measures $\dfrac{5}{16}\pi$ radians. What is the measure of minor arc XY?

A) $\dfrac{5}{16}\pi$

B) $\dfrac{5}{2}\pi$

C) 5π

D) 16π

3

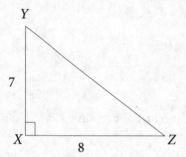

What is the value of tan $\angle XZY$?

A) $\dfrac{7\sqrt{115}}{115}$

B) $\dfrac{8\sqrt{115}}{115}$

C) $\dfrac{7}{8}$

D) $\dfrac{8}{7}$

10

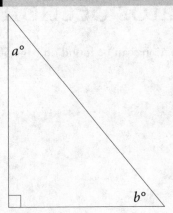

In the figure above, sin a = x. What is the value of cos b ?

A) x

B) $\dfrac{1}{x}$

C) $|1-x|$

D) $\dfrac{90-x}{90}$

15

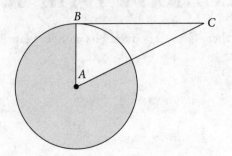

Note: Figure not drawn to scale.

The circle above with center A has an area of 21. BC is tangent to the circle with center A at point B. If $AC = 2AB$, then what is the area of the shaded region?

A) 3.5

B) 15.75

C) 17.5

D) 21

Geometry Drill 2: Calculator-Permitted Section

Calculator use is allowed on these questions, so use it to the best of your ability, but be sure to set up the questions on paper first. Answers and explanations can be found starting on page 509.

1

If a rectangular swimming pool has a volume of 16,500 cubic feet, a uniform depth of 10 feet, and a length of 75 feet, what is the width of the pool, in feet?

A) 22

B) 26

C) 32

D) 110

8

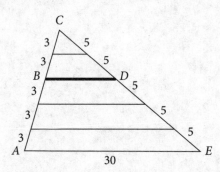

In the figure above, what is the length of $\overline{BD}$?

A) 8

B) 9

C) 12

D) 15

12

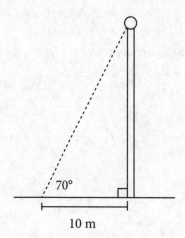

Martin wants to know how tall a certain flagpole is. Martin walks 10 meters from the flagpole, lies on the ground, and measures an angle of 70° from the ground to the base of the ball at the top of the flagpole. Approximately how tall is the flagpole from the ground to the base of the ball at the top of the flagpole?

A) 3 m

B) 9 m

C) 27 m

D) 29 m

26

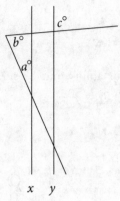

x   y

In the figure above, $x \parallel y$. What is the value of a ?

A) $b + c$

B) $2b - c$

C) $180 - b + c$

D) $180 - b - c$

29

A toy pyramid (not shown) is made from poly(methyl methacrylate), better known by its trade term Lucite. The toy pyramid has a regular hexagonal base of 15 cm² and a height of 4 cm. In the base of the pyramid, there is a semispherical indentation 2 cm in diameter. If the pyramid weighs 21.129 g, then what is the density of Lucite? (Density equals mass divided by volume.)

A) 1.06 g/cm³

B) 1.18 g/cm³

C) 2.09 g/cm³

D) 6.51 g/cm³

28

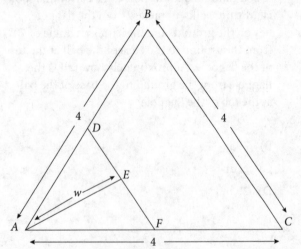

$\triangle ABC$ is equilateral and $\angle AEF$ is a right angle. D and F are the midpoints of AB and AC, respectively. What is the value of w ?

A) 1

B) $\sqrt{3}$

C) 2

D) $2\sqrt{3}$

CHAPTER DRILL ANSWERS AND EXPLANATIONS

Geometry Drill 1: No Calculator Section

2. **B** The question asks for the measure of minor arc *XY*. Since the question gives you the measure of the central angle in radians, you can use the formula $s = r\theta$ to find the arc length: $s = (8)\left(\dfrac{5}{16}\pi\right) = \dfrac{40}{16}\pi$, which reduces to $\dfrac{5}{2}\pi$. The correct answer is (B).

3. **C** The question asks for the tangent of an angle, which is defined as $\dfrac{\text{opposite}}{\text{adjacent}}$. The side opposite angle *XZY* is 7, and the side adjacent to this angle is 8, so the tangent of $\angle XZY = \dfrac{7}{8}$. The correct answer is (C).

10. **A** The question asks for the value of cos *b*. You can plug in when you're dealing with a geometry question with unknowns. When you're plugging in for a right triangle, use one of the special right triangles to make your life easier. Use a 3-4-5 right triangle. Make the side opposite *a* 3, the side adjacent to *a* 4, and the hypotenuse 5. Because sine is $\dfrac{\text{opposite}}{\text{hypotenuse}}$, $\sin a = \dfrac{3}{5}$, so $x = \dfrac{3}{5}$. Cosine is $\dfrac{\text{adjacent}}{\text{hypotenuse}}$, so $\cos b = \dfrac{3}{5}$. This is your target; circle it. Make $x = \dfrac{3}{5}$ in each answer choice and look for the answer that equals $\dfrac{3}{5}$. Only (A) works, so the correct answer is (A).

15. **C** The question asks for the area of the shaded region on the figure. The trick is to recognize that $\triangle ABC$ is a 30°-60°-90° right triangle. $\angle ABC$ must equal 90° since a tangent line must be perpendicular to the radius of a circle drawn to the point of tangency. Only a 30°-60°-90° has a hypotenuse (*AC*) equal to double the length of one of the sides (*AB*). (You can also use the Pythagorean Theorem to show this.) This means that $\angle BAC = 60°$, so the shaded region has a central angle measure of $360° - 60° = 300°$. To get the area, use the proportion $\dfrac{\text{central angle}}{360°} = \dfrac{\text{sector area}}{\text{circle area}}$, or $\dfrac{300°}{360°} = \dfrac{s}{21}$. Reduce, cross-multiply, and solve to get $s = 17.5$. The correct answer is (C).

Geometry Drill 2: Calculator-Permitted Section

1. **A** The question asks for the width of the pool. For this question, you need to know that volume equals *length* × *width* × *height*. You know that the volume is 16,500, the depth (or height) is 10, and the length is 75. Just put those numbers into the formula: $16{,}500 = 75 \times w \times 10$. Use your calculator to solve for *w*, which equals 22. The correct answer is (A).

8. **C** The question asks for the length of $\overline{BD}$. The 5 equal lengths that make up the two sides of the largest triangle tell you that you are dealing with 5 similar triangles. The largest triangle has sides 15:25:30, and the sides of all 5 triangles will have an equivalent ratio. Reduced, the ratio is 3:5:6, which happens to be the dimensions of the smallest triangle. You want to find the length of *BD*, the base of a triangle with sides of 6 and 10. This is twice as big as the smallest triangle, so the base *BD* must be $6 \times 2 = 12$. The correct answer is (C).

12.   **C**   The question asks how tall the flagpole is. Use SOHCAHTOA and your calculator to find the height of the flagpole. From the 70° angle, you know the adjacent side of the triangle, and you want to find the opposite side, so you need to use tangent. Tangent $= \dfrac{\text{opposite}}{\text{adjacent}}$, so $\tan 70° = \dfrac{x}{10\,\text{m}}$, where x is the height of the flagpole up to the ball. Isolate x by multiplying both sides by 10: $10 \tan 70° = x$. Use your calculator to find that $10 \tan 70° = 27.47$, which is closest to 27. The correct answer is (C).

26.   **D**   The question asks for the value of a, an angle measurement in the diagram. Don't forget that you can plug in numbers on geometry questions. Make $b = 70°$ and $a = 30°$. Therefore, the third angle in the triangle is 80°. You know that c would be 80° because it is opposite an 80° angle. Your target answer is $a = 30°$, so plug in 80° and 70° into the answer for c and b to find the one that equals 70. Choice (D) is the only one that works, since $180 - 70 - 80 = 30$. The correct answer is (D).

28.   **B**   The question asks for the value of w in the diagram. There is a lot going on in this question! Use Bite-Sized Pieces and start filling in information. First, the question says that triangle ABC is equilateral. Mark 60 degree angles on the figure. Next, you see that angle AEF is a right angle. Write that in as well. The question also conveniently tells you that D and F are the midpoints of AB and AC, respectively. Therefore, AD and AF are 2. Finally, the last piece of information reveals that E is the midpoint of DF; mark DE and EF as equal. Now you know that triangle AEF is a right triangle, with a hypotenuse of 2 and a leg of 1. Use the Pythagorean Theorem ($a^2 + b^2 = c^2$) to find that the other leg is $\sqrt{3}$. The correct answer is (B).

You may have also noticed that triangle ADE is a 30°-60°-90° triangle with hypotenuse 2, which means that DE is 1 and w, opposite the 60°, is the square root of 3. In geometry questions on the SAT, there will often be multiple ways to get to the answer. On the day of the test, use whichever method you are most comfortable with.

29.   **B**   The question asks for the density of Lucite. Work the problem in steps. You are given the mass, so to find density, you need to find the volume of the pyramid. The formula at the beginning of the section tells you that, for a pyramid, $V = \dfrac{1}{3} Bh$, where B is the area of the base of the pyramid and h is the height. Therefore, the volume of the pyramid is $\dfrac{1}{3}(15)(4) = 20$. However, you need to subtract the volume of the semispherical indentation in the base. Once again, the reference table found at the beginning of each Math section tells you that the volume of a sphere is given by the equation $V = \dfrac{4}{3}\pi r^3$. Because the diameter of the indentation is 2 cm, the radius of the hemisphere is 1 cm. If it were a whole sphere, the volume of the indentation would be $\dfrac{4}{3}\pi(1)^3 = 4.189$; you want only half, so dividing by 2 gives you 2.094 cm³ for the hemisphere. Subtracting 2.094 cm³ from the 20 cm³ of the pyramid gives you a total volume of $20 - 2.094 = 17.906$ cm³. Finally, you can find the density of Lucite by using the definition of density: Density $= \dfrac{21.129\ \text{g}}{17.906\ \text{cm}^3} \times 100 = 1.18$ g/cm³. The correct answer is (B).

Summary

○ **Degrees and angles**
- A circle contains 360 degrees.
- When you think about angles, remember circles.
- A line is a 180-degree angle.
- When two lines intersect, four angles are formed; the sum of their measures is 360 degrees.
- When two parallel lines are cut by a third line, the small angles are equal, the big angles are equal, and the sum of a big angle and a small angle is 180 degrees.

○ **Triangles**
- Every triangle contains 180 degrees.
- An isosceles triangle is one in which two of the sides are equal in length, and the two angles opposite the equal sides are equal in measure.
- An equilateral triangle is one in which all three sides are equal in length, and all three angles are equal in measure (60 degrees).
- The area of a triangle is $\frac{1}{2}bh$.
- The height must form a right angle with the base.
- The Pythagorean Theorem states that in a right triangle, the square of the hypotenuse equals the sum of the squares of the two legs. Remember the test-writers' favorite Pythagorean triplets (3-4-5 and 5-12-13).
- Remember the other special right triangles: 45°-45°-90° and 30°-60°-90°.
- Similar triangles have the same angles and their lengths are in proportion.

- For trigonometry questions, remember SOHCAHTOA:
  - $\sin \theta = \dfrac{\text{opposite}}{\text{hypotenuse}}$

  - $\cos \theta = \dfrac{\text{adjacent}}{\text{hypotenuse}}$

  - $\tan \theta = \dfrac{\text{opposite}}{\text{adjacent}}$

- o **Circles**
  - The circumference of a circle is $2\pi r$ or πd, where r is the radius of the circle and d is the diameter.
  - The area of a circle is πr^2, where r is the radius of the circle.
  - A tangent touches a circle at one point; any radius that touches that tangent forms a 90-degree angle.
  - Arcs are proportional to the circumference based on the central angle: $\dfrac{\text{central angle}}{360°} = \dfrac{\text{arc length}}{2\pi r}$.
  - Sectors are proportional to the area based on the central angle: $\dfrac{\text{central angle}}{360°} = \dfrac{\text{sector area}}{\pi r^2}$.
  - If the central angle is given in radians, the measure of the arc is given by $s = r\theta$.

- o **Rectangles and squares**
  - The perimeter of a rectangle is the sum of the lengths of its sides.
  - The area of a rectangle is *length × width*.
  - A square is a rectangle whose four sides are all equal in length.
  - Any polygon can be divided into triangles.
  - The volume of a rectangular solid is *length × width × height*. The formulas to compute the volumes of other three-dimensional figures are supplied in the instructions at the front of both Math sections.

- o When you encounter a geometry question on the SAT, ballpark the answer before trying to work it out.

- o You must be familiar with the size of certain common angles.

- o Most SAT geometry diagrams are drawn to scale. Use your eyes before you use your pencil. Try to eliminate impossible answers.

- o When a diagram is not drawn to scale, redraw it.

- o When no diagram is provided, make your own; when a provided diagram is incomplete, complete it.

- o When information is missing from a diagram, ballpark and plug in.

Chapter 20
Grid-Ins

On the SAT, 13 of the 58 Math questions will require you to produce your own answer. Although the format of these questions is different from that of the multiple-choice questions, the mathematical concepts tested aren't all that different. In this chapter, we will show you how to apply what you have learned in the previous chapters to these new questions.

WHAT IS A GRID-IN?

Both of the Math sections on the SAT will contain a group of questions without answer choices. There will be 5 of these in the No Calculator section and 8 in the Calculator section. The College Board calls these questions "student-produced responses." We call them Grid-Ins because you have to mark your answers on a grid printed on your answer sheet. The grid looks like this:

Despite their format, Grid-Ins are just like any other Math questions on the SAT, and many of the techniques that you've learned so far still apply. You can still use Plugging In and other great techniques, such as Bite-Sized Pieces. Your calculator will still help you out on many of these questions as well. So, Grid-Ins are nothing to be scared of. In fact, many of these are simply regular SAT multiple-choice math questions with the answer choices lopped off, so you have to arrive at your answer from scratch rather than choose from four possibilities.

You will need to be extra careful when answering Grid-In questions, however, because the grid format increases the likelihood of careless errors. It is vitally important that you understand how the Grid-In format works before you take the test. In particular, you'll need to memorize the College Board's rules about which kinds of answers receive credit and those that do not. The instructions may look complicated, but we've boiled them down to a few rules for you to memorize and practice.

Before we get into specifics, here are some basic rules about Grid-Ins to keep in mind.

- **Most answers for Grid-Ins are integers.** Take a look at the grid again. Because of the way it's arranged, only certain types of problems can be used for Grid-Ins. For example, you'll never see variables in your answer (though there can be variables in the question) because the grids can accommodate only numbers. You will also never have a π, square root, or negative number in your answer.

- **Your calculator can help you—if you use it carefully.** This means that your calculator will be useful on several questions. As always, be careful to set up the problem on paper before you (carefully) punch the numbers into your calculator. Because you have to write in the answer on the grid yourself, you need to be more careful than ever to avoid careless mistakes.

- **Be aggressive.** Just as with the multiple-choice questions, there is no penalty for wrong answers on the Grid-Ins. An incorrect answer on one of these questions is no worse for your score than a question left blank. And, by the same token, a blank is just as costly as an error. Therefore, you *should be very aggressive in answering these questions.* Don't leave a question blank just because you're worried that the answer you've found may not be correct. College Board's scoring computers treat incorrect answers and blanks like they're exactly the same. If you have arrived at an answer, you have a shot at earning points; and if you have a shot at earning points, you should take it. We're not saying you should guess blindly. But if you work a problem and are unsure of your answer, enter it anyway. There is no penalty for getting it wrong.

Take a Guess
Just like the multiple-choice questions, there is no penalty for wrong answers on the Grid-In questions.

THE INSTRUCTIONS

Here are the instructions for the Grid-In section as they will appear in the No Calculator section of the Math Test. The instructions for the Calculator section will look just like this, except they will start "For questions 31–38..."

DIRECTIONS

For questions 16–20, solve the problem and enter your answer in the grid, as described below, on the answer sheet.

1. Although not required, it is suggested that you write your answer in the boxes at the top of the columns to help you fill in the circles accurately. You will receive credit only if the circles are filled in correctly.

2. Mark no more than one circle in any column.

3. No question has a negative answer.

4. Some problems may have more than one correct answer. In such cases, grid only one answer.

5. **Mixed numbers** such as $3\frac{1}{2}$ must be gridded as 3.5 or 7/2. (If ⌐3 1 / 2⌐ is entered into the grid, it will be interpreted as $\frac{31}{2}$, not as $3\frac{1}{2}$.)

6. **Decimal Answers:** If you obtain a decimal answer with more digits than the grid can accommodate, it may be either rounded or truncated, but it must fill the entire grid.

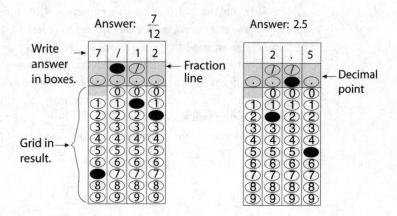

Answer: $\frac{7}{12}$ Answer: 2.5

Write answer in boxes. → Fraction line

Grid in result. → Decimal point

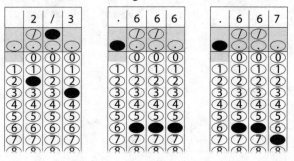

Acceptable ways to grid $\frac{2}{3}$ are:

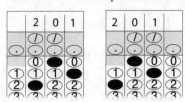

Answer: 201 – either position is correct

NOTE: You may start your answers in any column, space permitting. Columns you don't need to use should be left blank.

What the Instructions Mean

Of all the instructions on the SAT, these are the most important to understand thoroughly before you take the test. Pity the unprepared student who takes the SAT cold and spends 10 minutes of potential point-scoring time reading and puzzling over the confusing instructions. We've translated these unnecessarily complicated instructions into a few important rules. Make sure you know them all well.

Fill In the Boxes

Always write your answer in the boxes at the top of the grid before you darken the ovals below. Your written answers won't affect the scoring of your test; if you write the correct answer in the boxes and grid in the wrong ovals, you won't get credit for your answer (and you won't be able to appeal to the College Board). However, writing in the answers first makes you less likely to make an error when you grid in, and it also makes it easier to check your work.

Fill In the Ovals Correctly

As we just pointed out, you receive no credit for writing in the answer at the top of the grid. The scoring computer cares only whether the ovals are filled in correctly. For every number you write into the grid, make sure that you fill in the corresponding oval.

Stay to the Left

Although you'll receive credit no matter where you put your answer on the grid, you should always begin writing your answer in the far left column of the grid. This ensures that you will have enough space for longer answers when necessary. You'll also cut down on careless errors if you always grid in your answers the same way.

FRACTIONS OR DECIMALS: YOUR CHOICE

You can grid in an answer in either fraction or decimal form. For example, if your answer to a question is $\frac{1}{2}$, you can either grid in $\frac{1}{2}$ *or* .5. It doesn't matter to the College Board because $\frac{1}{2}$ equals .5; the computer will credit either form of the answer. That means you actually have a choice. If you like fractions, grid in your answers in fraction form. If you like decimals, you can grid in the decimal. If you have a fraction that doesn't fit in the grid, you can simply convert it to a decimal on your calculator or on paper and grid in the decimal.

Here's the bottom line: when gridding in fractions or decimals, use whichever form is easier and less likely to cause careless mistakes.

Watch Out
Negatives, π, and % cannot be gridded in! For a Grid-In question involving % or $, the SAT will tell you to ignore the % or $ symbol. But negative numbers, non-integer square roots, and π can't be gridded in, so they'll never be an answer for this type of problem.

Keep Left
No matter how many digits are in your answer, always start gridding in the left-most column. That way, you'll avoid omitting digits and losing points.

Decimal Places and Rounding

When you have a decimal answer of a value less than 1, such as .45 or .678, many teachers ask you to write a zero before the decimal point (for example, 0.45 or 0.678). On Grid-In questions, however, the College Board doesn't want you to worry about the zero. In fact, there is no 0 in the first column of the grid. If your answer is a decimal less than 1, just write the decimal point in the first column of the grid and then continue from there.

You should also notice that if you put the decimal point in the first column of the grid, you have only three places left to write in numbers. But what if your decimal is longer than three places, such as .87689? In these cases, you will get credit if you round off the decimal so that it fits in the grid. But you'll *also* get credit if you just enter as much of the decimal as will fit.

For example, if you had to grid in .87689, you could just write .876 (which is all that will fit) and then stop. You need to grid in only whatever is necessary to receive credit for your answer. Don't bother with extra unnecessary steps. You don't have to round off decimals, so don't bother.

If you have a long or repeating decimal, however, be sure to fill up all the spaces in the grid. If your decimal is .666666, you *must* grid in .666. Just gridding in .6 or .66 is not good enough.

Note: Very long decimal answers that don't equal a simple fraction are somewhat rare. Your answers will usually consist of integers or simple fractions.

Reducing Fractions

If you decide to grid in a fraction, the College Board doesn't care if you reduce the fraction or not. For example, if your answer to a question is $\frac{4}{6}$, you will get credit if you grid in $\frac{4}{6}$ or reduce it to $\frac{2}{3}$. So if you have to grid in a fraction, and the fraction fits in the grid, don't bother reducing it. Why give yourself more work (and another chance to make a careless error)?

The only time you might have to reduce a fraction is if it doesn't fit in the grid. If your answer to a question is $\frac{15}{25}$, it won't fit in the grid. You have two options: either reduce the fraction to $\frac{3}{5}$ and grid that in, or use your calculator to convert the fraction to .6. Choose whichever process makes you the most comfortable when calculator use is allowed, and make sure you know how to reduce fractions for the No Calculator section.

If Your Decimal Doesn't Fit...

Why do extra work? After all, it won't give you extra points. If your decimal doesn't fit in the grid, lop off the extra digits and grid in what does fit.

If Your Fraction Doesn't Fit...

If your answer is a fraction and it fits in the grid (fraction bar included), don't reduce it. Why bother? You won't get an extra point. However, if your fraction doesn't fit, reduce it or turn it into a decimal on your calculator, depending on the section you're working on.

Mixed Numbers

The scoring computer for the SAT does not recognize mixed numbers. If you try to grid in $2\frac{1}{2}$ by writing "2 1/2," the computer will read this number as $\frac{21}{2}$. You have to convert mixed numbers to fractions or decimals before you grid them in. To grid in $2\frac{1}{2}$, either convert it to $\frac{5}{2}$ or its decimal equivalent, which is 2.5. If you have to convert a mixed number to grid it in, be very careful not to change its value accidentally.

Don't Mix
Never grid in a mixed number. Change it into an improper fraction or its decimal equivalent.

Don't Worry

The vast majority of Grid-In answers will not be difficult to enter in the grid. The test-writers won't try to trick you by purposely writing questions that are confusing to grid in. Just pay attention to these guidelines and watch out for careless errors.

GRIDDING IN: A TEST DRIVE

To get a feel for this format, let's work through two examples. As you will see, Grid-In questions are just regular SAT Math problems.

16

If $a + 2 = 6$ and $b + 3 = 21$, what is the value of $\frac{b}{a}$?

Here's How to Crack It

The question asks for the value of $\frac{b}{a}$. You need to solve the first equation for a and the second equation for b. Start with the first equation, and solve for a. By subtracting 2 from both sides of the equation, you should see that $a = 4$.

Now move to the second equation, and solve for b. By subtracting 3 from both sides of the second equation, you should see that $b = 18$.

The question asked you to find the value of $\dfrac{b}{a}$. That's easy. The value of b is 18, and the value of a is 4. Therefore, the value of $\dfrac{b}{a}$ is $\dfrac{18}{4}$.

That's an ugly-looking fraction. How in the world do you grid it in? Ask yourself this question: "Does $\dfrac{18}{4}$ fit?" Yes! Grid in $\dfrac{18}{4}$.

Your math teacher wouldn't like it, but the scoring computer will. You shouldn't waste time reducing $\dfrac{18}{4}$ to a prettier fraction or converting it to a decimal. Spend that time on another question instead. The fewer steps you take, the less likely you will be to make a careless mistake.

───────○───────

Here's another example. This one is quite a bit harder.

───────○───────

34

Forty percent of the members of the sixth-grade class wore white socks. Twenty percent wore black socks. If twenty-five percent of the remaining students wore gray socks, what percent of the sixth-grade class wore socks that were not white, black, or gray? (Disregard the % when gridding your answer.)

Here's How to Crack It

The question asks for the percent of students that fit a certain requirement. The question doesn't tell you how many students are in the class, so you can plug in any number you like. This is a percentage question, so the easiest number to plug in is 100. Forty percent of 100 is 40; that means 40 students wore white socks. Twenty percent of 100 is 20. That means that 20 students wore black socks.

Your next piece of information says that 25 percent of the remaining students wore gray socks. How many students remain? Forty, because 60 students wore either white or black socks, and $100 - 60 = 40$. Therefore, 25 percent of these 40—10 students—wore gray socks.

How many students are left? 30. Therefore, the percentage of students not wearing white, black, or gray socks is 30 out of 100, or 30 percent. Grid it in, and remember to forget about the percent sign.

MORE POOD

Remember that the SAT no longer has a strict Order of Difficulty, but you do! You have your Personal Order of Difficulty, a strategy that encourages you to focus on the questions you know how to answer first. Don't spent too much time on questions you are unsure about.

Keep in mind, of course, that many of the math techniques that you've learned are still very effective on Grid-In questions. Plugging In worked very well on the previous question. If you're able to plug in or take an educated guess, go ahead and grid in that answer. Again, there is no penalty for getting it wrong.

Here's a challenging Grid-In question that you can answer correctly by using a technique you've learned before.

18

$$\frac{5}{a-4} - \frac{5a - 24}{\left(a - 4\right)^2}$$

The expression $\dfrac{k}{\left(a - 4\right)^2}$ is equivalent to the expression above.

What is the value of k if k is a positive constant and $a \neq 4$?

Watch Us Crack It

Here's How to Crack It

The question asks for an equivalent expression given an expression with a variable and a constant. When you see a question involving equivalent expressions and variables, think Plugging In! Choose a good number for a and plug it in to the first expression. Making $a = 5$ will work well because the denominators will equal 1. Plug in 5 and the expression becomes

$$\frac{5}{5-4} - \frac{5(5) - 24}{\left(5 - 4\right)^2}$$

Simplify.

$$\frac{5}{1} - \frac{25 - 24}{1^2}$$

Simplify some more.

$$5 - \frac{1}{1} = 5 - 1 = 4$$

Since the second expression is equivalent, set it equal to 4 and plug in 5 for a to get

$$\frac{k}{(5-4)^2} = 4$$

Simplify.

$$\frac{k}{1^2} = 4$$

Isolate k.

$$k = 4$$

The question asked for the value of k, so grid that in and you're done. The correct answer is 4.

Careless Mistakes

On Grid-In questions, you obviously can't use POE to get rid of bad answer choices, and Plugging In the Answers won't work either. In order to earn points on Grid-In questions, you're going to have to find the answer yourself, as well as be extremely careful when you enter your answers on the answer sheet. If you need to, double-check your work to make sure you have solved correctly. If you suspect that the question is a difficult one and you get an answer too easily, you may have made a careless mistake or fallen into a trap.

Try the example below with this in mind.

_____

20

A teacher is grading two assignments that each had to be a specific length: research papers and short stories. Each research paper has 5 more pages than each short story. How many pages are in a research paper if 7 research papers and 5 short stories have a total of 275 pages?

Watch Us Crack It

Here's How to Crack It

The question asks for the number of pages in a research paper given other information about two assignments. Use another skill from earlier in this book and translate English to math in bite-sized pieces. The question states that *each research paper has 5 more pages than each short story*. Let r represent the number of pages in a research paper. The word *has* translates to =. The phrase *5 more than* translates to 5 +. Finally, let s represent the number of pages in a short story. The sentence, therefore, translates to $r = 5 + s$. Do the same thing with the information that *7 research papers and 5 short stories have a total of 275 pages*. Use r and s again for the number of pages in a research paper and a short story, respectively. Translate *and* as + and *have a total of* as =, and the sentence translates to $7r + 5s = 275$. You now have two equations with the same two variables:

$$r = 5 + s$$

$$7r + 5s = 275$$

Substitute $5 + s$ for r in the second equation to get

$$7(5 + s) + 5s = 275$$

Distribute the 7.

$$35 + 7s + 5s = 275$$

Combine like terms on the left side, then subtract 35 from both sides.

$$12s = 240$$

Isolate *s*.

$$s = 20$$

It's tempting to grid in 20 and call it a day, but always read the final question! The question asks for the number of pages in a research paper, not in a short story. Plug 20 for *s* into the first equation to solve for *r*.

$$r = 5 + 20 = 25$$

Thus, *r* = 25, so grid in that value. The correct answer is 25.

RANGE OF ANSWERS

Some Grid-In questions will have many possible correct answers. It won't matter which correct answer you choose, as long as the one you choose really is correct.

Here's an example.

---○---

17

If $4 < 3x + 2 < 5$, what is one possible value of x ?

Here's How to Crack It

The question asks for a possible value of x. With double inequalities or equations, don't try to do the entire problem at once. It's much easier to split this problem into two smaller problems:

$$4 < 3x + 2 \text{ and } 3x + 2 < 5$$

Solve each one. For the first inequality, start by subtracting 2 from both sides, leaving $2 < 3x$. Divide by 3, leaving (approximately) $0.666 < x$. For the other inequality, start, as before, by subtracting 2 from both sides, leaving $3x < 3$. Divide by 3 to get $x < 1$. Combining both inequalities back together, you'll get that x is between 0.666 and 1.

So, what do you enter as your answer? Anything between .666 and 1. Really. Anything. .8, .954, .667, .999, 5/6, 7/8, 9/10, whatever. Any of these would count as a correct answer.

---○---

More Than One Answer

Some Grid-In questions have several possible correct answers. They are all equally correct, so grid in the first one you find and move on.

Extend Your Thinking

The last two Grid-Ins may be a pair of questions based on the same information. They can cover any of the previous math content, and they are still worth just one point each. Use your knowledge of your own test-taking skills to decide which of these you want to try, if you do them at all.

EXTENDED THINKING

The last two questions in the Calculator section may be a pair of Grid-Ins that the College Board refer to as Extended Thinking questions. It claims that these questions, drawn from real-world contexts, will assess a student's ability to apply "complex cognitive skills." Don't panic, though. Aside from being paired and sometimes more difficult, they are not any different than other Grid-Ins. Many of the same strategies will apply to the Extended Thinking questions. They can be drawn from pretty much any mathematical content, from problem solving to functions, and they are worth only one point each.

Let's look at a set.

Questions 37 and 38 refer to the following information.

$$KE = \frac{1}{2}mv^2$$

$$KE = \frac{p^2}{2m}$$

$$PE = mgh$$

A ball with a mass of 5 kg is to be rolled northward along the ground toward the edge of a cliff. The equations above describe the kinetic energy (*KE*) and potential energy (*PE*) of the ball as it moves along the level ground and falls off the cliff, where *m* is the mass of the ball in kilograms, *v* is the velocity in meters per second, *p* is the momentum of the ball in motion, *h* is the height of the ball above the ground, and *g* is the gravitational constant 9.8 meters per second squared.

37

What is the northward momentum, in kilogram-meters per second, of the ball as it rolls along the level ground at a velocity of 2.7 meters per second, assuming there is no friction?

The ball moving 2.7 meters per second has a potential energy of 22,050 Joules (kilogram meters squared per second squared) as it falls off the edge of the cliff. What is the vertical distance from the edge of the cliff to the ground below, in <u>kilometers</u>?
(1,000 meters = 1 kilometer)

Here's How to Crack It

As you can see, there is a lot going on here. You are faced with three equations, two questions, and a whole lot of variables. Go straight to the questions instead of spending time reading equations and information you may not need. The questions are equal in length, so read question 37 first to see if you can identify which equation to use. If it is not immediately obvious, you can move on to question 38 to see if that one is easier to sort through.

Question 37 asks for the momentum of the ball moving at a certain velocity. Look through the text to find a mention of *momentum*, which is defined by the variable p. Now find an equation that includes p. Only the second one does, so determine the other variables. KE is defined as kinetic energy. The variable m is the mass of the ball in kilograms. The text indicates that the ball has a mass of 5 kg, so plug this into the second equation to get $KE = \dfrac{p^2}{2(5)}$ or $KE = \dfrac{p^2}{10}$. In order to solve for p, you need the value of KE. The question gives velocity, so look for another equation that would give you kinetic energy with the information provided. The first equation also defines KE in

> **Tackling Extended Thinking Questions**
> Most Extended Thinking questions can be solved independent of each other, and one is often easier than the other. Consider doing the more straightforward one and skipping the more difficult or time-consuming one.

terms of *m*, the mass, and *v*, the velocity, of an object. Question 37 states that the velocity is 2.7 meters per second, so the first equation becomes $KE = \frac{1}{2}(5)(2.7)^2$ or $KE = 18.225$. Plug this value for *KE* into the second equation, $KE = \frac{p^2}{10}$, to get $18.225 = \frac{p^2}{10}$. Multiply both sides of the equation by 10 to get $182.25 = p^2$, then take the square root of both sides to get $13.5 = p$. The correct answer is 13.5.

Question 38 asks for *the vertical distance* between the top of the cliff and the ground below. The two equations you have already used did not have a variable for distance, and the question refers to *potential energy*, so look at the third equation. The third equation defines potential energy, *PE*, in terms of mass, height (distance), and the gravitational constant *g*. Plug the given values of *PE* = 22,050 and *g* = 9.8 into the equation *PE* = *mgh* to get 22,050 = (5)(9.8)*h*. This becomes 22,050 = 49*h*, so divide both sides of the equation by 49 to get 450 = *h*. Now, before you go gridding that in, check your units! The question specifically asks for the distance of value of *h* <u>in kilometers</u>. All the units for the energy equations are in meters, so the height is 450 *meters*. You need to convert this to kilometers using the given conversion. There are 1,000 meters in a kilometer, so set up a proportion, making sure to match up the units: $\frac{1 \text{ kilometers}}{1,000 \text{ meters}} = \frac{x}{450 \text{ meters}}$. Cross-multiply to get 1,000*x* = 450, then divide both sides by 1,000 to get *x* = 0.45. The correct answer is 0.45. You can't grid in a leading zero, so you would enter this as .45 in the Grid-In box.

Grid-In Drill 1: No Calculator Section

Work these Grid-Ins without your calculator. Answers and explanations can be found on page 534.

16

If $a^b = 4$, and $3b = 2$, what is the value of a ?

18

If $\dfrac{x^2 + x - 6}{x^2 - 8x + 12} = 4$, what is the value of x ?

17

If $4x + 2y = 24$ and $\dfrac{7y}{2x} = 7$, what is the value of x ?

19

If $-1 \le a \le 2$ and $-3 \le b \le 2$, what is the greatest possible value of $(a + b)(b - a)$?

Grid-In Drill 2: Calculator-Permitted Section

Work these Grid-Ins using your calculator as needed and applying the skills you've learned so far. Answers and explanations can be found starting on page 534.

32

$$n = 12 \times 2^{\frac{t}{3}}$$

The number of mice in a certain colony is shown by the formula above, such that n is the number of mice and t is the time, in months, since the start of the colony. If 2 *years* have passed since the start of the colony, how many mice does the colony contain now?

33

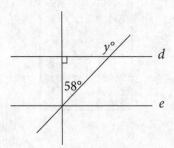

In the figure above, if d is parallel to e, what is the value of y ?

35

If Alexandra pays $56.65 for a table, and this amount includes a tax of 3% on the price of the table, what is the amount, in dollars, that she pays in tax? (Disregard the dollar sign when gridding your answer.)

36

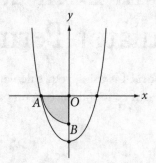

In the figure above, AB is the arc of the circle with center O. Point A lies on the graph of $y = x^2 - b$, where b is a constant. If the area of shaded region AOB is π, then what is the value of b?

Questions 37 and 38 refer to the following information.

A garden, measuring 10 feet by 12 feet, contains individual plots that measure 1 foot by 1 foot. 30% of the plots contain bell peppers, 30% contain cherry tomatoes, 25% contain squash, and the remaining 15% contain eggplants. Each bell pepper plot produces 2 bell peppers every 5 days, a tomato plot produces 4 cherry tomatoes every 6 days, a squash plot produces 1 squash every 15 days, and an eggplant plot produces 3 eggplants every 10 days.

37

In a 30-day month, how many vegetables are produced by the 10 × 12 foot garden?

38

An unusually warm and wet month causes the monthly production of eggplants to double. What is the daily average number of eggplants produced in the garden during a 30-day month at the new rate?

CHAPTER DRILL ANSWERS AND EXPLANATIONS

Grid-In Drill 1: No Calculator Section

16. **8** The question asks for the value of a. Using $3b = 2$, solve for b by dividing both sides by 3 to get $b = \frac{2}{3}$. That means $a^{\frac{2}{3}} = 4$. Fractional exponents tell you to use the denominator as the root and use the numerator as a regular exponent. So, $\sqrt[3]{a^2} = 4$. First, cube both sides to find $a^2 = 4^3 = 64$. Next, take the square root of both sides to find $a = 8$. This is the correct answer.

17. **3** The question asks for the value of x. You can solve this question using simultaneous equations because you have two equations with two variables. First, you need to rearrange the equations a bit: $4x + 2y = 24$ divided by 2 on both sides becomes $2x + y = 12$. $\frac{7y}{2x} = 7$, multiplied by $2x$ on both sides, becomes $7y = 14x$. This, divided by 7 on both sides, becomes $y = 2x$, which can be manipulated into $2x - y = 0$. Now you can add the equations:

$$
\begin{array}{r}
2x + y = 12 \\
+\ 2x - y = 0 \\
\hline
4x\ \ \ \ = 12
\end{array}
$$

Therefore, $x = 3$. This is the correct answer.

18. **9** The question asks for the value of x. Factor the numerator and the denominator into $\frac{(x-2)(x+3)}{(x-2)(x-6)} = 4$. The $(x - 2)$ cancels out of the top and bottom to leave $\frac{(x+3)}{(x-6)} = 4$. Multiply both sides by $(x - 6)$ to get $x + 3 = 4x - 24$. Subtract x from both sides: $3 = 3x - 24$. Add 24 to both sides: $27 = 3x$. Divide by 3 to get $x = 9$. This is the correct answer.

19. **9** The question asks for the largest possible value of $(a + b)(b - a)$. This looks suspiciously like a quadratic equation, and if you multiply it out, its equivalent is $b^2 - a^2$. You want to make this as large as possible, so you want b^2 to be large and a^2 to be small. If $b = -3$, $b^2 = 9$; if $a = 0$, $a^2 = 0$. So $b^2 - a^2$ can be as large as 9. This is the correct answer.

Grid-In Drill 2: Calculator-Permitted Section

32. **3,072** The question asks for the number of mice in the colony after 2 years. Because the t in $n = 12 \times 2^{\frac{t}{3}}$ represents the number of months, you cannot use the 2-year time frame given in the question in place of t. The colony has been growing for 24 months, which is evenly divisible by the

3 in the fractional exponent. The equation is much easier now that the fractional exponent is gone: $n = 12 \times 2^{\frac{24}{3}} = 12 \times 2^8 = 12 \times 256 = 3{,}072$. This is the correct answer.

33. **148** The question asks for the value of y, which is an angle measurement on the figure. A line crossing two parallel lines creates big angles and small angles. The big angle that matches y is split by a line perpendicular to d and e. The big angle is $58 + 90 = 148$, which is also the value for y. Another way to solve this is to find the third angle of the triangle: $180 - 90 - 58 = 32$. The $32°$ angle and the $y°$ angle make up a straight line, so $180 - 32 = 148$. This is the correct answer.

35. **1.65** The question asks for the amount that Alexandra pays in tax. The best way to approach this question is to set up an equation. There is some price such that if you add 3% of the price to the price itself, you get $56.65. This means that you can set up an equation: $x + 3\%$ of $x = 56.65$, or $x + 0.03x = 56.65$. Now you can just solve for x, and you get the original price, which was $55. Subtract this from $56.65 to get the tax $1.65. The correct answer is 1.65.

36. **4** The question asks for the value of b. This question looks tough, so work it one step at a time, and start with what you know. Sector AOB is a quarter-circle (it covers an angle of 90 out of 360 degrees), so multiplying its area (π) by 4 gives you the area of the whole circle (4π). Plugging this into the equation for the area of a circle, $A = \pi r^2$, gives you $4\pi = \pi r^2$, and the radius must be a positive value, so $r = 2$. This means that the coordinates of point A must be $(-2, 0)$. Because A is on both the circle and the parabola, you can plug its x- and y-coordinates into the given equation of the parabola, $y = x^2 - b$. This becomes $0 = (-2)^2 - b$, so $b = 4$. This is the correct answer.

37. **1,374** The question asks for the number of vegetables produced by the garden in 30 days. First, calculate the number of plots in the garden. Given that the garden measures 10 feet by 12 feet and each plot is one foot by one foot, there are $10 \times 12 = 120$ total plots. Next calculate the number of each type of vegetable plot as follows:

$120 \times 0.3 = 36$ bell pepper plots

$120 \times 0.3 = 36$ cherry tomato plots

$120 \times 0.25 = 30$ squash plots

$120 \times 0.15 = 18$ eggplant plots

According to the question, 2 bell peppers are grown every 5 days on each of the 36 pepper plots. That means that all the pepper plots together grow $2 \times 36 = 72$ peppers in 5 days. To determine how many peppers would grow in a month, set up a proportion.

$$\frac{72 \text{ peppers}}{5 \text{ days}} = \frac{x}{30 \text{ days}}$$

Cross-multiply, and then divide by 5 to find that the garden produces 432 peppers for the month. Repeat these steps with the other 3 vegetables. The 36 tomato plots produce 144 tomatoes every 6 days. Together, they produce 720 tomatoes in the month. The 30 squash plots produce 30 squash every 15 days, for a total of 60 squash in a month. Finally, the 18 eggplant plots grow 54 eggplants every 10 days, which means during a 30-day period, the garden will produce 162 eggplants. The total number of vegetables can be calculated as 432 bell peppers + 720 cherry tomatoes + 60 squash + 162 eggplants = 1,374 vegetables. The correct answer is 1,374.

38. **10.8** The question asks for the average number of eggplants produced each day in a 30-day month at the new rate. During a normal month, each eggplant plot produces 3 eggplants every 10 days. Therefore, if the production were to double, each plot would produce 6 eggplants every 10 days. Given that the garden measures 10 feet by 12 feet and each plot is one foot by one foot, there are 10 × 12 = 120 total plots, 15% of which are eggplant plots. Therefore, there are 120 × 0.15 = 18 eggplant plots. Calculate the total number of eggplants produced in 10 days as 18 × 6 = 108. In a 30-day month, there are three 10-day periods, so the entire garden would produce 108 × 3 = 324 total eggplants. To find the daily average production, divide 324 by 30 to get an average of 10.8 eggplants each day. The correct answer is 10.8.

Summary

o   Both of the Math sections on the SAT will contain a group of questions without answer choices. The College Board calls these questions "student-produced responses." We call them Grid-Ins, because you have to mark your answers on a grid printed on your answer sheet.

o   Despite their format, Grid-Ins are really just like other Math questions on the SAT, and many of the same techniques that you have learned still apply.

o   The grid format increases the likelihood of careless errors. Know the instructions and check your work carefully.

o   Just like the rest of the exam, there is no guessing penalty for Grid-Ins, so you should always grid in your answer, even if you're not sure whether it's correct.

o   Always write the numbers in the boxes at the top of the grid before you (carefully) fill in the corresponding ovals.

o   Grid in your answer as far to the left as possible.

o   If the answer to a Grid-In question contains a fraction or a decimal, you can grid in the answer in either form. When gridding in fractions or decimals, use whichever form is easier and least likely to cause careless mistakes.

o   There's no need to round decimals, even though it is permitted.

o   If you have a long or repeating decimal, be sure to fill up all the spaces in the grid.

o   If a fraction fits in the grid, you don't have to reduce the fraction before gridding it in.

o   The scoring computer does not recognize mixed numbers. Convert mixed numbers to fractions or decimals before gridding them in.

o   Some Grid-In questions will have more than one correct answer. It doesn't matter which answer you grid in, as long as it's one of the possible answers.

- Like all other questions on the SAT Math Test, Grid-In questions are arranged in a loose order of difficulty. Use your knowledge of your own strengths and weaknesses to decide which ones to tackle first and which ones, if any, to skip.

- The last two Grid-Ins in the Calculator section are usually Extended Thinking questions, a set of questions on the same information. Usually, they can be answered independently, and they are worth only 1 point each. Attempt both only if you are aiming for a top score.

- Negatives, π, square roots, %, $, and degree symbols cannot be gridded in.

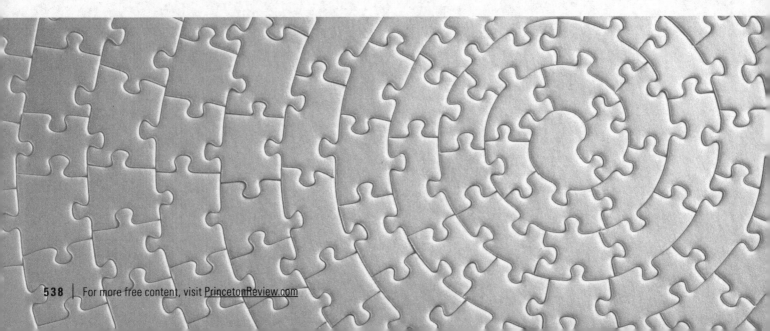

Part V
Taking the SAT

THE SAT IS A WEEK AWAY—WHAT SHOULD YOU DO?

First of all, you should practice the techniques we've taught you on lots of practice tests. If you haven't done so already, take and score the practice tests in this book and online. You can also download a practice test from the College Board's website, www.collegeboard.org.

If you want more practice, pick up a copy of our very own *10 Practice Tests for the SAT* at your local bookstore or through our website, at PrincetonReview.com/bookstore.

Perfect Your Skills
In addition to taking the practice tests in this book, you should register your book (See "Get More (Free) Content" on pages x–xi) to gain access to even more practice, as well as other fantastic resources to enhance your prep.

Getting Psyched

The SAT is a big deal, but don't let it scare you. Sometimes students get so nervous about doing well that they freeze up on the test and ruin their scores. The best thing to do is to think of the SAT as a game. It's a game you can get better at, and beating the test can be fun. When you go into the test center, just think about all those poor students who don't know how to plug in when they see variables in the answer choices.

The best way to keep from getting nervous is to build confidence in yourself and in your ability to remember and use our techniques. When you take practice tests, time yourself exactly as you will be timed on the real SAT. Develop a sense of how long 35 minutes is, for example, and how much time you can afford to spend on cracking difficult questions. If you know ahead of time what to expect, you won't be as nervous.

Of course, taking a real SAT is much more nerve-racking than taking a practice test. Prepare yourself ahead of time for the fact that 35 minutes will seem to go by a lot faster on a real SAT than it did on your practice tests.

It's all right to be nervous; the point of being prepared is to keep from panicking.

Veg Out
Although preparation is key to doing well on the test, you shouldn't exhaust yourself trying to cram information into your head. Take some breaks between study sessions to relax, unwind, and rest your mind.

Should You Sleep for 36 Hours?

Some guidance counselors tell their students to get a lot of sleep the night before the SAT. This probably isn't a good idea. If you aren't used to sleeping 12 hours a night, doing so will just make you groggy for the test. The same goes for going out all night: tired people are not good test-takers.

A much better idea is to get up early each morning for the entire week before the test and do your homework before school. This will get your brain accustomed to functioning at that hour of the morning. You want to be sharp at test time.

Before dinner the night before the test, spend an hour or so reviewing or doing a few practice problems. The goal here is to brush up on the material, not to exhaust yourself by over-cramming.

Furthermore...

Here are a few pointers for test day and beyond:

1. Eat a good breakfast before the test—your brain needs energy.

2. Work out a few SAT questions on the morning of the test to help dust off any cobwebs in your head and get you started thinking analytically.

3. Arrive at the test center early. Everyone is headed to the same place at the same time.

4. You must take acceptable identification to the test center on the day of the test. Acceptable identification must include a recognizable photograph and your name. Acceptable forms of ID include your driver's license, a school ID with a photo, or a valid passport. If you don't have an official piece of ID with your signature and your photo, you can have your school make an ID for you using a Student ID form provided by the College Board. Complete instructions for making such an ID are found on the College Board's website and in the Student Registration Booklet for the SAT. According to the College Board, the following forms of ID are *unacceptable:* a birth certificate, a credit card, or a Social Security card. Make sure you read all of the rules in the Student Registration Booklet, because conflicts with the College Board are just not worth the headache. Your only concern on the day of the test should be beating the SAT. To avoid hassles and unnecessary stress, make *absolutely certain* that you take your admissions ticket and your ID with you on the day of the test.

5. The only outside materials you are allowed to use on the test are No. 2 pencils, a wristwatch (an absolute necessity), and a calculator with fresh batteries. The latest rule is that mechanical pencils are not allowed. We're not sure why, but you should take lots of sharpened wooden No. 2 pencils just to be safe. Digital watches are best, but if it has a beeper, make sure you turn it off. Proctors will confiscate pocket dictionaries, word lists, portable computers, and the like. Proctors have occasionally also confiscated stopwatches and travel clocks. Technically, you should be permitted to use these, but you can never tell with some proctors. Take a watch and avoid the hassles.

6. Tablets and smartwatches are not allowed. Cell phones are permitted as long as they are away and turned off, but we recommend leaving them at home or in a car, if at all possible, because if it somehow makes a noise or you touch or look at it by accident, you could have your test canceled.

7. Some proctors allow students to bring food into the test room; others don't. Take a snack like a banana, which is sure to give you an energy boost. Save it until your break and eat outside the test room.

---

1. Eat Breakfast
You'll work better on a satisfied stomach.

2. Try Some Questions
Get your mind moving.

3. Show Up Early
Leave time for traffic.

4. Take Your ID
A driver's license, a passport, or a school photo ID will do.

5. Remember Supplies
A few sharpened No. 2 pencils, a watch, and a calculator.

6. No Technology
Don't bring smart devices to the SAT, and keep your phone at home or in the car if possible!

7. Take Fruit or Other Energy Food
Grapes or oranges can give you an energy boost if you need it.

8. Your Desk…
should be comfortable and suited to your needs.

9. Your Test…
should be printed legibly in your booklet.

10. Bubble In Carefully
A stray mark can hurt your score.

11. We're Here for You
The Princeton Review is proud to advise students who feel their exam was not administered properly.

8. You are going to be sitting in the same place for more than three hours, so make sure your desk isn't broken or unusually uncomfortable. If you are left-handed, ask for a left-handed desk. (The center may not have one, but it won't hurt to ask.) If the Sun is in your eyes, ask to move. If the room is too dark, ask someone to turn on the lights. Don't hesitate to speak up.

9. Make sure your booklet is printed legibly. Booklets sometimes contain printing errors that make some pages impossible to read. One year more than 10,000 students had to retake the SAT because of a printing error in their booklets. Also, check your answer sheet to make sure it isn't flawed.

10. Make sure you darken all your responses before the test is over. At the same time, erase any extraneous marks on the answer sheet. A stray mark in the margin of your answer sheet can result in correct responses being marked as wrong.

11. You deserve to take your SAT under good conditions. If you feel that your test was not administered properly (the high school band was practicing outside the window, or your proctor hovered over your shoulder during the test), don't hesitate to speak up.

Part VI
Practice Tests

Practice Test 2

Reading Test

65 MINUTES, 52 QUESTIONS

Turn to Section 1 of your answer sheet to answer the questions in this section.

Questions 1-10 are based on the following passage.

This passage is adapted from R. O'Grady, "But Once a Year." ©1917 by The Reilly & Britton Co.

A shabby little woman detached herself from the steadily marching throng on the avenue and paused before a shop window, from which solid rows of
Line electric bulbs flashed brilliantly into the December
5 twilight. The ever-increasing current of Christmas shoppers flowed on. Now and then it rolled up, like the waters of the Jordan, while a lady with rich warm furs about her shoulders made safe passage from her car to the tropic atmosphere of the great department store.
10 Wax figures draped with rainbow-tinted, filmy evening gowns caught her passing admiration, but she lingered over the street costumes, the silk-lined coats and soft, warm furs.

With her wistful gaze still fixed upon her favorite,
15 she had begun to edge her way through the crowd at the window. At the same instant, she caught the scent of fresh-cut flowers and looked up into the eyes of a tall young girl in a white-plumed velvet hat, with a bunch of English violets in her brown mink fur. As
20 their glances met, the shabby little woman checked a start, and half-defensively dropped her lids. There had flashed over the mobile face beneath the velvet hat a look of personal interest, an unmistakable impulse to speak.
25 The thrill of response that set the woman's pulses throbbing died suddenly. The red that mottled her grayish cheeks was the red of shame. Through the window, in a mirrored panel cruelly ablaze with light,

she saw herself: her made-over turban, her short,
30 pigeon-tailed jacket of a style long past, and her old otter cape with its queer caudal decorations and its yellowed cracks grinning through the plucked and ragged fur. As the white plume came nearer and nearer, the tremulous little woman regained her self-control.
35 It was but one of the coincidences of the city, she told herself, turning resolutely away.

The door slammed shut behind her. She glanced at her fingers, stained to an oily, bluish grime by the cheap dye of the garments that furnished her daily
40 work. Mechanically, she rose to wash. While her hands were immersed in the lather of rankly perfumed toilet soap, there came a gentle knock at the door.

"Come in," invited the woman, expecting some famine-pressed neighbor for a spoonful of coffee or a
45 drawing of tea.

The woman, having absently hung her towel on the doorknob, stared dazedly at the visitant. She could hardly credit her eyes. It was indeed the girl with the white ostrich plume and the bouquet of violets in her
50 brown mink fur.

"Do you know, I've such a silly excuse for coming." She laughed, and the laugh brought added music to her voice. "I noticed you had a rare fur-piece" her vivid glance returned to the pile of wraps on the chair "and
55 I want to ask a very great favor of you. Now please don't be shocked—I've been ransacking the city for something like it, and," with a determined air of taking the plunge, "I should like to buy it of you!"

CONTINUE

"It, it's a rare pattern, you know," groped the girl,
60 her sweet tones assuming an eloquent, persuasive
quiver, "and you don't know how glad I'd be to have it."

The indignant color faded out of the woman's face.
"If you really want the thing"—abruptly she put her
bizarre possession into her strange visitor's lap—"If
65 you really want it, but I don't see"—yearning crept into
her work-dimmed eyes, a yearning that seemed to
struggle with disillusionment. "Tell me," she broke off,
"is that all you came here for?"

Apparently oblivious to the question, the young
70 woman rose to her feet. "You'll sell it to me then!" she
triumphed, opening her gold-bound purse.

"But, see here," demurred the woman, "I can't, it
ain't worth…"

The girl's gloved hands went fumbling into her
75 purse, while the old fur cape hung limply across one
velvet arm.

"You leave it to me," she commanded, and smiled,
a radiant, winning smile. The girl was gone and all at
once the room seemed colder and dingier than it ever
80 had before. But the woman was not cold. As she sat
huddled on the cot, warmth and vitality glowed within
her, kindled by the memory of a recent kindly human
touch.

The following evening, after working hours, the
85 shabby woman, wearing a faded scarf about her neck
to replace the old fur collar, diffidently accosted a
saleslady at the Sixth Avenue department store.

It was unusual to sell expensive furs to such a
customer. But people might send what freaks of
90 servants they pleased to do their Christmas shopping,
provided they sent the money, too. In this case, the
shabby little woman was prepared. She produced three
crisp ten-dollar bills—the fabulous sum which the
girl had left in her hand at parting—and two dollars
95 more from the savings in her worn little purse. Then,
hugging the big flat box against the tight-fitting bosom
of her jacket, she triumphantly left the store.

CONTINUE

1

The author uses the image of the "waters of the
Jordan" (line 7) most likely to

A) claim the crowd approaching the window will
never ebb.

B) assert that the little woman was drowning in the
throng.

C) describe the method and magnitude of the crowd's
movement.

D) illustrate how a rich lady arrived at the
department store.

2

As used in line 16, "caught" most nearly means

A) chased.

B) grabbed.

C) stopped.

D) noticed.

3

Which choice best supports the claim that the shabby
little woman was at first excited by the tall young girl?

A) Lines 16–19 ("At the . . . fur")

B) Lines 19–21 ("As their . . . lids")

C) Lines 25–26 ("The thrill . . . suddenly")

D) Lines 29–33 ("she saw . . . fur")

4

According to the passage, why does the woman invite
the visitor to come in?

A) She plans to help someone in need.

B) No one has ever been refused entry.

C) She expects the young girl to drop by.

D) She is dazed and cannot see.

5

In the context of the conversation between the young girl and the woman, the girl's comments in lines 51–58 ("Do you . . . you!") mainly serve to

A) persuade the woman to sell the fur at a discount.

B) emphasize the desire that inspired the girl's action.

C) laugh at the shabby woman for being indignant.

D) demand that the shabby woman surrender her wrap.

6

The girl uses the word "ransacking" (line 56) mainly to emphasize that her search was

A) comprehensive.

B) disruptive.

C) shocking.

D) silly.

7

It can reasonably be inferred from the passage that the shabby woman initially declines to sell the fur mainly because

A) the young woman is only interested in rare fur pieces.

B) she yearns for the young woman to appreciate her work more.

C) the young woman offers too high of a price.

D) she doesn't believe that it has much value.

8

Which choice provides the best evidence for the answer to the previous question?

A) Lines 63–67 ("If you . . . disillusionment")

B) Lines 72–73 ("But, see . . . worth")

C) Lines 84–87 ("The following . . . store")

D) Lines 88–89 ("It was . . . customer")

9

The passage states that after the girl's departure the shabby woman felt

A) cold.

B) dingy.

C) tired.

D) warmth.

10

The main purpose of the last paragraph is to

A) claim that stores only reluctantly sold to people like the shabby woman.

B) contrast common occurrences with the shabby woman's experience.

C) highlight the shabby woman's greatest triumph.

D) show how servants like the shabby woman go Christmas shopping.

CONTINUE

Questions 11–20 are based on the following passage and supplementary material.

This passage is adapted from Nathan H. Lents, "In Humans and Animals, Social Learning Drives Intelligence." ©2018 by Sussex Publishers, LLC.

The human capacity to learn exceeds that of any other animal. Indeed, our massive memories and impressive computing power are the engines of all that
Line makes us different from other animals, rooted mostly,
5 but not entirely, in language. However, the way that humans and animals learn may not be as different as many people think.

We all know that humans do most of their learning socially, that is, we learn from others rather than
10 discovering things ourselves through trial-and-error. Formal schooling is entirely based on social learning. Even so-called self-directed learning and discovery is actually social because when we discover information in a book, someone else put it there.

15 Because animals do not go to school, we often think of their learning as entirely different. When we see a bird building a nest, for example, we assume that birds must have a built-in instinct to build nests and then learn to do it through trial-and-error. That may
20 be right, but there may also be a social component to animal learning.

It has long been known that most social animals that are reared artificially in captivity will be deficient in many skills that adult animals of that species are
25 generally proficient at. For example, chimpanzees raised without adult chimpanzees do not know how to build nests or care for young when they become parents themselves. Ring-tailed lemurs raised artificially do not show the "normal" food preferences
30 that wild lemurs display and instead will eat a larger variety of food.

Cross-fostering experiments, in which animals are raised by members of a different species, have also revealed the effects of social learning. For example,
35 Frans de Waal and Denise Johanowicz allowed some young rhesus macaques, which don't normally engage in social reconciliation following a conflict, to spend five months of their young lives with stump-tailed macaques, which are much more prone to reconciling
40 disputes peacefully. These fostered rhesus macaques learned the behavior of reconciliation, and it stuck with them even after they were placed back with other rhesus macaques. Surprisingly, this more conciliatory approach to conflict resolution remained even after
45 other habits they had picked up faded.

The continuing discovery that birds and mammals do a great deal of their learning socially, rather than individually, has important implications for how human intelligence evolved. It is well known that
50 the explosion of innovation and creativity in our lineage began well after our species had adopted our current anatomical form, including brain size, and is largely attributed to the acquisition of language and symbolic thinking around 65,000 years ago. From this
55 point forward, each generation of humans inherited the collected knowledge of the previous generation, which was transmitted socially through language. This steady accumulation of knowledge led to the eventual development of agriculture and everything else flowed
60 from that.

If we consider that our ape ancestors were already learning a great deal from each other, the evolutionary drive toward cognitive capacity was really just a drive for "more of the same." The great conundrum of
65 language and symbolic thought is that humans had to have evolved the capacity for these skills before they were actually used. You can't do something until you have the means to do it. When it comes to language and symbolism and culture, it could be that the means
70 to do it was social learning pure and simple. Over the last seven million years (and even going much further back than that, truth be told), the selective pressure was for increasing sociality, social cooperation, and social learning. If we view human evolution as a rising
75 tide of social learning, the emergence of language seems almost inevitable.

Of course, natural selection is involved in shaping anything and everything about us, and of course some animals really do have genetically programmed
80 behaviors that are complex, such as a beaver building a dam, a behavior that appears to be almost completely innate. But we are expecting too much of natural selection to think that all of the complex behaviors we see in animals are the product of pure genetics and
85 "survival of the fittest."

Social learning resolves this conundrum. Animal species didn't have to sit around and wait for random mutation to give them the innate knowledge of where to find food. They learned from their parents and
90 others. The role of evolution, then, was to continually select for better learners, and better social learners specifically, at least in some lineages.

CONTINUE ▶

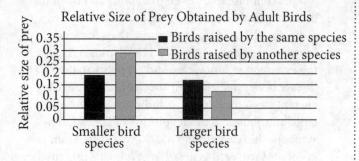

Relative Size of Prey Obtained by Adult Birds

■ Birds raised by the same species
▨ Birds raised by another species

Adapted from Tore Slagsvold and Karen L. Wiebe, "Social learning in birds and its role in shaping a foraging niche." ©2011 by The Royal Society.

Birds were either raised by their own species or cross-fostered by another species. When the birds reached adulthood, researchers measured the size of prey obtained by the birds for their own offspring.

11

The main purpose of the passage is to

A) chronicle the evolution of human intelligence through social learning.

B) provide evidence from human and animal observations to help explain knowledge and skill development across generations.

C) propose that humans are more intelligent than animals due to the different ways they learn.

D) show how birds and mammals learn social behaviors that humans do not understand.

12

Which choice best represents the different meanings of "back" as used in line 42 and line 72?

A) In exchange; behind

B) Earlier; dishonestly

C) Incorrectly; formerly

D) Again; previously

13

Based on the passage, which choice best describes what happened when the rhesus macaques in de Waal and Johanowicz's experiment were raised by stump-tailed macaques?

A) The rhesus macaques developed a behavior their species does not normally demonstrate.

B) The rhesus macaques became more violent when dealing with conflicts between members of their group.

C) The rhesus macaques became indistinguishable from the stump-tailed macaques that raised them.

D) The rhesus macaques became more intelligent and creative with their learned behaviors.

14

Based on the passage, de Waal and Johanowicz's experiment most likely ruled out which potential claim about social learning?

A) The habits an animal learns from another species will last only as long as they remain in close contact with that other species.

B) Individuals that are better at learning behaviors socially are more likely to pass on their beneficial traits to the next generation of their species.

C) Individuals that are raised by a different species are more likely to be ostracized by members of their own species.

D) Animals that learn behaviors from their own or a different species can pass those behaviors on to their offspring in the next generation of their own species.

CONTINUE →

15

Which choice provides the best evidence for the answer to the previous question?

A) Lines 22–25 ("It . . . proficient at")

B) Lines 43–45 ("Surprisingly . . . faded")

C) Lines 46–49 ("The continuing . . . evolved")

D) Lines 82–85 ("But we . . . fittest")

16

As presented in the passage, the author would most likely agree that human beings

A) have achieved the best methods of social learning possible by this time.

B) require a large brain size to retain their knowledge of learned behaviors.

C) are able to extend their creativity with the support of language.

D) should be learning behaviors from other species to improve their survival.

17

Which choice provides the best evidence for the answer to the previous question?

A) Lines 49–54 ("It is . . . ago")

B) Lines 54–57 ("From . . . language")

C) Lines 64–67 ("The great . . . used")

D) Lines 77–82 ("Of course . . . innate")

18

The author uses the terms "random mutation" and "innate knowledge" in the last paragraph of the passage most likely to

A) bring attention to the importance of natural selection for species survival.

B) stress the uncertainty with which the author views the benefits of social learning.

C) reinforce the contrast between genetic traits and social learning.

D) convey a serious tone regarding the scientific nature of socially learned behaviors.

19

According to the graph, what was the relative size of prey caught by the smaller birds that were raised by another species?

A) More than 0.25 but less than 0.3

B) More than 0.2 but less than 0.25

C) More than 0.15 but less than 0.2

D) More than 0.1 but less than 0.15

20

Information about which of the following is presented in the graph but NOT discussed in the passage?

A) Social learning within a species

B) Social learning from another species

C) Cross-fostering birds

D) Animal feeding behaviors

CONTINUE

Questions 21–31 are based on the following passages.

Passage 1 is adapted from Nicholas Weiler, "Birth of New Neurons in the Human Hippocampus Ends in Childhood." ©2018 by University of California San Francisco. Passage 2 is adapted from Laura C. Andreae, "Adult neurogenesis in humans: Dogma overturned, again and again?" ©2018 by Science Translational Medicine.

Passage 1

One of the liveliest debates in neuroscience over the past half century surrounds whether the human brain renews itself by producing new neurons throughout
Line life, and whether it may be possible to rejuvenate the
5 brain by boosting its innate regenerative capacity.

Now UC San Francisco scientists have shown that in the human hippocampus—a region essential for learning and memory and one of the key places where researchers have been seeking evidence that new
10 neurons continue to be born throughout the lifespan —neurogenesis declines throughout childhood and is undetectable in adults.

The lab's new research, based on careful analysis of 59 samples of human hippocampus from UCSF and
15 collaborators around the world, suggests new neurons may not be born in the adult human brain at all.

In the new study, Shawn Sorrells, PhD, a senior researcher in the Alvarez-Buylla lab, and Mercedes Paredes, PhD, a UCSF assistant professor of
20 neurology, led a team that collected and analyzed samples of the human hippocampus.

The researchers found plentiful evidence of neurogenesis in the dentate gyrus during prenatal brain development and in newborns, observing
25 an average of 1,618 young neurons per square millimeter of brain tissue at the time of birth. But the number of newborn cells sharply declined in samples obtained during early infancy.

"In young children, we were able to see that
30 substantial numbers of new neurons continue to be made and integrated into the dentate gyrus, but neurogenesis fades away completely by early adolescence," Paredes said. "The fact that we could compare newborn brains, where new neurons
35 were clearly present, to the adult, where we saw no evidence for young neurons, gave us added confidence that what we were seeing was correct."

The authors acknowledge that however comprehensively and carefully they searched, it would
40 be impossible to definitively show that there are never any new neurons in the adult hippocampus.

The absence of neurogenesis in the human brain may not be a bad thing, the researchers point out, but instead point the way to understanding what makes
45 the human brain distinct from other animals and set researchers on a better path to developing treatments for human brain diseases.

Passage 2

For most of the twentieth century, there was a general consensus that brain cells could not renew
50 themselves once the developmental period was over. Then, especially over the last two decades, overwhelming evidence gradually accumulated for the capacity of new neurons to be born in the adult brain in two clearly defined locations: the subventricular
55 zone and the dentate gyrus (DG) of the hippocampus.

Now, the near-simultaneous publication of two papers with opposing messages fuels this controversy and animates the debate. Sorrells *et al.* report that humans uniquely appear to lack
60 adult DG neurogenesis. They conducted a careful immunohistochemical study of hippocampal DG in 59 human subjects, and, using a series of well-known markers for neural progenitors and immature neurons, they hunted for evidence of newborn DG neurons
65 in brain tissue ranging from 14 gestational weeks to 77 years old. Neurogenesis, robust in embryos, rapidly decreased with advancing age, with none seen in samples from individuals older than 13 years. Conversely, Boldrini *et al.* find that hippocampal
70 neurogenesis not only occurs in adult humans but does not appear to decline with aging.

Although the two studies used very similar immunohistochemical approaches, including many of the same markers, the study by Boldrini *et al.* only
75 examined ages from 14 to 79 years, a time frame during which Sorrells *et al.* saw no dramatic changes. It is hard to directly compare the absolute numbers of newborn neurons reported by the two studies, as Boldrini *et al.* use a stereology approach to extrapolate
80 total cell numbers across entire DG regions.

However, they may not be so different: a few thousand cells in the whole anterior DG is arguably still relatively rare. Perhaps the question should be:

CONTINUE ➡

how rare is rare? And are rare newborn hippocampal
85 neurons enough to impact learning, mood, and even
brain repair? Further studies are clearly needed.

    What still seems likely is that if neurons are born in
human adulthood, they may be relatively few and far
between. Adult neurogenesis declines with age in most
90 species examined (and fascinatingly, may be absent in
whales and dolphins, also notable for longevity and
good memories), so perhaps we should be focusing
more on neurogenesis occurring in childhood/
adolescence, trying to understand whether this period
95 can be extended and whether juvenile newborn cells
can help treat neurological disorders.

21

According to Paredes in Passage 1, the researchers
had further confidence in their findings because they
were able to

A) collect brain samples from around the world.

B) prove no neurons are ever developed in the adult
hippocampus.

C) compare the brains of newborns to the brains of
adults.

D) observe 1,618 young neurons per square
millimeter.

22

The authors of the study in Passage 1 concede to
which shortcoming in their study?

A) They failed to measure a specific trait in all
humans.

B) They could not completely rule out the presence of
a certain biological structure.

C) Their sample size was smaller than it should have
been for completely accurate results.

D) The lab conditions were not representative of the
natural world.

23

Which choice provides the best evidence for the
answer to the previous question?

A) Lines 1–4 ("One of . . . life")

B) Lines 11–12 ("neurogenesis . . . adults")

C) Lines 22–26 ("The researchers . . . birth")

D) Lines 39–41 ("it would . . . hippocampus")

24

Which choice best supports the idea that the study
discussed in Passage 1 may have implications beyond
showing whether or not new neurons form later in
life?

A) Lines 13–16 ("The lab's . . . all")

B) Lines 26–28 ("But the . . . infancy")

C) Lines 29–33 ("In young . . . adolescence")

D) Lines 42–47 ("The absence . . . diseases")

25

In Passage 2, the phrase "general consensus" (line 49)
mainly serves to

A) provide historical context for the current debate
over learning in newborns.

B) establish researchers' certainty about the onset of
neurogenesis.

C) indicate the broad agreement about the decline of
neurogenesis that previously existed.

D) present a theory about the brain regions in which
neurogenesis takes place.

CONTINUE

26

In stating that the two papers' publication "animates the debate" (line 58), Andreae suggests that the papers

A) generated an unresolvable controversy.

B) energized a diminishing effort.

C) created interest in a dry subject.

D) presented seemingly contradictory evidence.

27

Based on Passage 2, Sorrells would most likely agree with which of the following statements about neurogenesis in the human dentate gyrus?

A) Its correlation with neurological disease has been overlooked.

B) It is not an elegant explanation for learning capacity.

C) Its frequency does not differ significantly between younger and older adults.

D) Its evolutionary purpose is not well understood.

28

In Passage 2, the fourth paragraph (lines 81–86) mainly serves to

A) point to difficulties in comparing the studies done by Boldrini and Sorrells.

B) highlight similarities between neurogenesis in various brain regions.

C) propose questions made salient by the scarcity of new hippocampal neurons in adults.

D) compare a recent study with one from the twentieth century.

29

The primary purpose of both passages is to discuss research that

A) explores the process by which the human brain creates new cells.

B) contradicts current beliefs about human neurogenesis.

C) compares the brain activity of newborns to that of older adults.

D) examines whether or not human brains continue to create certain cells as they age.

30

Based on Weiler's discussion of the research in Passage 1 and Andreae's discussion of the research in Passage 2, with which claim regarding neurogenesis would both authors most likely agree?

A) Recent studies have not brought any additional insight regarding adult neurogenesis.

B) Adult human neurogenesis is likely uncommon.

C) Brain region is not a factor in the rate of new neuron development.

D) The rate of new neuron development in humans increases just after birth.

31

In the passages, both research teams support their conclusions with

A) comparisons of samples from people of a range of ages.

B) experiments that replicate conditions in the body.

C) studies of human behavior in controlled settings.

D) evidence gathered from various textbooks and journals.

CONTINUE

Questions 32–42 are based on the following passage.

This passage is adapted from Washington Irving, *The Sketchbook of Geoffrey Crayon, Gent*. Originally published in 1819. "John Bull" is a satirical figure used to personify England, particularly the English middle class.

A stranger who wishes to study English peculiarities may gather much valuable information from the innumerable portraits of John Bull, as
Line exhibited in the windows of the caricature-shops. I
5 cannot resist the temptation to give a slight sketch of him, such as he has met my eye.

John Bull, to all appearance, is a plain downright matter-of-fact fellow, with much less of poetry about him than rich prose. There is little of romance in his
10 nature, but a vast deal of strong natural feeling. He excels in humor more than in wit; is jolly rather than gay; melancholy rather than morose. He is a boon companion, and he will stand by a friend in a quarrel, with life and purse, however soundly he may be
15 cudgeled[1]. In this last respect, he has a propensity to be somewhat too ready. He is a busy-minded personage, who thinks not merely for himself and family but for all the country round, and is most generously disposed to be everybody's champion. He is continually volunteering
20 his services to settle his neighbors' affairs. Though really a good-hearted, good-tempered old fellow, he is singularly fond of being in the midst of contention.

The secret of the matter is that John has a great disposition to protect and patronize. He thinks
25 it indispensable to the dignity of an ancient and honorable family, to be bounteous in its appointments and eaten up by dependents. The consequence is that like many other venerable family establishments, his manor is encumbered by old retainers whom he
30 cannot turn off, and an old style which he cannot lay down. Owls have taken possession of the dovecote, but they are hereditary owls, and must not be disturbed. In short, John has such a reverence for everything that has been long in the family that he will not hear even
35 of abuses being reformed, because they are good old family abuses.

All those whims and habits have concurred woefully to drain the old gentleman's purse. What is worst of all is the effect which these pecuniary
40 embarrassments have had on the poor man himself.

---
[1] A cudgel is a club-like stick.

Instead of strutting about as formerly, with his three-cornered hat on one side, flourishing his cudgel, he now goes about whistling thoughtfully to himself, with
45 his head drooping down, his cudgel tucked under his arm, and his hands thrust to the bottom of his breeches pockets, which are evidently empty.

Such is the plight of honest John Bull at present; yet for all this the old fellow's spirit is as tall and as gallant
50 as ever. If you drop the least expression of sympathy or concern, he takes fire in an instant; swears that he is the richest and stoutest fellow in the country; and talks of laying out large sums to adorn his house or buy another estate with a valiant swagger and grasping of
55 his cudgel.

I confess I cannot look upon John's situation without strong feelings of interest. He may not be so wonderfully fine a fellow as he thinks himself, but he is at least twice as good as his neighbors represent
60 him. His virtues are all his own; all plain, homebred, and unaffected. His very faults smack of the raciness of his good qualities. His extravagance savors of his generosity; his quarrelsomeness of his courage; his credulity of his open faith; his vanity of his pride;
65 and his bluntness of his sincerity. They are all the redundancies of a rich and liberal character. All that I wish is that John's present troubles may teach him more prudence in future. That he may cease to distress his mind about other people's affairs; that he may give
70 up the fruitless attempt to promote the good of his neighbors and the peace and happiness of the world by dint of the cudgel; that he may remain quietly at home; that he gradually get his house into repair and long enjoy, on his paternal lands, a green, an honorable, and a merry old age.

32

The author's descriptions of John Bull most directly support which larger claim?

A) Withdrawing from the public stage would only weaken an already threatened estate.

B) It is more difficult to abdicate a position of power than to safeguard it.

C) Financial stability is incompatible with ruling compassionately and maintaining shared traditions.

D) Having an overextended sphere of influence can jeopardize personal welfare.

CONTINUE →

33

During the course of the passage, the central focus shifts from

A) describing a symbolic figure to sounding a call for caution and consideration regarding future conduct.

B) celebrating the merits of a relatable hero to denouncing that hero as a national embarrassment.

C) making light of a character's flaws to casting doubt on his ability to improve a situation.

D) condemning a character for his unwise familial attitudes to mourning his fall from prominence.

34

According to the passage, there is a distinct contrast between

A) having well-meaning intentions and acting in one's best interest.

B) the responsibility to protect family and the duty to volunteer for one's country.

C) growing up as part of the aristocracy and earning a position of influence.

D) respecting ancestral traditions and choosing to neglect one's modern obligations.

35

As used in line 5, "sketch" most nearly means

A) account.

B) farce.

C) cartoon.

D) impersonation.

36

Which choice provides the best evidence for the idea that John Bull's core values include caring for others?

A) Lines 9–10 ("There . . . feeling")

B) Lines 16–19 ("He . . . champion")

C) Lines 47–49 ("yet . . . ever")

D) Lines 59–60 ("His . . . unaffected")

37

As used in line 35 and line 36, "abuses" most nearly means

A) violations.

B) assaults.

C) invasions.

D) impositions.

38

The repeated references to a "cudgel" throughout the second half of the passage mainly emphasize John Bull's

A) physical stature and fortitude.

B) reputation of power and authority.

C) capacity for violence and retaliation.

D) renown as a champion of England.

39

As used in line 56, "interest" most nearly means

A) suspicion.

B) care.

C) amusement.

D) curiosity.

CONTINUE

40

It can reasonably be inferred that John Bull suffers financial hardship primarily because

A) his family members feel entitled to their extravagances and refuse to economize.

B) his pursuit of restoring his family's social standing leads him into bad investments.

C) his support of local charities and community groups outpaces his diminished resources.

D) his pride in his family's holdings compromises his ability to manage them well.

41

Which choice provides the best evidence for the answer to the previous question?

A) Lines 12–16 ("He . . . ready")

B) Lines 27–31 ("The . . . down)

C) Lines 42–46 ("he now . . . empty")

D) Lines 61–65 ("His extravagance . . . character")

42

The author would most likely describe the public's attitude toward John Bull as

A) bitterly disappointed that he could not maintain financial stability.

B) affectionately nostalgic over his generous service to their communities.

C) overly critical of his faults.

D) coolly indifferent to his success or failure.

Questions 43–52 are based on the following passage and supplementary material.

This passage is adapted from Ed Yong, "Why We Sleep Badly on Our First Night in a New Place." ©2018 by The Atlantic Monthly Group.

When you check into a hotel room or stay with a friend, is your first night of sleep disturbed? Do you toss and turn, mind strangely alert, unable to shut
Line down in the usual way? If so, you're in good company.
5 This phenomenon is called the first-night effect, and scientists have known about it for over 50 years. "Even when you look at young and healthy people without chronic sleep problems, 99 percent of the time they show this first-night effect—this weird half-awake,
10 half-asleep state," says Yuka Sasaki from Brown University.

Other animals can straddle the boundaries between sleeping and wakefulness. Whales, dolphins, and many birds can sleep with just one half of their brains
15 at a time, while the other half stays awake and its corresponding eye stays open. In this way, a bottlenose dolphin can stay awake and alert for at least five days straight, and possibly many more.

Sasaki wondered if humans do something similar,
20 albeit to a less dramatic degree. Maybe when we enter a new environment, one half of our brain stays more awake than the other, so we can better respond to unusual sounds or smells or signs of danger. Maybe our first night in a new place is disturbed because half
25 our brain is pulling an extra shift as a night watchman. "It was a bit of a hunch," she says. "Maybe we'd find something interesting."

She invited 11 volunteers to spend a few nights at her laboratory. They slept in a hulking medical scanner
30 that measured their brain activity, while electrodes on their heads and hands measured their brain waves, eye movements, heart rate, and more.

While they snoozed, team members Masako Tamaki and Ji Won Bang measured their slow-wave
35 activity—a slow and synchronous pulsing of neurons that's associated with deep sleep. They found that this slow activity was significantly weaker in the left half of the volunteers' brains, but only on their first night. And the stronger this asymmetry, the longer the volunteers
40 took to fall asleep.

The team didn't find this slow-wave asymmetry over the entire left hemisphere. It wasn't noticeable in regions involved in vision, movement, or

attention. Instead, it only affected the default mode
45 network—a group of brain regions that's associated with spontaneous unfocused mental activity, like daydreaming or mind-wandering. These results fit with the idea of the first-night brain as a night watchman, in which the left default mode network is more
50 responsive than usual.

To test this idea, Sasaki asked more volunteers to sleep in a normal bed with a pair of headphones. Throughout the sessions, the team piped small beeps into one ear or the other, either steadily or
55 infrequently. They found that the participants' left hemispheres (but not the right) were more responsive to the infrequent beeps (but not the steady ones) on the first night (but not the second). The recruits were also better and quicker at waking up in response to the
60 beeps when the sounds were processed by their left hemispheres.

This shows how dynamic sleep can be, and how attuned it is to the environment. The same applies to many animals. In 1999, Niels Rattenborg from the Max
65 Planck Institute for Ornithology found that ducks at the edge of a flock sleep more asymmetrically than those in the safer center. "In this way, sleeping ducks avoid becoming sitting ducks," he says.

Lino Nobili from Niguarda Hospital in Milan adds
70 that these results fit with a "relatively new view of sleep" as a patchwork process, rather than a global one that involves the whole brain. Recent studies suggest that some parts can sleep more deeply than others, or even temporarily wake up. This might explain not only
75 the first-night effect but also other weird phenomena like sleepwalking or paradoxical insomnia, where people think they're getting much less sleep than they actually are.

To confirm the night watch hypothesis, Sasaki now
80 wants to use weak electric currents to shut down the left default mode network to see if people sleep faster in new environments. That would certainly support her idea that this region is behind the first night effect.

It won't help people sleep better in new places,
85 though. To do that, Sasaki tries to stay in the same hotel when she travels, or at least in the same chain. "I'm flying to England tomorrow and staying at a Marriott," she says. "It's not a completely novel environment, so maybe my brain will be a little more
90 at ease."

CONTINUE

Mean Brain Response to Deviant Sounds
during Slow-wave Sleep

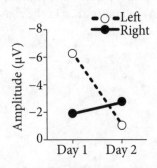

Figure 1

Response to Deviant Sounds during
Slow-wave Sleep over Time

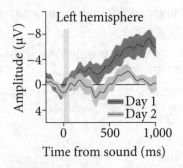

Figure 2

Figures adapted from Tamaki Masako, Ji Won Bang, Takeo Watanabe, and Yuka Sasaki, "Night Watch in One Brain Hemisphere during Sleep Associated with the First-Night Effect in Humans." ©2016 by Elsevier Ltd.

43

The primary purpose of the passage is to

A) describe a study on how slow-wave sleep activity causes sleep disorders.

B) analyze the neural underpinnings of slow-wave sleep activity.

C) propose solutions for difficulties sleeping in new places.

D) discuss research on a common phenomenon in sleep.

44

In the third paragraph (lines 19–27), the author uses the words "wondered" and "hunch" primarily to suggest that Sasaki and her colleagues

A) believed that the first-night effect would be most apparent in people who had greater awareness of their surroundings when going to sleep.

B) had not previously discovered evidence that part of the human brain responds to environmental stimuli when sleeping in a new place.

C) questioned whether the link between animal sleep patterns and the first-night effect in humans was related to similarities in their environment.

D) did not predict that slow-wave brain activity would have such a great influence on quality of sleep in various locations.

45

Which statement regarding subjects who had weaker left hemisphere slow-wave activity during the first night in the medical scanner can be most reasonably inferred from the passage?

A) They are more wakeful when presented with environmental stimuli while sleeping in a new place.

B) They are more restless sleepers overall and have trouble falling asleep in places other than their homes.

C) They are more likely to suffer from afflictions such as sleepwalking or paradoxical insomnia.

D) They are not able to sleep through the night unless their surroundings are silent.

46

Which choice provides the best evidence for the answer to the previous question?

A) Lines 38–40 ("And the . . . asleep")

B) Lines 58–61 ("The recruits . . . hemispheres")

C) Lines 74–78 ("This . . . are")

D) Lines 79–82 ("To confirm . . . environments")

CONTINUE

47

According to the passage, which statement best explains the hypothesis that Sasaki's group tested in their experiment with headphones?

A) Reducing left default mode network activity using an electric current can help individuals fall asleep.

B) Slow-wave brain activity during sleep depends on the ability to fall asleep quickly in a new place.

C) Brain activity in the left hemisphere default mode network is related to sleep disturbances during the first night in a new place.

D) Slow-wave asymmetry in the left default mode network only enhances neural responses to auditory stimuli.

48

The main purpose of the last paragraph is to

A) emphasize that the scientists could not provide useful applications for their sleep research.

B) suggest that people might be able to influence the severity of the first-night effect.

C) urge individuals to consider sleeping only in familiar places when they travel.

D) question the general significance of the first-night effect with regard to the new findings.

49

As used in line 84, "new" most nearly means

A) pristine.

B) singular.

C) inventive.

D) unfamiliar.

50

According to figure 1, the mean amplitude of brain responses to deviant sounds in the right hemisphere on Day 1 was closest to which value?

A) −8

B) −6

C) −4

D) −2

51

Figure 2 supports which statement about the relative amplitudes of left hemisphere brain responses to deviant sounds on Days 1 and 2?

A) They reached their most negative points 1,000 ms after sound onset.

B) They began to be increasingly negative 700 ms after sound onset.

C) They returned to their previous levels 1,000 ms after sound onset.

D) They became more negative between 400 ms and 700 ms after sound onset.

52

Based on the passage and figures 1 and 2, how would the plotted points in figure 1 most likely change if the left hemisphere data was focused on responses 400ms after sound onset?

A) The point for the left hemisphere on Day 1 only would be more positive.

B) The points for the right hemisphere would be more negative.

C) The points for the left hemisphere would be more positive.

D) The points on Day 2 would be greater than zero.

STOP

**If you finish before time is called, you may check your work on this section only.
Do not turn to any other section in the test.**

No Test Material On This Page

CONTINUE

Writing and Language Test

35 MINUTES, 44 QUESTIONS

Turn to Section 2 of your answer sheet to answer the questions in this section.

Each passage below is accompanied by a number of questions. For some questions, you will consider how the passage might be revised to improve the expression of ideas. For other questions, you will consider how the passage might be edited to correct errors in sentence structure, usage, or punctuation. A passage or a question may be accompanied by one or more graphics (such as a table or graph) that you will consider as you make revising and editing decisions.

Some questions will direct you to an underlined portion of a passage. Other questions will direct you to a location in a passage or ask you to think about the passage as a whole.

After reading each passage, choose the answer to each question that most effectively improves the quality of writing in the passage or that makes the passage conform to the conventions of standard written English. Many questions include a "NO CHANGE" option. Choose that option if you think the best choice is to leave the relevant portion of the passage as it is.

Questions 1–11 are based on the following passage.

The Dirt on Growing Plants Without Soil

With an average annual increase of approximately 83 million people, the current global population of over 7.5 billion represents a severe strain on the finite resources available on the planet. According to Jacques **1** Diouf, former Director-General of the United Nations' Food and Agriculture Organization, by 2050, the world will need to produce 70% more food to feed the additional 2.3 billion people expected by that year. And yet, this increase in food production could come at a great cost: conventional agriculture is one of the top contributors to water scarcity. One solution to this **2** more or less important issue is hydroponics, a method of growing plants without the use of soil.

1

A) NO CHANGE
B) Diouf former Director-General
C) Diouf former Director-General,
D) Diouf, former Director-General,

2

A) NO CHANGE
B) pressing
C) unusually significant
D) constantly thought about

CONTINUE ➡

Hydroponic systems use up to 10 times less water than conventional methods. When crops are planted in fields, the water [3] of the plants runs off into the environment, whereas in hydroponic systems, the water is captured and used again. Hydroponic systems come in several varieties, including ones in which the plant roots are submerged in nutrient-filled water and others in which a wick or pump provides water to the roots. [4]

[1] In addition to being stingy with water, hydroponic systems provide other benefits. [2] These systems use space more efficiently than do crop fields, so they can produce more fruits and vegetables per square foot and can even be built in cities. [3] Furthermore, indoor hydroponic systems can be used in almost any climate to grow plants year-round, which enhances access to fresh, local produce for people living in colder climates. [4] An added bonus is that since [5] there grown without soil, these plants are more visually appealing. [5] This reduces the environmental impact of transporting fruits and vegetables across the country from warmer regions. [6]

3

A) NO CHANGE
B) for the plants runs
C) from the plants running
D) within the plants runs

4

At this point, the writer is considering adding the following sentence.

> Lettuces, endives, and fresh herbs are a few types of produce that grow well with the use of hydroponics.

Should the writer make this addition here?

A) Yes, because it provides examples that support the previous point.
B) Yes, because it contradicts a statement made earlier in the passage.
C) No, because the information is given elsewhere in the passage.
D) No, because it is not relevant to the main point of the paragraph.

5

A) NO CHANGE
B) their
C) they're
D) its

6

To make this paragraph most logical, sentence 5 should be placed

A) where it is now.
B) after sentence 1.
C) after sentence 2.
D) after sentence 3.

CONTINUE

Although a few companies have had success producing and marketing hydroponic foods, the method still accounts for only a small part of American produce. Even though these systems **7** used less space, that space is more expensive in cities as compared to the relatively cheap farmland available in rural areas. And because the plants are grown in water with added nutrients instead of soil, some in the organic food industry **8** criticize hydroponics for being "unnatural" and claim that hydroponic produce has an inferior taste as compared to **9** conventional farms. Hydroponic operations can also be more energy intensive, **10** requiring specific types of building materials. Nonetheless, seeing as water scarcity was listed by the World Economic Forum in 2015 as the largest global risk over the next decade, **11** hydroponics farmers will likely fight to maintain the organic status of their produce.

7

A) NO CHANGE

B) are using

C) had used

D) use

8

A) NO CHANGE

B) criticize and condemn

C) criticize and also condemn

D) criticize and complain about

9

A) NO CHANGE

B) produce from conventional places.

C) farms that use soil.

D) conventionally grown produce.

10

Which choice most effectively supports the idea in the first part of the sentence?

A) NO CHANGE

B) since indoor systems may require a great deal of electricity for artificial lighting.

C) allowing different types of produce to grow in the same building.

D) since urban zoning laws may not allow for their construction.

11

The writer wants to conclude the passage by restating its main idea. Which choice best accomplishes this goal?

A) NO CHANGE

B) scientists will adjust the nutrients added to the water to create produce with a better taste.

C) the savings in water alone make hydroponics worthy of strong consideration.

D) experts predict that there may even be a world war related to the use of water.

CONTINUE

Questions 12–22 are based on the following passage.

Singing for Justice

In early 1939, Marian Anderson, a well-known African American singer, was invited by Howard University to come to Washington, D.C. and 12 have performed as part of the university's concert series. Because Anderson was so popular, the university attempted to hold the performance at Constitution Hall, the largest auditorium in the city, with a 13 volume of 4,000. This venue was owned by the Daughters of the American Revolution (DAR), an organization of female descendants of those involved in the Revolutionary War. The DAR refused to allow an African American artist to perform at the venue, 14 thrusting Anderson into the spotlight in the struggle against racial prejudice.

12

A) NO CHANGE
B) will perform
C) perform
D) performing

13

A) NO CHANGE
B) size
C) quantity
D) capacity

14

The writer wants to introduce one of the main ideas of the passage. Which choice best accomplishes this goal?

A) NO CHANGE
B) despite the fact that the organization would have earned money from the performance.
C) even though Anderson had just completed a very successful European tour.
D) which is something that unfortunately had happened to Anderson before.

CONTINUE

[15] Furthermore, First Lady and DAR member Eleanor Roosevelt, who had previously invited Anderson to sing at the White [16] House resigned from the organization in protest of its refusal to host Anderson. Thousands of other DAR members followed suit, but the group did not relent. Roosevelt, along with the President and others, [17] are able to arrange for the concert to be held on the steps of the Lincoln Memorial on Easter Sunday.

[18] Anderson was a modest and quiet person who valued community and wanted to bring people together. She believed that her pride and talent as a singer could eliminate prejudice. However, the change to an outdoor venue, as well as the publicity generated by the controversy, meant that Anderson would be performing for a much larger crowd than she had ever sung for before. Terrified, she even called her manager the night before, asking [19] did she really have to go through with the performance.

15

A) NO CHANGE
B) Nevertheless,
C) In addition,
D) DELETE the underlined portion.

16

A) NO CHANGE
B) House:
C) House—
D) House,

17

A) NO CHANGE
B) were
C) was
D) have been

18

The writer is considering deleting the underlined sentence. Should the sentence be kept or deleted?

A) Kept, because it supports the other claims made in the paragraph.
B) Kept, because it introduces an idea that the author later refutes.
C) Deleted, because it contradicts the author's claim that Anderson was a talented singer.
D) Deleted, because it provides information that is not relevant to the main idea of the paragraph.

19

A) NO CHANGE
B) whether she really had to go through with the performance.
C) did she really have to go through with the performance?
D) whether she really had to go through with the performance?

CONTINUE

On the day of the concert, the crowd numbered over 75,000 and reached from the Lincoln Memorial all the way to the Washington Monument. Despite her fears, Anderson went ahead with the concert, which included a patriotic song, two classical **20** songs; and several spirituals. Her performance was highly **21** acclaimed. She was praised for her rich and beautiful voice and for her powerful stand representing all those who faced racial discrimination.

Not wanting to take attention away from Anderson, Eleanor Roosevelt chose not to be publicly affiliated with the concert and in fact did not attend it due to other obligations. However, the two remained friends throughout their lives. Anderson's performance made her an international celebrity, and she is hailed for her role in cutting down barriers for African American performers. Later, the DAR changed its rules and apologized, and Anderson did eventually perform at Constitution Hall. **22**

20

A) NO CHANGE
B) songs and,
C) songs, and
D) songs, and,

21

Which choice most effectively combines the sentences at the underlined portion?

A) acclaimed; she was praised for her
B) acclaimed, both for her
C) acclaimed, having a
D) acclaimed, being praised by her

22

The writer wants to add a conclusion that reinforces the idea that Anderson focused on her singing as a way to fight intolerance. Which choice best accomplishes this goal?

A) She rarely spoke of her Lincoln Memorial performance and didn't express anger toward the injustice she had experienced that day and throughout her life, preferring to influence people through the power of her singing.

B) As a result of her 1939 performance, Anderson won the Spingarn Medal for outstanding achievement by an African American and later sang the National Anthem at President Kennedy's inauguration.

C) She paved the way for and inspired other African American artists such as singers Leontyne Price and Jessye Norman, the latter of whom performed at an anniversary concert in Anderson's honor in 2014.

D) She was a contralto, which is a type of classical singing voice that uses the lowest female vocal range, and while she was a talented singer even as a child, she did not have formal lessons until age fifteen.

CONTINUE

Questions 23–33 are based on the following passage and supplementary material.

Good Counsel for Now and Later

[23] Specialists who combine counseling training with financial planning acumen, a credit counselor can advise about issues such as student loans, mortgage payments, small business operations, and bankruptcy. Struggles with debt are common in American [24] society—the 2018 Consumer Financial Literacy Survey, revealed that one in four Americans admits to not paying all of his or her bills on time, while eight percent of respondents now have debts in collection. While a credit counselor's primary task may be to advise a client about resources that [25] mite help eliminate personal debt, this feedback can still involve many aspects of the client's life.

23
A) NO CHANGE
B) Acting as a specialist who combines
C) They who are specialists who combine
D) A specialist who combines

24
A) NO CHANGE
B) society: the 2018 Consumer Financial Literacy Survey
C) society, the 2018 Consumer Financial Literacy Survey,
D) society; the 2018 Consumer Financial Literacy Survey,

25
A) NO CHANGE
B) might help eliminate
C) mite help illuminate
D) might help illuminate

CONTINUE

26 Academic research provides insights into how people develop difficulties with debt. For example, some individuals struggle to make regular house or car payments while also trying to repay longstanding credit card or student loan debts. Credit counselors work with these individuals to assess their current situations, create budgets, and strategize about paying off existing debts. When individuals with more than one source of financial concern "come to credit counseling early in that process, there are more options at their disposal," explains Peter Klipa, vice president of creditor relations at the National Foundation for Credit Counseling. A counselor may propose **27** explanations that include a debt management plan, which involves paying a certain monthly amount toward the total sum owed.

Evidence suggests that when individuals go through financial counseling, the experience can affect both **28** resolutions of current debt crises and the habit's shaping future spending and credit use. For example, a 2016 study that analyzed the financial health outcomes associated with financial counseling indicates that those who don't receive credit counseling end up making their bad financial habits worse over time. The participants who

---

26

Which choice provides the best introduction to the main idea of the paragraph?

A) NO CHANGE

B) Struggles with debt can arise for people from all socioeconomic backgrounds.

C) It is particularly important for people to find a credit counselor who won't take advantage of their financial vulnerabilities.

D) Credit counseling can be particularly effective when people face multiple complicated financial situations at the same time.

27

A) NO CHANGE

B) answers

C) solutions

D) insights

28

A) NO CHANGE

B) resolution's of current debt crises and the habit's

C) resolutions of current debt crises and the habits

D) resolution's of current debt crises and the habits

CONTINUE

didn't receive counseling had, on average, not just failed to decrease their debt but had instead increased their overall debt levels **29** by $2,808 during the same period. **30** Despite the possible stigma of seeking counseling, clients who received counseling had, on average, decreased their total debt by almost $9,000 in the eighteen months after receiving that counseling. While both counseled and non-counseled individuals experienced an increase in their so-called open credit ratio, which measures how easily a person can pay off current debt obligations using currently available assets, the study found that people who received counseling experienced a greater bump: **31** on average, their final open credit ratio was 0.48.

Financial Outcomes for Clients
Who Did and Did Not Receive
"Sharpen Your Financial Focus" Counseling

Study Group + Financial Situation	Pre-Counseling (at the beginning of the study)	18 Months Later (at the end of the study)	Change
Counseled Individuals' Open Credit Ratio	0.31	0.57	+0.26
Non-Counseled Individuals' Open Credit Ratio	0.30	0.48	+0.18
Counseled Individuals' Total Debt	$81,059	$72,526	–$8,533
Non-Counseled Individuals' Total Debt	$84,130	$86,938	+$2,808

*Adapted from "Evaluation of Outcomes: The NFCC's Sharpen Your Financial Focus Program," National Foundation for Credit Counseling, 2018.

29

Which choice provides accurate information from the table to support the point made in the sentence?

A) NO CHANGE

B) by a ratio of 0.26

C) to a total of $72,526

D) by more than $8,533

30

Which choice provides the best transition from the previous sentence?

A) NO CHANGE

B) Although such counseling is not always successful,

C) Because personal finances are so complicated,

D) As proof of the success of credit counseling programs,

31

Which choice best uses information from the table to illustrate the claim made earlier in the sentence?

A) NO CHANGE

B) these clients' open credit ratio increased by 0.26.

C) there was an overall debt decrease of $8,533.

D) their pre-counseling ratio was already higher than that of the non-counseled group.

CONTINUE ➡

While a credit counselor may not be able to resolve an individual's financial difficulties **32** overnight; nevertheless, financial counseling provides valuable insights for people struggling with monetary commitments. Beyond helping individuals get out of **33** close-up financial distress, counselors also advise people on more sustainable budgeting and spending strategies for the future. That combination results in higher financial literacy and greater confidence moving forward.

32

A) NO CHANGE
B) overnight, but
C) overnight,
D) overnight; instead,

33

A) NO CHANGE
B) cutting
C) immediate
D) fierce

CONTINUE

Questions 34–44 are based on the following passage and supplementary material.

Protecting the People

In 1976, Congress passed the Toxic Substances Control Act (TSCA), which gave the Environmental Protection Agency (EPA) authority to regulate the manufacture and sale of chemicals for the purpose of preventing "unreasonable risk to human health or the environment." The act has **34** instituted and begun regulation of six dangerous chemicals since its inception, but this number is tiny in comparison to the more than 82,000 chemicals currently on the EPA chemical registry. Testing chemicals for toxicity is an expensive process, the burden of which is currently placed on the EPA rather than on the chemical manufacturers, and the EPA has extremely limited resources for testing. If the TSCA is to truly protect U.S. citizens from toxic chemicals, **35** and remove dangerous substances from the environment, the EPA must be provided with additional resources to ensure that chemicals are adequately tested for potential risk.

A company that manufactures new chemicals **36** are required only to register the chemicals with the EPA. Registration includes basic information about a new chemical, but toxicity data is only required if it is already known; companies are not required to make such studies. **37** Critics of the TSCA say that companies should be required to test new chemicals before they can be approved; in order to do so, it has only 90 days to perform extensive testing. As a result, the EPA has very little practical power to regulate any chemicals.

34

A) NO CHANGE
B) instituted
C) begun the institution
D) instituted by enacting

35

A) NO CHANGE
B) however,
C) for example,
D) DELETE the underlined portion.

36

A) NO CHANGE
B) have been
C) being
D) is

37

Which choice best introduces the topic of this sentence?

A) NO CHANGE
B) The EPA can only regulate a new chemical if it can prove that the chemical poses "unreasonable risk," but
C) Because there is controversy over which tests can best determine whether a chemical is safe,
D) It's hard to know whether the lack of regulation is more the fault of the TSCA, or the EPA itself needs reform, and

CONTINUE

Many states in the U.S., frustrated by the federal government's lack of action on toxic chemicals, have **38** passed stricter legislation that specifically targets chemicals in products designed for vulnerable populations, such as children and pregnant women. For example, the EPA regulates lead-based paints but does not place any restrictions on the use of lead **39** in other products. Such products might include toys or children's jewelry. Seventeen **40** states' have passed additional restriction's on lead to further reduce children's exposure. In what could be seen as evidence that there should be a federal policy regarding toxic chemicals, **41** over half of the fifty states have existing or pending legislation regulating the use of mercury.

Chemicals regulated by U.S. states beyond TSCA guidelines

	U.S. states with regulatory policies	U.S. states with pending policies	U.S. states without regulatory policies
Mercury	24	6	20
Lead	14	3	33
Fire Retardants	12	4	34
Bisphenol-A (BPA)	11	5	34
Cadmium	7	3	40
Phthalates	3	4	43
Formaldehyde	1	3	46
Triclosan	1	2	47

38

A) NO CHANGE

B) passed on

C) had a passing of

D) passed by

39

Which choice most effectively combines the sentences at the underlined portion?

A) in other products, such as

B) in other products:

C) in

D) in products such as

40

A) NO CHANGE

B) states have passed additional restrictions'

C) states have passed additional restrictions

D) states' have passed additional restrictions

41

Which information from the table provides the strongest evidence in support of the paragraph's main point?

A) NO CHANGE

B) ten states have existing or pending legislation regulating cadmium.

C) forty-six states have not yet taken any action to regulate formaldehyde.

D) at least eight chemicals are more strictly regulated by states than at the federal level.

CONTINUE ➔

The TSCA could be strengthened by [42] additional funding. The California Environmental Protection Agency (CalEPA), a state agency established in [43] 1991 has created a Green Chemistry Initiative that combines the efforts of lawmakers, the people of California, and the chemistry industry to create a market in which all products are evaluated for their impact on human health and the environment. The U.S. government could [44] become a trendsetter in environmental regulation by creating a similar, preemptive national initiative, rather than waiting for a substance to be proven toxic before restricting its use.

[42]

Which choice best introduces the discussion in the rest of the paragraph?
A) NO CHANGE
B) employing a cooperative model.
C) a reorganization of the EPA.
D) more rigorous chemical testing.

[43]

A) NO CHANGE
B) 1991,
C) 1991;
D) 1991—

[44]

Which choice best introduces the argument made in the final sentence of the paragraph?
A) NO CHANGE
B) appease state regulatory agencies
C) better protect its citizens and environment from toxic chemicals
D) save valuable taxpayer funds

STOP
If you finish before time is called, you may check your work on this section only.
Do not turn to any other section in the test.

No Test Material On This Page

CONTINUE

Math Test – No Calculator

25 MINUTES, 20 QUESTIONS

Turn to Section 3 of your answer sheet to answer the questions in this section.

DIRECTIONS

For questions 1–15, solve each problem, choose the best answer from the choices provided, and fill in the corresponding circle on your answer sheet. **For questions 16–20**, solve the problem and enter your answer in the grid on the answer sheet. Please refer to the directions before question 16 on how to enter your answers in the grid. You may use any available space in your test booklet for scratch work.

NOTES

1. The use of a calculator **is not permitted**.
2. All variables and expressions used represent real numbers unless otherwise indicated.
3. Figures provided in this test are drawn to scale unless otherwise indicated.
4. All figures lie in a plane unless otherwise indicated.
5. Unless otherwise indicated, the domain of a given function f is the set of all real numbers x for which $f(x)$ is a real number.

REFERENCE

$A = \pi r^2$
$C = 2\pi r$

$A = \ell w$

$A = \frac{1}{2} bh$

$c^2 = a^2 + b^2$

Special Right Triangles

$V = \ell wh$

$V = \pi r^2 h$

$V = \frac{4}{3}\pi r^3$

$V = \frac{1}{3}\pi r^2 h$

$V = \frac{1}{3}\ell wh$

The number of degrees of arc in a circle is 360.
The number of radians of arc in a circle is 2π.
The sum of the measures in degrees of the angles of a triangle is 180.

CONTINUE

1

$$(3x^4 + 2x^3 - 7) + (4x^6 - 5x^3 + 9)$$

Which of the following expressions is equivalent to the expression above?

A) $4x^6 + 3x^4 - 3x^3 + 2$

B) $4x^6 + 3x^4 + 7x^3 + 2$

C) $4x^6 + 3x^4 - 5x^3 + 2$

D) $7x^{10} - 3x^3 + 2$

2

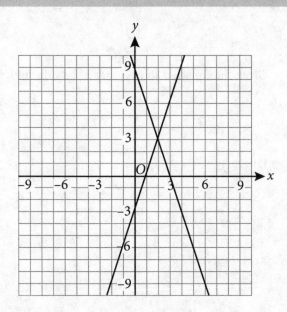

The lines graphed in the xy-plane above represent a system of two linear equations. What is the solution (x, y) to the system?

A) $(-1, -6)$

B) $(0, -3)$

C) $(2, 3)$

D) $(3, 0)$

3

Rosa has already eaten 10 pretzels from a bag that originally contained p pretzels. If Rosa is able to eat each remaining pretzel in 18 seconds, which of the following represents the amount of additional time, in seconds, needed for Rosa to eat all the pretzels in the bag?

A) $10(18 - p)$

B) $10(p - 18)$

C) $18(10 - p)$

D) $18(p - 10)$

4

$$0 = 7y - 5x + 9$$

What are the y-intercept and the slope of the line defined by the equation above?

A) The slope is $-\dfrac{5}{7}$, and the y-intercept is $-\dfrac{9}{7}$.

B) The slope is $-\dfrac{5}{7}$, and the y-intercept is $\dfrac{9}{7}$.

C) The slope is $\dfrac{5}{7}$, and the y-intercept is $-\dfrac{9}{7}$.

D) The slope is $\dfrac{5}{7}$, and the y-intercept is $\dfrac{9}{7}$.

CONTINUE ➡

5

If $5 + n = 9 - \frac{1}{3}n$, what is the value of n ?

A) 3

B) 4

C) 6

D) $\frac{21}{2}$

6

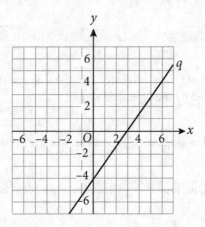

Line p (not shown) is perpendicular to line q shown above and passes through the point $(0, 4)$. Which of the following equations could represent line p ?

A) $y = -\frac{4}{3}x + 4$

B) $y = -\frac{3}{4}x + 4$

C) $y = \frac{3}{4}x + 4$

D) $y = \frac{4}{3}x + 4$

7

$$(4 + 7i) - (6 + 2i)$$

What complex number is equivalent to the expression above if $i = \sqrt{-1}$?

A)   2

B) $2 - 5i$

C) $-2 + 5i$

D) $-10 - 9i$

8

$$\frac{4}{n-3} = \frac{5}{n+2}$$

Given the equation above, what is the value of n ?

A) -7

B) -2

C)   8

D) 23

CONTINUE

9

What is the solution set to the equation
$0 = (3a + 1)^2(a - 4)$?

A) $\left\{\dfrac{1}{3}, -4\right\}$

B) $\left\{-\dfrac{1}{3}, 4\right\}$

C) $\left\{-\dfrac{1}{3}, \dfrac{1}{3}, -4\right\}$

D) $\left\{-\dfrac{1}{3}, \dfrac{1}{3}, 4\right\}$

10

What is the solution set to the equation

$\dfrac{2}{7-m} = \dfrac{4}{m} - \dfrac{5-m}{7-m}$?

A) $\{4, 7\}$

B) $\{4, 5\}$

C) $\{1, 7\}$

D) $\{4\}$

11

If 3 is a root of the function $f(x) = x^2 + 13x + c$ and c is a constant, what is the value of c ?

A) −48

B) −3

C) 5

D) 48

12

$$\dfrac{7}{12b^3} - \dfrac{3}{4b^3}$$

The above expression is equivalent to which of the following expressions for all $b > 0$?

A) $-\dfrac{1}{6b^3}$

B) $-\dfrac{1}{4b^3}$

C) $\dfrac{1}{4b^3}$

D) $\dfrac{1}{6b^3}$

CONTINUE

13

$$y = x^2 + 3$$
$$y = 15x - 33$$

The system of equations shown above is graphed in the xy-plane. If system has two solutions, what is the product of the x-coordinates of the two solutions?

A) 36

B) 4

C) −4

D) −36

14

$$\left(-27a^{10}\right)^{\frac{3}{5}}$$

For all values of a, which of the following is equivalent to the expression above?

A) $3a^6 \sqrt[5]{3}$

B) $-3a^6 \sqrt[5]{81}$

C) $3a^5 \sqrt[5]{81}$

D) $-3a^5 \sqrt[5]{3}$

15

The amount of carbon-15 in a given sample decays exponentially with time. If the function $C(m) = 100\left(\dfrac{1}{2}\right)^{24m}$ models the amount of carbon-15 remaining in the sample after m minutes, which of the following must be true?

A) The amount of carbon in the sample halves every minute.

B) The amount of carbon in the sample halves every 24 minutes.

C) The amount of carbon in the sample halves 24 times every minute.

D) The amount of carbon in the sample reduces by a factor of 24 every 2 minutes.

CONTINUE

DIRECTIONS

For questions 16–20, solve the problem and enter your answer in the grid, as described below, on the answer sheet.

1. Although not required, it is suggested that you write your answer in the boxes at the top of the columns to help you fill in the circles accurately. You will receive credit only if the circles are filled in correctly.

2. Mark no more than one circle in any column.

3. No question has a negative answer.

4. Some problems may have more than one correct answer. In such cases, grid only one answer.

5. **Mixed numbers** such as $3\frac{1}{2}$ must be gridded as 3.5 or 7/2. (If $3 \ 1 \ / \ 2$ is entered into the grid, it will be interpreted as $\frac{31}{2}$, not as $3\frac{1}{2}$.)

6. **Decimal Answers:** If you obtain a decimal answer with more digits than the grid can accommodate, it may be either rounded or truncated, but it must fill the entire grid.

Answer: $\frac{7}{12}$ Answer: 2.5

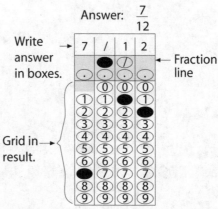

Write answer in boxes. ← Fraction line

Grid in result.

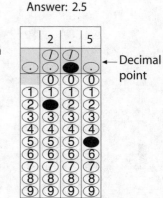

← Decimal point

Acceptable ways to grid $\frac{2}{3}$ are:

Answer: 201 – either position is correct

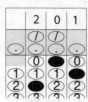

NOTE: You may start your answers in any column, space permitting. Columns you don't need to use should be left blank.

CONTINUE →

16

If $0 = \dfrac{2}{n-2} - \dfrac{6}{n+1}$, what is the value of n?

17

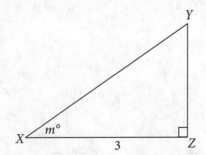

In the figure above, triangle XYZ is a right triangle with $XZ = 3$. If $\tan m = \sqrt{3}$, what is XY?

18

An angle in the xy-plane has measure 5π radians. What is the measure of the angle in degrees?

CONTINUE

19

Robert is selling televisions at an electronics store. The televisions normally cost $545 each but are being sold at an 8% discount. What is the minimum number of televisions Robert must sell if he wants to meet his quota of $100,000 in total sales?

20

The linear function $y = g(x)$ is graphed in the xy-plane. If $g(-3) = 4$ and $g(2) = 19$, what is the slope of line g?

S T O P
If you finish before time is called, you may check your work on this section only.
Do not turn to any other section in the test.

Math Test – Calculator

55 MINUTES, 38 QUESTIONS

Turn to Section 4 of your answer sheet to answer the questions in this section.

DIRECTIONS

For questions 1–30, solve each problem, choose the best answer from the choices provided, and fill in the corresponding circle on your answer sheet. **For questions 31–38**, solve the problem and enter your answer in the grid on the answer sheet. Please refer to the directions before question 31 on how to enter your answers in the grid. You may use any available space in your test booklet for scratch work.

NOTES

1. The use of a calculator **is permitted**.

2. All variables and expressions used represent real numbers unless otherwise indicated.

3. Figures provided in this test are drawn to scale unless otherwise indicated.

4. All figures lie in a plane unless otherwise indicated.

5. Unless otherwise indicated, the domain of a given function f is the set of all real numbers x for which $f(x)$ is a real number.

REFERENCE

$A = \pi r^2$
$C = 2\pi r$

$A = \ell w$

$A = \frac{1}{2} bh$

$c^2 = a^2 + b^2$

Special Right Triangles

$V = \ell w h$

$V = \pi r^2 h$

$V = \frac{4}{3} \pi r^3$

$V = \frac{1}{3} \pi r^2 h$

$V = \frac{1}{3} \ell w h$

The number of degrees of arc in a circle is 360.
The number of radians of arc in a circle is 2π.
The sum of the measures in degrees of the angles of a triangle is 180.

CONTINUE ➡

1

If the function g is defined by $g(x) = 3x + 5$, what is the value of $g(-5)$?

A) -20

B) -10

C) 20

D) 60

2

Number of Lightbulbs Produced at
Levington Lights in a Day

	Working	Defective	Total
60-Watt	1,230	127	1,357
100-Watt	2,384	271	2,655
Total	3,614	398	4,012

According to the table above, 100-Watt bulbs made up what fraction of the working lightbulbs?

A) $\dfrac{1,230}{3,614}$

B) $\dfrac{2,384}{3,614}$

C) $\dfrac{271}{398}$

D) $\dfrac{2,384}{2,655}$

3

The expression $(4n - 5)(5n - 4)$ is equivalent to which of the following?

A) $20n^2 - 41n + 20$

B) $20n^2 - 39n + 9$

C) $9n^2 - 41n + 20$

D) $4n^2 - 18n + 9$

4

The ratio of $\dfrac{2.7}{1.2}$ is equivalent to the ratio of $\dfrac{b}{4.8}$.

What is the value of b ?

A) 2.13

B) 4

C) 6.3

D) 10.8

CONTINUE

5

$$60 = 15mn + 20$$

What is the value of $3mn + 4$, according to the equation above?

A) 20

B) 15

C) 12

D) 4

6

A high school principal is seeking to determine the likelihood that students in Santana High School will attend the upcoming dance. Which of the following data collection methods is most likely to yield an accurate prediction by the principal?

A) Polling a randomly selected group of 1,500 teenagers in the town

B) Conducting a survey of 180 randomly selected students in the senior class at Santana High School

C) Polling a group of 250 randomly selected Santana High School students

D) Posting an Internet poll on the school's website open only to Santana High School students

Questions 7–9 refer to the following information.

Thomas was hired for a new job in 1977, with a starting salary of $40,000. Beginning in 1978, Thomas received an annual raise, increasing his salary by $2,300 each year.

7

If Thomas retired at the end of 1999, what was his salary in his final year?

A) $90,600

B) $76,000

C) $54,600

D) $40,000

8

Which of the following must be true, given that Thomas's salary after y years was between $54,000 and $60,000 ?

A) $3 < y < 6$

B) $6 < y < 9$

C) $9 < y < 12$

D) $y > 12$

CONTINUE

9

Which of the following graphs could represent Thomas's salary, S, in dollars, as a function of the number of years, y, after 1977 ?

A)

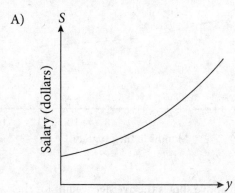

B)

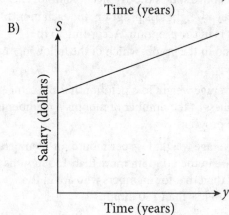

C)

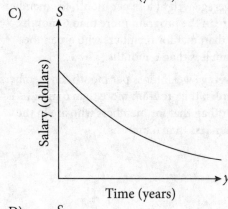

D)

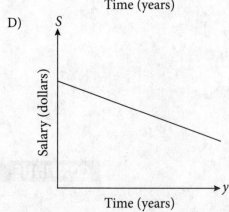

10

An investor is deciding between two options for a short-term investment. One option has a return R, in dollars, t months after investment, and is modelled by the equation $R = 100(3^t)$. The other option has a return R, in dollars, t months after investment, and is modeled by the equation $R = 350t$. After 4 months, how much less is the return given by the linear model than the return given by the exponential model?

A) $1,400

B) $4,050

C) $6,700

D) $8,100

11

$$n - \sqrt{2n + 22} = 1$$

Given the equation above, which of the following is a possible value of n ?

   I.   7

   II. −3

   III. −5

A) I only

B) III only

C) I and III only

D) II and III only

CONTINUE

12

$$3x - 6 = 5x - 2$$

Based on the equation above, what is the value of $2x - 4$?

A) −8

B) −2

C) 2

D) 6

13

Gas Mileage and Weight for Cars

The scatterplot above shows the relationship between gas mileage, in miles per gallon, and weight, in tons, for 10 cars selected at random. The line of best fit models the gas mileage based on the weight of the car. What is the weight, in tons, of the car for which the actual gas mileage was closest to the predicted value?

A) 2.5

B) 4.5

C) 15

D) 27

14

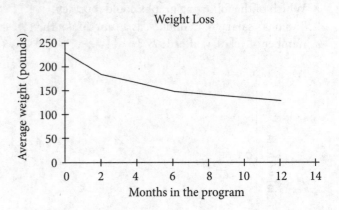

The graph above shows the average weight for the members of a weight loss program, for each month a member is in the program. According to the information in the graph, which of the following must be true?

A) The average weight loss per month is the same regardless of the number of months a member is in the program.

B) The average weight loss per month for members who are in the program more than 150 months is less than that for members who are in the program less than 150 months.

C) The average weight loss per month for members who are in the program more than 6 months is less than that for members who are in the program less than 6 months.

D) The average weight loss per month for members who are in the program more than 6 months is greater than that for members who are in the program less than 6 months.

CONTINUE

15

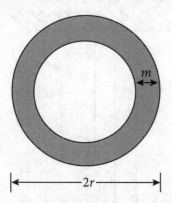

The figure above represents a circular lake with the walking path that is m meters wide. If the expression $\pi r^2 - \pi(r - m)^2$ represents the area of the walking path, in square meters, what does the quantity $(r - m)$ represent?

A) The radius of the lake

B) The combined radius of the lake and walking path

C) The combined area of the surface of the lake and walking path

D) The area of the surface of the lake

16

Kanaka took 8 tests for her social studies class. Each test has a maximum score of 100 and a minimum score of 0. On the 8 tests, Kanaka's mean score was 90. More than a quarter of her tests have scores less than 85. If the average of the remaining tests is x, which of the following must be true?

A) $x \le 85$

B) $85 < x < 90$

C) $x = 90$

D) $x > 90$

17

A poll of 400 randomly selected likely voters in Seanoa City was taken to determine the support for the mayoral candidates in the upcoming election. Of the likely voters selected, 190 stated that they are likely to vote for Candidate A. If the conclusion is drawn that "approximately 3,120 voters are likely to vote for Candidate A," which of the following is closest to the number of likely voters in Seanoa City?

A) 1,482

B) 3,120

C) 4,741

D) 6,568

18

$$y^2 = 21 - x$$
$$x = 5$$

The solutions to the system of equation above are (a_1, b_1) and (a_2, b_2). What are the values of b_1 and b_2?

A) −4 and 4

B) $-\sqrt{21}$ and $\sqrt{21}$

C) −5 and 5

D) $-\sqrt{26}$ and $\sqrt{26}$

CONTINUE

19

The function p is defined as $p(x) = x^2 - 3x$. If the function q is defined as $q(x) = p(x) - 4$, what is the value of $q(10)$?

A) −30

B)   6

C) 66

D) 70

20

If $c > 0$ and m and n are positive integers, which of the following is equivalent to $c^{\frac{m}{n}}$?

A) $\dfrac{c^m}{c^n}$

B) $cm - n$

C) $\left(\sqrt[m]{c}\right)^n$

D) $\left(\sqrt[n]{c}\right)^m$

21

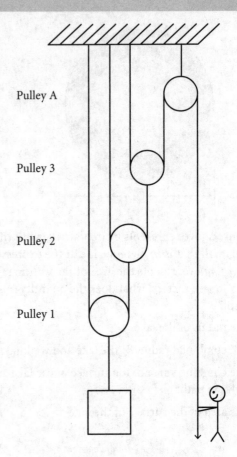

In the figure above, each pulley added to the pulley system after Pulley A reduces the amount of force required to lift an object to 50% of the original amount. If the system has three additional pulleys, what would be the approximate force, in Newtons, that is exerted to lift a weight that normally requires 200 pounds of force to lift? (1 Newton = 0.224 pounds)

A)   5.6

B)   11.2

C) 111.6

D) 223.2

CONTINUE

22

$$Q = 17.6T$$

The equation above shows the heat energy, Q, in Joules that is absorbed by a 10 g block of wood as temperature, T, in degrees Celsius, increases. Which of the following best describes the meaning of the number 17.6 in this equation?

A) The heat energy absorbed by the block of wood at a constant temperature

B) The heat energy absorbed by the block of wood with a change in temperature of $T°C$

C) The heat energy absorbed by the block of wood with every increase in temperature of 1°C

D) The heat energy absorbed by the block of wood when the temperature reaches 0°C

23

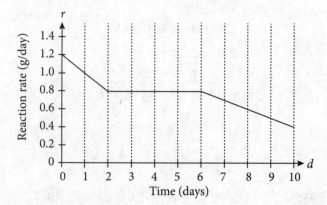

The graph above represents the reaction rate, r, at which an unfinished iron nail rusts in water during the first 10 days of an experiment, where d gives time measured in days. What was the total amount of rust produced from $d = 2$ to $d = 6$?

A) 0.8 grams

B) 1.6 grams

C) 2.4 grams

D) 3.2 grams

24

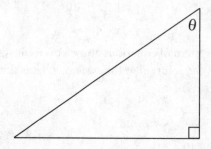

Note: Figure not drawn to scale.

In the figure above, if $\cos\theta = \dfrac{3}{5}$, what is the value of $\cos(90 - \theta)$?

A) $\dfrac{3}{5}$

B) $\dfrac{3}{4}$

C) $\dfrac{4}{5}$

D) $\dfrac{5}{4}$

CONTINUE

25

$$x + 7y = -10$$
$$3x - 4y = k$$

In the system of equations above, k is a constant. If (a, b) is the solution to the system, what is the value of a, in terms of k ?

A) $\dfrac{-k - 30}{25}$

B) $\dfrac{3k + 10}{25}$

C) $\dfrac{6k - 8}{25}$

D) $\dfrac{7k - 40}{25}$

26

According to the U.S. Department of Labor, the unemployment rate in January of 2012 in the United States was 8.3%. According to the same department, the unemployment rate in January of 2016 was 4.9%. According to the U.S. Department of Labor, how did the unemployment rate change from January 2012 to January 2016 ?

A) It decreased by 79%.

B) It decreased by 41%.

C) It decreased by 34%.

D) It increased by 41%.

Questions 27 and 28 refer to the following information.

In a particular college, the test scores of the most recent test given for a particular Physics class and a particular Literature class were studied. Both tests were scored from 0 to 100 and had a total of 20 questions, which were equally weighted with no partial credit. The Physics class had 128 students and the Literature class had 75 students. The test results are shown in the two graphs below.

Literature Test Results

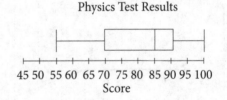

Physics Test Results

45 50 55 60 65 70 75 80 85 90 95 100
Score

27

The dean of the college is comparing the scores from the two classes and calculates the median for each class. If the dean labels the median score of the Physics class P and the median score of the Literature class L, what is the sum of P and L ?

A) 175

B) 170

C) 85

D) 80

CONTINUE

28

Which of the following box plots most accurately represents the result of the Literature test?

A)

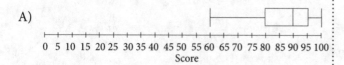

B)

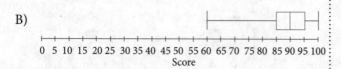

C)

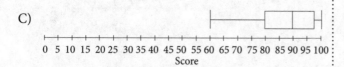

D)

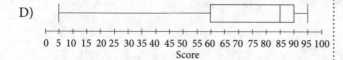

29

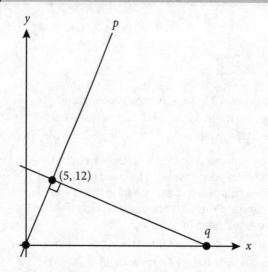

In the figure above, lines p and q are graphed on the xy-plane. What is the x-intercept of line q ?

A) 24

B) 27.6

C) 33.8

D) 38.4

30

$$y = x^2 + 16x + 28$$

The equation above represents the graph of a parabola in the xy-plane. Which of the following represents an equivalent form of the equation that includes the minimum value of y as a constant?

A) $y - 28 = x(x + 16)$

B) $y = x^2 + 2(8x + 14)$

C) $y = x(x + 16) + 28$

D) $y = (x + 8)^2 - 36$

CONTINUE

DIRECTIONS

For questions 31–38, solve the problem and enter your answer in the grid, as described below, on the answer sheet.

1. Although not required, it is suggested that you write your answer in the boxes at the top of the columns to help you fill in the circles accurately. You will receive credit only if the circles are filled in correctly.

2. Mark no more than one circle in any column.

3. No question has a negative answer.

4. Some problems may have more than one correct answer. In such cases, grid only one answer.

5. **Mixed numbers** such as $3\frac{1}{2}$ must be gridded as 3.5 or 7/2. (If  is entered into the grid, it will be interpreted as $\frac{31}{2}$, not as $3\frac{1}{2}$.)

6. **Decimal Answers:** If you obtain a decimal answer with more digits than the grid can accommodate, it may be either rounded or truncated, but it must fill the entire grid.

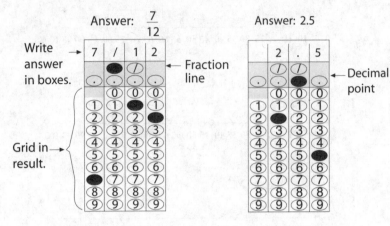

Answer: $\frac{7}{12}$ Answer: 2.5

Write answer in boxes. — Fraction line — Decimal point

Grid in result.

Acceptable ways to grid $\frac{2}{3}$ are:

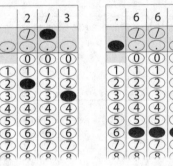

Answer: 201 – either position is correct

NOTE: You may start your answers in any column, space permitting. Columns you don't need to use should be left blank.

CONTINUE

31

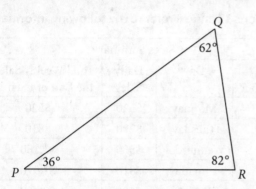

In the figure above, triangle *PQR* is similar to triangle *XYZ* (not shown). If *PQ:XY = QR:YZ = PR:XZ =* 4:5, what is the measure, in degrees, of angle *Y* ?

32

A new homeowner drew a floor plan of her new house, in which 1 inch on the floor plan is equivalent to 18 inches on the actual floor. If the actual longest side of the floor in one of the bedrooms is 153 inches, what is the length of the longest side of the same bedroom in the floor plan?

33

What is the number of pallets, each with an area of 60 square yards, that would be needed to cover a field that is 3 acres in area? (1 acre = 4,840 square yards)

34

If $b + \dfrac{22}{25} = \dfrac{7}{5}b$, what is the value of b ?

CONTINUE

35

The point $(p, 0)$ lies on a circle in the xy-plane. The points $(2, 3.5)$ and $(-2, 0.5)$ are the endpoints of a diameter of the circle. If $p > 0$, what is the value of p ?

36

$$7y = 11x$$

$$\frac{1}{5}x - \frac{1}{4}y = -\frac{81}{80}$$

If (x, y) is the solution to the system of equations above, what is the value of $\frac{y}{x}$?

Questions 37 and 38 refer to the following information.

Sales Summary			
Day Number	Day	Daily Sales	Total Weekly Sales at the End of Each Day
1	Monday	$520	$520
2	Tuesday	$290	$810
3	Wednesday	$350	$1,160
4	Thursday	$810	$1,970
5	Friday	$480	$2,450

A salesperson recorded her sales during a particular 5-day work week, shown in the table above, in order to study her daily sales.

37

The salesperson wants to increase her average sales per day by 20% in the following week. Given the information in the chart above, what should her daily sales average be for the following week?

38

During her eight-hour shift on Wednesday, the salesperson sold items that had an average price of $8.10. To the nearest tenth of an item, what is the number of items she sold per hour on Wednesday?

END OF TEST

DO NOT RETURN TO A PREVIOUS SECTION.

Practice Test 2:
Answers and
Explanations

PRACTICE TEST 2 ANSWER KEY

Section 1: Reading		Section 2: Writing and Language		Section 3: Math (No Calculator)		Section 4 : Math (Calculator)	
1. C	27. C	1. A	23. D	1. A	11. A	1. B	20. D
2. D	28. C	2. B	24. B	2. C	12. A	2. B	21. C
3. C	29. D	3. B	25. B	3. D	13. A	3. A	22. C
4. A	30. B	4. D	26. D	4. C	14. B	4. D	23. D
5. B	31. A	5. C	27. C	5. A	15. C	5. C	24. C
6. A	32. D	6. D	28. C	6. B	16. $\frac{7}{2}$	6. C	25. D
7. D	33. A	7. D	29. A	7. C	or	7. A	26. B
8. B	34. A	8. A	30. D	8. D	3.5	8. B	27. A
9. D	35. A	9. D	31. B	9. B	17. 6	9. B	28. A
10. B	36. B	10. B	32. C	10. D	18. 900	10. C	29. C
11. B	37. D	11. C	33. C		19. 200	11. A	30. D
12. D	38. B	12. C	34. B		20. 3	12. A	31. 62
13. A	39. B	13. D	35. A			13. A	32. 8.5
14. A	40. D	14. A	36. D			14. C	33. 242
15. B	41. B	15. D	37. B			15. A	34. $\frac{11}{5}$
16. C	42. C	16. D	38. A			16. D	or
17. A	43. D	17. C	39. C			17. D	2.2
18. C	44. B	18. A	40. C			18. A	35. 1.5
19. A	45. A	19. B	41. A			19. C	36. $\frac{11}{7}$
20. C	46. A	20. C	42. B				or
21. C	47. C	21. B	43. B				1.57
22. B	48. B	22. A	44. C				37. 588
23. D	49. D						38. 5.4
24. D	50. D						
25. C	51. D						
26. D	52. C						

PRACTICE TEST 2 EXPLANATIONS

Section 1: Reading

1. **C** The question asks why the author uses the image of the *waters of the Jordan*. Use the given line reference to find the window and read carefully. The answer should come from a window of approximately lines 1–10. The passage states that *The ever-increasing current of Christmas shoppers flowed on. Now and then it rolled up, like the waters of the Jordan*. The image is used to describe the movement of the crowd. Find an answer that matches this prediction. Choice (A) includes the word *never*, which is extreme language. The passage does not suggest that the crowd *will never ebb*. Eliminate (A). Choice (B) can be eliminated because there is no indication in the passage that *the little woman was drowning in the throng*. Choice (C) matches the prediction, so hang on to it. The image of the *waters of Jordan* is used to describe the movement of the crowd, not the movements of one person. Eliminate (D). The correct answer is (C).

2. **D** The question asks what the word *caught* means in line 16. Go back to the text, find the word *caught*, and mark it out. Carefully read the surrounding text to determine another word that would fit in the blank based on the context of the passage. The text says the woman *caught the scent of fresh-cut flowers*. In other words, the woman "became aware of" the scent. Find an answer that means something similar to becoming aware of. The only answer that matches this meaning is (D). The other answers might initially look attractive because they all relate to the word "caught," but none of the other three answers match the context of the passage. The correct answer is (D).

3. **C** The question asks about supporting the claim that *the shabby little woman was at first excited by the tall young girl*. Use the line references in the answer choices. The lines for (A) state that the shabby little woman *caught the scent of fresh-cut flowers and looked up into the eyes of a tall young girl in a white-plumed velvet hat, with a bunch of English violets in her brown mink fur*. These lines are an objective description of the young girl. There is no indication in these lines of how the woman feels. Eliminate (A). The lines for (B) state that *As their glances met, the shabby little woman checked a start, and half-defensively dropped her lids*. This description of the woman notes that she is startled and somewhat defensive. However, the question asks which lines show that the woman was excited. Eliminate (B). The lines for (C) state that the *thrill of response that set the woman's pulses throbbing died suddenly*. The phrase *thrill of response that sent the woman's pulses throbbing* indicates that the woman was initially excited. Keep (C). The lines for (D) describe how the woman saw herself. These lines do not relate to how the woman felt at meeting the tall young girl. Eliminate (D). The correct answer is (C).

4. **A** The question asks why the woman invites the visitor to come in. Use chronology to find the answer. The answer to question 3 was in the third paragraph, and the line reference for question 5 is in the seventh paragraph. Therefore, scan between the third and seventh paragraph for a description of the woman inviting a visitor. The fifth paragraph provides the following description. *"Come in," invited the woman, expecting some famine-pressed neighbor for a spoonful of coffee or a drawing of tea*. Look for an answer that matches the idea of the woman *expecting* someone in need. Choice (A) matches that idea, so keep it. Choice (B) can be eliminated because, though she does invite this person in, there's no evidence that the woman allows everyone in. Eliminate (C) because there is no indication that the woman expected *the young girl to drop by*. The passage also does not suggest that the woman *cannot see*, so eliminate (D). The correct answer is (A).

5.   **B**   The question asks about the purpose of the girl's comments in lines 51–58. The passage describes the young girl as saying *"I've such a silly excuse for coming.... I noticed you had a rare fur-piece... and I want to ask a very great favor of you. Now please don't be shocked—I've been ransacking the city for something like it, and...I should like to buy it of you."* Find an answer that matches the idea of the girl explaining why she has come to the apartment. Choice (A) can be eliminated: while the girl seeks to persuade the woman to sell her the fur, there is no indication that she wants *a discount*. Choice (B) is a solid paraphrase of the prediction, so keep it. The girl is not laughing at the shabby woman, nor does she demand *the shabby woman surrender her wrap,* so (C) and (D) can both be eliminated. The correct answer is (B).

6.   **A**   The question asks why the girl uses the word *ransacking.* In the passage, the young girl says *"I noticed you had a rare fur-piece...and I want to ask a very great favor of you. Now please don't be shocked—I've been ransacking the city for something like it, and...I should like to buy it of you."* In context, *ransacking the city* means that the girl has been looking everywhere in the city for a similar rare fur piece. Find an answer that matches this prediction. Only (A) matches the context of the passage. The girl has searched everywhere in the city for the same fur piece, so her search can be described as *comprehensive.* The correct answer is (A).

7.   **D**   The question asks why *the shabby woman initially declines to sell the fur.* In lines 72–73, the woman first expresses confusion about the girl's request, but then says, *"I can't, it ain't worth...."* The woman doesn't think the fur is worth anything. Eliminate (A) because the question asks about the woman's thoughts, not the young girl's. Choice (B) has nothing to do with the passage, so eliminate it. Choice (C) does mention the worth of the piece, but there is no discussion about the actual price. Eliminate (C). Choice (D) is a solid paraphrase of the prediction. The correct answer is (D).

8.   **B**   The question asks for the best evidence for the answer to the previous question. Lines 72–73 were used to answer Q8. The correct answer is (B).

9.   **D**   The question asks how the shabby woman felt after the girl's departure. Use chronology to find the answer. The answer to question 8 came from lines 72–73. Start reading after these lines to find how the woman felt. According to the passage, *As she sat huddled on the cot, warmth and vitality glowed within her, kindled by the memory of a recent kindly human touch.* Find an answer that is consistent with that prediction. The only answer that matches the positive feeling that the woman has after the young girl leaves is (D), *warmth.* The correct answer is (D).

10.   **B**   This question asks what the purpose of the last paragraph is. According to the last paragraph, *It was unusual to sell expensive furs to such a customer. But...[i]n this case, the shabby little woman was prepared. She produced three crisp ten-dollar bills...and two dollars more from the savings in her worn little purse.* Find an answer that matches the idea of the purchase being different than what normally happened. Choice (A) is a detail. Although the first sentence of the paragraph states that *it was unusual to sell expensive furs to such a customer,* this is not the purpose of the paragraph as a whole. Eliminate (A). Choice (B) matches the prediction, so keep it. Choice (C) uses extreme language. While the last paragraph describes the shabby woman as *triumphantly* leaving the store, there is no indication in the passage that the purchase was the shabby woman's *greatest triumph.* Eliminate (C). Choice (D) does not match the prediction. According to the passage, the sale of the furs to the shabby woman is described as *unusual.* Therefore, the last paragraph does not illustrate how servants *go Christmas shopping.* Eliminate (D). The correct answer is (B).

11. **B**   The question asks about the main purpose of the passage. Because this is a general question, it should be done after all the specific questions. The passage discusses social learning in animals and humans and its implications for the evolution of complex skills and language. Eliminate (A) because the passage is not a *chronicle* (an account of events in order of when they occurred), and because it discusses other animal species and qualities in addition to *human intelligence*. Keep (B) because it includes both *human and animal observations* and because *knowledge and skill development across generations* is a paraphrase for social learning. Eliminate (C) because the passage points out similarities between social learning in humans and animals; it does not try to explain why *humans are more intelligent than animals*. Eliminate (D) because the passage does not mention *social behaviors that humans do not understand*. The correct answer is (B).

12. **D**   The question asks about the meanings of *back* as used in lines 42 and 72. Go back to each reference in the text, find the word *back*, and cross it out. Carefully read the surrounding text to determine another word that would fit in each blank based on the context of the passage. The fifth paragraph mentions a group of macaques being *placed back with other rhesus macaques*. The first use of *back* conveys the sense of "to the place they came from." The reference from the seventh paragraph states, *Over the last seven million years (and even going much further back than that, truth be told)....* The second use of *back* conveys the sense of "earlier in time." Eliminate (A) because *in exchange* is not consistent with "to the place they came from," so that cannot be the right answer. Eliminate (B) because *earlier* is a match for the second use, not the first, and *dishonestly* is not consistent with either meaning. Eliminate (C) because *incorrectly* is not consistent with either meaning. Keep (D) because *again* is consistent with "to the place they came from," and *previously* is consistent with "earlier in time." The correct answer is (D).

13. **A**   The question asks for a description of *what happened when the rhesus macaques in de Waal and Johanowicz's experiment were raised by stump-tailed macaques*. Look for the lead words *rhesus macaques, stump-tailed macaques, de Waal*, and *Johanowicz* in the passage. The fifth paragraph describes an experiment in which *rhesus macaques* spent *five months of their young lives with stump-tailed macaques, which are much more prone to reconciling disputes peacefully. These fostered rhesus macaques learned the behavior of reconciliation*. The answer must have something to do with the newly learned behavior. Keep (A) because the rhesus macaques developed *a behavior their species does not normally demonstrate*. Eliminate (B) because it is a contradiction of what's stated in the passage: the *rhesus macaques learned the behavior of reconciliation;* they did not become *more violent*. Eliminate (C) because it is not supported: the rhesus monkeys adopted some of the behavior of the stump-tailed macaques, but they did not become *indistinguishable* from them. Eliminate (D) because it is not supported: the rhesus macaques did become *more conciliatory*, but not *more intelligent and creative*. The correct answer is (A).

14. **A**   The question asks *which potential claim about social learning* was *most likely ruled out* by *de Waal and Johanowicz's experiment*. Look for the lead words *de Waal and Johanowicz* in the passage. The fifth paragraph describes the experiment on *rhesus macaques* living *with stump-tailed macaques*. It goes on to say that the behaviors learned by the rhesus macaques *remained even after other habits they had picked up faded*. Keep (A) because the idea that the rhesus macaques' learned behavior *stuck with them even after they were placed back with other rhesus macaques* rules out the claim that learned *habits…will last only as long as they remain in close contact with that other species*. Eliminate (B) because de Waal and Johanowicz did not study passing on *traits to the next generation*. Eliminate (C) because there is no discussion of whether or not the rhesus macaques were *ostracized by members of their own species*. Eliminate (D) because de Waal and Johanowicz did not study passing *behaviors on to offspring in the next generation*. The correct answer is (A).

15. **B**   The question is the best evidence question in a paired set. Because Q14 was a specific question, simply look at the lines used to answer the previous question. Lines 40–45 were used to answer Q14. Of these lines, only lines 43–45 appear in an answer choice. The correct answer is (B).

16. **C**   The question asks what *the author would most likely agree* with about *human beings*. Notice that the following question is a best evidence question, so this question and Q17 can be done in tandem. Look at the answers for Q17 first. The lines in (17A) say that the human *explosion of innovation and creativity* is *largely attributed to the acquisition of language*. Look to see if those lines support any answers in Q16. Choice (16C) mentions that humans are *able to extend their creativity with the support of language*. Connect those two answers. Next, consider the lines for (17B). They say that human knowledge *was transmitted socially through language*. Consider the answers to Q16. Choice (16A) mentions *social learning*, but it says humans have *achieved the best methods*, which is not supported by (17B). Choice (16C) also mentions *language*, but (17B) doesn't mention *creativity*. Since no answer to Q16 is fully supported by (17B), eliminate it. The lines in (17C) mention evolving *the capacity for symbolic thought and language before they were actually used*, which is not referenced in any of the answers to Q16. Eliminate (17C). Choice (17D) mentions *natural selection* and *genetically programmed behaviors that are complex*, which are not referenced in any of the answers to Q16. Eliminate (17D). Without any support from Q17, (16A), (16B), and (16D) can be eliminated. The correct answers are (16C) and (17A).

17. **A**   (See explanation above.)

18. **C**   The question asks why the author uses the terms *random mutation* and *innate knowledge* in the last paragraph of the passage. Use the paragraph reference to find the window. The last paragraph says, *Social learning resolves this conundrum.* To understand the *conundrum*, look at the last sentence of the previous paragraph, which suggests that *the complex behaviors we see in animals* are not only due to *pure genetics and "survival of the fittest."* The last paragraph makes a distinction between social learning and *random mutation* or *innate knowledge:* the text suggests that social learning can explain *complex behaviors* that cannot be explained by *pure*

genetics. Eliminate (A) because these terms are used to show the importance of social learning, not *natural selection.* Eliminate (B) because the author does not show any *uncertainty* about the *benefits of social learning.* Keep (C) because it mentions a *contrast between genetic traits and social learning.* Eliminate (D) because conveying *a serious tone* is not the purpose of the two phrases that the question asks about. The correct answer is (C).

19. **A** The question asks for *the relative size of prey caught by the smaller birds that were raised by another species* in the graph. Look for the lead words *smaller birds* and *raised by another species* on the graph. The data about *smaller bird species* is in the columns on the left in the graph, and the gray columns show the data about the *birds raised by another species.* The gray column on the left is between 0.25 and 0.3, as shown on the left axis. Choice (A) matches the graph. Eliminate (B), (C), and (D), which do not match the information from the graph. The correct answer is (A).

20. **C** The question asks for a topic that *is presented in the graph but NOT discussed in the passage.* Look for lead words from each answer choice in the passage and the graph, and eliminate any that are mentioned in the passage or not included in the graph. Eliminate (A) because social learning from the same species is discussed in the passage, for example, in the second paragraph: *humans do most of their learning socially.* Eliminate (B) because social learning from other species is also discussed in the passage, for example, in the fifth paragraph, which discusses *cross-fostering experiments.* Keep (C) because while the graph presents data about birds that were *cross-fostered by another species,* the cross-fostering experiment discussed in the passage is about *macaques,* not *birds.* Eliminate (D) because *animal feeding behaviors* are mentioned in the fourth paragraph of the passage: *"normal" food preferences that wild lemurs display.* The correct answer is (C).

21. **C** The question asks, *according to Paredes,* what *the researchers* were able to do that gave them *further confidence in their findings* in Passage 1. Look for the lead word *confidence* in Passage 1. In the sixth paragraph, Paredes says, *"The fact that we could compare newborn brains…to the adult…gave us added confidence that what we were seeing was correct."* Eliminate (A) because, although the third paragraph mentions samples *from around the world,* this is not the reason given for the researchers' *added confidence.* Eliminate (B) because it is not the reason given; it is also contradicted in the next paragraph, which states that the researchers acknowledge that *it would be impossible to definitively show that there are never any new neurons in the adult hippocampus.* Keep (C) because to *compare the brains of newborns to the brains of adults* is a direct paraphrase of Paredes's quote. Eliminate (D) because, although *1,618 young neurons…* does appear elsewhere, this is not the reason given for their *confidence.* The correct answer is (C).

22. **B** The question asks for a *shortcoming in their study* to which the authors of the study in Passage 1 *concede.* Notice that the following question is a best evidence question, so this question and Q23 can be done in tandem. Look at the answers to Q23 first. The lines for (23A) reference *One of the liveliest debates in neuroscience;* they don't mention a *shortcoming* in the authors'

study, so eliminate (23A). The lines for (23B) state that *neurogenesis declines throughout childhood and is undetectable in adults;* this is a finding of the study, not a *shortcoming*, so eliminate (23B). The lines for (23C) state that *the researchers found plentiful evidence of neurogenesis;* this is also a finding of the study, not a *shortcoming*, so eliminate (23C). The lines for (23D) state that the *authors acknowledge…it would be impossible to definitively show that there are never any new neurons in the adult hippocampus.* This is a *shortcoming* of the study admitted by the authors, so look to see if those lines support any answers from Q22. They support (22B), *They could not completely rule out the presence of a certain biological structure,* so connect these two answers. Without support from Q23, (22A), (22C), and (22D) can be eliminated. The correct answers are (22B) and (23D).

23. **D** (See explanation above.)

24. **D** The question asks about *implications beyond showing whether or not new neurons form later in life* in Passage 1. Carefully read each line reference and eliminate any that don't answer the question. The lines in (A) describe the study's finding that *new neurons may not be born in the adult human brain at all;* however, these lines don't mention any *implications beyond* this finding, so eliminate (A). The lines in (B) mention an observation supporting the study's findings about *whether or not new neurons form later in life*, but they don't mention any *implications beyond* this finding, so eliminate (B). Similarly, the lines in (C) mention an observation supporting the study's findings about *whether or not new neurons form later in life*, but they don't mention any *implications beyond* this finding, so eliminate (C). The lines in (D) suggest that the study's findings may *point the way to understanding what makes the human brain distinct from other animals and set researchers on a better path to developing treatments for human brain diseases.* This is an *implication beyond showing whether or not new neurons form later in life*, so keep it. The correct answer is (D).

25. **C** The question asks for the purpose of the phrase *general consensus.* Use the given line reference to find the window. Lines 48–53 state, *For most of the twentieth century, there was a general consensus that brain cells could not renew themselves once the developmental period was over. Then, especially over the last two decades, overwhelming evidence gradually accumulated for the capacity of new neurons to be born in the adult brain.* The phrase *general consensus* describes the scientific community's agreement that neurogenesis (the creation of new neurons) stops after the human brain finishes developing—an agreement that existed until recent research gave evidence to the contrary. Look for an answer that matches this prediction. While it's true that the mention of the *general consensus* provides context for a *current debate*, it is not a debate about *learning in newborns.* Eliminate (A), which is a Mostly Right/Slightly Wrong trap answer. Choice (B) is also Mostly Right/Slightly wrong: the phrase does *establish researchers' certainty* about *neurogenesis*, but not about its *onset*, or beginning. Eliminate (B). Keep (C) because it matches the prediction. Eliminate (D) because the phrase *general consensus* is not related to *the brain regions in which neurogenesis takes place.* The correct answer is (C).

26. **D** The question asks what the author of Passage 2 suggests about the two papers when she says that their publication *animates the debate*. Use the given line reference to find the window. Lines 56–58 state, *Now, the near-simultaneous publication of two papers with opposing messages fuels this controversy and animates the debate*. The *debate* is discussed in the first paragraph—it is a debate over whether new neurons grow in adult human brains. The second paragraph goes on to describe the findings of the two papers—one found that new neurons do not grow in adult human brains, while the other found that new neurons do grow in adult human brains. The phrase *animates the debate* suggests that the two papers support opposing sides of this controversy. Look for an answer that matches this prediction. Choice (A) mentions an *unresolvable controversy*, but the passage does not indicate that the controversy cannot ever be resolved. This is a Mostly Right/Slightly Wrong trap answer; eliminate (A). Eliminate (B) because the passage does not mention a *diminishing effort*. Eliminate (C) because the text does not indicate that the subject of neurogenesis is a *dry* (which means "boring") *subject*. Keep (D) because it matches the prediction. The correct answer is (D).

27. **C** The question asks for a statement about *neurogenesis in the human dentate gyrus* that *Sorrells* would likely agree with. Since there is no line reference, use chronology and lead words to find the window for the question. Q26 asked about line 58, so the window for Q27 most likely comes after this line. Scan the second paragraph looking for the lead words *Sorrells*, *neurogenesis*, and *human dentate gyrus*. Lines 58–60 state that *Sorrells et al. report that humans uniquely appear to lack adult DG* (dentate gyrus) *neurogenesis*. This finding was based on a study of brain samples from subjects ranging in age from *14 gestational weeks to 77 years old*, which showed that *neurogenesis* occurred frequently in embryos, *rapidly decreased with advancing age*, and did not occur at all in *individuals older than 13 years*. Look for an answer that is consistent with these study results. Eliminate (A) because Sorrells's team did not study *neurological disease*. Eliminate (B) because the study was not about *learning capacity*. Choice (C) says that the frequency of neurogenesis *does not differ significantly between younger and older adults*. Sorrells's study found that there was no neurogenesis in people older than 13 years, which implies that there was no difference in frequency between younger adults and older adults. Keep (C). Eliminate (D) because Sorrells's team did not study the *evolutionary purpose* of neurogenesis. The correct answer is (C).

28. **C** The question asks for the main purpose of the fourth paragraph. Use the given line reference to find the window. In the fourth paragraph, the author argues that the two studies described in the previous paragraphs are similar, because both indicate that neurogenesis is relatively rare in adult humans. Then she suggests, *Perhaps the question should be: how rare is rare? And are rare newborn hippocampal neurons enough to impact learning, mood, and even brain repair? Further studies are clearly needed*. The main purpose of this paragraph is to suggest questions that should be studied, given the fact that neurogenesis is not common in adult humans. Look for an answer that matches this prediction. Choice (A) describes the purpose of the third paragraph, rather than the fourth paragraph; eliminate (A). The fourth paragraph indicates that the two studies are

somewhat similar, but it does not mention similarities *between neurogenesis in various brain regions*; eliminate (B). Keep (C) because it matches the prediction: *salient* means "relevant" or "important." Eliminate (D) because the paragraph compares two recent studies: earlier, the passage refers to the papers' *near-simultaneous publication*. The correct answer is (C).

29.   **D**   The question asks for the *primary purpose of both passages*. Because this is a question about both passages, it should be done after all the questions that ask about each passage individually. Passage 1 describes a study that found that *neurogenesis declines throughout childhood and is undetectable in adults*. Passage 2 discusses two studies with *opposing messages* about whether or not neurogenesis occurs in adult human brains. Look for an answer that matches this prediction. Eliminate (A) because neither passage discusses the *process* of neurogenesis. Eliminate (B) because both passages indicate that there is an ongoing *debate* about neurogenesis, so there is not one set of *current beliefs* that could be contradicted by the research. Additionally, Passage 2 presents studies that seem to support two different sets of beliefs. The study by Sorrells's team examined brain samples whose ages spanned the human lifespan (not just *newborns* and *older adults*), and Boldrini's team's study only examined samples from people aged 14 and older. Although neurogenesis in newborns and older adults is mentioned, comparing the brain activity of these two particular groups is not the focus of either of the studies discussed in the passages. Eliminate (C). Keep (D) because it matches the prediction. The correct answer is (D).

30.   **B**   The question asks for a claim about *neurogenesis* that *both authors* would likely agree with. Because this is a question about both passages, it should be done after all the questions that ask about each passage individually. Eliminate answers that misrepresent the perspective of either author. Eliminate (A) because neither of the authors dismisses the studies they discuss; they both mention insights gained from the studies. Keep (B) because it reflects the perspectives of both authors: the author of Passage 1 presents a study that shows that neurogenesis may not occur in adult humans. Passage 2 presents one study that found that neurogenesis may not occur in adult humans, and another which found that neurogenesis does occur in adult humans. However, the author of Passage 2 concludes, *What still seems likely is that if neurons are born in human adulthood, they may be relatively few and far between*. Eliminate (C) because both authors name particular brain regions where neurogenesis may take place, indicating that both authors would agree that brain region is a factor in the rate of new neuron development. Eliminate (D) because neither author indicates that neurogenesis *increases just after birth*. The study by Sorrells's team, discussed in both passages, indicates that the high rate of new growth found in embryos declines soon after birth. The correct answer is (B).

31.   **A**   The question asks what type of evidence is used by *both research teams* discussed in the passages. Because this is a question about both passages, it should be done after all the questions that ask about each passage individually. According to Passage 1, the team lead by Sorrells *collected and analyzed samples of the human hippocampus*. According to Passage 2, these samples were of *brain tissue ranging from 14 gestational weeks to 77 years old*. According to Passage 2, the team led by Boldrini used a similar approach, and *examined ages from 14*

to 79 years. Look for an answer that matches this prediction. Keep (A) because both teams did compare *samples from people of a range of ages*. Eliminate (B) because neither passage describes *experiments that replicate conditions in the body*. Instead, the researchers examined tissues taken from the body. Eliminate (C) because neither passage discusses *studies of human behavior*. Eliminate (D) because neither passage mentions the use of *textbooks* or *journals*. The correct answer is (A).

32. **D** The question asks for a *larger claim* supported by *the author's descriptions of John Bull*. Because this is a general question, it should be done after all the specific questions. In the third and fourth paragraphs, the author observes that the *secret of the matter is that John has a great disposition to protect and patronize. He thinks it indispensable to the dignity of an ancient and honorable family, to be bounteous in its appointments and eaten up by dependents. The consequence is that like many other venerable family establishments, his manor is encumbered by old retainers whom he cannot turn off, and an old style which he cannot lay down…All those whims and habits have concurred woefully to drain the old gentleman's purse.* In other words, John Bull tries to support many people and maintain a grand lifestyle, and that puts a financial strain on him. Eliminate (A) because the passage does not indicate that *withdrawing from the public stage* would *weaken* John Bull's *estate*. Eliminate (B) because the passage does not indicate that it would be *more difficult* for John Bull to give up or *abdicate* his position *than to safeguard it*. Eliminate (C): although it mentions *financial stability*, the passage does not argue that *financial stability is incompatible with ruling compassionately and maintaining shared traditions*. Keep (D) because *an overextended sphere of influence* refers to the *old retainers* that John Bull supports and the *old style* he maintains, and *jeopardize personal welfare* refers to the *drain* on *the old gentleman's purse*. The correct answer is (D).

33. **A** The question asks about the shift in the central focus over the course of the passage. Because this is a general question, it should be done after all the specific questions. The first paragraph states that a *stranger who wishes to study English peculiarities may gather much valuable information from the innumerable portraits of John Bull, as exhibited in the windows of the caricature-shops*. In other words, John Bull is not an actual individual, but a representation of a certain type of English person. (This is also stated in the blurb: *"John Bull" is a satirical figure used to personify England particularly the English middle class*.) The author describes John Bull and the troubles he faces and in the final paragraph says, *All that I wish is that John's present troubles may teach him more prudence in future*. Keep (A), since the first part of the passage is a description of *a symbolic figure* and the end of the passage is *a call for caution and consideration regarding future conduct*. Eliminate (B) because the author never denounces John Bull *as a national embarrassment*. Eliminate (C) because the author does not cast *doubt on* John Bull's *ability to improve* his *situation*. Eliminate (D) because the author does not *condemn* John Bull but rather says many positive things about him. The author does criticize some of John's extravagances, but these are not limited to *familial attitudes*. Finally, the passage does not end with *mourning* but with cautioning and a wish for John Bull's future. The correct answer is (A).

34. **A** The question asks for a *contrast* presented in the passage. Because this is a general question, it should be done after all the specific questions. The second and third paragraphs give examples of how John Bull tries to help others: *He is a boon companion, and he will stand by a friend in a quarrel, with life and purse,* and *He is a busy-minded personage, who thinks not merely for himself and family but for all the country round, and is most generously disposed to be everybody's champion.* The fourth paragraph describes how these generous tendencies have led to trouble for John Bull: *All those whims and habits have concurred woefully to drain the old gentleman's purse. What is worst of all is the effect which these pecuniary embarrassments have had on the poor man himself. Instead of strutting about as formerly…he now goes about whistling thoughtfully to himself, with his head drooping down.* Keep (A), since these lines present a contrast between John Bull's *well-meaning intentions* and his *own best interest.* Eliminate (B) because there is no discussion of *the duty to volunteer for one's country.* Eliminate (C) because the passage does not discuss *growing up a part of the aristocracy* or *earning a position of influence.* Eliminate (D) because these ideas are not contrasted; rather, John tries to respect *traditions* by honoring what he sees as his *modern obligations.* The correct answer is (A).

35. **A** The question asks what the word *sketch* means in line 5. Go back to the text, find the word *sketch,* and cross it out. Carefully read the surrounding text to determine another word that would fit in the blank based on the context of the passage. The first paragraph introduces *John Bull* and states, *I cannot resist the temptation to give a slight sketch of him, such as he has met my eye.* The next paragraph begins a description of John Bull. The correct answer should mean something like "description." Keep (A) because *account* is consistent with "description." Eliminate (B) because *farce* means "a sham" or "a mockery," not "description." Eliminate (C) because a *cartoon* could be a literal *sketch,* but the word does not mean "description." Eliminate (D) because *impersonation* means "imitation," not "description." The correct answer is (A).

36. **B** The question asks for the lines from the passage that support *the idea that John Bull's core values include caring for others.* Read each line reference in the answers and eliminate any that don't answer the question. The lines in (A) say that Bull has a *vast deal of strong natural feeling,* but there is no further information about what that feeling is or whether it includes *caring,* so eliminate (A). The lines in (B) say that John Bull *thinks not merely for himself and family but for all the country round, and is most generously disposed to be everybody's champion.* These lines support the idea that his *core values include caring for others,* so keep (B). The lines in (C) say *the old fellow's spirit is as tall and as gallant as ever* but do not reference *caring for others,* so eliminate (C). The lines in (D) reference his virtues—*plain, homebred, and unaffected*—but do not specifically reference *caring for others,* so eliminate (D). The correct answer is (B).

37. **D** The question asks what the word *abuses* means in line 35 and line 36. Go back to the text, find the word *abuses,* and cross it out. Carefully read the surrounding text to determine another word that would fit in the blank based on the context of the passage. The third paragraph describes John Bull's *great disposition to protect and patronize* and says, *He thinks it indispensable to the dignity of an ancient and honorable family, to be bounteous in its*

appointments and eaten up by dependents. The consequence is that like many other venerable family establishments, his manor is encumbered by old retainers whom he cannot turn off…In short, John has such a reverence for everything that has been long in the family that he will not hear even of abuses being reformed, because they are good old family abuses. In other words, John Bull is financially burdened by people who live at his house. The correct answer should mean something like "burdens." Eliminate (A) because, even though *violations* might initially seem consistent with *abuses,* that word is too strong based on the context of the passage. Eliminate (B) because no one in the family is physically attacking Bull. Eliminate (C) because the family members live in the house; there are no *invasions* occurring. Keep (D) because *impositions* is consistent with "burdens." The correct answer is (D).

38. **B** The question asks what the *repeated references to a "cudgel"…emphasize* about *John Bull.* Look for the lead word *cudgel* throughout the second half of the passage. The fourth paragraph contrasts John Bull's former *strutting about…flourishing his cudgel* with the way *he now goes about whistling thoughtfully to himself, with his head drooping down, his cudgel tucked under his arm.* In the last paragraph, the author hopes that John Bull *may cease to distress his mind about other people's affairs; that he may give up the fruitless attempt to promote the good of his neighbors and the peace and happiness of the world by dint of the cudgel.* The cudgel is associated with John Bull's former confidence and influence. Eliminate (A) because although a cudgel is a *physical* object, it is being used to represent non-physical attributes. Keep (B) because *reputation of power and authority* is consistent with the references to the *cudgel* and the idea of Bull's influence. Eliminate (C) because, although a cudgel can be used as a weapon, the author does not mention a *capacity for violence and retaliation* in Bull. The passage states that John Bull *thinks not merely for himself and family but for all the country round, and is most generously disposed to be everybody's champion;* however, this is a reference to his relationships with his family and neighbors; it does not literally mean that he was *a champion of England,* so eliminate (D). The correct answer is (B).

39. **B** The question asks what the word *interest* means in line 56. Go back to the text, find the word *interest,* and cross it out. Carefully read the surrounding text to determine another word or phrase that would fit in the blank based on the context of the passage. The final paragraph begins, *I confess I cannot look upon John's situation without strong feelings of interest.* The author describes John Bull's good qualities and says, *All that I wish is that John's present troubles may teach him more prudence in future. That he may cease to distress his mind about other people's affairs…that he gradually get his house into repair and long enjoy, on his paternal lands, a green, an honorable, and a merry old age.* The correct answer should mean something like "concern for his well-being." Eliminate (A) because *suspicion* is a negative definition for *interest* that isn't consistent with the context. Keep (B) because *care* is consistent with "concern for his well-being." Eliminate (C) because *amusement* does not mean "concern for his well-being." Eliminate (D) because *curiosity* and *interest* both involve wanting more information about a thing, but *curiosity* does not mean "concern for his well-being." The correct answer is (B).

40.   **D**   The question asks why John Bull suffers financial hardship. Notice that the following question is a best evidence question, so this question and Q41 can be answered in tandem. Look at the answers for Q41 first. The lines in (41A) mention that John Bull *will stand by a friend in a quarrel, with life and purse.* However, none of the answers for Q40 mentions supporting a *friend*, so eliminate (41A). The lines in (41B) state that the *consequence* [of allowing his family to maintain their lifestyle] *is that like many other venerable family establishments, his manor is encumbered by old retainers whom he cannot turn off, and an old style which he cannot lay down.* Look to see if those lines support any answers in Q40. Choice (40A) might initially look attractive, but the lines are about John and his motivations, not the actions and motivations of *his family members.* Choice (40D) says that John Bull suffers financial hardship because *his pride in his family's holdings compromises his ability to manage them well.* Connect those two answers. The lines in (41C) state that his pockets *are evidently empty,* but does not offer a reason for this, so eliminate (41C). The lines for (41D) include the statement that *His extravagance savors of his generosity,* but these lines do not directly support any of the answers for Q40, so eliminate (41D). Without support from Q41, (40A), (40B), and (40C) can be eliminated. The correct answers are (40D) and (41B).

41.   **B**   (See explanation above.)

42.   **C**   The question asks how the *author would most likely describe the public's attitude toward John Bull.* Look for references to the public in the passage. The final paragraph says that John Bull *is at least twice as good as his neighbors represent him.* This indicates that the author believes John Bull's neighbors, representing the public in the context of the passage, view him more negatively than he deserves. Eliminate (A) because there is no discussion of the public's view on John Bull's *financial stability.* Eliminate (B) because there is no mention of the public's view of his *service to their communities.* Keep (C) because the statement that the public is *overly critical of his faults* is supported by the statement about John Bull's neighbors. Eliminate (D) because there is no indication that the public is *indifferent to* John Bull's *success or failure.* The correct answer is (C).

43.   **D**   The question asks for the primary purpose of the passage. Because this is a general question, it should be done after all the specific questions. The passage describes research exploring the *first-night effect:* the tendency for people's sleep to be disturbed during their first night in an unfamiliar environment. Eliminate (A) because the first-night effect is not a *sleep disorder:* the first paragraph states that *healthy people…show this first-night effect.* The passage also describes more than one study. Eliminate (B) because it does not mention the *first-night effect.* Eliminate (C) because the passage offers reasons, not *solutions, for difficulties sleeping in new places.* Keep (D) because the description of *a common phenomenon in sleep* is consistent with the statement that *99 percent of the time they show this first-night effect.* The correct answer is (D).

44. **B** The question asks what the author is suggesting about *Sasaki and her colleagues* by using *the words "wondered" and "hunch"* in lines 19–27. Use the given line reference to find the window in the passage. The text says that *Sasaki wondered if humans do something similar…It was a bit of a hunch.* That similarity refers to the previous paragraph: *Other animals can straddle the boundaries between sleeping and wakefulness.* The words *wondered* and *hunch* indicate that Sasaki and her colleagues undertook the research based on curiosity and a guess that there might be a connection, rather than concrete evidence. Eliminate (A) because there's no indication that the researchers thought the first-night effect would be *most apparent* in particular people. Keep (B) because they had *not previously discovered evidence.* Eliminate (C) because although the passage brings up humans' and animals' *environments,* it does not mention *similarities* between them. Eliminate (D) because the author suggests that Sasaki did make some sort of prediction, not that the researchers failed to make a particular prediction. The correct answer is (B).

45. **A** The question asks about *subjects who had weaker left hemisphere slow-wave activity during the first night in the medical scanner.* Notice that the following question is a best evidence question, so this question and Q46 can be done in tandem. Look at the answers to Q46 first. The lines in (46A) indicate that *the stronger* the *asymmetry* between slow-wave activity in the left and right halves of the brain, *the longer the volunteers took to fall asleep.* Look to see if those lines support any answers from Q45. They support (45A), which states that those with weaker left hemisphere slow-wave activity were *more wakeful.* Connect these two answers. The lines in (46B) describe a later study and refer to all of the participants rather than just those with *weaker left hemisphere slow-wave activity,* so eliminate (46B). The lines in (46C) do not describe the *subjects* in the study, so eliminate (46C). The lines in (46D) do not describe the *subjects* in the study, so eliminate (46D). Without support from Q46, (45B), (45C), and (45D) can be eliminated. The correct answers are (45A) and (46A).

46. **A** (See explanation above.)

47. **C** The question asks for *the hypothesis that Sasaki's group tested in their experiment with headphones.* Look for the lead word *headphones* in the passage. The seventh paragraph begins, *To test this idea, Sasaki asked more volunteers to sleep in a normal bed with a pair of headphones.* To know what idea was tested, read just before, which states that results *fit with the idea of the first-night brain as a night watchman, in which the left default mode network is more responsive than usual.* The hypothesis should have to do with the left default mode network being more responsive. Eliminate (A) because there is no mention of *an electric current* related to the experiment with headphones. Eliminate (B) because the experiment with the *headphones* was not related to how *quickly* the subjects *fell asleep.* Keep (C) because it refers to *brain activity in the left hemisphere default mode network* and *sleep disturbances,* which fits the prediction. Choice (D) also mentions the *left default mode network.* However, the experiment with headphones specifically tested sounds, whereas the researchers would have to test other kinds of stimuli in order to see if they were also affected; eliminate (D). The correct answer is (C).

48. **B** The question asks for the main idea of the last paragraph. Carefully read the last paragraph. The text says that the research *won't help people sleep better in new places*, but then it brings up something the researcher does that she hopes will make her *brain a little more at ease* for sleeping somewhere new. Although this paragraph acknowledges that the research will not *help people sleep better in new places*, it does not *emphasize that the scientists could not provide useful applications for their sleep research*, so eliminate (A). Keep (B) because the paragraph does *suggest that people might be able to influence the severity of the first-night effect* by staying *in the same hotel* or *at least in the same chain* when they travel. Eliminate (C) because, although Sasaki says she stays *in the same hotel* or *at least in the same chain* in order to possibly *sleep better* when traveling, the main idea of the paragraph is not to *urge individuals to consider sleeping only in familiar places*. Eliminate (D) because this paragraph does not *question the general significance of the first-night effect;* it simply states that understanding the first-night effect alone will not help people sleep better. The correct answer is (B).

49. **D** The question asks what the word *new* means in line 84. Go back to the text, find the word *new*, and cross it out. Carefully read the surrounding text to determine another word that would fit in the blank based on the context of the passage. The last paragraph states the research *won't help people sleep better in new places, though. To do that, Sasaki tries to stay in the same hotel when she travels, or at least in the same chain. "I'm flying to England tomorrow and staying at a Marriott," she says. "It's not a completely novel environment, so maybe my brain will be a little more at ease."* The correct answer should mean something like "strange" or "different." Eliminate (A) because *pristine* is a different meaning of *new*, rather than another word for "strange." Eliminate (B) because *singular* means "extraordinary," not "strange." Choice (C) can be eliminated because *inventive* means "creative," not "strange" or "different." Keep (D) because *unfamiliar* is consistent with "different." The correct answer is (D).

50. **D** The question asks for *the mean amplitude of brain responses to deviant sounds in the right hemisphere on Day 1* in Figure 1. Look for the *right hemisphere, Day 1*, and *mean amplitude* on Figure 1. In the figure, *mean amplitude* is measured on the *y*-axis, and the solid line represents the right hemisphere. The mean amplitude for the right hemisphere on Day 1 is approximately –2. Eliminate (A), (B), and (C), which are inconsistent with this information. The correct answer is (D).

51. **D** The question asks *about the relative amplitudes of left hemisphere brain responses to deviant sounds on Days 1 and 2* in figure 2. Look for information about the *left hemisphere, Day 1*, and *Day 2* on figure 2, and eliminate any answer choices that are not consistent with the figure. Eliminate (A) because the relative amplitude for Day 2 reaches its *most negative* point about 700 ms after sound outset, not *1,000 ms after sound outset*. Eliminate (B) because the relative amplitude for Day 2 becomes increasingly positive after 700 ms, not *increasingly negative*. Eliminate (C) because the relative amplitude for Day 1 is still more negative than its *previous level 1,000 ms after sound outset*. Keep (D) because the relative amplitudes for both Day 1 and Day 2 *became more negative between 400 ms and 700 ms after sound onset*. The correct answer is (D).

52. **C** The question asks *how the plotted points in figure 1* would *change if the left hemisphere data was focused on responses 400 ms after sound onset,* referring to the passage and Figures 1 and 2. Read Figures 1 and 2 carefully to determine how they relate to one another. The title for Figure 2 indicates that it shows data for the *left hemisphere*. In Figure 2, *400 ms after sound onset,* the graph for Day 1 shows a relative amplitude of approximately –2, while the graph for Day 2 shows a relative amplitude of approximately 2. In Figure 1, the mean amplitude of the left on Day 1 is approximately –6, and the mean amplitude of the left on Day 2 is approximately –1. Therefore, if the left hemisphere data in Figure 1 was focused on responses 400 ms after sound onset, the points for both Day 1 and Day 2 would be more positive. Eliminate (A) because the points for the left hemisphere on both Day 1 and Day 2, not *on Day 1 only,* would be more positive. Eliminate (B) because the question is about a change in the left hemisphere data; there would be no effect on *the points for the right hemisphere.* Keep (C) because both *points for the left hemisphere would be more positive.* Eliminate (D) because the point for the right hemisphere on Day 2 would not change, so it would not be *greater than zero.* The correct answer is (C).

Section 2: Writing and Language

1. **A** Commas change in the answer choices, so this question tests comma usage. The phrase *former Director-General of the United Nations' Food and Agricultural Organization* is not necessary to the main meaning of the sentence, so it should be set off by commas. Choice (A) appropriately places commas both before and after the unnecessary phrase. Eliminate (B) and (C) because they lack a comma before the phrase. There is no need for a comma between *Director-General* and *of,* so eliminate (D). The correct answer is (A).

2. **B** Vocabulary changes in the answer choices, so this question tests precision of word choice. Look for a word or phrase with a definition that is consistent with the other ideas in the sentence. The number of words also changes in the answer choices, so this question could also test concision. Start with the most concise option, (B). The word *pressing* means "urgent and important," which matches with the sentence's meaning about *water scarcity,* so keep (B). Choice (A) is not as precise as (B) because *more or less important* does not correctly convey the idea of a *severe strain* on resources, so eliminate (A). Choice (C), *unusually significant,* is not as concise as (B), and there is no evidence from the sentence that water scarcity's significance is *unusual,* so eliminate it. Choice (D), *constantly thought about,* is not precise, because something can be constantly thought about but not necessarily be an important issue that needs to be dealt with. Eliminate (D). The correct answer is (B).

3. **B** Verbs change in the answer choices, so this question tests consistency of verbs. A verb must be consistent with the other verbs in the sentence. The other verbs in the sentence are *are planted* and *is captured,* which are in present tense, so the correct answer must also include a present-tense verb. Choices (A), (B), and (D) include the verb *runs,* which is correct. Eliminate

(C): *running* is not consistent with the other verbs in the sentence, and it makes the sentence incomplete. Prepositions also change in the answer choices, so this question may test idioms. Look at the phrase before the preposition to determine the correct idiom. Choice (A) describes the water as *of the plants*. The phrase *the water of* is not a correct idiom, so eliminate (A). Choice (B) suggests that the water is *for the plants*, which is a correct idiom and makes the meaning of the sentence clear, so keep (B). Choice (D) says that the water is *within the plants*. The phrase *the water within* could be a correct idiom, but in this case the phrase does not make sense because water that is *within* plants could not *run off into the environment*. Eliminate (D). The correct answer is (B).

4.   **D**   Note the question! The question asks whether a sentence should be added, so it tests consistency. If the content of the new sentence is consistent with the ideas surrounding it, then it should be added. The paragraph describes *hydroponic systems* and how they work. The new sentence explains *types of produce* that hydroponics can be used for, so it is not consistent with the ideas in the text; the new sentence should not be added. Eliminate (A) and (B). Eliminate (C) because this information is not given *elsewhere in the passage*. Keep (D) because it accurately states that *types of produce* are not *relevant* to the paragraph. The correct answer is (D).

5.   **C**   Pronouns change in the answer choices, so this question tests consistency of pronouns. A pronoun must be consistent in number with the noun it refers to. The underlined pronoun refers to the phrase *these plants*, which is plural. To be consistent, the underlined pronoun must also be plural. Eliminate (D) because *its* is singular. *There* refers to location, which does not make sense in this context, so eliminate (A). *They're* is a contraction of *they are*, which is needed in this sentence, so keep (C). The sentence does not indicate that *these plants* possess anything, so eliminate the possessive pronoun *their* in (B). The correct answer is (C).

6.   **D**   Note the question! The question asks where sentence 5 should be placed, so it tests consistency of ideas. The sentence must be consistent with the ideas that come both before and after it. Sentence 5 says *This reduces the environmental impact of transporting…from warmer regions*. The sentence needs to come after the idea that *this* refers to: something that reduces transporting food from warmer regions. Sentence 3 states that *indoor hydroponic systems can be used in almost any climate*, which means the plants don't have to come *from warmer regions*. Therefore, sentence 5 should follow sentence 3. Eliminate (A), (B), and (C). The correct answer is (D).

7.   **D**   Verbs change in the answer choices, so this question tests consistency of verbs. A verb must be consistent with other verbs in the sentence. The other verb in the sentence is *is*, which is in simple present tense. To be consistent, the underlined verb must also be in present tense, so eliminate (A) and (C) since they are both past tense. Choice (B), *are using*, is in present tense, but it is not consistent with the simple present tense *is*. Eliminate (B). The correct answer is (D).

8. **A** The number of words changes in the answer choices, so this question tests concision and precision. Check the shortest answer first: (A), *criticize,* provides a precise meaning, so keep it. Choices (B), (C), and (D) add the words *complain* or *condemn,* both of which are similar in meaning to *criticize.* There is no need to use more than one of those terms, so eliminate (B), (C), and (D). The correct answer is (A).

9. **D** The subject of the phrase changes in the answer choices. There is a comparison in the sentence, so this question tests consistency. When two things are compared, they should be consistent with each other. The first item in the comparison is *hydroponic produce.* Eliminate (A) and (C) because *farms* are not consistent with *produce.* Eliminate (B) because *from conventional places* is not consistent with *hydroponic* in the first part of the comparison, which describes how the produce is grown. *Conventionally grown* does describe how the produce is grown, so (D) makes the comparison consistent. The correct answer is (D).

10. **B** Note the question! The question asks which choice *most effectively supports the idea in the first part of the sentence,* so it tests consistency. Eliminate answers that are inconsistent with the purpose stated in the question. The first part of the sentence says that *hydroponic operations can…be more energy intensive,* so the underlined portion needs to match with the idea of being *energy intensive.* Eliminate (A) because *building materials* do not have a direct connection with *energy* use. Keep (B) because the statement that systems may *require a great deal of electricity* is consistent with their being *energy intensive.* Eliminate (C) because the ability to grow *different types of produce* isn't directly related to *energy* use. Eliminate (D) because *urban zoning laws* are also not consistent with the use of more *energy.* The correct answer is (B).

11. **C** Note the question! The question asks which choice would *conclude the passage by restating its main idea,* so it tests consistency of ideas. Determine the main idea of the passage and find the answer that is consistent with that idea. The passage is about *hydroponics,* which is described as a potential *solution* to *water scarcity.* Eliminate (A) because *organic status* is not consistent with the passage's main idea. Eliminate (B) because *better taste* also doesn't match the main idea that hydroponics can help with water scarcity. Keep (C) because *savings in water* and *worthy of consideration* match the tone and main idea of the passage. Eliminate (D) because the passage is about hydroponics specifically and not the consequences of *the use of water* in general. The correct answer is (C).

12. **C** Verbs change in the answer choices, so this question tests consistency of verbs. A verb must be consistent with the other verbs in the sentence. The sentence states that Marian Anderson *was invited…to come to Washington D.C. and,* so the underlined verb is in a list of two things and needs to be consistent with the verb *come.* In this case, *come* is part of the infinitive *to come,* and the *to* applies to both items in the list. The word *perform* completes the infinitive *to perform.* Eliminate (A), (B), and (D) because they do not use the correct form of *perform.* Keep (C) because *to come…and perform* is consistent. The correct answer is (C).

13. **D** Vocabulary changes in the answer choices, so this question tests precision of word choice. Look for a word that is consistent with the other ideas in the sentence. The sentence describes *the largest auditorium in the city* and says *of 4,000*. A large auditorium would normally be described in terms of the number of people it can hold, so the correct word should mean something like "number of people it can hold." Eliminate (A) because *volume* means "amount of space inside," which does not refer to the number of people a building can hold. Eliminate (B) because *size* means "spatial dimensions," which also does not refer to the number of people. Eliminate (C) because *quantity* means "number of things" and also does not refer to how many people can fit in the auditorium. Keep (D) because *capacity* means "how much or many something can hold," and it can be used to refer to people. The correct answer is (D).

14. **A** Note the question! The question asks which choice would *introduce one of the main ideas of the passage*, so it tests consistency of ideas. Determine the subject of the passage and find the answer that is consistent with that idea. The passage discusses how Marian Anderson wanted to *eliminate prejudice* and how her performance at the Lincoln Memorial is one example of why she *is hailed for her role in cutting down barriers*. Keep (A) because *the struggle against racial prejudice* is consistent with the main idea. Eliminate (B) because *the organization* and *money* are not related to the main idea about Anderson. Eliminate (C) because Anderson's *European tour* is not consistent with the passage's main idea. Eliminate (D) because Anderson's past performance experience is not consistent with the idea that her Lincoln Memorial performance helped her to *cut down barriers*. The correct answer is (A).

15. **D** Transitions change in the answer choices, so this question tests consistency of ideas. A transition must be consistent with the relationship between the ideas it connects. There is also the option to DELETE; consider this choice carefully, as it is often the correct answer. The sentence is precise without the underlined portion, so keep (D). The previous paragraph introduces Marian Anderson and describes how *the DAR refused to allow an African American artist to perform* at Constitution Hall. This paragraph introduces Eleanor Roosevelt and states that she *resigned* from the DAR *in protest of its refusal to host Anderson*. The information about Roosevelt's actions describes some of the consequences of the DAR's decision, so the correct answer should reflect that relationship between the ideas. There is no contrast between these ideas, so eliminate (B). Eliminate (A), *Furthermore,* and (C), *In addition*, because the information about Eleanor Roosevelt is part of the same story, rather than an additional point. No transition is necessary. The correct answer is (D).

16. **D** Punctuation changes in the answer choices, so this question tests STOP, HALF-STOP, and GO punctuation. Use the Vertical Line Test and identify the ideas as complete or incomplete. Draw the vertical line between the words *House* and *resigned*. The first part of the sentence, *First Lady and DAR member Eleanor Roosevelt, who had previously invited Anderson to sing at the White House*, is an incomplete idea. The second part of the sentence, *resigned from the organization in protest of its refusal to host Anderson*, is also an incomplete idea. Only GO punctuation can be used to connect two incomplete ideas. Eliminate (B) and (C) because

colons and dashes are both HALF-STOP punctuation, which must come after a complete idea. The phrase *who had previously invited Anderson to sing at the White House* is an unnecessary phrase, so it should be set off by commas. Eliminate (A) because it lacks a comma after *White House*. Choice (D) appropriately places a comma after *White House*. The correct answer is (D).

17. **C**   Verbs change in the answer choices, so this question tests consistency of verbs. A verb must be consistent with its subject. The subject of the sentence is *Roosevelt*, which is singular. To be consistent, the underlined verb must also be singular. Eliminate (A), (B), and (D) because they are all plural verbs. The correct answer is (C).

18. **A**   Note the question! The question asks whether a sentence should be deleted, so it tests consistency. If the sentence is not consistent with the ideas surrounding it, then it should be deleted. The underlined sentence provides specific information about Anderson's personality and what she *valued*. The paragraph goes on to tell about what Anderson *believed* and how she felt about the upcoming performance. The sentence is consistent with these ideas, so it should not be deleted. Eliminate (C) and (D). Choice (A) correctly states that the sentence *supports the other claims made in the paragraph*, so keep it. Eliminate (B) because the author does not *later refute* the ideas in the sentence. The correct answer is (A).

19. **B**   Punctuation changes in the answer choices, so this question tests STOP punctuation. A question mark should only be used at the end of a direct question. The writer is not directly asking a question in this sentence, so a question mark is not appropriate; eliminate (C) and (D). The wording of (A) would be appropriate for a question, but not for the description of events that this sentence contains; eliminate (A). Choice (B) correctly describes the phone call Anderson made to her manager. The correct answer is (B).

20. **C**   Punctuation changes in the answer choices, so this question could test STOP, HALF-STOP, and GO punctuation. The sentence contains a list of three things: 1) *a patriotic song*, 2) *two classical songs*, and 3) *several spirituals*. There should be a comma after each item in a list of three or more items. Eliminate (A) because it uses a semicolon instead of a comma. Eliminate (B) because it lacks a comma after *songs*. Keep (C) because it has a comma after each item in the list. Eliminate (D) because there should not be a comma after the word *and*. The correct answer is (C).

21. **B**   Note the question! The question asks how to effectively combine the underlined sentences, so it tests precision and concision. Eliminate (A) and (D) because the words *acclaimed* and *praised* mean the same thing, so these choices are repetitive. Keep (B) because it is concise and makes the sentence precise. Eliminate (C) because it does not precisely describe what elements of Anderson's performance were *acclaimed*. The correct answer is (B).

22. **A** Note the question! The question asks which choice *reinforces the idea that Anderson focused on her singing as a way to fight intolerance,* so it tests consistency. Eliminate answers that are inconsistent with the purpose stated in the question. Keep (A) because *preferring to influence people through the power of her singing* is consistent with the idea that she *focused on her singing as a way to fight intolerance.* Eliminate (B) because the fact that Anderson won the *Spingarn Medal for outstanding achievement* is not consistent with the idea that she was focused on *fighting intolerance.* Eliminate (C) because it focuses on the *other African American artists* Anderson inspired, not on what *Anderson* herself did to *fight intolerance.* Eliminate (D) because the description of Anderson's *type of classical singing voice* is not consistent with the idea of *fighting intolerance.* The correct answer is (A).

23. **D** Nouns change from singular to plural in the answer choices, so this question tests consistency of nouns. A noun must be consistent in number with the other nouns in the sentence. The non-underlined portion of the sentence contains the singular noun *a credit counselor;* the opening phrase of the sentence describes this noun, so the underlined portion must also be singular. Eliminate (A) and (C) because they both use the plural noun *specialists.* The phrase *acting as* does not make the sentence more precise, so eliminate (B). Choice (D) is concise and consistent with the rest of the sentence. The correct answer is (D).

24. **B** Punctuation changes in the answer choices, so this question tests STOP, HALF-STOP, and GO punctuation. Use the Vertical Line Test and identify the ideas as complete or incomplete. Draw the vertical line between the words *society* and *the.* The first part of the sentence, *Struggles with debt are common in American society,* is a complete idea. The second part of the sentence, *the 2018 Consumer Financial Literacy Survey revealed that one in four Americans admits to not paying all of his or her bills on time, while eight percent of respondents now have debts in collection,* is also a complete idea. To connect two complete ideas, STOP or HALF-STOP punctuation is needed. Eliminate (C) because a comma alone is GO punctuation. Eliminate (A) and (D) because there is no need for a comma between *the 2018 Consumer Financial Literacy Survey* and *revealed.* The correct answer is (B).

25. **B** Vocabulary changes in the answer choices, so this question tests precision of word choice. Look for a word with a definition that is consistent with the other ideas in the sentence. The word *mite* means "a small critter," while *might* is used to express possibility. The sentence suggests that it is possible that resources would help, so the word *might* is needed, not *mite.* Eliminate (A) and (C). The word *eliminate* means "get rid of," while *illuminate* means "light up." The sentence discusses *debt,* so it makes more sense to "get rid of" debt than to "light up" debt. Eliminate (D). The correct answer is (B).

26. **D** Note the question! The question asks which choice *provides the best introduction to the main idea of the paragraph,* so it tests consistency of ideas. Determine the subject of the paragraph and find the answer that is consistent with that idea. The paragraph describes how *some people struggle* with financial situations and explains how *credit counselors* can help. Eliminate (A)

because *academic research* is not consistent with information about *credit counselors*. Eliminate (B) because the fact that *people from all socioeconomic backgrounds* can struggle with *debt* is not consistent with the paragraph's focus on *credit counselors*. Choice (C) mentions *credit counselors*, but it suggests that some counselors *take advantage* of clients' *financial vulnerabilities*, which is not consistent with the paragraph's suggestion that credit counselors can help; eliminate (C). Keep (D) because the idea that credit counselors *can be particularly effective when people face multiple complicated financial situations* is consistent with the main idea of the paragraph. The correct answer is (D).

27. **C** Vocabulary changes in the answer choices, so this question tests precision of word choice. Look for a word with a definition that is consistent with the other ideas in the sentence. The underlined word must be something that *a counselor may propose* for someone who *struggles*, so the correct answer should be something like "method of help." Eliminate (A) because *explanations* means "meanings or reasons," which is not consistent with the idea of "help." Eliminate (B) because *answers* means "correct responses," which may help but aren't themselves a "method." Keep (C) because *solutions* means "solving problems," which is consistent with "method of help." Eliminate (D) because *insights* means "understandings," which is not consistent with the idea of a "method of help." The correct answer is (C).

28. **C** Apostrophes change in the answer choices, so this question tests apostrophe usage. When used with a noun, an apostrophe indicates possession. In this sentence, neither *resolutions* nor *habits* possesses anything, so an apostrophe is not needed in either word. Eliminate (A), (B), and (D) because they contain unnecessary apostrophes. The correct answer is (C).

29. **A** Note the question! The question asks which choice *provides accurate information from the table to support the point made in the sentence*, so it tests consistency. Read the labels on the table carefully, and look for an answer that is consistent with the information given in the table. The sentence states that *participants who didn't receive counseling...increased their overall debt levels*. Look for this information in the table. The row labeled *Non-Counseled Individuals' Total Debt* shows that their total debt had a change of +$2,808, which indicates a debt increase of that amount. Choice (A) provides this information, so keep it. Eliminate (B) because the number it includes is labeled in the table as a change in *open credit ratio* for counseled individuals, not an increase in debt for those who didn't receive counseling. Eliminate (C) because the number it provides is the total amount of debt for those who received counseling at the end of the study. Eliminate (D) because it shows the decrease in debt for individuals who received counseling. The correct answer is (A).

30. **D** Note the question! The question asks which choice *provides the best transition from the previous sentence*, so it tests consistency of ideas. Determine the ideas from the sentences before and after the underlined phrase, and look for an answer choice that is consistent with both. The previous sentence states that *participants who didn't receive counseling...increased their overall*

debt levels. The sentence that starts with the underlined phrase states that *clients who received counseling...decreased their total debt.* Eliminate (A) because the *stigma* is not consistent with these ideas. Eliminate (B) because the phrase *not always successful* is not consistent with the point the two sentences are making, which is that counseling can be successful. Eliminate (C) because the idea that *personal finances are so complicated* is not consistent with the idea that counseling can be helpful. Keep (D) because it introduces the second sentence as *proof of the success* of counseling programs, which is consistent with the idea that counseling can be helpful. The correct answer is (D).

31. **B**   Note the question! The question asks which choice *best uses information from the table to illustrate the claim made earlier in the sentence,* so it tests consistency. Read the labels on the table carefully, and look for an answer that is consistent with the information given in the table. The claim made earlier in the sentence is that *people who received counseling experienced a greater bump* in *open credit ratio.* Eliminate (A) because the group whose *final open credit ratio was 0.48* was the non-counseled individuals. Keep (B) because it describes an increase and refers to the correct group. Eliminate (C) because *overall debt increase* doesn't have to do with *open credit ratio.* Eliminate (D) because it talks only about a *pre-counseling ratio,* which does not show an increase. The correct answer is (B).

32. **C**   Punctuation changes in the answer choices, so this question tests STOP, HALF-STOP, and GO punctuation. Use the Vertical Line Test and identify the ideas as complete or incomplete. Draw the vertical line between the words *overnight* and *nevertheless.* The first part of the sentence, *While a credit counselor may not be able to resolve an individual's financial difficulties overnight,* is an incomplete idea. The second part of the sentence, *nevertheless, financial counseling provides valuable insights for people struggling with monetary commitments,* is a complete idea. To connect an incomplete idea to a complete idea, GO punctuation is needed. Eliminate (A) and (D) because a semicolon is STOP punctuation. Eliminate (B) because a comma with a FANBOYS word such as *but* is also STOP punctuation, and the first part of the sentence is still incomplete. Choice (C) correctly links the ideas with a comma. The correct answer is (C).

33. **C**   Vocabulary changes in the answer choices, so this question tests precision of word choice. Look for a word with a definition that is consistent with the other ideas in the sentence. The sentence describes how *credit counselors* can help people *get out of* some kind of *financial distress.* The word *beyond* indicates a contrast with the second part of the sentence, which describes long-term *strategies for the future.* Thus, the underlined portion needs to mean something like "short-term." Eliminate (A) because *close-up* means "physically nearby," which is not consistent with "short-term." Eliminate (B) because *cutting* means "harmful," which is not consistent with "short-term." Keep (C) because *immediate* means "happening right away," which is consistent with "short-term." Eliminate (D) because *fierce* means "intense or hostile," which is not consistent with "short-term." The correct answer is (C).

34. **B** The phrase containing *instituted* changes in the answer choices, so this question tests precision and concision. First determine whether the phrase is necessary. The words *instituted* and *begun* mean the same thing, so the additional word *begun* is not needed. Eliminate (A) and (C) because they repeat the same idea. *Enacting* also means the same thing as *instituting*, so eliminate (D). Choice (B) is concise and makes the meaning of the sentence precise. The correct answer is (B).

35. **A** Transitions change in the answer choices, so this question tests consistency of ideas. A transition must be consistent with the relationship between the ideas it connects. There is also the option to DELETE; consider this choice carefully as it is often the correct answer. A transition is necessary to make the sentence complete, so eliminate (D). The idea that the TSCA might *protect U.S. citizens from toxic chemicals* agrees with the statement that the act might *remove dangerous substances from the environment*, so a same-direction transition is needed. Eliminate (B) because *however* is an opposite-direction transition. The second idea adds on to the first, so eliminate (C) because the second idea is not an *example* of the first idea. Choice (A) appropriately links the ideas with the word *and*. The correct answer is (A).

36. **D** Verbs change in the answer choices, so this question tests consistency of verbs. A verb must be consistent with its subject. The subject of the verb is *A company*, which is singular. To be consistent, the underlined verb must also be singular. Eliminate (A) and (B) because they are plural. Choice (C), *being,* makes the sentence incomplete, so eliminate it. Choice (D) is singular and makes the sentence complete. The correct answer is (D).

37. **B** Note the question! The question asks which choice *best introduces the topic of this sentence*, so it tests consistency of ideas. Determine the subject of the sentence and find the answer that is consistent with that idea. The sentence says *in order to do so, it has only 90 days to do extensive testing*. The underlined portion needs to explain what has to be done through testing in 90 days and provide a noun that *it* refers to. Eliminate (A) because it does not contain a singular noun that *it* could refer to. Keep (B) because in this case *it* refers to *the EPA*, and *proving that the chemical poses "unreasonable risk"* could be the testing that needs to be done within 90 days. Eliminate (C) because it does not contain a singular noun that *it* could refer to. Eliminate (D) because it does not include something that needs to be done through *extensive testing* in 90 days. The correct answer is (B).

38. **A** Prepositions change in the answer choices, so this question tests idioms. Choice (A), *passed stricter legislation*, is a correct idiom, so keep it. Eliminate (B) because *passed on* means "rejected," and the sentence suggests that legislation has been passed in *many states*, not rejected. Eliminate (C) because *had a passing of stricter legislation* is not a correct idiom. The correct idiom is *passed legislation*. Eliminate (D) because *passed by* means "went past," and the sentence does not suggest that states have traveled past legislation. The correct answer is (A).

39.   **C**   Note the question! The question asks how to effectively combine the underlined sentences, so it tests precision and concision. Eliminate (A) and (D) because the sentence already says *for example*, so the phrase *such as* is not necessary. Eliminate (B) because it conveys the same idea as (C) but is less concise. Choice (C) is concise and effectively conveys that *toys or children's jewelry* are examples of products. The correct answer is (C).

40.   **C**   Apostrophes change in the answer choices, so this question tests apostrophe usage. When used with a noun, an apostrophe indicates possession. In this sentence, neither *states* nor *restrictions* possess anything, so no apostrophes are needed. Eliminate (A), (B), and (D) because they all use unnecessary apostrophes. The correct answer is (C).

41.   **A**   Note the question! The question asks which *information from the table provides the strongest evidence in support of the paragraph's main point*, so it tests consistency. Read the labels on the chart carefully, and look for an answer that is consistent with the information given in the chart. All answer choices are consistent with the chart, so identify the paragraph's main point, and look for an answer that is consistent with that. The paragraph states that *many states* are *frustrated by the federal government's lack of action on toxic chemicals* and that they have passed their own *stricter legislation*. The answer must be consistent with this idea. Keep (A) because the chart shows a total of 30 states with *existing or pending regulation regarding the use of mercury*, so this choice is consistent with the chart and with the main point of the paragraph. Eliminate (B) because *ten states* is not as consistent with *many states* as is (A). Eliminate (C) because the idea that *forty-six states have not yet taken any action* to regulate a specific chemical is not consistent with the main point of the paragraph. Eliminate (D) because the number of different chemicals that are *more strictly regulated by states* is not consistent with the main point that *many states* have taken legislative action—it could be that a small number of states regulated many different chemicals. The correct answer is (A).

42.   **B**   Note the question! The question asks which choice *best introduces the discussion in the rest of the paragraph*, so it tests consistency of ideas. Determine the subject of the rest of the paragraph and find the answer that is consistent with that idea. The rest of the paragraph describes the *Green Chemistry Initiative* and how it *combines the efforts* of different types of people. Eliminate (A) because *funding* is not consistent with the idea of combined efforts. Keep (B) because *a cooperative model* is consistent with the idea of combined efforts. Eliminate (C) and (D) because *reorganization* and *chemical testing* are not consistent with *combines the efforts*. The correct answer is (B).

43.   **B**   Punctuation changes in the answer choices, so this question tests STOP, HALF-STOP, and GO punctuation. Use the Vertical Line Test and identify the ideas as complete or incomplete. Draw the vertical line between the words *1991* and *has*. The first part of the sentence, *The California Environmental Protection Agency (CalEPA), a state agency established in 1991*, is an incomplete idea. The second part, *has created a Green Chemistry Initiative that combines the efforts of lawmakers, the people of California, and the chemistry industry to create a market in*

which all products are evaluated for their impact on human health and the environment, is also an incomplete idea. To connect two incomplete ideas, GO punctuation is needed. Keep (A) and (B) because they are both GO punctuation. Eliminate (C) and (D) because they are STOP and HALF-STOP punctuation, respectively. Now decide whether the sentence needs a comma. Because there is a comma before the unnecessary phrase *a state agency established in 1991*, there must be another comma after the phrase. Eliminate (A) because it does not have this comma. The correct answer is (B).

44.   **C**   Note the question! The question asks which choice *best introduces the argument made in the final sentence of the paragraph*, so it tests consistency of ideas. Determine the argument in the final sentence and find the answer that is consistent with that idea. The final sentence states that *The U.S. government could* accomplish a particular outcome *by creating a similar, preemptive national initiative, rather than waiting for a substance to be proven toxic before restricting its use*. The word *by* before the word *creating* in the second part of the sentence indicates that the underlined portion describes the imagined result of creating this initiative. The initiative that the *U.S. government* could replicate, according to the paragraph, is the *California* initiative that the previous sentence describes as producing *a market in which all products are evaluated for their impact on human health and the environment*. Eliminate (A) because *trendsetter* is not consistent with the idea that the U.S. government could create a *similar* initiative to the one in California. Eliminate (B) because *appease state regulatory agencies* is not consistent with the idea of creating a national initiative to evaluate chemicals. Keep (C) because *protect* the government's *citizens and environment from toxic chemicals* is consistent with the reason given by the paragraph for the initiative. Eliminate (D) because saving *taxpayer funds* is not consistent with the idea in the last sentence. The correct answer is (C).

Section 3: Math (No Calculator)

1. **A** The question asks for the expression that is equivalent to the expression $(3x^4 + 2x^3 - 7) + (4x^6 - 5x^3 + 9)$. Because the expression is the sum of two polynomials, combine like terms using Bite-Sized Pieces. Start by looking for differences in the choices. Choice (D) includes $7x^{10}$. Because there are no x^{10} terms in either polynomial, there can be no x^{10} term in the sum. This is a trap based on adding the exponents in the first terms, which is an improper use of exponent rules. Eliminate (D). All the remaining choices include $4x^6$, $3x^4$, and 2, so ignore the x^6, x^4, and constant terms. Combine the x^3 terms to get $2x^3 - 5x^3 = -3x^3$. Eliminate (B) and (C), which don't include $-3x^3$. The correct answer is (A).

2. **C** The question asks for the solution to the system of equations, which can be found by locating the intersection point of the two lines. The lines cross at $(2, 3)$, so the correct answer is (C).

3. **D** The question asks for the amount of additional time needed to eat all the pretzels. To find this, multiply the amount of time it takes to eat each pretzel by the number of pretzels remaining in the bag. It takes Rosa 18 seconds to eat each pretzel. Also, Rosa has already eaten 10 out of the p pretzels in the bag, so there are $p - 10$ pretzels remaining. Find the additional time needed by multiplying these two amounts to get $18(p - 10)$. The correct answer is (D).

4. **C** The question asks for the slope and y-intercept of the line. The equation given is very close to standard form. To get the equation in standard form, $Ax + By = C$, subtract 9 from both sides to get $-9 = 7y - 5x$, which can be rewritten as $-5x + 7y = -9$. In standard form, the slope is $-\frac{A}{B}$, so the slope of this line is $-\frac{A}{B} = -\frac{-5}{7} = \frac{5}{7}$. Eliminate (A) and (B). The y-intercept of a line in standard form is $\frac{C}{B}$, so the y-intercept of this line is $\frac{C}{B} = \frac{-9}{7} = -\frac{9}{7}$. Eliminate (D). The correct answer is (C).

5. **A** The question asks for the value of n, so solve the equation. To eliminate the fraction, multiply each term on both sides by 3 to get $15 + 3n = 27 - n$. Add n to both sides to get $15 + 4n = 27$. Subtract 15 from both sides to get $4n = 12$. Divide both sides by 4 to get $n = 3$. The correct answer is (A).

6. **B** The question asks for the equation that could represent line p. All of the equations are in the form $y = mx + b$, where m is the slope and b is the y-intercept. The b term is the same in all the choices, so ignore the y-intercept and find the slope. Line p is perpendicular to line q. Perpendicular lines have negative reciprocal slopes, so find the slope of q using the formula $\text{slope} = \frac{y_2 - y_1}{x_2 - x_1}$. Identify the points $(0, -4)$ and $(3, 0)$ on the graph and substitute them into the formula to get $\text{slope} = \frac{-4 - 0}{0 - 3} = \frac{-4}{-3} = \frac{4}{3}$. Since the slope of q is $\frac{4}{3}$, the slope of p is $-\frac{3}{4}$. Eliminate (A), (C), and (D), which have the wrong slope. The correct answer is (B).

7. **C** The question asks for the complex number that is equivalent to the given expression. To subtract complex numbers, subtract like terms. Subtracting the real parts results in $4 - 6 = -2$, and subtracting the imaginary parts results in $7i - 2i = 5i$. Therefore, $(4 + 7i) - (6 + 2i) = -2 + 5i$. The correct answer is (C).

8. **D** The question asks for the value of n. The given equation is a rational equation, so cross-multiply to get $4(n + 2) = 5(n - 3)$. Distribute to get $4n + 8 = 5n - 15$. Subtract $4n$ from both sides to get $8 = n - 15$. Add 15 to both sides to get $n = 23$. The correct answer is (D).

9. **B** The question asks for the solution set of the equation. There are numbers in the choices, so plug in the answers. Start by plugging $a = 4$ into the equation to get $0 = [3(4) + 1]^2(4 - 4)$, which simplifies to $0 = (13)^2(0)$ and $0 = 0$. Therefore, $a = 4$ is part of the solution set, so eliminate (A) and (C), which don't include 4. The remaining choices both include $-\frac{1}{3}$, so don't plug in that value. Instead plug in $a = \frac{1}{3}$ to get $0 = \left[3\left(\frac{1}{3}\right) + 1\right]^2\left(\frac{1}{3} - 4\right)$, which simplifies to $0 = (2)^2\left(-3\frac{2}{3}\right)$, or $0 = \frac{-44}{3}$. This is false, so $a = \frac{1}{3}$ is not part of the solution set. Eliminate (D), which includes $\frac{1}{3}$. The correct answer is (B).

10. **D** The question asks for the solution set to the equation. The equation is complicated to solve, but there are numbers in the choices, so plug in the answers. The number 7 appears in exactly two choices, so start there. Plug $m = 7$ into the equation. However, this will put a 0 in the denominator of two of the fractions, making them undefined. Therefore, 7 cannot be a solution to the equation. (Note that an algebraic solution will yield $m = 7$ as an extraneous solution.) Eliminate (A) and (C), which include 7. Both remaining choices include 4, so don't plug this in. Instead, plug in $m = 5$, which is in (B) but not (D). Plug $m = 5$ into the equation to get $\frac{2}{7-5} = \frac{4}{5} - \frac{5-5}{7-5}$. Simplify to get $\frac{2}{2} = \frac{4}{5} - \frac{0}{2}$, or $1 = \frac{4}{5}$. This is false, so 5 is not part of the solution set. Eliminate (B). The correct answer is (D).

11. **A** The question asks for the value of c in a quadratic function and states that 3 is a root of the function. A root is a value of x for which the function equals 0. Substitute $x = 3$ into the equation, and set the equation equal to 0 to get $3^2 + 13(3) + c = 0$. Simplify the left side to get $9 + 39 + c = 0$ and $48 + c = 0$. Subtract 48 from both sides to get $c = -48$. The correct answer is (A).

12. **A** The question asks for the expression that is equivalent to the given expression, which is the difference of two fractions. To subtract fractions, use common denominators. Multiply the second

fraction by $\dfrac{3}{3}$ to get $\dfrac{7}{12b^3} - \dfrac{3}{4b^3} \times \dfrac{3}{3} = \dfrac{7}{12b^3} - \dfrac{9}{12b^3}$. Now that the denominators are the same,

subtract the numerators to get $-\dfrac{2}{12b^3}$. Reduce the fraction by dividing the numerator and

denominator by 2 to get $-\dfrac{1}{6b^3}$. The correct answer is (A).

13.　**A**　The question asks for the product of the x-coordinates of the solutions to a system of equations in

the xy-plane. To get the solutions, set the two equations equal to each other to get $x^2 + 3 = 15x - 33$.

Now, get one side equal to 0. Subtract $15x$ from both sides to get $x^2 - 15x + 3 = -33$. Add 33 to

both sides to get $x^2 - 15x + 36 = 0$. The question asks for the product of the x-coordinates of

the solutions, so there is no need to actually get the solutions. The product of the solutions to a

quadratic equation in the form $ax^2 + bx + c = 0$ is $\dfrac{c}{a}$. In the equation $x^2 - 15x + 36 = 0$, $a = 1$ and

$c = 36$, so the product is $\dfrac{c}{a} = \dfrac{36}{1} = 36$. The correct answer is (A).

14.　**B**　The question asks for the choice that is equivalent to the given expression. Work using Bite-Sized

Pieces, starting with the most straightforward piece. When a product is raised to an exponent,

apply that exponent to both factors. Raising 27 to an exponent is difficult on the no calculator

section, so start with a. Raise a^{10} to the power of $\dfrac{3}{5}$ to get $\left(a^{10}\right)^{\frac{3}{5}}$. When an exponential expression

is raised to an exponent, multiply the exponents to get $\left(a\right)^{\frac{30}{5}} = a^6$. Eliminate (C) and (D), which

don't include a^6. Now work with the coefficients. An expression with a fractional exponent is

equivalent to a radical expression with the numerator of the exponent becoming the new exponent

and the denominator of the exponent becoming the index of the root. Therefore, the coefficient

on the answer will be the result of taking (-27) to the third power, then taking the fifth root of

that. Calculator use is not allowed here, and doing this work without one is tricky. However, the

remaining answers have different signs. A negative number taken to an odd power will be negative,

so eliminate (A). The correct answer is (B).

15.　**C**　The question asks what must be true about the amount of carbon-15 remaining in a sample, as

modeled by the function $C(m) = 100\left(\dfrac{1}{2}\right)^{24m}$. Exponential decay is modeled by the equation *final*

amount = original amount(*multiplier*)$^{number\ of\ changes}$. None of the choices deal with the final amount

or the original amount, so ignore these. The multiplier is $\dfrac{1}{2}$, so eliminate (D), which reduces the

amount of carbon-15 by a factor other than 2. The number of changes is $24m$. Eliminate (A), which doesn't include 24. To determine whether the amount halves every 24 minutes or 24 times every minute, plug and play. Let $m = 1$. In 1 minute, the number of changes is $24m = 24(1) = 24$. Therefore, it halves 24 times in 1 minute. Eliminate (B). The correct answer is (C).

16. $\dfrac{14}{4}$ or $\dfrac{7}{2}$ or **3.5**

The question asks for the value of n in the equation. Add $\dfrac{6}{n+1}$ to both sides to get $\dfrac{2}{n-2} = \dfrac{6}{n+1}$. Cross-multiply to get $2(n + 1) = 6(n - 2)$. Distribute to get $2n + 2 = 6n - 12$. Subtract $2n$ from both sides to get $2 = 4n - 12$. Add 12 to both sides to get $14 = 4n$. Divide both sides by 4 to get $n = \dfrac{14}{4}$. Grid-In questions do not require reduced fractions, so there is no further work to be done. The correct answer is $\dfrac{14}{4}$, $\dfrac{7}{2}$, or 3.5.

17. **6** The question asks for the length of XY and gives tan m. Since $\tan\theta = \dfrac{\text{opposite}}{\text{adjacent}}$, plugging in the given information results in $\sqrt{3} = \dfrac{YZ}{3}$. Multiply both sides by 3 to get $YZ = 3\sqrt{3}$. To find XY, either use the Pythagorean Theorem, or note that since one leg is $\sqrt{3}$ times another leg, this is a 30-60-90 right triangle, making the hypotenuse double the smaller leg. Therefore, $XY = 2 \times 3 = 6$. The correct answer is 6.

18. **900** The question asks for the measure of 5π radians in degrees. Use the formula $\dfrac{\text{radians}}{\text{degrees}} = \dfrac{\pi}{180}$. Substitute $radians = 5\pi$ and $degrees = d$ to get $\dfrac{5\pi}{d} = \dfrac{\pi}{180}$. Now solve for d. Cross-multiply to get $\pi d = 900\pi$. Divide both sides by π to get $d = 900$. The correct answer is 900.

19. **200** The question asks for the number of televisions Robert must sell to meet his quota of $100,000 in sales. Each computer normally costs $545 but has an 8% discount. Take 8% of 545, which is $\dfrac{8}{100} \times 545 = \dfrac{4,360}{100} = 43.6$. Since the discount is $43.60, the discounted price is $545 − $43.60 = $501.40. Let n be the number of televisions sold. The total amount of the sales of n televisions at $501.40 each is $501.40n$, so to meet the quota, $501.40n \geq 100,000$. To isolate n, divide by 501.40 to get $n \geq \dfrac{100,000}{501.40}$. However, this division is difficult without a calculator. Try Ballparking. Estimate 501.40 as 500 to get $\dfrac{100,000}{500} = 200$. Determine whether 200 televisions sold meets the quota by multiplying 200 by $501.40 to get $100,280. Since this is greater than $100,000, 200 televisions sold does meet the quota. However, the question asks for the minimum number, so consider whether fewer televisions sold can also meet the quota. Since each discounted television is sold for $501.40, selling one fewer television would mean $501.40 less in sales. Therefore, the total

amount of sales for 199 computers is \$100,280 – \$501.40, which is less than \$100,000. Therefore, 199 televisions sold would not meet the quota, and 200 is the minimum number of televisions Robert must sell. The correct answer is 200.

20.   **3**   The question asks for the slope of line g, which can be determined with the formula $\text{slope} = \dfrac{y_2 - y_1}{x_2 - x_1}$.

Let $(x_1, y_1) = (-3, 4)$ and $(x_2, y_2) = (2, 19)$. Substitute these points into the formula to get $\text{slope} = \dfrac{19 - 4}{2 - (-3)} = \dfrac{15}{5} = 3$. The correct answer is 3.

Section 4: Math (Calculator)

1.   **B**   The question asks for the value of $g(-5)$, so substitute the value -5 for x in the original function definition. Therefore, $g(-5) = 3(-5) + 5 = -15 + 5 = -10$. The correct answer is (B).

2.   **B**   The question asks what fraction of working lightbulbs were 100-Watt bulbs. Therefore, the denominator must be the total number of working lightbulbs, which is 3,614. Eliminate (C) and (D). The numerator is the number of working 100-Watt lightbulbs, which is 2,384. Eliminate (A). The correct answer is (B).

3.   **A**   The question asks for an expression that is equivalent to $(4n - 5)(5n - 4)$. All the answers are in expanded form, so expand the expression using Bite-Sized Pieces. Start with the n^2 term. To find the n^2 term, multiply the n terms in each factor to get $(4n)(5n) = 20n^2$. Eliminate (C) and (D), which don't have $20n^2$. The two remaining choices have different constant terms. To find the constant term of the expanded form, multiply the constant terms of the factored form to get $(-5)(-4) = 20$. Eliminate (B), which doesn't have 20. Only one choice remains. The correct answer is (A).

4.   **D**   The question asks for the value of b and gives equivalent ratios. Set the ratios equal to form a proportion: $\dfrac{2.7}{1.2} = \dfrac{b}{4.8}$. Cross-multiply to get $1.2b = 12.96$. Divide both sides by 1.2 to get $b = 10.8$. The correct answer is (D).

5.   **C**   The question asks for the value of $3mn + 4$. Since there is only one equation and two variables, it is not possible to solve for m or n individually. Instead, solve for the expression $3mn + 4$. Look for the most direct way to get to this expression from the given one. The right side of the equation is a multiple of $3mn + 4$, so divide both sides of the equation $60 = 15mn + 20$ by 5 to get $12 = 3mn + 4$. The correct answer is (C).

6.   **C**   The question asks which data collection method is most likely to yield an accurate prediction about students in Santana High School. Choose the method that produces a representative sample. Choice (A) would include teenagers who are not students at Santana High School, which could taint the results, so eliminate (A). Choice (B) would be a non-representative sample, since seniors

may not be representative of all classes, so eliminate (B). Choice (C) includes randomly selected students through the school, so keep (C). Choice (D) includes a self-selection bias, as not all students are equally likely to go to the website and answer the poll, so eliminate (D). The correct answer is (C).

7. **A** The question asks for Thomas's salary in 1999. Since his salary increases at a rate of $2,300 each year, determine the total amount of the increase by multiplying this rate by the number of years after 1977. Since 1999 − 1977 = 22 years after 1977, his salary increased by 22 × $2,300 = $50,600 from 1977 to 1999. Since his salary in 1977 was $40,000, his salary in 1999 is $40,000 + $50,600 = $90,600. The correct answer is (A).

8. **B** The question asks which of the ranges of values for y must be true if the range of salaries is $54,000 to $60,000. Translate the information into an equation. Thomas's salary increased by 2,300 per year for y years, so the total amount of the increase is $2,300y$. Since the starting salary was 40,000, the salary after y years is $2,300y + 40,000$. This salary must be between $54,000 and $60,000, so the full inequality is $54,000 < 2,300y + 40,000 < 60,000$. Subtract 40,000 from all parts of the inequality to get $14,000 < 2,300y < 20,000$, then divide all parts of the inequality by 2,300 to get about $6.09 < y < 8.7$. This is closest to $6 < y < 9$. Since the ranges in the answers on these questions don't overlap, it is also possible to solve this by plugging in numbers from the answers and using Process of Elimination. The correct answer is (B).

9. **B** The question asks which graph could represent Thomas's salary as a function of years. Since Thomas's salary *increases* each year, eliminate (C) and (D), which are decreasing functions. The difference between (A) and (B) is whether the function increases exponentially or linearly. Because the salary increased by a fixed amount each year rather than a fixed percentage, the increase is linear. Eliminate (A). The correct answer is (B).

10. **C** The question asks how much less the return of the option with the linear model is after 4 months than is that of the option with the exponential model. Find the returns for each option and subtract. For the exponential model, substitute $t = 4$ to get $R = 100(3^4) = 8,100$. For the linear model, substitute $R = 350(4) = 1,400$. Now subtract to get $8,100 − 1,400 = 6,700$. The correct answer is (C).

11. **A** The question asks for a possible value of n. Rather than algebraically solving a radical equation, notice that there are numbers in the statements and plug in the answers. Start with (I). Plug $n = 7$ into the equation to get $7 - \sqrt{2(7) + 22} = 1$. Simplify under the radical to get $7 - \sqrt{36} = 1$, which is $7 − 6 = 1$ and $1 = 1$. Therefore, 7 is a possible value of n, so eliminate (B) and (D), which don't include (I). Neither of the remaining choices include (II), so don't bother plugging in −3. Instead, go straight to (III) and plug in $n = −5$ to get $-5 - \sqrt{2(-5) + 22} = 1$. Simplify under the radical to get $-5 - \sqrt{12} = 1$. The left side of the equation will result in a negative, irrational number and therefore cannot equal 1. Thus, −5 is not a possible value of n, so eliminate (C), which includes (III). Only one choice remains. The correct answer is (A).

12. **A** The question asks for the value of $2x - 4$. Because the question asks for an expression rather than the value of x, it may not be necessary to find the value of x. Look for the most direct way to get to the expression $2x - 4$ from the given equation. Subtract $3x$ from both sides of the equation to get $-6 = 2x - 2$. Since the question asks for the value of $2x - 4$, subtract 2 from both sides to get $-8 = 2x - 4$. The correct answer is (A).

13. **A** The question asks for the weight of the car that accurately fits the model shown by the line of best fit. The car that most accurately fits the model is represented by the point that is closest to the line of best fit. Notice that one point is actually on the line of best fit. Find the weight of the car represented by the point by following the grid-line down to the horizontal axis, which represents weight. Since the weight is 2.5 tons, the correct answer is (A).

14. **C** The question asks which choice must be true based on the graph. All the choices ask about the average weight loss per month. Because weight loss is the change in y and number of months is the change in x, look at the slope. During the first 2 months, the slope is steeper than during the next 4 months. Furthermore, the slope in months 2 to 6 is steeper than the slope for the final 6 months. Therefore, the average weight loss during the first 2 months is greater than the average weight loss during the next 4 months, which is greater than the average weight loss during the final 6 months. Go to the choices. Eliminate (A), because the average weight loss changes. Eliminate (B), because nothing is known about 150 months. This is a trap answer based on confusing the axes. Choice (C) fits the prediction, so keep (C). Eliminate (D), because it reverses the prediction. The correct answer is (C).

15. **A** The question asks for the meaning of $(r - m)$ in the expression $\pi r^2 - \pi(r - m)^2$. Label the formula. Since the formula gives the area of an irregular shaded region, it is a form of the formula *Shaded = Total − Unshaded*. Therefore, πr^2 must be the total area and $\pi(r - m)^2$ must be the area of the unshaded region. The total area is the area of the surface of the lake and walking path combined. Since this is not $(r - m)$, eliminate (C). The unshaded area represents the area of the surface of the lake. Since this area is not $(r - m)$, eliminate (D). The formula for area of a circle is $A = \pi r^2$. Since $\pi(r - m)^2$ represents the area of the surface of the lake, $(r - m)$ represents the radius of the lake. The correct answer is (A).

16. **D** The question asks what must be true about x, which is the mean of the remaining tests. The mean of all 8 tests is 90. For questions involving a mean or average, use the formula $T = AN$, and plug in what you know. This becomes $T = (90)(8) = 720$. More than one-quarter of the tests have scores that were less than 85. Since one-quarter of 8 is $\frac{1}{4} \times 8 = 2$, more than 2 of the tests have scores less than 85. To find a possible value of x, say that 3 scores are equal to 80. The total of these scores is $80 + 80 + 80 = 240$. Since the question asks for the average of the remaining tests, get the number of remaining tests and the total of the remaining tests. To get the number of remaining tests, subtract the 3 tests from the 8 tests to get $8 - 3 = 5$. Similarly, get the total of the remaining tests

by subtracting the total of those 3 tests from the total of all tests to get $720 - 240 = 480$. Use the formula $T = AN$ again to get $480 = (A)(5)$. Divide 480 by 5 to get $A = 96$. The correct answer is (D).

17. **D** The question asks for the number of likely voters in Seanoa City. Since randomly selected likely voters were polled, the results of the poll are likely close to proportional to the general population. Since 190 out of 400 in the poll supported Candidate A and 3,120 voters in total are likely to vote for Candidate A, set up the proportion $\dfrac{190 \text{ for Candidate A}}{400 \text{ total}} = \dfrac{3,120 \text{ for Candidate A}}{x \text{ total}}$. Cross-multiply to get $190x = 1,248,000$. Divide both sides by 190 to get $x \approx 6,568$. The correct answer is (D).

18. **A** The question asks for b_1 and b_2, which are the y-values of the solutions to the system of equations. Solve the system for y. Substitute $x = 5$ from the second equation into the first equation to get $y^2 = 21 - 5$. Combine like terms to get $y^2 = 16$. Take the square root of both sides. Since the square of a negative is positive, both the positive and negative of the square root are solutions. Therefore, $y = \pm\sqrt{16} = \pm 4$. The correct answer is (A).

19. **C** The question asks for the value of $q(10)$. Since $q(x) = p(x) - 4$, substitute 10 for x to get $q(10) = p(10) - 4$. Now determine the value of $p(10)$. Since $p(x) = x^2 - 3x$, substitute 10 for x to get $p(10) = (10)^2 - 3(10) = 70$. Therefore, $q(10) = p(10) - 4 = 70 - 4 = 66$. The correct answer is (C).

20. **D** The question asks for the expression that is equivalent to $c^{\frac{m}{n}}$. By rule, fractional exponents correspond with radical expressions, so eliminate (A) and (B). The denominator of the exponent becomes the index of the root, and the numerator of the exponent stands alone as the new exponent. Therefore, $c^{\frac{m}{n}} = \sqrt[n]{c^m}$. The correct answer is (D).

21. **C** The question asks for the force required to lift a 200-pound weight using three additional pulleys in the pulley system. Each additional pulley reduces the amount of force needed to lift 50% of the original amount. Therefore, Pulley 1 reduces the force to $0.50 \times 200 = 100$ pounds, Pulley 2 reduces the force to $0.50 \times 100 = 50$ pounds, and Pulley 3 reduces the force to $0.50 \times 50 = 25$ pounds. The question asks for the force in Newtons and provides the conversion of 1 Newton = 0.224 pounds. Set up the proportion $\dfrac{0.224 \text{ pound}}{1 \text{ Newtons}} = \dfrac{25 \text{ pounds}}{x \text{ Newtons}}$. Cross-multiply to get $0.224x = 25$. Divide both sides by 0.224 to get $x = 111.6$. The correct answer is (C).

22. **C** The question asks for the meaning of 17.6 in the context of the equation. Label the formula. Q is the heat supplied, and T is the change in temperature. Eliminate any answers that don't fit the labels. Choice (B) matches the description of Q in the question, so eliminate (B). Choice (D) refers to a specific temperature, while the equation refers only to an increase in temperature, so eliminate

(D). Plug and play for the remaining two choices. Choice (A) says that 17.6 is the heat supplied when the temperature is constant. If the temperature is constant, the change in temperature is 0, so plug in $T = 0$ to get $Q = 17.6(0) = 0$. The heat supplied isn't 17.6, so eliminate (A). Choice (C) refers to an increase in temperature of 1°C, so plug in $T = 1$ to get $Q = 17.6(1) = 17.6$. The correct answer is (C).

23. **D** The question asks for the total amount of rust produced from $d = 2$ to $d = 6$. According to the graph, during that time period of $6 - 2 = 4$ days, the reaction rate is a constant 0.8 g/day. To find the total amount, multiply this constant rate by the time to get $0.8 \times 4 = 3.2$. The correct answer is (D).

24. **C** The question asks for the value of $\cos(90 - \theta)$ and states that $\cos \theta = \dfrac{3}{5}$. Since $\cos \theta = \dfrac{\text{adjacent}}{\text{hypotenuse}}$, the adjacent side of x is 3 and the hypotenuse is 5. The sum of the measures of the angles in any triangle is 180°. Therefore, the sum of the measures of the two non-right angles in a right triangle is $180° - 90° = 90°$. Since one of the non-right angles has measure θ, the other must have measure $(90 - \theta)$. Find the cosine of the other angle. The hypotenuse is 5, so eliminate (B) and (D), which don't have a denominator of 5. To find the adjacent side, either use the Pythagorean Theorem or recognize that it is a 3-4-5 right triangle. Either method results in an adjacent side equal to 4. Therefore, $\cos(90 - \theta) = \dfrac{4}{5}$. The correct answer is (C).

25. **D** The question asks for the value of a, which is the x-coordinate of the solution to the system of equations. The question uses the phrase *in terms of*, and there are variables in the choices, which are two signs to plug in. However, plugging for k still requires algebra that is just as complicated, so plug in for x and y. If $x = -3$ and $y = -1$, the first equation is true. Using these values, the second equation becomes $3(-3) - 4(-1) = k$ or $-9 + 4 = k$, so $k = -5$. Use this value in the answers to see which one is the value of a, the x-coordinate of the solution. Only (D) yields a value of -3, the original value of x. Another approach would be to solve the system using elimination. To find the x-coordinate of the solution, cancel the y-coordinates. Multiply both sides of the first equation by 4 and both sides of the second by 7 to get

$$4x + 28y = -40$$
$$21x - 28y = 7k$$

Add the two equations to get $25x = 7k - 40$. Divide both sides by 25 to get $x = \dfrac{7k - 40}{25}$. The correct answer is (D).

26. **B** The question asks how the unemployment rate changed over time, and there are percentages in the choices. Because the unemployment rate decreased over the time period, eliminate (D). To find a percent change, use the formula $\dfrac{\text{difference}}{\text{original}} \times 100$. The difference is $8.3 - 4.9 = 3.4$, and the original is 8.3. Substitute these values into the formula to get $\dfrac{3.4}{8.3} \times 100 \approx 41$. The correct answer is (B).

27. **A** The question asks for the sum of *P* and *L,* which are the medians of the scores of the Physics test and the Literature test, respectively. The median on a box plot is denoted by the line inside the box, so start with the Physics test scores. On that box plot, the line inside the box is at 85, so *P* = 85. Now find the median of the Literature test scores. Because the Literature class had 75 students, the median is the 38th score when the scores are listed in order. Find the 38th score from the chart. The first 2 scores are 60. The next 3 scores are 65, so the 3rd through 5th scores are 65. The next 5 scores are 70, so the 6th through 10th scores are 70. The next 4 scores are 75, so the 11th through 14th scores are 75. The next 10 scores are 80, so the 15th through 24th scores are 80. The next 12 scores are 85, so the 25th through 36th score are 85. The next 19 scores are 90, so the 37th through 55th scores are 90. Since the 38th score is 90, *L* = 90. The word "sum" means to add, so the sum of *P* and *L* is 90 + 85 = 175. The correct answer is (A).

28. **A** The question asks which box plot represents the scores of the Literature test. In a box plot, the endpoints of the whiskers, i.e., the horizontal lines outside the box, represent the minimum and maximum values of a set of data. According to the bar graph, the minimum score for the Literature class is 60. Eliminate (D), which has a minimum score of 5. All three remaining choices have the same maximum and the same median, so there is no need to determine these values. Find the interquartile range, which is represented by the endpoint of the box. The left endpoint represents the first quartile, which is the minimum score that is higher than 25% of the scores. There are 75 total scores, so the first quartile is the minimum score higher than $\frac{25}{100} \times 75 = 18.75$ scores, i.e., the 19th score. According to the bar graph, the first 2 scores are 60. The next 3 scores are 65, so the 3rd through 5th scores are 65. The next 5 scores are 70, so the 6th through 10th scores are 70. The next 4 scores are 75, so the 11th through 14th scores are 75. The next 10 scores are 80, so the 15th through 24th scores are 80. Therefore, the first quartile, which is the 19th score, is 80. Eliminate (B), which has a first quartile of 85. The right side of the box represents the third quartile, which is the minimum score that is greater than 75% of the scores. Since there are 75 scores, the third quartile is the minimum score higher than $\frac{75}{100} \times 75 = 56.25$ score, i.e., the 57th score. The easiest way to find this score is to count backward from the highest score. There are five 100's, so the 71st through 75th scores are 100. There are fifteen 95's, so the 56th through 70th scores are 95. Therefore, the third quartile, which is the 57th score, is 95. Eliminate (C), which has the wrong third quartile. The correct answer is (A).

29. **C** The question asks for the *x*-intercept of line *q*, which is perpendicular to line *p*. Perpendicular lines have slopes that are negative reciprocals, so find the slope of line *p*. The slope formula is slope $= \frac{y_2 - y_1}{x_2 - x_1}$. Since line *p* goes through both the origin and the point (5, 12), substitute (0, 0) for (x_1, y_1) and (5, 12) for (x_2, y_2) to get slope $= \frac{12 - 0}{5 - 0} = \frac{12}{5}$. Since the slope of *p* is $\frac{12}{5}$, the slope of *q* is its negative reciprocal, or $-\frac{5}{12}$. To find the *x*-intercept of line *q*, use the slope formula again with (5, 12) and (*x*, 0). This becomes $-\frac{5}{12} = \frac{12 - 0}{5 - x}$. Cross-multiply to get 12(12) = –5(5 – *x*) or 144 = –25 + 5*x*. Add 25 to both sides to get 169 = 5*x*, then divide both sides by 5 to get *x* = 33.8. The correct answer is (C).

30. **D** The question asks for the form of the equation that includes the minimum value of *y* as a constant. The minimum value of a positive, or upward-opening, parabola is the *y*-coordinate of the vertex, so the equation must be in vertex form: $y = (x - h)^2 + k$, where (*h*, *k*) is the vertex. Eliminate (A), (B), and (C), which are not in vertex form. Only one choice remains. The correct answer is (D).

31. **62** The question asks for the measure of angle *Y*, which is part of triangle *XYZ*. Since triangle *XYZ* is similar to triangle *PQR*, corresponding angles have equal measure and corresponding sides are proportional. Determine which angle from triangle *PQR* corresponds to angle *Y* by using the relationships given in the question. The sides that are in that proportion correspond. Therefore, *PQ* corresponds to *XY*, *YZ* corresponds to *QR*, and *PR* corresponds to *XZ*. Note that the actual value of the proportion was not important, only that there was a proportion. Sketch triangle *XYZ* with each side in the same position as its corresponding side in triangle *PQR*.

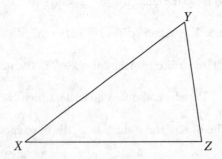

Since angle *Y* is in the same position as angle *Q*, the two angles correspond and thus have the same measure. Since angle *Q* has a measure of 62, so must angle *Y*. The correct answer is 62.

32. **8.5** The question asks for the longest side of the bedroom in the floor plan. Since the question provides a scale, use proportions. The length of the actual floor is 153 inches, so set up $\frac{1 \text{ inch floor plan}}{18 \text{ inch actual}} = \frac{x \text{ inch floor plan}}{153 \text{ inch actual}}$. Cross-multiply to get 18*x* = 153. Divide both sides by 18 to get *x* = 8.5. The correct answer is 8.5.

33. **242** The question asks for the number of 60-square-yard pallets that would be needed to cover a 3-acre field. Be sure to use like units. Start by converting the 3 acres to square yards using the proportion $\dfrac{1\text{ acre}}{4{,}840\text{ square yards}} = \dfrac{3\text{ acres}}{x\text{ square yards}}$. Cross-multiply to get $x = 14{,}520$. Since the field is 14,520 square yards, determine the number of pallets needed by setting up the proportion $\dfrac{1\text{ pallet}}{60\text{ square yards}} = \dfrac{y\text{ pallets}}{14{,}520\text{ square yards}}$. Cross-multiply to get $60y = 14{,}520$. Divide both sides by 60 to get $y = 242$. The correct answer is 242.

34. $\dfrac{11}{5}$ **or 2.2**

The question asks for the value of b, so solve the equation for b. Start by getting rid of the fractions. Multiply both sides by 25 to get $25b + 22 = 35b$. Combine like terms by subtracting $25b$ from both sides to get $22 = 10b$. Divide both sides by 10 to get $b = \dfrac{22}{10} = 2.2$. The possible correct answers are $\dfrac{11}{5}$ or 2.2.

35. **1.5** The question asks for the value of p, which is the x-coordinate of a point on the circle with y-coordinate 0. Find the equation of the circle, and substitute the point $(p, 0)$. The standard form of the equation of the circle is $(x - h)^2 + (y - k)^2 = r^2$, where (h, k) is the center of the circle and r is the radius. The center of the circle is the midpoint of the diameter. The midpoint formula is $\left(\dfrac{x_1 + x_2}{2}, \dfrac{y_1 + y_2}{2}\right)$, so $(h, k) = \left(\dfrac{2 + (-2)}{2}, \dfrac{3.5 + 0.5}{2}\right) = (0, 2)$. To find the radius, take half the length of the diameter, which is the distance between $(2, 3.5)$ and $(-2, 0.5)$. Either use the distance formula or notice that the difference in the x-coordinates is $2 - (-2) = 4$ and the difference in the y-coordinates is $3.5 - 0.5 = 3$, so the diameter is the hypotenuse of a 3-4-5 triangle. Therefore, the diameter is 5, and the radius is 2.5. As a result, the equation of the circle is $(x - 0)^2 + (y - 2)^2 = 2.5^2$ or $x^2 + (y - 2)^2 = 6.25$. Substitute $(p, 0)$ to get $p^2 + (0 - 2)^2 = 6.25$ or $p^2 + 4 = 6.25$. Subtract 4 from both sides to get $p^2 = 2.25$. Take the square root of both sides. Since $p > 0$, don't worry about the negative of the square root. Therefore, $p = \sqrt{2.25} = 1.5$. The correct answer is 1.5.

36. $\frac{11}{7}$ or **1.57**

The question asks for the value of $\frac{y}{x}$. When a question does not ask for the value of either variable but rather an expression involving both, it is not always necessary to solve for either variable individually. In this case, the first equation is enough to solve for $\frac{y}{x}$. Divide both sides of $7y = 11x$ by x to get $7\left(\frac{y}{x}\right) = 11$. Divide both sides by 7 to get $\frac{y}{x} = \frac{11}{7}$. The correct answer is $\frac{11}{7}$ or 1.57.

37.   **588**   The question asks what the salesperson's average sales per day should be during the following week to achieve her goal of increasing sales by 20%. To find her average daily sales, find the total sales for the week shown in the chart and divide by the number of days. Rather than adding the sales for each individual day, use the column that shows the *total week sales at the end of each day*. At the end of Friday, the total sales were \$2,450, making that amount the total sales for the week. There are 5 days in the week, so the average sales per day was \$2,450 ÷ 5 = \$490. Since the question is asking what the average daily sales would be if they increased by 20%, take 20% of \$490 to get $\frac{20}{100} \times \$490 = \$98$. Since the desired increase would be \$98, the desired average sales would be \$490 + \$98 = \$588. The correct answer is 588.

38.   **5.4**   The question asks for the number of items sold per hour on Wednesday. Since an average is given, use the formula $T = AN$. The question says that the items she sold on Wednesday averaged \$8.10 per item, so put that in for A. According to the table, her total sales for Wednesday are \$350, so put that in for T to get \$350 = (\$8.10)(N). The Number of Things can be found by dividing the Total by the Average. Divide 350 by 8.10 to get Number of Things ≈ 43.21. The question asks for the number of items sold per hour. Since her shift was 8 hours, divide 43.21 by 8 to get about 5.401. Since the question asks for the nearest tenth, the answer is 5.4.

RAW SCORE CONVERSION TABLE SECTION AND TEST SCORES

Raw Score (# of correct answers)	Math Section Score	Reading Test Score	Writing and Language Test Score	Raw Score (# of correct answers)	Math Section Score	Reading Test Score	Writing and Language Test Score
0	200	10	10	30	530	28	29
1	200	10	10	31	540	28	30
2	210	10	10	32	550	29	30
3	230	11	10	33	560	29	31
4	240	12	11	34	560	30	32
5	260	13	12	35	570	30	32
6	280	14	13	36	580	31	33
7	290	15	13	37	590	31	34
8	310	15	14	38	600	32	34
9	320	16	15	39	600	32	35
10	330	17	16	40	610	33	36
11	340	17	16	41	620	33	37
12	360	18	17	42	630	34	38
13	370	19	18	43	640	35	39
14	380	19	19	44	650	35	40
15	390	20	19	45	660	36	
16	410	20	20	46	670	37	
17	420	21	21	47	670	37	
18	430	21	21	48	680	38	
19	440	22	22	49	690	38	
20	450	22	23	50	700	39	
21	460	23	23	51	710	40	
22	470	23	24	52	730	40	
23	480	24	25	53	740		
24	480	24	25	54	750		
25	490	25	26	55	760		
26	500	25	26	56	780		
27	510	26	27	57	790		
28	520	26	28	58	800		
29	520	27	28				

Please note that the numbers in the table may shift slightly depending on the SAT's scale from test to test; however, you can still use this table to get an idea of how your performance on the practice tests will translate to the actual SAT.

CONVERSION EQUATION SECTION AND TEST SCORES

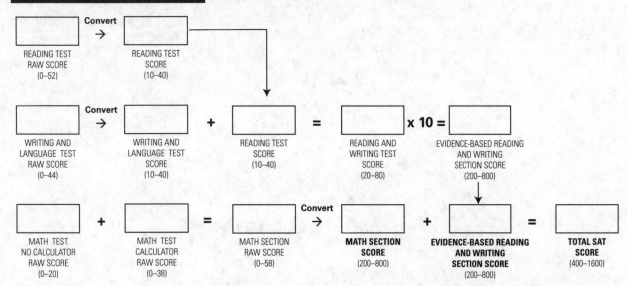

Practice Test 3

Reading Test

65 MINUTES, 52 QUESTIONS

Turn to Section 1 of your answer sheet to answer the questions in this section.

DIRECTIONS

Each passage or pair of passages below is followed by a number of questions. After reading each passage or pair, choose the best answer to each question based on what is stated or implied in the passage or passages and in any accompanying graphics (such as a table or graph).

Questions 1–10 are based on the following passage.

The passage that follows is adapted from an 1859 novel that follows the lives of both English and French characters during the French Revolution.

"You were very sound, Sydney, in the matter of those crown witnesses today. Every question told."

"I always am sound; am I not?"

Line "I don't gainsay it. What has roughened your
5 temper? Put some punch to it and smooth it again."

With a deprecatory grunt, Carton complied.

"The old Sydney Carton of old Shrewsbury School," said Stryver, nodding his head over him as he reviewed him in the present and the past, "the old seesaw
10 Sydney. Up one minute and down the next; now in spirits and now in despondency!"

"Ah!" returned the other, sighing: "Yes! The same Sydney, with the same luck. Even then, I did exercises for other boys, and seldom did my own."

15 "And why not?"

"God knows. It was my way, I suppose."

"Carton," said his friend, squaring himself at him with a bullying air, as if the fire-grate had been the furnace in which sustained endeavour was forged, and
20 the one delicate thing to be done for the old Sydney Carton of old Shrewsbury School was to shoulder him into it, "your way is, and always was, a lame way. You summon no energy and purpose. Look at me."

"Oh, botheration!" returned Sydney, with a lighter
25 and more good-humoured laugh, "don't *you* be moral!"

"How have I done what I have done?" said Stryver; "how do I do what I do?"

"Partly through paying me to help you, I suppose. But it's not worth your while to apostrophise me, or
30 the air, about it; what you want to do, you do. You were always in the front rank, and I was always behind."

"I had to get into the front rank; I was not born there, was I?"

"I was not present at the ceremony; but my opinion
35 is you were," said Carton. At this, he laughed again, and they both laughed.

"Before Shrewsbury, and at Shrewsbury, and ever since Shrewsbury," pursued Carton, "you have fallen into your rank, and I have fallen into mine. You were
40 always somewhere, and I was always nowhere."

"And whose fault was that?"

"Upon my soul, I am not sure that it was not yours. You were always driving and shouldering and passing, to that restless degree that I had no chance for my life
45 but in rust and repose. It's a gloomy thing, however, to talk about one's own past, with the day breaking. Turn me in some other direction before I go."

"Well then! Pledge me to the pretty witness," said Stryver, holding up his glass. "Are you turned in a
50 pleasant direction?"

"Pretty witness," he muttered, looking down into his glass. "I have had enough of witnesses today and tonight; who's your pretty witness?"

"The picturesque doctor's daughter, Miss Manette."
55 "*She* pretty?"

"Is she not?"

"No."

CONTINUE

"Why, man alive, she was the admiration of the whole Court!"

60 "Rot the admiration of the whole Court! Who made the Old Bailey a judge of beauty? She was a golden-haired doll!"

"Do you know, Sydney," said Mr. Stryver, looking at him with sharp eyes, and slowly drawing a hand across
65 his florid face: "do you know, I rather thought, at the time, that you sympathized with the golden-haired doll, and were quick to see what happened to the golden-haired doll?"

"Quick to see what happened! If a girl, doll or no
70 doll, swoons within a yard or two of a man's nose, he can see it without a perspective-glass. I pledge you, but I deny the beauty. And now I'll have no more drink; I'll get to bed."

When his host followed him out on the staircase
75 with a candle, to light him down the stairs, the day was coldly looking in through its grimy windows. When he got out of the house, the air was cold and sad, the dull sky overcast, the river dark and dim, the whole scene like a lifeless desert. And wreaths of dust were spinning
80 round and round before the morning blast, as if the desert-sand had risen far away, and the first spray of it in its advance had begun to overwhelm the city.

Climbing to a high chamber in a well of houses, he threw himself down in his clothes on a neglected bed,
85 and its pillow was wet with wasted tears. Sadly, sadly, the sun rose; it rose upon no sadder sight than the man of good abilities and good emotions, incapable of their directed exercise, incapable of his own help and his own happiness, sensible of the blight on him, and
90 resigning himself to let it eat him away.

1

The primary purpose of the passage as a whole is to

A) describe the history between Carton and Stryver.

B) characterize life at the Shrewsbury School.

C) reveal Carton's character.

D) show that Stryver has been exploiting Carton.

2

Based on the information in the passage, Carton is best characterized as

A) unsound.

B) mercurial.

C) unlucky.

D) imperceptive.

3

Which choice provides the best evidence for the answer to the previous question?

A) Lines 10–11 ("Up . . . despondency")

B) Lines 13–14 ("Even . . . own")

C) Lines 35–36 ("At this . . . laughed")

D) Lines 45–46 ("It's a . . . breaking")

4

As used in line 11, "spirits" most nearly means

A) soul.

B) liquor.

C) essence.

D) jubilation.

5

Based on lines 17–22 ("squaring . . . it"), it can be reasonably inferred that

A) Stryver is frustrated with Carton's behavior.

B) Stryver is planning to push Carton into the fireplace.

C) Stryver believes Carton to be comparatively older.

D) Stryver wishes to bully Carton as he did at Shrewsbury.

CONTINUE ➡

6

The use of italics in line 55 primarily serves to emphasize Carton's

A) incredulity.

B) confusion.

C) annoyance.

D) affection.

7

The passage suggests which of the following about Stryver?

A) He is in love with Miss Manette.

B) He believes that Carton lacks the intelligence required to be successful.

C) He does not believe that Carton finds Miss Manette unattractive.

D) He was born into a wealthy family.

8

Which choice provides the best evidence for the answer to the previous question?

A) Lines 32–33 ("I had . . . I")

B) Line 41 ("And whose . . . that")

C) Lines 58–59 ("Why . . . Court")

D) Lines 63–68 ("Do you . . . doll")

9

In context, "desert" in line 79 refers to

A) Stryver's cold demeanor.

B) London's landscape.

C) Carton's windows.

D) sunlit dunes.

10

The "tears" referred to in line 85 are "wasted" because

A) Miss Manette will never love Carton.

B) Carton is unlikely to change his ways.

C) Carton's home is one of squalor.

D) Stryver will continue to exploit Carton's labor.

CONTINUE ➡

Questions 11–21 are based on the following passage and supplementary material.

This passage is adapted from Priit Vesilind, *The Singing Revolution*. ©2008 by Sky Films Incorporated.

By the end of 1939 Soviet troops had forced their way into garrisons in the Baltic states of Estonia, Latvia, and Lithuania. In 1940 the Soviets forcibly annexed the three Baltic states into the USSR. But in 1941 Hitler double-crossed Stalin: he launched an attack on the Soviet Union. The Baltic nations were caught in the middle of the treachery. In 1945, when the war ended, Estonia remained occupied by the Soviets.

After nearly 50 years of Soviet occupation, when agitations for independence came in the late 1980s, the protestors pointed back to the Molotov-Ribbentrop Pact, a secret non-aggression treaty between the Soviet Union and Nazi Germany. If the Kremlin were to acknowledge the existence of this protocol, they reasoned, it would be admitting that the Baltic States had no legal "marriage" with Moscow, but that these nations were forcibly abducted with the collusion of the world's most heinous fascist regime. So the occupied nations had every right to ask for their freedom, and with no need for a legal "divorce."

The Baltic states had been morally supported with the firm stand taken in 1940 by the United States not to recognize the legality of the forceful annexation of Estonia, Latvia, and Lithuania. But politics were effective only if the Estonians had some other leverage. A nation of barely one million, burdened with half a million foreign settlers and 100,000 Soviet troops, could not threaten the Soviet Union militarily or economically, so it had to do it with the force of its culture. Estonia had always been a nation of singers. Its wealth of folk songs gave rhythm to village life and work, and its earnest anthems often invoked the longing for self-determination. Estonians had lived for centuries in servitude, and the themes of their music were often grim: sorrow, slavery, soil, blood, birch forests, and sacrifice. But there was always hope in their hearts.

Early in their national awakening, about 140 years ago, Estonians established a history of mass song festivals, held when money and politics allowed— celebrations that would kindle and fortify the courage to express their love of language and nation, and their reluctance to be absorbed by anyone. The festivals were a nationwide phenomenon, as were similar festivals held in Latvia and Lithuania.

In Tallinn the massive modern song stage held some 30,000 singers and the outdoor amphitheater could accommodate as many as 300,000. Often, 30 percent of all Estonians would be there—at a single concert. During the Soviet years the festivals were forced to pay tribute to Communist icons and the solidarity of the Soviet peoples. Choirs from other parts of the vast empire would come and all would whip up a rousing tribute to Stalin or Lenin. To these mandatory performances Estonians would introduce patriotic songs disguised as love songs or folk music. An unofficial national anthem, by the popular choir director Gustav Ernesaks, established itself in 1947, and survived the entire Soviet occupation despite a serious attempt by officials to eliminate it in 1969.

By the late 1980s the nation was simmering. A movement of young historians was already defying Soviet authority in speeches that laid history bare under the cover of Gorbachev's policy of glasnost, or "free speech." And the burden of protest songs had passed to rock-and-rollers, young men whose energized patriotic tunes blared from every radio.

Momentum built to a crescendo in the summer of 1988 when a rock concert in Tallinn's Old Town spilled into the Song Festival grounds and massive crowds gathered for six straight nights to lift arms, sway in unison, and sing patriotic songs. Emboldened, Estonians brought out forbidden blue-and-black-and-white national flags, some from attics and basements where they had been hidden since 1940. Shockingly, no one stopped them. For the finale of these "Night Song Festivals" more than 200,000 Estonians gathered.

This was the heart of "The Singing Revolution," a spontaneous, non-violent, but powerful political movement that united Estonians with poetry and music. After that there was no backing up. Sedition hung in the wind, waiting to be denied.

CONTINUE

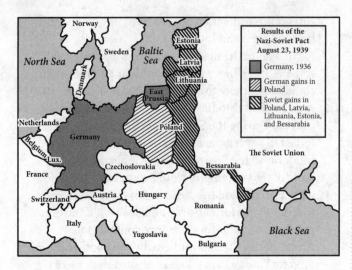

Diagram of Europe following the Nazi-Soviet Pact of 1939, also known as the Molotov-Ribbentrop Pact. Image adapted from CQ Researcher.

11

The point of view from which the passage is written is best described as

A) condemnatory of the Soviet Union's treacherous actions.

B) sympathetic to the Baltic states' struggle for freedom.

C) dismissive of the idea of non-violent revolution.

D) conflicted about the underlying cause of the revolution.

12

In lines 34–38, the author draws a distinction between

A) the tone of Estonian songs and the people's true feelings.

B) the themes of Estonian folk songs and anthems.

C) the military strength of Estonia and that of the Soviet Union.

D) song festivals in Estonia and those in Latvia and Lithuania.

13

In the context of the passage, the phrase "their reluctance to be absorbed" suggests that Estonians

A) refused to speak Russian with the many foreign settlers in Estonia.

B) wanted to have an independent nation.

C) worked to ensure their culture stayed distinct from those of the other Baltic states.

D) were unwilling to devote the amount of concentration to song festivals that the Soviets demanded.

14

Which choice best supports the claim that the Soviet Union perceived Estonia's culture as a threat?

A) Lines 31–34 ("Estonia . . . self-determination")

B) Lines 39–44 ("Early . . . anyone")

C) Lines 51–53 ("During . . . peoples")

D) Lines 58–61 ("An unofficial . . . 1969")

CONTINUE ➤

15

As used in line 66, "burden" most nearly means

A) weight.

B) travail.

C) responsibility.

D) need.

16

The primary rhetorical effect of the last sentence of the passage is to

A) convey the sense of dread that hung over Estonia at the height of the Singing Revolution.

B) indicate the depth of disagreement between violent and non-violent revolutionaries.

C) show how crucial music and poetry were to Estonia's fight for independence.

D) communicate the sense of optimistic tension that Estonians felt after the Night Song Festivals.

17

The author implies which of the following about Estonian song festivals?

A) They afforded Estonians a medium through which national and cultural pride could be expressed.

B) They were started during the Soviet occupation to preserve Estonian culture and language.

C) They were unique in size and format to the country where they were founded.

D) They provided an opportunity to sing songs that were more uplifting than those sung while working.

18

Which choice provides the best evidence for the answer to the previous question?

A) Lines 19–21 ("So . . . 'divorce'")

B) Lines 44–46 ("The festivals . . . Lithuania")

C) Line 62 ("By the . . . simmering")

D) Lines 79–82 ("This . . . music")

19

Which of the following claims is supported by the diagram?

A) In the 1939 pact, Germany gained the entirety of Poland.

B) The Soviet Union doubled in size after the pact.

C) Lithuania and Estonia are contiguous countries.

D) The Soviet Union's gains stretched from the Baltic Sea to the Black Sea.

20

Which statement from the passage is most directly reflected by the information presented on the diagram?

A) Lines 1–3 ("By the . . . Lithuania")

B) Lines 3–4 ("In 1940 . . . USSR")

C) Lines 10–14 ("After . . . Germany")

D) Lines 22–25 ("The Baltic . . . Lithuania")

21

What purpose does the diagram serve in relation to the passage as a whole?

A) It clarifies Estonia's relationship to the Soviet Union.

B) It illustrates the results of a non-aggression treaty that shaped the region.

C) It shows the impact of the Singing Revolution on surrounding countries.

D) It emphasizes the importance of Estonia's role in the region.

CONTINUE ➡

Questions 22–31 are based on the following passage.

This passage is an excerpt adapted from a speech given in 1917 by American Senator Robert LaFollette. In the speech, LaFollette explains the special importance of free speech during times of war and the relation between free speech and democratic governance.

Since the declaration of war the triumphant war press has pursued those Senators and Representatives who voted against war with malicious falsehood and
Line recklessly libelous attacks, going to the extreme limit of
5 charging them with treason against their country.

I have in my possession numerous affidavits establishing the fact that people are being unlawfully arrested, thrown into jail, held incommunicado for days, only to be eventually discharged without ever
10 having been taken into court, because they have committed no crime. Private residences are being invaded, loyal citizens of undoubted integrity and probity arrested, cross-examined, and the most sacred constitutional rights guaranteed to every American
15 citizen are being violated.

It appears to be the purpose of those conducting this campaign to throw the country into a state of terror, to coerce public opinion, to stifle criticism, and suppress discussion of the great issues involved in this
20 war.

I think all men recognize that in time of war the citizen must surrender some rights for the common good which he is entitled to enjoy in time of peace. But sir, the right to control their own Government
25 according to constitutional forms is not one of the rights that the citizens of this country are called upon to surrender in time of war.

Rather in time of war the citizen must be more alert to the preservation of his right to control his
30 Government. He must be most watchful of the encroachment of the military upon the civil power. He must beware of those precedents in support of arbitrary action by administrative officials, which excused on the plea of necessity in war time, become
35 the fixed rule when the necessity has passed and normal conditions have been restored.

More than all, the citizen and his representative in Congress in time of war must maintain his right of free speech. More than in times of peace it is necessary that
40 the channels for free public discussion of governmental policies shall be open and unclogged. I believe, Mr. President, that I am now touching upon the most

important question in this country today—and that is the right of the citizens of this country and their
45 representatives in Congress to discuss in an orderly way frankly and publicly and without fear, from the platform and through the press, every important phase of this war; its causes, the manner in which it should be conducted, and the terms upon which peace should
50 be made. I am contending, Mr. President, for the great fundamental right of the sovereign people of this country to make their voice heard and have that voice heeded upon the great questions arising out of this war, including not only how the war shall be prosecuted but
55 the conditions upon which it may be terminated with a due regard for the rights and the honor of this Nation and the interests of humanity.

I am contending for this right because the exercise of it is necessary to the welfare, to the existence, of this
60 Government to the successful conduct of this war, and to a peace which shall be enduring and for the best interest of this country.

Suppose success attends the attempt to stifle all discussion of the issues of this war, all discussion
65 of the terms upon which it should be concluded, all discussion of the objects and purposes to be accomplished by it, and concede the demand of the war-mad press and war extremists that they monopolize the right of public utterance upon these
70 questions unchallenged, what think you would be the consequences to this country not only during the war but after the war?

It is no answer to say that when the war is over the citizen may once more resume his rights and feel some
75 security in his liberty and his person. As I have already tried to point out, now is precisely the time when the country needs the counsel of all its citizens. In time of war even more than in time of peace, whether citizens happen to agree with the ruling administration or
80 not, these precious fundamental personal rights—free speech, free press, and right of assemblage so explicitly and emphatically guaranteed by the Constitution should be maintained inviolable.

CONTINUE ➤

22

The position that LaFollette takes is best described as that of

A) a law-maker suggesting a new piece of legislation.

B) an impartial observer arbitrating a legal issue.

C) a dissenter arguing for a cause.

D) a pacifist arguing against international conflicts.

23

In the passage, LaFollette draws a distinction between

A) rights that are appropriately and inappropriately sacrificed during war.

B) moments when free speech is and is not necessary.

C) just wars and wars fought for economic interest.

D) the interests of the Nation and the interests of humanity.

24

Which choice provides the best evidence for the answer to the previous question?

A) Lines 6–11 ("I have . . . crime")

B) Lines 21–27 ("I think . . . war")

C) Lines 30–31 ("He must . . . power")

D) Lines 50–57 ("I am . . . humanity")

25

Based on the information in the passage, those criticized by the press are

A) members of Congress standing in opposition to the war.

B) citizens who have committed treason against their country.

C) government officials seeking to stifle free speech.

D) Senators and Representatives who have committed libel.

26

As used in line 22, "surrender" most nearly means

A) declare defeat.

B) throw away.

C) set aside.

D) submit to.

27

Lines 32–36 suggest that

A) some rights are necessarily given up during war time.

B) restrictions on civil powers are always arbitrary.

C) the Government must be watchful of the military.

D) temporary restrictions may become permanent.

28

As used in line 49, "terms" most nearly means

A) periods.

B) conversations.

C) definitions.

D) conditions.

29

The principal rhetorical effect of the phrase in lines 48–50 ("its causes . . . made") is to

A) argue against granting free speech during war by emphasizing the difficulties faced by the military and the President.

B) suggest the numerous points at which citizens should exercise their free speech during times of war.

C) discuss three reasons members of the press are currently unable to speak frankly without fear.

D) show that LaFollette believes that the citizens understand the dynamics of war far better than the President.

CONTINUE

30

Which choice provides the best evidence for the answer to the previous question?

A) Lines 11–15 ("Private . . . violated")

B) Lines 16–20 ("It appears . . . war")

C) Lines 30–36 ("He must . . . restored")

D) Lines 37–41 ("More . . . unclogged")

31

The author's attitude toward "the attempt to stifle" (line 63) can be described as

A) sympathetic.

B) apathetic.

C) frustrated.

D) morose.

CONTINUE

Questions 32–41 are based on the following passage and supplementary material.

This passage is adapted from Joe Turner, "Fill Up Your Gas Tank with Bamboo?" ©2015 by *Science*.

2014 was a banner year for making automotive fuel from nonfood crops, with a series of major new production plants opening in the United States.
Line However, producing this so-called cellulosic ethanol
5 remains considerably more expensive than gasoline. So researchers are always on the lookout for new ways to trim costs. Now they have a new lead, a microbe that can use abundant nitrogen gas as the fertilizer it needs to produce ethanol from plants.

10 The discovery is "a major commercial accomplishment for biofuel production," says Steven Ricke, a microbiologist and editor of a textbook on biofuel production at the University of Arkansas, Fayetteville, who was not involved in the study.

15 Scientists have long eyed biofuels as a cleaner and more sustainable alternative to traditional fossil fuels. Instead of pumping oil from the ground, researchers harvest plants like cassava and sugarcane, grind them up, add enzymes to break down the plant matter, and
20 sprinkle in yeast. The microbe ferments sugars in the plants to produce ethanol, a form of alcohol, which is now commonly mixed with gasoline and used in cars and buses around the world.

But biofuels are controversial. The majority are
25 derived from food crops, like corn. Critics say the increased demand for these crops could increase food prices. And although direct emissions of carbon dioxide from burning biofuels are less than those from traditional fuels, some scientists now argue
30 that once indirect emissions from land use changes and producing the crop are considered, the overall emissions from some biofuels can actually be higher.

So in recent years, researchers have turned to nonfood crops—like trees and bamboo—for biofuel
35 production. These crops need less fertilizer than traditional biofuel crops, and they often have less detrimental impact on the land. In an ideal world, biofuels would be produced only from plant materials that cannot be eaten, such as trees and parts of plants
40 that are left in fields after harvest, like straw.

But there are problems. The enzymes needed to break down plants' primary structural components— cellulose and hemicellulose—into simple sugars are expensive. To ferment the simple sugars, the microbes

45 also need nitrogen to grow and divide. So researchers add fertilizer to their fermentation vats to boost the ethanol yields. It is estimated that an ethanol production plant may be spending more than $1 million on this a year.

50 Instead of using yeast to ferment their plants into fuel, microbiologists at Indiana University, Bloomington, turned to *Zymomonas mobilis*, a bacterium also capable of doing the job. So the researchers looked at the amount of ethanol that the
55 microbe could produce with and without additional nitrogen fertilizer being supplied and found that it did better without it. The study, published in the *Proceedings of the National Academy of Sciences*, even showed that the bacterium produces ethanol
60 more quickly and uses more of the plant material when it uses nitrogen gas than when it is fed nitrogen in fertilizer. If the same holds true in a production plant, this could reduce biofuel production costs, the authors say. The process is also more environmentally friendly,
65 they add, because there are greenhouse gas emissions associated with producing nitrogen fertilizer.

However, questions remain about how well this process will work in a large biofuel plant. Whereas using *Z. mobilis* might make it cheaper for producers
70 to use inexpensive, nonfood crops, there could also be added costs and problems.

The overall environmental benefits may also be slim. Even if nitrogen fertilizers are not used in the fermentation process, they might still be needed to
75 grow the crops. And the new advance doesn't address other environmental impacts from biofuels, such as the greenhouse gas emissions from growing, harvesting, and transporting the plants. According to Fengqi You, a chemical engineer at Northwestern University in
80 Evanston, Illinois, further studies would be needed to consider all the environmental and economic costs and benefits of doing this on an industrial scale so that it can be compared with existing systems.

CONTINUE

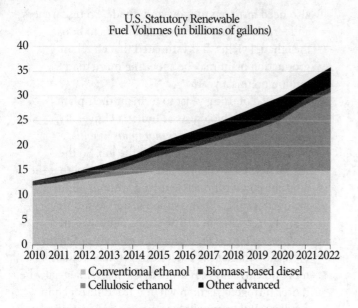

U.S. Statutory Renewable
Fuel Volumes (in billions of gallons)

Conventional ethanol   Biomass-based diesel
Cellulosic ethanol   Other advanced

Figure 1

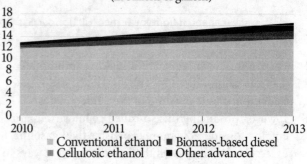

Final EPA Renewable Fuel Volume Mandates
(in billions of gallons)

Conventional ethanol   Biomass-based diesel
Cellulosic ethanol   Other advanced

Figure 2

Figures adapted from data by Center for Climate and Energy Solutions.

32

The passage is written from the perspective of an

A) advocate arguing for more project funding.

B) educator explaining textbook chemistry concepts.

C) expert lauding the successes of an industry.

D) objective observer evaluating new research.

33

The last sentence of the first paragraph primarily serves to

A) assess recent commercial accomplishments.

B) explain why one fuel is more expensive than another.

C) propose a potential solution to a known problem.

D) restate the results of a banner year.

34

According to the passage, nonfood crops produce fewer indirect land use emissions by

A) occupying land that would otherwise produce corn.

B) curtailing sudden increases in food prices.

C) limiting the fertilizer required to produce biofuels.

D) stopping the proliferation of fossil fuel use.

35

Which choice provides the best evidence for the answer to the previous question?

A) Lines 35–37 ("These . . . land")

B) Lines 37–40 ("In an . . . straw")

C) Lines 41–44 ("The enzymes . . . expensive")

D) Lines 47–49 ("It is . . . year")

CONTINUE

36

As used in line 37, "ideal world" most nearly means

A) best-case scenario.

B) dream sequence.

C) perfect model.

D) utopian society.

37

It can most reasonably be inferred from the results of the Indiana University study involving *Zymomonas mobilis* that

A) all bacteria can ferment corn and trees into fuel.

B) total greenhouse gas emissions will remain unchanged.

C) researchers would prefer biofuels to be used as a food source.

D) using nitrogen gas may reduce biofuel production costs.

38

Which choice provides the best evidence for the answer to the previous question?

A) Lines 59–63 ("the bacterium . . . costs")

B) Lines 64–66 ("The process . . . fertilizer")

C) Lines 68–71 ("Whereas . . . problems")

D) Lines 73–75 ("Even . . . crops")

39

As used in line 73, "slim" most nearly means

A) brittle.

B) negligible.

C) skinny.

D) useless.

40

According to figure 1, in what year is the required statutory volume of conventional ethanol closest to that of another fuel type?

A) 2010

B) 2012

C) 2018

D) 2022

41

According to figure 2, which of the following fuels is least likely to meet the volume requirements shown in figure 1?

A) Biomass-based diesel

B) Cellulosic ethanol

C) Conventional ethanol

D) Other advanced renewable fuels

CONTINUE

Questions 42–52 are based on the following passages.

Passage 1 is adapted from Theodore S. Melis, Ed., "Effects of Three High-Flow Experiments on the Colorado River Ecosystem Downstream from Glen Canyon Dam, Arizona," published in 2011 by the U.S. Geological Survey. Passage 2 is adapted from Paul E. Grams, "A Sand Budget for Marble Canyon, Arizona—Implications for Long-Term Monitoring of Sand Storage Change," published in 2013 by the U.S. Geological Survey.

Passage 1

At the time Glen Canyon Dam was constructed (1956–63), little consideration was given to how dam operations might affect downstream resources
Line in Grand Canyon National Park. In fact, the dam
5 was completed before enactment of the National Environmental Policy Act of 1969 and the Endangered Species Act of 1973. By the late 1950s, public values began to shift, and throughout the 1960s and 1970s recognition of the environmental consequences of
10 Glen Canyon Dam and its operation grew. National Park Service and U.S. Geological Survey scientists and river recreationists observed the physical transformation of the river in Grand Canyon, including the loss of large beaches used for camping,
15 narrowing of rapids so as to reduce navigability, and changes in the distribution and composition of riparian vegetation. The humpback chub and Colorado pikeminnow, species found only in the Colorado River Basin, were listed as endangered in 1967 by
20 the U.S. Fish and Wildlife Service, which concluded in 1978 that the dam and its operation jeopardized the continued existence of humpback chub in Grand Canyon.

Annual spring snowmelt floods were the defining
25 attribute of the pre-dam flow regime. Before the Colorado River was regulated by dams, streamflow gradually increased from mid-December to March, precipitously increased in April and May, and reached its peak in early June.
30 Pre-dam floods disturbed the aquatic ecosystem, and native fish species developed strategies to survive periods when the velocity in the main part of the channel was high and large amounts of suspended sediment were being transported. For example, several
35 of the native fish species share unusual body shapes, including a large adult body size, small depressed skulls, large humps on their backs, and small eyes, which presumably developed as adaptations to life in a turbid and seasonally variable riverine environment.
40 Sandbars, riverbanks, and their accompanying aquatic habitats were reshaped during floods. Additionally, the increased elevation of the river surface during floods provided water to native riparian vegetation otherwise principally dependent on precipitation.

Passage 2

45 Decline in the size and abundance of sandbars since the pre-Glen Canyon Dam era has been documented by analysis of old aerial and ground-level photographs and by topographic surveys that began in the mid-1970s. Scientists have estimated that sandbar
50 area in the upstream 100 miles of Glen, Marble, and Grand Canyons was 25 percent less in 2000 than in average pre-dam years. This decline occurred because releases of water from Lake Powell are virtually free of sediment. The tributaries that enter the Colorado River
55 downstream from the dam supply only a fraction of the pre-dam sand supply, and the capacity of the post-dam river to transport that sand greatly exceeds this limited supply. Normal dam operations, therefore, tend to erode, rather than build, sandbars.
60 By experimentation, scientists have learned that controlled floods, if released from the reservoir immediately following large inputs of sand from tributaries, can build sandbars. These sandbars are built during controlled floods when sand is carried
65 from the riverbed and temporarily suspended at high concentration in the flow. The suspended sand is transported into eddies where it is then deposited in areas of low stream-flow velocity. Sandbars enlarged by this process provide larger camping beaches for
70 river-rafting trips and create backwater habitats used by native fish. Newly deposited sandbars also provide areas for riparian vegetation to grow and are a source of windblown sand. Windblown sand carried upslope from sandbars helps to cover and potentially preserve
75 some of the culturally significant archeological sites in Grand Canyon.

Scientists have also learned that controlled floods may erode sandbars if the concentration of suspended sand during a controlled flood is too low.
80 The concentration of sand during a flood is directly proportional to the amount of the riverbed covered by sand and the size of that sand. Higher concentrations of suspended sand occur when the sand is relatively

CONTINUE ➡

fine and large amounts of the riverbed are covered by
85 sand. These findings are incorporated in the current
reservoir-release management strategy for Glen
Canyon Dam, which involves releasing controlled
floods—administratively referred to as High Flow
Experiments (HFEs)—whenever the Paria River
90 has recently delivered large amounts of sand to the
Colorado River. The magnitude and duration of the
controlled floods is adjusted to transport just the
amount of sand that has recently been delivered from
the Paria River.

42

The author of Passage 1 most likely believes that the
Glen Canyon Dam

A) is a useful tool for managing scarce water
resources.

B) was built with a lack of foresight.

C) has decimated native fish populations.

D) has had a calming effect on the aquatic ecosystem.

43

Which choice provides the best evidence for the
answer to the previous question?

A) Lines 1–4 ("At the . . . Park")

B) Lines 17–23 ("The humpback . . . Canyon")

C) Lines 24–25 ("Annual . . . regime")

D) Lines 30–34 ("Pre-dam . . . transported")

44

The author of Passage 1 mentions scientists and river
recreationists primarily to

A) provide support for the idea that the post-dam
river looks drastically different.

B) draw a contrast between scientific observations
and casual observations of river conditions.

C) emphasize the spirit of collaboration between the
science community and the public in conservation
efforts.

D) prove that the Glen Canyon Dam has had a
ruinous effect on the river.

45

Passage 1 suggests that the humpback chub

A) is now extinct in the Grand Canyon.

B) has a small, depressed skull.

C) can survive in changing environments.

D) thrives in high velocity river channels.

46

As used in line 25, "regime" most nearly means

A) government.

B) tenure.

C) system.

D) management.

47

As used in line 65, "suspended" most nearly means

A) stopped.

B) mixed.

C) withheld.

D) hanging.

48

It is reasonable to conclude that controlled floods

A) successfully simulate pre-dam snowmelt floods.

B) contain large amounts of suspended sediment.

C) may be detrimental to the health of the Colorado
River.

D) should be carried out during the months when
snowmelt floods typically occur.

CONTINUE

49

Which choice provides the best evidence for the answer to the previous question?

A) Lines 58–59 ("Normal . . . sandbars")

B) Lines 66–68 ("The suspended . . . velocity")

C) Lines 71–73 ("Newly . . . sand")

D) Lines 77–79 ("Scientists . . . low")

50

The author of Passage 1 would most likely respond to the High Flow Experiments described in Passage 2 by

A) appreciating the efforts of scientists to maintain the sand supply below the dam.

B) warning of the calamity of interfering with the river ecosystem.

C) questioning the ability of controlled floods to build up sandbars.

D) worrying that reshaped habitats will harm native fish.

51

Which of the following best describes the structure of the two passages?

A) Passage 1 introduces a problem, and Passage 2 proposes a solution to the problem.

B) Passage 1 offers a historical discussion, and Passage 2 describes the implications of a scientific practice.

C) Passage 1 discusses general principles, and Passage 2 examines practical applications.

D) Passage 1 describes an experiment, and Passage 2 offers suggestions for future action.

52

Which of the following statements is true of Passage 1, but not of Passage 2?

A) The passage gives details of scientific studies conducted on the river.

B) The passage offers documented evidence of topographic change in the river.

C) The passage indicates the importance of floods to the river ecosystem.

D) The passage gives specific examples of species affected by the dam.

STOP
If you finish before time is called, you may check your work on this section only.
Do not turn to any other section in the test.

No Test Material On This Page

CONTINUE

Writing and Language Test

35 MINUTES, 44 QUESTIONS

Turn to Section 2 of your answer sheet to answer the questions in this section.

Questions 1–11 are based on the following passage.

And Justice for All

Her father got her the job. Amanda was between semesters at college, and her **[1]** work at the mall wouldn't do much for her when she got out of school. It was time to do something more serious, something that meant more to her. Many of her friends were getting internships in the city, working for this or that publishing house or TV studio. Amanda, however, wanted something different. She would start applying to law schools **[2]** soon and she wanted to know what the law looked like in action.

1

A) NO CHANGE
B) work, at the mall, wouldn't do much for her
C) work at the mall wouldn't do much for her,
D) work, at the mall, wouldn't do much for her,

2

A) NO CHANGE
B) soon and,
C) soon, and
D) soon,

CONTINUE →

Fortunately, her dad knew someone from high school, a friend **3** named Ellen, who had then gone on to study at Duke University. It was a thankless job, and although the Department building itself covered almost one hundred acres (in New York City, there was an entire island devoted to it), no one paid the Department of Corrections much mind. Most people never come near a jail cell, so **4** it's easy for them to dismiss inmates as totally removed from society.

[1] At the Department, however, Amanda learned about prisoners' rights. [2] Or, by the same token, when was the use of force appropriate from the officers? [3] There is a clear provision in the Constitution that prohibits "cruel and unusual punishment." [4] The meaning of these four words **5** were nowhere more ambiguous than in prisons. [5] Everyone within these walls had been convicted of a crime and was now paying **6** they're debt to society, but how could a government ensure that the place would deliver the "reform" in a reformatory or the "penitence" in a penitentiary?

3

Which of the following true statements contains information most in keeping with the main idea of this passage?

A) NO CHANGE

B) who had gone on to law school and now worked at the County Department of Corrections.

C) with whom he had not spoken in twenty-five years, though with whom he still felt very close.

D) DELETE the underlined portion.

4

Which of the following best concludes this paragraph by reinforcing ideas presented in this sentence and the preceding one?

A) NO CHANGE

B) people often know literally nothing about prison life, though they are endlessly fascinated.

C) movie studios are famous for their sordid but often wrong depictions of prison life.

D) incarceration rates in the United States are some of the highest in the world.

5

A) NO CHANGE

B) have been

C) are

D) is

6

A) NO CHANGE

B) their

C) there

D) his or her

CONTINUE

[6] Should inmates with, for example, mental illnesses be treated differently from others? **7**

While Amanda did not gain any answers from her summer at the Department of Corrections, she **8** gathered together a whole new set of questions. She had uncovered questions and conundrums about the prison system itself, but she had begun to see prisoners' rights as central to the question of free rights as well. She began to wonder exactly what it was that a government owed its people and how much freedom was too much. Her internship that summer made her realize that politics and the law **9** was a living thing. As she applied to law schools the following fall, Amanda wrote passionately about what she had uncovered. "Although law has long

7

In the sequence of the paragraph, the best placement for sentence 2 would be

A) where it is now.

B) before sentence 1.

C) after sentence 3.

D) after sentence 6.

8

A) NO CHANGE

B) gathered up

C) collected up

D) gathered

9

A) NO CHANGE

B) were living things.

C) was a thing that was alive.

D) were things that were living.

CONTINUE

been considered a profession of privilege and prestige," she concluded her essay, "I have seen firsthand how it affects the lives of all of us. We may believe that we never come into contact with the **10** law; however, it is written into everything around us, including how we see ourselves." **11**

10

A) NO CHANGE

B) law, however

C) law, however;

D) law, however,

11

At this point, the writer is considering adding the following sentence.

> Amanda was accepted into three law schools and chose the one with the strongest coursework on the prison system.

Should the writer make this addition here?

A) Yes, because it explains how students can use their interests to choose the right school.

B) Yes, because it reveals the conclusion to a dilemma mentioned earlier in the paragraph.

C) No, because it distracts from the passage's focus on how an experience can affect one's view of the world.

D) No, because it does not indicate whether Amanda actually graduated from law school and became a lawyer.

CONTINUE ➡

Questions 12–22 are based on the following passage and supplementary material.

Alexander's Empire of Culture

Alexander the Great is a name known to all, but not all know the extent of Alexander's accomplishments. Now that the study of the "classics" (mainly Roman and Greek civilizations) has **12** disappeared both from high-school and college curricula, Alexander the Great's legend is not on the tongue of every schoolboy, though his accomplishments have not **13** diminished for all that.

Alexander was born in Pella, Macedonia, in 356 BCE. His father, King Philip II, a strong military king **14** in his own write, believed that his son was born part man and part god. Alexander came to cultivate the image himself, bolstered by his keen intellect and learning, quickened in part by his tutor, the great Greek philosopher Aristotle. Pella was at that time a backwater of Greek culture, and **15** his arrival announced a new era of what historians would later call "enlightened monarchy," **16** even though that term is used much more to describe monarchies in the eighteenth century.

12

A) NO CHANGE
B) disappeared from both
C) disappeared both
D) from both disappeared

13

A) NO CHANGE
B) ameliorated
C) gone down
D) subsided

14

A) NO CHANGE
B) in his own right,
C) in his own rite,
D) by his own rite,

15

A) NO CHANGE
B) Aristotle's
C) their
D) the

16

Which of the following true statements would best conclude the paragraph by emphasizing the change that Alexander's rule brought to Macedonia?

A) NO CHANGE
B) although those who suffered defeat at Alexander's hands might not have seen it that way.
C) suggesting a style for the reigns of both Julius Caesar and Napoleon Bonaparte.
D) underlining further that Philip's former militaristic state was entering a new age.

CONTINUE

Still, the age was not entirely new. Alexander spent nearly all his time abroad, first uniting the Greek kingdom that threatened to fall apart at Philip's death, then moving on to broader military conquests. **17** Alexander had conquered an incredible amount of land by the time of his death in 323 BCE, **18** as his empire stretched from Greece to modern-day India, some two million square miles. When his armies conquered Persia (now Iran and Iraq) once and for all, he took on the title by which he is still known today: King of Babylon, King of Asia, King of the Four Quarters of the World.

17

The author wants to insert an introductory phrase or clause at the beginning of this sentence that will emphasize the continuity Alexander's reign had with the previous one. Which of the following choices would most effectively give this emphasis?

A) In what must have been truly exhausting,

B) With great ambition,

C) As his father had before him,

D) Just as historians have noted,

18

Which of the following choices gives information consistent with the map shown below?

A) NO CHANGE

B) while he traveled on foot throughout most of modern-day Europe,

C) because he circled the entire Mediterranean Sea and much of the Indian Ocean,

D) as he conquered all of Italy hundreds of years before Caesar had done so,

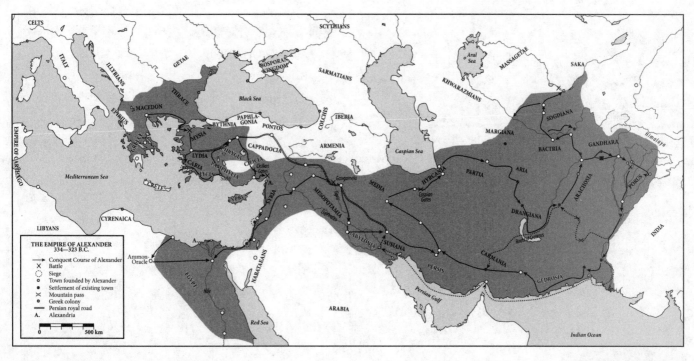

Extent of the empire of Alexander the Great

CONTINUE

Alexander's historical importance is not merely one of military might, however. **19** He moved to these different parts of the world, he brought Greek culture with him. His reign marks an unprecedented **20** instance of contact, between the ancient East and West. Over twenty cities throughout the empire bear his name. Alexandria, Egypt, perhaps the most famous of these cities, continues to **21** thrive. It is the second-largest city in the modern nation of Egypt.

Perhaps history is the wrong place to understand the accomplishments of Alexander the Great. Epic poetry seems more suitable. After all, Alexander's great teacher Aristotle showed him Homer's *Iliad* and *Odyssey*, and it seems that Alexander himself understood his life as a shuttling back and forth between man and god, the individual and the world, and the natural **22** and the unnatural.

19
A) NO CHANGE
B) As he
C) Although he
D) Moreover, he

20
A) NO CHANGE
B) instance, of contact, between the ancient East
C) instance of contact between the ancient East
D) instance of contact between the ancient East,

21
Which of the following is the most effective way to combine these two sentences?
A) thrive; it is
B) thrive, is
C) thrive. It's
D) thrive and is

22
A) NO CHANGE
B) versus
C) from
D) but

CONTINUE ➡

Questions 23–33 are based on the following passage.

Brother, Can You Spare a Dime?

Although printed cheaply and for quick consumption, **23** today's experience of culture is largely shaped by dime novels. For much of the nineteenth century, Americans consumed fiction, poetry, and non-fiction by way of literary periodicals. Some of our best-known authors from this period, **24** though there were also some notable exceptions, published something close to their complete works between the pages of countless periodicals.

23

A) NO CHANGE

B) we experience culture the way we do because of dime novels.

C) dime novels have shaped the way we experience culture today.

D) the shape of dime novels influences of cultural experiences.

24

Which of the following true phrases gives the most specific information in the context?

A) NO CHANGE

B) some of the best-known authors of all time,

C) and some who were not so well-known,

D) especially Edgar Allan Poe and Nathaniel Hawthorne,

CONTINUE

Things started to change around the Civil War. Harriet Beecher Stowe's great [25] novel, *Uncle Tom's Cabin* had been an enormously popular serial novel in the abolitionist periodical *The National Era*. By the time the novel's forty-week run had concluded, however, publishers were clamoring for an actual [26] book. That book went on to become the first American bestseller. And it showed that Americans were willing to pay for books, which had, to that point, been too expensive to print and subsequently to buy. [27]

[25]

A) NO CHANGE
B) novel, *Uncle Tom's Cabin*,
C) novel *Uncle Tom's Cabin*,
D) novel *Uncle Tom's Cabin*

[26]

A) NO CHANGE
B) book, rather than a series from a magazine.
C) book written by Stowe.
D) book that could be sold to Americans.

[27]

At this point, the writer is considering adding the following true statement:

> The average annual income for men in New England from 1820–1850 was a mere $323.25.

Should the writer make this addition here?

A) Yes, because it makes clear how expensive books must have been in the period.
B) Yes, because it shows that even those in New England could not afford books printed there.
C) No, because it strays from the paragraph's focus on the changes in book publishing.
D) No, because it suggests that people in New England were not wealthy enough to read.

CONTINUE

In 1860, Irwin and Erastus Beadle published the first in a long series of what **28** would become known as Beadle's Dime Novels. The first was called *Malaeska, The Indian Wife of the White Hunter*. By the turn of the nineteenth century, dime novels were everywhere.

The **29** affects are difficult to chart, but we can actually see the influence of these dime novels everywhere. Much of the mythology of the Old West, for example, was concretized in these dime novels, and William Bonney and James Butler Hickok became the folk heroes Billy the Kid and Wild Bill Hickok as the dime novels charted their (largely imagined) adventures. **30**

28

A) NO CHANGE

B) becomes

C) is

D) would have become

29

A) NO CHANGE

B) effects

C) effect's

D) affect's

30

The author is considering deleting the names "Billy the Kid and Wild Bill Hickok" from the preceding sentence. Should the names be kept or deleted?

A) Kept, because they are specific names in a sentence that speaks in generalities.

B) Kept, because they demonstrate the transformation described in the sentence.

C) Deleted, because they are nicknames of people whose true names are already listed in the sentence.

D) Deleted, because they encourage the frontier behavior that made the Wild West such a violent place.

CONTINUE

The new media of the twentieth-century—film, radio, and comic books—may have replaced the dime novel, but they did so with much they had **31** been taught from the dime novel's popularity. All three media, for instance, borrowed characters that had become popular in dime novels—characters such as Frank Reade and Nick Carter, Master Detective. Then, in comic books and radio, a new generation of superheroes—The Shadow, Superman, and Popeye—was created in the mold of the old swashbuckling romanciers of the dime-novel era.

So today, as we enjoy superhero action films or boy-wizard series of novels, we should be aware that there is nothing new under the Sun. Indeed, **32** for our hopelessly mass-media universe, this now forgotten form laid the foundation, pushing the same books onto countless readers. Such a feat may be commonplace as films gross many billions of dollars at the box office, but in the nineteenth century, the dime novel brought a new **33** integration and a belief that the small world was getting larger bit by bit.

31

A) NO CHANGE
B) got
C) learned
D) brought

32

If the punctuation is adjusted accordingly, the best placement for the underlined portion would be

A) where it is now.
B) after the word *form*.
C) after the word *foundation*.
D) at the end of the sentence.

33

A) NO CHANGE
B) framework
C) plan
D) composition

CONTINUE

Questions 34–44 are based on the following passage and supplementary material.

The Tiger Moth's Phantom Target

— 1 —

Bats have always seemed mysterious predators. While many other animal predators use methods **34** similar to human hunters, bats have evolved a series of unique methods of capturing prey. **35** The main curiosity among the bat's weaponry is its use of echolocation, or sonar.

— 2 —

Because bats hunt in the dark, they are not often able to see their prey. Instead, they use a process wherein they emit sounds and listen for the echoes. If **36** they are, say, standing atop a mountain and shout, you can figure out the distance across the canyon using the speed of sound waves and a series of precise calculations. Using its innate senses, a bat does these same **37** calculations instinctively. With extreme precision, a bat can identify its prey's location and size in the dark and capture its prey. While a bat does have relatively acute vision, **38** though not nearly as acute as some species of shrimp, its echolocation is what makes it such an effective predator.

34

A) NO CHANGE
B) similar to that of human hunters,
C) similar to those of human hunters,
D) like human hunters,

35

A) NO CHANGE
B) The echolocation, sonar, of the bat's weaponry is its main curiosity.
C) The bat has a curious weaponry, main among which is its echolocation and sonar.
D) The bat's weaponry is mainly curious in its use of echolocation of sonar.

36

A) NO CHANGE
B) they're,
C) one is,
D) you are,

37

A) NO CHANGE
B) calculations by instinct.
C) calculations with its instincts.
D) calculations.

38

The writer intends to insert a phrase or clause that emphasizes a common misunderstanding about bats' vision. Which of the following would best suit that intention?

A) NO CHANGE
B) undermining the cliché "blind as a bat,"
C) despite the pitch darkness in which it hunts,
D) in addition to its incredible hearing,

CONTINUE

— 3 —

However, scientists have recently discovered a species that can disrupt the bat's usually failsafe echolocation. The tiger moth, a victim of bat predation for over 50 million years, has figured out a way to "jam" **39** its system of echolocation. Most tiger moths can emit clicks that warn bats away from the **40** moths; suggesting that the moths might be inedible toxic compounds.

— 4 —

In the long history of bat research, scientists have never seen the like of these tiger moths. Although human methods of warfare have used sonic deception for as long as such warfare has existed, the tiger moth and **41** their sonar jamming provide one of the first instances of aural camouflage in the animal kingdom that scientists have discovered. It seems that no matter how ancient the conflict, bats and tiger moths continue to attack, **42** counterattack, and adapt in a war as old as time.

39

A) NO CHANGE
B) the bats'
C) the bat's
D) the bats

40

A) NO CHANGE
B) moths, suggesting
C) moths suggesting
D) moths. Suggesting

41

A) NO CHANGE
B) it's
C) its
D) its'

42

A) NO CHANGE
B) counterattack, and, adapt
C) counterattack and adapt
D) counterattack and adapt,

CONTINUE

— 5 —

One species, the tiger moth *Bertholdia trigona*, has done even better. This species emits a high-frequency clicking noise that throws off the bat's sonar altogether. While no one is certain exactly how these clicks camouflage the *B. trigona*, the clicks have been remarkably successful in defending the moths from bat attacks. Some suggest that the clicks force bats to misinterpret their sensory data, taking the moth clicks for their own echoes. As a result, bats **43** miss their prey at the moment of attempted capture, and the tiger moths flit away unharmed. **44**

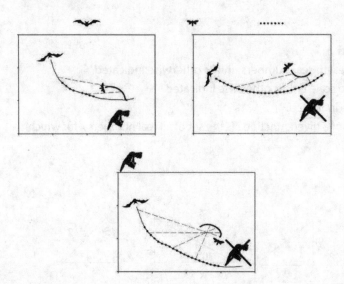

This image is adapted from the *Journal of Experimental Biology* © 2011.

43

Which of the following provides accurate information based on the diagrams?

A) NO CHANGE

B) attack other animals they find easier to detect,

C) fly after one another, bonking their heads together,

D) hear no sounds at all,

44

In the context of the passage as a whole, the best placement for paragraph 5 would be

A) where it is now.

B) after paragraph 1.

C) after paragraph 2.

D) after paragraph 3.

STOP
**If you finish before time is called, you may check your work on this section only.
Do not turn to any other section in the test.**

Math Test – No Calculator

25 MINUTES, 20 QUESTIONS

Turn to Section 3 of your answer sheet to answer the questions in this section.

DIRECTIONS

For questions 1–15, solve each problem, choose the best answer from the choices provided, and fill in the corresponding circle on your answer sheet. **For questions 16–20,** solve the problem and enter your answer in the grid on the answer sheet. Please refer to the directions before question 16 on how to enter your answers in the grid. You may use any available space in your test booklet for scratch work.

NOTES

1. The use of a calculator **is not permitted**.
2. All variables and expressions used represent real numbers unless otherwise indicated.
3. Figures provided in this test are drawn to scale unless otherwise indicated.
4. All figures lie in a plane unless otherwise indicated.
5. Unless otherwise indicated, the domain of a given function f is the set of all real numbers x for which $f(x)$ is a real number.

REFERENCE

$A = \pi r^2$
$C = 2\pi r$

$A = \ell w$

$A = \frac{1}{2} bh$

$c^2 = a^2 + b^2$

Special Right Triangles

$V = \ell wh$

$V = \pi r^2 h$

$V = \frac{4}{3} \pi r^3$

$V = \frac{1}{3} \pi r^2 h$

$V = \frac{1}{3} \ell wh$

The number of degrees of arc in a circle is 360.
The number of radians of arc in a circle is 2π.
The sum of the measures in degrees of the angles of a triangle is 180.

CONTINUE

1

Which of the following equations has a vertex of (3, –3) ?

A) $y = 5(x - 3)^2 - 3$

B) $y = 5(x + 3)^2 - 3$

C) $y = 5(x - 3)^2 + 3$

D) $y = 5(x + 3)^2 + 3$

2

A beverage store charges a base price of x dollars for one keg of root beer. A sales tax of a certain percentage is applied to the base price, and an untaxed deposit for the keg is added. If the total amount, in dollars, paid at the time of purchase for one keg is given by the expression $1.07x + 17$, then what is the sales tax, expressed as a percentage of the base price?

A)   0.07%

B)   1.07%

C)   7%

D) 17%

3

Syed took out a cash advance of d dollars from a financing company. The company deducts a fee of $\frac{1}{3}$ of the original advanced amount along with a wire transfer fee of $30.00. Which of the following represents the final advanced amount that Syed receives after all applied fees, in dollars?

A) $\frac{1}{3}d - 30$

B) $\frac{1}{3}(d - 30)$

C) $\frac{2}{3}(d - 30)$

D) $\frac{2}{3}d - 30$

4

What is the equation of a line that contains the point (1, 6) and has a y-intercept of 4 ?

A) $y = \frac{1}{2}x + 4$

B) $y = x + 4$

C) $y = 2x + 4$

D) $y = 4x + 2$

CONTINUE

5

The number of bonus points, $B(p)$, that a credit card holder receives is given by the function $B(p) = 4p + 7$, where p represents the number of purchases made. If the number of purchases is increased by 3, by how much does the number of bonus points increase?

A) 3

B) 4

C) 12

D) 19

6

Jeff tests how the total volume occupied by a fluid contained in a graduated cylinder changes when round marbles of various sizes are added. He found that the total volume occupied by the fluid, V, in cubic centimeters, can be found using the equation below, where x equals the number of identical marbles Jeff added, one at a time, to the cylinder, and r is the radius of one of the marbles.

$$V = 24\pi + x\left(\frac{4}{3}\pi r^3\right)$$

If the volume of the graduated cylinder is 96π cubic centimeters, then, what is the maximum number of marbles with a radius of 3 centimeters that Jeff can add without the volume of the fluid exceeding that of the graduated cylinder?

A) 1

B) 2

C) 3

D) 4

7

If b is two more than one-third of c, which of the following expresses the value of c in terms of b ?

A) $c = \dfrac{b - 2}{3}$

B) $c = \dfrac{b + 2}{3}$

C) $c = 3(b - 2)$

D) $c = 3(b - 6)$

8

The rotation rate of a mixing blade, in rotations per second, slows as a liquid is being added to the mixer. The blade rotates at 1,000 rotations per second when the mixer is empty. The rate at which the blade slows is four rotations per second less than three times the square of the height of the liquid. If h is the height of liquid in the mixer, which of the following represents $R(h)$, the rate of rotation?

A) $4 - 9h^2$

B) $1,000 - (4 - 3h)$

C) $1,000 - (9h - 4)$

D) $1,000 - (3h^2 - 4)$

CONTINUE

9

A dental hygiene company is creating a new 24-ounce tube of toothpaste by combining its most popular toothpastes, Cavity Crusher and Bad Breath Obliterator. Cavity Crusher contains 0.25% of sodium fluoride as its active ingredient, and Bad Breath Obliterator contains 0.30% of triclosan as its active ingredient for a total of 0.069 ounces of active ingredients in both toothpastes. Solving which of the following systems of equations yields the number of ounces of Cavity Crusher, c, and the number of ounces of Bad Breath Obliterator, b, that are in the new toothpaste?

A)
$$c + b = 0.069$$
$$0.25c + 0.3b = 24$$

B)
$$c + b = 24$$
$$0.0025c + 0.003b = 0.069$$

C)
$$c + b = 24$$
$$0.025c + 0.03b = 0.069$$

D)
$$c + b = 24$$
$$0.25c + 0.3b = 0.069$$

10

$$\frac{2d^2 - d - 10}{d^2 + 7d + 10} = \frac{d^2 - 4d + 3}{d^2 + 2d - 15}$$

In the equation above, what is the value of d ?

A) −4

B) 2

C) 4

D) 6

11

Which of the following is a possible equation for a circle that is tangent to both the x-axis and the line $x = 4$?

A) $(x + 2)^2 + (y + 2)^2 = 4$

B) $(x + 2)^2 + (y - 2)^2 = 4$

C) $(x - 2)^2 + (y + 4)^2 = 4$

D) $(x - 6)^2 + (y - 2)^2 = 4$

CONTINUE

12

Reactant A is placed in a beaker, to which Reactant B will be added. Reactants A and B will not react unless B gets to a certain concentration. Once the reaction starts, both concentrations decrease until B has been consumed. Which of the following graphs, showing concentration in moles as a function of time in seconds, represents the reaction?

A)

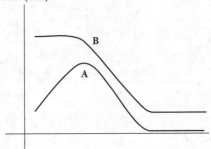

B)

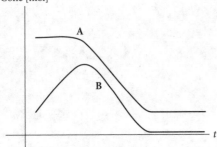

C)

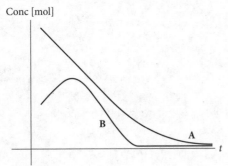

D)

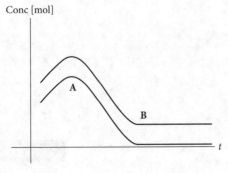

13

$$-2y \leq 8$$
$$y - 3 \leq x$$
$$-\frac{1}{3}y + 1 \geq x$$

Which of the following graphs shows the solution to the system of inequalities above?

A)

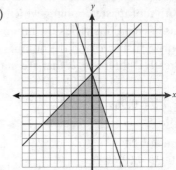

B)

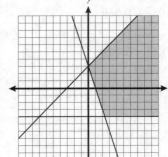

C)

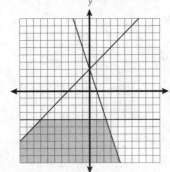

D)

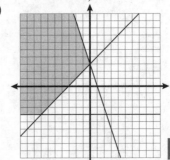

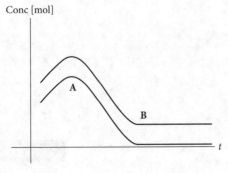

14

If rectangle *ABCD* has an area of 48 and the tangent

of ∠*BCA* (not shown) is $\dfrac{3}{4}$, then which of the

following is the length of $\overline{BD}$ (not shown)?

A)   5

B)   10

C)   13

D)   It cannot be determined from the given information.

15

Which of the following is equivalent to

$$\frac{2m + 6}{4} \times \frac{6m - 36}{3m + 9} ?$$

A) $\dfrac{12m^2 - 216}{12m + 36}$

B) $\dfrac{8m - 30}{3m + 13}$

C) $\dfrac{m - 6}{4}$

D) $m - 6$

CONTINUE

DIRECTIONS

For questions 16–20, solve the problem and enter your answer in the grid, as described below, on the answer sheet.

1. Although not required, it is suggested that you write your answer in the boxes at the top of the columns to help you fill in the circles accurately. You will receive credit only if the circles are filled in correctly.

2. Mark no more than one circle in any column.

3. No question has a negative answer.

4. Some problems may have more than one correct answer. In such cases, grid only one answer.

5. **Mixed numbers** such as $3\frac{1}{2}$ must be gridded as 3.5 or 7/2. (If [3 1 / 2] is entered into the grid, it will be interpreted as $\frac{31}{2}$, not as $3\frac{1}{2}$.)

6. **Decimal Answers:** If you obtain a decimal answer with more digits than the grid can accommodate, it may be either rounded or truncated, but it must fill the entire grid.

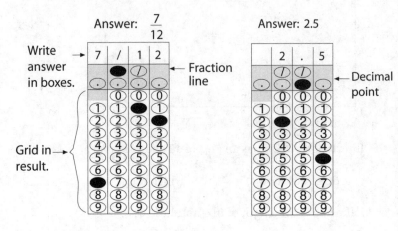

NOTE: You may start your answers in any column, space permitting. Columns you don't need to use should be left blank.

CONTINUE →

16

A rectangular box has sides 3, 4, and x and a volume of 18. What is the value of x?

17

Jeanne babysits Chuy one day each week. Jeanne charges a $20 fee for the day, plus $5.50 for every 30 minutes of babysitting. How much has Jeanne earned after three hours of babysitting? (Disregard the $ sign when gridding your answer.)

18

The parabola $y = -x^2 + 5x + 6$ is intersected by the line $y = -\dfrac{1}{2}x + 12$. What is the y-coordinate of the intersection closest to the x-axis?

CONTINUE

19

$$13r + 8v = 47$$
$$22v = 63 - 17r$$

Based on the system of equations above, what is the sum of r and v ?

20

A gardener has a cultivated plot that measures 4 feet by 6 feet. Next year, she wants to double the area of her plot by increasing the length and width by x feet. What is the value of x ?

STOP
If you finish before time is called, you may check your work on this section only.
Do not turn to any other section in the test.

No Test Material On This Page

CONTINUE

Math Test – Calculator

55 MINUTES, 38 QUESTIONS

Turn to Section 4 of your answer sheet to answer the questions in this section.

DIRECTIONS

For questions 1–30, solve each problem, choose the best answer from the choices provided, and fill in the corresponding circle on your answer sheet. **For questions 31–38**, solve the problem and enter your answer in the grid on the answer sheet. Please refer to the directions before question 31 on how to enter your answers in the grid. You may use any available space in your test booklet for scratch work.

NOTES

1. The use of a calculator **is permitted**.
2. All variables and expressions used represent real numbers unless otherwise indicated.
3. Figures provided in this test are drawn to scale unless otherwise indicated.
4. All figures lie in a plane unless otherwise indicated.
5. Unless otherwise indicated, the domain of a given function f is the set of all real numbers x for which $f(x)$ is a real number.

REFERENCE

$A = \pi r^2$
$C = 2\pi r$

$A = \ell w$

$A = \frac{1}{2} bh$

$c^2 = a^2 + b^2$

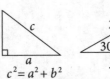
Special Right Triangles

$V = \ell wh$

$V = \pi r^2 h$

$V = \frac{4}{3}\pi r^3$

$V = \frac{1}{3}\pi r^2 h$

$V = \frac{1}{3}\ell wh$

The number of degrees of arc in a circle is 360.
The number of radians of arc in a circle is 2π.
The sum of the measures in degrees of the angles of a triangle is 180.

CONTINUE

1

The population, P, of Town Y since 1995 can be estimated by the equation $P = 1.0635x + 3{,}250$, where x is the number of years since 1995 and $0 \le x \le 20$. In the context of this equation, what does the number 1.0635 most likely represent?

A) The estimated population of town Y in 1995

B) The estimated population of town Y in 2015

C) The factor by which the population of town Y increased yearly

D) The factor by which the population of town Y decreased yearly

2

If $x^2 + 12x = 64$ and $x > 0$, what is the value of x ?

A) 2

B) 4

C) 8

D) 16

3

Sai is ordering new shelving units for his store. Each unit is 7 feet in length and extends from floor to ceiling. The total length of the walls in Sai's store is 119 feet, which includes a length of 21 feet of windows along the walls. If the shelving units cannot be placed in front of the windows, which of the following inequalities includes all possible values of r, the number of shelving units that Sai could use?

A) $r \le \dfrac{119 - 21}{7}$

B) $r \le \dfrac{119 + 21}{7}$

C) $r \le 119 - 21 + 7r$

D) $r \ge 119 + 21 - 7r$

CONTINUE

Truffula Tree Fruit Weight

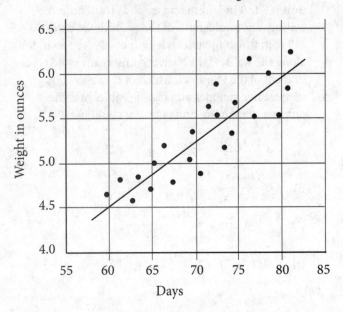

The scatterplot above shows the weight, in ounces, of the fruits on a certain truffula tree from days 55 to 85 after flowering. According to the line of best fit in the scatterplot above, which of the following is the closest approximation of the number of days after flowering of a truffula fruit that weighs 5.75 ounces?

A) 63

B) 65

C) 77

D) 81

Hannah placed an online order for shirts that cost $24.50 per shirt. A tax of 7% is added to the cost of the shirts, before a flat, untaxed shipping rate of $6 is charged. Which of the following represents Hannah's total cost for s shirts, in dollars?

A) $0.07(24.50s + 6)$

B) $1.07(24.50 + 6)s$

C) $1.07(24.50s) + 6$

D) $1.07(24.50 + s) + 6$

Once a certain plant begins to grow, its height increases at a linear rate. After six weeks, the plant is 54 centimeters tall. Which of the following functions best models the relationship between $h(w)$, the height, in centimeters, of the plant, and w, the number of weeks that the plant has been growing?

A) $h(w) = 6w$

B) $h(w) = 9w$

C) $h(w) = 54w$

D) $h(w) = 54 + w$

CONTINUE

7

Which of the following is equivalent to $(12x^2 + 4x + 5y) + (3x^2 - 2x + 3y)$?

A) $2x^2 - 2x + 8y$

B) $2x^2 + 15x + 8y$

C) $15x^2 - 2x + 8y$

D) $15x^2 + 2x + 8y$

8

An advertisement for Royal Rat Rations states: "7 out of 8 veterinarians recommend Royal Rat Rations for your fancy rat." No other information about the data is provided by the company.

Based on this data, which of the following inferences is most valid?

A) Royal Rat Rations provides the best nutrition for fancy rats.

B) If you do not feed your rat Royal Rat Rations, your rat will be unhealthy.

C) Only one veterinarian does not recommend Royal Rat Rations for your fancy rat.

D) Of the veterinarians surveyed by Royal Rat Rations, the majority recommend Royal Rat Rations for your fancy rat.

9

$$\frac{1}{2}t + 4 = \frac{3}{4}t - 5$$

In the equation above, what is the value of t ?

A) 4

B) 9

C) 18

D) 36

10

Dogs need 8.5 to 17 ounces of water each day for every 10 pounds of their weight. Everett has two dogs—Ringo is a 35-pound black lab mix, and Elvis is a 55-pound beagle. Which of the following ranges represents the approximate total number of ounces of water, w, that Elvis and Ringo need in a week?

A) $77 \leq w \leq 153$

B) $109 \leq w \leq 218$

C) $536 \leq w \leq 1{,}071$

D) $765 \leq w \leq 1{,}530$

CONTINUE

11

Priya is planning to send her favorite dry rub recipe to a friend who lives in France. Before sending the recipe, Priya wants to convert the American customary units in the instructions into metric units so that her friend will easily be able to understand the measurements. If the recipe calls for a ratio of four ounces of paprika to every seven ounces of chili powder, and if Priya's friend is planning to make a large batch of dry rub with 91 total ounces of chili powder, approximately how many total grams of paprika and chili powder will the recipe require? (1 ounce = 28.3 grams)

A) 4,047 grams

B) 4,521 grams

C) 4,925 grams

D) 5,149 grams

12

Luciano measured the amount of water that evaporated over a period of time from a container holding w ounces of water, where w is greater than 12. By the end of the first day, the cup had lost 2 ounces of water. By the end of the 7th day, the cup had lost an additional 8 ounces of water. By the end of the 11th day, the cup had lost half of the water that remained after the 7th day. Which of the following represents the remaining amount of water, in ounces, in Luciano's container at the end of the 11th day?

A) $\dfrac{w-2}{8}$

B) $\dfrac{w-2}{2} - 10$

C) $\dfrac{1}{2}w - 10$

D) $\dfrac{w-10}{2}$

CONTINUE

Questions 13 and 14 refer to the following information.

In the 1990s, the park rangers at Yellowstone National Park implemented a program aimed at increasing the dwindling coyote population in Montana. Results of studies of the coyote population in the park are shown in the scatterplot below.

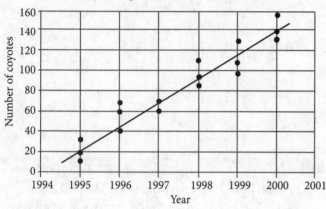

Coyote Population in Yellowstone Park

13

Based on the line of best fit in the scatterplot above, which of the following is the closest to the average annual increase in coyotes in Yellowstone Park between 1995 and 2000 ?

A) 22

B) 24

C) 26

D) 28

14

According to the data in the scatterplot, which of the following best represents the percent increase between the median of the results of the studies from 1995 and the median of the results of the studies from 1996 ?

A) 50%

B) 100%

C) 150%

D) 200%

CONTINUE

15

Bailey's Boutique Clothing is having a 20% off sale during which shirts cost $30.00 and pants cost $60.00. On the day of the sale, Bailey's sells a total of 60 shirts and pants and earned a total of $2,250. On a regular day, Bailey's sells $\frac{2}{3}$ the number of shirts and pants sold during the sale and earns a total of $1,875. Solving which of the following systems of equations yields the number of shirts, s, and the number of pants, p, sold during a regular day?

A) $s + p = 40$
       $37.5s + 75p = 1,875$

B) $s + p = 40$
       $30s + 60p = 2,250$

C) $s + p = 60$
       $30s + 60p = 2,250$

D) $s + p = 2,250$
       $30s + 60p = 60$

16

Bryan, who works in a high-end jewelry store, earns a base pay of $10.00 per hour plus a certain percent commission on the sales that he helps to broker in the store. Bryan worked an average of 35 hours per week over the past two weeks and helped to broker sales of $5,000.00 worth of jewelry during that same two-week period. If Bryan's earnings for the two-week period were $850.00, what percent commission on sales does Bryan earn?

A) 1%

B) 2%

C) 3%

D) 4%

17

If $\dfrac{(C+x)}{x-3} = \dfrac{x+8}{3}$, which of the following could be an expression of C in terms of x ?

A) $3(1 + x)$

B) $x^2 + 2x - 24$

C) $\dfrac{1}{3}(x+6)(x-4)$

D) $\dfrac{1}{3}(x-3)(x+8)$

18

Lennon has 6 hours to spend in Ha Ha Tonka State Park. He plans to drive around the park at an average speed of 20 miles per hour, looking for a good trail to hike. Once he finds a trail he likes, he will spend the remainder of his time hiking it. He hopes to travel more than 60 miles total while in the park. If he hikes at an average speed of 1.5 miles per hour, which of the following systems of inequalities can be solved for the number of hours Lennon spends driving, d, and the number of hours he spends hiking, h, while he is at the park?

A) $1.5h + 20d > 60$
       $h + d \leq 6$

B) $1.5h + 20d > 60$
       $h + d \geq 6$

C) $1.5h + 20d < 60$
       $h + d \geq 360$

D) $20h + 1.5d > 6$
       $h + d \leq 60$

CONTINUE

19

In a certain sporting goods manufacturing company, a quality control expert tests a randomly selected group of 1,000 tennis balls in order to determine how many contain defects. If this quality control expert discovered that 13 of the randomly selected tennis balls were defective, which of the following inferences would be most supported?

A) 98.7% of the company's tennis balls are defective.

B) 98.7% of the company's tennis balls are not defective.

C) 9.87% of the company's tennis balls are defective.

D) 9.87% of the company's tennis balls are not defective.

20

If $-\dfrac{20}{7} < -3z + 6 < -\dfrac{11}{5}$, what is the greatest possible integer value of $9z - 18$?

A) 6

B) 7

C) 8

D) 9

21

$$-24 - 8j = 12k$$
$$3 + \frac{5}{3}k = -\frac{7}{6}j$$

Which of the following ordered pairs (j, k) is the solution to the system of equations above?

A) $(6, -6)$

B) $(3, 0)$

C) $(0, 2)$

D) $(-4, 1)$

CONTINUE

22

United States Investment in
Alternative Energy Sources

	Actual 2007 Investment	Projected 2017 Investment
Biofuels	0.31	0.34
Wind	0.40	0.32
Solar	0.27	0.30
Fuel Cells	0.02	0.04
Total	1.00	1.00

The table above shows the relative investment in alternative energy sources in the United States by type. One column shows the relative investment in 2007 of $75 million total invested in alternative energy. The other column shows the projected relative investment in 2017 given current trends. The total projected investment in alternative energy in 2017 is $254 million. Suppose that a new source of alternative energy, Cold Fusion, is perfected. It is projected that by 2017 that $57 million will be invested in Cold Fusion in the United States, without any corresponding reduction in investment for any other form of alternative energy. What portion of the total investment of alternative energy in the United States will be spent on biofuels?

A) 0.18

B) 0.22

C) 0.28

D) 0.34

23

$$(x - 2)^2 + y^2 = 36$$
$$y = -x + 2$$

The equations above represent a circle and a line that intersects the circle across its diameter. What is the point of intersection of the two equations that lies in Quadrant II ?

A) $\left(-3\sqrt{2}, 3\sqrt{2}\right)$

B) $(-4, 2)$

C) $\left(2 + \sqrt{3}, 2\right)$

D) $\left(2 - 3\sqrt{2}, 3\sqrt{2}\right)$

CONTINUE

24

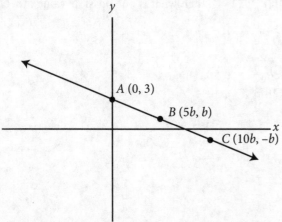

The graph of $f(x)$ is shown above in the xy-plane. The points $(0, 3)$, $(5b, b)$, and $(10b, -b)$ are on the line described by $f(x)$. If b is a positive constant, what are the coordinates of point C ?

A) $(5, 1)$

B) $(10, -1)$

C) $(15, -0.5)$

D) $(20, -2)$

25

Melanie puts $1,100 in an investment account that she expects will make 5% interest for each three-month period. However, after a year she realizes she was wrong about the interest rate and she has $50 less than she expected. Assuming the interest rate the account earns is constant, which of the following equations expresses the total amount of money, x, she will have after t years using the actual rate?

A) $x = 1,100(1.04)^{4t}$

B) $x = 1,100(1.05)^{4t-50}$

C) $x = 1,100(1.04)^{t/3}$

D) $x = 1,100(1.035)^{4t}$

26

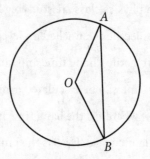

If the radius of the circle above is x, $\angle AOB = 120°$, and O is the center of the circle, what is the length of chord AB, in terms of x ?

A) $\sqrt{2}x$

B) $\sqrt{3}x$

C) $\dfrac{x}{\sqrt{2}}$

D) $\dfrac{x}{\sqrt{3}}$

CONTINUE

27

Students in a physics class are studying how the angle at which a projectile is launched on level ground affects the projectile's hang time and horizontal range. Hang time can be calculated using the formula $t = \dfrac{2v \cdot \sin(\theta)}{g}$, where t is the hang time in seconds, v is the initial launch velocity, θ is the projectile angle with respect to level ground, and g is the acceleration due to gravity, defined as 9.8 m/s². Horizontal range can be calculated using the formula $R = \dfrac{v^2 \sin(2\theta)}{g}$, where R is the distance the projectile travels from the launch site, in feet. Which of the following gives the value of v, in terms of R, t, and θ?

A) $v = \dfrac{t \sin(\theta)}{2R \sin(\theta)}$

B) $v = \dfrac{2t \sin(\theta)}{R \sin(\theta)}$

C) $v = \dfrac{2R \sin(\theta)}{t \sin(2\theta)}$

D) $v = \dfrac{2R \sin(2\theta)}{t \sin(\theta)}$

28

If $(i^{413})(i^x) = 1$, then what is one possible value of x?

A) 0

B) 1

C) 2

D) 3

CONTINUE

29

The function g is defined by $g(x) = 2x^2 - dx - 6$, where d is a constant. If one of the zeros of g is 6, what is the value of the other zero of g ?

A) 2

B) $\dfrac{1}{2}$

C) $-\dfrac{1}{2}$

D) -2

30

The flu shot for a flu season is created from four strains of the flu virus, named Strain A, B, C, and D, respectively. Medical researchers use the following data to determine the effectiveness of the vaccine over the flu season. Table 1 shows the effectiveness of the vaccine against each of these strains individually. The graph below the table shows the prevalence of each of these strains during each month of the flu season, represented as a percentage of the overall cases of flu that month.

Table 1

Strain	Effectiveness
A	35%
B	13%
C	76%
D	68%

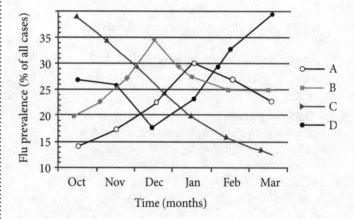

For the strain against which the flu shot was the most effective, approximately how effective was the shot overall during the month that strain was least prevalent?

A) 13%

B) 20%

C) 27%

D) 48%

CONTINUE

DIRECTIONS

For questions 31–38, solve the problem and enter your answer in the grid, as described below, on the answer sheet.

1. Although not required, it is suggested that you write your answer in the boxes at the top of the columns to help you fill in the circles accurately. You will receive credit only if the circles are filled in correctly.

2. Mark no more than one circle in any column.

3. No question has a negative answer.

4. Some problems may have more than one correct answer. In such cases, grid only one answer.

5. **Mixed numbers** such as $3\frac{1}{2}$ must be gridded as 3.5 or 7/2. (If $\boxed{3\,1\,/\,2}$ is entered into the grid, it will be interpreted as $\frac{31}{2}$, not as $3\frac{1}{2}$.)

6. **Decimal Answers:** If you obtain a decimal answer with more digits than the grid can accommodate, it may be either rounded or truncated, but it must fill the entire grid.

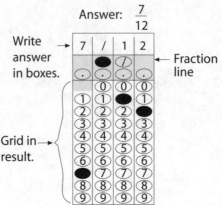

Answer: $\frac{7}{12}$ — Write answer in boxes. — Fraction line — Grid in result.

Answer: 2.5 — Decimal point

Acceptable ways to grid $\frac{2}{3}$ are:

Answer: 201 – either position is correct

NOTE: You may start your answers in any column, space permitting. Columns you don't need to use should be left blank.

CONTINUE

31

If $9 > 3v - 3$, what is the greatest possible integer value of v?

32

In the expression $\dfrac{\dfrac{6}{5}}{\dfrac{12}{2y} - \dfrac{5}{y}} = 1$, what is the value of y?

33

During a presidential election, a high school held its own mock election. Students had the option to vote for Candidate A, Candidate B, or several other candidates. They could also choose to spoil their ballot. The table below displays a summary of the election results.

	Candidate A	Candidate B	Other	Total
10th grade	0.32	0.58	0.10	1.00
11th grade	0.50	0.42	0.08	1.00
12th grade	0.63	0.32	0.05	1.00
Total	0.48	0.44	0.08	1.00

614 students voted for Candidate A. Approximately how many students attend the school?

34

If $\tan \theta = \dfrac{12}{5}$, then $\cos \theta =$

CONTINUE

35

Marcellus is traveling abroad in Ghana and using traveler's checks, which he has acquired from Easy Traveler's Savings Bank. Easy Traveler's Savings Bank charges a 7% fee on traveler's checks, which can then be used like cash at any location overseas at the same exchange rate, and any change will then be returned to Marcellus in local currency. For this trip, Marcellus bought a 651 Cedi traveler's check and paid a fee of 32.30 USD (United States dollars) for the check.

While in Ghana, Marcellus finds Leon's Pawnshop and Barter, which offers store credit for Marcellus's briefcase equal to its value in Cedis. If Marcellus's briefcase is worth 5,000 USD at the same exchange rate at which he bought his traveler's check, then how much store credit, to the closest Cedi, will Marcellus receive for the briefcase?

36

A square is inscribed in a circle. The area of the square is what percent of the area of the circle? (Disregard the percent symbol when gridding your answer.)

CONTINUE

Questions 37 and 38 refer to the following information.

Professor Malingowski, a chemist and teacher at a community college, is organizing his graduated cylinders in the hopes of keeping his office tidy and setting a good example for his students. He has beakers with diameters, in inches, of $\frac{1}{2}$, $\frac{3}{4}$, $\frac{4}{5}$, 1, and $\frac{5}{4}$.

37

Professor Malingowski notices one additional cylinder lying on the ground, and can recall certain facts about it, but not its actual diameter. If he knows that the value of the additional graduated cylinder's diameter, x, will not create any modes and will make the mean of the set equal to $\frac{5}{6}$, what is the value of the additional cylinder's diameter?

38

With his original five cylinders, Professor Malingowski realizes that he is missing a cylinder necessary for his upcoming lab demonstration for Thursday's class. He remembers that the cylinder he needs, when added to the original five, will create a median diameter value of $\frac{9}{10}$ for the set of six total cylinders. He also knows that the measure of the sixth cylinder will exceed the value of the range of the current five cylinders by a width of anywhere from $\frac{1}{4}$ inches to $\frac{1}{2}$ inches, inclusive. Based on the above data, what is one possible value of y, the diameter of this missing sixth cylinder?

END OF TEST

DO NOT RETURN TO A PREVIOUS SECTION.

Practice Test 3:
Answers and
Explanations

PRACTICE TEST 3 ANSWER KEY

Section 1: Reading		Section 2: Writing and Language		Section 3: Math (No Calculator)		Section 4: Math (Calculator)	
1. C	27. D	1. A	23. C	1. A	11. D	1. C	20. C
2. B	28. D	2. C	24. D	2. C	12. B	2. B	21. A
3. A	29. B	3. B	25. D	3. D	13. A	3. A	22. C
4. D	30. D	4. A	26. A	4. C	14. B	4. C	23. D
5. A	31. C	5. D	27. C	5. C	15. D	5. C	24. B
6. A	32. D	6. D	28. A	6. B	16. 1.5	6. B	25. A
7. C	33. C	7. D	29. B	7. C	or	7. D	26. B
8. D	34. C	8. D	30. B	8. D	$\frac{3}{2}$	8. D	27. C
9. B	35. A	9. B	31. C	9. B		9. D	28. D
10. B	36. A	10. A	32. C	10. C		10. C	29. C
11. B	37. D	11. C	33. B		17. 53	11. A	30. D
12. A	38. A	12. B	34. C		18. 10	12. D	31. 3
13. B	39. B	13. A	35. A		19. $\frac{11}{3}$	13. B	32. $\frac{5}{6}$ or
14. D	40. D	14. B	36. D		or	14. D	.83
15. C	41. B	15. B	37. D		3.66	15. A	
16. D	42. B	16. D	38. B		or	16. C	33. 1,279
17. A	43. A	17. C	39. C		3.67	17. C	34. $\frac{5}{13}$
18. D	44. A	18. A	40. B		20. 2	18. A	or
19. D	45. C	19. B	41. C			19. B	.384
20. A	46. C	20. C	42. A				or
21. B	47. B	21. D	43. A				.385
22. C	48. C	22. A	44. D				
23. A	49. D						35. 7,054
24. B	50. A						36. 63.6
25. A	51. B						or
26. C	52. D						63.7
							37. $\frac{7}{10}$
							or .7
							38. $1 \leq$
							$y \leq$
							1.25

PRACTICE TEST 3 EXPLANATIONS

Section 1: Reading

1. **C** The question asks about the primary purpose of the passage. Since this is a general question, it should be answered after the specific questions. The main focus of the passage is Sydney Carton. Lines 9–10 describe him during his school days as *the old seesaw Sydney. Up one minute and down the next.* Lines 30–31 state that his friend Stryver was *always in the front rank, and I [Sydney] was always behind.* The passage concludes with a description of Carton's mood. Look for an answer choice about Carton. Choice (A) describes the purpose of a section of a passage, but it is too specific and does not describe the purpose of the passage as a whole. This is a Right Answer, Wrong Question trap answer; eliminate (A). Similarly, while the speakers briefly discuss the Shrewsbury School, the discussion is not the main point of the passage. Eliminate (B). Because the passage focuses on Carton, it is accurate to say that its purpose is to reveal his character, so keep (C). Because there is no evidence in the passage that Stryver has exploited Carton, eliminate (D). The correct answer is (C).

2. **B** The question asks how to best characterize *Carton*. Notice that this is the first question in a paired set, so it can be done in tandem with Q3. Look at the answer choices for Q3 first. The lines for (3A) say that Carton is *up one minute and down the next, now in spirits and now in despondency.* Look to see whether these lines support any of the answer choices for Q2. The word *mercurial* is used to describe someone whose mood changes a lot. Draw a line connecting (3A) and (2B). The lines for (3B) say that Carton *did exercises for other boys, and seldom did [his] own.* These lines don't support any of the answer choices in Q2; eliminate (3B). The lines for (3C) mention that Carton and Stryver laughed together, which doesn't support any of the answer choices in Q2. Eliminate (3C). The lines for (3D) say, *It's a gloomy thing…to talk about one's own past.* This statement doesn't support any of the answer choices in Q2, so eliminate (3D). Without any support in the answers from Q3, (2A), (2C), and (2D) can be eliminated. The correct answers are (2B) and (3A).

3. **A** (See explanation above.)

4. **D** The question asks what the word *spirits* most nearly means in line 11. Go back to the text, find the word *spirits*, and cross it out. Then read the window carefully, using context clues to determine another word that would fit in the text. Lines 10–11 say that Sydney is *up one minute and down the next; now in spirits and now in despondency.* Therefore, *spirits* must mean something like "happiness." *Soul* means "the immaterial part of a person;" it doesn't match "happiness," so eliminate (A). *Liquor* refers to alcoholic drinks; it doesn't mean "happiness," so eliminate (B). *Essence* means "the most significant quality of something;" it doesn't match "happiness," so eliminate (C). Choices (A), (B), and (C) are Could Be True trap answers based on other meanings of *spirits* that do not fit the context in the passage. *Jubilation* matches "happiness," so keep (D). The correct answer is (D).

5. **A** The question asks what can be inferred from Stryver's statement in lines 17–22. Use the given line reference to find the window. In this paragraph, Stryver tells Carton, *"your way is, and always was, a lame way. You summon no energy and purpose,"* so it is clear that Stryver dislikes Carton's behavior. Look for an answer that matches this information. Choice (A) matches the prediction, so keep it. Choice (B) uses the Right Words with the Wrong Meaning; Stryver does not want to literally push Carton into the fireplace. Eliminate (B). Similarly, (C) has the Right Words but the Wrong Meaning; *the old Sydney Carton* is not used in reference to his literal age but rather is a term of endearment. Eliminate (C). While the passage states that Stryver had *a bullying air*, there is no evidence that Stryver ever bullied Sydney at school, so eliminate (D). The correct answer is (A).

6. **A** The question asks why the author uses *italics in line 55*. Use the given line reference to find the window. In line 48, Stryver tells Carton, *"Pledge me to the pretty witness,"* whom he reveals to be Miss Manette. Carton responds with a question: *"She pretty?"* Therefore, he is in disbelief that Stryver is describing Miss Manette as pretty. Look for something that matches this information. Because *incredulity* means "disbelief," (A) is a good description of Carton's attitude; keep it. Carton is not confused. He knows what he thinks and what Stryver thinks; eliminate (B). There is no indication that Carton is annoyed by Stryver in the lines in question, so eliminate (C). Carton is indicating his belief that Miss Manette is not pretty, not that he feels *affection* toward her. Eliminate (D). The correct answer is (A).

7. **C** The question asks what the passage suggests *about Stryver*. Notice that this is the first question in a paired set, so it can be done in tandem with Q8. Look at the answer choices for Q8 first. In the lines for (8A), Stryver states, *"I had to get into the front rank; I was not born there, was I?"*, which suggests he was not born into privilege. Look to see whether these lines support any of the answers for Q7. They do not, so eliminate (8A). The line in (8B) asks simply, *"And whose fault was that?"*, which doesn't suggest anything about Stryver, nor correspond to any of the answer choices in Q7. Eliminate (8B). The lines for (8C) say that Miss Manette was *the admiration of the whole court*. These lines refer only to her looks; they don't suggest that Stryver is in love with her. These lines don't support any of the answer choices in Q7, so eliminate (8C). The lines for (8D) say that Stryver thought Carton *sympathized with the golden-haired doll*, which indicates that Stryver believes Carton was paying attention to her and saw what happened to her at court. This is a response to Carton's statement, *"She pretty?"* which was Carton's way of saying that he did not find Miss Manette attractive. Stryver's response indicates that he thought Carton was paying attention to Miss Manette because he did think she was pretty, so he does not believe Carton finds Miss Manette unattractive. Draw a line connecting (8D) and (7C). Without any support in the answers from Q8, (7A), (7B), and (7D) can be eliminated. The correct answers are (7C) and (8D).

8. **D** (See explanation above.)

9. **B** The question asks what the word *desert* refers to in line 79. Read a window around the line reference. Lines 76–79 say that *the air was cold and sad, the dull sky overcast, the river dark and dim, the whole scene like a lifeless desert.* The author is describing the setting in the city. Choices (A) and (C) do not describe a setting, so eliminate them. *London's landscape* matches the prediction, so keep (B). Choice (D) refers to a feature seen in literal deserts, but the author uses the word figuratively. This is a Right Words, Wrong Meaning answer; eliminate (D). The correct answer is (B).

10. **B** The question asks why the *"tears"* in line 85 are described as *wasted*. Use the given line reference to find the window. Lines 83–90 say that Carton *threw himself down in his clothes on a neglected bed, and its pillow was wet with wasted tears,* and that *there is no sadder sight than the man of good abilities and good emotions, incapable of their directed exercise, incapable of his own help and his own happiness, sensible of the blight on him, and resigning himself to let it eat him away.* Since the passage says that Carton cannot help himself and is resigned, it can be inferred that he will not try to change anything about his circumstances. His tears are *wasted* because they will not prompt him to make a change for the better. There is no indication of Miss Manette's feelings, positive or negative, toward Carton, so eliminate (A). Choice (B) matches the prediction, so keep it. The passage mentions only one detail about Carton's apartment, and the neglected bed is not the focus of Carton's tears, so eliminate (C). There is no indication that Stryver is exploiting Carton, so eliminate (D). The correct answer is (B).

11. **B** The question asks for the best description of the *point of view* of the passage. Since this is a general question, it should be answered after the specific questions. The author views Estonia's Singing Revolution in a positive light, and describes Estonia, Latvia, and Lithuania's right to independence from the Soviet Union. Eliminate (A) because *condemnatory* is too strong; the passage is focused mostly on Estonia's Singing Revolution rather than on criticism of the Soviet Union's actions. Keep (B) because *sympathetic* matches the positive point of view toward the Baltic states (Estonia, Latvia, and Lithuania). Eliminate (C) and (D) because *dismissive* and *conflicted* are negative and do not match the positive point of view. The correct answer is (B).

12. **A** The question asks what the author *draws a distinction between*. Use the given line reference to find the window. Lines 35–38 say that *the themes of their music were often grim,* but *there was always hope in their hearts.* Keep (A) because the author makes a distinction between the songs' tone, which was *grim*, and the people's feelings of *hope*. Eliminate (B) because, although *folk songs* and *anthems* are both mentioned, there is no distinction drawn between them. Eliminate (C) because there is no mention of *military strength* in lines 34–38. The author contrasts the military strength of the two in lines 27–30, making this the Right Answer to the Wrong Question. Eliminate (D) because there is no mention of *song festivals in Latvia and Lithuania* in these lines, and when the author mentions them (lines 45–46), they are described as *similar* to Estonia's. The correct answer is (A).

13. **B**   The question asks what the phrase *"their reluctance to be absorbed"* suggests about the Estonians. Since there is no line reference, use chronology and lead words to find the window for the question. Q12 asked about lines 34–38, so the window for Q13 most likely begins after line 38. Scan the passage beginning with line 39, looking for the phrase *"their reluctance to be absorbed."* Lines 40–44 state that *Estonians established a history of mass song festivals, celebrations that would kindle and fortify the courage to express their love of language and nation, and their reluctance to be absorbed by anyone.* Eliminate (A) because there is no mention of speaking *Russian*. Keep (B) because wanting *to have an independent nation* matches *their love of language and nation* and *their reluctance to be absorbed by anyone.* Eliminate (C) because the paragraph states that there were *similar festivals held in Latvia and Lithuania.* Eliminate (D) because the passage indicates that the Estonian song festivals started before the *Soviets* arrived. The correct answer is (B).

14. **D**   The question asks which choice *best supports the claim that the Soviet Union perceived Estonia's culture as a threat.* Notice that the answer choices are lines from the passage. Use the lines given to answer the question. The lines for (A) say that *Estonia had always been a nation of singers* and discusses the importance of *folk songs.* However, there is no mention of the *Soviet Union* in these lines, so eliminate (A). The lines for (B) say *Estonians established a history of mass song festivals* and discusses those *celebrations.* Again there is no mention of the *Soviet Union*, so eliminate (B). The lines for (C) say *the festivals were forced to pay tribute to Communist icons and the solidarity of the Soviet peoples*, which was not threatening to the Soviet Union, so eliminate (C). The lines for (D) mention *an unofficial national anthem* and that it *survived the entire Soviet occupation despite a serious attempt by officials to eliminate it*; the fact that the Soviet officials tried to eliminate the Estonian anthem indicates that they saw the anthem as a threat, so keep (D). The correct answer is (D).

15. **C**   The question asks what the word *burden* most nearly means in line 66. Go back to the text, find the word *burden*, and cross it out. Then read the window carefully, using context clues to determine another word that would fit in the text. Lines 62–68 say, *A movement of young historians was already defying Soviet authority in speeches* and that the *burden of protest songs had passed to rock-and-rollers, young men whose energized patriotic tunes blared from every radio.* Therefore, *burden* must mean something like "duty" or "leadership." Eliminate (A) because *weight* means "mass" and does not match "duty." This is a Could Be True trap answer based on another meaning of *burden* that does not fit the context in the passage. Eliminate (B) because *travail* means "painful effort" and does not match "duty." This is another Could Be True trap answer. Keep (C) because *responsibility* matches "duty" and "leadership." Eliminate (D) because *need* does not match "duty." The correct answer is (C).

16. **D**   The question asks for the *primary rhetorical effect of the last sentence.* Read a window around the sentence that is referenced. The last paragraph begins, *This was the heart of "The Singing Revolution," a spontaneous, non-violent, but powerful political movement that united Estonians with poetry and music.* The last sentence says *Sedition hung in the wind, waiting to be denied.*

Sedition means "disobeying the government;" this sentence figuratively describes the sense that revolution was about to occur. Eliminate (A) because there is no *sense of dread*; the words *united* and *powerful* indicate a sense of hopefulness about the revolution. Eliminate (B) because there is no discussion of *disagreement between violent and non-violent revolutionaries.* Eliminate (C) because although it's true that music and poetry were important in the fight for independence, that is not the focus of the last sentence; this is a Right Answer, Wrong Question trap answer. Keep (D) because communicating *the sense of optimistic tension* is a rhetorical effect and matches *sedition hung in the wind.* The correct answer is (D).

17. **A** The question asks what the author implies about the *Estonian song festivals.* Notice that this is the first question in a paired set, so it can be done in tandem with Q18. Look at the answer choices for Q18 first. The lines for (18A) say that *the occupied nations had every right to ask for their freedom, and with no need for a legal "divorce."* There is no mention of *Estonian song festivals*, so these lines do not address Q17; eliminate (18A). The lines for (18B) say, *The festivals were a nationwide phenomenon, as were similar festivals held in Latvia and Lithuania.* Look to see whether these lines support any of the answers for Q17. Although the lines mention the *festivals*, they don't provide specifics to support any of the answers in Q17, so eliminate (18B). The lines for (18C) say, *By the late 1980s the nation was simmering.* There is no mention of *Estonian song festivals*, so these lines do not address Q17; eliminate (18C). The lines for (18D) say that *This was the heart of "The Singing Revolution," a spontaneous, non-violent, but powerful political movement that united Estonians with poetry and music.* These lines mention *"The Singing Revolution,"* which began with the *song festivals.* Look to see whether these lines support any of the answers for Q17. They support (17A) since the festivals *united Estonians* and gave them *a medium through which national and cultural pride could be expressed.* Draw a line connecting (18D) with (17A). Without any support in the answers from Q18, (17B), (17C), and (17D) can be eliminated. The correct answers are (17A) and (18D).

18. **D** (See explanation above.)

19. **D** The question asks which claim is *supported by the diagram.* Work through each answer choice using the diagram. Eliminate (A) because the diagram shows both German and Soviet gains in *Poland.* Eliminate (B) because the Soviet Union did not double in size after the pact; the area of Soviet gains is smaller than the area of the Soviet Union shown in the diagram. Eliminate (C) because *contiguous* means "having a border in common," and Estonia and Lithuania do not border each other. Keep (D) because the diagram shows that the Soviet gains did stretch from the *Baltic Sea* to the *Black Sea.* The correct answer is (D).

20. **A** The question asks which statement in the passage is supported by the diagram. Work through each answer choice using the diagram. Keep (A) because the diagram shows Soviet gains in *the Baltic states of Estonia, Latvia, and Lithuania.* Eliminate (B) because the diagram shows the results of a 1939 pact and not what happened *in 1940.* Eliminate (C) because *agitations for independence came in the late 1980s,* which is much later than the time depicted on the diagram.

Eliminate (D) because *the firm stand taken in 1940 by the United States* is not shown on the diagram. The correct answer is (A).

21. **B**   The question asks what *purpose* the diagram serves *in relation to the passage*. Since this is a general question, it should be answered after the specific questions. Make sure to read the note under the figure. The diagram shows *Europe following the Nazi-Soviet Pact of 1939, also known as the Molotov-Ribbentrop Pact*. Work through each answer choice using the figure. Although the diagram shows that the Soviet Union made gains in Estonia, the diagram does not give any more information about the relationship beyond what is in the passage; eliminate (A). The diagram does show the results of the Molotov-Ribbentrop Pact, which the passage calls a *secret non-aggression treaty* (lines 11–14), so keep (B). The diagram does not show anything about the *Singing Revolution*; eliminate (C). The diagram does show Estonia and the countries surrounding it, but there is no information on the diagram about Estonia's *role* in the region; eliminate (D). The correct answer is (B).

22. **C**   The question asks how to best describe *the position that LaFollette takes*. Because this is a general question, it should be done after all the specific questions. Lines 21–29 state that LaFollette disagrees with some of his colleagues, arguing against the restriction of citizens' *right to control their own government*, so look for an answer that has to do with LaFollette arguing for something with which others disagree. While LaFollette is a lawmaker, no *new piece of legislation* is being considered in the passage, so (A) is a Mostly Right/Slightly Wrong answer. Eliminate it. Choice (B) is also incorrect: as a senator, LaFollette is not *an impartial observer*, and he isn't *arbitrating a legal issue* in this passage, so eliminate (B). LaFollette can certainly be described as *a dissenter arguing for a cause* as he is discussing an issue with which some of his colleagues disagree, so keep (C). Nowhere in the text does LaFollette claim to be against war in general, as *a pacifist* would, so eliminate (D). The correct answer is (C).

23. **A**   The question asks which *distinction* LaFollette draws in the passage. Because this is the first question in a paired set, it can be done in tandem with Q24. Consider the answers for Q24 first. The lines for (24A) mention LaFollette being aware of people *being unlawfully arrested* and otherwise detained even though they *committed no crime*. Check the answers for Q23 to see if any of the answers are supported by those lines. These lines don't support any of the answers for Q23, so eliminate (24A). The lines for (24B) introduce LaFollette's idea that people *must surrender some rights for the common good* during war, and LaFollette draws a distinction here, noting that *the right to control their own Government…is not one of the rights* that citizens are *called upon to surrender in time of* war. This matches with (23A), so draw a line connecting those two answers. The lines for (24C) and (24D) don't include distinctions, nor do they match any of the answers for Q23, so eliminate those answers. The correct answers are (23A) and (24B).

24. **B**   (See explanation above.)

25.   **A**   The question asks who is *criticized by the press*. Since there is no line reference, use chronology and lead words to find the window for the question. This is the first specific question, and Q26 asks about line 22, so the window for Q25 is most likely in the first three paragraphs. Scan the passage beginning with line 1, looking for the lead word *press*. Lines 1–5 state that *the triumphant war press has pursued those Senators and Representatives who voted against war with malicious falsehood and recklessly libelous attacks, going to the extreme limit of charging them with treason against their country.* Choice (A) matches this prediction, so keep it. Choice (B) is a Right Words, Wrong Meaning trap answer: the passage states that the press has accused the Senators and Representatives of treason, but it doesn't say that these people actually committed treason. Eliminate (B). Eliminate (C) because the passage states that the Congress members have spoken out against the war; they have not tried to *stifle free speech*. Choice (D) is a Right Words, Wrong Meaning trap answer: the passage suggests that the press has committed libel against the Senators and Representatives, not that the Senators and Representatives have committed libel. Eliminate (D). The correct answer is (A).

26.   **C**   The question asks what the word *surrender* most nearly means in line 22. Go back to the text, find the word *surrender*, and mark it out. Carefully read the surrounding text to determine another word that would fit in the blank based on the context of the passage. In line 22, LaFollette states that *in time of war the citizen must surrender some rights for the common good which he is entitled to enjoy in time of peace*, so *surrender* means something like "give up temporarily." *Declare defeat* does not match "give up temporarily." This is a Could Be True trap answer based on another meaning of *surrender* that does not fit the context in the passage. Eliminate (A). *Throw away* doesn't mean to "give up temporarily," so eliminate (B). Choice (C), *set aside*, matches the meaning of "give up temporarily," so keep it. *Submit to* doesn't match "give up temporarily," so eliminate (D). The correct answer is (C).

27.   **D**   The question asks what is suggested by lines 32–36. Read a window around the line reference. Lines 32–36 state that citizens *must beware of those precedents in support of arbitrary action by administrative officials, which excused on the plea of necessity in war time, become the fixed rule when the necessity has passed and normal conditions have been restored.* Thus, LaFollette is concerned that officials may restrict free speech during times of war but then fail to remove those restrictions when the war is over. While LaFollette does grant that *the citizen must surrender some rights*, this is not mentioned in lines 32–36; this is the Right Answer to the Wrong Question, so eliminate (A). While LaFollette does say that some restrictions are *arbitrary* (meaning not based on reason or necessity), he explicitly denies that all restrictions are arbitrary in lines 21–29, so (B) can be eliminated. Choice (C) is never mentioned in the passage, so eliminate it. Choice (D) matches the prediction: *temporary restrictions* placed during war time may not be removed when the war is over, becoming *permanent,* so keep (D). The correct answer is (D).

28.   **D**   The question asks what the word *terms* most nearly means in line 49. Go back to the text, find the word *terms*, and mark it out. Carefully read the surrounding text to determine another

word that would fit in the blank based on the context of the passage. Lines 43–50 discuss the citizens' right to discuss *every important phase of this war*, which include its causes, the way it should be carried out, and *the terms upon which peace should be made*. Therefore, "terms" must mean something like "requirements." *Periods* doesn't match "requirements." This is a Could Be True trap answer based on another meaning of *terms* that does not fit the context in the passage. Eliminate (A). *Conversations* doesn't match "requirements," so eliminate (B). *Definitions* doesn't match "requirements;" (C) is another Could Be True trap answer. Eliminate it. *Conditions* matches "requirements," so keep (D). The correct answer is (D).

29.   **B**   The question asks what the *principal rhetorical effect* of the phrase in lines 48–50 is. This is the first question in a paired set, but it is a specific question, so it can be done on its own. Read a window around the line reference. In lines 37–41, the speaker defends the right of free speech. Then, the speaker specifies the citizen's right to discuss *every important phase of this war*. Lines 48–50 list the various phases of the war that people should be free to discuss. Eliminate (A) because the speaker is arguing for free speech, not *against* it, and these lines do not mention *difficulties faced by the military and the President*. Keep (B) because it matches the prediction. Eliminate (C) because lines 48–50 list topics that citizens should be free to discuss, not reasons members of the press are not able to speak freely. Eliminate (D) because there is no discussion about who understands war best. The correct answer is (B).

30.   **D**   The question is the best evidence question in a paired set. Because Q29 was a specific question, simply look at the lines used to answer the previous question. Lines 37–47 were used to answer the question. Of these lines, only lines 37–41 are given in an answer choice. The correct answer is (D).

31.   **C**   The question asks how the author's attitude toward *"the attempt to stifle"* in line 63 can be described. Read a window around the line reference. In lines 63–72, LaFollette ponders the consequences that would occur if *the attempt to stifle all discussion of the issues of this war* were successful. Throughout the passage, he argues that people should have free speech during war time, and in this paragraph he describes the attempt to stifle free speech as *the demand of the war-mad press and war extremists that they monopolize the right of public utterance*. Look for an answer that reflects LaFollette's negative view of the attempt to stifle free speech. He is not *sympathetic* to efforts to stifle discussion of the war, so eliminate (A). He is not *apathetic*, or "uncaring," so eliminate (B). *Morose* means "gloomy," which doesn't describe LaFollette's attitude in line 63, so eliminate (D). He is actively speaking out about the issue, which indicates that he believes change can be made; therefore, he is upset, but not *morose*. Keep (C) because *frustrated* matches the prediction. The correct answer is (C).

32.   **D**   This question asks about the perspective from which the passage is written. Because this is a general question, it should be done after all of the specific questions. Overall, the passage discusses new research findings in biofuel production. Find an answer that matches this prediction. Choice (A) can be eliminated because while the passage concludes that *further*

studies would be needed to determine the environmental impacts of biofuels, there is no request for *project funding*. Eliminate (B) because the entire passage is about research in biofuel production, not *chemistry concepts*. Choice (C) can be eliminated because *lauding* means "praising," and, while the research discussed in the passage yielded some promising results, according to the last paragraph, *further studies would be needed* to determine the environmental impacts of biofuel. Therefore, the entire passage is not *lauding the successes of an industry*. Eliminate (C). *An objective observer evaluating new research* matches the discussion about biofuel production. The correct answer is (D).

33. **C** This question asks about the function of the last sentence of the first paragraph. Use the first paragraph as the window. According to the first paragraph, producing ethanol *remains considerably more expensive than gasoline. So researchers are always on the lookout for new ways to trim costs.* According to the last sentence of the first paragraph, researchers *have a new lead, a microbe that can use abundant nitrogen gas as the fertilizer it needs to produce ethanol from plants*. In other words, the microbe may solve the production cost problem. Find an answer that matches this prediction. Choice (A) may seem tempting because the last sentence describes a recent discovery—the microbe. However, the microbe is not a *commercial accomplishment*. For this reason, eliminate (A). Choice (B) may seem tempting because the paragraph discusses the relative production costs of ethanol and gasoline. However, the last sentence of the first paragraph does not provide a reason as to *why one fuel is more expensive than another*. Eliminate (B). Choice (C) is consistent with the prediction. The last sentence of the first paragraph proposes that the microbe may be a potential solution for the problem of the high cost of producing ethanol. Eliminate (D) because the final sentence of the paragraph does not *restate the results* of that year. The correct answer is (C).

34. **C** This question asks how *nonfood crops produce fewer indirect land use emissions*. Because this is this first question in a paired set, this question can be done in tandem with Q35. Look at the answer choices for Q35 first. The lines for (35A) state that nonfood crops such as trees and bamboo *need less fertilizer than traditional biofuel crops*. This matches (34C). Connect answers (35A) and (34C). The lines in (35B) state that *in an ideal world, biofuels would be produced only from plant materials that cannot be eaten*. This information does not explain *how nonfood crops produce fewer indirect land use emissions*. Eliminate (35B). The lines for (35C) state that *the enzymes needed to break down plants' primary structural components…are expensive*. It may be tempting to connect this answer with (34B), since (34B) discusses prices. However, this answer does not explain *how nonfood crops produce fewer indirect land use emissions*. Eliminate (35C). The lines in (35D) explain that *an ethanol production plant may be spending more than $1 million on* fertilizer a year. It may be tempting to connect this answer with (34B), since (34B) discusses prices. However, this information does not explain *how nonfood crops produce fewer indirect land use emissions*. Eliminate (35D). The correct answers are (34C) and (35A).

35. **A** (See explanation above.)

36.   **A**   The question asks what the phrase *ideal world* most nearly means in line 37. Go back to the text, find the phrase *ideal world*, and cross it out. Then read the window carefully, using context clues to determine another word that would fit in the text. The text says that *researchers have turned to nonfood crops...for biofuel production* because these crops need less fertilizer and they often have a less detrimental impact on the land. The phrase *an ideal world* is used to introduce the idea that *biofuels would be produced only from plant materials that cannot be eaten.* In context, the phrase *an ideal world* means something along the lines of "in the best situation." Find an answer that matches this prediction. *Best-case scenario* matches "in the best situation," so keep (A). *Dream sequence* may seem tempting, but producing *biofuels* from *only plant materials that cannot be eaten* is realistic and not a *dream sequence*; eliminate (B). Choice (C) may seem tempting, but *biofuels* are not a *model* for anything. Choice (D) may also seem tempting, since a *utopian society* is one that possesses highly desirable or perfect qualities. However, the definition of a utopian society has to do with a society having an ideal social, political, and moral climate, not producing *biofuels...only from plant materials that cannot be eaten*; eliminate (D). The correct answer is (A).

37.   **D**   This question asks what can *be inferred from the results of the Indiana University study involving Zymomonas mobilis*. Because this is this first question in a paired set, this question can be done in tandem with Q38. Look at the "best evidence" answer choices for Q38 first. The lines for (38A) state that the research showed that *the bacterium produces ethanol more quickly and uses more of the plant material when it uses nitrogen gas than when it is fed nitrogen in fertilizer. If the same holds true in a production plant, this could reduce biofuel production costs.* This supports answer (37D). Connect answers (38A) and (37D). The lines for (38B) state that *the process is also more environmentally friendly...because there are greenhouse gas emissions associated with producing nitrogen fertilizer.* It may be tempting to connect this answer with (37B), since (37B) mentions greenhouse gases. However, (37B) is a reversal. According to the lines in (37B), the amount of greenhouse gases would change. Eliminate both (38B) and (37B). The lines for (38C) state that *whereas using Z. mobilis might make it cheaper for producers to use inexpensive, nonfood crops, there could also be added costs and problems.* This information does not match any of the possible answers for Q37. Eliminate (38C). The lines for (38D) state that *even if nitrogen fertilizers are not used in the fermentation process, they might still be needed to grow the crops.* This information matches none of the answers in Q37. Eliminate (38D). The correct answers are (37D) and (38A).

38.   **A**   (See explanation above.)

39.   **B**   This question asks what the word *slim* most nearly means, as used in line 73. Read the window, cross out the world *slim,* and replace it with another word or phrase that makes sense based on the context of the passage. Then, eliminate anything that does not match the prediction. The passage states that *questions remain* about using *Z. mobilis,* that *there could also be added costs and problems*, and that overall benefits to the environment *may also be slim.* In context, the

word *slim* means something along the lines of "small" or "low in number." Find an answer that matches this prediction. *Brittle* and *useless* do not mean "small" or "low in number." Eliminate (A) and (D). *Negligible* matches "small," so keep (B). Choice (C) may seem tempting, but *skinny* does not match "small" or "low in number." The correct answer is (B).

40. **D** This question asks *in what year is the required statutory volume of conventional ethanol closest to that of another fuel type,* according to figure 1. Look at figure 1. First, locate the *statutory volume of conventional ethanol.* The statutory renewable fuel volume for conventional ethanol holds steady at approximately 12–15 billion gallons for each of the years shown. Then, look for a year that has *another fuel type* around 12–15 billion gallons. The only fuel that matches that volume is Cellulosic ethanol in the year 2022. Therefore, the correct answer is (D).

41. **B** This question asks which fuel *is least likely to meet the volume requirements shown in figure 1,* according to figure 2. Work through each answer choice by comparing the *volume requirements shown* in figure 1 to the volumes in figure 2. *Biomass-based diesel* has a consistent requirement of around 1 billion gallons in figure 1 and is consistently around 1 billion gallons in figure 2. This would meet the requirements, and the question wants the fuel that is *least likely.* Eliminate (A). *Cellulosic ethanol* in figure 1 goes from approximately zero gallons in 2011 to over 15 billion gallons by 2022 but doesn't even appear on figure 2. This discrepancy means that it is unlikely to meet the volume requirements in figure 1; keep (B). *Conventional ethanol* in figure 1 increases to 15 billion gallons by 2015; in figure 2 it is already close to 14 billion gallons in 2013. It looks as if *conventional ethanol* will meet the requirements; eliminate (C). *Other advanced renewable fuels* in figure 1 start at 0 gallons in 2010 and end at around 5 billion gallons in 2022. In figure 2, these fuels are slowly increasing, ending at around 2 billion gallons in 2013. This increase means that *other advanced renewable fuels* are on pace to meet the requirements in figure 1. Eliminate (D). The correct answer is (B).

42. **B** The question asks what *the author of Passage 1 most likely believes* about *the Glen Canyon Dam.* Notice that this is the first question in a paired set, so it can be done in tandem with Q43. Look at the answer choices for Q43 first. The lines for (43A) say that *At the time Glen Canyon Dam was constructed (1956–63), little consideration was given to how dam operations might affect downstream resources in Grand Canyon National Park.* Look to see whether these lines support any of the answers for Q42. They support the statement in (42B) that Glen Canyon Dam *was built with a lack of foresight.* Draw a line connecting (43A) and (42B). The lines for (43B) say that *humpback chub and Colorado pikeminnow were listed as endangered in 1967* and *the dam and its operation jeopardized the continued existence of humpback chub.* Although these lines may seem to support (42C), this is a Mostly Right/Slightly Wrong trap answer, as the phrase *decimated native fish populations* is too extreme to describe endangering two species. Eliminate (43B). The lines for (43C) say, *Annual spring snowmelt floods were the defining attribute of the pre-dam flow regime.* This information is not about the dam itself, so it does not answer Q42; eliminate (43C). The lines for (43D) say that *Pre-dam floods disturbed the aquatic ecosystem* and *native fish species developed strategies to survive* those floods. Although it may seem reasonable

that if the pre-dam floods disturbed the ecosystem, the dam would calm the ecosystem (42D), this is a Could Be True trap answer since there is not concrete support in the passage that the dam *has had a calming effect on the aquatic ecosystem*. Eliminate (43D). Without any support in the answers from Q43, (42A), (42C), and (42D) can be eliminated. The correct answers are (42B) and (43A).

43.   **A**   (See explanation above.)

44.   **A**   The question asks why the author of Passage 1 mentions *scientists and river recreationists*. Since there is no line reference, use chronology and lead words to find the window for the question. Q46 asks about line 25, so the window for Q44 most likely comes from before line 25. Scan the first paragraph, looking for the lead words *scientists* and *river recreationists*. Starting at line 10, the passage states *National Park Service and U.S. Geological Survey scientists and river recreationists observed the physical transformation of the river in Grand Canyon* and then includes details about the *physical transformation*. Keep (A) because the window gives details on how the area *looks drastically different*. Eliminate (B) because there is no *contrast between scientific observations and casual observations*: the scientists and recreationists noticed the same changes. Eliminate (C) because there is no mention of *collaboration* between the *scientists* and *recreationists*. Eliminate (D) because, although the scientists and recreationists did observe harmful changes, the words *prove* and *ruinous* are too strong to match the evidence in the passage, and so (D) is a Mostly Right/Slightly Wrong trap answer. The correct answer is (A).

45.   **C**   The question asks what Passage 1 suggests about *humpback chub*. Since there is no line reference, use chronology and lead words to find the window for the question. Q46 asks about line 25, so the window for Q46 most likely begins before line 25. Scan the first paragraph, looking for the lead words *humpback chub*. Starting at line 17, the passage states that *humpback chub...were listed as endangered in 1967 by the U.S. Fish and Wildlife Service* and *the dam and its operation jeopardized the continued existence of humpback chub*. Lines 30–34 give more information that applies to the humpback chub, saying that *native fish species developed strategies to survive periods when the velocity in the main part of the channel was high and large amounts of suspended sediment were being transported*. Eliminate (A) because the passage says that the *humpback chub* were endangered, not *extinct*. Although the passage does say that *several of the native fish species share unusual body shapes, including...small depressed skulls*, this is a Could Be True trap answer because the passage doesn't state that the *humpback chub* is one of the species that has a *small, depressed skull*. Eliminate (B). Keep (C) because the *humpback chub* does *survive in changing environments*, both changes from the dam and changes due to flooding. Eliminate (D) because *thrive* is too strong to match what is indicated by the passage; the text says that the fish can *survive* in high velocity river channels, but not that they *thrive* there. This is a Mostly Right/Slightly Wrong trap answer. The correct answer is (C).

46.   **C**   The question asks what the word *regime* most nearly means in line 25. Go back to the text, find the word *regime*, and cross it out. Then read the window carefully, using context clues to determine another word that would fit in the text. The text says that *Annual spring snowmelt*

floods were the defining attribute of the pre-dam flow regime. Therefore, *regime* must mean something like "process." Eliminate (A) because *government* does not match "process." This is a Could Be True trap answer based on another meaning of *regime* that does not fit the context in the passage. Eliminate (B) because *tenure* means "holding office, land, or a position" and does not match "process." Keep (C) because *system* matches "process." Eliminate (D) because *management* means "dealing with or controlling people or things" and does not match "process." The correct answer is (C).

47. **B** Go to the second sentence of the second paragraph in Passage 2 and cross out the word *suspended*. Replace it with your own word using the context of the paragraph. The paragraph mentions that sand is included *at high concentration in the flow*, so a good replacement would be "combined." Choice (B) is the best match and therefore the correct answer.

48. **C** The question asks what can be concluded about *controlled floods*. Notice that this is the first question in a paired set, so it can be done in tandem with Q49. Look at the answer choices for Q49 first. The lines for (49A) say that *Normal dam operations, therefore, tend to erode, rather than build, sandbars;* since there is no mention of *controlled floods*, these lines do not answer Q48; eliminate (49A). The lines for (49B) say, *The suspended sand is transported into eddies where it is then deposited in areas of low stream-flow velocity.* This paragraph is about *controlled floods*, so look to see if these lines support any of the answers to Q48. They do not: although the previous sentence mentions a *high concentration* of sand and might seem to support (48B), lines 66–68 do not mention the amount of sediment, so eliminate (49B). The lines for (49C) say, *Newly deposited sandbars also provide areas for riparian vegetation to grow and are a source of windblown sand.* These lines do not support any of the answers choices for Q48, so eliminate (49C). The lines for (49D) say, *Scientists have also learned that controlled floods may erode sandbars if the concentration of suspended sand during a controlled flood is too low.* Eroding sandbars is *detrimental*, so these lines support (48C). Draw a line connecting (49D) and (48C). Without any support in the answers from Q49, (48A), (48B), and (48D) can be eliminated. The correct answers are (48C) and (49D).

49. **D** (See explanation above.)

50. **A** The question asks how *the author of Passage 1 would most likely respond to the High Flow Experiments described in Passage 2.* Because this is a question about both passages, it should be done after all the questions about individual passages. Look for the lead words *High Flow Experiments* in Passage 2. Lines 86–92 indicate that the *High Flow Experiments* are the name for the controlled floods at the *Glen Canyon Dam*. The main focus of Passage 2 is the decline of sandbars after the Glen Canyon Dam was built and how controlled floods *can build sandbars* (lines 60–63). Look for statements about *sandbars* and *floods* in Passage 1. The last two paragraphs discuss *pre-dam floods*, and lines 40–41 state, *Sandbars, riverbanks, and their accompanying aquatic habitats were reshaped during floods.* Since the controlled floods can mimic the pre-dam floods and build sandbars, the author of Passage I would view the High

Flow Experiments positively. Keep (A) because *appreciating* is a positive view. Eliminate (B) and (D) because *warning* and *worrying* are both negative. Eliminate (C) because *questioning* is neutral, or somewhat negative. The correct answer is (A).

51. **B** The question asks for the statement that *best describes the structure of the two passages*. Because this is a question about both passages, it should be done after all the questions about individual passages. Consider the relationship between the two passages. Passage 1 discusses the environmental changes due to the installment of the *Glen Canyon Dam*. Passage 2 focuses on sandbars and how controlled floods can build sandbars. Eliminate (A) because Passage 2 doesn't address the problem introduced in Passage 1. Passage 1 discusses several problems, including *the loss of large beaches*, *narrowing of rapids*, *changes in the distribution and composition of riparian vegetation*, and endangered species. Passage 2 only focuses on a solution to the problem of declining sandbars. Additionally, Passage 2 discusses a solution that is already part of the *current reservoir-release management strategy for Glen Canyon Dam*, so it is incorrect to say that it *proposes* a solution. Keep (B) because Passage 1 includes a *historical discussion* of the *Glen Canyon Dam*, and Passage 2 discusses *a scientific practice* of controlled floods. Eliminate (C) because Passage 1 discusses changes that occurred within a particular ecosystem (the *Colorado River Basin*) due to the construction of a dam; it does not discuss *general principles*. Eliminate (D) because Passage 1 does not discuss an *experiment*, and Passage 2 focuses on strategies that have already been implemented, rather than *offering suggestions* for the *future*. The correct answer is (B).

52. **D** The question asks for a statement that is true for Passage 1, but not Passage 2. Because this is a question about both passages, it should be done after all the questions about individual passages. Consider the main focus of each passage. Eliminate (A) because Passage 2 does give details of scientific studies of controlled flooding on the river, and because Passage 1 does not explicitly mention studies on the river. Eliminate (B) because both Passage 1 and Passage 2 offer *evidence of topographic change*. Eliminate (C) because both passages discuss *the importance of floods to the river ecosystem*. Keep (D) because only Passage 1 mentions specific species, like *the humpback chub and Colorado pikeminnow*. The correct answer is (D).

Section 2: Writing and Language

1. **A** If you can't cite a reason to use a comma, don't use one. In this case, commas are not necessary because the fact that she works at the mall is important as a contrast to *more serious*. Therefore, the answer is (A).

2. **C** The idea before the punctuation *(She would start applying to law schools soon)* is complete. The idea after the comma and conjunction *(she wanted to know what the law looked like in action)* is also complete. Remember the STOP punctuation rules. Choices (A) and (D) can be eliminated because two complete ideas cannot be joined with just a conjunction or just a comma; both are needed. The comma in (B) is in the wrong place, so the answer is (C).

3. **B** Notice the question! It asks which statement is most in keeping with the main idea. The passage centers on the Department of Corrections, and the only choice that introduces this information is (B). The next sentence doesn't even make sense without the specific information in (B).

4. **A** Notice the question! It asks for a statement that reinforces ideas in this sentence as well as the preceding sentence. The ideas in these sentences are about no one paying much attention to the Department of Corrections. Choice (B) contradicts this idea. Choices (C) and (D) contain the wrong focus. Therefore, (A) is the answer.

5. **D** The subject of this sentence is *meaning,* which is singular. Eliminate the choices with plural verbs—(A), (B), and (C)—because they are inconsistent. The correct answer is (D).

6. **D** The underlined pronoun refers to *Everyone,* which is singular. Choice (D) is the only possible answer because it is consistent in number.

7. **D** The sentence should come after another question about the treatment of inmates in order to make sense of the phrase *by the same token.* This question appears in sentence 6, so this sentence should go after sentence 6, as (D) suggests.

8. **D** Choices (A), (B), (C), and (D) all say essentially the same thing, but (D) does so in the most concise way possible. Therefore, (D) is correct.

9. **B** The subject of this verb is *politics and the law*, which is plural, thus eliminating (A) and (C). Choice (B) is the correct answer because it is more concise than (D).

10. **A** The idea before the conjunction *(We may believe that we never come into contact with the law)* is complete, and the idea after the conjunction *(it is written into everything…ourselves)* is also complete. When a conjunctive adverb connects two complete ideas in one sentence, it is preceded by a semicolon and followed by a comma. Therefore, (A) is correct.

11. **C** The essay focuses on the transformational experience Amanda had working at the prison, so a single detail about something that happened to her later on is not consistent with the passage. Eliminate (A) and (B). Choice (D) is incorrect because the detail still wouldn't be consistent if it had included information whether Amanda graduated. The correct answer is (C).

12. **B** The correct idiom is *disappear from.* The sentence as written implies two things have disappeared when it should be just the *study of the classics.* Eliminate (A). Choices (C) and (D) are not the correct form of the idiom. Choice (B) is the correct answer.

13. **A** This sentence is correct as written. Although the phrase *for all that* might sound foreign, it is being used correctly here. Choice (B) does not make sense. Choices (C) and (D) are basically the same as (A), and remember, if there is no grammatical reason to change the original, don't. Therefore, (A) is correct.

14. **B** The correct idiom uses the words *in* and *right*, so (A), (C), and (D) can be eliminated. Choice (B) is correct.

15. **B** The correct answer will feature words or phrases that are as precise as possible. The sentence as written does not make clear to whom the pronoun is referring: Alexander or Aristotle. Choice (B) clears up this pronoun ambiguity. Choice (C) can be eliminated because Alexander was born in Pella, and his arrival as a newborn would not have announced an enlightened era, nor is it likely they arrived together. Choice (D) can also be eliminated because it does not clear up the ambiguity problem.

16. **D** Notice the question! It asks for a concluding statement that emphasizes the change brought about by Alexander's rule. Choices (A), (B), and (C) do not address the change from militaristic Philip to enlightened Alexander. Only (D) has the correct emphasis.

17. **C** Notice the question! It asks for an introductory phrase that emphasizes continuity from the previous rule. The only choice that refers to the previous rule and explains how the second sentence connects to the first in the paragraph is (C).

18. **A** Check the answer choices against the map, and make sure that the information is consistent with the figure. Choices (B) and (D) contain information that cannot be gleaned from the map, while (C) contains information that contradicts the map. Choice (A) is consistent with the map, so it is the correct answer.

19. **B** As written, the first part of the sentence creates a comma splice, wherein a comma separates two complete ideas. Choice (A) can be eliminated. Choice (B) is the best of the remaining answer choices because it is the most concise. A conjunction such as *although* or *moreover* is not needed due to the *however* in the preceding sentence. This sentence's purpose is to explain the preceding sentence.

20. **C** All of the information in this part of the sentence is necessary, so there is no reason to use any commas. Eliminate (A), (B), and (D) because they all have unnecessary commas. The correct answer is (C).

21. **D** The idea before the period (*Alexandria, Egypt, perhaps the most...continues to thrive*) is a complete idea. The idea after the period (*It is the second...of Egypt*) is also a complete idea. Therefore, the two cannot be joined together with only a comma. (Remember your STOP punctuation rules.) Eliminate (B). Of the remaining answer choices, (D) is the most effective way to combine the two sentences because it eliminates the need to repeat the subject, which makes the sentence flow better. Therefore, (D) is correct.

22. **A** The sentence as written is consistent in structure with *between man and god* and *the individual and the world,* both of which use the conjunction *and.* As the last item in this list, *and* should be used between *the natural and the unnatural.* All other choices are not consistent and change the meaning. Therefore, (A) is the answer.

23. **C** The correct answer will contain phrases that are as precise as possible. It is the dime novel that was *printed cheaply and for quick consumption*, so the words *dime novel* need to be placed

immediately next to the modifier phrase. Choices (A), (B), and (D) all include this misplaced modifier. Only (C) makes the sentence precise.

24. **D** Notice the question! It asks for the phrase that gives the most specific information. Choice (D) provides specific names of authors who wrote by way of literary periodicals. Choices (A), (B), and (C) refer to the authors only in vague terms.

25. **D** The title of Stowe's book is necessary information, which means it should not be surrounded by commas, so eliminate (B). Choices (A) and (C) have other unnecessary commas. The correct answer is (D) because it contains no commas at all.

26. **A** Choices (B), (C), and (D) all add more information after *book*, so consider whether that information is necessary to the meaning of the sentence. For (B), the word *actual* already implies the difference between a *book* and Stowe's previous works in a magazine, so the additional words aren't needed. Eliminate (B). Eliminate (C) because it is already clear that the book would be written by Stowe. Eliminate (D) because it does not need to be stated that the book *could be sold to Americans* as it is already implied. Choice (A) is concise and clear. The correct answer is (A).

27. **C** The average annual income of a man in this period is not in line with the main idea of the paragraph, which discusses the shift from periodicals to novels. To add this statement would be inconsistent with the paragraph's focus, which is stated in (C).

28. **A** Choices (B) and (D) use the wrong verb tense. Choice (C) is not in line with the focus of the paragraph. Additionally, since you do not know if the series is still known this way, (A) is the correct answer.

29. **B** *Effect* is generally a noun, while *affect* is a verb except in certain unusual circumstances. The underlined portion needs to be a noun, so *affects* is incorrect. Eliminate (A) and (D). The sentence discusses multiple effects, not something belonging to the effects, so the plural form of the verb is needed, not the possessive form. Eliminate (C). This leaves (B), which is the correct answer.

30. **B** The correct answer will feature words or phrases that make the passage as precise as possible. Without the actual names, the phrase *William Bonney and James Butler Hickcock became the folk heroes* does not make sense. You need the names of transformed folk heroes in order to make sense of the sentence. Eliminate (C) and (D). Choice (A) is incorrect because the rest of sentence does not speak in generalities; it provides two names already. Choice (B) is correct.

31. **C** The correct idiom is *learned from*, not *taught from*, so eliminate (A). The new media has not brought anything from the dime novel's popularity because it is something entirely new, so eliminate (D). *Learned* is more precise than *got*, so the correct answer is (C).

32. **C** As written, the sentence is unclear for whom or what the foundation is being laid, so eliminate (A). The underlined portion needs to follow the word *foundation* in order to clarify this. The correct answer will make the passage as precise as possible. This is (C).

33. **B** The passage is about the *dime novel* and how it provided a popular *mold* or *form*. The answer should mean something like "form." *Integration* means mixing together, so eliminate (A). *Framework* matches with "form," so keep (B). *Plan* means preparing for the future, which doesn't match with "form," so eliminate (C). *Composition* means "something made up," which doesn't match with "form" or "mold," so eliminate (D). The correct answer is (B).

34. **C** Be sure to compare similar things to maintain consistency and precision. The sentence as written compares *methods* to *humans*. Compare methods to methods, or change the construction of the sentence. Eliminate (A) and (D) because both make the same mistake. Choice (B) uses the singular pronoun *that* to refer to the plural *methods,* so eliminate it. Choice (C) uses the correct comparison and the plural pronoun, so it is correct.

35. **A** All four choices use similar words. Choose the one that expresses the idea most clearly. In this case, the clearest choice is (A). Choice (B) is passive and contains unnecessary commas. Choice (C) contains the awkward phrase *main among which is its*. Choice (D) uses *curious* as an adjective instead of a noun, implying that the weaponry is curious about something instead of being a curiosity itself.

36. **D** This sentence does not refer to the bats (bats cannot shout). Eliminate (A) and (B). The sentence uses the word *you* later, so this underlined portion should be consistent with the rest of the sentence. Eliminate (C). Choice (D) correctly replaces *they* with *you*.

37. **D** All four choices use similar words. Choose the one that expresses the idea most clearly and concisely. In this case, the answer is (D). *Instincts* does not need to be repeated because the word *innate* was already used.

38. **B** Notice the question! The question asks for a phrase that emphasizes a common misunderstanding about bats' vision. Choice (A) compares bats' vision to shrimp, which is not a common misunderstanding. Choices (C) and (D) describe aspects of bats' hunting but do not emphasize a common misunderstanding. Only (B) discusses the common thought (or cliché) about bats being blind.

39. **C** The pronoun *its* is ambiguous, as it is unclear whether it refers to the tiger moth or the bat. The correct choice features words that are as precise as possible, so eliminate (A). The other choices clear up the ambiguity, but only (C) has the correct possessive singular pronoun needed. Choice (B) uses a plural pronoun, but since only a single system of echolocation is referred to, the singular *bat's* is appropriate.

40. **B** Use the Vertical Line Test. The first part of the sentence, *Most tiger moths can emit clicks that warn bats away from the moths*, is a complete idea. The second part of the sentence, *suggesting*

that the moths might be inedible toxic compounds, is an incomplete idea. To connect these ideas, GO or HALF-STOP punctuation is needed. Eliminate (A) and (D) because they are STOP punctuation. Now decide whether a comma is needed. There is a shift in ideas, so a comma is needed. Also, without the comma, it could sound like the moths are *suggesting* something. Eliminate (C). The correct answer is (B).

41. **C** The pronoun refers to *the tiger moth,* which is the name of a species and therefore a collective noun. Collective nouns are singular, so eliminate (A) because it is inconsistent. When dealing with pronouns, remember that possessives do not use apostrophes, while contractions do use apostrophes. Choice (B) contains a contraction. It would not make sense to say *the tiger moth and it is sonar jamming,* so eliminate (B). There is no such word as *its',* so eliminate (D). The sonar jamming belongs to the tiger moth, so a possessive pronoun is needed, as in (C).

42. **A** The commas is correct as written. There should be a comma after each item in a list of three or more items. A comma is needed after *counterattack*, but not after *and* or *adapt.* Choices (B) and (D) contain unnecessary commas, while (C) does not contain any; therefore, (A) is the answer.

43. **A** Check the answer choices against the figures. Only (A) can be supported by the diagram. There is no indication of other animals, as in (B); what sounds are or are not heard, as in (D); or bats running into each other, as in (C).

44. **D** Paragraph 5 does not fit as a conclusion, so eliminate (A). This paragraph should come after the discussion of the tiger moth and its tactics and before the conclusion of the essay. This indicates the best placement is after the third paragraph, so (D) is the answer.

Section 3: Math (No Calculator)

1. **A** The vertex form of a parabola is $y = a(x - h)^2 + k$, where (h, k) denotes the vertex. Plug in the point $(3, -3)$ into the vertex form to get $y = a(x - 3)^2 - 3$. The correct answer is (A).

2. **C** You can plug in to make sense of this equation. Say that $x = \$100$. The amount of the keg would then be $\$107 + \$17$. The $\$17$ must be the untaxed deposit since it is a flat fee rather than percentage based. Therefore, the tax is $\$7$, which is 7% of the original $\$100$ base price. The answer is (C).

3. **D** Whenever there are variables in the question, plug in. Be sure to plug in a number that is divisible by 3. Let $d = 300$. $\frac{1}{3}$ of the original amount of $\$300$ is $\$100$, and that is deducted by the company, leaving Syed with $\$200$. Then, subtract the wire transfer fee to get $\$200 - \$30 = \$170$, which is the target number. Plug in 300 for d in the answer choices

to see which one is equal to the target number of 170. In (A), $\frac{1}{3}$ (300) − 30 = 70. This is

not the target number, so eliminate (A). Likewise in (B), $\frac{1}{3}$ (300 − 30) = 90, and in (C),

$\frac{2}{3}$ (300 − 30) = 180. Neither of these is the target number, so eliminate (B) and (C). In (D),

$\frac{2}{3}$ (300) − 30 = 170, which is the target number. The correct answer is (D).

4. **C** All of the answers are written in the slope-intercept form $y = mx + b$, where b is the y-intercept

and x and y are points on the line. Eliminate (D) because the y-intercept in that equation is

2. For the remaining answer choices, plug in the x- and y-values to determine which equation

works. If $x = 1$ and $y = 6$, (A) becomes $6 = \frac{1}{2}(1) + 4$. Solve both sides of the equation to get

$6 = 4\frac{1}{2}$. Eliminate (A). Choice (B) becomes 6 = 1 + 4, so eliminate (B). Choice (C) becomes

6 = 2(1) + 4, or 6 = 6. Therefore, the correct answer is (C).

5. **C** Whenever there are variables in the question and the answer choices, think Plugging In. If 2

purchases were made, then $p = 2$, and the number of bonus points can be calculated as 4(2) + 7 =

8 + 7 = 15. If the number of purchases were then increased by 3, the new p equals 5 and the num-

ber of bonus points can be calculated as 4(5) + 7 = 27. The bonus points increased by 27 − 15 = 12.

The correct answer is (C).

6. **B** This is a good PITA question. Start with (B) and plug in 2 for x and 3 for r in the equation to

get $V = 24\pi + 2\left(\frac{4}{3}\pi 3^3\right)$, which is equal to the target amount of 96π, so (B) is correct.

7. **C** Whenever there are variables in the question and in the answers, think Plugging In. Let $c = 30$.

Therefore, $b = 2 + \frac{1}{3}(30) = 2 + 10 = 12$. Plug 12 in for b in the answers to see which answer

equals the target number of 30. Choice (A) becomes $\frac{12 - 2}{3} = \frac{10}{3} = 3.\overline{3}$. Eliminate (A), since

it does not equal the target number. Choice (B) becomes $\frac{12 + 2}{3} = \frac{14}{3} = 4.\overline{6}$. Eliminate (B).

Choice (C) becomes 3(12 − 2) = 3(10) = 30. Keep (C), but check (D) just in case it also works.

Choice (D) becomes 3(12 − 6) = 3(6) = 18. Eliminate (D). The correct answer is (C).

8. **D** Treat this question as a translation problem. According to the question, $R(h)$ = four rotations

per second less than three times the square of the height of the liquid. The height of the liquid

is represented by h. Therefore, three times the square of the height of the liquid = $3h^2$. Four less

than this amount is $3h^2 - 4$. Since the original speed was 1,000, subtract this value from 1,000

to get the current rate of rotation. The correct answer is (D).

9. **B** Start with the easier equation and use Process of Elimination. The easier equation is related to the total number of ounces, $c + b$, in the tube. According to the question, the tube has 24 ounces, so $c + b = 24$. Eliminate (A), since it does not include this equation. The other equation in the set is related to the amount of active ingredients. According to the question, c includes 0.25% of sodium fluoride and b contains 0.30% triclosan. 0.25% = 0.0025 and 0.30% = 0.003. Therefore, in the correct equation, c should be associated with 0.0025 and b should be associated with 0.003. Eliminate (C) and (D) because both of these equations get the percentages wrong. The correct answer is (B).

10. **C** Whenever the question includes variables and the answer choices are numbers, think PITA. In (A), $d = -4$, and the equation becomes $\frac{2(-4)^2 - (-4) - 10}{(-4)^2 + 7(-4) + 10} = \frac{(-4)^2 - 4(-4) + 3}{(-4)^2 + 2(-4) - 15}$.

    Solve both sides of the equation to get $\frac{2(16) + 4 - 10}{16 - 28 + 10} = \frac{16 + 16 + 3}{16 - 8 - 15}$, or $\frac{26}{-2} = \frac{35}{-7}$. Reduce

    both fractions to get $-13 = -5$. This is not true, so eliminate (A). In (B), $d = 2$, and the equa-

    tion becomes $\frac{2(2)^2 - 2 - 10}{2^2 + 7(2) + 10} = \frac{2^2 - 4(2) + 3}{2^2 + 2(2) - 15}$. Solve both sides of the equation to get

    $\frac{2(4) - 2 - 10}{4 + 14 + 10} = \frac{4 - 8 + 3}{4 + 4 - 15}$, or $\frac{-4}{28} = \frac{-1}{-7}$. Reduce both fractions to get $\frac{-1}{7} = \frac{1}{7}$. Eliminate

    (B). In (C), $d = 4$ and the equation becomes $\frac{2(4)^2 - 4 - 10}{4^2 + 7(4) + 10} = \frac{4^2 - 4(4) + 3}{4^2 + 2(4) - 15}$. Solve both

    sides of the equation to get $\frac{2(16) - 4 - 10}{16 + 28 + 10} = \frac{16 - 16 + 3}{16 + 8 - 15}$, or $\frac{18}{54} = \frac{3}{9}$. Reduce both fractions

    to get $\frac{1}{3} = \frac{1}{3}$. The correct answer is (C).

11. **D** All the answer choices are equal to 4 (which is r^2, making $r = 2$), so you need to focus on where the center of the circle lies. If the circle is tangent to both the x-axis (which is equivalent to the line $y = 0$) and the line $x = 4$, then the center must be 2 units from $y = 0$ and 2 units from $x = 4$. Choices (A) and (B) both have centers with an x-value of -2 (remember the standard form of the circle equation is $(x - h)^2 + (y - k)^2 = r^2$, where (h, k) is the center and r is the radius), which is 6 units from $x = 4$. Eliminate (A) and (B). Choice (C) has a center at $(2, -4)$. The x-value is 2 units from $x = 4$; however, the y-value is 4 units from $y = 0$. Eliminate (C) and choose (D).

12. **B** According to the question, Reactant A does not react unless B gets to a certain concentration. Therefore, the correct answer will have an initial flat line for A while the line for B is rising. Only graph (B) shows this initial relationship. Therefore, the correct answer is (B).

13. **A** All of the answer choices have the same lines graphed, so this question is really about the shading. Plugging In is probably the easiest way to approach this question. Start with $(0, 0)$ because this is an easy value to check. This works in all three equations since $0 \le 8$, $-3 \le 0$, and $1 \ge 0$. Therefore, this value needs to be shaded as a possible answer. Eliminate (B), (C), and (D) because they do not include this point. The correct answer is (A).

14. **B** The question says that tan $\angle BCA$ is $\dfrac{3}{4}$, so draw segment CA. Since tan $= \dfrac{\text{opposite}}{\text{adjacent}}$, $\dfrac{AB}{BC} = \dfrac{3}{4}$. Let $AB = 3x$ and $BC = 4x$. The question says that the area of the rectangle is 48. The formula for the area of the rectangle is $A = lw$. Plug in $A = 48$, $l = 3x$, and $w = 4x$ into the formula to get $48 = (3x)(4x)$. Simplify the right side to get $48 = 12x^2$. Divide both sides by 12 to get $4 = x^2$. Then take the square root of both sides to get $x = 2$. Therefore, $AB = 3x = 3(2) = 6$, and $BC = 4x = 4(2) = 8$. The question asks for the length of $\overline{BD}$, which is the diagonal of the rectangle and equal to diagonal AC. The diagonal of the rectangle is the hypotenuse of a right triangle. Since the two legs are 6 and 8, this is 6-8-10 right triangle, so the hypotenuse is 10. The answer is (B).

15. **D** Whenever there are variables in the question and answers, think Plugging In. If $m = 2$, the expression becomes $\dfrac{2(2) + 6}{4} \times \dfrac{6(2) - 36}{3(2) + 9} = \dfrac{4 + 6}{4} \times \dfrac{12 - 36}{6 + 9} = \dfrac{-24}{15} \times \dfrac{10}{4} = \dfrac{-240}{60} = -4$.

Plug 2 in for m in the answer choices to see which one equals the target number of -4. Choice (A) becomes $\dfrac{12(2)^2 - 216}{12(2) + 36} = \dfrac{12(4) - 216}{24 + 36} = \dfrac{48 - 216}{60} = \dfrac{-168}{60} = -2.8$. This does not match the target number, so eliminate (A). Choice (B) becomes $\dfrac{8(2) - 30}{3(2) + 13} = \dfrac{16 - 30}{6 + 13} = \dfrac{-14}{19}$. Eliminate (B). Choice (C) becomes $\dfrac{2 - 6}{4} = \dfrac{-4}{4} = -1$. Eliminate (C). Choice (D) becomes $m - 6 = 2 - 6 = -4$. The correct answer is (D).

16. $\dfrac{3}{2}$ or **1.5**

Plug the given values into the equation for the volume of a rectangular solid: $18 = (3)(4)(x)$.

Multiply the right side of the equation to find that $18 = 12x$. Divide both sides by 12 to find that $x = \dfrac{18}{12}$. Both 18 and 12 are divisible by 6, so this fraction reduces to $\dfrac{3}{2}$ or 1.5.

17. **53** Jeanne charges $5.50 \times 2 = \$11$ per hour for babysitting. Therefore, her entire earnings for three hours can be calculated as $(3 \times 11) + 20 = 53$. The correct answer is 53.

18. **10** To solve the problem without a graphing calculator, set the two equations equal to each other: $-x^2 + 5x + 6 = -\dfrac{1}{2}x + 12$. Multiply the entire equation by 2 to get $-2x^2 + 10x + 12 = -x + 24$. Rewrite the equation to equal 0, so it becomes $-2x^2 + 11x - 12 = 0$. Multiply the entire equation by -1 to get $2x^2 - 11x + 12 = 0$. Then factor the quadratic to get $(2x - 3)(x - 4) = 0$. Solve for the two possible values of x: if $2x - 3 = 0$, then $x = \dfrac{3}{2}$, and if $x - 4 = 0$, then $x = 4$. Because the slope of the line is negative, the x-value of the point that is farthest to the right along the x-axis must also be closer to the x-axis. Plug 4 in for x in the second equation to get $y = -\dfrac{1}{2}(4) + 12 = -2 + 12 = 10$. The correct answer is 10.

19. $\dfrac{11}{3}$ or **3.66** or **3.67**

   Whenever there are two equations with the same two variables, the equations can be solved simultaneously by adding or subtracting them. Take the second equation and rewrite it so that the variables are on the left side of the equation: $17r + 22v = 63$. Stack the equations and add them together.

   $$
   \begin{array}{r}
   13r + 8v = 47 \\
   \underline{17r + 22v = 63} \\
   30r + 30v = 110
   \end{array}
   $$

   Divide the entire equation by 30 to get $r + v = \dfrac{110}{30}$. This is too big to grid in, so reduce it to $\dfrac{11}{3}$ or 3.66 or 3.67.

20. **2** The area of the current plot is $4 \times 6 = 24$ square feet, so the new plot will be $24 \times 2 = 48$ square feet. According to the question, x feet will be added to each side to obtain the new area of 48 feet. Since the length is only 2 feet more than the width, you need two factors of 48 that differ by 2. You may recognize that these factors are 6 and 8. So, the increase was 2 feet in each direction. Alternatively, you can write a quadratic: $(4 + x)(6 + x) = 48$. Expand the right side of the equation to get $x^2 + 10x + 24 = 48$. Set the equation to 0 by subtracting 48 from both sides to get $x^2 + 10x - 24 = 0$. Factor the equation to get $(x + 12)(x - 2) = 0$. Therefore, $x = -12$ or $x = 2$. Since lengths can never be negative, the only possible value is $x = 2$. The correct answer is 2.

Section 4: Math (Calculator)

1. **C** Use Process of Elimination. According to the question, P represents the population, so the outcome of the entire equation has something to do with the population. Therefore, eliminate both (A) and (B) because 1.0635 can't represent the population if P does. In the given equation, the only operations are multiplication and addition, which means that over time the population would increase. Therefore, eliminate (D). The correct answer is (C).

2. **B** To solve the quadratic equation, first set the equation equal to 0. The equation becomes $x^2 + 12x - 64 = 0$. Next, factor the equation to get $(x + 16)(x - 4) = 0$. Therefore, the two possible solutions for the quadratic equation are $x + 16 = 0$ and $x - 4 = 0$, so $x = -16$ or 4. Since the question states that $x > 0$, $x = 4$ is the only possible solution. Another way to approach this question is to use PITA. Start with (B), $x = 4$. Plug 4 into the equation to get $4^2 + 12(4) = 64$. Solve the left side of the equation to get $16 + 48 = 64$, or $64 = 64$. Since this is a true statement, the correct answer is (B).

3. **A** To figure out the total number of shelving units Sai could use, find the total available wall space and divide by the length of the units. The total amount of wall space can be calculated as $119 - 21$. Because the length of each unit is 7 feet, the maximum number of units Sai could put up can be calculated as $\dfrac{119 - 21}{7}$. Because this is the maximum number of units Sai could put up, r has to be less than or equal to this number. Therefore, the correct answer is (A).

4. **C** Weight is shown on the vertical axis of the graph, given in ounces. Make your own mark indicating 5.75 on this axis; then draw a horizontal line from that mark to the line of best fit. Once you hit it, draw a vertical line straight down to the horizontal axis. It should hit between 75 and 80 days, slightly closer to the mark for 75. This makes (C) the correct answer. Draw your lines carefully, using your answer sheet as a straightedge if necessary.

5. **C** Whenever the question includes variables, plug in. If $s = 2$, the shirts cost 2($24.50) = $49. The tax on the shirts is 0.07($49) = $3.43. So, the shirts with tax and the $6 shipping fee cost $49 + $3.43 + $6 = $58.43. Plug in 2 for s in the answers to see which answer equals the target number of $58.43. In (A), 0.07[24.50(2) + 6] = 3.85. This is not the target number, so eliminate (A). In (B), 1.07(24.50 + 6)(2) = 65.25. Again, this is not the target number, so eliminate (B). In (C), 1.07[24.50(2)] + 6 = 58.43. This is the target number, so keep it, but be sure to check the remaining answer choice. In (D), 1.07(24.50 + 2) + 6 = 34.355, which is not the target number. Therefore, the correct answer is (C).

6. **B** The question states that after 6 weeks the plant is 54 centimeters tall. Therefore, when $w = 6$, $h(w) = 54$. Plug in 6 for w in the answer choices to see which one equals the target number of 54. In (A), $h(w) = 6(6) = 36$. Eliminate (A). In (B), $h(w) = 9(6) = 54$. The correct answer is (B).

7. **D** Because the operation between the parentheses is addition, the parentheses can be removed, and the resulting expression becomes $12x^2 + 4x + 5y + 3x^2 - 2x + 3y$. Reorder the terms so that like terms are next to each other: $12x^2 + 3x^2 + 4x - 2x + 5y + 3y$. Combine like terms to get $15x^2 + 2x + 8y$. The correct answer is (D).

8. **D** You do not know how the survey is conducted, nor do you know how many veterinarians were surveyed (it may be the case that only 8 were surveyed). Therefore, you cannot infer that the survey accurately measures all veterinarians' beliefs about Royal Rat Rations. Choice (A) is not supported. First, you do not know what veterinarians believe in general, and second, veterinarians may be recommending Royal Rat Rations for a reason other than its nutrition. Choice (B) is similarly not supported: besides not knowing veterinarians' beliefs, this choice assumes that no other rat food is acceptable. Choice (C) is not supported because you do not know the sample size of the survey, nor is there any indication that there is only one veterinarian who does not recommend Royal Rat Rations. Choice (D) is the correct answer: you know the opinions only of the veterinarians surveyed by Royal Rat Rations.

9. **D** Use a calculator to translate the fractions into decimals. $\frac{1}{2}t + 4 = \frac{3}{4}t - 5$ becomes $0.5t + 4 = 0.75t - 5$. Subtract $0.5t$ from both sides to get $4 = 0.25t - 5$, and then add 5 to both sides. This results in $9 = 0.25t$. Use a calculator to divide: $t = 36$; therefore, the correct answer is (D).

10. **C** Taking the two dogs together, Everett has $35 + 55 = 90$ pounds of dog. Set up the following proportion to determine the lowest amount of water the dogs need per day: $\frac{8.5 \text{ ounces}}{10 \text{ lbs}} = \frac{x}{90 \text{ lbs}}$. Cross-multiply to get $10x = 765$, so $x = 76.5$. Multiply by 7 days to get the weekly amount of water the dogs need: $76.5 \times 7 = 535.5$ ounces, or approximately 536 ounces. Only (C) includes 536 as the low-end amount. Therefore, the correct answer is (C).

11. **A** In order to answer this question, you need to deal with the ratio as well as the unit conversion. For the large batch of dry rub, Priya's friend is planning to use 91 ounces of chili powder. Since the paprika and the chili powder must be used in a ratio of 4 to 7, you can set up a proportion to determine how much paprika is needed: $\frac{4}{7} = \frac{x}{91}$. Cross-multiply and solve for x to determine that x (i.e., paprika) = 52 ounces. So you have 52 ounces of paprika and 91 ounces of chili powder for a total of 143 ounces. Multiply that by your conversion number, 28.3, to determine that this is equivalent to 4,046.9 grams, which is closest to (A).

12. **D** Whenever there are variables in the problem and in the answer choices, plug in. If $w = 20$, then Luciano's cup has $20 - 2 = 18$ ounces at the end of day 1. At the end of 7 days, Luciano's cup would have $18 - 8 = 10$ ounces. After 11 days, Luciano's cup would hold $10 - 5 = 5$ ounces. Plug in 20 for w in the answer choices to see which answer is equal to the target number of 5. Choice (A) becomes $\frac{20 - 2}{8} = \frac{18}{8} = 2.25$. This does not match the target number of 5, so eliminate (A). Choice (B) becomes $\frac{20 - 2}{2} - 10 = \frac{18}{2} - 10 = 9 - 10 = -1$. Eliminate (B). Choice (C) becomes $\left(\frac{1}{2}\right)(20) - 10 = 10 - 10 = 0$. Eliminate (C). Choice (D) becomes $\frac{20 - 10}{2} = \frac{10}{2} = 5$. This matches the target number; therefore, the correct answer is (D).

13. **B** According to the line of best fit, in 1995 there were 20 coyotes in the park. In 2000, there were 140 coyotes in the park. This is an increase of 120 coyotes over a period of 5 years, so $\frac{120}{5}$ = an average increase of 24 coyotes per year, which is (B).

14. **D** The median number of coyotes in the park in 1995 was 20, and the median number of coyotes in the park in 1996 was 60. (Be careful to RTFQ; the question wants the median, not the line of best fit!) In order to calculate the percent increase, it is necessary to use the percent change formula: $\frac{\text{difference}}{\text{original}} \times 100$. The calculation here will be $\frac{60 - 20}{20} \times 100 = \frac{40}{20} \times 100 = 2 \times 100 = 200\%$, which is (D).

15. **A** Start with the easier equation and use Process of Elimination. The easier equation is related to the total number of shirts and pants, $s + p$, sold on a regular day. The question states that on a regular day Bailey's sells $\frac{2}{3}$ the number of pants and shirts sold during a sale. $\frac{2}{3}(60) = 40$. Therefore, one of the equations in the correct answer will be $s + p = 40$. Eliminate (C) and (D) since neither includes this equation. The other equation is related to the money Bailey's earns on a regular day. According to the question, Bailey's earns a total of \$1,875 on a regular day, so the equation must equal \$1,875. Eliminate (B) because the total in the money equation is incorrect. The correct answer is (A).

16. **C** There are a few different ways to approach this question. In any approach, the best first step is to figure out how much income Bryan earned during the two-week period without the commission. Since he worked an average of 35 hours per week for two weeks, he worked a total of 70 hours. At a rate of $10.00 per hour base pay, this would add up to $700.00 ($70 \times 10 = 700$). Since Bryan's earnings were actually $850.00, that means he must have earned $150.00 of commission ($850 - 700 = 150$). At this point, you can calculate the percent commission algebraically or simply work backward from the answer choices. Algebraically, you know that $150.00 is equal to a certain percent of $5,000.00 in sales, which can be represented as follows: $150 = \frac{x}{100} (5,000)$. Solve for x, and you get 3, which is (C). If instead you wish to work backward from the answer choices, you can take each choice and calculate what 1%, 2%, etc. of $5,000.00 would be, and then add that back to $700.00 to see which choice matches your target of $850.00: (C).

17. **C** Cross-multiply to get $3(C + x) = (x - 3)(x + 8)$. Expand the right side of the equation to get $3(C + x) = x^2 + 5x - 24$. Distribute the 3 to get $3C + 3x = x^2 + 5x - 24$. Subtract $3x$ from both sides of the equation to get $3C = x^2 + 2x - 24$. Factor the right side of the equation to get $3C = (x + 6)(x - 4)$. Divide both sides by 3 to get $C = \frac{(x + 6)(x - 4)}{3} = \frac{1}{3}(x + 6)(x - 4)$. The correct answer is (C). Alternatively, you can plug in for x to get a target value for C, and then use Process of Elimination.

18. **A** Start with the easiest piece of information first, and use Process of Elimination. Since h is the number of hours spent hiking and d is the number of hours driving, the total number of hours Lennon spends in the park can be calculated as $h + d$. The question states that Lennon has up to 6 hours to spend in the park—"up to" means ≤. So, $h + d \le 6$. Eliminate (B), (C), and (D). The correct answer is (A).

19. **B** The quality control expert discovered that 13 out of 1,000 randomly selected tennis balls were defective. $\frac{13}{1,000} = 0.013$, which is equivalent to 1.3%. This means that $100 - 1.3 = 98.7\%$ of tennis balls tested were not defective, and this data most supports (B), which is the correct answer.

20. **C** When solving inequalities, the natural impulse is to isolate the variable. In this case, though, look at what the question is asking. The question doesn't want you to find just the value of z, but rather the value of $9z - 18$. To get from the value of $-3z + 6$ given in the inequality to

this new value, the original inequality must be multiplied by –3. Just multiply the entire inequality by this value, making sure to flip the inequality signs when multiplying by a negative number. The equation becomes $-3\left(-\dfrac{20}{7}\right) > -3(-3z + 6) > -3\left(-\dfrac{11}{5}\right)$ or $\dfrac{60}{7} > 9z - 18 > \dfrac{33}{5}$. The question asks for the greatest possible integer value, so focus on the high end of the given values. The value at that end, $\dfrac{60}{7}$, equals 8.57, so the greatest integer less than that is 8. The answer is (C).

21. **A** Whenever there are variables in the question and numbers in the answer choices, think PITA. In (A), $j = 6$, and $k = -6$. Plug these two values into the first equation to get $-24 - 8(6) = 12(-6)$. Solve for both sides of the equation to get $-24 - 48 = -72$, or $-72 = -72$. Therefore, the values work for the first equation. Plug the values into the second equation to get $3 + \dfrac{5}{3}(-6) = -\dfrac{7}{6}(6)$. Solve both sides of the equation to get $3 + (-10) = -7$, or $-7 = -7$. Since the values given in (A) work in both equations, the correct answer is (A).

22. **C** You know the new proportion must be less than the current 0.34 for biofuels (because the total amount spent on alternative energy is increasing, but the amount spent on biofuels is remaining the same), so you can eliminate (D). Next, determine the amount that will be spent on biofuels in 2017 by multiplying 0.34 by the total of $254 million: $0.34 \times 254 = \$86.36$ million. Because 57 million new dollars will be spent on alternative energy, the new total will be 254 + 57 = $311 million. Divide $86.36 million by $311 million to get the new proportion: $\dfrac{86.38}{311} = 0.28$, which is (C).

23. **D** In Quadrant II, the x-coordinate is negative, and the y-coordinate is positive. Therefore, eliminate (C). Whenever the question includes variables and the answer choices are numbers, think PITA. Of the remaining choices, (B) is easiest to work with. In (B), the x-value is –4 and the y-value is 2. Plug these values into the second equation to get $-4 = -2 + 2$. Since this is not a true statement, eliminate (B). Try the values in (A) in the second equation to get $3\sqrt{2} = -(-3\sqrt{2}) + 2$. This is also not true, so the correct answer is (D).

24. **B** Right away, (A) can be eliminated, since point C has a negative y-coordinate. Given any two points, the slope of the line can be determined using the equation $\dfrac{y_2 - y_1}{x_2 - x_1}$. Use this formula to find the value of b by setting the slope of $\overline{AB}$ equal to the slope of $\overline{BC}$. Use points (0, 3) and

(5*b*, *b*) in the left side of the equation and points (5*b*, *b*) and (10*b*, –*b*) in the right side of the equation to get $\dfrac{3-b}{0-5b} = \dfrac{-b-b}{10b-5b}$. Simplify both sides of the equation to get $\dfrac{3-b}{-5b} = \dfrac{-2b}{5b}$, or $\dfrac{3-b}{-5b} = \dfrac{-2}{5}$. Cross-multiply to get 5(3 – *b*) = 10*b*. Divide both sides by 5 to get 3 – *b* = 2*b*. Add *b* to both sides to get 3 = 3*b*. Divide both sides by 3 to get *b* = 1. Plug in *b* =1 for point *C* to get [10(1), – (1)], or (10, –1). Therefore, the correct answer is (B).

25. **A** The formula for compound interest is $A = P(1 + r)^t$, where *P* is the starting principle, *r* is the rate expressed as a decimal, and *t* is the number of times the interest is compounded. Melanie received less than 5% interest, so you can eliminate (B) because 1.05 = 1 + 0.05, which indicates that she was receiving 5% interest. You can also eliminate (C) because over the course of a year, the interest is compounded 4 times, not $\dfrac{1}{3}$ of a time. Because Melanie invested $1,100 at what she thought was 5% compounded 4 times (12 months in a year ÷ 3 months per period), she expected $1,100(1 + 0.05)^4 = \$1,337.06$ after a year. Instead, she has 1,337.06 – 50 = $1,287.06 after one year. Because *t* is in years in the answer choices, make *t* = 1 in (A) and (D) and eliminate any choice that does not equal 1,287.06. Only (A) works.

26. **B** You can start by plugging in a value for *x;* try *x* = 4. Because angle *AOB* is 120° and the triangle is isosceles, angles *A* and *B* are each 30°. Cut triangle *AOB* in half to make two 30-60-90 triangles with a hypotenuse of 4 and legs of 2 and $2\sqrt{3}$. The leg with length $2\sqrt{3}$ lies on chord *AB*. Double it to get the total length: $4\sqrt{3}$ or just $\sqrt{3}x$, which is (B) when you put *x* = 4 into the answer choices.

27. **C** Whenever there are variables in the question and in the answer choices, think Plugging In.

The question states the value of *g*, but it is a constant and a weird one at that. Pick numbers for all the variables that will make the math more straightforward. If *v* = 4 and *g* = 2, then

$$t = \frac{2(4) \cdot \sin(\theta)}{2} = \frac{8 \cdot \sin(\theta)}{2} = 4 \cdot \sin(\theta), \quad \text{and} \quad R = \frac{4^2 \cdot \sin(2\theta)}{2} = \frac{16 \cdot \sin(2\theta)}{2} = 8 \cdot \sin(2\theta).$$

Plug these values into the answer choices to see which equation works. Choice (A) becomes

$4 = \dfrac{4 \cdot \sin(\theta) \cdot \sin(\theta)}{2[8\sin(2\theta)\sin(\theta)]}$. Simplify the right side of the equation to get $4 = \dfrac{4 \cdot \sin(\theta) \cdot \sin(\theta)}{16\sin(2\theta)\sin(\theta)}$,

or $4 = \dfrac{\sin(\theta)}{4\sin(2\theta)}$. This will not simplify further, so eliminate (A). Choice (B) becomes

$4 = \dfrac{2[4\sin(\theta)]\sin(\theta)}{8\sin(2\theta)(\sin(\theta))}$. Simplify the right side of the equation to get $4 = \dfrac{8\sin(\theta)(\sin(\theta))}{8\sin(2\theta)(\sin(\theta))}$ or

$4 = \dfrac{\sin(\theta)}{\sin(2\theta)}$. Eliminate (B). Choice (C) becomes $4 = \dfrac{2[8\sin(2\theta)]\sin(\theta)}{(4\sin(2\theta))(\sin(2\theta))}$. Distribute the 2 to get

$4 = \dfrac{16\sin(2\theta)\sin(\theta)}{(4\sin(\theta))(\sin(2\theta))}$. Reduce the equation to get $4 = \dfrac{16}{4}$ or $4 = 4$. The correct answer is (C).

28. **D** $i^a = 1$ when a is a multiple of 4. Use the exponents rule to determine that $413 + x$ must also be a multiple of 4. Plug in the answers and look for what makes $413 + x$ a multiple of 4. Only (D) works.

29. **C** The zero of g is the value of the variable, in this case x, when the equation is set to 0. This is also called the root or solution of an equation. Set the equation to 0 to get $0 = 2x^2 - dx - 6$. Plug 6 in for x to get $0 = 2(6^2) - d(6) - 6$. Simplify the equation to get $0 = 72 - 6d - 6$, or $0 = 66 - 6d$. Solve for d to get $-66 = -6d$, so $11 = d$. Plug 11 in for d and set the quadratic to 0 to get $0 = 2x^2 - 11x - 6$. Factor the equation to get $0 = (x - 6)(2x + 1)$. The other zero of the equation is when $2x + 1 = 0$. Solve for x to get $2x = -1$, or $x = \dfrac{-1}{2}$. The correct answer is (C).

30. **D** The flu shot is most effective against Strain C, which is least prevalent in March. To determine the overall efficacy of the flu shot at this time, multiply the prevalence of each strain of flu by the efficacy of the flu shot against that strain, and then add those products to get a weighted average of the efficacy of the shot: $(0.23 \times 0.35) + (0.25 \times 0.13) + (0.13 \times 0.76) + (0.39 \times 0.68) = 0.477 = 47.7\%$, which is closest to (D).

31. **3** Solve the equation for v. Take $9 > 3v - 3$ and add 3 to both sides to get $12 > 3v$. Now divide both sides by 3 to find that $4 > v$. Therefore, the largest integer that v could be is 3. Grid in 3.

32. $\dfrac{5}{6}$ **or .83**

Start by multiplying the second fraction in the denominator of the equation by $\dfrac{2}{2}$ to get

$\dfrac{\frac{6}{5}}{\frac{12}{2y} - \frac{10}{2y}} = 1$. Combine the fractions in the denominator to get $\dfrac{\frac{6}{5}}{\frac{2}{2y}} = 1$. Reduce the fraction in

the denominator to get $\dfrac{\frac{6}{5}}{\frac{1}{y}} = 1$. Dividing by a number is the same as multiplying by its reciprocal,

so the equation becomes $\dfrac{6}{5} \times y = 1$. Multiply both sides of the equation by $\dfrac{5}{6}$ to get $y = \dfrac{5}{6}$. The

correct answer is $\dfrac{5}{6}$ or .83.

33. **1,279** 614 students voting for Candidate A represents 0.48 of the population out of 1. Set up a proportion: $\frac{0.48}{1.00} = \frac{614}{x}$, where x is the total number of students in the school. Cross-multiply: $0.48x = 614$. Divide both sides by 0.48 and you get approximately 1,279.

34. $\frac{5}{13}$ or **.384** or **.385**

Draw a right triangle and label a non-right angle θ. SOHCAHTOA tells you that tangent is $\frac{\text{opposite}}{\text{adjacent}}$, so the leg opposite θ is 12 and the leg adjacent to θ is 5. Cosine is $\frac{\text{adjacent}}{\text{hypotenuse}}$, so you need to find the hypotenuse of the triangle. You can use the Pythagorean Theorem, or you can recognize this as a 5-12-13 Pythagorean triplet. The hypotenuse is therefore 13. The leg adjacent to θ is still 5, so $\cos \theta = \frac{5}{13}$ or .384 or .385.

35. **7,054** First, you need to determine the current exchange rate. The 7% fee is the same (relative to the exchange rate), whether it was applied to the Cedi or USD. Therefore, 7% of 651 Cedi is equal to 32.30 USD. Translate English to math: $0.07(651) = 32.30$, or 45.57 Cedi = 32.30 USD. Next, you want the value of an item worth 5,000 USD in Cedi, so set up a proportion: $\frac{45.57 \text{ Cedi}}{32.30 \text{ USD}} = \frac{x \text{ Cedi}}{5,000 \text{ USD}}$. Cross-multiply: $(45.57)(5,000) = 32.30x$, or $227,850 = 32.30x$. Divide both sides by 32.30 and you get $x = 7,054.18$ USD, which rounds to 7,054.

36. **63.6** or **63.7**

First, draw a square inscribed in a circle. Because the diameter of the circle is equal to the diagonal of the square, you can plug in a number like $2\sqrt{2}$ for the length of the diameter. Because the diameter forms a 45⁰-45⁰-90⁰ triangle, each side of the square has a length of 2. Using the area formula for a square ($A = s^2$), plug in 2 for the s to get $A = 2^2$, which simplifies to $A = 4$. The area of the square is 4. To find the area of the circle, use the formula $A = \pi r^2$. Because the diameter of the circle is $2\sqrt{2}$, $r = \sqrt{2}$. Plug that into the area formula to see that $A = \pi(\sqrt{2})^2$, which simplifies to $A = 2\pi$. To find the solution, translate the question from English into math. The area of the square is what percent of the area of the circle becomes: $4 = \frac{x}{100} \cdot 2\pi$. Solve for x. First, divide each side by 2π, and then multiply each side by 100. The answer is a non-repeating decimal beginning 63.66197…. When entering your answer, simply cut off the decimal so it takes up four spaces. You should enter 63.6 or 63.7.

37. $\dfrac{7}{10}$ or .7

If the mean of the new set is $\dfrac{5}{6}$, then the sum of the diameters of the cylinders divided by the number of cylinders must equal $\dfrac{5}{6}$. Set up the equation: $\dfrac{5}{6} = \dfrac{\dfrac{1}{2} + \dfrac{3}{4} + \dfrac{4}{5} + 1 + \dfrac{5}{4} + x}{6}$, where x is the unknown cylinder. Multiply both sides by 6 to simplify: $5 = \dfrac{1}{2} + \dfrac{3}{4} + \dfrac{4}{5} + 1 + \dfrac{5}{4} + x$.

Combine like terms (use your calculator, but be careful with parentheses!): $5 = \dfrac{43}{10} + x$. Subtract $\dfrac{43}{10}$ from both sides and you get $\dfrac{7}{10}$ or .7.

38.   **$1 \leq y \leq 1.25$**

A set with an even number of elements will have as its median the average of the middle two terms. In the current set, $\dfrac{4}{5}$ and 1 have an average of $\dfrac{9}{10}$, so the new cylinder must be equal to or greater than 1, so the median will be the average of $\dfrac{4}{5}$ and 1. The range of the set of five cylinders is the greatest minus the least: $\dfrac{5}{4} - \dfrac{1}{2} = \dfrac{3}{4}$. Because the new cylinder must be $\dfrac{1}{4}$ inches to $\dfrac{1}{2}$ greater than $\dfrac{3}{4}$, the cylinder must be between 1 and $\dfrac{5}{4}$ inches in diameter. Therefore, in the grid for this question, you can enter 1.1, 1.11, 1.2, 1.21, or any other number between 1 and 1.25.

RAW SCORE CONVERSION TABLE SECTION AND TEST SCORES

Raw Score (# of correct answers)	Math Section Score	Reading Test Score	Writing and Language Test Score
0	200	10	10
1	200	10	10
2	210	10	10
3	230	11	10
4	240	12	11
5	260	13	12
6	280	14	13
7	290	15	13
8	310	15	14
9	320	16	15
10	330	17	16
11	340	17	16
12	360	18	17
13	370	19	18
14	380	19	19
15	390	20	19
16	410	20	20
17	420	21	21
18	430	21	21
19	440	22	22
20	450	22	23
21	460	23	23
22	470	23	24
23	480	24	25
24	480	24	25
25	490	25	26
26	500	25	26
27	510	26	27
28	520	26	28
29	520	27	28

Raw Score (# of correct answers)	Math Section Score	Reading Test Score	Writing and Language Test Score
30	530	28	29
31	540	28	30
32	550	29	30
33	560	29	31
34	560	30	32
35	570	30	32
36	580	31	33
37	590	31	34
38	600	32	34
39	600	32	35
40	610	33	36
41	620	33	37
42	630	34	38
43	640	35	39
44	650	35	40
45	660	36	
46	670	37	
47	670	37	
48	680	38	
49	690	38	
50	700	39	
51	710	40	
52	730	40	
53	740		
54	750		
55	760		
56	780		
57	790		
58	800		

Please note that the numbers in the table may shift slightly depending on the SAT's scale from test to test; however, you can still use this table to get an idea of how your performance on the practice tests will translate to the actual SAT.

CONVERSION EQUATION SECTION AND TEST SCORES

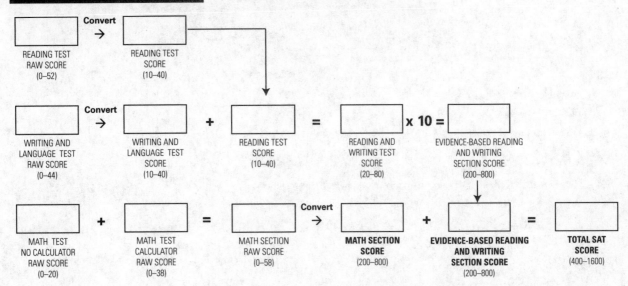

Practice Test 4

Reading Test

65 MINUTES, 52 QUESTIONS

Turn to Section 1 of your answer sheet to answer the questions in this section.

DIRECTIONS

Each passage or pair of passages below is followed by a number of questions. After reading each passage or pair, choose the best answer to each question based on what is stated or implied in the passage or passages and in any accompanying graphics (such as a table or graph).

Questions 1–10 are based on the following passage.

This passage is adapted from Charlotte Brontë, *Jane Eyre,* originally published in 1847.

While he spoke my very conscience and reason turned traitors against me, and charged me with crime in resisting him. They spoke almost as loud as Feeling:
Line and that clamored wildly. "Oh, comply!" it said.
5 "Think of his misery; think of his danger—look at his state when left alone; remember his headlong nature; consider the recklessness following on despair—soothe him; save him; love him; tell him you love him and will be his. Who in the world cares for you or who will be
10 injured by what you do?"

Still indomitable was the reply—"I care for myself. The more solitary, the more friendless, the more unsustained I am, the more I will respect myself. I will keep the law given by God; sanctioned by man. I will
15 hold to the principles received by me when I was sane, and not mad—as I am now. Laws and principles are not for the times when there is no temptation: they are for such moments as this, when body and soul rise in mutiny against their rigor; stringent are they; inviolate
20 they shall be. If at my individual convenience I might break them, what would be their worth? They have a worth—so I have always believed; and if I cannot believe it now, it is because I am insane—quite insane: with my veins running fire, and my heart beating faster
25 than I can count its throbs. Preconceived opinions, foregone determinations, are all I have at this hour to stand by: there I plant my foot."

I did. Mr. Rochester, reading my countenance, saw I had done so. His fury was wrought to the highest:
30 he must yield to it for a moment, whatever followed; he crossed the floor and seized my arm and grasped my waist. He seemed to devour me with his flaming glance: physically, I felt, at the moment, powerless as stubble exposed to the draught and glow of a furnace:
35 mentally, I still possessed my soul, and with it the certainty of ultimate safety. The soul, fortunately, has an interpreter—often an unconscious, but still a truthful interpreter—in the eye. My eye rose to his; and while I looked in his fierce face I gave an involuntary
40 sigh; his gripe was painful, and my over-taxed strength almost exhausted.

"Never," said he, as he ground his teeth, "never was anything at once so frail and so indomitable. A mere reed she feels in my hand!" And he shook me with
45 the force of his hold. "I could bend her with my finger and thumb: and what good would it do if I bent, if I uptore, if I crushed her? Consider that eye: consider the resolute, wild, free thing looking out of it, defying me, with more than courage—with a stern triumph.
50 Whatever I do with its cage, I cannot get at it—the savage, beautiful creature! If I tear, if I rend the slight prison, my outrage will only let the captive loose. Conqueror I might be of the house; but the inmate would escape to heaven before I could call myself
55 possessor of its clay dwelling-place. And it is you, spirit—with will and energy, and virtue and purity— that I want: not alone your brittle frame. Of yourself

CONTINUE ➡

you could come with soft flight and nestle against my
heart, if you would: seized against your will, you will
60 elude the grasp like an essence—you will vanish ere I
inhale your fragrance. Oh! Come, Jane, come!"

As he said this, he released me from his clutch, and
only looked at me. The look was far worse to resist
than the frantic strain: only an idiot, however, would
65 have succumbed now. I had dared and baffled his fury;
I must elude his sorrow: I retired to the door.

"You are going, Jane?"

"I am going, sir."

"You are leaving me?"

70 "Yes."

"You will not come? You will not be my comforter,
my rescuer? My deep love, my wild woe, my frantic
prayer, are all nothing to you?"

What unutterable pathos was in his voice! How
75 hard it was to reiterate firmly, "I am going."

1

Jane's attitude toward Mr. Rochester is best
characterized as

A) sympathetic.

B) uncaring.

C) despising.

D) reckless.

2

Based on the information in the passage, it can
be inferred that Jane refuses Rochester's advances
because

A) she does not love him as much as he loves her.

B) it would violate her personal ideals.

C) he thinks that she is weak and frail.

D) she wishes to cause him injury.

3

Which choice provides the best evidence for the
answer to the previous question?

A) Lines 1–3 ("While . . . him")

B) Lines 13–16 ("I will . . . now")

C) Lines 36–38 ("The soul . . . eye")

D) Lines 50–51 ("Whatever . . . creature")

4

In context, the phrase "I am insane—quite insane"
in line 23 refers chiefly to

A) a severe mental illness that Jane suffers from.

B) a mental state brought on by God's law.

C) a feeling that currently urges Jane to reject
Rochester.

D) a reduction of judgment due to emotion.

5

As used in line 29, "wrought" most nearly means

A) hammered.

B) made.

C) excited.

D) wrung.

6

The fourth paragraph (lines 42–61) provides a
contrast between

A) Jane's body and her will.

B) Rochester's love and anger toward Jane.

C) a bird and its cage.

D) Jane's purity and impurity.

7

The inmate Rochester mentions in line 53 refers to

A) a criminal locked away in jail.

B) Rochester trapped in his emotions.

C) Jane stuck in the traditions of her time.

D) the possible behavior of Jane's spirit.

CONTINUE

8

Which choice provides the best evidence for the answer to the previous question?

A) Lines 38–41 ("My eye . . . exhausted")

B) Lines 45–47 ("I could . . . her")

C) Lines 55–57 ("And it . . . frame")

D) Lines 63–65 ("The look . . . now")

9

As used in line 63, "worse" most nearly means

A) less desirable.

B) more difficult.

C) of lower quality.

D) unskillful.

10

Based on the information in the final paragraph, it can be reasonably inferred that Jane values

A) her emotions over her reason.

B) freedom over social convention.

C) her principles over her feelings.

D) true love above all else.

CONTINUE

Questions 11–21 are based on the following passage and supplementary material.

This passage is adapted from Hillary Clinton's remarks to the U.N. Fourth World Conference on Women Plenary Session in 1995 in Beijing, China.

There are some who question the reason for this conference. Let them listen to the voices of women in their homes, neighborhoods, and workplaces. There
Line are some who wonder whether the lives of women and
5 girls matter to economic and political progress around the globe. Let them look at the women gathered here and at Huairou—the homemakers and nurses, the teachers and lawyers, the policymakers and women who run their own businesses. It is conferences like
10 this that compel governments and peoples everywhere to listen, look, and face the world's most pressing problems. Wasn't it after all—after the women's conference in Nairobi ten years ago that the world focused for the first time on the crisis of domestic
15 violence?

The great challenge of this conference is to give voice to women everywhere whose experiences go unnoticed, whose words go unheard. Women comprise more than half the world's population, 70 percent of
20 the world's poor, and two-thirds of those who are not taught to read and write. We are the primary caretakers for most of the world's children and elderly. Yet much of the work we do is not valued—not by economists, not by historians, not by popular culture, not by
25 government leaders.

At this very moment, as we sit here, women around the world are giving birth, raising children, cooking meals, washing clothes, cleaning houses, planting crops, working on assembly lines, running
30 companies, and running countries. Women also are dying from diseases that should have been prevented or treated. They are watching their children succumb to malnutrition caused by poverty and economic deprivation. They are being denied the right to go to
35 school by their own fathers and brothers. They are being forced into prostitution, and they are being barred from the bank lending offices and banned from the ballot box.

Those of us who have the opportunity to be here
40 have the responsibility to speak for those who could not. As an American, I want to speak for those women in my own country, women who are raising children on the minimum wage, women who can't afford health care or child care, women whose lives are threatened
45 by violence, including violence in their own homes.

Speaking to you today, I speak for them, just as each of us speaks for women around the world who are denied the chance to go to school, or see a doctor, or own property, or have a say about the direction of their
50 lives, simply because they are women. The truth is that most women around the world work both inside and outside the home, usually by necessity.

We need to understand there is no one formula for how women should lead their lives. That is why
55 we must respect the choices that each woman makes for herself and her family. Every woman deserves the chance to realize her own God-given potential. But we must recognize that women will never gain full dignity until their human rights are respected and protected.

60 Tragically, women are most often the ones whose human rights are violated. Even now, in the late twentieth-century, the rape of women continues to be used as an instrument of armed conflict. Women and children make up a large majority of the world's
65 refugees. And when women are excluded from the political process, they become even more vulnerable to abuse. I believe that now, on the eve of a new millennium, it is time to break the silence. It is time for us to say for the world to hear that it is no longer
70 acceptable to discuss women's rights as separate from human rights.

If there is one message that echoes forth from this conference, let it be that human rights are women's rights and women's rights are human rights once and
75 for all. Let us not forget that among those rights are the right to speak freely—and the right to be heard.

Women must enjoy the rights to participate fully in the social and political lives of their countries, if we want freedom and democracy to thrive and endure. It
80 is indefensible that many women in nongovernmental organizations who wished to participate in this conference have not been able to attend—or have been prohibited from fully taking part.

As long as discrimination and inequities remain
85 so commonplace everywhere in the world, as long as girls and women are valued less, fed less, fed last, overworked, underpaid, not schooled, subjected to violence in and outside their homes—the potential of the human family to create a peaceful, prosperous
90 world will not be realized.

CONTINUE ▶

Poverty Rates by Age and Gender: 2012
(in percent)

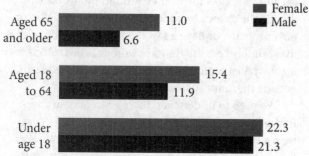

Poverty rates in the United States, divided by age and gender. Image courtesy the U.S. Census Bureau.

11

The position that Clinton takes in her speech can best be described as that of

A) a critic countering a series of arguments.

B) a scholar analyzing social phenomena.

C) an advocate seeking a particular outcome.

D) a mediator seeking a fair compromise.

12

As used in line 23, "valued" most nearly means

A) increased.

B) considered.

C) bought.

D) insured.

13

In lines 12–13, what is the most likely reason that Clinton mentions the prior "women's conference in Nairobi"?

A) To provide an example of a previous, failed attempt to solve the problem of domestic violence

B) To disagree with those who question the reason for the current conference

C) To contend that a great number of women and their experiences have gone unnoticed

D) To offer evidence for the claim that conferences compel people to address problems

---

14

Which choice provides the best evidence for the answer to the previous question?

A) Lines 1–2 ("There . . . conference")

B) Lines 9–12 ("It is . . . problems")

C) Lines 21–22 ("We are . . . elderly")

D) Lines 30–32 ("Women . . . treated")

15

In lines 39–45, Clinton draws a distinction between

A) those who work at schools and hospitals.

B) people who can and cannot speak out.

C) employed and unemployed women.

D) women who can and cannot vote.

16

Based on the information in the passage, women face each of the following challenges EXCEPT

A) lack of access to health care.

B) violence in their homes.

C) limited financial resources.

D) widespread unemployment.

CONTINUE

17

The principal rhetorical effect of the phrase in lines 73–75 ("let it … all") is to

A) argue against attempts to understand women's rights as distinct from other rights.

B) show that many women who should be at the conference are unable to attend.

C) emphasize the special nature of women's rights as they relate to human rights at large.

D) suggest that the need to focus on the specific problems of women is now past.

18

Which choice provides the best evidence for the answer to the previous question?

A) Lines 57–59 ("But we . . . protected")

B) Lines 68–71 ("It is . . . rights")

C) Lines 75–76 ("Let us . . . heard")

D) Lines 79–83 ("It is . . . part")

19

Based on the information presented in Clinton's speech, it can be inferred that some of those who have important positions of authority in the world

A) are actively working against the prosperity of women.

B) do not consider the labor done by women to be of serious import.

C) are ready to ensure that men and women have equal legal rights.

D) have made it unacceptable to discuss women's rights.

20

According to the figure, in the United States in 2012,

A) people aged 18 to 64 were more likely to live in poverty than were people under 18 years of age.

B) the greatest poverty rates existed among people over the age of 65.

C) the smallest gender disparity in poverty rates existed among people under the age of 18.

D) the gender disparity in poverty rates among those aged 18 to 64 was greater than that among people aged 65 and older.

21

Using information in the graph and the passage, it can be reasonably inferred that

A) in America and across the world the greatest gender disparity in poverty rates is among those 65 and older.

B) women 18 to 64 comprise 15.4 percent of the world's poor.

C) while a high percentage of children are poor in America, the opposite is true worldwide.

D) poverty rates in America are in line with a worldwide gender disparity.

CONTINUE

Questions 22–31 are based on the following passages.

Passage 1 is adapted from *Gardner's Art Through the Ages.* ©1991 by Harcourt Brace Jovanovich, Inc. Passage 2 is adapted from John Boardman, "The Parthenon Frieze—Another View. "©1977 by John Boardman. Both passages discuss the Parthenon Frieze, a band of sculpture that once encircled all four walls of the Parthenon, a temple to the goddess Athena. The naos is the inner sanctuary of the temple.

Passage 1

The inner Ionic frieze of figures was seen from below in reflected light against a colored ground. It enriched the plain wall and directed attention
Line toward the entrance to the temple. Though its subject
5 is still a matter of scholarly dispute ("the riddle of the Parthenon frieze"), it probably represents the Panathenaic procession that took place every four years when the citizens of Athens gathered in the marketplace and carried the *peplos*, or robe, for the
10 statue of Athena to the Parthenon. The robe was not for Phidias' ivory and gold statue, but for an older, archaic one, kept, ultimately, in the Erechtheion of the Acropolis. This is the first known representation of a nonmythological subject in Greek temple reliefs.
15 The Panathenaic frieze is unique in the ancient world for its careful creation of the impression of the passage of time, albeit a brief fragment of time. The effect is achieved by the use of a sequence of figures posed to present a gradation of motion. In the part of
20 the frieze that decorated the western side of the naos, the viewer can see the procession forming: youths are lacing their sandals and holding or mounting their horses; they are guided by marshals who stand at intervals, and particularly at the corners, to slow
25 movement and guide the horsemen at the turn. In the friezes of the two long sides of the naos, the procession moves in parallel lines, a cavalcade of spirited youths, chariots, elders, jar carriers, and animals for sacrifice. Seen throughout the procession
30 is that balance of the monumentally simple and the actual, of the tactile and the optical, of the "ideal" and the "real," of the permanent and the momentary that is characteristically Greek and the perfect exemplification of the "inner concord of opposites" that Heraclitus,
35 the philosopher, wrote of in the sixth century B.C. The movement of the procession becomes slower and more solemn as it nears the eastern side of the naos, when, after turning the corner, it approaches the seated divinities, who appear to be guests of Athena at her

40 great festival. Standing figures face against the general movement at ever-closer intervals, slowing the forward motion of the procession.

Passage 2

There are many representations of festival or sacrifice in classical Greek art but it is unparalleled to
45 find them attended by a number of guest deities, let alone the complete pantheon. And here we see Athena herself in their number; and they seem to be ignoring the handling of the peplos, which is the nearest we get to the culminating act of the procession. Finally,
50 there is the choice of subject. In Lawrence's words, "Never before has a contemporary subject been treated on a religious building and no subsequent Greek instance is known, with the doubtful exception of the Erechtheum. The flagrant breach with tradition
55 requires explanation."

It is unthinkable that a classical Athenian, looking up at the frieze, could have said to himself "there I go," or even more vaguely "there we go." The subject must be, in some respect, more than mortal and
60 the explanation must lie in the frieze itself and in knowledge of the background to its carving and the building on which it was placed. Moreover the explanation must have been apparent to the classical Athenian who knew this background. We cannot
65 exempt the frieze from the conventions of classical art.

We must rule out, then, the explanation that it is a contemporary or generic statement of the Panathenaic procession conducted by the citizens of Periclean Athens.
70 In classical Athens of these years there was one group of mortal Athenian citizens who, by their actions, had acquired the right to depiction on public buildings and in the company of the gods: these are the men who fought at Marathon.
75 Pausanias tells us that the people of Marathon worshipped the Athenian men who died as heroes, and a Hellenic inscription records that young Athenian men lay wreaths at their tomb. The heroising of the dead at Marathon is a fact which cannot be called
80 into dispute, and it was appropriate that they should have been celebrated on the Parthenon, in a position secondary to that of the purely divine and heroic subjects.

CONTINUE ▶

My suggestion is that the frieze shows the fighters
85 of Marathon celebrating the prime festival of the
goddess Athena, on the temple dedicated to her as a
thanksgiving for her aid at Marathon and afterwards,
and in a manner which indicates the heroic status of
those who fell there.

22

The author of Passage 1 references a quote from
Heraclitus (lines 29–35) primarily to

A) reinforce the sense of the passage of time present
in the frieze.

B) suggest that opposing qualities of the carving
present a sense of overall balance.

C) prove that the style of the frieze is
characteristically Greek.

D) emphasize the contrast between the men in the
procession and the goddess Athena at its end.

23

Which of the following best describes the structure of
Passage 1?

A) A purpose for the frieze is proposed and then a
description is given

B) An interpretation of the frieze is questioned and a
new solution is offered

C) The frieze is described in detail, with emphasis on
its unique qualities

D) A historical overview is given that helps explain
the layout of the frieze

24

As used in line 44, "unparalleled" most nearly means

A) crooked.

B) normal.

C) unsurpassed.

D) unprecedented.

25

The first two paragraphs of Passage 2 primarily serve
to

A) reject the idea that the frieze depicts the
Panathenaic procession.

B) argue against the idea that the frieze represents the
passage of time.

C) suggest that the frieze represents the heroes of
Marathon.

D) outline problems in the traditional interpretation
of the frieze.

26

As used in line 59, "mortal" most nearly means

A) human.

B) deadly.

C) terrible.

D) common.

27

In the context of the passage, the author's use of the
phrase "there I go" (lines 57–58) is primarily meant to
convey the idea that

A) figures in the frieze were not meant to be portraits
of individual citizens.

B) the frieze cannot be a representation of a human
event.

C) the citizens of Athens did not participate in the
Panathenaic procession.

D) the subject of the frieze should be obvious to
modern viewers.

CONTINUE

28

Which choice provides the best evidence for the answer to the previous question?

A) Lines 46–49 ("And here . . . procession")

B) Lines 54–55 ("The flagrant . . . explanation")

C) Lines 62–64 ("Moreover . . . background")

D) Lines 66–69 ("We must . . . Athens")

29

The author of Passage 2 would most likely argue that the "youths" (line 21) described in Passage 1 are

A) citizens of Athens from around the time the Parthenon was built.

B) Athenian men who died in battle at Marathon.

C) people of Marathon who were worshipped as heroes in Athens.

D) purely divine participants in the celebration of a festival of Athena.

30

Passage 2 differs from Passage 1 in that Passage 1

A) focuses on determining the subject of the frieze.

B) gives a detailed description of the figures in the frieze.

C) considers how Greek citizens might have viewed the frieze.

D) entirely rejects the traditional interpretation of the frieze.

31

Which choice provides the best evidence for the answer to the previous question?

A) Lines 4–10 ("Though . . . Parthenon")

B) Lines 13–14 ("This . . . reliefs")

C) Lines 15–17 ("The Panathenaic . . . time")

D) Lines 19–25 ("In the . . . turn")

CONTINUE

Questions 32–42 are based on the following passage.

The passage is adapted from Elsa Youngsteadt, "Free Upgrades, Unfortunately." ©2006 by *American Scientist*.

Contrary to infectious-disease dogma, the mutations that enable bacteria to resist antibiotics do not always result in weaker strains, according
Line to a study published in the June 30 issue of the
5 journal *Science*. This is bad news for public-health efforts, especially because the germ in question is the tuberculosis-causing *Mycobacterium tuberculosis,* once the leading cause of death in the United States.

Classic laboratory experiments once suggested
10 that bacteria pay a price for antibiotic resistance—that resistant bacteria are weaker than their susceptible counterparts and should not spread through the human population when forced to compete with hardier strains.

15 But the new study, headed by scientists at Stanford University, has undermined this comforting conventional wisdom. It shows that in real human patients, tuberculosis bacteria can evolve resistance to antibiotics and still be just as aggressive as their
20 susceptible ancestors.

"It's generally bad news for the world that some tuberculosis strains can get something for nothing," said Sebastien Gagneux, one of the lead authors of the study and a research associate at the Institute of
25 Systems Biology. "Even though many drug-resistant strains are less hardy than susceptible strains, others evolve over the course of treatment and remain virulent."

The investigators looked at the evolution of
30 resistance to the drug rifampin, one of the preferred first-line treatments for the disease. Rifampin binds to the molecule that makes, or polymerizes, bacterial RNA. The drug disables the so-called polymerase molecule and prevents the crucial flow of information
35 from DNA to RNA. Without RNA, bacteria can't make the proteins they need to survive. But simple mutations in the gene that encodes RNA polymerase can change its structure. The different shape decreases the drug's ability to bind and allows *M. tuberculosis* to
40 persist in the face of antibiotic onslaught. Classic studies suggested that such a change would carry some cost, such as decreased efficiency of the polymerase molecule. Such a penalty would cause the mutants to grow more slowly than unmodified strains, thereby
45 retarding the spread of the antibiotic-resistant mutation in the population.

Not so, according to the new study, which found that some resistant bugs are every bit as robust as unmodified strains. The Stanford group collected
50 tuberculosis bacteria from the sputum of patients, first at the beginning of their infections, and a second time after some of those patients developed rifampin-resistant infections. The investigators then pitted the resistant strains against their susceptible counterparts
55 in antibiotic-free competition assays. These tests force the two strains to compete for limited resources in a common culture flask, so the hardier bug should take over as the weaker one gets crowded out. Contrary to expectations, five of the ten resistant strains held their
60 own in these tests, and one actually dominated its antibiotic-susceptible ancestor.

Just how clinical isolates outperform lab-generated strains with identical mutations remains a mystery. Some changes simply have a low cost to begin with,
65 and, the study also found, the cost depends on the strain in which the mutation occurs. However, the real key is likely to be compensatory mutation— one or more additional changes, in the same RNA polymerase gene or in related genes, that make up
70 for the diminished function caused by the original mutation. Gagneux is planning future studies to find these putative compensatory mutations and learn how they restore the performance of strains that acquire antibiotic-resistance mutations.

75 The authors don't want their study to fuel an alarmist panic. Indeed, the data don't call for it, says Bruce Levin, an expert on the evolution of antibiotic resistance at Emory University who was not involved with the study. Levin points out that "the spread of
80 tuberculosis does not depend solely on the efficacy or lack of efficacy of antibiotics." He cites public-health practices and better nutrition as bulwarks against 19th-century-style epidemics.

However, the paper does highlight a sobering trend
85 in human epidemiology. Drug-resistant bacteria are here to stay, even if society stopped abusing antibiotics right now. Furthermore, evolution doesn't just work on bacteria. Levin explains, "The drug-resistant mutations that aren't costly are the ones that will take over, not
90 only in the bacteria responsible for tuberculosis but also in [organisms] responsible for other diseases."

CONTINUE

32

The primary purpose of the passage is to

A) support the findings of classic laboratory experimentation.

B) assert that controversial findings should cause alarm.

C) present concerns raised by the results of a study.

D) criticize the methodology of an existing study.

33

What did the scientists in the Stanford University study discover about tuberculosis bacteria that "undermined this comforting conventional wisdom" (lines 16–17)?

A) Bacteria have shown the ability to resist antibiotics through mutation without losing strength.

B) *Mycobacterium tuberculosis* has become the leading cause of death in the United States.

C) RNA and DNA interchangeability in tuberculosis has led to stronger antibiotics.

D) Rifampin can no longer be used to treat disease due to proliferation of polymerase molecules.

34

Which choice provides the best evidence for the answer to the previous question?

A) Lines 35–36 ("Without . . . survive")

B) Lines 49–53 ("The Stanford . . . infections")

C) Lines 58–61 ("Contrary . . . ancestor")

D) Lines 64–66 ("Some . . . occurs")

35

As used in line 26, "hardy" most nearly means

A) difficult.

B) strong.

C) terrible.

D) thick.

36

Which statement about rifampin can be most reasonably inferred from the passage?

A) It stopped tuberculosis from being the leading cause of death in the United States.

B) It has successfully inhibited protein production in bacteria.

C) It makes RNA for tuberculosis bacteria compatible with other DNA.

D) It is the most effective known treatment for tuberculosis.

37

As presented in the passage, the Stanford University study relied on which type of evidence?

A) Anecdotal opinion

B) Secondhand observation

C) Animal studies

D) Clinical testing

38

The author indicates that prior to the Stanford University study the scientists generally believed that antibiotic-resistant strains of tuberculosis

A) had a better chance of survival than their antibiotic-susceptible ancestors.

B) would once again become the most deadly of diseases.

C) resulted in lowered amounts of sputum in those they infect.

D) did not have a survival rate equal to that of non-resistant strains.

CONTINUE

39

According to the passage, Sebastien Gagneux plans to conduct further studies to answer which of the following questions?

A) Are more virulent strains of tuberculosis likely to cause a panic?

B) Do drug-resistant bacteria cost more to treat?

C) How do antibiotic-resistant bacteria compensate for deficiencies caused by mutation?

D) Why are some strains of bacteria more likely to resist antibiotics than others?

40

Which choice provides the best evidence for the answer to the previous question?

A) Lines 71–74 ("Gagneux . . . mutations")

B) Lines 79–81 ("the spread . . . antibiotics")

C) Lines 85–87 ("Drug-resistant . . . now")

D) Lines 88–89 ("The drug-resistant . . . over")

41

The author mentions an "alarmist panic" (line 76) most likely in order to

A) bring attention to the threat posed by antibiotic-resistant bacteria.

B) state that 19th century public-health practices were unable to halt the spread of tuberculosis.

C) identify the inevitable result of rampant societal antibiotic abuse.

D) draw a contrast between an undesirable reaction and a reasonable response.

42

The primary function of the final paragraph (lines 84–91) is to

A) reevaluate the hypothesis of the Stanford University study.

B) provide a warning supported by results of the Stanford University study.

C) credit the Stanford University study with changing society.

D) explain the methodology of the Stanford University study.

CONTINUE

Questions 43–52 are based on the following passage and supplementary material.

This passage is adapted from David P. Hill, Roy A. Bailey, James W. Hendley II, Peter H. Stauffer, Mae Marcaida, "California's Restless Giant: The Long Valley Caldera." ©2014 by U.S. Geological Survey.

About 760,000 years ago a cataclysmic volcanic eruption in the Long Valley area of eastern California blew out 150 cubic miles—600 cubic kilometers
Line (km³)—of magma (molten rock) from a depth of about
5 4 miles (6 km) beneath the Earth's surface. Rapid flows of glowing hot ash (pyroclastic flows) covered much of east-central California, and airborne ash fell as far east as Nebraska. The Earth's surface sank more than 1 mile (1.6 km) into the space vacated by the erupted magma,
10 forming a large volcanic depression that geologists call a caldera.

Long Valley Caldera is part of a large volcanic system in eastern California that also includes the Mono-Inyo Craters chain. This chain extends from
15 Mammoth Mountain at the southwest rim of the caldera northward 25 miles (40 km) to Mono Lake. Eruptions along this chain began 400,000 years ago, and Mammoth Mountain was formed by a series of eruptions ending 58,000 years ago. The volcanic
20 system is still active—eruptions occurred in both the Inyo Craters and Mono Craters parts of the volcanic chain as recently as 600 years ago, and small eruptions occurred in Mono Lake sometime between the mid-1700s and mid-1800s.

25 Although no volcanic eruptions are known to have occurred in eastern California since those in Mono Lake, earthquakes occur frequently. These are caused by movement along faults and by the pressure of magma rising beneath the surface, two closely
30 related geologic processes. In 1872, a magnitude 7.4 earthquake centered 80 miles (125 km) south of Long Valley was felt throughout most of California, and moderate (magnitude 5 to 6) earthquakes have shaken the Long Valley area since 1978.

35 In 1978, a magnitude 5.4 earthquake struck 6 miles southeast of the caldera, heralding a period of geologic unrest in the Long Valley area that is still ongoing. That temblor ended two decades of low quake activity in eastern California. The area has since experienced
40 numerous swarms of earthquakes, especially in the southern part of the caldera and the adjacent Sierra Nevada.

The most intense of these swarms began in May 1980 and included four strong magnitude 6 shocks,
45 three on the same day. Following these shocks, scientists from the U.S. Geological Survey (USGS) began a reexamination of the Long Valley area, and they soon detected other evidence of unrest—a dome-like uplift within the caldera. Measurements showed
50 that the center of the caldera had risen almost a foot (30 centimeters) since the summer of 1979—after decades of stability. This swelling, which by 2014 totaled more than 2.5 feet (75 centimeters) and affected more than 100 square miles (250 km²), is caused by
55 new magma rising beneath the caldera.

In response to this increased unrest, USGS intensified its monitoring in the Long Valley region. Today, a state-of-the-art network of seismometers and geodetic equipment closely monitors earthquake
60 activity and the swelling in the caldera. Data from these instruments help scientists to assess the volcanic hazard in the Long Valley area and to recognize early signs of possible eruptions.

During the early 1990s, trees began dying at several
65 places on Mammoth Mountain on the southwest edge of Long Valley Caldera. Studies conducted by USGS and U.S. Forest Service scientists showed that the trees are being killed by large amounts of carbon dioxide (CO_2) gas seeping up through the soil from magma
70 deep beneath Mammoth Mountain. Such emissions of volcanic gas, as well as earthquake swarms and ground swelling, commonly precede volcanic eruptions. When they precede an eruption of a "central vent" volcano, such as Mount St. Helens, Washington, they normally
75 last only a few weeks or months. However, symptoms of volcanic unrest may persist for decades or centuries at large calderas, such as Long Valley Caldera. Studies indicate that only about one in six such episodes of unrest at large calderas worldwide actually culminates
80 in an eruption.

Over the past 4,000 years, small to moderate eruptions have occurred somewhere along the Mono-Inyo volcanic chain every few hundred years, and the possibility remains that the geologic unrest in the
85 Long Valley area could take only weeks to escalate to an eruption. Nonetheless, geologists think that the chances of an eruption in the area in any given year are quite small.

CONTINUE

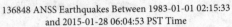

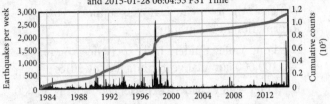

136848 ANSS Earthquakes Between 1983-01-01 02:15:33
and 2015-01-28 06:04:53 PST Time

Long Valley Caldera cumulative earthquakes between 1983 and 2015, USGS.
The vertical bars on the graphs above correspond with the left-side y-axis
and represent the number of earthquakes per week. The thicker gray line
indicates the cumulative number of earthquakes and corresponds with
the right-side y-axis.

43

As used in line 10, "depression" most nearly means

A) dejection.

B) decrease.

C) crater.

D) trouble.

44

The authors use the phrase "as recently as 600 years
ago" (line 22) primarily to

A) suggest that there will be another eruption this
century.

B) convey a sense of the magnitude of geologic time.

C) communicate irony, because 600 years ago is not
recent.

D) indicate that the word "recently" is a relative term.

45

As used in line 38, "temblor" most nearly means

A) drum.

B) earthquake.

C) eruption.

D) caldera.

46

What is the reason geologists have increased their
monitoring of the Long Valley Caldera?

A) It has been more than 150 years since the last
eruption.

B) Eruptions happen frequently in volcanic chains of
such size.

C) The area is experiencing geologic activity
indicative of an impending eruption.

D) The swelling of the caldera may damage the
sensitive geodetic equipment.

47

Which choice provide the best evidence for the
answer to the previous question?

A) Lines 19–24 ("The volcanic . . . mid-1800s")

B) Lines 38–39 ("That . . . California")

C) Lines 58–60 ("Today, . . . caldera")

D) Lines 70–72 ("Such . . . eruptions")

48

In the context of the passage as a whole, what is the
primary purpose of the last paragraph?

A) To suggest that geologists believe danger from an
eruption is not imminent

B) To explain how quickly geologic unrest can turn
into a catastrophic eruption

C) To warn of the dire impact of another eruption
like Mount St. Helens

D) To emphasize the impact of the earthquakes
discussed earlier in the passage

CONTINUE

49

It can be inferred from the passage that Mammoth Mountain

A) erupted most recently around 600 years ago.

B) is an active volcano that the USGS is monitoring for early signs of eruption.

C) shows signs that the larger volcanic system to which it belongs is still active.

D) was formed 760,000 years ago by pyroclastic flows from a volcanic eruption.

50

Which choice provides the best evidence for the answer to the previous question?

A) Lines 1–5 ("About . . . surface")

B) Lines 19–24 ("The volcanic . . . mid-1800s")

C) Lines 25–27 ("Although . . . frequently")

D) Lines 75–77 ("However . . . Caldera")

51

Which of the following situations is most analogous to the recent swelling of the Long Valley Caldera?

A) Many small tremors along a particular fault precede a large, magnitude 8 earthquake.

B) A scientist discovers a new species of insect by chance while observing snakes in the Amazon rainforest.

C) Bad road conditions cause a collision between two cars, and poor visibility contributes to a multi-car pile-up.

D) A doctor is unable to give a definitive diagnosis to a patient after assessing symptoms typical of a particular disease.

52

Which of the following claims is supported by information in the graph?

A) Long Valley Caldera had experienced more than 100,000 cumulative earthquakes by 2015.

B) Long Valley Caldera experienced roughly 30,000 earthquakes per week in 1990.

C) By 2012, Long Valley Caldera had experienced 1.2 million cumulative earthquakes.

D) By 1988, Long Valley Caldera had experienced over 25,000 cumulative earthquakes.

STOP
If you finish before time is called, you may check your work on this section only.
Do not turn to any other section in the test.

No Test Material On This Page

CONTINUE

Writing and Language Test

35 MINUTES, 44 QUESTIONS

Turn to Section 2 of your answer sheet to answer the questions in this section.

Questions 1–11 are based on the following passage and supplementary material.

Park Rangers, Naturally

Of the many parks that are part of the American heritage, the National Park Service (NPS) is easily the most majestic. From the moment of the first European settlements in the fifteenth and sixteenth centuries, visitors and residents alike have **1** gawked at the natural beauty and diversity of the **2** American landscape's attractiveness. As part of a commitment to preserving these national treasures against the forward movement of industrialization, the National Park Service was founded in 1916 during the presidency of Woodrow Wilson.

1

A) NO CHANGE

B) marveled

C) pondered

D) stared

2

A) NO CHANGE

B) pulchritudinous American landscape.

C) pretty American landscape.

D) American landscape.

CONTINUE

Today, there are over 400 parks in the service, and these parks are run and overseen by the Department of the Interior. The day-to-day operations, **3** including maintenance and tours, are the work of park rangers. These park rangers are responsible for the upkeep of the **4** parks, their main responsibility is to maintain the balance between the wildlife and plant species and the human visitors that come to the parks every day.

5 Without park rangers, the parks would be overrun with pollution. Some are scientists who revel in the ecological aspects of maintaining the parts. Some are educators **6** helping visitors to understand the unique aspects and historical significance of the parks. Still others come from law enforcement and firefighting, given that their posts are often very far indeed from the municipal bodies that typically provide **7** them.

3

The writer wants to include a detail that will clarify the phrase "day-to-day operations." Which of the following would best fulfill this goal?

A) NO CHANGE

B) and some that are more long-term,

C) often repetitive tasks,

D) not the political decisionmaking,

4

A) NO CHANGE

B) parks their

C) parks—their

D) parks, their—

5

Which of the following would best introduce the topic of this paragraph?

A) NO CHANGE

B) Park rangers can come from all walks of life.

C) Many millions visit the National Parks every year.

D) The most successful park rangers usually have some background in ecology.

6

A) NO CHANGE

B) that are helping

C) who are helping

D) who help

7

A) NO CHANGE

B) these services.

C) those.

D) it.

CONTINUE

There are nearly 4,000 park rangers in service with the NPS today. **8** Visitors are on the rise, poising that number for growth. **9** Although park visitation numbers peaked before the 2020 pandemic, the general trend has been a steady rise. The numbers continue to be high, with over 230 million visitors in 2020. It seems that as economic conditions in the country are uncertain, more and more people turn to parks for economical, **10** educational; and enlightening alternatives to the more costly tourist activities and trips. Now, too, that climate science has foretold difficult times, the NPS is seen to be protecting the last vestiges of our green world before it slips away.

Visitors to America's National Parks, 1990–2020 (in millions)

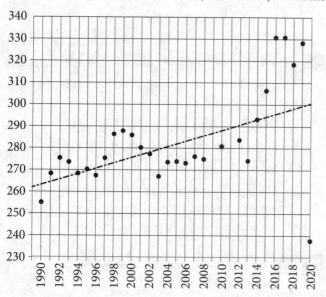

8

A) NO CHANGE

B) Visitation numbers are poised on the rise for significant growth.

C) That number is poised to grow, as visitation numbers are on the rise.

D) Poised on the rise, visitation numbers are growing.

9

Which of the following gives accurate information based on the graph?

A) NO CHANGE

B) Park visitation peaked in the late 1990s and has tapered off since then.

C) Park visitation reached record lows in 2003.

D) Park visitation has risen in a linear progression since the early 1990s.

10

A) NO CHANGE

B) educational, and

C) educational—and,

D) educational and,

CONTINUE ➡

11 The park-ranger workforce is so diverse, there are actually a few common attributes among park rangers. Park rangers need at least a two-year degree and some experience working in parks. Many seasonal park workers and volunteers go on to become park rangers. Ultimately, attaining work as a park ranger is less about a skill-set than a particular mindset. Park rangers must honor and revere the natural world: they spend their entire careers learning about and living in the places they work. Park rangers have special jobs, so it naturally takes a group of special people to do those jobs.

A) NO CHANGE

B) Truly, the

C) Because the

D) Although the

CONTINUE

Questions 12–22 are based on the following passage and supplementary material.

The Ferry Godfather

[1] For much of the early part of American history, Pennsylvania and Virginia, two major early colonies and states, shared a border. [2] This part of Virginia became the modern state of West Virginia on June 20, 1863. [3] Then came the Civil War. [4] Amid the furor of secession and conflict, President Abraham Lincoln granted a special provision for that part of Virginia that was loyal to the Union. **12**

Although this region is not in the news quite so often today, in America's early history one part of it was on the tip of everyone's tongue. The town of Harpers Ferry played a crucial role in the pre–Civil War era. George Washington proposed that the United States station one of **13** their two major armories there, and by 1799, Harpers Ferry became **14** one of the major industrial towns, in the United States. Its position about 60 miles from Washington, D.C., and Baltimore put it close enough to major cities, but its place **15** in the hills at the meeting of the Potomac and Shenandoah Rivers made it difficult to access and easy to defend.

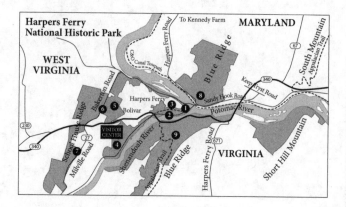

12

For the sake of the logic and coherence of this paragraph, sentence 2 should be placed

A) where it is now.

B) before sentence 1.

C) after sentence 3.

D) after sentence 4.

13

A) NO CHANGE

B) they're

C) its

D) it's

14

A) NO CHANGE

B) one, of the major industrial towns,

C) one, of the major industrial towns

D) one of the major industrial towns

15

Which of the following gives accurate information based on the map?

A) NO CHANGE

B) approximately 20 miles northeast of the town of Bolivar

C) across the Shenandoah River from Maryland

D) at the foot of the Adirondack Mountains

CONTINUE

Because it was situated on the borderline between the Union and the Confederacy, and because its armory was full of the weapons being manufactured to fight the Civil War, **16** the Confederacy took it four times and the Union did also, and both sides saw it as a pivotal strategic base.

In the popular imagination today, Harpers Ferry is still seen as a crucial **17** place of great importance during the Civil War but mainly for events that occurred there before the war had even started. In 1859, radical abolitionist John Brown led a raid on Harpers Ferry, seeking to free slaves and begin a guerilla campaign to free slaves all over the country. While Brown's raid was ultimately a dismal failure and Brown was executed for treason, **18** his raid began a national conversation.

16

A) NO CHANGE

B) the war saw Harpers Ferry change hands eight times,

C) Harpers Ferry changed hands eight times during the war,

D) eight was the number of times Harpers Ferry changed hands,

17

A) NO CHANGE

B) place

C) place that was important

D) place where a great deal happened

18

The writer wants to include an idea here that shows that Brown's raid still had major importance. Which of the following true ideas would best fulfill this goal?

A) NO CHANGE

B) Herman Melville's poem about John Brown is very well-known.

C) the raid was based on some earlier well-known slave revolts.

D) he could not have chosen a more central location.

CONTINUE

Abolitionists in the North saw him as a hero and a freedom fighter, while those in the South saw him as a **19** filthy terrorist. **20** The Civil War and the nation's movement toward it used John Brown's name as both sides' rallying cry.

Today, Harpers Ferry is a sleepy town in the mountains of West Virginia. Much of its heritage remains **21** intact. Historical tours run every day. Above all, Harpers Ferry is a living reminder that the crucial events in history are not limited to the big places and the major players. Without the catalyzing effect of this small **22** town: American history as we know it might have been much different.

19

A) NO CHANGE

B) heroic

C) janky

D) vile

20

A) NO CHANGE

B) Brown's name became a rallying cry for both sides as the nation moved toward Civil War.

C) Brown's cry was the rally that both sides named as the Civil War moved in on the nation.

D) Both sides used Brown's name as the nation's Civil War was moving toward it.

21

A) NO CHANGE

B) intact, historical

C) intact historical

D) intact; and historical

22

A) NO CHANGE

B) town;

C) town.

D) town,

CONTINUE ➡

Questions 23–33 are based on the following passage.

Stefan Zweig's Return

Stefan Zweig's name has been showing up a lot lately. In addition to a large amount of recently republished works, Wes Anderson cites Zweig as the major influence on Anderson's recent film **23** (*The Grand Budapest Hotel* 2014). It seems that Zweig has suddenly become **24** revelant again after nearly 75 years of obscurity. Why this sudden interest? What can he offer that our culture seems to need?

23

A) NO CHANGE

B) *The Grand Budapest Hotel* 2014.

C) (*The Grand Budapest Hotel*), 2014.

D) *The Grand Budapest Hotel* (2014).

24

A) NO CHANGE

B) relevant

C) irrelevant

D) irrevelant

CONTINUE

Stefan Zweig was born in 1881. **25** His parents were part of the Jewish cultural elite in Vienna at the time. Stefan was afforded every possible luxury and privilege. By 1904, Zweig had earned a doctoral degree from the University of Vienna, and he formed the connections that would allow his entry into the **26** city's cultural elite. Zweig went on to publish a near infinitude of works of fiction, drama, journalism, and biography, and enjoyed a period of major celebrity in the 1920s and 1930s. **27**

25

The author would like to combine the two sentences reproduced below:

> His parents were part of the Jewish cultural elite in Vienna at the time. Stefan was afforded every possible luxury and privilege.

Which of the following gives the best combination of the two sentences?

A) His parents were part of the Jewish cultural elite in Vienna at the time; Stefan was afforded every possible luxury and privilege.

B) Zweig was afforded every possible luxury and privilege because his parents were part of the Jewish cultural elite in Vienna at the time.

C) Born to parents who were part of Vienna's Jewish cultural elite, Stefan was afforded every possible luxury and privilege.

D) His parents were part of the Jewish cultural elite in Vienna at the time, and so Stefan benefited from their eliteness with luxury.

26

A) NO CHANGE

B) cities

C) citie's

D) cities'

27

The writer is considering deleting the phrase "of fiction, drama, journalism, and biography" and placing a comma after the word *works*. Should the phrase be kept or deleted?

A) Kept, because it shows that Zweig had no problem finding work after he left Vienna.

B) Kept, because it demonstrates the range of Zweig's talents.

C) Deleted, because it is implausible that a single writer could work well in so many forms.

D) Deleted, because it presents information given in numerous places throughout the essay.

CONTINUE

Still, Zweig's relationship with his homeland was always tenuous. While he did support the German side in World War I, Zweig remained a committed pacifist and participated only in the Archives of the Ministry of War. By the second war, [28] however, Zweig's pacifism was no longer looked on with such understanding. Zweig and his wife fled Nazi Germany in 1939 and spent their remaining years in the Americas. Only a few short years after their escape, Zweig and his wife took their own lives out of despair over what had become of Europe. Zweig's ancestral home, [29] which, you'll recall, was in Vienna, insisted on tearing itself apart, and Jewish men like himself were being slaughtered by the millions.

For many years, cultural critics saw Zweig's work as a historical curiosity. His decision to flee Europe was seen as an act of quaint pacifism, and his ultimate decision to end his own life was seen as the act of a privileged man for [30] which everyday realities were simply too much to bear. Much more popular in the post–WWII era were more traditionally "masculine" figures, who not only went to war but treated writing, painting, and filmmaking [31] like competitive sports.

28

A) NO CHANGE
B) indeed,
C) on the one hand,
D) although,

29

Which of the following choices would best emphasize the personal stake that Zweig had in the conflict in Europe?

A) NO CHANGE
B) not the Americas to which he had moved,
C) in which he had such pride,
D) the land of Goethe and Beethoven,

30

A) NO CHANGE
B) who
C) whose
D) whom

31

Which of the following conclusions to this sentence would best support the idea presented at the beginning in the sentence?

A) NO CHANGE
B) with a pacifist bent.
C) like proper gentlemen.
D) as the province of veterans.

Today, however, Zweig's sensibility makes a good deal more sense. Like Zweig, many of us were alive and aware before the great catastrophes of [32] his own age, and our longing for a "simpler time" is not pure nostalgia. We know that things cannot be as they once were, but we [33] have sensed the injustice in the world being so complicated, and in the power just a few people have to take it all away from us.

[32]

A) NO CHANGE

B) their

C) her

D) our

[33]

A) NO CHANGE

B) are sensing

C) sense

D) sensed

CONTINUE →

Questions 34–44 are based on the following passage.

For Figs? The Chimps Aren't Chumps

Sometimes as you fall asleep, you're thinking about what to eat for breakfast the next morning. "When I get up, I'll go to the fridge. I'll have an egg, a 34 piece of toast, and a few strips of bacon while I'm making coffee." Even though you may know where your food is coming from, you plan breakfast as a way to plan the day.

Our species may have been doing this kind of breakfast planning long before refrigerators, long before our species was even our species. A team of researchers recently followed groups of chimpanzees through three periods of fruit scarcity in West Africa. 35 For a chimpanzee, every day during a fruit-poor season can be like Black Friday, where all the "shoppers" want the same hot item.

34

A) NO CHANGE
B) piece of toast, and a few strips of bacon,
C) piece, of toast, and a few strips, of bacon,
D) piece of toast and a few strips of bacon

35

At this point, the author wants to add a sentence that accurately summarizes the scientists' research in a way that is consistent with other information in the passage. Which sentence would most effectively achieve that goal?

A) They wanted to see whether the chimps would prefer new, high-yield fruits like figs to their traditional diet of bananas.
B) They wanted to discover where chimps spent the time between waking and sleep.
C) They wanted to know how the chimps acquired highly sought-after fruits, like figs, when the trees that bear these fruits are depleted so quickly.
D) They wanted to uncover the secrets of human evolution and how chimps would operate in a retail environment.

CONTINUE

36 Why does everyone freak out during Black Friday when the deals aren't even that good? If you want to be sure to get the new, say, plasma TV, what do you have to do? Camp out in front of the store! Well, that's exactly what the researchers found the chimpanzees to do with the coveted fruits. In fruit-poor seasons, the nomadic **37** chimpanzees set up their campsites within striking distance of the ripe fruits. When the fruits were **38** "lively," or quick to disappear, the female chimpanzees set up their sleeping nests more pointedly in the direction of the fruit **39** than the fruit was plentiful. Moreover, in order to ensure that the fruit supply would not be **40** gobbled by the time the chimps got there, they woke up early, often before sunrise, when the forests were still dark.

36

Which of the following would provide the best transition from the previous paragraph and introduction to this paragraph?

A) NO CHANGE

B) The similarity to Black Friday shoppers goes even a bit further than this.

C) For a monkey, every day of the year is like Black Friday, but without Thanksgiving.

D) Black Friday is the day after the American Thanksgiving, and it is often characterized by heavy retail traffic.

37

A) NO CHANGE

B) chimpanzee sets up their

C) chimpanzee sets up its

D) chimpanzees set up its

38

Which of the following provides the most precise word given the definition that immediately follows?

A) NO CHANGE

B) "desiccated,"

C) "ephemeral,"

D) "eternal,"

39

A) NO CHANGE

B) then

C) than if

D) than when

40

A) NO CHANGE

B) depleted

C) chomped

D) ate

CONTINUE

The findings about the chimp [41] has led scientists to reopen a number of heated questions. The first has to do with animals' existence outside the present moment: how much do they remember, and how much do they plan? In other words, is "consciousness" really only [42] the province of humans? The other set of questions has to do with the lines of evolution. It has been firmly established that chimpanzees are our evolutionary ancestors, but now we have to wonder if we've inherited even more [43] than we thought from them initially. Have the lives of chimpanzees conditioned the small, day-to-day patterns of our own lives?

While such questions may seem purely academic and conceptual, they actually have a good deal to do with our lived experience. We learn more and more about what we share with other [44] animals and with each discovery, we learn a new way to relate to the world around us.

41

A) NO CHANGE
B) have lead
C) have led
D) has lead

42

A) NO CHANGE
B) the providence of
C) the provenance of
D) providential for

43

A) NO CHANGE
B) from them than we initially thought.
C) then initially thought.
D) than we had been thinking from them initially.

44

A) NO CHANGE
B) animals,
C) animals and:
D) animals—and

STOP

If you finish before time is called, you may check your work on this section only.
Do not turn to any other section in the test.

Math Test – No Calculator

25 MINUTES, 20 QUESTIONS

Turn to Section 3 of your answer sheet to answer the questions in this section.

DIRECTIONS

For questions 1–15, solve each problem, choose the best answer from the choices provided, and fill in the corresponding circle on your answer sheet. **For questions 16–20,** solve the problem and enter your answer in the grid on the answer sheet. Please refer to the directions before question 16 on how to enter your answers in the grid. You may use any available space in your test booklet for scratch work.

NOTES

1. The use of a calculator **is not permitted**.
2. All variables and expressions used represent real numbers unless otherwise indicated.
3. Figures provided in this test are drawn to scale unless otherwise indicated.
4. All figures lie in a plane unless otherwise indicated.
5. Unless otherwise indicated, the domain of a given function f is the set of all real numbers x for which $f(x)$ is a real number.

REFERENCE

$A = \pi r^2$
$C = 2\pi r$

$A = \ell w$

$A = \frac{1}{2}bh$

$c^2 = a^2 + b^2$

Special Right Triangles

    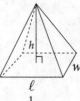

$V = \ell wh$

$V = \pi r^2 h$

$V = \frac{4}{3}\pi r^3$

$V = \frac{1}{3}\pi r^2 h$

$V = \frac{1}{3}\ell wh$

The number of degrees of arc in a circle is 360.
The number of radians of arc in a circle is 2π.
The sum of the measures in degrees of the angles of a triangle is 180.

CONTINUE

1

If two times a number is equal to that number minus 4, what is the number?

A) −7

B) −6

C) −4

D) −3

2

The number of soil samples, *s*, that Sonal needs for an experiment must be greater than 6 but less than or equal to 13. Which of the following represents an acceptable number of soil samples for Sonal's experiment?

A) $6 < s < 13$

B) $6 \leq s < 13$

C) $6 < s \leq 13$

D) $6 \leq s \leq 13$

3

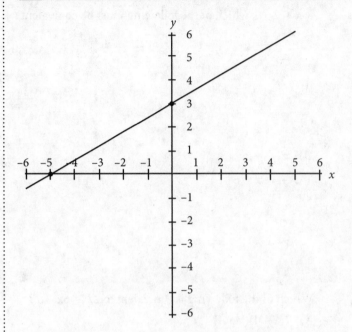

In the figure above, the graph of $y = f(x)$ is shown. Which of the following could be the equation of $f(x)$?

A) $f(x) = -\dfrac{3}{5}x + 3$

B) $f(x) = -\dfrac{3}{5}x - 3$

C) $f(x) = \dfrac{3}{5}x - 3$

D) $f(x) = \dfrac{3}{5}x + 3$

CONTINUE

4

If $x + y = 0$, which of the following must be equivalent to $x - y$?

A) $-2y$

B) $\dfrac{x}{y}$

C) x

D) x^2

5

Which of the following is equivalent to $2x^2 - 6x - 8$?

A) $2(x - 4)(x + 1)$

B) $3(x + 4)(x - 1)$

C) $2(x - 3)(x + 2)$

D) $3(x - 4)(x - 2)$

6

Ryan and Allison build a ramp to help their elderly cat, Simms, walk up to their bed. They need the ramp to make a 35° angle with their bedroom floor. How long must the ramp be to reach the top of their bed that is exactly three feet off the ground?

A) $\dfrac{\sin 35°}{3}$

B) $\dfrac{\sin 55°}{3}$

C) $\dfrac{3}{\sin 55°}$

D) $\dfrac{3}{\sin 35°}$

7

If $3a + 2b = 24$ and $4a + 5b = 53$, what is the value of $a + b$?

A) 2

B) 7

C) 9

D) 11

CONTINUE

8

Given the equation $y = 3x^2 + 4$, what is the function of the coefficient of 3 ?

A) It moves the graph of $y = 3x^2 + 4$ three units higher than the graph of $y = x^2 + 4$.

B) It moves the graph of $y = 3x^2 + 4$ three units lower than the graph of $y = x^2 + 4$.

C) It makes the graph of $y = 3x^2 + 4$ wider than the graph of $y = x^2 + 4$.

D) It makes the graph of $y = 3x^2 + 4$ narrower than the graph of $y = x^2 + 4$.

9

Steven needs to buy t theme park tickets for himself and his family. Each ticket costs \$80, and the number of tickets he needs to buy can be modeled by the expression $t^2 - 4t - 90 = 6$ when $t > 0$. What is the total cost of the theme park tickets that Steven purchased?

A) \$640

B) \$800

C) \$960

D) \$1,120

10

$$2c + 3d = 17$$
$$6c + 5d = 39$$

In the system of linear equations above, what is the value of $4c - 4d$?

A) −4

B) 1

C) 4

D) 13

11

If $x^2 + 2xy + y^2 = 64$ and $y - x = 12$, which of the following could be the value of x ?

A) −10

B) −4

C) 2

D) 10

CONTINUE

12

Samantha offers two different packages of yoga classes at her yoga studio. She offers two hot yoga sessions and three zero gravity yoga sessions at a total cost of $400. She also offers four hot yoga sessions and two zero gravity sessions at a price of $440. Samantha wants to offer a larger package for long-time clients in which the cost must exceed $800. If Samantha does not wish to include more than 13 sessions for the long-time client package, will she be able to create this package for her clients?

A) No, because the closest package that she can offer consists of three hot yoga and three zero gravity yoga sessions.

B) No, because the closest package that she can offer consists of four hot yoga and four zero gravity yoga sessions.

C) Yes, because she can offer five hot yoga and five zero gravity yoga sessions.

D) Yes, because she can offer six hot yoga and six zero gravity yoga sessions.

13

Cuthbert is conducting a chemistry experiment that calls for a number of chemicals to be mixed in various quantities. The one amount of which he is unsure is grams of potassium, p. If Cuthbert is certain that $(3p^2 + 14p + 24) - 2(p^2 + 7p + 20) = 0$, what is one possible value of $3p + 6$, the exact number of grams of potassium that Cuthbert would like to use for this experiment?

A) 20

B) 18

C) 12

D) 10

14

What is the value of $(2 + 8i)(1 - 4i) - (3 - 2i)(6 + 4i)$? (Note: $i = \sqrt{-1}$)

A) 8

B) 26

C) 34

D) 50

15

If $2\sqrt{x} = x - 3$, which of the following is the solution set for x?

A) $\{-1, 9\}$

B) $\{1, -9\}$

C) $\{9\}$

D) $\{1, 9\}$

CONTINUE

DIRECTIONS

For questions 16–20, solve the problem and enter your answer in the grid, as described below, on the answer sheet.

1. Although not required, it is suggested that you write your answer in the boxes at the top of the columns to help you fill in the circles accurately. You will receive credit only if the circles are filled in correctly.

2. Mark no more than one circle in any column.

3. No question has a negative answer.

4. Some problems may have more than one correct answer. In such cases, grid only one answer.

5. **Mixed numbers** such as $3\frac{1}{2}$ must be gridded as 3.5 or 7/2. (If ⌷3⌷1⌷/⌷2⌷ is entered into the grid, it will be interpreted as $\frac{31}{2}$, not as $3\frac{1}{2}$.)

6. **Decimal Answers:** If you obtain a decimal answer with more digits than the grid can accommodate, it may be either rounded or truncated, but it must fill the entire grid.

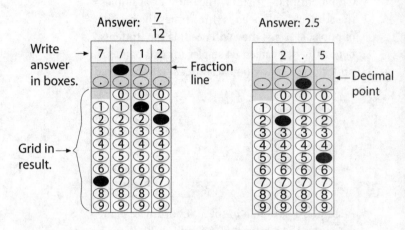

Answer: $\frac{7}{12}$ — Write answer in boxes. — Fraction line — Grid in result.

Answer: 2.5 — Decimal point

Acceptable ways to grid $\frac{2}{3}$ are:

Answer: 201 – either position is correct

NOTE: You may start your answers in any column, space permitting. Columns you don't need to use should be left blank.

CONTINUE

16

A group of students at Omega High School is using staples and popsicle sticks to build a scale model of the Great Wall of China as part of a project detailing China's military history. The number of staples the students will need is three times the number of popsicle sticks they will need. If the students determine they need 84 staples for this particular project, how many popsicle sticks will they need?

17

A standard parabola in the xy-coordinate plane intersects the x-axis at (5, 0) and (–5, 0). What is the value of the x-coordinate of this parabola's line of symmetry?

18

Danielle is a civil engineer for Dastis Dynamic Construction, Inc. She must create blueprints for a wheelchair accessible ramp leading up to the entrance of a mall that she and her group are building. The ramp must be exactly 100 meters in length and make a 20° angle with the level ground. What is the horizontal distance, in meters, from the start of the ramp to the point level with the start of the ramp immediately below the entrance of the mall, rounded to the nearest meter? (Note: Disregard units when inputting your answer, sin 20° ≈ 0.324, cos 20° ≈ 0.939, tan 20° ≈ 0.364)

CONTINUE

19

If twice a number is equal to that number minus five, what is three times that number plus seventeen minus that number?

20

Given that the equation $3x^2 + 2x - 8 = 0$ has two distinct solutions, what is the value of the smaller solution subtracted from the larger solution?

STOP
If you finish before time is called, you may check your work on this section only.
Do not turn to any other section in the test.

Math Test – Calculator

55 MINUTES, 38 QUESTIONS

Turn to Section 4 of your answer sheet to answer the questions in this section.

DIRECTIONS

For questions 1–30, solve each problem, choose the best answer from the choices provided, and fill in the corresponding circle on your answer sheet. **For questions 31–38**, solve the problem and enter your answer in the grid on the answer sheet. Please refer to the directions before question 31 on how to enter your answers in the grid. You may use any available space in your test booklet for scratch work.

NOTES

1. The use of a calculator **is permitted**.
2. All variables and expressions used represent real numbers unless otherwise indicated.
3. Figures provided in this test are drawn to scale unless otherwise indicated.
4. All figures lie in a plane unless otherwise indicated.
5. Unless otherwise indicated, the domain of a given function f is the set of all real numbers x for which $f(x)$ is a real number.

REFERENCE

$A = \pi r^2$
$C = 2\pi r$

$A = \ell w$

$A = \frac{1}{2} bh$

$c^2 = a^2 + b^2$

$2x$ $60°$ x
$30°$
$x\sqrt{3}$

s $45°$ $s\sqrt{2}$
$45°$
s

Special Right Triangles

$V = \ell wh$

$V = \pi r^2 h$

$V = \frac{4}{3}\pi r^3$

$V = \frac{1}{3}\pi r^2 h$

$V = \frac{1}{3}\ell wh$

The number of degrees of arc in a circle is 360.
The number of radians of arc in a circle is 2π.
The sum of the measures in degrees of the angles of a triangle is 180.

CONTINUE

1

A pencil-making machine is slowly filling a bin with pencils. After about five minutes, the machine jams, preventing pencils from falling into the bin. A technician notices the problem ten minutes later and clears the jam, causing all of the backed-up pencils to fall into the bin. In order to make up for lost time, the technician then increases the rate at which the machine operates. Which of the following graphs could represent this situation?

A)

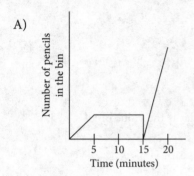

B)

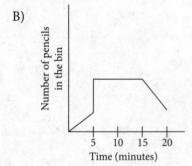

C)

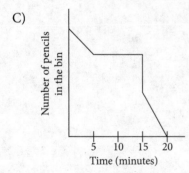

D)

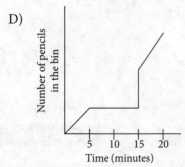

2

A submarine currently operating at 100 feet below the surface of the ocean begins to dive to increased depths at a rate of 30 feet per minute. Which of the following equations represents the submarine's depth below the surface, d, in feet, m minutes after beginning to dive?

A) $d = 100 + 30m$

B) $d = 100 - 30m$

C) $d = 100 - 30$

D) $d = 100m - 30$

CONTINUE

3

A craft store sells specialty beads for $1.00 for a single bead but will give a discount if a customer buys more than one bead. For each bead after the first, the price per bead goes down until it reaches 75 cents per bead, the lowest possible price, once 5 or more beads are purchased. Which of the following graphs represents the cost per bead in cents, y, of buying x beads in a single visit?

A)

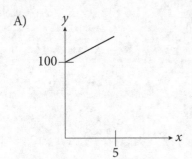

B)

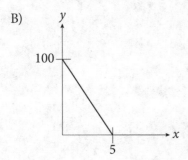

C)

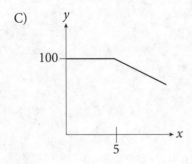

D)

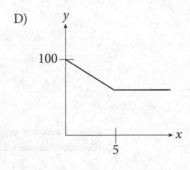

4

For the function defined as $g(x) = \frac{x-2}{3}$, what is the value of $g(-4)$?

A) −2

B) $-\frac{2}{3}$

C) $\frac{2}{3}$

D) 2

5

If $18 + d = 12$, what is the value of $5d$?

A) −30

B) −18

C) −6

D) 6

CONTINUE

6

The principal at a large high school in a major city believes that the math teachers for each class assign drastically different amounts of homework to their respective students. Which method of sampling would be best to estimate the average number of hours of homework assigned to students by the different math teachers?

A) Select one math teacher at random and survey the number of assigned homework hours in each of his or her classes.

B) Post an online poll to the school's social media account that asks students how much math homework they get each night.

C) Select 5 students from each math class in the high school and then record the number of hours assigned to each student selected.

D) Select the student with the highest grade in each math class and then survey those students to see how much homework they do each night.

7

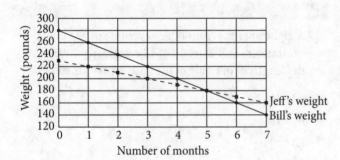

Bill and Jeff are participating in two different weight loss programs. The graphs above show how much weight each one has lost over a number of months. On average, how many more pounds did Bill lose per month than did Jeff?

A) 5

B) 10

C) 20

D) 50

8

Which of the following is equivalent to $9y^4 + 6y^3 + 3$?

A) $3y^2(3y^2 + 6y + 3)$

B) $3y^2(3y^2 + 2y) + 3$

C) $3y^2(6y^2 + 3y + 1)$

D) $15y^7 + 3$

9

A recent biological study performed on a large random sample of North American birds found that 46% of birds' nests experienced full or partial nest predation, in which some type of predator raided the nest before the hatchlings had flown off. The margin of error for the study was 3%. Which of the following is the best interpretation of the margin of error for this study?

A) The percentage of North American birds whose nests get raided by predators is likely somewhere between 43% and 49%.

B) There is a 3% chance that the study's finding about nest predation for North American birds is incorrect.

C) It is unlikely that fewer than 43% of birds' nests will get raided this coming year.

D) The research indicates that no more than 49% of birds' nests will likely get raided by predators.

CONTINUE

10

The function $g(x) = 16^x$ is defined for all real values of x. What is $g\left(\dfrac{1}{2}\right) + g\left(\dfrac{1}{4}\right)$?

A) 2

B) 6

C) 8

D) 16

11

A customer bought a clock for $27.50, which included a 10% sales tax. What was the price of the clock before tax?

A) $2.75

B) $25.00

C) $30.25

D) $30.56

12

List X	List Y
5	9
8	10
13	11
13	15
15	19
18	20

Which of the following answers is a true statement about the two lists in the table above?

A) The means are the same, and the medians are different.

B) The means are the same, and the standard deviations are the same.

C) The medians are the same, and the standard deviations are the same.

D) The medians are different, and the means are different.

13

A right square pyramid has a volume of 324 cubic centimeters and a height of 12 centimeters. What is the length of one side of the base, in centimeters?

A) $18\sqrt{2}$

B) 18

C) 9

D) $3\sqrt{3}$

CONTINUE

Questions 14 and 15 refer to the following information.

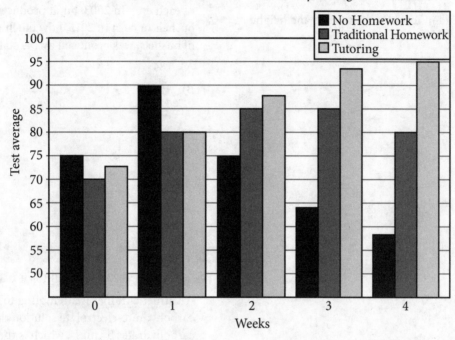

Student Performance for Three Study Strategies

A researcher is studying the effectiveness of various study strategies on student performance. The researcher has randomly assigned the 30 students equally into one of three groups: a "no homework" group that learns only in class, a "traditional homework" group that receives assignments as they usually do in this class, and a "tutoring" group in which students come to the researcher for a 10-minute tutoring session twice per week. Each week, the researcher administers the same test to all students and tracks their average score. The results are shown in the table above.

14

Which of the following groups showed an increase in test performance in each week of the study?

    I. Tutoring

    II. Traditional Homework

    III. No Homework

A) I only

B) II only

C) I and III only

D) I, II, and III

15

Which of the following best approximates the ratio of the improvement in test average for students in the Traditional Homework group to the students in the Tutoring group from the start of the study to week 4 of the study?

A) 3 to 4

B) 1 to 3

C) 2 to 5

D) 1 to 2

CONTINUE

16

For a right rectangular pyramid with height h and a square base with side length s, the volume is $V = \frac{1}{3}hs^2$. Which of the following defines the side length of the base of the pyramid in terms of the volume and height of the pyramid?

A) $\sqrt{\dfrac{3V}{h}}$

B) $\sqrt{\dfrac{h}{3V}}$

C) $\dfrac{3V}{h}$

D) $\dfrac{h}{3V}$

17

Breakfast Drink of Choice

Hot		Cold		
Tea	Coffee	Water	Milk	Juice
5.3%	26.9%	18.8%	17.2%	31.8%

A national survey determined the breakfast beverage of choice for American high school students. The results are summarized in the table above. Based on this information, which of the following is closest to the probability that a student drinks coffee, given that she does not drink a cold drink at breakfast?

A) 0.84

B) 0.66

C) 0.32

D) 0.27

18

From the year 2005 to the year 2015, the production of corn in a certain state has increased by 15%. During the same interval, the production of wheat has fallen by 40%. If the state produced identical amounts of each crop in 2005, but it produced 161 million bushels of corn in 2015, how much wheat, in millions of bushels, was produced by the state in 2015 ?

A) 84

B) 111.09

C) 233.33

D) 350

19

$$0.27(a + b) = 0.15a + 0.35b$$

An athletic trainer is attempting to produce a carbohydrate-electrolyte solution that is at 27% carbohydrates by mass, which is the maximum amount of saturation allowed by her league. A supply company provides solutions that are at 15% and 35% carbohydrates by mass, respectively. Based on the equation above, if the trainer uses 10 quarts of the 15% solution, how many quarts of the 35% solution will she need?

A) 180

B) 90

C) 30

D) 15

CONTINUE

20

$$f(x) = (x - b)^2 - 4$$

In the function above, b is a constant. When plotted in the xy-plane, the function is a parabola with a vertex at $(b, 4)$. Which of the following is true of the parabola?

A) Its y-intercept is at $(-b, 0)$.

B) Its y-intercept is at $(0, -b)$.

C) Its y-intercept is at $(0, b^2 - 4)$.

D) Its y-intercept is at $(b^2 - 4, 0)$.

21

A teacher is looking at the set of recent test scores from her class. After investigating, she realized that she transposed two different test grades. The 19 should be 91, while another student who had an 86 should have had a 68. After correcting these two mistakes, which of the following must increase in the updated data set?

A) The range

B) The standard deviation

C) The median

D) The mean

22

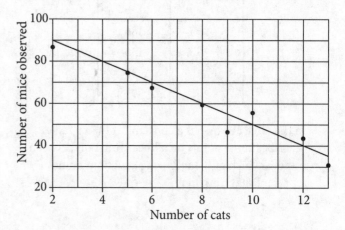

A researcher is studying the use of cats to control mice populations in granaries. The scatterplot above shows the numbers of cats owned, x, and the number of mice observed, y, for several different farms. A line of best fit is plotted for the data. Which of the following could be the equation of that line?

A) $y = -0.2x + 100$

B) $y = 0.2x + 100$

C) $y = 5x + 100$

D) $y = -5x + 100$

23

An online survival game begins a marathon session with over 65,000 players active on the server. Every hour, the half of the active players whose scores are the lowest get eliminated from the game. If $g(t)$ is the number of players remaining in the game after t hours, which of the following best describes the function g ?

A) The function g increases exponentially.

B) The function g decreases exponentially.

C) The function g increases linearly.

D) The function g decreases linearly.

CONTINUE

x	y
$-3b$	$18b$
$-2b$	$13b$
0	$3b$
$2b$	$-7b$

In the table above, b is a constant. If the xy-table describes some points on a linear function between x and y, which of the following equations could represent that function?

A) $5x + y = 2b$

B) $x - 5y = -3b$

C) $5x + y = 3b$

D) $x - 5y = -7b$

$$8a + 20 = 7 + \frac{3}{4}(8a + 20)$$

Based on the equation above, which of the following is equal to $2a + 5$?

A) -7

B) $-\dfrac{5}{2}$

C) 7

D) 10

$$1.3x - 0.6y = -0.7$$
$$6.5x - 1.5y = -0.5$$

When two equations above are graphed in the xy-plane, there is a single solution at (x, y). What is the y-coordinate of that solution?

A) -1.33

B) -1.125

C) 2

D) 3.25

Sally is modeling the change in diets among Native American populations around the Great Lakes by looking at the change over time of goosefoot seed remains in midden heaps. Midden heaps were locations where early peoples would dump the remains of food. She notices that the number of goosefoot seeds deposited in midden heaps has decreased by roughly 7% per century, c, since the earliest time period she studies. She estimates there were roughly 500 goosefoot seed remains deposited initially. Which of the following functions models $S(c)$, the number of seeds found per century?

A) $S(c) = 500\,(1.07)^c$

B) $S(c) = 500\,(0.93)^c$

C) $S(c) = 500^{0.93c}$

D) $S(c) = 500^c$

CONTINUE

28

$$C = 0.0045P + 5.22$$

A production line manager uses the equation above to predict the production cost per item produced in dollars, *C*, based on the number of products made, *P*. In the context of the model, what is the meaning of 5.22 ?

A) The initial production cost, in dollars, of each product made

B) The approximate production cost increase, in dollars per item, for each item made

C) The approximate production cost, in dollars per item, for every 0.0045 products made

D) The approximate production cost decrease, in dollars per item, for every 0.0045 products made

29

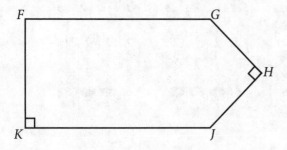

In the figure above, $\overline{FG} \parallel \overline{JK}$, $FG = JK$, and $GH = HJ$. What is the measure of angle *J* if $FK = HJ\left(\sqrt{2}\right)$?

A) 90°

B) 120°

C) 135°

D) 160°

30

The function $h(x)$ is defined as $h(x) = a(x - 2)(x + 5)$ for all real values of *x*. If *a* is a negative number, which one of the following could be a graph of $h(x)$?

A)
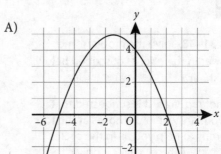

B)
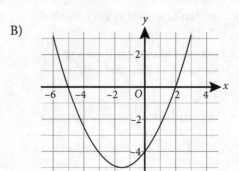

C)
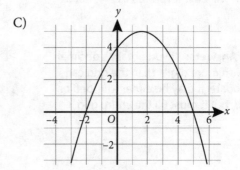

D)
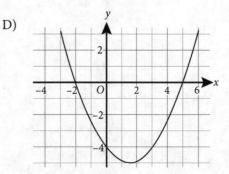

CONTINUE ➡

DIRECTIONS

For questions 31–38, solve the problem and enter your answer in the grid, as described below, on the answer sheet.

1. Although not required, it is suggested that you write your answer in the boxes at the top of the columns to help you fill in the circles accurately. You will receive credit only if the circles are filled in correctly.

2. Mark no more than one circle in any column.

3. No question has a negative answer.

4. Some problems may have more than one correct answer. In such cases, grid only one answer.

5. **Mixed numbers** such as $3\frac{1}{2}$ must be gridded as 3.5 or 7/2. (If is entered into the grid, it will be interpreted as $\frac{31}{2}$, not as $3\frac{1}{2}$.)

6. **Decimal Answers:** If you obtain a decimal answer with more digits than the grid can accommodate, it may be either rounded or truncated, but it must fill the entire grid.

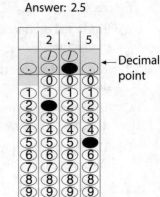

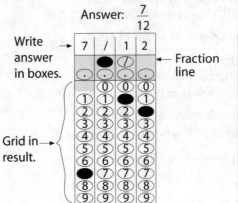

Acceptable ways to grid $\frac{2}{3}$ are:

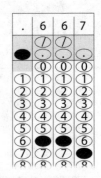

Answer: 201 – either position is correct

NOTE: You may start your answers in any column, space permitting. Columns you don't need to use should be left blank.

31

650, *a*, 1550, 1750, 2300, 2650

If the mean of the list above is 1650, what is the value of *a* ?

32

John is buying some burgers and fries for his friends. Burgers cost $4.30 each and fries cost $3.10 per order. There is no tax on the food. If he has $50 and buys 6 orders of fries, what is the maximum number of burgers he can buy?

33

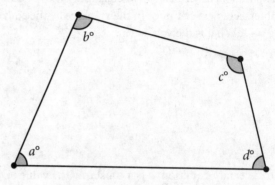

Note: Figure not drawn to scale.

If *a* = 118 and *b* = 67 in the quadrilateral above, what is the value of *c* + *d* ?

34

$$-3x + 2 = p(x - q)$$

In the equation above, *p* and *q* are constants. If there are infinitely many solutions to the equation, what is the value of *q* ?

CONTINUE

35

A parabola described by the equation $y = x^2 - 6x + c$ is intersected exactly once in the xy-plane by the equation $y = -1$. What is the value of c ?

36

In a certain function, a is a constant. The value of the function is 5 when $x = b$. If the function can be modeled using the equation $f(x) = ax^2$, what is the value of the function when $x = 3b$?

Questions 37 and 38 refer to the following information.

To leave the Moon's gravity well, a shuttle must reach speeds of 8568 kilometers per hour. This speed is known as escape velocity because, if not reached, the shuttle would not be able to escape the Moon's gravity and return to Earth.

37

If the space shuttle traveling at escape velocity has 150 km left before reaching lunar orbit, in approximately how many seconds will the shuttle reach orbit? (Round your answer to the nearest second).

38

What is the space shuttle's escape velocity in meters per second, rounded to the nearest hundred? (1 kilometer = 1000 meters)?

END OF TEST

DO NOT RETURN TO A PREVIOUS SECTION.

Practice Test 4:
Answers and
Explanations

PRACTICE TEST 4 ANSWER KEY

Section 1: Reading		Section 2: Writing and Language		Section 3: Math (No Calculator)		Section 4: Math (Calculator)	
1. A	27. B	1. B	23. D	1. C	11. A	1. D	18. A
2. B	28. D	2. D	24. B	2. C	12. D	2. A	19. D
3. B	29. B	3. A	25. C	3. D	13. B	3. D	20. C
4. D	30. B	4. C	26. A	4. A	14. A	4. A	21. D
5. C	31. D	5. B	27. B	5. A	15. C	5. A	22. D
6. A	32. C	6. D	28. A	6. D	16. 28	6. C	23. B
7. D	33. A	7. B	29. C	7. D	17. 0	7. B	24. C
8. C	34. C	8. C	30. D	8. D	18. 94	8. B	25. C
9. B	35. B	9. A	31. A	9. C	19. 7	9. A	26. C
10. C	36. B	10. B	32. D	10. C	20. $\frac{10}{3}$	10. B	27. B
11. C	37. D	11. D	33. C			11. B	28. A
12. B	38. D	12. D	34. A			12. C	29. C
13. D	39. C	13. C	35. C			13. C	30. A
14. B	40. A	14. D	36. B			14. A	31. 1000
15. B	41. D	15. A	37. A			15. D	32. 7
16. D	42. B	16. C	38. C			16. A	33. 175
17. A	43. C	17. B	39. D			17. A	34. $\frac{2}{3}$ or 0.66 or 0.67
18. B	44. B	18. A	40. B				
19. B	45. B	19. D	41. C				35. 8
20. C	46. C	20. B	42. A				36. 45
21. D	47. D	21. A	43. B				37. 63
22. B	48. A	22. D	44. D				38. 2400
23. A	49. C						
24. D	50. D						
25. D	51. D						
26. A	52. A						

PRACTICE TEST 4 EXPLANATIONS

Section 1: Reading

1. **A** Although Jane resists Mr. Rochester, the first sentence of the passage indicates that her conscience and emotions are actually favorably inclined toward Mr. Rochester. Because she has positive feelings toward him, (A) is an accurate description of her attitude. While Mr. Rochester perceives Jane to be *uncaring,* (B) is incorrect because the narration indicates that she does care but resists her own feelings. Similarly, (C) is incorrect because the first sentence tells you she has positive feelings for Rochester. Because Jane acts calmly, ignoring her emotions, she cannot accurately be described as *reckless.* Therefore, (D) is also incorrect, so (A) is the correct answer.

2. **B** Because Q2 and Q3 are general paired questions, consider Q2 and the textual evidence given in Q3 at the same time. Q2 asks for the reason Jane refused Rochester's advances. Consider the lines referenced in the answer choices for Q3 and whether they support any of the answers in Q2. Choices (A), (C), and (D) in Q3 do not support any of the answer choices in Q2, so they can be eliminated. However, (3B), *I will hold to the principles received by me when I was sane, and not mad—as I am now,* provides support for only (2B), so (B) must be the answer to both Q2 and Q3. These answers make sense because they indicate that Jane resists Rochester because she wishes to hold to her principles.

3. **B** (See explanation above.)

4. **D** There is no evidence that Jane is literally insane. Rather, she is speaking metaphorically about the conflict between her reason and her desires. Therefore, (A) is wrong. Because Jane says the law (not her mental state) has been given by God, (B) is incorrect. Jane says that her insanity tempts her to disregard the worth of her principles, and it is her principles that are preventing her from giving in to Mr. Rochester, so her insanity is tempting her to give in to Rochester. Therefore, (C) is wrong; her insanity does not urge her to *reject* Rochester, but rather to accept his advances. Choice (D) is correct because her feeling of insanity is directly related to her emotions, as evidenced by the phrase *with my veins running fire, and my heart beating faster than I can count its throbs,* which Jane provides to explain why she feels insane.

5. **C** Because *wrought* describes Mr. Rochester's fury, and the passage says that his fury has reached its highest, *wrought* must mean something like "increased." Because *hammered* has nothing to do with increasing fury, (A) is incorrect. Choice (B) also does not have anything to do with "increased," so eliminate it. Because *excited* could mean "increased" when applied to someone's emotions, (C) accurately describes the passage's use of *wrought.* Since *wrung* means *squeezed and twisted,* (D) does not describe the passage's use of *wrought.* The correct answer is (C).

6. **A** Choice (A) is correct because Mr. Rochester describes Jane's soul as strong and her body as weak in paragraph 5. While paragraph 1 states that Rochester loves Jane, and paragraph 4 states that he is angry with her for refusing his advances, Rochester is angry for the entirety of paragraph 5. Therefore, it does not contrast his love with his anger, and (B) is incorrect. Though Rochester speaks of a cage, he never actually mentions a *bird;* eliminate (C). Similarly, Rochester refers only to Jane's purity. Because he never calls Jane *impure,* (D) is not correct.

7. **D** Rochester is speaking metaphorically, not about a literal convict, so (A) is incorrect. Because he is talking about Jane, not himself, (B) cannot be correct. When Rochester refers to breaking the prison and Jane's body, you can tell that the inmate's prison refers to Jane's body, not the ideals of the time. Therefore, (C) is incorrect. The inmate refers to Jane's soul, so (D) accurately describes Rochester's use of *inmate* and is the correct answer.

8. **C** Think about the evidence in the passage that helped you answer the previous question: Rochester is using the word *inmate* to refer to Jane's soul trapped in her body. Because (A) mentions neither soul nor body, (A) is incorrect. Choice (B) refers only to Jane's body, so it cannot be correct. Choice (C) mentions both Jane's spirit and body (her *brittle frame*), providing good support for the answer to the previous question. Choice (D) makes no mention of either soul or body, so it is incorrect. The correct answer is (C).

9. **B** Because Jane is having a harder time resisting Rochester now that he is sad, *worse* means something close to "harder." Because *less desirable, of lower quality,* and *unskillful* all mean things other than "harder," you can eliminate (A), (C), and (D). Because "harder" matches *more difficult,* (B) accurately describes the passage's use of *worse* and is the correct answer.

10. **C** *Pathos* refers to Jane's emotions, so the paragraph depicts Jane overcoming her emotions. Therefore, (A) cannot be correct. Jane makes no allusion to *social conventions,* which makes (B) incorrect. However, because the paragraph depicts Jane overcoming her emotions, (C) is a good description of Jane's values. Since Jane battles to overcome her feelings, (D) is not an accurate description of her values. Choice (C) is the answer.

11. **C** Clinton's speech speaks out against gender inequality all over the world and advocates in favor of these injustices being amended. Choice (C) best reflects this idea. Although Clinton criticizes how women are treated worldwide, she does not *counter any arguments,* so eliminate (A). She does not take a *scholarly approach* to analyze women's place in society, so eliminate (B). Clinton is not *mediating* between two parties, so eliminate (D).

12. **B** Although women play different roles in society, many of these roles are not appreciated. Choice (B) most accurately reflects this meaning. Choices (A), (C), and (D) have meanings that are related to the word *valued* but are not used in the context of the word's use in the passage.

13. **D** Clinton discusses the importance of conferences in *compelling people to consider important issues.* She then mentions the conference in Nairobi as helping to bring to light the crisis of domestic violence. Therefore, (D) is the correct answer. The passage does not claim that the crisis of domestic violence was not *solved,* so eliminate (A). The passage does not discuss anyone questioning the reason for holding the *current conference,* so eliminate (B). Although Clinton mentions the fact that the experiences of women tend to go *unnoticed,* this is not her reason for mentioning the conference in Nairobi. Eliminate (C).

14. **B** Think about the evidence in the passage that helped you answer the previous question: *It is conferences like this that compel governments and peoples everywhere to listen, look, and face the world's most*

pressing problems. She then mentions the conference in Nairobi as helping to bring to light the crisis of domestic violence. Choice (B) provides the most support for why Clinton mentions the conference in Nairobi. The current conference was not held because of the conference in Nairobi, so eliminate (A). Women being the primary caretakers of the world is not the reason for mentioning the conference in Nairobi, so eliminate (C). Women dying from preventable diseases is not the reason for mentioning the conference in Nairobi, so eliminate (D).

15. **B** Clinton discusses how some women are able to attend a conference that speaks out against the inequalities against women, while others are not able to do so. Choice (B) most accurately reflects this idea. Clinton does not differentiate between people *who work at schools and hospitals,* so eliminate (A). Clinton does not mention *employed women, unemployed women,* or *women who can or cannot vote,* so eliminate (C) and (D).

16. **D** Choices (A), (B), and (C) are each discussed in paragraph 4, so eliminate them. The passage does not discuss women suffering from *widespread unemployment,* so (D) is the correct answer.

17. **A** In paragraph 8, Clinton argues that women's rights are also human rights, which matches (A). Women's attendance at the conference is not discussed in this paragraph, so eliminate (B). Clinton does not claim that women's rights have a *special nature,* just that these rights are the same as human rights, so eliminate (C). Clinton does not suggest that we *no longer need to focus on women's problems;* this is the opposite of what is discussed in the passage, so eliminate (D).

18. **B** Think about the evidence in the passage that helped you answer the previous question. In paragraph 8, Clinton argues that women's rights are also human rights. Choice (B) provides the most support for the rhetorical effect of the phrase discussed in the previous question. Although Clinton discusses the respect and protection of women's rights, this is not the phrase that best supports the rhetorical effect of the discussed phrase, so eliminate (A). Giving examples of the specific rights in question does not provide the best support for the rhetorical effect of the discussed phrase, so eliminate (C). The attendance of women at the conference is not related to the discussed phrase, so eliminate (D).

19. **B** In paragraph 2, Clinton discusses the experiences of women throughout the world: *Yet much of the work we do is not valued—not by economists, not by historians, not by popular culture, not by government leaders.* Choice (B) most accurately reflects this idea. Clinton does not state that these leaders are purposely *working against the prosperity of women,* so eliminate (A). Choice (C) is contradicted by what the passage states, so eliminate this choice. Although these leaders may not value the work of women, the passage does not state that these leaders *have made it unacceptable to discuss women's rights,* so eliminate (D).

20. **C** The question asks for a statement about *the United States in 2012* that is supported by the figure. Work through each answer choice using the figure. Eliminate (A) because the figure shows *people under 18 years of age* were more likely to live in poverty than were *people aged 18 to 64.* Eliminate (B) because the figure shows that *people over the age of 65* experienced the lowest poverty rates.

Keep (C) because the disparity in poverty rates between males and females under age 18 was only 1 percent (22.3 percent – 21.3 percent), while the disparity among those ages 18 to 64 was 3.5 percent (15.4 percent – 11.9 percent), and the disparity among those over age 65 was 4.4 percent (11.0 percent – 6.6 percent). For the same reason, eliminate (D). The correct answer is (C).

21.　**D**　The graphic shows poverty rates in America divided by gender and age. Across all age groups, women experience higher rates of poverty than their male counterparts. This falls in line with the passage's assertion that women comprise 70 percent of the world's poor. Therefore, (D) is correct. Choice (A) is incorrect because, while the graphic shows a high gender disparity among those 65 and older, it refers only to American poverty rates. The graphic actually states that 15.4 percent of American women 18 to 65 are impoverished, not that they make up that percentage of the world's poor. Therefore, (B) is incorrect. And there is no mention of how many children are impoverished worldwide in either the graphic or the passage, so (C) is incorrect.

22.　**B**　The third-to-last sentence of the passage states that *Seen throughout the procession is that balance of the monumentally simple and the actual,* and goes on to list several more types of balance, *that Heraclitus, the philosopher, wrote of in the sixth century B.C.* This is support for (B). While the author does discuss the representation of the passage of time in the frieze, this idea is not connected to Heraclitus, so (A) can be eliminated. The mention of Heraclitus also does not support the idea that the frieze is *characteristically Greek,* so (C) is incorrect. Choice (D) is tempting, if the entirety of the sentence mentioning Heraclitus isn't included; however, the balance mentioned isn't between mortals and the goddess Athena.

23.　**A**　In the first paragraph of Passage 1, the author proposes his idea of what the frieze *probably represents.* In the second paragraph, he describes the frieze. This matches (A). Choice (B) may seem close at first because the author does indicate that the subject of the frieze *is still a matter of scholarly dispute.* However, he does not *question* someone else's interpretation, so (B) is incorrect. Choice (C) falls into the category of "too narrow": the author does describe the frieze, but only in paragraph 2. Choice (C) doesn't take paragraph 1 into account. Since no *historical overview* is given, (D) is also incorrect.

24.　**D**　By using the word *unparalleled,* the author is saying that it is unusual to see a representation of a festival in classical Greek art that shows deities in attendance. Choices (A), (B), and (C) do not match the meaning of "unusual," but (D) does. Therefore, (D) is the answer.

25.　**D**　Passage 2 begins with the first paragraph describing ways that the particular piece of art in question is unusual in the world of classical Greek art: it shows deities attending a festival, including Athena, and they are ignoring the peplos. This represents a *flagrant breach with tradition* that *requires explanation.* Paragraph 2 continues with an explanation of what it cannot represent. Since the author does not say that the frieze cannot *depict the Panathenaic procession,* (A) is incorrect. The author also does not discuss *the passage of time,* so (B) is incorrect. While the author goes on to describe the *heroes of Marathon,* the question is asking about the purpose of the first two paragraphs, so (C) is a tempting trap answer but must be eliminated. Choice (D) comes the closest to what the author is doing in the first two paragraphs, describing *problems in the traditional interpretation of the frieze.*

26. **A** Paragraph 2 begins by discussing what a *classical Athenian,* or resident of Athens, would not have thought as he looked at the frieze, that is, that it was a representation of himself. In the second sentence, *mortal* could be replaced by *classical Athenian,* because the subject must be something greater than a resident of Athens. Therefore, (B), (C), and (D) do not fit, and (A) is the correct answer.

27. **B** Paragraph 2 begins by discussing what a *classical Athenian,* or resident of Athens, would not have thought as he looked at the frieze: *"there I go" or even more vaguely "there we go."* The next sentence mentions that the subject of the frieze must be *more than mortal,* or more than about the *classical Athenian* looking at it. Putting these together, you can surmise that when the author says that the *classical Athenian* wouldn't say *"there I go,"* he means that the frieze is not about the *classical Athenian.* Paragraph 3 confirms this idea by saying *we must rule out...that it is a contemporary or generic statement of the Panathenaic procession conducted by the citizens....* Since there was never a discussion of the figures themselves and whether they represented *individual citizens,* (A) is incorrect. Choice (B) does match pretty closely, so keep it. Choice (C) has more to do with who participated in the procession rather than the subject of the frieze, so eliminate (C). Choice (D) goes too far because the author never says that the *subject of the frieze should be obvious to modern viewers.* Choice (B) is the correct answer.

28. **D** Think about the evidence in the passage that helped you answer the previous question: support for (B) in Q27 comes from paragraphs 2 and 3, so (A) and (B) can be eliminated. While it may be true that *the explanation must have been apparent to the classical Athenian who knew this background,* this does not support the idea that the frieze cannot represent a human event, so eliminate (C). Choice (D) directly supports (B) in Q27 and is therefore the correct answer.

29. **B** The author of Passage 2 proposes that the frieze *shows the fighters of Marathon celebrating the prime festival of the goddess Athena...as a thanksgiving for her aid at Marathon and afterwards.* This ties into (B), *Athenian men who died in battle at Marathon.* There is no indication that the author believes the *youths* were *from around the time the Parthenon was built,* so eliminate (A). Choice (C) is too broad because it includes all *people of Marathon who were worshipped as heroes,* whereas the author specifies the fighters of Marathon, so eliminate (C). Choice (D) contradicts the author's description that the frieze is a representation of the fighters, not *purely divine participants,* so eliminate it. Choice (B) is the answer.

30. **B** Passage 1 does not *focus on determining the subject of the frieze*—that's only in the first paragraph. Eliminate (A). Passage 2 considers *how Greek citizens might have viewed the frieze,* but Passage 1 does not. Eliminate (C). Passage 1 also does not *entirely reject* the traditional perspective, so eliminate (D). Passage 1 does give *a detailed description of the figures* in the second paragraph, so (B) is the correct answer.

31. **D** Think about the evidence in the passage that helped you answer the previous question: Passage 1 gives a *detailed description of the figures* in the frieze in the second paragraph. Only (D) references lines that give a detailed description of figures in the frieze, so (D) is the correct answer.

32. **C** This question asks about the primary purpose of the passage. Because this is a general question, it should be done after the specific questions. The passage describes the results of a Stanford University study that showed that antibiotic-resistant strains of tuberculosis evolve over the course of treatment and remain virulent. The passage goes on to discuss the concerns raised by the study. The passage concludes by stating that drug-resistant bacteria are here to stay. Find an answer that matches this prediction. Choice (A) can be eliminated because, while the passage does mention *classic laboratory experiments,* it does not support those findings. Choice (B) can be eliminated because the idea that the findings *should cause alarm* is the opposite of what the passage says in the last two paragraphs. The passage does review the Stanford University study and discusses the *concerns raised by the study.* Keep (C). Eliminate (D) because the passage does not *criticize the methodology* of any study. The correct answer is (C).

33. **A** This question asks what *the scientists in the Stanford University study* discovered *about tuberculosis bacteria that "undermined this comforting conventional wisdom."* Notice that this is a paired question with best evidence answers that cover a large part of the text. Therefore, Q33 and Q34 can be done in tandem. Look at the "best evidence" answer choices for Q34 first. The lines for (34A) state that *Without RNA, bacteria can't make the proteins they need to survive.* This does not support any of the answers in Q33. Eliminate (34A). The lines in (34B) provide information about when the Stanford group collected tuberculosis bacteria from the sputum of patients. This does not support any of the answers in Q33. Eliminate (34B). The lines in (34C) state that *five of the ten resistant strains held their own in these tests, and one actually dominated its antibiotic-susceptible ancestor.* This supports the idea in (33A) that bacteria can *resist antibiotics* without *losing strength.* Connect (34C) with (33A). The lines for (34D) state that *Some changes simply have a low cost to begin with, and, the study also found, the cost depends on the strain in which the mutation occurs.* This does not support any of the answers in Q33. Without any support in the answers from Q34, (33B), (33C), and (33D) can be eliminated. The correct answers are (33A) and (34C).

34. **C** (See explanation above.)

35. **B** This question asks what the word *hardy* most nearly means, as used in line 26. Read the window, cross out the word *hardy,* and replace it with another word or phrase that makes sense based on the context of the passage. Then, eliminate anything that does not match the prediction. In the passage, the word *hardy* is used in connection with drug-resistant strains that *remain virulent.* In other words, these are potent strains that keep their strength. Look for a word that means "strong" or "tough." *Difficult* and *thick* do not match "strong" or "tough." Eliminate (A) and (D). *Strong* matches the prediction; keep (B). While (C) may be tempting since a virulent strain would be *terrible,* no such value judgment about the drug-resistant strains is made in the passage; eliminate (C). The correct answer is (B).

36. **B** This question asks what *statement about rifampin can be most reasonably inferred from the passage.* Use the lead word *rifampin* and chronology to find the window. The answer to Q35 was in line 26. Therefore, start looking for *rifampin* after line 26. The first mention of rifampin is in line 30.

According to the passage, *rifampin…disables the so-called polymerase molecule and prevents the crucial flow of information from DNA to RNA. Without RNA, bacteria can't make the proteins they need to survive.* Find an answer that matches this prediction. Choice (A) may be tempting at first because the passage states that rifampin is one of the preferred first-line treatments for the disease. However, the passage does not say that this drug *stopped tuberculosis from being the leading cause of death in the United States.* Eliminate (A). Choice (B) is a good paraphrase of the prediction, so keep it. Choice (C) can be eliminated because there is no suggestion in the passage that rifampin makes RNA *compatible with DNA.* Choice (D) can be eliminated because there is no mention in the passage as to whether rifampin is *more effective* than other drugs. The correct answer is (B).

37. **D** This question asks which type of evidence the Stanford University study relied on. Use the lead word *Stanford* and chronology to find the window. The answer to Q36 was in line 35, so the answer to this question should come somewhere after line 35. Line 49 contains the word *Stanford.* According to the passage, *the Stanford group collected tuberculosis bacteria from the sputum of patients, first at the beginning of their infections, and a second time after some of those patients developed rifampin-resistant infections.* Look for an answer that matches this prediction. Given that the Stanford group did research using human patients, *anecdotal opinion, secondhand observations,* and *animal studies* do not match the prediction. *Clinical testing* matches the prediction. The correct answer is (D).

38. **D** This question asks about what scientists *believed* about *antibiotic-resistant strains of tuberculosis prior to the Stanford study.* Remember to use answers to questions from earlier in the passage if they are relevant. Q33 asked about *conventional wisdom,* which thought antibiotic-resistant bacteria were weaker than their non-resistant counterparts. Find an answer that matches this prediction. Choice (A) can be eliminated because prior to the study, the scientists believed the antibiotic-resistant strains had a worse chance of survival. Eliminate (B) because prior to the study, the scientists expected the antibiotic-resistant strains to be less likely to survive. Therefore, it is unlikely that they expected the antibiotic-resistant strains to become *the most deadly of diseases.* Choice (C) can be eliminated because, while sputum was mentioned earlier in the passage, it was mentioned in relation to how the scientists collected the study samples, not in relation to the scientists' expectations of the study outcomes. Given that the scientists discovered the resistant bacteria were not weaker than their counterparts and the results of the study were *contrary to expectations,* it can be concluded that prior to the study, the scientists expected the antibiotic-resistant strains not to survive. The correct answer is (D).

39. **C** This question asks what question *Sebastien Gagneux* plans to answer through *further studies.* Because this is the first question in a paired set, this question can be done in tandem with Q40. Look at the "best evidence" answer choices for Q40 first. The lines for (40A) state that *Gagneux is planning future studies to find these putative compensatory mutations and learn how they restore the performance of strains that acquire antibiotic-resistant mutations.* This supports the question in (39C). Connect answers (40A) and (39C). The lines in (40B) quote Levin as saying that "*the spread of tuberculosis does not depend solely on the efficacy or lack of efficacy of antibiotics.*" This information

is unrelated to Gagneux's future research plans. Eliminate (40B). The lines for (40C) state that *drug-resistant bacteria are here to stay*. This information is unrelated to Gagneux's future research plans and does not support any of the answers for Q39. Eliminate (40C). The lines for (40D) quote Levin as saying that *the drug-resistant mutations that aren't costly are the ones that will take over*. It may be tempting to connect (40D) with (39B) since (39B) includes the word *cost*. However, the information in the lines for (40D) is unrelated to Gagneux's future research plans. Eliminate (40D). Without any support in the answers from Q40, (39A), (39B), and (39D) can be eliminated. The correct answers are (39C) and (40A).

40. **A** (See explanation above.)

41. **D** This question asks why the author mentions the *alarmist panic* in line 76. Use the given line reference to find the window. According to the passage, *the authors don't want their study to fuel an alarmist panic...the data don't call for it*. The passage goes on to quote Levin as saying "*the spread of tuberculosis does not depend solely on the efficacy or lack of efficacy of antibiotics.*" Therefore, the *alarmist panic* is related to the public's reaction to the study results. Find an answer that matches this prediction. Choice (A) can be eliminated because the passage states that the data does not call for an alarmist panic. Therefore, the author is not using the term to *bring attention to a threat*. Eliminate (B) because there is no mention of *19th century public-health practices* in the window. The author is not identifying *an inevitable result* of antibiotic use, so eliminate (C). Choice (D) matches the prediction. The author is drawing a contrast between the study data (*an undesirable reaction*) and *a reasonable response*, which is not alarmist panic, as *the data don't call for it*. The correct answer is (D).

42. **B** This question asks about the primary function of the final paragraph. Use the final paragraph as the window. The final paragraph broadly summarizes the study findings and makes a general prediction about future bacteria mutations. Find an answer that matches this prediction. Choice (A) can be eliminated because the paragraph does not *reevaluate the Stanford University study*. Choice (B) is consistent with the prediction, so keep it. Choice (C) can be eliminated because there is no indication that the author believes that the Stanford University study *changed society*. Eliminate (D) because the last paragraph does not *explain the methodology of the Stanford University study*. The correct answer is (B).

43. **C** Look earlier in the sentence for the phrase the *Earth's surface sank more than 1 mile*. Go through the answer choices to find the one that matches this description. Choice (C) is correct because a *crater* is a "large, bowl-shaped cavity in the earth." Eliminate (A), (B), and (D), as none of them match this physical description.

44. **B** The second paragraph primarily discusses the extensive time range of volcanic eruptions, starting *as far back as 400,000 years ago* and *as recently as 600 years ago*. Use POE to find the answer choice that matches this information. There is no evidence of *another eruption this century* based on the passage, so eliminate (A). Choice (B) works because it shows the large range of time in geologic terms. Choice (C) almost works, but the author is not just trying to be ironic. The information

is not relevant to the paragraph, so eliminate (C). Choice (D) is incorrect because a relative term doesn't fit; *recently* isn't being compared to any other variables. Choice (B) is the answer.

45. **B** The pronoun *that* precedes *temblor*, so it must refer to something earlier in the previous sentence. The first sentence discusses *a magnitude 5.4 earthquake struck 6 miles southeast of the caldera*, so (B) is correct because the *temblor ended two decades of low quake activity*.

46. **C** The third sentence in paragraph 7 states that the geologists studied trees that were dying on Mammoth Mountain from carbon dioxide, and that this would often *precede volcanic eruptions*. This information suggests the possibility of a volcanic eruption. Choice (C) is a good match for this information. There is no evidence to support (A) and (B), so eliminate them. There is no mention of *geodetic equipment* in this paragraph, so eliminate (D) as well. Choice (C) is the answer.

47. **D** Think about the evidence in the passage that helped you answer the previous question: the geologists are monitoring the caldera to try to predict a future eruption. Use POE to find the best reference from the passage to the previous question. Eliminate (A) because that sentence refers to eruptions from centuries ago. Choice (B) does not reference geologist activity at all, so get rid of it. Eliminate (C) because it discusses the equipment, not the geologists. Choice (D) works because it details studies from the USGS regarding forms of evidence that often *precede volcanic eruptions*.

48. **A** The final sentence in the last paragraph states that *geologists think that the chances of an eruption in the area in any given year are quite small*. This contradicts the information in (B) and (C), so eliminate them. *Earthquakes* are only a small part of the overall passage, so eliminate (D) because it is too limited. Choice (A) is correct.

49. **C** Use POE to find the answer choice that is best supported by the passage. Choice (A) is incorrect since it was *both the Inyo Craters and Mono Craters* that erupted 600 years ago. Choice (B) almost works, but the passage never suggests that Mammoth Mountain is actually active, as opposed to the larger chain—the Long Valley Caldera—it's part of. Choice (C) is a good fit because the seventh paragraph states that *symptoms of volcanic unrest may persist for decades or centuries at large calderas, such as Long Valley Caldera*. The information in (D) is mentioned in the first paragraph, but there is no evidence that refers to Mammoth Mountain, so eliminate it. Choice (C) is correct.

50. **D** Think about the evidence in the passage that helped you answer the previous question: the seventh paragraph states that *symptoms of volcanic unrest may persist for decades or centuries at large calderas, such as Long Valley Caldera*. This sentence is referenced by (D), while the other choices do not relate to the correct answer to the previous question. Therefore, (D) is the answer.

51. **D** The last few sentences of the seventh paragraph state that *symptoms of volcanic unrest may persist for decades or centuries at large calderas, such as Long Valley Caldera. Studies indicate that only about one in six such episodes of unrest at large calderas worldwide actually culminates in an eruption.* The swelling of the Long Valley Caldera is part of these symptoms, so this basically says that there is no definitive outcome that results from them. Choice (D) is a good analogy for this information and therefore the correct answer.

52. **A** 2015 is at the far right end of the graph, at which point the line indicating the number of cumulative earthquakes hits above the 1.2 line. However, each number on the right y-axis needs to be multiplied by one hundred thousand (100,000), so the number of cumulative earthquakes is actually *greater than 120,000*. Therefore, (A) is the correct answer. Choice (B) is incorrect because earthquakes per week are tracked on the right axis, not the left. Choice (C) is incorrect because 1.2 needs to be multiplied by one hundred thousand (100,000), not one million (1,000,000). Choice (D) is incorrect because cumulative earthquakes for 1988 were at less than 0.2 hundred thousand, or 20,000.

Section 2: Writing and Language

1. **B** Use POE to compare the vocabulary options. *Gawked* means "stared in a confused or negative way," but the passage mentions *natural beauty*, so a more positive word is needed. Eliminate (A). *Marveled* means "looked at with wonder," which is consistent with the subject of the sentence, so keep (B). *Pondered* means "thought about," but "pondered at" isn't a correct phrasing, so eliminate (C). *Stared* is not as precise as *marveled* because *stared* simply means "looked at for a period of time" and does not express the wonder at the *natural beauty* that is implied by the sentence. Eliminate (D). The correct answer is (B).

2. **D** Use POE here, since there doesn't seem to be a common thread being tested on this question. Eliminate (B) and (C) because *pulchritudinous* and *pretty* basically mean the same thing, making these choices interchangeable and impossible to choose between. Go back to the passage and notice that it already uses the phrase *marveled at the natural beauty*, so using another word to describe its beauty again would be redundant. Therefore, eliminate (A). Choice (D) is the most concise response, and therefore the correct answer.

3. **A** Notice the question! You're asked for a choice that will include detail to clarify *day-to-day operations*. Look at the next sentence, which describes the activities of the *park rangers*. It states that they are in charge of the park's *upkeep* and *maintain the balance between the wildlife and plant species and the human visitors*. Both of these correspond with the underlined portion of *maintenance and tours*. Nothing is stated about the *length* of the tasks, whether or not they are *repetitive,* or the *political* aspects of them, so eliminate (B), (C), and (D). Choice (A) provides the detail the question asks for and is the correct answer.

4. **C** The idea before the punctuation, *These park rangers are responsible for the upkeep of the parks*, is a complete idea, as is the clause, *their main responsibility is to maintain the balance between the wildlife and plant species and the human visitors that come to the parks every day*, that follows it. Therefore, a comma alone cannot separate two complete ideas, so eliminate (A) and (D). Eliminate (B) as well, because punctuation is needed to separate two complete ideas. Choice (C) is the correct answer because a dash (HALF-STOP punctuation) can be used to separate these complete ideas.

5. **B** The paragraph describes the *park rangers* as *scientists*, *educators*, and professionals with backgrounds in *law enforcement* and *firefighting*. Look for the answer choice that is consistent with this type of diversity. Eliminate (A) because *pollution* is not talked about in the paragraph, as well as (C) because the paragraph is not interested in the *visitors* to the park. *Ecology* is too limited for (D), so eliminate it. You're left with (B), which is the correct answer.

6. **D** Look to the previous sentence, which describes some of the park rangers, and notice the phrase *Some are scientists who revel*. Since the next sentence is also describing the park rangers, it needs to be consistent and parallel with the previous sentence, so it should be *Some are educators who help*. Choice (D) is the correct response.

7. **B** Notice that the answer choices are pronouns, so look at the current sentence to determine what the pronoun *them* refers to; this might be unclear because both *posts* and *municipal services* are used in the sentence. Eliminate (A) and (C), which are ambiguous, and (D) because it's singular and ambiguous. Choice (B) is the clearest, most precise choice and is therefore correct.

8. **C** Use POE to find the clearest and most concise response. Choice (A) is awkward because *visitors are on the rise* doesn't necessarily refer to their numbers, so eliminate it. Choice (B) is incorrect, as *poised on the rise* is an idiom error and should be *poised to rise*. Choice (D) is awkward, unclear, and redundant, as *poised on the rise* seems to be referring to the *numbers*, which are also described as *growing*. (Note that like (B), (D) also contains an idiom error.) Choice (C) is the answer.

9. **A** Check the underlined portion of this sentence, which states that the *visitation numbers peaked before the 2020 pandemic,* and compare it with the chart. This information is true, as is the second phrase, *the general trend has been on a steady rise*, so keep (A). Eliminate (B) because the high point in the late 1990s isn't the highest portion of the graph and visitation has not *tapered off*. Choice (C) is not true because the lowest point was in 1990, and (D) can be eliminated because the growth has been somewhat erratic and not *linear*. Choice (A) is correct.

10. **B** Punctuation in a list of three things is changing in the answer choices. In a list of three or more things, there must be a comma after every item. Eliminate (A), (C), and (D) because they do not have a comma after the word *educational*. The correct answer is (B).

11. **D** The idea before the punctuation, *The park-ranger workforce is so diverse*, is a complete idea, as is the clause that follows it, *there are actually a few common attributes among park rangers*. A comma cannot separate two complete ideas, so eliminate (A). Choice (B), *Truly, the park-ranger,* simply adds emphasis to the sentence. It does nothing to point out the contrast between the beginning and the end of the sentence. Therefore, (B) is incorrect. Look at (C) and (D), since the transition words *because* and *although* are exact opposites, and then refer back to the sentence to see if the two ideas are complimentary or contrasting. The words used in the sentence are *diverse* and *a few common*, so pick the transition word that indicates a contrast. Choice (D) is the answer.

12. **D** Sentence 2 begins with the phrase *This part*. Because a pronoun is used, go back and find the noun it refers to. Sentence 4 states that *Lincoln granted a special provision for that part of Virginia*, so the

pronoun *this* refers to the *part of Virginia*. Therefore, sentence 2 should go after sentence 4, so (D) is the correct answer.

13. **C** The answer choices here suggest that this question is testing pronouns. Go back earlier in the sentence to find what the pronoun refers to. It's *the United States*, which is a collective noun and therefore singular. Eliminate (A) and (B). Eliminate (D) as well because a contraction is not necessary here. Choice (C), which is a singular possessive pronoun, is the correct answer.

14. **D** This question is testing comma usage, so check to see if the comma is separating two complete ideas or if it's necessary to break up the incomplete ideas. Neither appears to be the case, and this sentence does not need a break. Remember, if you don't have a good reason to add a comma, don't use one. Choice (D) is correct.

15. **A** Use POE to determine whether the information in the map is consistent with the answer choices. Choice (A) seems like a good choice because Harpers Ferry is directly at the meeting point of the Shenandoah and Potomac Rivers, so keep it. Eliminate (B) because there is not enough information to support the 20-mile northeast approximation from Bolivar to Harpers Ferry. Choice (C) is also unsupported because Harpers Ferry is across the Shenandoah from Virginia, not Maryland, so eliminate (C). Choice (D) is incorrect because the Adirondack Mountains are not even on the map (they are actually in upstate New York). Choice (A) is correct.

16. **C** Use POE for this question, as there doesn't seem to be a specific rule being tested. Eliminate (A) because *it* is an ambiguous pronoun that could refer to either the *armory* or *the Civil War*. Choice (B) is incorrect because *war* should not be the subject of this phrase as though it *saw Harpers Ferry* literally *change hands*. Same goes for (D), as *eight* should not be the subject of the phrase. Choice (C) makes it clear that it was *Harpers Ferry* that *changed hands*, making it the most precise answer choice and the correct answer.

17. **B** If you look at the answer choices, you may notice that there isn't a huge difference between them; watch out for redundancy and try to be concise. The sentence uses the word *crucial* already, so eliminate (A), (C), and (D), which add words that mean the same thing as *crucial*. The answer is (B).

18. **A** Notice the question! Use POE to find an answer choice that is consistent with the *major importance* of Brown's raid. *A national discussion* started because of the raid, so keep (A). Choice (B) suggests the raid's importance, but *Herman Melville* is not mentioned anywhere else in the passage, so eliminate (B). Eliminate (C) and (D) because neither deals with the impact of the raid after the fact. Choice (A) is the answer.

19. **D** The correct answer to this question needs to contrast the positive terms of *hero* and *freedom fighter*, so eliminate (B), which is also positive. Eliminate (A) because, taken literally, *filthy* means "unclean" and doesn't really contrast *hero*. Choice (C) is slang, and therefore incorrect. Choice (D) works because *vile* is consistent with *terrorist* and contrasts the positive tone of *hero*.

20. **B** Use POE to find the clearest and most concise answer choice. Eliminate (A) and (D) because both use the ambiguous pronoun *it*. Choice (C) is incorrect because it's unclear how *Brown's rally* was named. This would change the overall meaning of the sentence. Choice (B) is the clearest and most concise, and therefore the correct answer.

21. **A** The underlined portion uses a period, so check for complete and incomplete ideas. The period here separates two complete ideas, so the period is STOP punctuation that is being used correctly. Eliminate (B) because it uses GO punctuation, and eliminate (C) because it uses no punctuation at all and therefore creates a run-on sentence. Eliminate (D) because the transition *and* is used after the semicolon, turning the complete idea into an incomplete one. Choice (A) is correct.

22. **D** The underlined portion uses HALF-STOP punctuation (a colon) to separate the two ideas, so the first idea must be complete in order for the colon to work. The first idea is incomplete, so eliminate (A). Also eliminate (B) and (C), as STOP punctuation can be used only between two complete ideas. Choice (D) is the answer because it correctly uses GO punctuation between an incomplete idea and a complete idea.

23. **D** Use POE to evaluate the use of punctuation. Since 2014 is not in italics, it must not be part of the name of the film. Thus, it needs to be separated from the name of the film, not directly following it. Eliminate (A) and (B) because 2014 appears right next to *The Grand Budapest Hotel* without a separation. Choice (C) separates 2014 with a comma, but by putting the name of the movie in parentheses, this choice suggests that the name of the movie is unnecessary. Removing the name of the movie makes the sentence say ...*Anderson's recent film, 2014,* which is not correct. Eliminate (C). Choice (D) correctly puts the date in parentheses, which separates it from the name of the film. The correct answer is (D).

24. **B** In the following sentence, the author wonders about the *sudden interest* in Zweig's work after its *obscurity*, so an acceptable alternative to the underlined word would be something similar to *important*. *Relevant* is the best match, so (B) is the correct answer. Choice (A) is an incorrect spelling, so it is incorrect. Choice (C) is the opposite of what's needed, and (D) is a misspelling of the opposite of the required term.

25. **C** Notice the question! The best way to combine these two sentences would be to turn it into one concise sentence. Choice (A) can be eliminated because the only difference is the semicolon, which basically serves the same purpose as a period. Choice (D) is awkward because *eliteness* is an improper form of the word *elite*. Comparing (B) and (C), (C) is more concise. Therefore, (C) is the answer because it's grammatically correct and concise.

26. **A** This question is testing the use of apostrophes, and since the phrase *city's cultural elite* indicates possession, check to see whether or not the noun is singular or plural. Since *city* is singular, then the *'s* is correct, so (A) is the correct answer.

27. **B** The passage states that Zweig *published a near infinitude of works* and then goes on to list what the works are. Therefore, the examples of those works are necessary to the sentence. Eliminate (C) and

(D). Also get rid of (A) since the examples are not for other types of work Zweig could get. Choice (B) is the correct answer.

28. **A** The paragraph opens by describing Zweig's relationship with Vienna as *tenuous* and then goes on to describe him as a *committed pacifist*. The next sentence states that his *pacifism was no longer looked on with such understanding*, which means that the conjunction must show a contrast. Eliminate (B) and (C) because they do not indicate a contrast. Eliminate (D) because *although* should be used to start an incomplete thought (a dependent clause). As used here it creates an incomplete sentence. Choice (A) is correct because *however* shows a clear shift to a new idea.

29. **C** The answer to this question needs to address Zweig's personal stake in the European conflict, so eliminate (A) and (D), as neither choice addresses Zweig himself. Also eliminate (B) because the emphasis is on his ancestral home, not the Americas. Choice (C) is correct because it states Zweig has such *pride* in his home country of Vienna.

30. **D** Based on the answer choices, this question is testing pronoun uses. Since the pronoun in the sentence refers to the *privileged man*, eliminate (A); *which* cannot be used to refer to a person. The correct answer will be an object pronoun, so eliminate (B) because it's a subject pronoun, and (C) because it's possessive. Choice (D) is the answer.

31. **A** Notice that the question asks for the choice that best supports the idea presented at the beginning of the sentence, which emphasizes more *"masculine" figures. Competitive sports* might be something that is traditionally considered *"masculine."* Therefore, the sentence seems to make sense as is, so (A) is the correct answer. The other choices can be eliminated because none of them refer to *masculine* behavior or activities.

32. **D** Based on the answer choices, this question is testing pronouns. Be careful, however, because the underlined portion is not addressing Zweig, but rather *many of us*. You can eliminate (A) and (C) because those are singular pronouns and therefore inconsistent. The next phrase states *our longing*, so the use of *our* in (D) creates consistency.

33. **C** Check out the answer choices, which show that verb tense is the concept being tested here. Look at the earlier part of the sentence that states *We know that things cannot be* and select the choice that is consistent with the verb *know*. Choice (C) is consistent and therefore the correct response.

34. **A** Based on the answer choices, the question is testing comma usage. In a list of three or more items, a comma must be used after each item in the list and before *and*, so eliminate (D). Also, (B) and (C) use unnecessary commas after *bacon* and *strips,* and there is no reason to slow down the flow of ideas in this sentence. Choice (A) is correct.

35. **C** Notice the question and use POE. Although the passage is ultimately concerned with *chimpanzees* seeking *fruit*, there is no information that suggests the *banana* was its *traditional diet*. Eliminate (A). The *chimps' waking and sleeping* habits are never discussed in the passage, so get rid of (B). Choice (C) works because the following paragraph discusses how *the nomadic chimpanzees set up*

their campsites within striking distance of the ripe fruits. Therefore, keep (C) because it's consistent with this paragraph. *Human evolution* isn't discussed anywhere in the passage, so eliminate (D). The correct answer is (C).

36. **B** Notice the question! Look for the choice that serves as a transition and introduction. The previous paragraph ends with *for a chimpanzee, every day during a fruit-poor season can be like Black Friday where all the "shoppers" want the same hot item.* Use POE to find the choice that correlates with this statement. Eliminate (A) because the value of the *deals* is irrelevant. Eliminate (C) and (D) because *Thanksgiving* isn't necessary for the comparison between how *chimpanzees* get food and *Black Friday.* Choice (B) is the answer because it connects the reference to Black Friday in the previous paragraph and at the same time introduces the topic of the current paragraph.

37. **A** Look out for the pronoun changes in the answer choices, specifically *its* and *their.* The subject of the sentence should be *chimpanzees,* a plural noun, to match the plural noun in the previous sentence. Therefore, you can eliminate (B) and (C), which have singular nouns. Eliminate (D) because it incorrectly joins a plural noun (*chimpanzees*) with a singular pronoun (*its*). Choice (A) correctly uses both a plural noun (*chimpanzees*) and the plural pronoun (*their*).

38. **C** The definition in the sentence is *quick to disappear,* so use POE to find the word that most directly matches the meaning. Eliminate (B) and (D) because *desiccated* means to "dry up," and *eternal* would be the opposite of *quick to disappear.* Eliminate (A) because *lively* means "energetic" or "animated." *Ephemeral* means "brief" or "fleeting," so it's a good match, making (C) the correct answer.

39. **D** The word *than,* a comparison word, is used several times in the answer choices. Figure out what is being compared and eliminate answer choices that don't match. The sentence begins with *when the fruits were,* so the answer is going to have to compare to a time period. Only (D) does this, so it's the correct answer.

40. **B** Use POE to find a word that is consistent with the paragraph, which is a lack of food. *Gobbled, chomped,* and *ate* all refer to the consumption of food, but not necessarily a lack of food, so eliminate (A), (C), and (D). *Depleted* would fit because it means "used up completely." Choice (B) is correct.

41. **C** The answer choices split between the verbs *have* and *has,* so find the subject and pick the verb that is consistent. The subject in this case is *findings,* which is plural, so eliminate (A) and (D), since *has* is singular. Eliminate (B) because the verb *lead* is present tense. With the helping verb *have,* the past participle is necessary. Choice (C) correctly uses the past participle of the verb *lead.*

42. **A** This question is testing diction, so find the word that is consistent with the context of the sentence. *Province,* (A), means "type of learning," which would fit well with the previous sentence, so keep it. *Providence* means "goodwill from a higher power," so it doesn't fit; eliminate (B). Choice (C) can be eliminated because *provenance* means "origin." Finally, eliminate (D) since *providential* means "lucky." Choice (A) is the answer.

43. **B** The answer choices don't seem to indicate that a clear grammatical rule is being tested here, so use POE. Choice (A) seems to change the intended meaning, since the adverb *initially* comes after what it's supposed to be modifying instead of before, which it should; eliminate (A). Choice (D) makes the same mistake, so eliminate it as well. Choice (B) is much clearer and more concise, so hold onto it. Choice (C) uses *then*, which is the wrong word choice (it indicates time) and should therefore be eliminated. Choice (B) is correct.

44. **D** Use the Vertical Line Test, drawing lines around the FANBOYS word *and*. The first part of the sentence, *We learn more and more about what we share with other animals*, is a complete idea. The second part of the sentence, *with each discovery, we learn a new way to relate to the world around us*, is also a complete idea. Because both ideas are complete, STOP or HALF-STOP punctuation is needed. Eliminate (A) and (C) because a FANBOYS word with no comma isn't STOP punctuation. Choice (B) uses a comma but gets rid of the word *and*. A comma alone is GO punctuation, so eliminate (B). Choice (D) correctly uses HALF-STOP punctuation to link the two complete ideas. The correct answer is (D).

Section 3: Math (No Calculator)

1. **C** Translate the question into an equation. Let x equal the number, and then $2x = x - 4$. Solving for x, you find that $x = -4$. The answer is (C).

2. **C** Sonal needs s soil samples. If according to the question, he must have more than 6 samples, then $s > 6$. Also according to the question, he may have no more than 13 samples, so $s \leq 13$. Combining these two expressions, you find that $6 < s \leq 13$. The answer is (C).

3. **D** The graph of $f(x)$ has a y-intercept at $y = 3$. Because of this, you know that when $y = 3$, $x = 0$. $f(x)$ must then satisfy the condition that $f(0) = 3$. This is true only for (A) and (B). Alternatively, by recognizing that each equation is in the slope-intercept form: $f(x) = y = mx + b$, where b is the y-intercept, you can reach the same conclusion. Next, notice that the slope of the line is positive. That is, as the value of x increases, so too does y. Returning to the slope-intercept form, m gives the slope of the line. Only (D) has a positive coefficient (m). Choice (D), then, is the correct function.

4. **A** If $x + y = 0$, then $x = -y$. Using this relationship and substituting into the expression $x - y$, you find that $x - y = -y - y = -2y$. This is (A).

5. **A** This question requires factoring the expression $2x^2 - 6x - 8$. Begin by factoring 2 from the expression: $2(x^2 - 3x - 4)$. This expression is further factorable, giving $2(x - 4)(x + 1)$, which is (A).

6. **D** The question describes a ramp that forms a triangle, the length of which is the hypotenuse of the triangle. The height of the ramp (3 feet) is the length of the side of the triangle opposite the 35° angle. In general, for some angle θ, $\sin\theta = \dfrac{\text{opposite}}{\text{hypotenuse}}$. In the question, this corresponds to $\sin 35° = \dfrac{\text{opposite}}{\text{hypotenuse}} = \dfrac{3}{\text{length of ramp}}$, so length of ramp $= \dfrac{3}{\sin 35°}$. This is (D).

7. **D** This question requires evaluating both equations to determine the values of a and b. You can begin by solving either of the two equations for a or b, and then substituting the solution into the other equation. But note that the question asks for the value of $a + b$, so check to see if there's a faster way. Can you stack and add (or subtract) the equations? If you stack and add the equations, you get $7a + 7b = 77$. Now divide both sides of the equation by 7, resulting in $a + b = 11$. This is (D).

8. **D** When a function $f(x)$ is transformed into a function of the form $f(ax)$, where a is a constant, if $a > 0$, the function will be compressed horizontally by a factor of a. Here, $y = x^2 + 4$ can be represented as the parent function, and $y = 3x^2 + 4$ as the transformed function compressed horizontally versus the parent function, and thus narrower, by a factor of 3. This is (D). If you're not sure, try plugging values into each equation to construct a rough graph of each equation and compare them.

9. **C** Rearranging and factoring the expression provided in the question, you have $t^2 - 4t - 90 = 6 \Rightarrow t^2 - 4t - 96 = 0 \Rightarrow (t - 12)(t + 8) = 0$. Therefore, $t - 12 = 0$ and $t + 8 = 0$. t must then equal 12 or -8. If t represents the number of tickets Steven buys, then only $t = 12$ is consistent with the context of the question. If each ticket costs $80, Steven must have spent $\$80 \times 12 = \$960$. This is (C).

10. **C** Find values of c and d by solving the system of equations in order to determine the value of $4c - 4d$. There are several ways to go about this. One way is to multiply the terms of the equation $2c + 3d = 17$ by -3 to get $-6c - 9d = -51$. If you stack and add this equation with the second equation, the result is $-4d = -12$, which solves to $d = 3$. Plug this value for d into the equation $6c + 5d = 39$ to get $6c + 15 = 39$, so $6c = 24$ and $c = 4$. Therefore, $4c - 4d = 4(4) - 4(3) = 16 - 12 = 4$. This is (C).

11. **A** Factoring the left side of the equation $x^2 + 2xy + y^2 = 64$ gives $(x + y)^2 = 64$. Taking the square root of both sides of the equation, you find that $x + y = 8$ or -8. The other equation provides that $y - x = 12$, so $y = x + 12$. Substitute this value of y into the first equation: either $x + (x + 12) = 8$, so $2x + 12 = 8$, $2x = -4$, and $x = -2$, or else or $x + (x + 12) = -8$, so $2x + 12 = -8$, so $2x = -20$, and $x = -10$. Therefore, x could be either -2 or -10, and only -10 is an option in the answers, so (A) is correct.

12. **D** Translate from English to math using Bite-Sized Pieces. Make the price of a hot yoga lesson h and the price of a zero gravity yoga session z. If she offers 2 hot yoga and 3 zero gravity yoga sessions for $400, then $2h + 3z = 400$. Similarly, if 4 hot yoga and 2 zero gravity yoga sessions are $440, then $4h + 2z = 440$. Now, be sure to read the final question. You want to know whether Samantha can create a package that's greater than $800 but has fewer than 13 sessions. If you stack the two equations and then add them together, you get $6h + 5z = 880$. In other words, she can offer 6 hot yoga and 5 zero gravity yoga sessions (11 total sessions) for $880. This satisfies her requirements, so you know the answer is "Yes"; eliminate (A) and (B). For (C), because you don't know the price of each lesson individually, you don't know yet whether 5 hot yoga and 5 zero gravity yoga sessions will be over $800; leave (C) for now. For (D), if 6 hot yoga and 5 zero gravity yoga sessions were over $800, then adding a zero gravity yoga session will still be over $800. Given what you already know, (D) must be true; choose (D).

13. **B** Begin by simplifying the given equation: $(3p^2 + 14p + 24) - 2(p^2 + 7p + 20) = 3p^2 + 14p + 24 - 2p^2 - 14p - 40 = p^2 - 16 = 0$. Factoring the left side of the simplified equation, you find that $(p - 4)(p + 4) = 16$. Solving for p, you find that $p = \pm4$. The value of $3p + 6$ must then be either $3(-4) + 6 = -6$ or $3(4) + 6 = 18$. The latter value is (B).

14. **A** Taking note that $i = \sqrt{-1}$, the expression $(2 + 8i)(1 - 4i) - (3 - 2i)(6 + 4i)$ becomes $(2 + 8\sqrt{-1})(1 - 4\sqrt{-1}) - (3 - 2\sqrt{-1})(6 + 4\sqrt{-1})$. Expanding, this becomes $2 - 8\sqrt{-1} + 8\sqrt{-1} - 32(\sqrt{-1})^2 - (18 + 12\sqrt{-1} - 12\sqrt{-1} - 8(\sqrt{-1})^2) = 2 - 32(\sqrt{-1})^2 - 18 + 8(\sqrt{-1})^2 = 8(\sqrt{-1})^2 - 32(\sqrt{-1})^2 - 16$. This further simplifies to $-8 + 32 - 16 = 8$. This is (A).

15. **C** Plug in the answers! The answer choices aren't in any particular order, and some numbers appear more than once, so you don't need to start in the middle. Instead, start with 9 because it is in three of the four choices. If $x = 9$, then $2\sqrt{9} = 9 - 3$. Since $\sqrt{9} = 3$, the left side of the equation is $2 \times 3 = 6$, and the right side of the equation is $9 - 3 = 6$. This works, so 9 is part of the solution set; eliminate (B) because it doesn't include 9. Next, try $x = 1$: $2\sqrt{1} = 1 - 3$, which solves to $2 = -2$. This isn't true, so 1 is not part of the solution set; eliminate (D). Lastly, try $x = -1$: $2\sqrt{-1} = -1 - 3$. You cannot take the square root of a negative number, so this doesn't work. Eliminate (A) and choose (C).

16. **28** Let s equal the number of staples required by the students and let p be the number of popsicle sticks required. If the number of staples the students will need is three times the number of popsicle sticks they will need, then $s = 3p$. If the students need 84 staples for this project, then $s = 84$. Substitute 84 for s to get $84 = 3p$. Divide both sides by 3 to get $28 = p$. The students will need 28 popsicle sticks.

17. **0** If a parabola intersects the x-axis at the points $(5, 0)$ and $(-5, 0)$, it must be symmetric about the x-axis and centered at $x = 0$. The x-coordinate of its vertical axis of symmetry must then be 0.

18. **94** The question describes a 100-meter ramp that forms a triangle. The length of this ramp corresponds to the hypotenuse of a triangle. The height of the ramp is the length of the side of the triangle opposite the 20° angle; the horizontal distance from the start of the ramp immediately below the entrance of the mall is the side of the triangle adjacent to the 20° angle. The function that relates adjacent and hypotenuse is cosine: $\cos\theta = \dfrac{\text{adjacent}}{\text{hypotenuse}}$. In this problem, $\cos 20° = \dfrac{x}{100}$, where x is the horizontal distance. Solve by multiplying both sides by 100: $\cos 20° = x$. Next, replace $\cos 20°$ with 0.939, the value given in the problem: $100(0.939) = x$. Multiply 100 by 0.939 to get $x = 93.9$, which rounds to 94.

19.   **7**   Let x equal the number. Then, $2x = x - 5 \Rightarrow x = -5$. Three times that number plus seventeen minus that number is $3(-5) + 17 - (-5) = 7$.

20. $\dfrac{10}{3}$ $3x^2 + 2x - 8 = (x + 2)(3x - 4) = 0$. Solving $x + 2 = 0$ and $3x - 4 = 0$ for x, you find that the two solutions for x are -2 and $\dfrac{4}{3}$. The question asks you to subtract the value of the smaller solution from the larger solution. This difference is $\dfrac{4}{3} - (-2) = \dfrac{4}{3} + \dfrac{6}{3} = \dfrac{10}{3}$.

Section 4: Math (Calculator)

1.   **D**   The question asks for a graph that represents a specific situation. Translate the question using Bite-Sized Pieces and eliminate after each piece. One piece of information says that the machine *is slowly filling a bin with pencils*. The graph will show an increase for the first 5 minutes or so. Eliminate (C), as it shows a decrease during this time. Another piece of information says that a jam occurs, *preventing pencils from falling into the bin*. The graph will show a line with a slope of zero starting at 5 minutes. Eliminate (B), as it shows a vertical line here, which would indicate a number of pencils being dumped into the bin at that instant. Compare the remaining answer choices. The difference between (A) and (D) is whether the number of pencils in the bins decreases to 0 or continues increasing. Since the technician *clears the jam* and then *increases the rate* of operation, the number of pencils in the bin will only increase. Eliminate (A). The correct answer is (D).

2.   **A**   The question asks for an equation that models the submarine's depth below the surface. Translate the information using Bite-Sized Pieces and eliminate after each piece. One piece of information says that the submarine starts at a depth of 100 feet. This has nothing to do with m, the number of minutes after the dive begins, so 100 should not be multiplied by m. Eliminate (D). The depth of the submarine is *increased* after the dive begins, so something should be added to 100. Eliminate (B) and (C), which subtract from 100, meaning that the submarine is at a smaller depth and closer to the surface and not at *increased depths*. The correct answer is (A).

3.   **D**   The question asks for a graph that represents a specific situation. Translate the question using Bite-Sized Pieces and eliminate after each piece. One piece of information says that the store charges *$1.00 for a single bead*. The cost per bead, y, is shown on the vertical axis in cents, so the graph will start at 100 cents. All four graphs in the answer choices do that. From there, the question says that *the price per bead goes down*. Eliminate (A), as it shows an initial increase, and (C), which shows a flat line initially. Another piece of information says that there is a *lowest possible price* of *75 cents per bead* starting at 5 beads purchased. The graph will show a line with a slope of zero starting at 5 beads on the horizontal axis. Eliminate (B), as it does not level off at some set price but shows a continued price decrease until the price goes down to 0. The correct answer is (D).

4.   **A**   The question asks for the value of $g(-4)$. In function notation, the number inside the parentheses is the x-value that goes into the function, and the value that comes out of the function is the y-value. Plug $x = -4$ into the function to get $g(-4) = \dfrac{-4 - 2}{3} = \dfrac{-6}{3} = -2$. The correct answer is (A).

5. **A** The question asks for the value of 5*d*. Use the given equation to solve for *d*. Subtract 18 from both sides of the equation to get $d = -6$. Multiply both sides of this equation by 5 to get $5d = -30$. The correct answer is (A).

6. **C** The question asks for an appropriate sampling method to estimate information about a population. Read each answer carefully and use Process of Elimination. For a study to be reliable, it needs a large sample size that is representative of the population being studied. The question asks for an estimate for *the average number of hours of homework assigned to students by the math teachers,* so the survey should include a wide variety of participants across different math classes. Choice (A) refers to *one math teacher,* so it will not provide information about the students who have other math teachers. Eliminate (A). Choice (B) refers to an *online poll* on *the school's social media,* but no information is given about how many math students might see and answer that poll. Keep (B) for now, but check whether there is a better choice. Choice (C) refers to *5 students from each math class,* so it will provide a good amount of information about the math classes across the school. This is a better method than an online poll, so keep (C) and eliminate (B). Choice (D) refers to *the student with the highest grade in each math class,* which may or may not be a representative sample from the entire school. Perhaps those students have higher grades because they spend many more hours studying than their peers. Eliminate (D). The correct answer is (C).

7. **B** The question asks for a comparison of Bill and Jeff's monthly weight loss based on a graph. *Number of months* is listed along the horizontal axis, and *Weight* is listed on the vertical axis. For Bill, represented by the solid line, he started at 280 pounds and went down to 140 pounds for a loss of $280 - 140 = 140$ pounds. The question asks about *pounds...per month,* so divide 140 pounds by 7 months to get 20 pounds per month. For Jeff, represented by the dashed line, he started at 230 pounds and went down to 160 pounds for a loss of $230 - 160 = 70$ pounds. This was over the same 7 months, so Jeff's weight loss per month is 10 pounds. The difference is $20 - 10 = 10$ pounds. The correct answer is (B).

8. **B** The question asks for an equivalent form of an expression. There are variables in the answer choices, so one option is to plug in. Make $y = 2$. The expression becomes $9(2^4) + 6(2^3) + 3 = 9(16) + 6(8) + 3 = 144 + 48 + 3 = 195$. This is the target value; circle it. Now plug $y = 2$ into the answer choices to see which one matches the target value. Choice (A) becomes $3(2^2)[3(2)^2 + 6(2) + 3] = 3(4)[3(4) + 12 + 3] = (12)(12 + 15) = (12)(27) = 324$. This does not match the target, so eliminate (A). Choice (B) becomes $3(2^2)[3(2)^2 + 2(2)] + 3 = 3(4)[3(4) + 4] + 3 = (12)(12 + 4) + 3 = (12)(16) + 3 = 192 + 3 = 195$. Keep (B), but check the remaining choices just in case. Choice (C) becomes $3(2^2)[6(2)^2 + 3(2) + 1] = 3(4)[6(4) + 6 + 1] = (12)(24 + 7) = (12)(31) = 372$. Eliminate (C). Choice (D) becomes $15(2^7) + 3 = 15(128) + 3 = 1,920 + 3 = 1,923$. Eliminate (D). Another option is to use Bite-Sized Pieces and Process of Elimination to tackle this question. The first term in the given expression is $9y^4$. Choice (D) does not have any term with y^4, so eliminate (D). For each remaining answer, multiply the number outside the parentheses by the first term inside the parentheses to see if it results in $9y^4$. For (A) and (B), this becomes $3y^2(3y^2) = 9y^4$. For (C), this becomes $3y^2(6y^2) = 18y^4$. Eliminate (C). The next term in the given expression is $6y^3$, so determine the second term when distributing in (A) and (B). For (A), this becomes $3y^2(6y) = 18y^3$, so eliminate (A). Either way, the correct answer is (B).

9. **A** The question asks for an appropriate conclusion regarding the results of a study that was conducted. Read each answer carefully and use Process of Elimination. A margin of error expresses the amount of random sampling error in a survey's results. The survey provides an estimate of the percentage of *birds' nests* that *experienced full or partial nest predation*. The margin of error is 3%, meaning that results within a range of 3% above and below the estimation are reasonable. The study found that 46% of nests experienced predation, so the reasonable results for this study are between 43% and 49%. Choice (A) says that *percentage of North American birds whose nests get raided by predators is likely somewhere between 43% and 49%*. This does match the range of reasonable results, so keep (A), but check the remaining answers just in case. Choice (B) says that *there is a 3% chance that the study's finding about nest predation…is incorrect*. This is a misunderstanding of *margin of error*, which is not how likely the study is to be correct but is how far off the results may be. Eliminate (B). Choice (C) refers to the percentage *of birds' nests* that *will get raided this coming year*. This answer may be tempting, but it refers to all birds, not just the North American birds from the study. A correct prediction about all birds cannot be made, so eliminate (C). Choice (D) has the same issue with making a prediction about all birds based on a study of one type of bird, so eliminate (D). The correct answer is (A).

10. **B** The question asks for the value of $g\left(\dfrac{1}{2}\right) + g\left(\dfrac{1}{4}\right)$. In function notation, the number inside the parentheses is the x-value that goes into the function, and the value that comes out of the function is the y-value. Plug $x = \dfrac{1}{2}$ into the function to get $g\left(\dfrac{1}{2}\right) = 16^{\frac{1}{2}}$. With a fractional exponent, the numerator is the power and the denominator is the root, so this can be rewritten as $g\left(\dfrac{1}{2}\right) = \sqrt{16} = 4$. Now plug $x = \dfrac{1}{4}$ into the function to get $g\left(\dfrac{1}{4}\right) = 16^{\frac{1}{4}} = \sqrt[4]{16} = 2$. Finally, add the results to get $4 + 2 = 6$. The correct answer is (B).

11. **B** The question asks for the price of the clock before tax. Since the question asks for a specific value and the answers contain numbers in increasing order, plug in the answers. Begin by labeling the answers as "clock price" and start with (B), $25.00. The tax is 10% of this price, and *ten percent* can be written as $\dfrac{10}{100}$. To take a percent of a number, multiply the percent by the number, so the tax is $\dfrac{10}{100}(\$25.00) = \$2.50$. Add this to the price of the clock to get a total cost of $25.00 + $2.50 = $27.50. This matches the value given in the question, so stop here. The correct answer is (B).

12. **C** The question asks for a true statement about two lists of numbers. The answers refer to mean, median, and standard deviation. Of these, the median is the easiest to calculate, so start there. The median of a list of numbers is the middle number when all values are arranged in order. In lists with an even number of items, the median is the average of the middle two numbers. For List X, the middle two numbers are both 13, so there is no need to average to find the median—it is 13. For List Y, the two middle numbers are 11 and 15, so the median is $\dfrac{11 + 15}{2} = \dfrac{26}{2} = 13$. Use this

to eliminate answers before calculating anything else. Choices (A) and (D) can be eliminated, as those both say that the medians are different. Compare the remaining choices—both indicate that the standard deviations are the same, so focus on the means of the two lists. For means (averages), use the formula $T = AN$, in which T is the total, A is the average, and N is the number of things. For List X, the *Total* is $5 + 8 + 13 + 13 + 15 + 18 = 72$. The *Number of things* is 6, so the formula becomes $72 = (A_X)(6)$. Divide both sides by 6 to get $12 = A_X$. Follow the same steps to calculate the mean of List Y. The *Total* is $9 + 10 + 11 + 15 + 19 + 20 = 84$, the *Number of things* is 6, and the formula is $84 = (A_Y)(6)$. Divide both sides by 6 to get $14 = A_Y$. The averages are not the same, so eliminate (B). The correct answer is (C).

13. **C** The question asks for the length of one side of the base of a pyramid. Use the geometry basic approach. Start by drawing a figure and labeling it with the given information. The pyramid has a height of 12 and a square base. Label each side of the base as *s*.

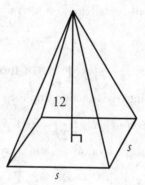

The formula for the volume of a pyramid $V = \frac{1}{3}lwh$, which becomes $V = \frac{1}{3}s^2h$ for a pyramid with a square base. Plug in the given information to get $324 = \frac{1}{3}s^2(12)$, which simplifies to $324 = 4s^2$. Divide both sides of the equation by 4 to get $81 = s^2$, then take the square root of both sides to get $9 = s$. The correct answer is (C).

14. **A** The question asks for which data sets display an increasing trend in test performance on a graph. Check the items in the Roman numerals one at a time and look for a study strategy that shows this trend throughout the experiment. Eliminate after each one. All three Roman numerals appear in at least two answer choices, so start with (I). This is Tutoring, which is represented by the light gray bars. The *Weeks* are listed along the horizontal axis, and the *Test average* is listed on the vertical axis. As the weeks increase, the test average for students in the tutoring group increases throughout the entire period. The tutoring group matches the trend, so eliminate (B), as it does not include (I). As the weeks increase, the test average for students in the traditional homework group, represented by the dark gray bars, increases then decreases. The traditional homework group does NOT match the trend, so eliminate (D), as it includes (II). As the weeks increase, the test average for the no homework group, represented by the black bars, increases then decreases. This does NOT match the trend, so eliminate (C), as it includes (III). The correct answer is (A).

15. **D** The question asks for the ratio of one group's test average improvement to that of another group over the same period of time. Read the graph carefully to find the correct numbers to make the ratio. The *Traditional Homework* group is represented by the dark gray bars. The *start of the study* is week 0, and this group showed a test average of 70 that week. In week 4, the same group had a test average of 80. The improvement for the group with traditional homework was 80 − 70 = 10 points over this time frame. Repeat the steps for the *Tutoring* group, represented by the light gray bars. In week 0, the test average was about 73 and in week 4, the test average was 95. This is an improvement of 95 − 73 = 22 points. The ratio of the test average improvement for the traditional homework group to the tutoring group is 10 to 22 or approximately 1 to 2. The correct answer is (D).

16. **A** The question asks for the side length of the square base of a pyramid in terms of the pyramid's volume and height. Although there are variables in the answer choices, plugging in on this question may not be the fastest approach, given that the equation is easy to manipulate. Instead, solve for s. To begin to isolate s, multiply both sides of the equation by 3 to get $3V = hs^2$. Divide both sides by h to get $\frac{3V}{h} = s^2$. Take the square root of both sides to get $\sqrt{\frac{3V}{h}} = s$. The correct answer is (A).

17. **A** The question asks for a probability, which is defined as $\frac{\text{\# of outcomes that fit requirements}}{\text{total \# of outcomes}}$. Read the table carefully to find the numbers to make the probability. The question asks for a student that *drinks coffee*, of which 26.9% do, so that is the *# of outcomes that fit requirements*. It doesn't matter that this is a percent not a number, as all the categories on the chart are percents of the same whole. The chosen coffee drinker is selected from among those who do *not drink a cold drink at breakfast*. This means that the *total # of outcomes* is all those who drank hot drinks, or 5.3% + 26.9% = 32.2%. Therefore, the probability is $\frac{26.9\%}{32.2\%} \approx 0.84$. The correct answer is (A).

18. **A** The question asks for how much wheat was produced in 2015 based on a percent decrease in wheat production and a percent increase in corn production. Percent change is calculated using the equation *percent change* $= \frac{difference}{original} \times 100$. Start by plugging the information provided about corn into the percent change equation to calculate the production of corn in 2005, in millions of bushels, which can be called c. The equation for corn becomes $15 = \frac{161 - c}{c} \times 100$. Multiply both sides of the equation by c to get $15c = (161 - c) \times 100$, and then distribute on the right side to get $15c = 16,100 - 100c$. Add $100c$ to both sides to get $115c = 16,100$, and then divide both sides by 115 to get $c = 140$ million bushels. The question says that *the state produced identical amounts of each crop in 2005*, so the production of wheat in 2005 was also 140 million bushels. This production *decreased by 40%* from 2005 to 2015, so the 2015 production of wheat must be less than 140. Eliminate (C) and (D), as these show an increase in production over this time. Since the

question asks for a specific value and the answers contain numbers, plug in the remaining answers. Label the answers as "wheat 2015." Start with (A), 84, since it does not have a decimal. Plug this value into the percent change equation to see if it makes the equation true. The equation for wheat becomes $40 = \dfrac{140 - 84}{140} \times 100$. Simplify the numerator on the right to get $40 = \dfrac{56}{140} \times 100$. Multiply both sides by 140 and simplify on the right side to get $5{,}600 = 5{,}600$. This is true, so stop here. The correct answer is (A).

19. **D** The question asks for the amount of a solution to mix with another solution in order to create a certain concentration. Since the question asks for a specific value and the answers contain numbers, plug in the answers. Test each value in the equation from the question and look for a value that makes the equation true. The question states that the trainer will use 10 quarts of the 15% solution, and the a on the right side of the equation is multiplied by 0.15, so $a = 10$. Begin by labeling the answers as b and start with (B), 90. The equation becomes $0.27(10 + 90) = 0.15(10) + 0.35(90)$, or $0.27(100) = 1.5 + 31.5$. This simplifies to $27 = 33$, which is not true, so eliminate (B). A smaller quantity of the higher percent solution is needed to make the equation true, so eliminate (A) and try (C) next. If $b = 30$, the equation becomes $0.27(10 + 30) = 0.15(10) + 0.35(30)$, or $0.27(40) = 1.5 + 10.5$. This simplifies to $10.8 = 12$, which is much closer but is still not true. Eliminate (C). The correct answer is (D).

20. **C** The question asks for a true statement about a parabola given the function $f(x) = (x - b)^2 - 4$ with a vertex of $(b, 4)$. There are variables in the answer choices, so one way to approach this would be to plug in for b. Make $b = 2$, so the function becomes $f(x) = (x - 2)^2 - 4$. Calculator use is allowed, so graph this on a calculator. It will look like this:

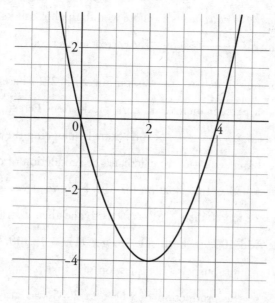

The answer choices refer to the y-intercept, which is where the graph crosses the y-axis. At this point, $x = 0$, so (A) and (D) can be eliminated. Now plug $b = 2$ into the points in the remaining answer choices to see which matches $(0, 0)$. The point in (B) becomes $(0, -2)$, so eliminate (B). The point in (C) becomes $(0, 2^2 – 4)$ or $(0, 4 – 4)$, which is $(0, 0)$. Another option is to plug $x = 0$ into the function. Because all the answer choices refer to the y-intercept, plugging in this value for x will give the y-coordinate of the y-intercept. The function becomes $f(0) = (0 – b)^2 – 4 = (–b)^2 – 4 = b^2 – 4$. Either way, the correct answer is (C).

21. **D** The question asks for the statistical measure that would increase when changes are made to a set of numbers. Only 2 numbers are given in the original set, so plug in a few more to see what would happen. Make the original set {19, 30, 86, and 90}. Once the teacher corrects the mistakes, the set will be {30, 68, 90, and 91}. To compare the lists, start with range, which is easy to calculate. The range of a list of values is the greatest value minus the least value. For the original set, the range is $90 – 19 = 71$, and for the new set, it is $91 – 30 = 61$. The range did not increase, so eliminate (A). Another easy calculation is the median. The median of a list of numbers is the middle number when all values are arranged in order. In lists with an even number of items, the median is the average of the middle two numbers. For the original set, the median is $\frac{30 + 86}{2} = \frac{116}{2} = 58$, and for the new set, it is $\frac{68 + 90}{2} = \frac{158}{2} = 79$. The median did increase, so keep (C) for now. For means (averages), use the formula $T = AN$, in which T is the total, A is the average, and N is the number of things. For the original set, the *Total* is 225 and the *Number of things* is 4, so $225 = A(4)$. Divide both sides by 4 to get $56.25 = A$. For the new set, *Total* is 279, so $279 = A(4)$ and $A = 69.75$. The average also increased, so keep (D). Choice (B) refers to the standard deviation of the sets. Standard deviation is a measure of the amount of variation or dispersion of a set of values. There is no way to tell that based on only 2 values from the set, so this cannot be the answer. Eliminate (B). The remaining choices are median and mean. Because the median is the middle number in the list, it may increase or decrease depending on where 19 and 86 appear in the original list. Not enough information is given to determine this. However, there will always be the same number of items in the original list and the new list, so changes in *Total* will affect the average. When the 19 becomes a 91, the *Total* increases by 72. When the 86 becomes a 68, the *Total* decreases by 18. These two changes together cause a new increase in the *Total* of $72 – 18 = 54$, meaning the average *must* increase. The correct answer is (D).

22. **D** The question asks for an equation of the line of best fit on a graph. To find the best equation, compare features of the graph to the answer choices. The graph for this question has a negative slope. The answer choices are in $y = mx + b$ form, in which m is the slope and b is the y-intercept. Eliminate answer choices that do not have a negative value for m. Eliminate (B) and (C), then compare the remaining choices. The difference between (A) and (D) is the slope, so calculate slope

using the formula $slope = \dfrac{y_2 - y_1}{x_2 - x_1}$. The graph goes through the points (2, 90) and (12, 40), so $slope = \dfrac{40 - 90}{12 - 2} = \dfrac{-50}{10} = -5$. Eliminate (B). The correct answer is (D).

23. **B** The question asks for the best description of the function g. Compare the answer choices. Two choices describe a linear increase or decrease, which is an increase or decrease by the same amount each unit of time, and two choices describe an exponential increase or decrease, which is an increase or decrease by the same percent or fraction each unit of time. Each hour, one half of the remaining players are eliminated, so the number of players is decreasing, not increasing. Eliminate (A) and (C). After one hour, there will be $\dfrac{65,000}{2} = 32,500$ players remaining. After another hour, half the remaining players will be eliminated, so there will be $\dfrac{32,500}{2} = 16,250$ players remaining. The first decrease was 32,500 players, and the second was 16,250 players, so the decrease is not linear. Eliminate (D). The correct answer is (B).

24. **C** The question asks for the equation that represents the relationship between two variables. When given a table of values and asked for the correct equation, plug values from the table into the answer choices to see which one works. It won't matter that the points also have a variable in them, but it will be easiest to use the point with only one variable. According to the table, $x = 0$ when $y = 3b$. Plug $x = 0$ and $y = 3b$ into the answer choice equations to see which is true. Choice (A) becomes $5(0) + 3b = 2b$, which simplifies to $0 + 3b = 2b$. This is not true, so eliminate (A). Choice (B) becomes $0 - 5(3b) = -3b$, which simplifies to $0 - 15b = -3b$. Eliminate (B). Choice (C) becomes $5(0) + 3b = 3b$, which simplifies to $0 + 3b = 3b$. This is true, so keep (C), but check (D) just in case. Choice (D) becomes $0 - 5(3b) = -7b$, which simplifies to $0 - 15b = -7b$. Eliminate (D). The correct answer is (C).

25. **C** The question asks for the value of an expression based on an equation. Although the answers contain numbers, the question asks for the value of an expression instead of a specific value, so plugging in the answers may be tricky. Another way to approach this is by solving the equation for the value of a. To solve for a, distribute on the right side of the equation to get $8a + 20 = 7 + 6a + 15$. Simplify the right side to get $8a + 20 = 6a + 22$. Subtract $6a$ from both sides to get $2a + 20 = 22$, then subtract 20 from both sides to get $2a = 2$. The question asks for the value of $2a + 5$, so add 5 to the value of $2a$ to get $2 + 5 = 7$. The correct answer is (C).

26. **C** The question asks for the value of the y-coordinate of the solution to a system of equations. The best way to solve the system of y is to find a way to make the x-coordinates disappear when stacking and adding the equations. The larger x coefficient, 6.5, is 5 times the smaller one, 1.3. Multiply the entire the first equation by -5 to get the same coefficient with opposite signs on the x terms. The first equation becomes $-5(1.3x - 0.6y) = -5(-0.7)$ and then $-6.5x + 3y = 3.5$. Now stack and add the two equations.

$$-6.5x + \quad 3y = \quad 3.5$$
$$\underline{+ \ 6.5x - 1.5y = -0.5}$$
$$\quad\quad\quad 1.5y = \quad 3.0$$

Divide both sides of the resulting equation by 1.5 to get $y = 2$. The correct answer is (C).

27. **B** The question asks for the function that represents a specific situation. The number of goosefoot seeds deposited decreased by a certain percent over time, so this question is about exponential decay. Knowing the parts of the growth and decay formula can help with this question. That formula is *final amount* = (*original amount*)(1 ± *rate*)^*number of changes*. In this case, $S(c)$ is the final amount, and the question states that the original amount was 500. All four choices have 500 as the original amount, but (C) and (D) have 500 raised to an exponent instead of a (1 ± *rate*) in parentheses raised to an exponent. This is not the proper form, so eliminate (C) and (D). The original amount must be multiplied by (1 − *rate*), because the numbers are decreasing, and the *rate* here is 7%. This can be expressed as 0.07, so the value in parentheses should be (1 − 0.07) or (0.93). Eliminate (A) because it does not have this rate. The only remaining answer is (B), and it matches the decay formula. Without this formula, it is still possible to answer this question. Plug in a value of c to see how the number of seeds deposited decreased over time. After 1 century, the number of seeds deposited would have decreased by 7% of the initial 500. The number of seeds would then be 500 − (0.07)(500) = 500 − 35 = 465. Plug $c = 1$ into the answer choices to see which gives a value of 465 for $S(c)$. Only (B) will work. Either way, the correct answer is (B).

28. **A** The question asks for the meaning of a number in the context of a model for production cost per item. Start by reading the final question, which asks for the meaning of the number 5.22. Then label the parts of the equation with the information given. The question states that C is the *production cost per item* and P is *the number of products made*. The number 5.22 is added to the term with P, so it must be a cost that is unrelated to the number of items produced. Next, use Process of Elimination to get rid of answer choices that are not consistent with the labels. Choice (A) refers to the initial production cost, which is consistent with the labels. At the start of production, $P = 0$, and plugging this into the equation results in $C = 0.0045(0) + 5.22 = 0 + 5.22$. Therefore, when 0 products are made, the cost is still 5.22, so keep (A). Choice (B) refers to the cost increase, *in dollars per item*, but this is inconsistent with the labels, as 5.22 is not related to P. Eliminate (B). Choices (C) and (D) also refer to cost *in dollars per item*, so eliminate (C) and (D). The correct answer is (A).

29. **C** The question asks for the measurement of an angle on the figure. Use the geometry basic approach. Start by ballparking—the angle is larger than 90°, so eliminate (A). Label the figure with the given information that $FG = JK$ and $GH = HJ$. If $\overline{FG} \parallel \overline{JK}$, then angle F is also a right angle. Label this as well. No measurements are given, but the relationship between FK and HJ is given. When there is a relationship between numbers, plug in. Make $HJ = 2$, so $GH = 2$ and $FK = 2\sqrt{2}$. Label these on the figure as well, which should look like this:

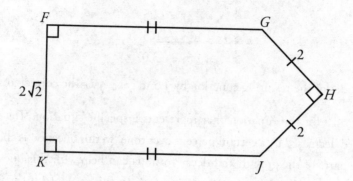

Now the figure is starting to look like a rectangle and a triangle. Draw line *GJ* to better see this. Because *FG* and *JK* are parallel and congruent, *FGJK* is a rectangle. This means that angle *GJK* is a right angle, and *GJ* is $2\sqrt{2}$ because it is opposite *FK*. Now focus on finding angle *GJH*, which is part of the triangle. When there is a $\sqrt{2}$ in a triangle question, the triangle is likely a 45°-45°-90° triangle. In those triangles, the legs are *x* and the hypotenuse is $x\sqrt{2}$. Triangle *GHJ* has this relationship of the sides, so angle *GJH* is a 45° angle. Therefore, angle *J* is angle *GJK* + angle *GJH* or *J* = 90 + 45 = 135°. The correct answer is (C).

30. **A** The question asks for the graph of the given parabola. One option would be to plug in a value for *a* and graph the parabola on a graphing calculator. If *a* = –1, the function becomes *h*(*x*) = –(*x* – 2)(*x* + 4). In function notation, *f*(*x*) or *h*(*x*) = *y*, and the graph of *y* = –(*x* – 2)(*x* + 5) will look like this:

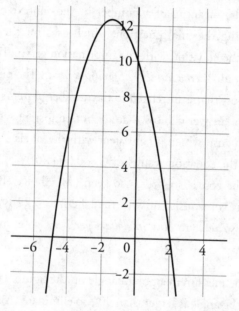

None of the graphs match this exactly, but the graphs in (B) and (D) open up and this one opens down. If the value of *a* is negative, the parabola will open down. Eliminate (B) and (D). The intercepts on this graph are at *x* = –5 and *x* = 2. These will be the intercepts no matter what the value of *a* is, because *a* determines the direction of the parabola and how narrow or wide it is. The correct answer graph must also have these intercepts, so eliminate (C), which has the wrong signs on the intercepts. Without a graphing calculator, it is still possible to answer this question. The function is given in factored form. If $(x - a)$ is a factor of a polynomial, then a is a solution, and the graph will cross the x-axis at a. The equation has factors of $(x - 2)$ and $(x + 5)$, so the roots must be at 2 and –5. This eliminates (C) and (D), which do not have these roots. To determine if it is (A) or (B), it is necessary to know how the sign of a affects the shape of the parabola. Either way, the correct answer is (A).

31. **1000** The question asks about the value of a in a set of numbers with a mean of 1,650. For means (averages), use the formula $T = AN$, in which T is the total, A is the average, and N is the number of things. The *Total* is 650 + a + 1,550 + 1,750 + 2,300 + 2,650 = 8,900 + a, and the *Number of things* is 6. The formula becomes 8,900 + a = (1,650)(6), which simplifies to 8,900 + a = 9,900. Subtract 8,900 from both sides of the equation to get a = 1,000. The correct answer is 1000.

32. **7** The question asks for the maximum number of burgers John can buy in a specific situation. Translate the English to math using Bite-Sized Pieces to solve. The question states that John *buys 6 orders of fries*, which cost *$3.10 per order*. "Per" means to multiply, so the fries cost John 6($3.10) = $18.60. John has $50, so his remaining money is $50 – $18.60 = $31.40. The question states the burgers *cost $4.30 each*, so divide $31.40 by $4.30 to find that John can buy about 7.3 burgers. The number of burgers must be an integer, so round this down to 7 burgers. The correct answer is 7.

33. **175** The question asks for the value of $c + d$, which represent two angles on a figure. Use the geometry basic approach. Start by labeling the figure with the given information. Mark a = 118 and b = 67. There are 360° in a quadrilateral, so $a + b + c + d$ = 360. Plug in the values of a and b to get 118 + 67 + $c + d$ = 360, then simplify to get 185 + $c + d$ = 360. Subtract 185 from both sides of the equation to get $c + d$ = 175. The correct answer is 175.

34. $\frac{2}{3}$, **.666, or .667**

The question asks for the value of a variable in an equation with infinitely many solutions. When an equation has infinitely many solutions, the two sides of the equation must represent the same expression. Distribute p on the right side of the equation to get $-3x + 2 = px - pq$. If the two sides are the same expression, then $-3x = px$. Divide both sides by x to get $-3 = p$. The equation then becomes $-3x + 2 = -3x - (-3)q$. Subtract $-3x$ from both sides to get 2 = 3q, and then divide both sides by 3 to get $\frac{2}{3} = q$. The correct answer can be entered as $\frac{2}{3}$, .666, or .667.

35. **8** The question asks for the value of a constant in the equation of a parabola that intersects the line $y = -1$ at exactly one point. To intersect at only one point, the line must intersect only the vertex of the parabola. One way to determine the equation of such a parabola is to graph the line $y = -1$ and the parabola $y = x^2 - 6x$ on a graphing calculator. It will look like this:

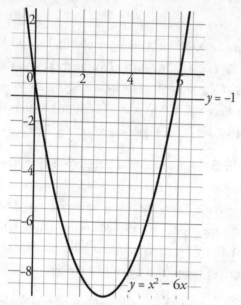

The vertex of the parabola with no value for c is at $(3, -9)$, so the vertex must move up 8 units to be at $(3, -1)$. To move a function up 8 units, add an 8 to the function, which becomes $y = x^2 - 6x + 8$ in this case. This means that $c = 8$. Another approach is to solve the equation algebraically. For the parabola to intersect the line exactly once, there must be only one solution to this equation. The factored form must look like $(x - a)^2$. The coefficient on the x term is -6, so the parabola must be $(x - 3)^2$. Using FOIL, multiply this out to get $x^2 - 3x - 3x + 9$, which simplifies to $x^2 - 6x + 9$. To compare this to the original equation, plug in -1 for y to get $-1 = x^2 - 6x + c$. Add 1 to both sides to get $0 = x^2 - 6x + c - 1$. The x^2 and x terms match in both equations, so the remaining constants must also match. Therefore, $9 = c + 1$, and $c = 8$. Either way, the correct answer is 8.

36. **45** The question asks for the value of a function. In function notation, the number inside the parentheses is the x-value that goes into the function, and the value that comes out of the function is the y-value. The question says that the *value of the function is 5 when* $x = b$, so $f(b) = 5$ and $f(b) = ab^2$. This can be written as $5 = ab^2$. To make this easier to solve, plug in for either of these variables and then solve for the other. To plug in for b, use a value such as 5 to make the math easier. The equation becomes $5 = a(5^2)$, which simplifies to $5 = 25a$. Divide both sides by 25 to get $\frac{1}{5} = a$. The function can now be defined as $f(x) = \frac{1}{5}x^2$. The question asks for the value of $3b$, which is $3(5) = 15$ when $b = 5$. Plug $x = 15$ into the f function to get $f(15) = \frac{1}{5}(15)^2$, which simplifies to $f(15) = \frac{225}{5}$. This becomes $f(15) = 45$. The correct answer is 45.

37.   **63**   The question asks for the time it will take in seconds for the shuttle to travel 150 kilometers. Begin by reading the question to find information on the shuttle's speed. The question states that the speed is 8,568 kilometers per hour. To determine the speed in seconds, divide this by the number of seconds in one hour. There are 60 minutes in an hour and 60 seconds in a minute, so there are $(60)(60) = 3,600$ seconds in an hour. The speed is $\frac{8,568}{3,600} = 2.38$ km/s. To find the time it takes to travel 150 kilometers at this speed, use the formula $D = RT$, in which D is distance, R is rate, and T is time. The formula becomes $150 = 2.38T$. Divide both sides by 2.38 to get $63.025 = T$. Round this to the nearest second, as indicated by the question, which is 63. The correct answer is 63.

38.   **2400**   The question asks for a space shuttle's escape velocity in meters per second based on the escape velocity in kilometers per hour. When dealing with conflicting units, make a proportion, being sure to match up units. To convert hours to seconds, determine the number of seconds in an hour. There are 60 minutes in an hour and 60 seconds in a minute, so there are $(60)(60) = 3,600$ seconds in an hour. Now convert kilometers to meters using the information in the note. The proportion is $\frac{1 \text{ kilometer}}{1,000 \text{ meters}} = \frac{8,568 \text{ kilometers}}{x \text{ meters}}$. Cross-multiply to get $x = 8,568,000$ meters. The speed *in meters per second* becomes $\frac{8,568,000 \text{ meters}}{3,600 \text{ seconds}} = 2,380$ m/s. Round this to the nearest hundred, as indicated by the question, which is 2,400. The correct answer is 2400.

RAW SCORE CONVERSION TABLE SECTION AND TEST SCORES

Raw Score (# of correct answers)	Math Section Score	Reading Test Score	Writing and Language Test Score
0	200	10	10
1	200	10	10
2	210	10	10
3	230	11	10
4	240	12	11
5	260	13	12
6	280	14	13
7	290	15	13
8	310	15	14
9	320	16	15
10	330	17	16
11	340	17	16
12	360	18	17
13	370	19	18
14	380	19	19
15	390	20	19
16	410	20	20
17	420	21	21
18	430	21	21
19	440	22	22
20	450	22	23
21	460	23	23
22	470	23	24
23	480	24	25
24	480	24	25
25	490	25	26
26	500	25	26
27	510	26	27
28	520	26	28
29	520	27	28

Raw Score (# of correct answers)	Math Section Score	Reading Test Score	Writing and Language Test Score
30	530	28	29
31	540	28	30
32	550	29	30
33	560	29	31
34	560	30	32
35	570	30	32
36	580	31	33
37	590	31	34
38	600	32	34
39	600	32	35
40	610	33	36
41	620	33	37
42	630	34	38
43	640	35	39
44	650	35	40
45	660	36	
46	670	37	
47	670	37	
48	680	38	
49	690	38	
50	700	39	
51	710	40	
52	730	40	
53	740		
54	750		
55	760		
56	780		
57	790		
58	800		

Please note that the numbers in the table may shift slightly depending on the SAT's scale from test to test; however, you can still use this table to get an idea of how your performance on the practice tests will translate to the actual SAT.

CONVERSION EQUATION SECTION AND TEST SCORES

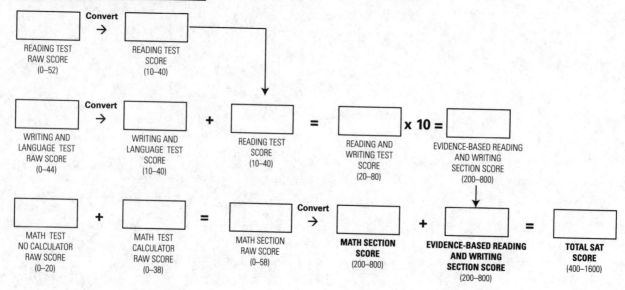

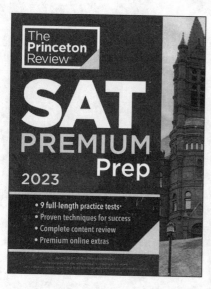

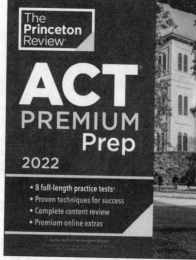